PROGRAMMING IN

Ada ^{95}

INTERNATIONAL COMPUTER SCIENCE SERIES

Consulting Editor   **A D McGettrick**   University of Strathclyde

SELECTED TITLES IN THE SERIES

PROGRAMMING IN

Ada ^{95}

JOHN BARNES

ADDISON-WESLEY PUBLISHING COMPANY

WOKINGHAM, ENGLAND • READING, MASSACHUSETTS • MENLO PARK, CALIFORNIA • NEW YORK
DON MILLS, ONTARIO • AMSTERDAM • BONN • SYDNEY • SINGAPORE
TOKYO • MADRID • SAN JUAN • MILAN • PARIS • MEXICO CITY • SEOUL • TAIPEI

Cover designed by Designers & Partners of Oxford
and printed by The Riverside Printing Co. (Reading) Ltd.
The cover depicts part of the rings of Saturn which make Saturn the most complex planet in the Solar System. This echoes the theme that Ada 95 is the appropriate language for major applications in our modern complex world.
Typeset by John Barnes Informatics.
Printed in Great Britain by T. J. Press (Padstow) Ltd, Padstow, Cornwall.

First printed 1995.

ISBN 0-201-87700-7

British Library Cataloguing in Publication Data
A catalogue record for this book is available from the British Library.

Library of Congress Cataloging in Publication Data applied for.

To Barbara

Foreword

John Barnes' *Programming in Ada* has been the classic text on Ada since it was first published 14 years ago. Now that Ada 95, the new revision of Ada, has been officially approved as an ISO and ANSI standard, this new book seems destined to become the classic text on Ada 95.

Ada 95 is first and foremost still Ada, and the original Ada standard (Ada 83) has turned out to be a remarkably good language for the production of high-quality, highly reliable, industrial strength software. Inasmuch as every language seems to build up a surrounding culture, the Ada programming culture has developed as one that values highly readable programs where both the overall architecture of the system and the more detailed design, are captured explicitly in the structure, abstractions, and nomenclature of the source code. Subsystem interfaces, as embodied in package specifications, have become critical design elements in themselves, providing the stable framework around which the whole program is built.

But no technology stands still, and the last decade has been a particularly active period of development in the areas of programming language technology and software development methodologies. Ada helped spearhead the development of object-oriented methodologies, fostered by its excellent support for data abstraction and program modularization, with information hiding and a strong separation of interface and implementation. Yet Ada 83 is fundamentally a static language; all data types and all subprogram bindings are fully determined prior to execution. Over the past decade, the software industry has moved toward a more dynamic model of program composition. The concepts of inheritance and polymorphism have emerged as mechanisms that can guarantee interface compatibility at compile time, while deferring the binding to particular data types or subprogram implementations to run time. This combination can preserve the reliability associated with compile time interface checking, while supporting more flexible composition and reuse of independently built subsystems.

Ada 95 builds on the excellent Ada 83 foundation of data abstraction and modularity, enhancing it to support type extension as part of inheritance, class-wide programming for polymorphism, and a hierarchical library unit name space. Together these enable a better representation within the language of the subsystem and abstraction hierarchies inherent in component-based, object-oriented programming. Accompanying these enhancements to the data abstraction and program structuring building blocks of the language, are enhancements to the concurrent programming facilities. Support has been added for efficient data-oriented synchronization, complementing the rendezvous-based synchronization model of Ada 83, and for asynchronous signaling, complementing the synchronous interaction model of Ada 83.

The publication of this new book focused on Ada 95 indicates that Ada 95 is truly here, and that the 'Ada 9X' revision process has come to a successful conclusion. This revision process actually began in 1988 with an initial call for user input on the goals for the revision, and the Ada 9X design team worked full time from March of 1990 until February 1995 to meet those goals (so now we know the 'X' in Ada 9X is '5'). John Barnes was active in the process from the beginning, as an individual reviewer and sage, as head of the UK delegation to the ISO working group on Ada (WG9), where he made critical contributions toward building consensus for the object-oriented features of Ada 95, and ultimately as the author of the Ada 95 Rationale that accompanied the various drafts of the standard during its ISO and ANSI ballots.

Throughout this period, John's insight, perseverance, and indomitable good humor helped ensure the success of this process. With the publication of this new book, John helps to celebrate the completion of the 9X design process, while doing his own part to start the essential process of integrating the new Ada 95 features into the Ada culture. The Ada 95 Reference Manual can tell a programmer what are the features of Ada 95. However, only an author with John's unique style can reveal not just what is there, but also why it is there and how it can be used in the development of highly reliable, highly flexible, and highly adaptable software systems.

S. Tucker Taft
Cambridge, Mass
July 1995

Preface

This book is about programming in Ada 95 – the new ISO standard which was published in February 1995. It is interesting to observe that Ada 95 is the first ISO standard to incorporate the dynamic features which go under the banner of Object Oriented Programming (OOP).

But Ada 95 is not just about OOP. It also includes better tasking facilities, a structured library especially useful for building a system out of independent subsystems as well as more flexible means of communication with other languages and systems.

Moreover, Ada 95 defines a number of optional annexes as well as a core language. These optional annexes define additional specialized facilities for six distinct application areas. These areas are Systems Programming, Real-Time Systems, Distributed Systems, Information Systems, Numerics, and Safety and Security. Thus Ada 95 extends the domain of Ada out from the embedded systems area for which Ada 83 was originally designed in order to cover a broader spectrum of programming activity.

Ada 95 has also been designed to preserve the investment in existing Ada 83 programs. With minor and usually obscure exceptions, an Ada 83 program will run as an Ada 95 program with identical behaviour.

The overall essence of Ada 95 is that it adds the flexibility of OOP and related techniques to the firm strongly typed and secure foundation provided by the Software Engineering approach of Ada 83.

One might think of Smalltalk as being flexible and secure but not efficient, of C++ as being flexible and efficient but not secure, and of Ada 83 as being secure and efficient but not flexible. Ada 95 brings the best of all worlds, it is secure, efficient and flexible. And moreover, compilers are becoming widely and freely available enabling Ada 95 to be used by a wider community who found access to Ada 83 not so easy.

This book follows the tradition of its predecessor, *Programming in Ada*. It presents an overall description of Ada 95 as a language. Some knowledge of the principles of programming is assumed and an acquaintance with languages such as Pascal or C would be helpful but by no means necessary. This book is not about how to design a program or about the wonders of OOP as such but such matters are inevitably addressed from time to time.

Although this book draws on material from its predecessor where appropriate, nevertheless it presents Ada 95 as a language in its own right with little reference to Ada 83 other than a brief checklist at the end of each chapter outlining the main changes in the area concerned. The book comprises 23 chapters grouped into four parts as follows

- Chapters 1 to 4 provide an overview which should give the reader an understanding of the overall scope of the language as well as the ability to run significant programs as examples;
- Chapters 5 to 10 discuss the small-scale aspects roughly corresponding to the domain addressed by languages such as Pascal and C; these chapters cover the lexical details, scalar, array and simple record types, control structures, subprograms and access types;
- Chapters 11 to 19 cover the large-scale aspects including packages, separate compilation, abstraction, OOP and tasking as well as exceptions and the details of numerics; this is the main part of the book and contains much exciting new material;
- Chapters 20 to 23 complete the story by discussing the predefined library, interfacing to the outside world and the specialized annexes; there is then a finale concluding with some ruminations over design.

It is interesting to observe that the book concludes, as did its predecessor, *Programming in Ada*, with the fantasy customer in the shop trying to buy reusable software components and whose dream now seems as far away or indeed as near at hand as it did nearly fifteen years ago when I first toiled at this book. So much and yet so little progress has been made in those fifteen years.

Those familiar with *Programming in Ada* will find that much of the old material has been retained but rearranged and updated where necessary. For example, access types are introduced much earlier since they are very important for OOP. The chapters on packages, private types and separate compilation have been completely restructured because of the introduction of the hierarchical library and the loosening of the rules regarding the redefinition of equality. The chapter on tasking is rather different since the introduction of protected types and the requeue statement has meant that much old discussion was obsolete.

Apart from the obsolete tasking examples, the only other material to have disappeared is the lengthy discussion on model numbers. This is because it no longer applies to the core language but only to implementations supporting the Numerics annex.

There are of course many more exercises covering the new ground but a few less interesting old ones have been removed. Full answers and associated discussion are included as before.

I have also taken the opportunity to polish existing material where necessary and the identifiers in some examples have been changed where it seems to increase understanding.

The material on the potentially bearded man and the woman who can bear children has been retained and built upon as an interesting example of the use of type extension and abstraction. Some have commented that this is sexist and politically incorrect. However, it is a biological fact of life that only females have wombs and only males can have (serious) beards. I have continued to attribute the children and parenthood in a traditional manner but that is because it makes the example more interesting rather than because of a desire to take a sexist view. If this offends any reader, then I apologize but this is a book about programming and not social science and using such intuitive examples makes the material much easier to understand.

And now I must take this opportunity to thank all those who have helped with this new book. The reviewers included Colin Atkinson, Ben Brosgol, Alan Burns, Colin Carter, Fred Ives, John Savage, Pat Rogers, Andy Wellings and Salih Yurttas, all of whom made some very useful comments and detected a number of embarrassing errors. Extra special thanks go to Tucker Taft to whom I am especially grateful for his patient explanation of some of the details and help with improving the explanation of more obscure parts such as visibility.

Big thanks are due to Bill Carlson of Intermetrics and to Christine Anderson of the USDoD for encouraging and enabling me to work with the Ada 9X design team on writing material for the Ada 9X Rationale. I am particularly grateful for their permission to use some of that material as the foundation for some examples.

I must also thank all those who responded to my request for advice on Comp.Lang.Ada regarding the presentation of floating point types. As a result of their replies the text has been written in terms of the type Float rather than the hypothetical type Real used in *Programming in Ada*. I do hope that this change will make the text more accessible to the novice while not discouraging the declaration of one's own types for portability.

Finally, many thanks to my wife Barbara for help in typesetting and proof-reading (and for allowing me to abuse her name in Chapter 20), and to my daughter Janet for spotting many errors in the examples and exercises and to friends at Addison-Wesley for their continued help and guidance.

John Barnes
Caversham, England
July 1995

Major examples of programs, including answers to exercises and the syntax from this book may be accessed (Autumn, 1995) via anonymous ftp at: ftp.aw.com under aw.computer.science in a file entitled Barnes95. The code is also available on disk from Addison-Wesley Publishing Company; send requests to Barnes95@aw.com. Comments to the author can also be sent to this same address.

Contents

Part 1

An Overview

This first part comprises four chapters which cover the background to the language and an overview of most of the features. Enough material is presented here to enable a programmer to write complete simple programs.

Chapter 1 contains a historical account of the origins of both Ada 95 and Ada 83 and a brief discussion of how the evolution of abstraction has been an important key to the development of programming languages in general.

Broadly speaking, the other three chapters in this part provide an overview of the material in the corresponding other parts of the book. Thus Chapter 2 describes the simple concepts familiar from languages such as C and Pascal and which form the subject of the six chapters which comprise Part 2. Similarly Chapter 3 covers the important topic of abstraction which is the main theme of Part 3. And then Chapter 4 rounds off the overview by showing how a complete program is put together and corresponds to Part 4 which covers material such as the predefined library.

Chapter 3 includes a discussion of the popular topic of Object Oriented Programming and illustrates the key concepts of classes as groups of related types, of type extension and inheritance as well as static polymorphism (genericity) and dynamic polymorphism leading to dynamic binding. It also includes a brief comparison between the terminology used by Ada and that used by some other languages. This chapter concludes with an introduction to tasking which is an important aspect of Ada and is a topic not addressed by most languages at all.

Those familiar with Ada 83 can skip Chapter 2 but will find much new material in Chapters 3 and 4.

Those not familiar with Ada will find that this part will give them a fair idea of Ada's capabilities and lays the foundation for understanding the details presented in the remainder of the book.

1 Introduction

Ada 95 is a comprehensive high level programming language especially suited for the professional development of large or critical programs for which correctness and robustness are major considerations. In this introductory chapter we briefly trace the development of Ada 95 (and its predecessor Ada 83), its place in the overall language scene and the general structure of the remainder of this book.

1.1 History

Ada 95 is a direct descendant of and highly compatible with Ada 83 which was originally sponsored by the US Department of Defense for use in the so-called embedded system application area. (An embedded system is one in which the computer is an integral part of a larger system such as a chemical plant, missile or dishwasher.)

The story of Ada goes back to about 1974 when the United States Department of Defense realized that it was spending far too much on software, especially in the embedded systems area. To cut a long story short the DoD sponsored the new language through a number of phases of definition of requirements, competitive and parallel development and evaluation which culminated in the issue of the ANSI standard for Ada in 1983 which is referred to as *RM83 (Reference Manual for Ada 83)*[1].

The final requirements for Ada 83 are defined in the Steelman document[2] and the team that developed Ada was based at CII Honeywell Bull in France under the leadership of Jean D Ichbiah. Fuller details of the development of Ada 83 will be found in the introductory chapter of the predecessor to this book.

The language is named after Augusta Ada Byron, Countess of Lovelace (1815–52). Ada, the daughter of Lord Byron, was the assistant and patron of Charles Babbage and worked on his mechanical analytical engine. In a very real sense she was therefore the world's first programmer.

ANSI then proposed to the International Standards Organization (ISO) that Ada become an ISO standard. This resulted in the establishment of an ISO working group which performed the required activities. Ada became ISO standard 8652 in 1987. During this process (and since) a large number of technical queries were analysed by the so-called Ada Rapporteur Group (ARG). The recommendations resulting from these queries are known as Ada Issues (AIs). An annotated form of *RM83* is available containing the summaries of the AIs[3].

Time and technology do not stand still and accordingly, after several years' use, it was decided that the Ada 83 language standard should be revised in the light of experience and changing requirements. One major change was that Ada was now being used for many areas of application other than the embedded systems for which it was originally designed. Much had also been learnt about new programming paradigms such as Object Oriented Programming.

The DoD, as the agent of ANSI, the original proposers of the standard to ISO, established the Ada 9X project in 1988 under the management of Christine M Anderson. The revision comprised a number of stages: the gathering of requests from the user community, the consolidation of these into a number of requirements, and then the mapping of these requirements into a revised language definition.

The requirements document was published in 1990[4]. It describes 41 specific Requirements plus 22 Study Topics which, as the name implies, cover areas that were not so well understood. The general goal of the revision was thus to satisfy all the Requirements and as many of the Study Topics as possible.

An interesting aspect of the requirements is that they cover a number of specialized application areas. It seemed likely that it would be too costly to implement a language meeting all these requirements in its entirety on every architecture. On the other hand, one of the strengths of Ada is its portability and the last thing wanted was the anarchy of uncontrolled subsets. As a consequence, Ada 95 comprises a Core language plus a small number of specialized Annexes. All compilers have to implement the core language and vendors can choose to implement zero, one or more annexes according to the needs of their markets.

Having established the requirements, the revised language design was contracted to Intermetrics Inc under the technical leadership of S Tucker Taft with continued strong interaction with the user community.

The revised ISO standard was published on 15th February 1995 and so Ada 9X is Ada 95. The first compilers started to emerge in 1993 and it is thus now appropriate to consider the use of Ada 95 as a language in its own right and not just as an evolution of Ada 83.

However, evolution is important and Ada 95 has been designed so that the great majority of Ada 83 programs will behave identically as Ada 95 programs. Indeed the theme of the whole 9X project was 'maximum positive impact' with 'minimum negative impact'. Nevertheless, no language revision has ever been totally upward compatible and indeed Ada 95 could not meet its requirements and be completely compatible. So although this book is primarily about Ada 95 it contains indications of the main differences from Ada 83 so that programmers are guided in the migration of existing Ada 83 programs.

The official definition of Ada 95 is the *Reference Manual for the Ada Programming Language* (*RM95*)[5]. An annotated version of *RM95* containing detailed explanatory information is available as the *AARM*[6]. There is also an accompanying *Rationale* document[7] giving a broad overview of the language and especially the reasons for the changes from Ada 83.

1.2   Software engineering

It should not be thought that Ada is just another programming language. Ada is about Software Engineering, and by analogy with other branches of engineering it can be seen that there are two main problems with the development of software: the need to reuse software components as much as possible and the need to establish disciplined ways of working.

As a language, Ada (and hereafter by Ada we mean Ada 95) largely solves the problem of writing reusable software components (or at least through its excellent ability to prescribe interfaces, provides an enabling technology in which reusable software can be written).

Concerning the establishment of a disciplined way of working, it was realized twenty years ago that the language is just one component, although an important one, of the toolkit that every programmer (and manager) should have available. It was therefore felt that additional benefit would be achieved if a uniform programming environment could also be established. This Holy Grail continues to be sought and has resulted in a number of so-called CASE (Computer Aided Software Engineering) tools and PCTE+ (Portable Common Tools Environment); the latter focuses on the establishment of Public Tool Interfaces which are intended to allow tools to be moved between different environments. However, environments are really another story outside the scope of this book.

Returning to the consideration of Ada as a language, it is now clear after many years' use of Ada 83 that Ada is living up to its promise of providing a language which can reduce the cost of both the initial development of software and its later maintenance. The main advantage of Ada is simply that it is reliable. The strong typing and related features ensure that programs contain few surprises; most errors are detected at compile time and of those that remain many are detected by run-time constraints. This aspect of Ada considerably reduces the costs and risks of program development compared for example with C and its derivatives such as C++. Moreover an Ada compilation system includes the facilities found in separate tools such as lint and make for C. Even if Ada is seen as just another programming language, it reaches parts of the software development process that other languages do not reach.

The essence of Ada 95 is that it adds extra flexibility to the inherent reliability of Ada 83, thereby producing an outstanding language suitable for the development needs of applications that matter well into the next century.

Two kinds of application stand out where Ada is particularly relevant. The very large and the very critical.

Very large applications, which inevitably have a long lifetime, require the cooperative effort of large teams. The information hiding properties of Ada and especially the way in which integrity is maintained across compilation unit boundaries are invaluable in enabling such developments to progress smoothly. Furthermore, if and when the requirements change and the program has to be modified, the structure and especially the readability of Ada enable rapid understanding of the original program even if it is modified by a different team.

Very critical applications are those that just have to be correct otherwise people or the environment get damaged. Obvious examples occur in avionics, railway signalling, process control and medical applications. Such programs may not be large but have to be very well understood and often mathematically proven to be correct. The full flexibility of Ada is not appropriate in this case but the intrinsic reliability of the strongly typed kernel of the language is exactly what is required. Indeed many certification agencies dictate the properties of acceptable languages and whereas they do not always explicitly demand a subset of Ada, nevertheless the properties are not provided by any other practically available language.

Ada is thus very appropriate for many application domains. Ada 95 with its extra facilities and specialized annexes extends the domain further thereby making this professional language applicable to a wider community.

1.3 Evolution and abstraction

The evolution of programming languages has apparently occurred in a rather *ad hoc* fashion but with hindsight it is now possible to see a number of major advances. Each advance seems to be associated with the introduction of a level of abstraction which removes unnecessary and harmful detail from the program.

The first advance occurred in the early 1950s with high level languages such as Fortran and Autocode which introduced 'expression abstraction'. It thus became possible to write statements such as

```
X = A + B(I)
```

so that the use of the machine registers to evaluate the expression was completely hidden from the programmer. In these early languages the expression abstraction was not perfect since there were somewhat arbitrary constraints on the complexity of expressions; subscripts had to take a particularly simple form for instance. Later languages such as Algol 60 removed such constraints and completed the abstraction.

The second advance concerned 'control abstraction'. The prime example was Algol 60 which took a remarkable step forward; no language since then has made such an impact on later developments. The point about control abstraction is that the flow of control is structured and individual control points do not have to be named or numbered. Thus we write

    if X = Y **then** P := Q **else** A := B

and the compiler generates the gotos and labels which would have to be explicitly used in early versions of languages such as Fortran. The imperfection of early expression abstraction was repeated with control abstraction. In this case the obvious flaw was the horrid Algol 60 switch which has now been replaced by the case statement of languages such as Pascal. (The earlier case clause of Algol 68 had its own problems.)

The third advance was 'data abstraction'. This means separating the details of the representation of data from the abstract operations defined upon the data.

Older languages take a very simple view of data types. In all cases the data is directly described in numerical terms. Thus if the data to be manipulated is not really numerical (it could be traffic light colours) then some mapping of the abstract type must be made by the programmer into a numerical type (usually integer). This mapping is purely in the mind of the programmer and does not appear in the written program except perhaps as a comment. It is probably a consequence of this fact that software component libraries have not emerged except in numerical analysis. (Note that although much software is now sold it is at a different level and inevitably comprises whole programs and not components.) Numerical algorithms, such as those for finding eigenvalues of a matrix, are directly concerned with manipulating numbers and so these languages, whose data values are numbers, have proved appropriate. The point is that the languages provide the correct abstract values in this case only. In other cases, libraries are not successful because there is unlikely to be agreement on the required mappings. Indeed different situations may best be served by different mappings and these mappings pervade the whole program. A change in mapping usually requires a complete rewrite of the program.

Pascal introduced a certain amount of data abstraction as instanced by the enumeration type. Enumeration types allow us to talk about the traffic light colours in their own terms without our having to know how they are represented in the computer. Moreover, they prevent us from making an important class of programming errors – accidentally mixing traffic lights with other abstract types such as the names of fish. When all such types are described in the program as numerical types, such errors can occur.

Another form of data abstraction concerns visibility. It has long been recognized that the traditional block structure of Algol and Pascal is not adequate. For example, it is not possible in Pascal to write two procedures to operate on some common data and make the procedures accessible without also making the data directly accessible. Many languages have provided control of visibility through separate compilation; this technique is adequate for medium-sized systems, but since the separate compilation facility usually depends upon some external system, total control of visibility is not gained. The module of Modula is an example of an appropriate construction.

Ada was probably the first practical language to bring together these various forms of data abstraction.

Another language which made an important contribution to the development of data abstraction is Simula 67 with its concept of class. This leads us into the paradigm now known as Object Oriented Programming which is currently in vogue. There seems to be no precise definition of OOP, but its essence is a flexible form of data abstraction providing the ability to define new data abstractions in terms of old ones and allowing dynamic selection of types.

All types in Ada 83 are static and thus Ada 83 is not classed as a truly Object Oriented language but as an Object Based language. However, Ada 95 includes the essential functionality associated with OOP such as polymorphism and type extension.

We are, as ever, probably too close to the current scene to achieve a proper perspective. Data abstraction in Ada 83 seems to have been not quite perfect, just as Fortran expression abstraction and Algol 60 control abstraction were imperfect in their day. It remains to be seen just how well Ada 95 provides what we might call 'object abstraction'. Indeed it might well be that inheritance and other aspects of OOP turn out to be unsatisfactory by obscuring the details of types although not hiding them completely; this could be argued to be an abstraction leak making the problems of program maintenance even harder.

A brief survey of how Ada relates to other languages would not be complete without mention of C and C++. These have a completely different evolutionary trail to the classic Algol–Pascal–Ada route.

The origin of C can be traced back to the CPL language devised by Strachey, Barron and others in the early 1960s. This was intended to be used on major new hardware at Cambridge and London universities but proved hard to implement. From it emerged the simple system programming language BCPL and from that B and then C. The essence of BCPL was the array and pointer model which abandoned any hope of strong typing and (with hindsight) a proper mathematical model of the mapping of the program onto a computing engine. Even the use of := for assignment was lost in this evolution which reverted to the confusing use of = as in Fortran. About the only feature of the elegant CPL remaining in C is the unfortunate braces {} and the associated compound statement structure which has now been abandoned by all other languages in favour of the more reliable bracketed form originally proposed by Algol 68.

Of course there is a need for a low level systems language with functionality like C. It is, however, unfortunate that the interesting structural ideas in C++ have been grafted onto the fragile C foundation. As a consequence although C++ has many important capabilities for data abstraction, including inheritance and polymorphism, it is all too easy to break these abstractions and create programs that violently misbehave or are exceedingly hard to understand and maintain.

The designers of Ada 95 have striven to incorporate the positive dynamic facilities of the kind found in C++ onto the firm foundation provided by Ada 83.

Ada 95 is thus an important advance along the evolution of abstraction. It incorporates full object abstraction in a way that is highly reliable without incurring excessive run-time costs.

1.4   From Ada 83 to Ada 95

In this section (and especially for the benefit of those familiar with Ada 83), we briefly survey the main changes from Ada 83 to Ada 95. As we said above, one of the great strengths of Ada 83 is its reliability. The strong typing ensures that most errors are detected at compile time while many of those remaining are detected by various checks at run time. Moreover, the compile-time checking extends across compilation unit boundaries. This reliability aspect of Ada considerably reduces the costs and risks of program development (especially for large programs) compared with weaker languages which do not have such a rigorous type model.

However, after a number of years' experience it became clear that some improvements were necessary in order to completely satisfy the present and the future needs of users from a whole variety of application areas. Four main areas were perceived as needing attention.

*   Object oriented programming.   Recent experience with other languages has shown the benefits of the object oriented paradigm. This gives much flexibility and, in particular, it enables a program to be extended without editing or recompiling existing and tested parts of it.

*   Program libraries.   The library mechanism is one of Ada's great strengths. Nevertheless the flat structure in Ada 83 is a hindrance to fine visibility control and to program extension without recompilation.

*   Interfacing.   Although Ada 83 does have facilities to enable it to interface to external systems written in other languages, these have not proved as flexible as they might. For example, it has proved particularly awkward to program call-back mechanisms which are very useful especially when using Graphical User Interfaces.

*   Tasking.   The Ada 83 rendezvous model provides an advanced description of many paradigms. However, it has not proved entirely appropriate for shared data problems where a static monitor like approach brings performance benefits. Furthermore, Ada 83 has a rather rigid approach to priorities and it is not easy to take advantage of recent deeper understanding of scheduling theory which has emerged since Ada was first designed.

The first three topics are really all about flexibility and so a prime goal of the design of Ada 95 has been to give the language a more open and extensible feel without losing the inherent integrity and efficiency of Ada 83. That is to keep the Software Engineering but allow more flexibility.

As we shall see, the additions to Ada 95 which contribute to this more flexible feel are the extended or tagged types, the hierarchical library and the greater ability to manipulate pointers or references. The tagged types and hierarchical library together provide very powerful tools for programming by extension.

As a consequence, Ada 95 incorporates the benefits of object oriented languages without incurring the pervasive overheads of languages such as Smalltalk or the insecurity brought by the weak C foundation in the case of C++. Ada 95 remains a very strongly typed language but provides the prime benefits of all key aspects of the object oriented paradigm.

In the case of the tasking model, the introduction of protected types allows a more efficient implementation of standard paradigms of shared data access. This brings the benefits of speed provided by low level primitives such as semaphores without the risks incurred by the use of such unstructured primitives. Moreover, the clearly data-oriented view brought by the protected types fits in naturally with the general spirit of the object oriented paradigm. Other improvements to the tasking model allow a more flexible response to interrupts and other changes of state.

Another area which sees considerable change is that of generics. These are largely consequences of changes to the type model but nevertheless deserve special mention because generics are one of the key facilities of Ada 83 which promote reuse.

Ada 95 also incorporates numerous other minor improvements reflecting feedback from the use of existing features. Finally there are a number of specific new features addressing the needs of specialized applications and communities.

1.5 Structure and objectives of this book

Learning a programming language is a bit like learning to drive a car. Certain key things have to be learnt before any real progress is possible. Although we need not know how to use the windscreen washer, nevertheless we must at least be able to start the engine, engage gears, steer and brake. So it is with programming languages. We do not need to know all about Ada before we can write useful programs but quite a lot must be learnt. Moreover many virtues of Ada become apparent only when writing large programs just as many virtues of a Rolls-Royce are not apparent if we only use it to drive to the local shop.

This book is not an introduction to programming but an overall description of programming in Ada. It is assumed that the reader will have significant experience of programming in some high level language. A knowledge of Pascal would be helpful but is certainly not necessary. A knowledge of C is probably an equally good background.

It should also be noted that this book strives to remain neutral regarding methods of program design and should therefore prove useful whatever techniques are used. However, certain features of Ada naturally align themselves with different design concepts such as Functional Decomposition (based on control flow) and Object Oriented Design (based on data abstraction) and will be mentioned as appropriate.

This book is primarily about programming in Ada 95, but in order to aid transition from Ada 83 most chapters contain a summary of where Ada 95 differs from Ada 83 in the area concerned.

This book is in four main parts. The first part, Chapters 1 to 4, is an extensive overview of most of the language and covers enough material to enable a wide variety of programs to be written; it also lays the foundation for understanding the rest of the material. The second part, Chapters 5 to 10, covers in detail the traditional algorithmic parts of the language and roughly corresponds to Pascal or C. The third part, Chapters 11 to 19, covers modern and exciting material associated with data abstraction, programming in the large, OOP and parallel processing.

Finally, the fourth part, Chapters 20 to 23, completes the story by discussing the predefined environment, interfacing to the outside world and the specialized annexes; the concluding chapter also pulls together a number of threads that are slightly dispersed in the earlier chapters.

Most sections contain exercises. It is important that the reader does most, if not all, of these since they are an integral part of the discussion and later sections often use the results of earlier exercises. Solutions to all the exercises will be found at the end of the book.

Most chapters conclude with a short checklist of key points to be remembered. Although incomplete, these checklists should help to consolidate understanding. Furthermore, the reader is encouraged to refer to the syntax in Appendix 3 which is organized to correspond to the order in which the topics are introduced.

This book covers all aspects of Ada but does not explore every pathological situation. Its purpose is to teach the reader the effect of and intended use of the features of Ada. In three areas the discussion is incomplete; these are system dependent programming, input–output, and the specialized annexes. System dependent programming (as its name implies) is so dependent upon the particular implementation that only a brief overview seems appropriate. Input–output, although important, does not introduce new concepts but is rather a mass of detail; again a simple overview is presented. And, as their name implies, the specialized annexes address the very specific needs of certain communities; to cover them in detail would make this book excessively long and so only an overview is provided. Further details of these areas can be found in the *Ada Reference Manual* (the *ARM* or *RM95*)[5] which is referred to from time to time.

Various appendices are provided in order to make this book reasonably self-contained; they are mostly based upon material drawn from the *ARM*. Access to the *ARM* is recommended but should not be absolutely essential.

1.6 References

1 United States Department of Defense. *Reference Manual for the Ada Programming Language* (ANSI/MIL-STD-1815A). Washington DC, 1983.
2 Defense Advanced Research Projects Agency. *Department of Defense Requirements for High Order Computer Programming Languages – 'STEELMAN'*. Arlington, Virginia, 1978.
3 Karl A Nyberg, ed. *The Annotated Ada Reference Manual*. 3rd edn. Grebyn Corporation, 1994.
4 Office of the Under Secretary of Defense for Acquisition. *Ada 9X Requirements*. Washington DC, 1990.
5 International Organization for Standardization. *Information technology – Programming languages – Ada. Ada Reference Manual*. ISO/IEC 8652:1995(E).
6 *Annotated Ada 95 Reference Manual, Version 6.0*. Intermetrics Inc, 1995.
7 *Ada 95 Rationale*. Intermetrics Inc, 1995.

2 Simple Concepts

This is the first of three chapters covering in outline the main goals, concepts and features of Ada. Enough material is given in these chapters to enable the reader to write significant programs. It also allows the reader to create a framework in which the exercises and other fragments of program can be executed, if desired, before all the required topics are discussed in depth.

The material covered in this chapter corresponds approximately to that in simple languages such as Pascal and C.

2.1 Key goals

Ada is a large language since it addresses many important issues relevant to the programming of practical systems in the real world. It is, for instance, much larger than Pascal, which, unless extended in some way, is really only suitable for training purposes (for which it was designed) and for small personal programs. Ada is similarly much larger than C although perhaps of the same order of size as C++. But a big difference is the stress which Ada places on integrity and readability. Some of the key issues in Ada are

- Readability – it is recognized that professional programs are read much more often than they are written. It is important therefore to avoid an over terse notation such as in APL which, although allowing a program to be written down quickly, makes it almost impossible to be read except perhaps by the original author soon after it was written.

- Strong typing – this ensures that each object has a clearly defined set of values and prevents confusion between logically distinct concepts. As a consequence many errors are detected by the compiler which in other languages (such as C) would have led to an executable but incorrect program.

- Programming in the large – mechanisms for encapsulation, separate compilation and library management are necessary for the writing of portable and maintainable programs of any size.

- Exception handling – it is a fact of life that programs of consequence are rarely perfect. It is necessary to provide a means whereby a program can be constructed in a layered and partitioned way so that the consequences of unanticipated events in one part can be contained.

- Data abstraction – as mentioned earlier, extra portability and maintainability can be obtained if the details of the representation of data can be kept separate from the specifications of the logical operations on the data.

- Object oriented programming – in order to promote the reuse of tested code, the type flexibility associated with OOP is important. Type extension (inheritance), polymorphism and late binding are all desirable especially if achieved without loss of type integrity.

- Tasking – for many applications it is important that the program be conceived as a series of parallel activities rather than just as a single sequence of actions. Building appropriate facilities into a language rather than adding them via calls to an operating system gives better portability and reliability.

- Generic units – in many cases the logic of part of a program is independent of the types of the values being manipulated. A mechanism is therefore necessary for the creation of related pieces of program from a single template. This is particularly useful for the creation of libraries.

- Interfacing – programs do not live in isolation and it is important to be able to communicate with systems possibly written in other languages.

An overall theme in the design of Ada was concern for the programming process. Programming is a human activity and a language should be designed to be helpful. An important aspect of this is enabling errors to be detected early in the overall process. For example, care has been taken that wherever possible a single typographical error results in a program that does not compile rather than a program that still compiles but does the wrong thing. Examples are the distinct use of := for assignment as opposed to = for equality and the control structures with distinct closing brackets; the accidental omission of a colon or semicolon is then detected by the compiler rather than producing a program that does the wrong thing as so often happens with C.

2.2   **Overall structure**

One of the most important objectives of Software Engineering is to reuse existing pieces of program so that the effort of detailed new coding is kept to a minimum. The concept of a library of program components naturally emerges and an important aspect of a programming language is therefore its ability to express how to use the items in a library.

Ada recognizes this situation and introduces the concept of library units. A complete Ada program is conceived as a main subprogram (itself a library unit) which calls upon the services of other library units. These library units can be thought of as forming the outermost lexical layer of the total program.

The main subprogram takes the form of a procedure of an appropriate name. The service library units can be subprograms (procedures or functions) but they are more likely to be packages. A package is a group of related items such as subprograms but may contain other entities as well.

Suppose we wish to write a program to print out the square root of some number such as 2.5. We can expect various library units to be available to provide us with a means of computing square roots and producing output. Our job is merely to write a main subprogram to use these services as we wish.

For the sake of argument we will suppose that the square root can be obtained by calling a function in our library whose name is Sqrt. In addition we will suppose that our library includes a package called Simple_IO containing various simple input–output facilities. These facilities might include procedures for reading numbers, printing numbers, printing strings of characters and so on.

Our program might look like

```
with Sqrt, Simple_IO;
procedure Print_Root is
   use Simple_IO;
begin
   Put(Sqrt(2.5));
end Print_Root;
```

The program is written as a procedure called Print_Root preceded by a with clause giving the names of the library units which it wishes to use. The body of the procedure contains the single statement

```
Put(Sqrt(2.5));
```

which calls the procedure Put in the package Simple_IO with a parameter which in turn is the result of calling the function Sqrt with the parameter 2.5.
Writing

```
use Simple_IO;
```

gives us immediate access to the facilities in the package Simple_IO. If we had omitted this use clause we would have had to write

```
Simple_IO.Put(Sqrt(2.5));
```

in order to indicate where Put was to be found.

We can make our program more useful by making it read in the number whose square root we require. It might then become

```
with Sqrt, Simple_IO;
procedure Print_Root is
   use Simple_IO;
   X: Float;
begin
   Get(X);
   Put(Sqrt(X));
end Print_Root;
```

The overall structure of the procedure is now clearer. Between **is** and **begin** we can write declarations, and between **begin** and **end** we write statements. Broadly speaking, declarations introduce the entities we wish to manipulate and statements indicate the sequential actions to be performed.

We have now introduced a variable X of type Float which is a predefined language type. Values of this type are a set of certain floating point numbers and the declaration of X indicates that X can have values only from this set. In our example a value is assigned to X by calling the procedure Get which is also in our package Simple_IO.

Some small-scale details should be noted. The various statements and declarations all terminate with a semicolon; this is unlike some other languages such as Algol and Pascal where semicolons are separators rather than terminators. The program contains various identifiers such as **procedure**, Put and X. These fall into two categories. A few (69 in fact) such as **procedure** and **is** are used to indicate the structure of the program; they are reserved and can be used for no other purpose. All others, such as Put and X, can be used for whatever purpose we desire. Some of these, notably Float in our example, have a predefined meaning but we can nevertheless reuse them if we so wish although it might be confusing to do so. For clarity in this book we write the reserved words in lower case bold and capitalize the others. This is purely a notational convenience; the language rules do not distinguish the two cases except when we consider the manipulation of characters themselves. Note also how the underline character is used to break up long identifiers into meaningful parts.

Finally, observe that the name of the procedure, Print_Root, is repeated between the final **end** and the terminating semicolon. This is optional but is recommended so as to clarify the overall structure although this is obvious in a small example such as this.

Our program is still very simple; it might be more useful to enable it to cater for a whole series of numbers and print out each answer on a separate line. We could stop the program somewhat arbitrarily by giving it a value of zero.

```
with Sqrt, Simple_IO;
procedure Print_Roots is
   use Simple_IO;
   X: Float;
begin
   Put("Roots of various numbers");
   New_Line(2);
   loop
      Get(X);
      exit when X = 0.0;
      Put(" Root of ");
      Put(X);
      Put(" is ");
      if X < 0.0 then
         Put("not calculable");
      else
         Put(Sqrt(X));
      end if;
      New_Line;
   end loop;
   New_Line;
   Put("Program finished");
   New_Line;
end Print_Roots;
```

The output has been enhanced by the calls of further procedures New_Line and Put in the package Simple_IO. A call of New_Line will output the number of new lines specified by the parameter (which is of the predefined type Integer); the procedure New_Line has been written in such a way that if no parameter is supplied then a default value of one is assumed. There are also calls of Put with a string as argument. This is in fact a different procedure from the one that prints the number X. The compiler knows which is which because of the different types of parameters. Having more than one procedure with the same name is known as overloading. Note also the form of the string; this is a situation where the case of the letters does matter.

Various new control structures are also introduced. The statements between **loop** and **end loop** are repeated until the condition X = 0.0 in the **exit** statement is found to be true; when this is so the loop is finished and we immediately carry on after **end loop**. We also check that X is not negative; if it is we output the message 'not calculable' rather than attempting to call Sqrt. This is done by the if statement; if the condition between **if** and **then** is true, then the statements between **then** and **else** are executed, otherwise those between **else** and **end if** are executed.

The general bracketing structure should be observed; **loop** is matched by **end loop** and **if** by **end if**. All the control structures of Ada have this closed form rather than the open form of Pascal and C which can lead to poorly structured and incorrect programs. .

We will now consider in outline the possible general form of the function Sqrt and the package Simple_IO that we have been using.

The function Sqrt will have a structure similar to that of our main subprogram; the major difference will be the existence of parameters.

```
function Sqrt(F: Float) return Float is
   R: Float;
begin
   -- compute value of Sqrt(F) in R
   return R;
end Sqrt;
```

We see here the description of the formal parameters (in this case only one) and the type of the result. The details of the calculation are represented by the comment which starts with a double hyphen. The return statement is the means by which the result of the function is indicated. Note the distinction between a function which returns a result and is called as part of an expression, and a procedure which does not have a result and is called as a single statement.

The package Simple_IO will be in two parts: the specification which describes its interface to the outside world, and the body which contains the details of how it is implemented. If it just contained the procedures that we have used, its specification might be

```
package Simple_IO is
   procedure Get(F: out Float);
   procedure Put(F: in Float);
   procedure Put(S: in String);
   procedure New_Line(N: in Integer := 1);
end Simple_IO;
```

The parameter of Get is an **out** parameter because the effect of calling Get as in

```
Get(X);
```

is to transmit a value out from the procedure to the actual parameter X. The other parameters are all **in** parameters because the value goes in to the procedures.

Only a part of the procedures occurs in the package specification; this part is known as the procedure specification and just gives enough information to enable the procedures to be called.

We see also the two overloaded specifications of Put, one with a parameter of type Float and the other with a parameter of type String. Finally, note how the default value of 1 for the parameter of New_Line is indicated.

The package body for Simple_IO will contain the full procedure bodies plus any other supporting material needed for their implementation and is naturally hidden from the outside user. In vague outline it might look like

```
with Ada.Text_IO;
package body Simple_IO is
   ...
```

```
        procedure Get(F: out Float) is
           ...
        begin
           ...
        end Get;
        -- other procedures similarly
     end Simple_IO;
```

The with clause shows that the implementation of the procedures in
Simple_IO uses the more general package Ada.Text_IO. The notation indicates
that Text_IO is a *child* package of the package Ada. It should also be noticed
how the full body of Get repeats the procedure specification which was given
in the corresponding package specification. (The procedure specification is the
bit up to but not including **is**.) Note that the package Text_IO really exists
whereas Simple_IO is a figment of our imagination made up for the purpose of
our example. We will say more about Text_IO in Chapter 4.

The example in this section has briefly revealed some of the overall
structure and control statements of Ada. One purpose of this section has been
to stress that the idea of packages is one of the most important concepts in Ada.
A program should be conceived as a number of components which provide
services to and receive services from each other.

Perhaps this is an appropriate point to mention the special package
Standard. This is a package which exists in every implementation and contains
the declarations of all the predefined identifiers such as Float and Integer. We
can assume access to Standard automatically and do not have to give its name
in a with clause. It is discussed in detail in Chapter 20.

EXERCISE 2.2

1   In practice it is likely that the function Sqrt will not be in the library on its own but
    in a package along with other mathematical functions. Suppose this package has the
    identifier Simple_Maths and other functions are Log, Ln, Exp, Sin and Cos. By
    analogy with the specification of Simple_IO, write the specification of such a
    package. How would our program Print_Roots need to be changed?

2.3   Errors and exceptions

We introduce this topic by considering what would have happened in the
example in the previous section if we had not tested for a negative value of X
and consequently called Sqrt with a negative argument. Assuming that Sqrt has
itself been written in an appropriate manner then it clearly cannot deliver a
value to be used as the parameter of Put. Instead an exception will be raised.

The raising of an exception indicates that something unusual has happened and the normal sequence of execution is broken. In our case the exception might be Constraint_Error which is a predefined exception declared in the package Standard. If we did nothing to cope with this possibility then our program would be terminated and no doubt the Ada Run Time System will give us a rude message saying that our program has failed and why. We can, however, look out for an exception and take remedial action if it occurs. In fact we could replace the conditional statement

```
if X < 0.0 then
   Put("not calculable");
else
   Put(Sqrt(X));
end if;
```

by

```
begin
   Put(Sqrt(X));
exception
   when Constraint_Error =>
      Put("not calculable");
end;
```

This fragment of program is an example of a block. If an exception is raised by the sequence of statements between **begin** and **exception**, then control immediately passes to the one or more statements following the handler for that exception and these are obeyed instead. If there were no handler for the exception (it might be another exception such as Storage_Error) then control passes up the flow hierarchy until we come to an appropriate handler or fall out of the main subprogram, which then becomes terminated as we mentioned with a rude message from the Run Time System.

The above example is not a good illustration of the use of exceptions since the event we are guarding against can easily be tested for directly. Nevertheless it does show the general idea of how we can look out for unexpected events and leads us into a brief consideration of errors in general.

There are two underlying causes of errors in software as perceived externally: an incorrect software specification in which a possible sequence of external events has not been taken into consideration, and an incorrect implementation of the software specification itself. The first type of error can be allowed for to some extent by exception handlers. The second type leads to an incorrect Ada program.

From the linguistic viewpoint, an Ada program may be incorrect for various reasons. There are four categories according to how they are detected.

- Many errors are detected by the compiler – these include simple punctuation mistakes such as leaving out a semicolon or attempting to violate the type rules such as mixing up colours and fish. In these cases the program is said to be illegal and will not be executed.

- Other errors are detected when the program is executed. An attempt to find the square root of a negative number or divide by zero are examples of such errors. In these cases an exception is raised as we have just seen and we have an opportunity to recover from the situation.

- There are also certain situations where the program breaks the language rules but there is no simple way in which this violation can be detected. For example a program should not use a variable before a value is assigned to it. In cases like this the behaviour is not predictable but will nevertheless lie within certain bounds. Such errors are called bounded errors.

- In more extreme situations there are some kinds of errors which can lead to quite unpredictable behaviour. In these (quite rare) cases we say that the behaviour is erroneous.

Finally there are situations where, for implementation reasons, the language does not prescribe the order in which things are to be done. For example the order in which the parameters of a procedure call are evaluated is not specified. If the behaviour of a program does depend on such an order then it is not considered to be incorrect but just not portable.

Care must be taken to avoid writing programs whose behaviour is not predictable. In practice if we avoid clever tricks then all will usually be well.

2.4   The scalar type model

We have said that one of the key benefits of Ada is its strong typing. This is well illustrated by the enumeration type. Consider

```
declare
   type Colour is (Red, Amber, Green);
   type Fish is (Cod, Hake, Plaice);
   X, Y: Colour;
   A, B: Fish;
begin
   X := Red;              -- ok
   A := Hake;             -- ok
   B := X;                -- illegal
   ...
end;
```

Here we have a block which declares two enumeration types Colour and Fish, and two variables of each type, and then performs various assignments. The declarations of the types gives the allowed values of the types. Thus the variable X can only take one of the three values Red, Amber or Green. The fundamental rule of strong typing is that we cannot assign a value of one type to a variable of a different type. So we cannot mix up colours and fish and thus our (presumably accidental) attempt to assign the value of X to B is illegal and will be detected during compilation.

There are three enumeration types predefined in the package Standard. One is

type Boolean **is** (False, True);

which plays a fundamental role in control flow. Thus the predefined relational operators such as < produce a result of this type and such a value follows **if** as we saw in the construction

if X < 0.0 **then**

in the example of Section 2.2. The other predefined enumeration types are Character and Wide_Character. The values of these types are the 8-bit ISO Latin-1 characters and the 16-bit ISO Basic Multilingual Plane characters; these types naturally play an important role in input–output. The literal values of these types include the printable characters and these are represented by placing them in single quotes thus 'X' or 'a' or indeed '''.

The other fundamental types are the numeric types. One way or another, all other data types are built out of enumeration types and numeric types. The two major classes of numeric types are the integer types and floating point types (there are also fixed point types which are rather obscure and deserve no further mention in this brief overview). The integer types in fact are subdivided into signed integer types (such as Integer) and unsigned or modular types. All implementations will have the types Integer and Float used in Section 2.2. In addition, if the architecture is appropriate, an implementation may have other predefined numeric types, Long_Integer, Long_Float, Short_Float and so on. There will also be specific integer types for an implementation depending upon the supported word lengths such as Integer_16 and corresponding unsigned types such as Unsigned_16.

One of the problems of numeric types is how to obtain both portability and efficiency in the face of variation in machine architecture. In order to explain how this is done in Ada it is convenient to introduce the concept of a derived type. (We will deal with derived types in more detail in the next chapter when we come to object oriented programming.)

The simplest form of derived type introduces a new type which is almost identical to an existing type except that it is logically distinct. If we write

type Light **is new** Colour;

then Light will, like Colour, be an enumeration type with literals Red, Amber and Green. However, values of the two types cannot be arbitrarily mixed since they are logically distinct. Nevertheless, in recognition of the close relationship, a value of one type can be converted to the other by explicitly using the destination type name. So we can write

declare
   type Light **is new** Colour;
   C: Colour;
   L: Light;
begin

```
        L := Amber;              -- the light amber, not the colour
        C := Colour(L);          -- explicit conversion
        ...
    end;
```

whereas a direct assignment

```
        C := L;                  -- illegal
```

would violate the strong typing rule and this violation would be detected
during compilation.

Returning now to our numeric types, if we write

type My_Float **is new** Float;

then My_Float will have all the operations (+, – etc.) of Float and in general can
be considered as equivalent. Now suppose we transfer the program to a
different computer on which the predefined type Float is not so accurate and
that Long_Float is necessary. Assuming that the program has been written
using My_Float rather than Float then replacing the declaration of My_Float by

type My_Float **is new** Long_Float;

is the only change necessary. We can actually do better than this by directly
stating the precision that we require, thus

type My_Float **is digits** 7;

will cause My_Float to be based on the smallest predefined type with at least 7
decimal digits of accuracy.

A similar approach is possible with integer types so that rather than using
the predefined types Integer or Long_Integer we can give the range of values
required thus

type My_Integer **is range** –1000_000 .. +1000_000;

The point of all this is that it is not good practice to use the predefined
numeric types directly when writing professional programs which may need to
be portable. However, for simplicity, we will generally use the types Integer
and Float in examples in most of this book. We will say no more about numeric
types for the moment except that all the expected operations apply to all integer
and floating types.

EXERCISE 2.4

1   Declare a type Month_Name suitable for manipulating months.

2.5 Arrays and records

Ada naturally enables the creation of composite array and record types. Arrays may actually be declared without giving a name to the underlying type (the type is then said to be anonymous) but records always have a type name.

As an example of the use of arrays suppose we wish to compute the successive rows of Pascal's triangle. This is usually represented as shown in Figure 2.1. The reader will recall that the rows are the coefficients in the expansion of $(1 + x)^n$ and that a neat way of computing the values is to note that each one is the sum of the two diagonal neighbours in the row above.

Suppose that we are interested in the first ten rows. We could declare an array to hold such a row by

```
Pascal: array (0 .. 10) of Integer;
```

and now assuming that the current values of the array Pascal correspond to row $n-1$, with the component Pascal(0) being 1 then the next row could be computed in a similar array Next by

```
Next(0) := 1;
for I in 1 .. N-1 loop
   Next(I) := Pascal(I-1) + Pascal(I);
end loop;
Next(N) := 1;
```

and then the array Next could be copied into the array Pascal.

This illustrates another form of loop statement where a controlled variable I takes successive values from a range; the variable is automatically declared to be of the type of the range which in this case is Integer. Note that the intermediate array Next could be avoided by iterating backwards over the array; we indicate this by writing **reverse** in front of the range thus

```
Pascal(N) := 1;
for I in reverse 1 .. N-1 loop
   Pascal(I) := Pascal(I-1) + Pascal(I);
end loop;
```

We can also declare arrays of several dimensions. So if we wanted to keep all the rows of the triangle we might declare

```
Pascal2: array (0 .. 10, 0 .. 10) of Integer;
```

and then the loop for computing row n would be

```
Pascal2(N, 0) := 1;
for I in 1 .. N-1 loop
   Pascal2(N, I) := Pascal2(N-1, I-1) + Pascal2(N-1, I);
end loop;
Pascal2(N, N) := 1;
```

```
                    1
                  1   1
                1   2   1
              1   3   3   1
            1   4   6   4   1
          1   5  10  10   5   1
```

Figure 2.1   Pascal's triangle.

We have declared our arrays without giving a name to their type. We could alternatively have written

> **type** Row **is array** (0 .. Size) **of** Integer;
> Pascal, Next: Row;

where we have given the name Row to the type and then declared the two arrays Pascal and Next. There are advantages to this approach as we will see later. Incidentally the bounds of an array do not have to be constant, they could be any computed values such as the value of some variable Size.

We conclude this brief discussion of arrays by observing that the type String which we encountered in Section 2.2 is in fact an array whose components are of the enumeration type Character. Its declaration (in the package Standard) is

> **type** String **is array** (Positive **range** <>) **of** Character;

and this illustrates a form of type declaration which is said to be indefinite because it does not give the bounds of the array; these have to be supplied when an object is declared

> Buffer: String(1 .. 80);

Incidentally the identifier Positive in the declaration of the type String denotes what is known as a subtype of Integer; values of the subtype Positive are the positive integers and so the bounds of all arrays of type String must also be positive – the lower bound is of course typically 1 but need not be.

A record is an object comprising a number of named components typically of different types. We always have to give a name to a record type. If we were manipulating a number of buffers then it would be convenient to declare a record type containing the buffer and an indication of the start and finish of that part of the buffer actually containing useful data.

> **type** Buffer **is**
>   **record**
>   Data: String(1 .. 80);
>   Start, Finish: Integer;
>   **end record**;

An individual buffer could then be declared by

My_Buffer: Buffer;

and the components of the buffer can then be manipulated using a dotted notation to select the individual components

My_Buffer.Start := 1;
My_Buffer.Finish := 3;
My_Buffer.Data(1 .. 3) := "XYZ";

Note that this assigns values to the first three components of the array using a so-called slice.

Whole array and record values can be created using aggregates which are simply a set of values in brackets separated by commas.

Thus we could assign appropriate values to Pascal and to Buffer by

Pascal(0 .. 4) := (1, 4, 6, 4, 1);
Buffer := (('X', 'Y', 'Z', others => ' '), 1, 3);

where in the latter case we have in fact assigned all 80 values to the array Buffer.Data and used **others** to indicate that after the three useful characters the remainder of the array is padded with spaces. Note also the nesting of brackets.

This concludes our brief discussion on simple arrays and records. In the next chapter we will show how record types can be extended.

EXERCISE 2.5

1   Write statements to copy the array Next into the array Pascal.

2   Write a nested loop to compute all the rows of Pascal's triangle in the two-dimensional array Pascal2.

3   Using the type Month_Name from Exercise 2.4(**1**) declare a type Date with components giving the day, month and year. Then declare a variable Today and assign Queen Victoria's date of birth to it (or your own).

2.6 Access types

The last section showed how the scalar types (numeric and enumeration types) may be composed into arrays and records. The other vital means for creating structures is through the use of access types (the Ada name for pointer types); access types allow list processing and are typically used with record types.

The explicit manipulation of pointers or references has been an important feature of most languages since Algol 68. References rather dominated Algol

68 and caused problems and the corresponding pointer facility in Pascal is rather austere. The pointer facility in C on the other hand provides raw flexibility which is open to abuse and quite insecure and thus the cause of many wrong programs.

Ada provides both a high degree of reliability and considerable flexibility through access types. A full description will be found in Chapter 10 but the following brief description will be useful for discussing polymorphism in the next chapter.

Ada access types must explicitly indicate the type of data to which they refer. The most general form of access types can refer to any data of the type concerned but we will restrict ourselves in this overview to those which just refer to data declared in a storage pool (the Ada term for a heap).

For example suppose we wanted to declare various buffers of the type in the previous section. We might write

```
type Buffer_Ptr is access Buffer;
Handle: Buffer_Ptr;
...
Handle := new Buffer;
```

This allocates a buffer in the storage pool and sets a reference to it into the variable Handle. We can then refer to the various components of the buffer indirectly using the variable Handle

```
Handle.Start := 1;
Handle.Finish := 3;
```

and we can refer to the complete record as Handle.**all**. Note that Handle.Start is strictly an abbreviation for Handle.**all**.Start.

Access types are of particular value for list processing where one record structure contains an access value to another record structure. The classic example which we will encounter in many forms is typified by

```
type Cell;
type Cell_Ptr is access Cell;

type Cell is
   record
      Value: Data;
      Next: Cell_Ptr;
   end record;
```

The type Cell is a record containing a component of some type Data plus a component Next which can refer to another similar record. Note the partial declaration of the type Cell. This is required in the declaration of the type Cell_Ptr because of the inherent nature of the circularity of the declarations. An example of the use of this sort of construction will be found in the next chapter.

Access types can be used to refer to any type although records are common. Access types may also be used to refer to subprograms and this is particularly important when communicating with programs in other languages.

2.7 Terminology

We conclude this first introductory chapter with a few remarks on terminology. Every subject has its own terminology or jargon and Ada is no exception. (Indeed in Ada an exception is a kind of error as we have seen!) A brief glossary of terms will be found in Appendix 2.

Terminology will generally be introduced as required but before starting off with the detailed description of Ada it is convenient to mention a few concepts which will occur from time to time.

The term *static* refers to things that can be determined at compilation, whereas *dynamic* refers to things determined during execution. Thus a static expression is one whose value can be determined by the compiler such as

    2 + 3

and a statically constrained array is one whose bounds are known during compilation.

The term *real* comes up from time to time in the context of numeric types. The floating point types and fixed point types are collectively known as real types. (Fixed point types are rather specialized and not discussed until Chapter 15.) Literals such as 2.5 are known as real literals since they can be used to denote values of both floating and fixed point types. Other uses of the term real will occur in due course.

Sometimes it is necessary to make a parenthetic remark to the compiler where the remark is often not a part of the program as such but more a useful hint. This can be done by means of a construction known as a *pragma*. As an example we can indicate that we wish the compiler to optimize our program with emphasis on saving space by writing

    pragma Optimize(Space);

inside the region of program to which it is to apply. Alternatively we could write

    pragma Optimize(Time);

which indicates that speed of execution is the primary criterion. Or even

    pragma Optimize(Off);

to indicate that optional optimization should be turned off.

Generally a pragma can appear anywhere that a declaration or statement can appear and in some other contexts also. Sometimes there may be special rules regarding the position of a particular pragma. For fuller details on pragmas see Appendix 1.

Object oriented programming has its own rather specialized terminology and a section is devoted to this in the next chapter.

3 Abstraction

As mentioned in Chapter 1, abstraction in various forms seems to be the key to the development of programming languages. In this chapter we survey various aspects of abstraction with particular emphasis on the object oriented paradigm.

3.1 Packages and private types

In the last chapter we declared a type for the manipulation of a buffer

```
type Buffer is
   record
      Data: String(1 .. 80);
      Start: Integer;
      Finish: Integer;
   end record;
```

in which the component Data actually holds the characters in the buffer and Start and Finish index the ends of the part of the buffer containing useful information. We also saw how the various components might be updated and read using normal assignment.

However, such direct assignment is often unwise since the user could inadvertently set inconsistent values into the components or read nonsense

29

components of the array. A much better approach is to create an Abstract Data Type (ADT) so that the user cannot see the internal details of the type but can only access it through various subprogram calls which define an appropriate protocol.

This can be done using a package containing a private type. Let us suppose that the protocol allows us to reload the buffer (possibly not completely full) and to read one character at a time. Consider the following

```
package Buffer_System is                      -- visible part

   type Buffer is private;

   procedure Load(B: out Buffer; S: in String);
   procedure Get(B: in out Buffer; C: out Character);

private                                        -- private part
   Max: constant Integer := 80;
   type Buffer is
      record
         Data: String(1 .. Max);
         Start: Integer := 1;
         Finish: Integer := 0;
      end record;

end Buffer_System;

package body Buffer_System is

   procedure Load(B: out Buffer; S: in String) is
   begin
      B.Start := 1;
      B.Finish := S'Length;
      B.Data(B.Start .. B.Finish) := S;
   end Load;

   procedure Get(B: in out Buffer; C: out Character) is
   begin
      C := B.Data(B.Start);
      B.Start := B.Start + 1;
   end Get;

end Buffer_System;
```

With this formulation the client can only access the information in the visible part of the specification which is the bit before the word **private**. In this visible part the declaration of the type Buffer merely says that it is private and the full declaration then occurs in the private part. There are thus two views of the type Buffer; the external client just sees the partial view whereas within the package the code of the server subprograms can see the full view. The specifications of the server subprograms are naturally also declared in the visible part.

The net effect is that the user can declare and manipulate a buffer by simply writing

```
My_Buffer: Buffer;
...
Load(My_Buffer, Some_String);
...
Get(My_Buffer, A_Character);
```

but the internal structure is quite hidden. There are two advantages: one is that the user cannot inadvertently misuse the buffer and the second is that the internal structure of the private type could be rearranged if necessary and provided that the protocol is maintained the user program will not need to be changed.

This hiding of information and consequent separation of concerns is very important and illustrates the benefit of data abstraction. The design of appropriate interface protocols is the key to the development and subsequent maintenance of large programs.

The astute reader will note that we have not bothered to ensure that the buffer is not loaded when there is still unread data in it or the string is too long to fit, nor read from when it is empty. We could rectify this by declaring our own exception called perhaps Error in the visible part of the specification thus

```
Error: exception;
```

and then check within Load by for example

```
if S'Length > Max or B.Start <= B.Finish then
    raise Error;
end if;
```

This causes our own exception to be raised if the buffer is overloaded.

As a minor point note the use of the constant Max so that the literal 80 only appears in one place. Note also the attribute Length which applies to any array and gives the number of its components. The upper and lower bounds of an array S are incidentally given by S'First and S'Last.

Another point is that the parameter Buffer of Get is marked as **in out** because the procedure both reads the initial value of Buffer and updates it.

Finally note that the components Start and Finish of the record have initial values in the declaration of the record type; these ensure that when a buffer is declared these components are assigned sensible values and thereby indicate that the buffer is empty. An alternative would of course be to provide a procedure Reset but the user might forget to call it.

EXERCISE 3.1

1   Extend the package Buffer_System to include the exception Error in its specification and appropriate checks in the subprogram bodies. Also add a function Is_Empty visible to the user.

3.2 Objects and inheritance

The term object oriented programming is currently in vogue. A precise definition is hard and is made somewhat worse by a complete lack of agreement on appropriate terminology. Ada 95 uses carefully considered terminology which is rather different from that in some languages such as C++ but avoids the ambiguities which can arise from the confusing overuse of some terms such as class.

As its name suggests, object oriented programming concerns the idea of programming around objects. A good example of an object in this sense is the variable My_Buffer of the type Buffer in the previous section. We conceive of the object such as a buffer as a coordinated whole and not just as the sum of its components. (Corresponding to a holistic rather than reductionist view to use terminology from Quantum Mechanics.) Indeed the external user cannot see the components at all but can only manipulate the buffer through the various subprograms associated with the type.

Certain operations upon a type are called the primitive operations of the type. In the case of the type Buffer they are the subprograms declared in the package specification along with the type itself and which have parameters or a result of the type. In the case of a type such as Integer, the primitive operations are those such as + and – which are predefined for the type (and indeed they are declared in Standard along with the type Integer itself and so fit the same model). Such operations are called methods in some languages.

Other important ideas in OOP are

- the ability to define one type in terms of another and especially as an extension of another; this is type extension,
- the ability for such a derived type to inherit the primitive operations of its parent and also to add to and replace such operations; this is inheritance,
- the ability to distinguish the specific type of an object at run time from among several related types and in particular to select an operation according to the specific type; this is (dynamic) polymorphism.

In the previous chapter we showed how the type Light was derived from Colour and also showed how numeric portability could be aided by deriving a numeric type such as My_Float from one of the predefined types. These were very simple forms of inheritance; the new types inherited the primitive operations of the parent; however, the types were not extended in any way and underneath were really the same type. The main benefit of such derivation is simply to provide a different name and thereby to distinguish the different uses of the same underlying type in order to prevent us from inadvertently using a Light when we meant to use a Colour.

The more general case is where we wish to extend a type in some way and also to distinguish objects of different types at run time. The most natural form of type for the purposes of extension is of course a record where we can consider extension as simply the addition of further components. The other point is that if we need to distinguish the type at run time then the object must contain an indication of its type. This is provided by a hidden component called

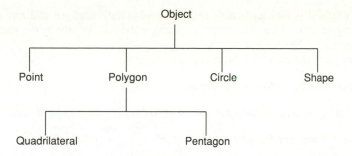

Figure 3.1   A hierarchy of geometrical objects.

the tag. Type extension in Ada is thus naturally carried out using tagged record types.

As a simple example suppose we wish to manipulate various kinds of geometrical objects. We can imagine that the kinds of objects form a hierarchy as shown in Figure 3.1.

All objects will have a position given by their *x*- and *y*-coordinates. So we declare the root of the hierarchy as

```
type Object is tagged
  record
    X_Coord: Float;
    Y_Coord: Float;
  end record;
```

Note carefully the introduction of the reserved word **tagged**. This indicates that values of the type carry a tag at run time and that the type can be extended. The other types of geometrical objects will be derived (directly or indirectly) from this type. For example we could have

```
type Circle is new Object with
  record
    Radius: Float;
  end record;
```

and the type Circle then has the three components X_Coord, Y_Coord and Radius. It inherits the two coordinates from the type Object and the component Radius is added explicitly.

Sometimes it is convenient to derive a new type without adding any further components. For example

```
type Point is new Object with null record;
```

In this last case we have derived Point from Object but naturally not added any new components. However, since we are dealing with tagged types we have to explicitly add **with null record**; to indicate that we did not want any new components. This has the advantage that it is always clear from a declaration whether a type is tagged or not.

A private type can also be marked as tagged

```
type Shape is tagged private;
```

and the full type declaration must then (ultimately) be a tagged record

```
type Shape is tagged
   record ...
```

or derived from a tagged record such as Object. On the other hand we might wish to make visible the fact that the type Shape is derived from Object and yet keep the additional components hidden. In this case we would write

```
package Hidden_Shape is
   type Shape is new Object with private;      -- client view
      ...
private
   type Shape is new Object with              -- server view
      record
         -- the private components
      end record;
end Hidden_Shape;
```

In this last case it is not necessary for the full declaration of Shape to be derived directly from the type Object. There might be a chain of intermediate derived types (it could be derived from Circle); all that matters is that Shape is ultimately derived from Object.

The primitive operations of a type are those declared in the same package specification as the type and that have parameters or result of the type. On derivation these operations are inherited by the new type. They can be overridden by new versions and new operations can be added and these then become primitive operations of the new type and are themselves naturally inherited by any further derived type.

Thus we might have declared a function giving the distance from the origin

```
function Distance(O: in Object) return Float is
begin
   return Sqrt(O.X_Coord**2 + O.Y_Coord**2);
end Distance;
```

The type Circle would then sensibly inherit this function. If however, we were concerned with the area of an object then we might start with

```
function Area(O: in Object) return Float is
begin
   return 0.0;
end Area;
```

which returns zero since a raw object has no area. The abstract concept of an area applies also to a circle and so it is appropriate that a function **Area** be defined for the type **Circle**. However, to inherit the function from the type **Object** is clearly inappropriate and so we explicitly declare

```
function Area(C: in Circle) return Float is
begin
   return Pi*C.Radius**2;
end Area;
```

which then overrides the inherited operation. We can perhaps summarize these ideas by saying that the specification is always inherited whereas the implementation may be inherited but can be replaced.

It is possible to convert a value from the type **Circle** to **Object** and vice versa. From circle to object is straightforward, we simply write

```
O: Object := (1.0, 0.5);
C: Circle := (0.0, 0.0, 34.7);
...
O := Object(C);
```

which effectively ignores the third component. However, conversion in the other direction requires the provision of a value for the extra component and this is done by an extension aggregate thus

```
C := (O with 41.2);
```

where the expression **O** is extended after **with** by the values of the extra components written just as in a normal aggregate. In this case we only had to give a value for the radius.

EXERCISE 3.2

1   Declare the type **Object** and the functions **Distance** and **Area** in a package **Objects**. Then declare a package **Shapes** containing the types **Circle** and **Point** and also a type **Triangle** with sides A, B and C and appropriate functions returning the area.

3.3   Classes and polymorphism

In the last section we showed how to declare a hierarchy of types derived from the type **Object**. We saw how on derivation further components and operations could be added and that operations could be replaced.

However, it is very important to note that an operation cannot be taken away nor can a component be removed. As a consequence we are guaranteed that all the types derived from a common ancestor will have all the components and operations of that ancestor.

So in the case of the type Object, all types in the hierarchy derived from Object will have the common components such as their coordinates and the common operations such as Distance and Area. Since they have these common properties it is natural that we should be able to manipulate a value of any type in the hierarchy without knowing exactly which type it is provided that we only use the common properties. Such general manipulation is done through the concept of a class.

Ada carefully distinguishes between the set of types such as Object plus all its derivatives on the one hand and an individual type such as Object itself on the other hand. A set of such types is known as a class. Associated with each class is a type called the class wide type which for the set rooted at Object is denoted by Object'Class. The type Object is referred to as a specific type when we need to distinguish it from a class wide type.

We can of course have subclasses, for example Polygon'Class represents the set of all types derived from and including Polygon. This is a subset of the class Object'Class. All the properties of Object'Class will also apply to Polygon'Class but not vice versa. For example, although we have not shown it, the type Polygon will presumably contain a component giving the length of the sides. Such a component will belong to all types of the class Polygon'Class but not to Object'Class.

As a simple example of the use of a class wide type consider the following function

```
function Moment(OC: Object'Class) return Float is
begin
    return OC.X_Coord * Area(OC);
end Moment;
```

Those who recall their school mechanics will remember that the moment of a force about a fulcrum is the product of the weight by the distance from the fulcrum. So in our example, taking the x-axis as being horizontal, the moment of a geometrical object about the origin is the x-coordinate multiplied by the weight which we can take as being proportional to the area (and for simplicity we have assumed is just the area).

This function has a formal parameter of the class wide type Object'Class. This means it can be called with an actual parameter whose type is any specific type in the class comprising the set of all types derived from Object. Thus we could write

```
C: Circle...
M: Float;
...
M := Moment(C);
```

Within the function Moment we can naturally refer to the specific object as OC. Since we know that the object must be of a specific type in the Object class, we are guaranteed that it will have a component OC.X_Coord. Similarly we are guaranteed that the function Area will exist for the type of the object since it is a primitive operation of the type Object and will have been inherited by (and possibly overridden for) every type derived from Object. So the appropriate function Area is called and the result multiplied by the x-coordinate and returned as the result of the function Moment.

Note carefully that the particular function Area to be called is not known until the program executes. The choice depends upon the specific type of the parameter and this is determined by the tag of the object passed as actual parameter; remember that the tag is a sort of hidden component of the tagged type. This selection of the particular subprogram according to the tag is known as dispatching and is a vital aspect of the dynamic behaviour provided by polymorphism.

Dispatching only occurs when the actual parameter is of a class wide type; if we call Area with an object of a specific type such as C of type Circle then the choice is made at compile time. Dispatching is often called late binding because the call is only bound to the called subprogram late in the compile-link-execute process. The binding to a call of Area with the parameter C of type Circle is called static binding because the subprogram to be called is determined at compile time.

Observe that the function Moment is not a primitive operation of any type; it is just an operation of Object'Class and it happens that a value of any specific type derived from Object can be implicitly converted to the class wide type. Class wide types do not have primitive operations and so no inheritance is involved.

It is interesting to consider what would have happened if we had written

```
function Moment(O: Object) return Float is
begin
   return O.X_Coord * Area(O);
end Moment;
```

where the formal parameter is of the specific type Object. This always returns zero because the function Area for an Object always returns zero. If this function Moment were declared in the same package as Object then it would be a primitive operation of Object and thus inherited by the type Circle. However, the internal call would still be to the function Area for the type Object and not to the type Circle and so the answer would still be zero. This is because the binding is static and inheritance simply passes on the same code. The code mechanically works on a Circle because it only uses the Object part of the circle (we say it sees the Object view of the Circle); but unfortunately it is not what we want. We could of course override the inherited operation by writing

```
function Moment(C: Circle) return Float is
begin
   return C.X_Coord * Area(C);
end Moment;
```

but this is both tedious and causes unnecessary duplication of similar code. The proper approach for such general situations is to use the original class wide version with its internal dispatching; this can be shared by all types without duplication and always calls the appropriate function Area.

A major advantage of using a class wide operation such as Moment is that a system using it can be written, compiled and tested without knowing all the specific types to which it is to be applied. Moreover we can then add further types to the system without recompilation of the existing tested system.

For example we could add a further type

```
type Pentagon is new Object with...
function Area(P: Pentagon) return Float;
...
Star: Pentagon := ...
...
Put("Moment of star is ");
Put(Moment(Star));
```

and then the old existing tried and tested Moment will call the new Area for the Pentagon without being recompiled. (It will of course have to be relinked.)

This works because of the mechanism used for dynamic binding; the essence of the idea is that the class wide code has dynamic links into the new code and this is accessed via the tag of the type. Naturally enough this creates a very flexible and extensible interface ideal for building up a system from reusable components. Details of how this apparent magic might be implemented will be given when we discuss OOP in detail in Chapter 13.

One difficulty with the flexibility provided by class wide types is that we cannot know how much space might be occupied by an arbitrary object of the type because the type might be extended. So although we can declare an object of a class wide type it has to be initialized and thereafter that object can only be of the specific type of that initial value. Note that a formal parameter of a class wide type such as in Moment is allowed because the space is provided by the actual parameter.

Another similar restriction is that we cannot have an array of class wide components (even if initialized) because the components might be of different specific types of different sizes and thus impossible to index efficiently.

One consequence of these necessary restrictions is that it is very natural to use access types with object oriented programming since there is no problem with pointing to objects of different sizes at different times.

Thus suppose we wanted to manipulate a series of geometrical objects; it is very natural to declare these in free storage as required. They can then be chained together on a list for processing. Consider

```
type Pointer is access Object'Class;
type Cell;
type Cell_Ptr is access Cell;

type Cell is
   record
      Element: Pointer;
      Next: Cell_Ptr;
   end record;
```

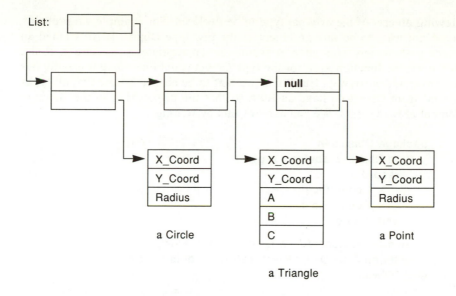

Figure 3.2 A chain of objects.

which enables us to create cells which can be linked together; each cell has an element which is a pointer to any geometrical object.

We can now imagine that a number of objects have been created and linked together to form a list as in Figure 3.2. We assume that this chain is accessed through a variable called List of the type Cell_Ptr.

We can now easily process the objects on the list and might for example compute the total moment of the set of objects by calling the following function

```
function Total_Moment(The_List: Cell_Ptr) return Float is
   Local: Cell_Ptr := The_List;
   Result: Float := 0.0;
begin
   loop
      if Local = null then      -- end of list
         return Result:
      end if;
      Result := Result + Moment(Local.Element.all);
      Local := Local.Next;
   end loop:
end Total_Moment;
```

We conclude this brief survey of the OOP facilities in Ada by considering abstract types. It is sometimes the case that we would like to declare a type as the foundation for a class of types with certain common properties but without allowing objects of the original type to be declared. For example we probably would not want to declare an object of the raw type Object. If we wanted an object without any area then it would be appropriate to declare a Point. Moreover, the function Area for the type Object is dubious since it usually has to be overridden anyway. But it is important to be able to ensure that all types derived from Object do have an Area so that the dispatching in the function Moment always works. We can achieve this by writing

```
package Objects is
   type Object is abstract tagged
      record
         X_Coord: Float;
         Y_Coord: Float;
      end record;

   function Distance(O: in Object) return Float;
   function Area(O: in Object) return Float is abstract;
end Objects;
```

In this formulation the type Object and the function Area are marked as abstract. It is illegal to declare an object of an abstract type and an abstract subprogram has no body and so cannot be called. On deriving a concrete (that is, nonabstract) type from an abstract type any abstract inherited operations must be overridden by concrete operations. Note that we have declared the function Distance as not abstract; this is largely because we know that it will be appropriate anyway.

This approach has a number of advantages; we cannot declare a raw Object by mistake, we cannot inherit the silly function Area and we cannot make the mistake of declaring the function Moment for the specific type Object (why?).

But despite the type being abstract we can declare the function Moment for the class wide type Object'Class. This always works because of the rule that we cannot declare an object of an abstract type; any actual object passed as parameter must be of a concrete type and will have an appropriate function Area to which it can dispatch.

EXERCISE 3.3

1 Declare a procedure Add_To_List which takes a Cell_Ptr and (an access to) any object of the type Object'Class and adds it to the list pointed to by the Cell_Ptr.

2 Write the body of the package Objects for the version with the abstract type.

3 How would the package Shapes of Exercise 3.2(1) need to be modified using the package Objects with the abstract type?

4 Why could we not declare the function Moment for the abstract type Object?

5 The moment of inertia of an object about the origin M_O is equal to its moment of inertia about its centre M_I plus MR^2 where M is its mass and R its distance from the origin. Assuming that we have functions MI for each specific type declare a class wide function MO returning the moment of inertia about the origin.

3.4 Genericity

We have seen how class wide types provide us with dynamic polymorphism. This means that we can manipulate several types with a single construction and that the specific type is determined dynamically, that is at run time. In this section we introduce the complementary concept of static polymorphism where again we have a single construction for the manipulation of several types but in this case the choice of type is made statically at compile time.

At the beginning of Section 2.2 we said that an important objective of Software Engineering is to reuse existing software components. However, the strong typing model of Ada (even with class wide types) sometimes gets in the way unless we have a method of writing software components which can be used for various different types. For example, the program to do a sort is largely independent of what it is sorting – all it needs is a rule for comparing the values to be sorted. Record input–output is another example – the actions are quite independent of the contents of the records.

So we need a means of writing pieces of software which can be parameterized as required for different types. In Ada this is done by the generic mechanism. We can make a package or subprogram generic with respect to one or more parameters which can include types. Such a generic unit provides a template from which we can create genuine packages and subprograms by so-called instantiation. The full details of Ada generics are quite extensive and will be dealt with in Chapter 17. However, in the next chapter we will be discussing input–output and other aspects of the predefined library which make significant use of the generic mechanism and so a brief introduction is appropriate.

The standard package for the input and output of floating point values in text form is generic with respect to the actual floating type. This is because we want a single package to cope with all the possible floating types such as the underlying machine types Float and Long_Float as well as the portable type My_Float. Its specification is

```
generic
   type Num is digits <>;
package Float_IO is

   ...
   procedure Get(Item: out Num; ... );
   procedure Put(Item: in Num; ... );

   ...
end Float_IO;
```

where we have omitted various details relating to the format. The one generic parameter is Num and the notation **digits** <> indicates that it must be a floating point type and echoes the declaration of My_Float using **digits** 7 that we briefly mentioned in Section 2.4.

In order to create an actual package to manipulate values of the type My_Float, we write

> **package** My_Float_IO **is new** Float_IO(My_Float);

which creates a package with the name My_Float_IO where the formal type Num has been replaced throughout with our actual type My_Float. As a consequence, procedures Get and Put taking parameters of the type My_Float are created and we can then call these as required. But we are straying into the next chapter.

The kind of parameterization provided by genericity is similar but rather different to that provided through class wide types. In both cases the parameterization is over a related set of types with a set of common properties. Such a related set of types is termed a class.

A common form of class is a derivation class where all the types are derived from a common ancestor such as the type Object. Tagged derivation classes form the basis of dynamic polymorphism as we have seen.

But there are also broader forms of class such as the set of all floating point types which are allowed as actual parameters for the generic package Float_IO. The parameters of generic units use these broader classes. For example, a very broad class is the set of all types having assignment. Such a class would be a suitable basis for writing a generic sort routine.

In due course we will see that the two forms of polymorphism work together; a common form of generic package is one which takes as a parameter a type from a tagged derivation class. As we shall see in Chapter 19, this may be used to provide important capabilities such as multiple inheritance.

3.5   Object oriented terminology

It is perhaps convenient at this point to compare the Ada terminology with that used by other object oriented languages such as Smalltalk and C++. Those not familiar with such languages could skip this section before they get confused.

About the only term in common is inheritance. Ada 83 has always had inheritance although not type extension which only occurs with tagged record types. Untagged record types are called structs in some languages.

Ada actually uses the term object to denote variables and constants in general whereas in the OO sense an object is an instance of an Abstract Data Type (ADT).

Many languages use *class* to denote what Ada calls a specific tagged type (or more strictly an ADT consisting of a tagged type plus its primitive operations). The reason for this difference is that Ada uses the word class exclusively to refer to a group of related types. Indeed Ada has used the term class for this purpose since before Ada was called Ada. Ada classes are not just those groups of types related by derivation but also groups with broader correspondence as used for generic parameter matching.

The Ada approach clarifies the distinction between the group of types and a single type and strengthens that clarification by introducing class wide types as such. Some languages use the term class for both specific types and the group of types with much resulting confusion both in terms of description but also in understanding the behaviour of the program and keeping track of the real nature of an object.

Primitive operations of Ada tagged types are often called methods or virtual functions. The call of a primitive operation in Ada is bound statically or dynamically according to whether the parameter is of a specific type or class wide. The rules in C++ are more complex and depend upon the whether the parameter is a pointer and also whether the call is prefixed by its class name. In Ada, an operation with class wide formal parameters is always bound statically although it applies to all types of the class.

Dispatching is the Ada term for calling a primitive operation with dynamic binding and indeed subprogram calls through access types are also a form of dynamic binding.

Abstract types correspond to abstract class in many languages. Abstract subprograms are pure virtual member functions in C++. Note that Eiffel uses the term deferred rather than abstract.

Ancestor or parent type and descendant or derived type become superclass and subclass. The Ada concept of subtype (which we have not yet discussed) has no correspondence in other languages which do not have range checks and has no relationship to subclass. As we will see later, a subtype can never have more values than its base type, whereas a descendant type (subclass to other languages) can never have fewer values than its parent type.

Generic units are templates but in Ada they carry type checking with them whereas many languages treat templates as raw macros.

Another important point is that many languages have no encapsulation mechanism other than so-called classes whereas Ada has the package largely unrelated to type extension and inheritance and the private type. The effect of private and protected operations in C++ is provided in Ada by a combination of private types and child packages; the latter are kinds of friends.

3.6   Tasking

No survey of abstraction in Ada would be complete without a brief mention of tasking. It is often necessary to write a program as a set of parallel activities rather than just as one sequential program.

Most programming languages do not address this issue at all. Some argue that the underlying operating system provides the necessary mechanisms and that they are therefore unnecessary in a programming language. Such arguments do not stand up to careful examination for two main reasons.

- Built-in syntactic constructions provide a degree of reliability which cannot be obtained through a series of individual operating system calls.

- General operating systems do not provide the degree of control and timing required by many applications.

An Ada program can thus be written as a series of interacting tasks. There are two main ways in which tasks can communicate: directly by sending messages to each other and indirectly by accessing shared data.

Direct communication between Ada tasks is achieved by one task calling an entry in another task. The calling (client) task waits while the called (server) task executes an accept statement in response to the call; the two tasks are closely coupled during this interaction which is called a rendezvous.

Controlled access to shared data is vital in tasking applications if interference is to be avoided. For example, returning to the character buffer example in Section 3.1, it would be a disaster if a task started to read the buffer while another task was updating it with further information since the component B.Start could be changed and a component of the Data array read by Get before the buffer had been correctly updated by Load. Ada prevents such interference by a construction known as a protected object.

The general syntactic form of both tasks and protected objects is similar to that of a package. They have a specification part prescribing the interface, a private part containing hidden details of the interface and a body stating what they actually do. The general client–server model can thus be expressed as

```
task Server is
   entry Some_Service(Formal: Data);
end;

task body Server is
begin
   ...
   accept Some_Service(Formal: Data) do
      -- statements providing the service
      ...
   end;
   ...
end Server;

task Client;

task body Client is
begin
   ...
   Server.Some_Service(Actual);
   ...
end Client;
```

A good example of the form of a protected object is given by the buffer example which could be rewritten as follows

```
protected type Buffer(Max: Integer) is       -- visible part

  procedure Load(S: in String);
  procedure Get(C: out Character);

private                                       -- private part

  Data: String(1 .. Max);
  Start: Integer := 1;
  Finish: Integer := 0;

end Buffer;

protected body Buffer is

  procedure Load(S: in String) is
  begin
    Start := 1;
    Finish := S'Length;
    Data(Start .. Finish) := S;
  end Load;

  procedure Get(C: out Character) is
  begin
    C := Data(Start);
    Start := Start + 1;
  end Get;

end Buffer;
```

This construction uses a slightly different style to the package. It is a type in its own right whereas the package exported the type. As a consequence, the calls of the procedures do not need to pass explicitly the parameter referring to the buffer and moreover within their bodies the references to the private data are naturally taken to refer to the current instance. Note also that the type is parameterized by the discriminant **Max** and so we can supply the actual size of a particular buffer when it is declared. Statements using the protected type might thus look like

```
B: Buffer(80);
...
B.Load(Some_String);
...
B.Get(A_Character);
```

Although this formulation prevents disastrous interference between several clients nevertheless it does not prevent a call of Load from overwriting unread data. As before we could insert tests and raise an exception. But the proper approach is to cause the tasks to wait if circumstances are not appropriate. We will see how to do this when we discuss tasking in detail in Chapter 18.

Programs and Libraries

In this final introductory chapter we consider the important topic of putting together a complete program. Such a program will inevitably use predefined material such as that for input and output and we therefore also briefly survey the structure and contents of the extensive predefined library.

4.1   The hierarchical library

A complete program is put together out of various separately compiled units. In developing a very large program it is inevitable that it will be conceived as a number of subsystems themselves each composed out of a number of separately compiled units.

We see at once the risk of name clashes between the various parts of the total. It would be all too easy for the designers of different parts of the system to reuse popular package names such as Error_Messages or Debug_Info and so on.

In order to overcome this and other related problems, Ada has a hierarchical naming scheme at the library level. Thus a package Parent may have a child package with the name Parent.Child.

We immediately see that if our total system breaks down into a number of major parts such as acquisition, analysis and report then name clashes will be avoided if it is mapped into three corresponding library packages plus appropriate child units. There is then no risk of a clash between

Analysis.Debug_Info and Report.Debug_Info because the names are quite distinct.

The naming is hierarchical and can continue to any depth. A good example of the use of this hierarchical naming scheme is found in the standard libraries which are provided by every implementation of Ada.

We have already mentioned the package Standard which is an intrinsic part of the language. All library units can be considered to be children of Standard and it should never be necessary to explicitly mention Standard at all (unless you do something crazy like redefine Integer to mean something else; the original could then still be referred to as Standard.Integer).

In order to reduce the risk of clashes with user's own names the predefined library comprises just three packages each of which have a number of children. The three packages are System, which is concerned with the control of storage and similar implementation matters; Interfaces, which is concerned with interfaces to other languages and the intrinsic hardware types; and finally Ada which contains the bulk of the predefined library.

The packages System and Interfaces are described in detail in Chapter 21. In this chapter we will briefly survey the main package Ada; a fuller description will be found in Chapter 20.

The package Ada itself (herself?) is simply

```
package Ada is
   pragma Pure(Ada);      -- as white as driven snow!
end Ada;
```

and the various predefined units are children of Ada. The pragma indicates that Ada has no variable state; (this concept is important for sharing in distributed systems, a topic outside the scope of this book).

Important child packages of Ada are

Numerics; this contains the mathematical library providing the various elementary functions, random number generators and facilities for complex numbers.

Characters; this contains various packages for classifying and manipulating characters as well as the names of all the characters in the Latin-1 set.

Strings; this contains packages for the manipulation of strings of various kinds: fixed length, bounded and unbounded.

Text_IO, Sequential_IO and Direct_IO; these and other packages provide a variety of input–output facilities.

There are many other children of Ada and these will be mentioned as required.

Those familiar with Ada 83 will note that the predefined library units of Ada 83 have now all become child units of Ada. Compatibility is achieved because of the predefined renamings of these child units as library units such as

```
with Ada.Text_IO;
package Text_IO renames Ada.Text_IO;
```

although it should be noted that these renamings are considered obsolescent and thus could be removed in a future version. Renaming is a useful feature and is discussed in Chapter 12.

Most library units are packages and it is easy to think that all library units must be packages; indeed only a package can have child units. But of course the main subprogram is a library subprogram and any library package can have child subprograms. A library unit can also be a generic package or subprogram and even an instantiation of a generic package or subprogram; this latter fact is often overlooked.

We have introduced the hierarchical library as simply a naming mechanism. It also has important information hiding and sharing properties which will be dealt with in detail in Chapter 12. An important example is that a child unit can access the information in the private part of its parent; but of course other units cannot see into the private part of a package. This and related facilities enable a group of units to share private information while keeping the information hidden from external clients.

It should also be noted that a child package does not need to have a with clause or use clause for its parent; this emphasizes the close relationship of the hierarchical structure and parallels the fact that we never need a with clause for Standard because all units are children of Standard.

4.2   Input–output

The Ada language is defined in such a way that all input and output is performed in terms of other language features. There are no special intrinsic features just for input and output. In fact input–output is just a service required by a program and so is provided by one or more Ada packages. This approach runs the attendant risk that different implementations will provide different packages and program portability will be compromised. In order to avoid this, the *ARM* describes certain standard packages that will be available in all implementations. Other, more elaborate, packages may be appropriate to special circumstances and the language does not prevent this. Indeed very simple packages such as our purely illustrative Simple_IO may also be appropriate. Full consideration of input and output is deferred until Chapter 20. However, we will now briefly describe how to use some of the features so that the reader will be able to run some simple exercises. We will restrict ourselves to the input and output of simple text.

Text input–output is performed through the use of the standard package Ada.Text_IO. Unless we specify otherwise, all communication will be through two standard files, one for input and one for output, and we will assume that (as is likely for most implementations) these are such that input is from the keyboard and output is to the screen. The full details of Text_IO cannot be described here but if we restrict ourselves to just a few useful facilities it looks a bit like

```
with Ada.IO_Exceptions;
package Ada.Text_IO is
   type Count is ...            -- an integer type
   ...
   procedure New_Line(Spacing: in Count := 1);
   procedure Set_Col(To: in Count);
   function Col return Count;
   ...
   procedure Get(Item: out Character);
   procedure Put(Item: in Character);
   procedure Put(Item: in String);
   ...
   -- the package Float_IO outlined in Section 3.4
   -- plus a similar package Integer_IO
   ...
end Ada.Text_IO;
```

Note first that this package commences with a with clause for the package Ada.IO_Exceptions. This further package contains the declaration of a number of different exceptions relating to a variety of things which can go wrong with input–output. For toy programs the most likely to arise is probably Data_Error which would occur for example if we tried to read in a number from the keyboard but then accidentally typed in something which was not a number at all or was in the wrong format.

The next thing to note is the outline declaration of the type Count. This is an integer type having similar properties to the type Integer and almost inevitably with the same implementation (just as the type My_Integer might be based on Integer). The parameter of New_Line is of the type Count rather than plain Integer, although since the parameter will typically be a literal such as 2 (or be omitted so that the default of 1 applies) this will not be particularly evident.

The procedure Set_Col and function Col are useful for tabulation. The character positions along a line of output are numbered starting at 1. So if we write (assuming **use** Ada.Text_IO;)

```
Set_Col(10);
```

then the next character output will go at position 10. A call of New_Line naturally sets the current position to 1 so that output commences at the beginning of the line. The function Col returns the current position and so

```
Set_Col(Col + 10);
```

will move the position on by 10 and thereby leave 10 spaces. Note that Col is an example of a function that has no parameters.

A single character can be output by for example

```
Put('A');
```

and a string of characters by

> Put("This Is a string of characters");

A value of the type My_Float can be output in various formats. But first we have to instantiate the package Float_IO mentioned in Section 3.4 and which is declared inside Ada.Text_IO. Having done that we can call Put with a single parameter, the value of type My_Float to be output, in which case a standard default format is used, or we can add further parameters controlling the format. This is best illustrated by a few examples and we will suppose that the type My_Float was declared to have 7 decimal digits as in the example in Section 2.4.

If we do not supply any format parameters then an exponent notation is used with 7 significant digits, 1 before the point and 6 after (the 7 matches the precision given in the declaration of My_Float). There is also a leading space or minus sign. The exponent consists of the letter E followed by the exponent sign (+ or –) and then a two digit decimal exponent. The effect is shown by the following statements with the output given as a comment. For clarity the output is surrounded by quotes and s designates a space; in reality there are no quotes and spaces are spaces.

> Put(12.34);   -- "s1.234000E+01"
> Put(-987.65);   -- "-9.876500E+02"
> Put(0.00289);   -- "s2.890000E-03"

We can override the default by providing three further parameters which give respectively, the number of characters before the point, the number of characters after the point, and the number of characters after E. However, there is still always only one digit before the point. So

> Put(12.34, 3, 4, 2);   -- "ss1.2340E+1"

If we do not want exponent notation then we simply specify the last parameter as zero and we then get normal decimal notation. So

> Put(12.34, 3, 4, 0);   -- "s12.3400"

The output of values of integer types follows a similar pattern. In this case we similarly instantiate the generic package Integer_IO inside Ada.Text_IO which applies to all integer types with the particular type such as My_Integer.

We can then call Put with a single parameter, the value of type My_Integer, in which case a standard default field is used, or we can add a further parameter specifying the field. The default field is the smallest that will accommodate all values of the type My_Integer allowing for a leading minus sign. Thus for the range of My_Integer, the default field is 8. It should be noticed that if we specify a field which is too small then it is expanded as necessary. So

> Put(123);   -- "sssss123"
> Put(-123);   -- "ssss-123"

```
Put(123, 4);              -- "s123"
Put(123, 0);              -- "123"
```

That covers enough output for simple toy programs. The only input likely to be needed is of integer and floating point values and perhaps single characters. This is easily done by a call of Get with a parameter that must be a variable of the appropriate type, just as we wrote Get(X); in the simple program in Section 2.2.

A call of Get with a floating or integer parameter will expect us to type in an appropriate number at the keyboard; this must have a decimal point if the parameter is of a floating type. It should also be noted that leading blanks (spaces) and newlines are skipped. A call of Get with a parameter of type Character will read the very next character, and this can be neatly used for controlling the flow of an interactive program, thus

```
C: Character;
...
Put("Do you want to stop?  Answer Y if so. ");
Get(C);
if C = 'Y' then
    ...
```

For simple programs that do not have to be portable, the effort of doing the instantiations is not necesssary if we just use the predefined types Integer and Float since the predefined library contains nongeneric versions with the names Ada.Integer_Text_IO and Ada.Float_Text_IO respectively. So all we need write is

```
use Ada.Integer_Text_IO, Ada.Float_Text_IO;
```

and then we can call Put and Get without more ado.

That concludes our brief introduction to input–output which has inevitably been of a rather cookbook nature. Hopefully it has provided enough to enable the reader to drive such trial examples as desired as well as giving some further flavour to the nature of Ada.

EXERCISE 4.2

1   Which of the calls of Put discussed above would produce different results if we had used the type Integer rather than My_Integer? Consider both a 16-bit and a 32-bit implementation of Integer.

4.3   Numeric library

The numeric library comprises the package Ada.Numerics plus a number of
child packages. The package Ada.Numerics is as follows

```
package Ada.Numerics is
   pragma Pure(Numerics);
   Argument_Error: exception;
   Pi: constant := 3.14159_26535_89793_23846_26433_83279_
                                  50288_41971_69399_37511;
   e : constant := 2.71828_18284_59045_23536_02874_71352_
                                  66249_77572_47093_69996;
end Ada.Numerics;
```

This contains the exception Argument_Error which is raised if something is
wrong with the argument of a numeric function (such as attempting to take the
square root of a negative number) and the two useful constants Pi and e. These
constants are given to 50 decimal places and technically of course the literals
must all be on a single line but the page width of this book (unlike that of the
ARM) cannot cope.

One child package of Ada.Numerics provides the familiar elementary
functions such as Sqrt and is another illustration of the use of the generic
mechanism. Its specification is

```
generic
   type Float_Type is digits <>;
package Ada.Numerics.Generic_Elementary_Functions is
   function Sqrt(X: Float_Type'Base) return Float_Type'Base;
   ...   -- and so on
end;
```

Again there is a single generic parameter giving the floating type. In order to
call the function Sqrt we must first instantiate the generic package much as we
did for Float_IO, thus (assuming appropriate with and use clauses)

```
package My_Elementary_Functions is
      new Generic_Elementary_Functions(My_Float);
use My_Elementary_Functions;
```

and we can then write a call of Sqrt directly.

The reader may wonder at the enormity of the name My_Elementary_
Functions. This follows the recommended practice in the *ARM*. In fact it should
be noted that there is a nongeneric version for the type Float with just the name
Elementary_Functions for the convenience of those using the predefined type
Float.

A little point to note is that the parameter and result of Sqrt is written as
Float_Type'Base; the reason for this is explained in Chapter 15 when we look
at numeric types in more detail.

We emphasize that the exception Ada.Numerics.Argument_Error is raised if the parameter of a function such as Sqrt is unacceptable. This contrasts with our hypothetical function Sqrt introduced earlier which we assumed raised the predefined exception Constraint_Error when given a negative parameter. We will see later when we deal with exceptions in detail in Chapter 14 that it is generally better to declare and raise our own exceptions rather than use the predefined ones.

Two other important child packages are those for the generation of random numbers. One returns a value of the type Float within the range zero to one and the other returns a random value of a discrete type (a discrete type is an integer type or an enumeration type). We will look superficially at the latter and refer the reader to Chapter 20 for full details of both.

The specification is as follows

```
generic
   type Result_Subtype is (<>);
package Ada.Numerics.Discrete_Random is
   type Generator is limited private;
   function Random(Gen: Generator) return Result_Subtype;
   ...   -- plus other facilities
end Ada.Numerics.Discrete_Random;
```

This introduces a number of new points. The most important is the form of the generic formal parameter which indicates that the actual type must be a discrete type. The pattern echoes that of an enumeration type in much the same way as that for the floating generic parameter in Generic_Elementary_Functions echoed the declaration of a floating type. Thus we see that the discrete types are another example of a class of types as discussed in Section 3.4.

A small point is that the type Generator is declared as limited. This simply means that assignment is not available for the type (or at least not for the partial view as seen by the client).

The random number generator is used as in the following fragment which illustrates the simulation of tosses of a coin

```
use Ada.Numerics;
type Coin is (Heads, Tails);
package Random_Coin is new Discrete_Random(Coin);
use Random_Coin;
G: Generator;
C: Coin;
...
loop
   C := Random(G);
   ...
end loop;
...
```

Having declared the type Coin we then instantiate the generic package. We then declare a generator and use it as the parameter of successive calls of Random.

The generator technique enables us to declare several generators and thus run several independent random sequences at the same time.

This concludes our brief survey of the standard numeric packages; further details will be found in Chapter 20.

4.4   Running a program

We are now in a position to put together a complete program using the proper input–output facilities. As an example we will rewrite the procedure Print_Roots of Section 2.2 and also use the standard mathematical library. For simplicity we will first use the predefined type Float. The program becomes

```ada
with Ada.Text_IO;
with Ada.Float_Text_IO;
with Ada.Numerics.Elementary_Functions;
procedure Print_Roots is
  use Ada.Text_IO;
  use Ada.Float_Text_IO;
  use Ada.Numerics.Elementary_Functions;

  X: Float;
begin
  Put("Roots of various numbers");

  ...   -- and so on as before

end Print_Roots;
```

Note that we can put the use clauses inside the procedure Print_Roots as shown or we can place them immediately after the with clauses.

If we want to write a portable version then the general approach would be

```ada
with Ada.Text_IO;
with Ada.Numerics.Generic_Elementary_Functions;
procedure Print_Roots is
  type My_Float is digits 7;
  package My_Float_IO is new Ada.Text_IO.Float_IO(My_Float);
  use My_Float_IO;
  package My_Elementary_Functions is
      new Ada.Numerics.Generic_Elementary_Functions(My_Float);
  use My_Elementary_Functions;

  X: My_Float;
begin
  Put("Roots of various numbers");

  ...   -- and so on as before

end Print_Roots;
```

To have to write all that introductory stuff each time is rather a burden, so we will put it in a standard package of our own and then compile it once so that it is permanently in our program library and can then be accessed without more ado. We include the type My_Integer as well and write

```
with Ada.Text_IO;
with Ada.Numerics.Generic_Elementary_Functions;
package Etc is
   type My_Float is digits 7;
   type My_Integer is range –1000_000 .. +1000_000;

   package My_Float_IO is new Ada.Text_IO.Float_IO(My_Float);
   package My_Integer_IO is
                      new Ada.Text_IO.Integer_IO(My_Integer);

   package My_Elementary_Functions is
        new Ada.Numerics.Generic_Elementary_Functions(My_Float);
end Etc;
```

and having compiled Etc our typical program can look like

```
with Ada.Text_IO, Etc;
use Ada.Text_IO, Etc;
procedure Program is
   use My_Float_IO, My_Integer_IO, My_Elementary_Functions;
   ...
   ...
end Program;
```

The reader will realize that the author had great difficulty in identifying an appropriate and short name for the package Etc and hopes that he is forgiven for the pun on etcetera.

An alternative approach, rather than declaring everything in the one package Etc, is to first compile a tiny package just containing the types My_Float and My_Integer and then to compile the various instantiations as individual library packages (remember that we said in Section 4.1 that a library unit can be just an instantiation).

```
package My_Numerics is
   type My_Float is digits 7;
   type My_Integer is range –1000_000 .. +1000_000;
end My_Numerics;

with My_Numerics; use My_Numerics;
with Ada.Text_IO;
package My_Float_IO is new Ada.Text_IO.Float_IO(My_Float);

with My_Numerics; use My_Numerics;
with Ada.Text_IO;
package My_Integer_IO is new Ada.Text_IO.Integer_IO(My_Integer);
```

```
with My_Numerics; use My_Numerics;
with Ada.Numerics.Generic_Elementary_Functions;
package My_Elementary_Functions is
      new Ada.Numerics.Generic_Elementary_Functions(My_Float);
```

With this approach we only need to include (via with clauses) the particular packages as required and our program is thus likely to be smaller if we do not need them all. We could even arrange the packages as an appropriate hierarchy.

The reader should now be in a position to write complete simple programs. The exercises in this book have been written as fragments rather than complete programs for two reasons; one is that complete programs would take up a lot of space (and actually be rather repetitive) and the other is that Ada is really all about software components anyway.

One important matter remains to be addressed and that is how to build a complete program. A major benefit of Ada is that consistency is maintained between separately compiled units so that the integrity of strong typing is preserved across compilation unit boundaries. It is therefore illegal to build a program out of inconsistent units. The exact means whereby this is achieved will depend upon the implementation.

A related issue is the order in which units are compiled. This is dictated by the idea of dependency. There are three main causes of dependency

* a body depends upon the corresponding specification
* a child depends upon the specification of its parent
* a unit depends upon the specifications of those it mentions in a with clause.

The key rule is that a unit can only be compiled if all those on which it depends are present in the library environment.

An important consequence is that although a specification and body can be compiled separately, the specification must always be present before the body can be compiled.

Similarly if a unit is modified, then typically all those which depend on it will also have to be recompiled in order to preserve consistency of the total program.

Unfortunately it is not possible to explain how to call the Ada compiler and manipulate the library environment or indeed how to call our Ada program because this depends upon the implementation and so we must leave the reader to find out how to do these last vital steps from the documentation for the implementation concerned.

This brings us to the end of our brief survey of the main features of Ada. We have in fact encountered most of the main concepts although very skimpily in some cases. One notable omission is any significant mention of subtypes which concern the imposition of constraints on types thereby reducing the range of allowed values.

Hopefully the reader will have grasped the key structural concepts and especially the forms of abstraction discussed in Chapter 3. The remainder of this book takes us through various topics in considerable detail starting with the small-scale aspects. In looking at these aspects we should not lose sight of the big picture to which we will return in Chapter 11. Moreover, we will generally use the types Integer and Float for simplicity but the reader will no doubt remember that they are not portable.

EXERCISE 4.4

1   Write a program to output the multiplication table up to ten. Make each column of the table 5 characters wide.

2   Write a program to output a table of square roots of numbers from 1 up to some limit specified by the user in response to a suitable question. Print the numbers as integers and the square roots to 6 decimal places in two columns. Use Set_Col to set the second column position so that the program can be easily modified. Note that a value N of type Integer can be converted to the corresponding My_Float value by writing My_Float(N).

3   Declare the packages My_Float_IO, My_Integer_IO and My_Elementary_Functions as child packages of My_Numerics. Avoid unnecessary with and use clauses.

4   Write a program to generate 100 random days of the week and count how many of them are Sundays. Output the answer in a suitable format.

5   Write a program to print out Pascal's triangle described in Section 2.5. Read in the value of an Integer variable Size which gives the final row number. Ensure that the triangle is properly aligned and has a suitably aligned caption. Print each number in a field of width 4; this will neatly accommodate values of Size up to 12. Note that a value N of type Integer can be converted to type Count by writing Count(N).

Part 2

Algorithmic Aspects

This second part covers the small-scale algorithmic features of the language in detail. These correspond to the areas covered by simple languages such as Pascal and C although Ada has richer facilities in these areas.

Chapter 5 deals with the lexical detail which needs to be described but can perhaps be skimmed on a first reading and just referred to when required.

Chapter 6 is where the story really begins and covers the type model and illustrates that model by introducing most of the scalar types. Chapter 7 then discusses the control structures which are very straight-forward. Chapter 8 covers arrays in full but only the most simple forms of records; it is also convenient to introduce characters and strings in this chapter since strings in Ada are treated as arrays of characters. Chapter 8 is quite long compared with a corresponding discussion on Pascal or C largely because of the named notation for array aggregates which is an important feature for writing readable programs.

Subprograms are discussed in Chapter 9 and at this point we can write serious lumps of program. Again the named notation enriches the discussion and includes the mechanism for default parameters.

Finally, Chapter 10 concludes this part of the book with a discussion on access types which correspond to pointers in Pascal and C. Although the concept of an access type is easy to understand, nevertheless the rules regarding accessibility might be found difficult on a first reading. These rules give much greater flexibility than Pascal but nevertheless are carefully designed to prevent dangling references which can so easily cause a program to crash in C.

Those familiar with Ada 83 will find little changed in Chapters 5 to 9 apart from the easier rules for array aggregates. However, Chapter 10 contains important new material such as general access types and access to subprogram types. Access to subprogram types are particularly important for writing programs that interface with systems in other languages.

5 Lexical Style

In the previous chapters, we introduced some concepts of Ada and illustrated the general appearance of Ada programs with some simple examples. However, we have so far only talked around the subject. In this chapter we get down to serious detail.

Regrettably it seems best to start with some rather unexciting but essential material – the detailed construction of things such as identifiers and numbers which make up the text of a program. However, it is no good learning a human language without getting the spelling sorted out. And as far as programming languages are concerned, compilers are usually very unforgiving regarding such corresponding and apparently trivial matters.

We also take the opportunity to introduce the notation used to describe the syntax of Ada language constructs. In general we will not use this syntax notation to introduce concepts but, in some cases, it is the easiest way to be precise. Moreover, if the reader wishes to consult the *ARM* then knowledge of the syntax notation is necessary. For completeness and easy reference the full syntax is given in Appendix 3.

5.1   Syntax notation

The syntax of Ada is described using a modified version of Backus-Naur Form (BNF). In this, syntactic categories are represented by lower case names; some of these contain embedded underlines to increase readability. A category is defined in terms of other categories by a sort of equation known as a production. Some categories are atomic and cannot be decomposed further – these are known as terminal symbols. A production consists of the name being defined followed by the special symbol ::= and its defining sequence.

Other symbols used are

[ ]   square brackets enclose optional items,

{ }   braces enclose optional items which may be omitted, appear once or be repeated many times,

| a vertical bar separates alternatives.

In some cases the name of a category is prefixed by a word in italics. In such cases the prefix is intended to convey some semantic information and can be treated as a form of comment as far as the context free syntax is concerned. Sometimes a production is presented in a form that shows the recommended layout.

5.2   Lexical elements

An Ada program is typically written as a sequence of lines of text containing the following characters

*   the alphabet A–Z
*   the digits 0–9
*   various special characters " # & ' ( ) * + , – . / : ; < = > _ |
*   the space character

The lower case alphabet may be used instead of or in addition to the upper case alphabet, but the two are generally considered the same. (The only exception is where the letters stand for themselves in character strings and character literals.)

The international standard describes the language in terms of the ISO 8-bit Latin-1 set which means that the various accented characters are also allowed in identifiers. Other graphic characters such as ! may also be used in strings and literals. Comments may contain almost anything.

The *ARM* does not prescribe how one proceeds from one line of text to the next. This need not concern us. We can just imagine that we type our Ada program as a series of lines using whatever mechanism the keyboard provides for starting a new line.

A line of Ada text can be thought of as a sequence of groups of characters known as lexical elements. We have already met several forms of lexical elements in previous chapters. Consider for example

Age := 21;   -- John's age

This consists of five such elements

- the identifier   Age
- the compound symbol   :=
- the number   21
- the single symbol   ;
- the comment   -- John's age

Other classes of lexical element are strings and character literals; they are dealt with in Chapter 8.

Individual lexical elements may not be split by spaces but otherwise spaces may be inserted freely in order to improve the appearance of the program. A most important example of this is the use of indentation to reveal the overall structure. Naturally enough a lexical element must fit on one line. Special care should be taken that the following compound delimiters do not contain spaces

=>	used in aggregates, cases, etc.
..	for ranges
**	exponentiation
:=	assignment
/=	not equals
>=	greater than or equals
<=	less than or equals
<<	label bracket
>>	the other label bracket
<>	the 'box' for type parameterization

However, spaces may occur in strings and character literals where they stand for themselves, and also in comments. Note that adjacent words and numbers must be separated from each other by spaces otherwise they would be confused. Thus we must write **end loop** rather than **endloop**.

5.3   Identifiers

We met numerous identifiers in the simple examples in previous chapters. As an example of the use of the syntax notation we now consider the following definition of an identifier

identifier ::= identifier_letter {[underline] letter_or_digit}

letter_or_digit ::= identifier_letter | digit

This states that an identifier consists of an identifier_letter followed by zero, one or more instances of letter_or_digit optionally preceded by a single underline. A letter_or_digit is, as its name implies, either a letter or a digit. As far as this example is concerned the categories underline, digit, and identifier_letter are not decomposed further and so are considered to be terminal symbols.

In plain English this merely says that an identifier consists of a letter possibly followed by one or more letters or digits with embedded isolated underlines. Either case of letter can be used. What the syntax does not convey is that the meaning attributed to an identifier does not depend upon the case of the letters. So identifiers which differ only in the case of corresponding letters are considered to be the same. But, on the other hand, the underline characters are considered to be significant.

Ada does not impose any limit on the number of characters in an identifier. Moreover all are significant. There may however be a practical limit since an identifier must fit onto a single line and an implementation is likely to impose some maximum line length. However, this maximum must be at least 200 and so identifiers of up to 200 characters will always be accepted. Programmers are encouraged to use meaningful names such as Time_Of_Day rather than cryptic meaningless names such as T. Long names may seem tedious when first writing a program but in the course of its lifetime a program is read much more often than it is written and clarity aids subsequent understanding both by the original author and by others who may be called upon to maintain the program. Of course, in short mathematical or abstract subprograms, identifiers such as X and Y may be appropriate.

Identifiers are used to name all the various entities in a program. However, some words are reserved for special syntactic significance and may not be used as identifiers. We have already encountered several of these such as **if**, **procedure** and **end**. There are 69 reserved words; they are listed in Appendix 1. For readability they are printed in boldface in this book, but that is not important. In program text they could, like identifiers, be in either case or indeed in a mixture of cases – procedure, PROCEDURE and Procedure are all acceptable. Nevertheless, some discipline aids understanding, and a useful convention is to use lower case for the reserved words and leading upper case for all others. But this is a matter of taste.

There are minor exceptions regarding the reserved words **access**, **delta**, **digits** and **range**. As will be seen later, they are also used as attributes Access, Delta, Digits and Range. However, when so used they are always preceded by a single quote character and so there is no confusion.

Some identifiers such as Integer and True have a predefined meaning from the package Standard. These are not reserved and can be reused although to do so is usually unwise since the program could become very confusing.

EXERCISE 5.3

1   Which of the following are not legal identifiers and why?

(a) Ada	(d) UMO164G	(g) X_
(b) fish&chips	(e) Time__Lag	(h) tax rate
(c) RATE–OF–FLOW	(f) 77E2	(i) goto

5.4   Numbers

Numbers (or numeric literals to use the proper jargon) take two forms according to whether they denote an integer (an exact whole number) or a real (an approximate and not usually whole number). The important distinguishing feature is that real literals always contain a decimal point whereas integer literals never do. Real literals can be used as values of any real type which we recall covers both floating point and fixed point types. Ada is strict on mixing up types. It is illegal to use an integer literal where the context demands a real literal and vice versa. Thus

        Age: Integer := 21.0;

and

        Weight: Float := 150;

are both illegal.
     The simplest form of integer literal is just a sequence of decimal digits. If the literal is very long it may be convenient to split it up into groups of digits by inserting isolated underlines thus

        123_456_789

In contrast to identifiers such underlines are, of course, of no significance other than to make the literal easier to read.
     The simplest form of real literal is a sequence of decimal digits containing a decimal point. Note that there must be at least one digit on either side of the decimal point. Again, isolated underlines may be inserted to improve legibility provided they are not adjacent to the decimal point; thus

        3.14159_26536

     Unlike most languages both integer and real literals can have an exponent. This takes the form of the letter E (either case) followed by a signed or unsigned decimal integer. This exponent indicates the power of ten by which the preceding simple literal is to be multiplied. The exponent cannot be negative in the case of an integer literal – otherwise it might not be a whole number. (As a trivial point an exponent of –0 is not allowed for an integer literal but it is for a real literal.)
     Thus the real literal 98.4 could be written with an exponent in any of the following ways

        9.84E1   98.4e0   984.0e–1   0.984E+2

Note that 984e–1 would not be allowed.
     Similarly, the integer literal 1900 could also be written as

        19E2   190e+1   1900E+0

but not as 19000e-1 nor as 1900E-0.

The exponent may itself contain underlines if it consists of two or more digits but it is unlikely that the exponent would be so large as to make this necessary. However, the exponent may not itself contain an exponent!

A final facility is the ability to express a literal in a base other than 10. This is done by enclosing the digits between # characters and preceding the result by the base. Thus

    2#111#

is a based integer literal of value $4 + 2 + 1 = 7$.

Any base from 2 to 16 inclusive can be used and, of course, base 10 can always be expressed explicitly. For bases above 10 the letters A to F are used to represent the extended digits 10 to 15. Thus

    14#ABC#

equals $10 \times 14^2 + 11 \times 14 + 12 = 2126$.

A based literal can also have an exponent. But note carefully that the exponent gives the power of the base by which the simple literal is to be multiplied and not a power of ten – unless, of course, the base happens to be ten. The exponent itself, like the base, is always expressed in normal decimal notation. Thus

    16#A#E2

equals $10 \times 16^2 = 2560$ and

    2#11#E11

equals $3 \times 2^{11} = 6144$.

A based literal can be real. The distinguishing mark is again the point. (We can hardly say 'decimal point' if we are not using a decimal base! A better term is radix point.) So

    2#101.11#

equals $4 + 1 + \frac{1}{2} + \frac{1}{4} = 5.75$ and

    7#3.0#e-1

equals $\frac{3}{7} = 0.\dot{4}2857\dot{1}$.

The reader may have felt that the possible forms of based literal are unduly elaborate. This is not really so. Based literals are useful – especially for fixed point types since they enable the programmer to represent values in the form in which he or she thinks about them. Obviously bases 2, 8 and 16 will be the most useful. But the notation is applicable to any base and the compiler can compute to any base, so why not?

Finally note that a numeric literal cannot be negative. A form such as –3 consists of a literal preceded by the unary minus operator.

EXERCISE 5.4

1   Which of the following are not legal literals and why? For those that are legal, state
    whether they are integer or real literals

    (a) 38.6   (e) 2#1011   (i) 16#FfF#
    (b) .5   (f) 2.71828_18285   (j) 1_0#1_0#E1_0
    (c) 32e2   (g) 12#ABC#   (k) 27.4e_2
    (d) 32e–2   (h) E+6   (l) 2#11#e–1

2   What are the values of the following?

    (a) 16#E#E1   (c) 16#F.FF#E+2
    (b) 2#11#E11   (d) 2#1.1111_1111_111#E11

3   How many different ways can you express the following as an integer literal?

    (a) the integer 41   (b) the integer 150

    (Forget underlines, distinction between E and e, nonsignificant leading zeros and
    optional + in an exponent.)

5.5   Comments

It is important to add appropriate comments to a program to aid its
understanding by someone else or yourself at a later date.

A comment in Ada is written as an arbitrary piece of text following two
hyphens (or minus signs – the same thing). Thus

        –– this is a comment

The comment extends to the end of the line. There is no facility in Ada to
insert a comment into the middle of a line. Of course, the comment may be the
only thing on the line or it may follow some other Ada text. A long comment
needing several lines is merely written as successive comments.

        –– this comment
        –– is spread
        –– over
        –– several
        –– lines.

It is important that the leading hyphens are adjacent and are not separated by
spaces.

EXERCISE 5.5

1   How many lexical elements are there in each of the following lines of text?

   (a) X := X+2; -- add two to X
   (b) -- that was a silly comment
   (c) -----------------------
   (d) - - - - - - - - - - - -

2   Distinguish

   (a) **delay** 2.0;
   (b) **delay**2.0;

CHECKLIST 5

The case of a letter is immaterial in all contexts except strings and character literals.

Underlines are significant in identifiers but not in numeric literals.

Spaces are not allowed in lexical elements, except in strings, character literals and comments.

The presence or absence of a point distinguishes real and integer literals.

An integer may not have a negative exponent.

Numeric literals cannot be signed.

Nonsignificant leading zeros are allowed in all parts of a numeric literal.

Changes from Ada 83

Ada 95 has six more reserved words than Ada 83 namely **abstract**, **aliased**, **protected**, **requeue**, **tagged** and **until**.

Ada 83 permitted certain other characters as alternatives to |, # and ". Although also allowed in Ada 95 they are considered obsolescent.

Ada 95 has some more predefined identifiers in Standard.

6 Scalar Types

6.1 Object declarations and assignments	6.5 Simple numeric types
6.2 Blocks and scopes	6.6 Enumeration types
6.3 Types	6.7 The Boolean type
6.4 Subtypes	6.8 Type classification
	6.9 Expression summary

This chapter lays the foundations for the small-scale aspects of Ada. We start by considering the declaration of objects and the assignment of values to them and briefly discuss the ideas of scope and visibility. We then introduce the important concepts of type, subtype and constraints. As examples of types, the remainder of the chapter discusses the numeric types Integer and Float, enumeration types in general, the type Boolean in particular, and the operations on them.

6.1 Object declarations and assignments

Values can be stored in objects which are declared to be of a specific type. Objects are either variables, in which case their value may change (or vary) as the program executes, or they may be constants, in which case they keep their same initial value throughout their life.

A variable is introduced into the program by a declaration which consists of the name (that is, the identifier) of the variable followed by a colon and then the name of the type. This can then optionally be followed by the := symbol and an initial value. The declaration terminates with a semicolon. Thus we might write

```
I: Integer;
P: Integer := 38;
```

This introduces the variable I of type Integer but gives it no particular initial value, and then the variable P and gives it the specific initial value of 38.

We can introduce several variables at the same time in one declaration by separating them by commas thus

```
I, J, K: Integer;
P, Q, R: Integer := 38;
```

In the second case all of P, Q and R are given the initial value of 38.

If a variable is declared and not given an initial value then great care must be taken not to use the undefined value of the variable until one has been properly given to it. If a program does use the undefined value in an uninitialized variable, its behaviour will be unpredictable; the program is said to have a bounded error as described in Section 2.3.

A common way to give a value to a variable is by using an assignment statement. In this, the identifier of the variable is followed by := and then some expression giving the new value. The statement terminates with a semicolon. Thus

```
I := 36;
```

and

```
P := Q+R;
```

are both valid assignment statements and place new values in I and P, thereby overwriting their previous values.

Note that := can be followed by any expression provided that it produces a value of the type of the variable being assigned to. We will discuss all the rules about expressions later, but it suffices to say at this point that they can consist of variables and constants with operations such as + and round brackets (parentheses) and so on just like an ordinary mathematical expression.

There is a lot of similarity between a declaration containing an initial value and an assignment statement. Both use := before the expression and the expression can be of arbitrary complexity.

An important difference, however, is that although several variables can be declared and given the same initial value together, it is not possible for an assignment statement to give the same value to several variables. This may seem odd but in practice the need to give the same value to several variables usually only arises with initial values anyway.

Perhaps we should remark at this stage that strictly speaking a multiple declaration such as

```
A, B: Integer := E;
```

is really a shorthand for

```
A: Integer := E;
B: Integer := E;
```

This means that in principle the expression E is evaluated for each variable. This is a subtle point and does not usually matter, but we will encounter some examples later where the effect is important.

A constant is declared in a similar way to a variable by inserting the reserved word **constant** after the colon. Of course, a constant must be initialized in its declaration otherwise it would be useless. Why? An example might be

```
Pi: constant Float := 3.14159_26536;
```

In the case of numeric types, and only numeric types, it is possible to omit the type from the declaration of a constant thus

```
Pi: constant := 3.14159_26536;
```

It is then technically known as a number declaration and merely provides a name for the number. The distinction between integer and real named numbers is made by the form of the initial value. In this case it is real because of the presence of the decimal point. It is usually good practice to omit the type when declaring numeric constants for reasons which will appear later. We will therefore do so in future examples. But note that the type cannot be omitted in numeric variable declarations even when an initial value is provided.

There is an important distinction between the allowed forms of initial values in constant declarations (with a type) and number declarations (without a type). In the former case the initial value may be any expression and is evaluated when the declaration is encountered at run time whereas in the latter case it must be static and so evaluated at compile time. Full details are deferred until Chapter 12.

EXERCISE 6.1

1   Write a declaration of a floating point variable F giving it an initial value of one.

2   Write appropriate declarations of constants Zero and One of type Float.

3   What is wrong with the following declarations and statements?

(a) **var** I: Integer;
(b) G: **constant** := 981
(c) P, Q: **constant** Integer;
(d) P := Q := 7;
(e) MN: **constant** Integer := M*N;
(f) 2Pi: **constant** := 2.0*Pi;

6.2 Blocks and scopes

Ada carefully distinguishes between declarations which introduce new identifiers and statements which do not. It is clearly only sensible that the declarations which introduce new identifiers should precede the statements which manipulate them. Accordingly, declarations and statements occur in separate places in the program text. The simplest fragment of text which includes declarations and statements is a block.

A block commences with the reserved word **declare**, some declarations, **begin**, some statements and concludes with the reserved word **end** and the terminating semicolon. A trivial example is

```
declare
    I: Integer := 0;          -- declarations here
begin
    I := I + 1;               -- statements here
end;
```

A block is itself an example of a statement and so one of the statements in its body could be another block. This textual nesting of blocks can continue indefinitely.

Since a block is a statement it can be executed like any other statement. When this happens the declarations in its declarative part (the bit between **declare** and **begin**) are elaborated in order, and then the statements in the body (between **begin** and **end**) are executed in the usual way. Note the terminology: we elaborate declarations and execute statements. All that the elaboration of a declaration does is make the thing being declared come into existence and then evaluate and assign any initial value to it. When we come to the **end** of the block all the things which were declared in the block automatically cease to exist.

We can now see that the above simple example of a block is rather foolish; it introduces I, adds 1 to it but then loses it before use is made of the resulting value.

Another point to note is that the objects used in an initial value must, of course, already exist. They could be declared in the same declarative part but the declarations must precede their use. For example

```
declare
    I: Integer := 0;
    K: Integer := I;
begin
```

is allowed. This idea of elaborating declarations in order is important; the jargon is 'linear elaboration of declarations'.

Like other block structured languages, Ada also has the idea of hiding. Consider

```
declare
   I, K: Integer;
begin
   ...                          -- here I is the outer one
   declare
      I: Integer;
   begin
      ...                       -- here I is the inner one
   end;
   ...                          -- here I is the outer one
end;
```

In this, a variable I is declared in an outer block and then redeclared in an inner block. This redeclaration does not cause the outer I to cease to exist but merely makes it temporarily hidden. In the inner block I refers to the new I, but as soon as we leave the inner block, this new I ceases to exist and the outer one again becomes directly visible.

We distinguish the terms 'scope' and 'visibility'. The scope is the region of text where the entity has some effect. In the case of a block the scope of a variable (or constant) extends from the start of its declaration until the end of the block. We say it is visible at a given point if its identifier can be used to refer to it at that point. A fuller discussion has to be left until Chapter 9 when we distinguish visibility and direct visibility but the following simple rules will suffice for the moment

- an object is never visible in its own declaration,
- an object is hidden by the declaration of a new object with the same identifier from the start of the declaration.

Thus the inner declaration of I in the above example could never be

```
   I: Integer := I;              -- illegal
```

because we cannot refer to the inner I in its own declaration and the outer I is already hidden by the inner I.

EXERCISE 6.2

1   How many errors can you see in the following?

```
declare
   I: Integer := 7;
   J, K: Integer
begin
   J := I+K;
```

```
declare
   P: Integer=I;
   I, J: Integer;
begin
   I := P+Q;
   J := P−Q;
   K := I*J;
end;
Put(K);          −− output value of K
end;
```

6.3   Types

'A type is characterized by a set of values and a set of primitive operations ...' (*ARM* 3.2).

In the case of the built-in type Integer, the set of values is represented by

..., −3, −2, −1, 0, 1, 2, 3, ...

and the primitive operations include

+, −, * and so on.

With minor exceptions to be discussed later (arrays, tasks and protected objects) every type has a name which is introduced in a type declaration. (The built-in types such as Integer are considered to be declared in the package Standard.) Moreover, every type declaration introduces a new type quite distinct from any other type.

The set of values belonging to two distinct types are themselves quite distinct, although in some cases the actual lexical form of the values may be identical – which one is meant at any point is determined by the context. The idea of one lexical form representing two or more different things is known as overloading.

Values of one type cannot be assigned to variables of another type. This is the fundamental rule of strong typing. Strong typing, correctly used, is an enormous aid to the rapid development of *correct* programs since it ensures that many errors are detected at compile time. (Overused, it can tie one in knots; we will discuss this thought in Chapter 23.)

A type declaration uses a somewhat different syntax to an object declaration in order to emphasize the conceptual difference. It consists of the reserved word **type**, the identifier to be associated with the type, the reserved word **is** and then the definition of the type followed by the terminating semicolon. We can imagine that the package Standard contains type declarations such as

    type Integer **is** ... ;

The type definition between **is** and ; gives in some way the set of values
belonging to the type. As a concrete example consider the following

    type Colour **is** (Red, Amber, Green);

(This is an example of an enumeration type and will be dealt with in more
detail in a later section in this chapter.)
   This introduces a new type called Colour. Moreover, it states that there are
only three values of this type and they are denoted by the identifiers Red,
Amber and Green.
   Objects of this type can then be declared in the usual way

    C: Colour;

An initial value can be supplied

    C: Colour := Red;

or a constant can be declared

    Default: **constant** Colour := Red;

We have stated that values of one type cannot be assigned to variables of
another type. Therefore one cannot mix colours and integers and so

    I: Integer;
    C: Colour;
    ...
    I := C;

is illegal. In older languages it is often necessary to implement concepts such
as enumeration types by more primitive types such as integers and give values
such as 0, 1 and 2 to variables named Red, Amber and Green. Thus in Algol 60
one could write

    integer Red, Amber, Green;
    Red := 0; Amber := 1; Green := 2;

and then use Red, Amber and Green as if they were literal values. Obviously
the program would be easier to understand than if the code values 0, 1 and 2
had been used directly. But, on the other hand, the compiler could not detect
the accidental assignment of a notional colour to a variable which was, in the
mind of the programmer, just an ordinary integer. In Ada, as we have seen, this
is detected during compilation thus making a potentially tricky error quite
trivial to discover. It should be noted that C also has no enumeration types and
is thus prone to error.

6.4   Subtypes

We now introduce subtypes and constraints. A subtype, as its name suggests, characterizes a set of values which is just a subset of the values of some type. The subset is defined by means of a constraint. Constraints take various forms according to the category of the type. As is usual with subsets, the subset may be the complete set. There is, however, no way of restricting the set of operations of the type. The subtype takes all the operations; subsetting applies only to the values.

(In Ada 83, the type of the subtype was known as the base type and we will sometimes continue to use that term in an informal way. In Ada 95, the type name is strictly considered to denote an unconstrained subtype of the type. Such a subtype is then called the first subtype. One advantage of this apparently pedantic approach is that the *ARM* can use the term subtype rather than having to say type or subtype all the time.)

As an example suppose we wish to manipulate dates; we know that the day of the month must lie in the range 1 .. 31 so we declare a subtype thus

subtype Day_Number **is** Integer **range** 1 .. 31;

We can then declare variables and constants using the subtype identifier in exactly the same way as a type identifier.

D: Day_Number;

We are then assured that the variable D can only be assigned integer values from 1 to 31 inclusive. The compiler will insert run-time checks if necessary to ensure that this is so; if a check fails then the Constraint_Error exception is raised.

It is important to realize that a subtype declaration does not introduce a new distinct type. An object such as D is of type Integer, and so the following is perfectly legal from the syntactic point of view.

D: Day_Number;
I: Integer;
...
D := I;

Of course, on execution, the value of I may or may not lie in the range 1 .. 31. If it does, then all is well; if not then Constraint_Error will be raised. Assignment in the other direction

I := D;

will, of course, always work.

It is not always necessary to introduce a subtype explicitly in order to impose a constraint. We could equally have written

D: Integer **range** 1 .. 31;

Furthermore a subtype need not impose a constraint. It is perfectly legal to write

> **subtype** Day_Number **is** Integer;

although in this instance it is not of much value.

A subtype (explicit or not) may be defined in terms of a previous subtype

> **subtype** Feb_Day **is** Day_Number **range** 1 .. 29;

Any additional constraint must of course satisfy existing constraints

> Day_Number **range** 0 .. 10

would be incorrect and cause Constraint_Error to be raised.

The above examples have shown constraints with static bounds. This is not necessarily the case; in general the bounds can be given by arbitrary expressions and so the set of values of a subtype need not be static, that is known at compile time. However, it is an important fact that a type is always static.

In conclusion then, a subtype does not introduce a new type but is merely a shorthand for an existing type or subtype with an optional constraint. However, in later chapters we will encounter several contexts in which an explicit constraint is not allowed; a subtype has to be introduced for these cases. We refer to a subtype name as a subtype mark and to the form consisting of a subtype mark followed by an optional constraint as a subtype indication as shown by the syntax

> subtype_mark ::= *subtype*_name
>
> subtype_indication ::= subtype_mark [constraint]

Thus we can restate the previous remark as saying that there are situations where a subtype mark has to be used whereas, as we have seen here, the more general subtype indication (which includes a subtype mark on its own) is allowed in object declarations.

The sensible use of subtypes has two advantages. It can ensure that programming errors are detected earlier by preventing variables from being assigned inappropriate values. It can also increase the execution efficiency of a program. This particularly applies to array subscripts as we shall see later.

We conclude this section by summarizing the assignment statement and the rules of strong typing. Assignment has the form

> Variable := expression;

and the two rules are

- both sides must have the same type,
- the expression must satisfy any constraints on the variable; if it does not, the assignment does not take place, and Constraint_Error is raised instead.

Note carefully the general principle that type errors (violations of the first rule) are detected during compilation whereas subtype errors (violations of the second rule) are detected during execution by the raising of Constraint_Error. (A clever compiler might give a warning during compilation.)

We have now introduced the basic concepts of types and subtypes. The remaining sections of this chapter illustrate these concepts further by considering in more detail the properties of the simple types of Ada.

EXERCISE 6.4

1   Given the following declarations

   I, J: Integer **range** 1 .. 10;
   K: Integer **range** 1 .. 20;

which of the following assignment statements could raise Constraint_Error?

   (a) I := J;   (b) K := J;   (c) J := K;

6.5   Simple numeric types

Perhaps surprisingly, a full description of the numeric types of Ada is deferred until much later in this book. The problems of numerical analysis (error estimates and so on) are complex and Ada is correspondingly rich in this area so that it can cope in a reasonably complete way with the needs of the numerical specialist. For our immediate purposes such complexity can be ignored. Accordingly, in this section, we merely consolidate a simple understanding of the two predefined numeric types Integer and Float.

First a reminder. We recall from Section 2.4 that the predefined numeric types are not portable and should be used with caution. However, all the operations described here apply to all integer and floating point types, both predefined and those defined by the user such as My_Integer and My_Float.

As we have seen, a constraint may be imposed on the type Integer by using the reserved word **range**. This is then followed by two expressions separated by two dots which, of course, must produce values of integer type. These expressions need not be literal constants. One could have

   P: Integer **range** 1 .. I+J;

A range can be null as would happen in the above case if I+J turned out to be zero. Null ranges may seem pretty useless but they often automatically occur in limiting cases, and to exclude them would mean taking special action in such cases.

The minimum value of the type Integer is given by Integer'First and the maximum value by Integer'Last. These are our first examples of attributes. Ada contains various attributes denoted by a single quote followed by an identifier.

The value of Integer'First will depend on the implementation but will always be negative. On a two's complement machine it will be –Integer'Last–1 whereas on a one's complement machine it will be –Integer'Last. So on a minimal 16-bit two's complement implementation we will have

```
Integer'First = -32768
Integer'Last = +32767
```

Of course, we should always write Integer'Last rather than +32767 if that is what we logically want. Otherwise program portability could suffer.

Two useful subtypes are

```
subtype Natural is Integer range 0 .. Integer'Last;
subtype Positive is Integer range 1 .. Integer'Last;
```

These are so useful that they are declared for us in the package Standard.

The attributes First and Last also apply to subtypes so

```
Positive'First = 1
Natural'Last = Integer'Last
```

We turn now to a brief consideration of the type Float. It is possible to apply a constraint to the type Float in order to reduce the range such as

```
subtype Chance is Float range 0.0 .. 1.0;
```

where the range of course is given using expressions of the type Float. There are also attributes Float'First and Float'Last. It is not really necessary to say any more at this point.

The other predefined operations that can be performed on the types Integer and Float are much as one would expect in a modern programming language. They are summarized below.

+, –   These are either unary operators (that is, taking a single operand) or binary operators taking two operands.

In the case of a unary operator, the operand can be either Integer or Float; the result will be of the same type. Unary + effectively does nothing. Unary – changes the sign.

In the case of a binary operator, both operands must be of the same type; the result will be of that type. Normal addition or subtraction is performed.

*   Multiplication; both operands must be of the same type; again the result is of the same type.

/   Division; both operands must be of the same type; again the result is of the same type. Integer division truncates towards zero.

rem   Remainder; in this case both operands must be Integer and the result is Integer. It is the remainder on division.

mod   Modulo; again both operands must be Integer and the result is Integer. This is the mathematical modulo operation.

abs   Absolute value; this is a unary operator and the single operand may be Integer or Float. The result is again of the same type and is the absolute value. That is, if the operand is positive, the result is the same but if it is negative, the result is the corresponding positive value.

**   Exponentiation; this raises the first operand to the power of the second. If the first operand is of type Integer, the second must be a positive integer or zero. If the first operand is of type Float, the second can be any integer. The result is of the same type as the first operand.

In addition, we can perform the operations =, /=, <, <=, > and >= which return a Boolean result True or False. Again both operands must be of the same type. Note the form of the not equals operator /=.

Although the above operations are mostly straightforward a few points are worth noting.

It is a general rule that mixed mode arithmetic is not allowed. One cannot, for example, add an integer value to a floating point value; both must be of the same type. A change of type from Integer to Float or vice versa can be done by using the desired type name (or indeed subtype name) followed by the expression to be converted in brackets.

So given

    I: Integer := 3;
    F: Float := 5.6;

we cannot write

    I + F

but we must write

    Float(I) + F

which uses floating point addition to give the floating point value 8.6, or

    I + Integer(F)

which uses integer addition to give the integer value 9.

Conversion from Float to Integer always rounds rather than truncates, thus

1.4	becomes	1
1.6	becomes	2

and a value midway between two integers, such as 1.5, is always rounded away from zero so that 1.5 always becomes 2 and –1.5 becomes –2.

There is a subtle distinction between **rem** and **mod**. The **rem** operation produces the remainder corresponding to the integer division operation /.

Figure 6.1   Behaviour of I **rem** 5 around zero.

Figure 6.2   Behaviour of I **mod** 5 around zero.

Integer division truncates towards zero; this means that the absolute value of the result is always the same as that obtained by dividing the absolute values of the operands. So

```
  7 / 3 = 2
(–7) / 3 = –2
  7 / (–3) = –2
(–7) / (–3) = 2
```

and the corresponding remainders are

```
  7 rem  3 = 1
(–7) rem  3 = –1
  7 rem (–3) = 1
(–7) rem (–3) = –1
```

The remainder and quotient are always related by

$$(I/J) * J + I \textbf{ rem } J = I$$

and it will also be noted that the sign of the remainder is always equal to the sign of the first operand I (the dividend).

However, **rem** is not always satisfactory. If we plot the values of I **rem** J for a fixed value of J (say 5) for both positive and negative values of I we get the pattern shown in Figure 6.1. As we can see, the pattern is symmetric about zero and consequently changes its incremental behaviour as we pass through zero. The **mod** operation, on the other hand, does have uniform incremental behaviour as shown in Figure 6.2.

The **mod** operation enables us to do normal modulo arithmetic. For example

(A+B) **mod** n = (A **mod** n + B **mod** n) **mod** n

for all values of A and B both positive and negative. For positive n, A **mod** n is always in the range 0 .. n–1; for negative n, A **mod** n is always in the range n+1 .. 0. Of course, modulo arithmetic is only usually performed with a positive value for n. But the **mod** operator gives consistent and sensible behaviour for negative values of n also.

We can look upon **mod** as giving the remainder corresponding to division with truncation towards minus infinity. So

```
  7 mod   3 =  1
(–7) mod   3 =  2
  7 mod (–3) = –2
(–7) mod (–3) = –1
```

In the case of **mod** the sign of the result is always equal to the sign of the second operand whereas with **rem** it is the sign of the first operand.

The reader may have felt that this discussion has been somewhat protracted. In summary, it is perhaps worth saying that integer division with negative operands is rare. The operators **rem** and **mod** only differ when just one operand is negative. It will be found that in such cases it is almost always **mod** that is wanted. Moreover, note that if we are performing modular arithmetic in general then we should perhaps being using modular types; these are unsigned integer types with automatic range wraparound and are discussed in detail in Chapter 15.

Finally some notes on the exponentiation operator **. For a positive second operand, the operation corresponds to repeated multiplication. So

```
3**4 = 3*3*3*3 = 81
3.0**4 = 3.0*3.0*3.0*3.0 = 81.0
```

A very subtle point is that the repeated multiplications can be performed by appropriate squarings as an optimization although as we shall see in Section 22.5 there can be slight differences in accuracy in the floating point case.

The second operand can be 0 and, of course, the result is then always the value one

```
3**0 = 1
3.0**0 = 1.0
0**0 = 1
0.0**0 = 1.0
```

The second operand cannot be negative if the first operand is an integer, as the result might not be a whole number. In fact, the exception Constraint_Error would be raised in such case. But it is allowed for a floating point first operand and produces the corresponding reciprocal

$$3.0**(-4) = 1.0/81.0 = 0.0123456780123 \ldots$$

We conclude this section with a brief discussion on combining operators in an expression. As is usual, the operators have different precedence levels and the natural precedence can be overruled by the use of brackets. Operators of the same precedence are applied in order from left to right. A subexpression in brackets obviously has to be evaluated before it can be used. But note that the order of evaluation of the two operands of a binary operator is not specified. The precedence levels of the operators we have met so far are shown below in increasing order of precedence

```
=   /=  <   <=   >   >=
+   -                          (binary)
+   -                          (unary)
*   /   mod   rem
**   abs
```

Thus

A/B*C	means	(A/B)*C
A+B*C+D	means	A+(B*C)+D
A*B+C*D	means	(A*B)+(C*D)
A*B**C	means	A*(B**C)

In general, as stated above, several operations of the same precedence can be applied from left to right and brackets are not necessary. However, the syntax rules forbid multiple instances of the exponentiation operator without brackets. Thus we cannot write

A**B**C

but must explicitly write either

(A**B)**C   or   A**(B**C)

This restriction avoids the risk of accidentally writing the wrong thing. Note however that the well established forms

A-B-C   and   A/B/C

are allowed. The syntax rules similarly prevent the mixed use of **abs** and ****** without brackets.

The precedence of unary minus needs care

-A**B   means   -(A**B)   rather than   (-A)**B

as in Algol 68 and C. Also

A**-B   and   A*-B

are illegal. Brackets are necessary.

Note finally that the precedence of **abs** is, confusingly, not the same as that of unary minus. As a consequence we can write

   – abs X   but not   **abs** – X

EXERCISE 6.5

1 Evaluate the expressions below given the following

   I: Integer := 7;
   J: Integer := –5;
   K: Integer := 3;

(a) I*J*K   (d) J + 2 **mod** I   (g) –J **mod** 3
(b) I/J*K   (e) J + 2 **rem** I   (h) –J **rem** 3
(c) I/J/K   (f) K**K**K

2 Rewrite the following mathematical expressions in Ada. Use suitable identifiers of appropriate type.

(a) Mr^2 – moment of inertia of black hole
(b) b^2-4ac – discriminant of quadratic
(c) $^4/_3\pi r^3$ – volume of sphere
(d) $p\pi a^4/8l\eta$ – viscous flowrate through tube

6.6 Enumeration types

Here are some examples of declarations of enumeration types starting with Colour which we introduced when discussing types in general.

      type Colour **is** (Red, Amber, Green);
      type Day **is** (Mon, Tue, Wed, Thu, Fri, Sat, Sun);
      type Stone **is** (Amber, Beryl, Quartz);
      type Groom **is** (Tinker, Tailor, Soldier, Sailor,
                      Rich_Man, Poor_Man, Beggar_Man, Thief);
      type Solo **is** (Alone);

This introduces an example of overloading. The literal Amber can represent a Colour or a Stone. Both meanings of the same name are visible together and the second declaration does not hide the first whether they are declared in the same declarative part or one is in an inner declarative part. We can usually tell which is meant from the context, but in those odd cases when we cannot we can always qualify the literal by placing it in brackets and preceding it by an

appropriate subtype mark (that is its type name or a relevant subtype name) and
a single quote. Thus

> Colour'(Amber)
> Stone'(Amber)

Examples where this is necessary will occur later.

Although we can use Amber as an enumeration literal in two distinct
enumeration types, we cannot use it as an enumeration literal and the identifier
of a variable at the same time. The declaration of one would hide the other and
they could not both be declared in the same declarative part. Later we will see
that an enumeration literal can be overloaded with a subprogram.

There is no upper limit on the number of values in an enumeration type but
there must be at least one. An empty enumeration type is not allowed.

Constraints on enumeration types and subtypes are much as for integers.
The constraint has the form

> **range** lower_bound_expression .. upper_bound_expression

and this indicates the set of values from the lower bound to the upper bound
inclusive. So we can write

> **subtype** Weekday **is** Day **range** Mon .. Fri;
> D: Weekday;

or

> D: Day **range** Mon .. Fri;

and then we know that D cannot be Sat or Sun.

If the lower bound is above the upper bound then we get a null range, thus

> **subtype** Colourless **is** Colour **range** Amber .. Red;

Note the curious anomaly that we cannot have a null subtype of a type such as
Solo (since it only has one value).

The attributes First and Last apply to enumeration types and subtypes, so

> Colour'First = Red
> Weekday'Last = Fri

There are built-in functional attributes to give the successor or predecessor of
an enumeration value. These consist of Succ or Pred following the type name
and a single quote. Thus

> Colour'Succ(Amber) = Green
> Stone'Succ(Amber) = Beryl
> Day'Pred(Fri) = Thu

Of course, the thing in brackets can be an arbitrary expression of the
appropriate type. If we try to take the predecessor of the first value or the

successor of the last then the exception Constraint_Error is raised. In the absence of this exception we have, for any type T and any value X,

    T'Succ(T'Pred(X)) = X

and vice versa.

Another functional attribute is Pos. This gives the position number of the enumeration value, that is the position in the declaration with the first one having a position number of zero. So

    Colour'Pos(Red) = 0
    Colour'Pos(Amber) = 1
    Colour'Pos(Green) = 2

The opposite to Pos is Val. This takes the position number and returns the corresponding enumeration value. So

    Colour'Val(0) = Red
    Day'Val(6) = Sun

If we give a position value outside the range, as for example

    Solo'Val(1)

then Constraint_Error is raised.

Clearly we always have

    T'Val(T'Pos(X)) = X

and vice versa. We also note that

    T'Succ(X) = T'Val(T'Pos(X) + 1)

they either both give the same value or both raise an exception.

It should be noted that these four attributes Succ, Pred, Pos and Val may also be applied to subtypes but are then identical to the same attributes of the corresponding base type.

It is probably rather bad practice to mess about with Pos and Val when it can be avoided. To do so encourages the programmer to think in terms of numbers rather than the enumeration values and hence destroys the abstraction.

The operators =, /=, <, <=, > and >= also apply to enumeration types. The result is defined by the order of the values in the type declaration. So

    Red < Green   is   True
    Wed >= Thu   is   False

The same result would be obtained by comparing the position values. So

    T'Pos(X) < T'Pos(Y)   and   X < Y

are always equivalent (except that X < Y might be ambiguous).

EXERCISE 6.6

1   Evaluate

(a) Day'Succ(Weekday'Last)
(b) Weekday'Succ(Weekday'Last)
(c) Stone'Pos(Quartz)

2   Write suitable declarations of enumeration types for

(a) the colours of the rainbow,
(b) typical fruits.

3   Write an expression that delivers one's predicted bridegroom after eating a portion
of pie containing N stones. Use the type Groom declared at the beginning of this
section.

4   If the first of the month is in D where D is of type Day, then write an assignment
replacing D by the day of the week of the Nth day of the month.

5   Why might X < Y be ambiguous?

6.7   The Boolean type

The Boolean type is a predefined enumeration type whose declaration can be
considered to be

> **type** Boolean **is** (False, True);

Boolean values are used in constructions such as the if statement which we
briefly met in Chapter 2. Boolean values are produced by the operators =, /=,
<, <=, > and >= which have their expected meaning and apply to many types.
So we can write constructions such as

> **if** Today = Sun **then**
>   Tomorrow := Mon;
> **else**
>   Tomorrow := Day'Succ(Today);
> **end if**;

The Boolean type (we capitalize the name in memory of the mathematician
Boole) has all the normal properties of an enumeration type, so, for instance

> False < True = True !!
> Boolean'Pos(True) = 1

We could even write the curious

> **subtype** Always **is** Boolean **range** True .. True;

and	F	T		or	F	T		xor	F	T
F	F	F		F	F	T		F	F	T
T	F	T		T	T	T		T	T	F

Figure 6.3   Operator tables for **and**, **or** and **xor**.

The Boolean type also has other operators which are as follows

not   This is a unary operator and changes True to False and vice versa. It has the same precedence as **abs**.

and   This is a binary operator. The result is True if both operands are True, and False otherwise.

or   This is a binary operator. The result is True if one or other or both operands are True, and False only if they are both False.

xor   This is also a binary operator. The result is True if one or other operand but not both are True. (Hence the name – eXclusive OR.) Another way of looking at it is to note that the result is True if and only if the operands are different. (The operator is known as 'not equivalent' in some languages.)

The effects of **and**, **or** and **xor** are summarized in the usual operator tables shown in Figure 6.3.

The precedences of **and**, **or** and **xor** are equal to each other but lower than that of any other operator. In particular they are of lower precedence than the relational operators =, /=, <, <=, > and >=. This is unlike Pascal and as a consequence brackets are not needed in expressions such as

P < Q **and** I = J

However, although the precedences are equal, **and**, **or** and **xor** cannot be mixed up in an expression without using brackets (unlike + and – for instance). So

B **and** C **or** D   is illegal

whereas

I + J – K   is legal

We have to write

B **and** (C **or** D)   or   (B **and** C) **or** D

in order to emphasize which meaning is required.

The reader familiar with other programming languages will remember that **and** and **or** usually have a different precedence. The problem with this is that the programmer often gets confused and writes the wrong thing. It is to prevent this that Ada makes them the same precedence and insists on brackets. Of course, successive applications of the same operator are permitted so

> B **and** C **and** D   is legal

and as usual evaluation goes from left to right although, of course, it does not matter in this case since the operator **and** is associative.

Take care with **not**. Its precedence is higher than **and**, **or** and **xor** as in other languages and so

> **not** A **or** B

means

> (**not** A) **or** B

rather than

> **not** (A **or** B)

which those familiar with logic will remember is the same as

> (**not** A) **and** (**not** B)

Boolean variables and constants can be declared and manipulated in the usual way.

> Danger: Boolean;
> Signal: Colour;
> ...
> Danger := Signal = Red;

The variable Danger is then True if the signal is Red. We can then write

> **if** Danger **then**
>   Stop_Train;
> **end if**;

Note that we do not have to write

> **if** Danger = True **then**

although this is perfectly legal; it just misses the point that Danger is already a Boolean and so can be used directly as the condition.

A worse sin is to write

```
    if Signal = Red then
        Danger := True;
    else
        Danger := False;
    end if;
```

rather than

```
    Danger := Signal = Red;
```

The literals True and False could be overloaded by declaring for example

```
    type Answer is (False, Dont_Know, True);
```

but to do so might make the program rather confusing.

Finally, it should be noted that it is often clearer to introduce our own two-valued enumeration type rather than use the type Boolean. Thus instead of

```
    Wheels_OK: Boolean;
    ...
    if Wheels_OK then
```

it is much better (and safer!) to write

```
    type Wheel_State is (Up, Down);
    Wheel_Position: Wheel_State;
    ...
    if Wheel_Position = Up then
```

since whether the wheels are OK or not depends upon the situation. OK for landing is different to being OK for cruising. The enumeration type removes any doubt as to which is meant.

EXERCISE 6.7

1   Write declarations of constants T and F having the values True and False.

2   Using T and F from the previous exercise, evaluate

(a) T **and** F **and** T   (d) (F = F) = (F = F)
(b) **not** T **or** T   (e) T < T < T < T
(c) F = F = F = F

3   Evaluate

   (A /= B) = (A **xor** B)

for all combinations of values of Boolean variables A and B.

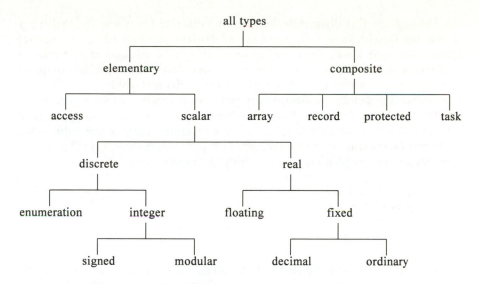

Figure 6.4   Ada type hierarchy.

6.8   Type classification

At this point we pause to consolidate the material presented in this chapter so far.

The types in Ada can be classified as shown in Figure 6.4. The broad classification is into elementary types and composite types. Ultimately everything is essentially made up of elementary types.

Elementary types are divided into access types which are dealt with in Chapter 10 and the scalar types some of which we have discussed in this chapter. In Chapter 8 we will deal with arrays and simple records but the other composite types (task and protected types) will be dealt with much later. Record types themselves take various forms; they may be tagged as we saw in Chapter 3 and these are dealt with in detail in Chapter 13 when we discuss Object Oriented Programming. Record types and task and protected types may also be parameterized with so-called discriminants and these are discussed in Chapter 16.

The scalar types themselves can be subdivided into real types and discrete types. The real types are subdivided into floating point types and fixed point types. Our sole example of a real type has been the floating point type Float – the other real types are discussed in Chapter 15. The other types discussed in this chapter, Integer, Boolean and enumeration types in general are discrete types – the only other kinds of discrete types to be introduced are other integer types again dealt with in Chapter 15, and character types which are in fact a form of enumeration type and are dealt with in Chapter 8. Note that the integer types are subdivided into signed integer types such as Integer and the modular types.

The key abstract distinction between the discrete types and the real types is that the former have a clear-cut set of distinct separate (that is, discrete) values. The type Float, on the other hand, should be thought of as having a continuous set of values – we know in practice that a finite digital computer must implement a real type as actually a set of distinct values but this is an implementation detail, the abstract concept is of a continuous set of values.

The attributes Pos, Val, Succ and Pred apply to all discrete types (and subtypes) because the operations reflect the discrete nature of the values. We explained their meaning with enumeration types in Section 6.6. In the case of type Integer the position number is simply the number itself so

```
Integer'Pos(N) = N
Integer'Val(N) = N
Integer'Succ(N) = N+1
Integer'Pred(N) = N–1
```

The application of these attributes to integers does at first sight seem pretty futile, but when we come to the concept of generic units in Chapter 17 we will see that it is convenient to allow them to apply to all discrete types.

Furthermore, despite our previous remarks about the continuous nature of real types, the attributes Pred and Succ (but not Pos and Val) also apply to all real types. They return the adjacent implemented number.

The attributes First and Last also apply to all scalar types and subtypes including real types. The attribute Range provides a useful shorthand since S'Range is equivalent to S'First .. S'Last.

There are two other functional attributes for all scalar types and subtypes. These are Max and Min which take two parameters and return the maximum or minimum value of the base type respectively. Thus

```
Integer'Min(5, 10) = 5
```

Again we emphasize that Max, Min, Pos, Val, Succ and Pred for a subtype are identical to the corresponding operations on the base type, whereas in the case of First, Last and Range this is not so.

Finally we note the difference between a type conversion and a type qualification.

```
Float(I)            -- conversion
Integer'(I)         -- qualification
```

In the case of a conversion we are changing the type, in the second, we are just stating it (usually to overcome an ambiguity). As a mnemonic aid *q*ualification uses a *q*uote.

In both cases we can use a subtype name and Constraint_Error could consequently arise. Thus

```
Positive(F)
```

would convert the value of the floating point variable F to integer and then
check that it was positive, whereas

>   Positive'(I)

would just check that the value of I was positive. In both cases, of course, the
result is the checked value and is then used in an overall expression; these
checks cannot just stand alone.

EXERCISE 6.8

1   Evaluate

>   (a) Boolean'Min(True, False)   (b) Weekday'Max(Tue, Sat)

6.9   Expression summary

All the operators introduced so far are shown in Table 6.1 grouped by
precedence level. In all the cases of binary operators except for ******, the two
operands must be of the same type.

We have actually now introduced all the operators of Ada except for one
(&) although as we shall see there are further possible meanings to be added.

There are also two membership tests which apply to all scalar types (among
others). These are **in** and **not in**. They are technically not operators although
their precedence is the same as that of the relational operators =, **/**= and so on.
They enable us to test whether a value lies within a specified range (including
the end values) or satisfies a constraint implied by a subtype. The first operand
is therefore a scalar expression, the second is a range or a subtype mark and the
result is, of course, of type Boolean. Examples are

>   I **not in** 1 .. 10
>   I **in** Positive
>   Today **in** Weekday

Note that this is one of the situations where we have to use a subtype mark
rather than a subtype indication. We could not replace the last example by

>   Today **in** Day **range** Mon .. Fri

although we could write

>   Today **in** Mon .. Fri

Ada seems a bit curious here!

Table 6.1   Simple scalar operators.

Operator	Operation	Operand(s)	Result
and	conjunction	Boolean	Boolean
or	inclusive or	Boolean	Boolean
xor	exclusive or	Boolean	Boolean
=	equality	any	Boolean
/=	inequality	any	Boolean
<	less than	scalar	Boolean
<=	less than or equals	scalar	Boolean
>	greater than	scalar	Boolean
>=	greater than or equals	scalar	Boolean
+	addition	numeric	same
–	subtraction	numeric	same
+	identity	numeric	same
–	negation	numeric	same
*	multiplication	Integer	Integer
		Float	Float
/	division	Integer	Integer
		Float	Float
mod	modulo	Integer	Integer
rem	remainder	Integer	Integer
**	exponentiation	Integer, Natural	Integer
		Float, Integer	Float
not	negation	Boolean	Boolean
abs	absolute value	numeric	same

The test **not in** is equivalent to using **in** and then applying **not** to the result, but **not in** is usually more readable. So the first expression above could be written as

> **not** (I **in** 1 .. 10)

where the brackets are necessary.

The reason that **in** and **not in** are not technically operators is explained in Chapter 9 when we deal with subprograms.

There are also two short circuit control forms **and then** and **or else** which like **in** and **not in** are also not technically classed as operators.

The form **and then** is closely related to the operator **and**, whereas **or else** is closely related to the operator **or**. They may occur in expressions and have the same precedence as **and**, **or** and **xor**. The difference lies in the rules regarding the evaluation of their operands.

In the case of **and** and **or**, both operands are always evaluated but the order is not specified. In the case of **and then** and **or else** the left hand operand is always evaluated first and the right hand operand is only evaluated if it is necessary in order to determine the result.

So in

   X **and then** Y

X is evaluated first. If X is false, the answer is false whatever the value of Y so Y is not evaluated. If X is true, Y has to be evaluated and the value of Y is the answer.

Similarly in

   X **or else** Y

X is evaluated first. If X is true, the answer is true whatever the value of Y so Y is not evaluated. If X is false, Y has to be evaluated and the value of Y is the answer.

The forms **and then** and **or else** should be used in cases where the order of evaluation matters. A common circumstance is where the first condition protects against the evaluation of the second condition in circumstances that could raise an exception.

Suppose we need to test

   I/J > K

and we wish to avoid the risk that J is zero. In such a case we could write

   J /= 0 **and then** I/J > K

and we would then know that if J is zero there is no risk of an attempt to divide by zero. The observant reader will realize that this is not a very good example because one could usually write I>K*J (assuming J positive) – but even here we could get overflow. Better examples occur with arrays and access types and will be mentioned in due course.

Like **and** and **or**, the forms **and then** and **or else** cannot be mixed without using brackets.

We now summarize the primary components of an expression (that is the things upon which the operators operate) that we have met so far. They are

- identifiers   such as Colour
- literals   such as 4.6, 2#101#
- type conversions   such as Integer(F)
- qualified expressions   such as Colour'(Amber)
- attributes   such as Integer'Last
- function calls   such as Day'Succ(Today)

A full consideration of functions and how they are declared and called has to be deferred until later. However, it is worth noting at this point that a function with one parameter is called by following its name by the parameter in brackets. The parameter can be any expression of the appropriate type and could include further function calls. We will assume for the moment that we have available a simple mathematical library containing familiar functions such as

Sqrt	square root
Log	logarithm to base 10
Ln	natural logarithm
Exp	exponential function
Sin	sine
Cos	cosine

In each case they take an argument of type Float and deliver a result of type Float.

We are now in a position to write statements such as

```
Root := (–B+Sqrt(B**2–4.0*A*C)) / (2.0*A);
Sin2x := 2.0*Sin(X)*Cos(X);
```

Finally a note on errors although this is not the place to deal with them in depth. The reader will have noticed that whenever anything could go wrong we have usually stated that the exception Constraint_Error will be raised. This is a general exception which applies to all sorts of violations of ranges. Constraint_Error is also raised if something goes wrong with the evaluation of an arithmetic expression itself before an attempt is made to store the result. An obvious example is an attempt to divide by zero.

As well as exceptions there are erroneous constructs and bounded errors as mentioned in Chapter 2. The use of a variable before a value has been assigned to it is an important example of a bounded error. In addition there are situations where the order is not defined and which could give rise to a nonportable program. Two cases which we have encountered so far where the order is not defined are

- The destination variable in an assignment statement may be evaluated before or after the expression to be assigned.
- The order of evaluation of the two operands of a binary operator is not defined.

(In the first case it should be realized that the destination variable could be an array component such as A(I+J) and so the expression I+J has to be evaluated as part of evaluating the destination variable; we will deal with arrays in Chapter 8.) Examples where these orders matter cannot be given until we deal with functions in Chapter 9.

EXERCISE 6.9

1   Rewrite the following mathematical expressions in Ada.

   (a) $2\pi\sqrt{l/g}$ – period of a pendulum

   (b) $\dfrac{m_0}{\sqrt{1-v^2/c^2}}$ – mass of relativistic particle

   (c) $\sqrt{2\pi n.n^n.e^{-n}}$ – Stirling's approximation for $n!$ (integral n)

2   Rewrite **1**(c) replacing n by the real value x.

CHECKLIST 6

Declarations and statements are terminated by a semicolon.

Initialization, like assignment uses :=.

Any initial value is evaluated for each object in a declaration.

Elaboration of declarations is linear.

The identifier of an object may not be used in its own declaration.

Each type definition introduces a quite distinct type.

A subtype is not a new type but merely a shorthand for a type with a possible constraint.

A type is always static, a subtype need not be.

No mixed mode arithmetic.

Distinguish **rem** and **mod** for negative operands.

Exponentiation with a negative exponent only applies to real types.

Take care with the precedence of the unary operators.

A scalar type cannot be empty, a subtype can.

Max, Min, Pos, Val, Succ and Pred on subtypes are the same as on the base type.

First and Last are different for subtypes.

Qualification uses a quote.

Order of evaluation of binary operands is not defined.

Distinguish **and, or** and **and then, or else**.

Changes from Ada 83

Max and **Min** did not exist in Ada 83.

Pred and **Succ** did not apply to real types in Ada 83.

Incorrect arithmetic could raise **Numeric_Error** in Ada 83; this is an obsolescent renaming of **Constraint_Error** in Ada 95.

Rounding of exact halves was not defined in Ada 83.

7 Control Structures

7.1	If statements	7.4	Goto statements and labels
7.2	Case statements	7.5	Statement classification
7.3	Loop statements		

This chapter describes the three bracketed sequential control structures of Ada. These are the if statement, the case statement and the loop statement. It is well known that these three control structures are sufficient to be able to write programs with a clearly discernible flow of control without recourse to goto statements and labels. However, for pragmatic reasons, Ada does have a goto statement and this is also described in this chapter.

The three control structures exhibit a similar bracketing style. There is an opening reserved word **if**, **case** or **loop** and this is matched at the end of the structure by the same reserved word preceded by **end**. The whole is, as usual, terminated by a semicolon. So we have

if	**case**	**loop**
...	...	...
end if;	**end case**;	**end loop**;

In the case of the loop statement the word **loop** can be preceded by an iteration scheme commencing with **for** or **while**.

7.1 If statements

The simplest form of if statement starts with the reserved word **if** followed by a Boolean expression and the reserved word **then**. This is then followed by a

99

sequence of statements which will be executed if the Boolean expression turns out to be True. The end of the sequence is indicated by the closing **end if**. The Boolean expression can, of course, be of arbitrary complexity and the sequence of statements can be of arbitrary length.

A simple example is

```
if Hungry then
   Eat;
end if;
```

In this, Hungry is a Boolean variable and Eat is a subprogram describing the details of the eating activity. The statement Eat; merely calls the subprogram (subprograms are dealt with in detail in Chapter 9).

The effect of this if statement is that if variable Hungry is True then we call the subprogram Eat and otherwise we do nothing. In either case we then obey the statement following the if statement.

As we have said there could be a long sequence between **then** and **end if**. Thus we might break down the process into more detail

```
if Hungry then
   Cook;
   Eat;
   Wash_Up;
end if;
```

Note how we indent the statements to show the flow structure of the program. This is most important since it enables the program to be understood so much more easily. The **end if** should be underneath the corresponding **if** and the **then** is best placed on the same line as the **if**.

Sometimes, if the whole statement is very short it can all go on one line

```
if X < 0.0 then X := -X; end if;
```

Note that **end if** will always be preceded by a semicolon. This is because the semicolons terminate statements rather than separate them as in Algol and Pascal. Readers familiar with those languages will probably feel initially that the Ada style is irksome. However, it is consistent and makes line by line program editing so much easier.

Often we will want to do alternative actions according to the value of the condition. In this case we add **else** followed by the alternative sequence to be obeyed if the condition is False. We saw an example of this in the last chapter

```
if Today = Sun then
   Tomorrow := Mon;
else
   Tomorrow := Day'Succ(Today);
end if;
```

Algol and C users should note that Ada is not an expression language and so conditional expressions are not allowed. We cannot write something like

```
Tomorrow :=
        if Today = Sun then Mon else Day'Succ(Today) end if;
```

The statements in the sequences after **then** and **else** can be quite arbitrary and so could be further nested if statements. Suppose we have to solve the quadratic equation

$$ax^2 + bx + c = 0$$

The first thing to check is a. If $a = 0$ then the equation degenerates into a linear equation with a single root $-c/b$. (Mathematicians will understand that the other root has slipped off to infinity.) If a is not zero then we test the discriminant $b^2 - 4ac$ to see whether the roots are real or complex. We could program this as

```
if A = 0.0 then
        -- linear case
else
   if B**2 – 4.0*A*C >= 0.0 then
        -- real roots
   else
        -- complex roots
   end if;
end if;
```

Observe the repetition of **end if**. This is rather ugly and occurs sufficiently frequently to justify an additional construction. This uses the reserved word **elsif** as follows

```
if A = 0.0 then
        -- linear case
elsif B**2 – 4.0*A*C >= 0.0 then
        -- real roots
else
        -- complex roots
end if;
```

This construction emphasizes the essentially equal status of the three cases and also the sequential nature of the tests.

The **elsif** part can be repeated an arbitrary number of times and the final **else** part is optional. The behaviour is simply that each condition is evaluated in turn until one that is True is encountered; the corresponding sequence is then obeyed. If none of the conditions turns out to be True then the else part, if any, is taken; if there is no else part then none of the sequences is obeyed.

Note the spelling of **elsif**. It is the only reserved word of Ada that is not an English word (apart from operators such as **xor**). Note also the layout – we align **elsif** and **else** with the **if** and **end if** and all the sequences are indented equally.

As a further example, suppose we are drilling soldiers and they can obey four different orders described by

> **type** Move **is** (Left, Right, Back, On);

and that their response to these orders is described by calling subprograms Turn_Left, Turn_Right and Turn_Back or by doing nothing at all respectively. Suppose that the variable Order of type **Move** contains the order to be obeyed. We could then write the following

```
if Order = Left then
   Turn_Left;
else
   if Order = Right then
      Turn_Right;
   else
      if Order = Back then
         Turn_Back;
      end if;
   end if;
end if;
```

But it is far clearer and neater to write

```
if Order = Left then
   Turn_Left;
elsif Order = Right then
   Turn_Right;
elsif Order = Back then
   Turn_Back;
end if;
```

This illustrates a situation where there is no **else** part. However, although better than using nested if statements, this is still a bad solution because it obscures the symmetry and mutual exclusion of the four cases ('mutual exclusion' means that by their very nature only one can apply). We have been forced to impose an ordering on the tests which is quite arbitrary and not the essence of the problem. The proper solution is to use the case statement as we shall see in the next section.

Contrast this with the quadratic equation. In that example, the cases were not mutually exclusive and the tests had to be performed in order. If we had tested $b^2 - 4ac$ first then we would have been forced to test a against zero in each alternative if we were using the normal formula.

There is no directly corresponding contraction for **then if** as in Algol 68. Instead the short circuit control form **and then** can often be used.

So, rather than

```
if J > 0 then
  if I/J > K then
    Action;
  end if;
end if;
```

we can, as we have seen, write

```
if J > 0 and then I/J > K then
  Action;
end if;
```

EXERCISE 7.1

1   The variables Day, Month and Year contain today's date. They are declared as

```
Day: Integer range 1 .. 31;
Month: Month_Name;
Year: Integer range 1901 .. 2099;
```

where

```
type Month_Name is (Jan, Feb, Mar, Apr, May, Jun,
                    Jul, Aug, Sep, Oct, Nov, Dec);
```

Write statements to update the variables to contain tomorrow's date. What happens if today is 31 Dec 2099?

2   X and Y are two variables of type Float. Write statements to swap their values, if necessary, to ensure that the larger value is in X. Use a block to declare a temporary variable T.

7.2   Case statements

A case statement allows us to choose one of several sequences of statements according to the value of an expression. For instance, the example of the drilling soldiers should be written as

```
case Order is
  when Left => Turn_Left;
  when Right => Turn_Right;
  when Back => Turn_Back;
  when On => null;
end case;
```

All possible values of the expression must be provided for in order to guard against accidental omissions. If, as in this example, no action is required for one or more values then the null statement has to be used.

The null statement, written

    null;

does absolutely nothing but its presence indicates that we truly want to do nothing. The sequence of statements here, as in the if statement, must contain at least one statement. (There is no empty statement as in Algol 60 and Pascal.)

It often happens that the same action is desired for several values of the expression. Consider the following

```
case Today is
   when Mon | Tues | Wed | Thu => Work;
   when Fri                    => Work; Party;
   when Sat | Sun              => null;
end case;
```

This expresses the idea that on Monday to Thursday we go to work. On Friday we also go to work and then go to a party. At the weekend we do nothing. The alternative values are separated by the vertical bar character. Note again the use of a null statement.

If several successive values have the same action then it is more convenient to use a range

```
when Mon .. Thu => Work;
```

Sometimes we wish to express the idea of a default action to be taken by all values not explicitly stated; this is provided for by the reserved word **others**. The above example could be rewritten

```
case Today is
   when Mon .. Thu => Work;
   when Fri        => Work; Party;
   when others     => null;
end case;
```

It is possible to have ranges as alternatives. In fact this is probably a situation where the clearest explanation of what is allowed is given by the formal syntax (note that in the production for discrete_choice_list, the vertical bar stands for itself and is not a metasymbol).

```
case_statement ::=
     case expression is
       case_statement_alternative
       {case_statement_alternative}
     end case;

case_statement_alternative ::=
     when discrete_choice_list => sequence_of_statements
```

discrete_choice_list ::= discrete_choice { | discrete_choice}

discrete_choice ::= expression | discrete_range | **others**

discrete_range ::= *discrete*_subtype_indication | range

subtype_indication ::= subtype_mark [constraint]

subtype_mark ::= *subtype*_name

range ::= range_attribute_reference
                        | simple_expression .. simple_expression

We see that **when** is followed by one or more discrete choices separated by vertical bars and that a discrete choice may be an expression, a discrete range or **others**. An expression, of course, just gives a single value – Fri being a trivial example. A discrete range offers several possibilities. It can be the syntactic form range which the syntax tells us can be two simple expressions separated by two dots – Mon .. Thu is a simple example; a range can also be given by a range attribute which we will meet in the next chapter. A discrete range can also be a discrete subtype indication which as we know is a subtype mark followed optionally by an appropriate constraint. In this case the constraint has to be a range constraint which is merely the reserved word **range** followed by the syntactic form range. Examples of discrete ranges are

> Mon .. Thu
> Day **range** Mon .. Thu
> Weekday
> Weekday **range** Mon .. Thu

All these possibilities may seem unnecessary, but as we shall see later the form, discrete range, is used in other contexts as well as the case statement. In the case statement there is not usually much point in using the type name since this is known from the context anyway. Similarly there is not much point in using the subtype name followed by a constraint since the constraint alone will do. However, it might be useful to use a subtype name alone when that exactly corresponds to the range required. So we could rewrite the example as

```
case Today is
   when Weekday => Work;
                        if Today = Fri then
                           Party;
                        end if;
      when others     => null;
   end case;
```

although this solution feels untidy.

There are various other restrictions that the syntax does not tell us. One is that if we use **others** then it must appear alone and as the last alternative. As stated earlier it covers all values not explicitly covered by the previous alternatives (one can write **others** even if there are no other cases left).

Another very important restriction is that all the choices must be static so that they can be evaluated at compile time. Thus all expressions in discrete choices must be static – in practice they will usually be literals as in our examples. Similarly, if a choice is simply a subtype such as Weekday then it too must be static.

Finally we return to the point made at the beginning of this section that all possible values of the expression after **case** must be provided for. This usually means all values of the type of the expression. This is certainly the case of a variable declared as of a type without any constraints (as in the case of Today). However, if the expression is of a simple form and belongs to a static subtype (that is one whose constraints are static expressions and so can be determined at compile time) then only values of that subtype need be provided for. In other words, if the compiler can tell that only a subset of values is possible then only that subset need and must be covered. The simple forms allowed for the expression are the name of an object of the static subtype (and that includes a function call whose result is of the static subtype) or a qualified or converted expression whose subtype mark is that of the static subtype.

In the case of our example, if Today had been of subtype Weekday then we would know that only the values Mon .. Fri are possible and so only these can and need be covered. Even if Today is not constrained we can still write our expression as a qualified expression Weekday'(Today) and then again only Mon .. Fri is possible. So we could write

```
case Weekday'(Today) is
   when Mon .. Thu => Work;
   when Fri         => Work; Party;
end case;
```

but, of course, if Today happens to take a value not in the subtype Weekday (that is, Sat or Sun) then Constraint_Error will be raised. Mere qualification cannot prevent Today from being Sat or Sun. So this is not really a solution to our original problem.

As further examples, suppose we had variables

```
I: Integer range 1 .. 10;
J: Integer range 1 .. N;
```

where N is not static. Then we know that I belongs to a static subtype (albeit anonymous) whereas we cannot say the same about J. If I is used as an expression in a case statement then only the values 1 .. 10 have to be catered for, whereas if J is so used then the full range of values of type Integer (Integer'First .. Integer'Last) have to be catered for.

The above discussion on the case statement has no doubt given the reader the impression of considerable complexity. It therefore seems wise to summarize the key points which will in practice need to be remembered

- Every possible value of the expression after **case** must be covered once and once only.
- All values and ranges after **when** must be static.
- If **others** is used it must be last and on its own.

EXERCISE 7.2

1 Rewrite Exercise 7.1(**1**) to use a case statement to set the correct value in End_Of_Month.

2 A vegetable gardener digs in winter, sows seed in spring, tends the growing plants in summer and harvests the crop in the autumn or fall. Write a case statement to call the appropriate subprogram Dig, Sow, Tend or Harvest according to the month M. Declare appropriate subtypes if desired.

3 An improvident man is paid on the first of each month. For the first ten days he gorges himself, for the next ten he subsists and for the remainder he starves. Call subprograms Gorge, Subsist and Starve according to the day D. Assume End_Of_Month has been set and that D is declared as

    D: Integer **range** 1 .. End_Of_Month;

7.3   Loop statements

The simplest form of loop statement is

    loop
        sequence_of_statements
    end loop;

The statements of the sequence are then repeated indefinitely unless one of them terminates the loop by some means. So immortality could be represented by

    loop
        Work;
        Eat;
        Sleep;
    end loop;

As a more concrete example consider the problem of computing the base e of natural logarithms from the infinite series

$$e = 1 + 1/1! + 1/2! + 1/3! + 1/4! + ...$$

where

$$n! = n \times (n-1) \times (n-2) ... 3 \times 2 \times 1$$

A possible solution is

```
declare
  E: Float := 1.0;
  I: Integer := 0;
  Term: Float := 1.0;
begin
  loop
    I := I + 1;
    Term := Term / Float(I);
    E := E + Term;
  end loop;
  ...
```

Each time around the loop a new term is computed by dividing the previous term by I. The new term is then added to the sum so far which is accumulated in E. The term number I is an integer because it is logically a counter and so we have to write Float(I) as the divisor. The series is started by setting values in E, I and Term which correspond to the first term (that for which I = 0).

The computation then goes on for ever with E becoming a closer and closer approximation to *e*. In practice, because of the finite accuracy of the computer, Term will become zero and continued computation will be pointless. But in any event we presumably want to stop at some point so that we can do something with our computed result. We can do this with the statement

exit;

If this is obeyed inside a loop then the loop terminates at once and control passes to the point immediately after **end loop**.

Suppose we decide to stop after *N* terms of the series – that is when I = N. We can do this by writing the loop as

```
loop
  if I = N then exit; end if;
  I := I + 1;
  Term := Term / Float(I);
  E := E + Term;
end loop;
```

The construction

if condition **then exit**; **end if**;

is so common that a special shorthand is provided

exit when condition;

So we now have

```
loop
  exit when I = N;
  I := I + 1;
```

```
    Term := Term / Float(I);
    E := E + Term;
  end loop;
```

Although an exit statement can appear anywhere inside a loop – it could be in the middle or near the end – a special form is provided for the frequent case where we want to test a condition at the start of each iteration. This uses the reserved word **while** and gives the condition for the loop to be continued. So we could write

```
  while I /= N loop
    I := I + 1;
    Term := Term / Float(I);
    E := E + Term;
  end loop;
```

The condition is naturally evaluated each time around the loop.

The final form of loop allows for a specific number of iterations with a loop parameter taking in turn all the values of a discrete range. Our example could be recast as

```
  for I in 1 .. N loop
    Term := Term / Float(I);
    E := E + Term;
  end loop;
```

where I takes the values 1, 2, 3, ... N.

The parameter I is implicitly declared by its appearance in the iteration scheme and does not have to be declared outside. It takes its type from the discrete range and within the loop behaves as a constant so that it cannot be changed except by the loop mechanism itself. When we leave the loop (by whatever means) I ceases to exist (because it was implicitly declared by the loop) and so we cannot read its final value from outside.

We could leave the loop by an exit statement – if we wanted to know the final value we could copy the value of I into a variable declared outside the loop thus

```
  if condition_to_exit then
    Last_I := I;
    exit;
  end if;
```

The values of the discrete range are normally taken in ascending order. Descending order can be specified by writing

```
  for I in reverse 1 .. N loop
```

but the range itself is always written in ascending order.

It is not possible to specify a numeric step size of other than 1. This should not be a problem since the vast majority of loops go up by steps of 1 and almost all the rest go down by steps of 1. The very few which do behave otherwise can be explicitly programmed using the while form of loop.

The range can be null (as for instance if N happened to be zero or negative in our example) in which case the sequence of statements will not be obeyed at all. Of course, the range itself is evaluated only once and cannot be changed inside the loop.

Thus

```
N := 4;
for I in 1 .. N loop
    ...
    N := 10;
end loop;
```

results in the loop being executed just four times despite the fact that N is changed to ten.

Our examples have all shown the lower bound of the range being 1. This, of course, need not be the case. Both bounds can be arbitrary dynamically evaluated expressions. Furthermore the loop parameter need not be of integer type. It can be of any discrete type, as determined by the discrete range.

We could, for instance, simulate a week's activity by

```
for Today in Mon .. Sun loop
    case Today is
        ...
    end case;
end loop;
```

This implicitly declares Today to be of type Day and obeys the loop with the values Mon, Tue, ... Sun in turn.

The other forms of discrete range (using a type or subtype name) are of advantage here. The essence of Mon .. Sun is that it embraces all the values of the type Day. It is therefore better to write the loop using a form of discrete range that conveys the idea of completeness

```
for Today in Day loop
    ...
end loop;
```

And again since we know that we do nothing at weekends anyway we could write

```
for Today in Day range Mon .. Fri loop
```

or better

```
for Today in Weekday loop
```

It is interesting to note a difference regarding the determination of types in the case statement and for statement. In the case statement, the type of a discrete range after **when** is determined from the type of the expression after **case**. In the for statement, the type of the loop parameter is determined from the type of the discrete range after **in**. The dependency is the other way round.

It is therefore necessary for the type of the discrete range to be unambiguous in the for statement. This is usually the case but if we had two enumeration types with two overloaded literals such as

> **type** Planet **is** (Mercury, Venus, Earth, Mars, Jupiter,
>   Saturn, Uranus, Neptune, Pluto);
> **type** Roman_God **is** (Janus, Mars, Jupiter, Juno, Vesta,
>   Vulcan, Saturn, Mercury, Minerva);

then

> **for** X **in** Mars .. Saturn **loop**

would be ambiguous and the compiler would not compile our program. We could resolve the problem by qualifying one of the expressions

> **for** X **in** Planet'(Mars) .. Saturn **loop**

or (probably better) by using a form of discrete range giving the type explicitly

> **for** X **in** Planet **range** Mars .. Saturn **loop**

When we have dealt with numerics in more detail we will realize that the range 1 .. 10 is not necessarily of type Integer (it might be Long_Integer). A general application of our rule that the type must not be ambiguous in a for statement would lead us to have to write

> **for** I **in** Integer **range** 1 .. 10 **loop**

However, this would be very tedious and so in such cases the type Integer can be omitted and is then implied by default. We can therefore conveniently write

> **for** I **in** 1 .. 10 **loop**

More general expressions are also allowed so that we could also write

> **for** I **in** −1 .. 10 **loop**

although we recall that −1 is not a literal as explained in Section 5.4. We will return to this topic in Section 15.1.

Finally we reconsider the exit statement. The simple form encountered earlier always transfers control to immediately after the innermost embracing loop. But of course loops may be nested and sometimes we may wish to exit from a nested construction. As an example suppose we are searching in two dimensions

```
      for I in 1 .. N loop
        for J in 1 .. M loop
          -- if values of I and J satisfy
          -- some condition then leave nested loop
        end loop;
      end loop;
```

A simple exit statement in the inner loop would merely take us to the end of that loop and we would have to recheck the condition and exit again. This can be avoided by naming the outer loop and using the name in the exit statement thus

```
    Search:
    for I in 1 .. N loop
      for J in 1 .. M loop
        if condition_OK then
          I_Value := I;
          J_Value := J;
          exit Search;
        end if;
      end loop;
    end loop Search;
    -- control passes here
```

A loop is named by preceding it with an identifier and colon. (It looks remarkably like a label in other languages but it is not and cannot be 'gone to'.) The identifier must be repeated between the corresponding **end loop** and the semicolon. The conditional form of exit can also refer to a loop by name

```
    exit Search when condition;
```

EXERCISE 7.3

1   The statement Get(I); reads the next value from the input file into the integer variable I. Write statements to read and add together a series of numbers. The end of the series is indicated by a dummy negative value.

2   Write statements to determine the power of 2 in the factorization of N. Compute the result in Count but do not alter N.

3   Compute

$$g = \sum_{p=1}^{n} 1/p - \log n$$

(As $n \to \infty$, $g \to \gamma = 0.577215665...$)

7.4   Goto statements and labels

Many will be surprised that a modern programming language should contain a goto statement at all. It is now considered to be extremely bad practice to use goto statements because of the resulting difficulty in proving correctness of the program, maintenance and so on. And indeed Ada contains adequate control structures so that it should not normally be necessary to use a goto at all.

So why provide a goto statement? The main reason concerns automatically generated programs. If we try to transliterate (by hand or machine) a program from some other language into Ada then the goto will probably be useful. Another example might be where the program is generated automatically from some high level specification. Finally there may be cases where the goto is the neatest way – perhaps as a way out of some deeply nested structure – but the alternative of raising an exception (see Chapter 14) could also be considered.

In order to put us off using gotos and labels (and perhaps so that our manager can spot them if we do) the notation for a label is unusual and stands out like a sore thumb. A label is an identifier enclosed in double angled brackets thus

    <<The_Devil>>

and a goto statement takes the expected form of the reserved word **goto** followed by the label identifier and semicolon

    goto The_Devil;

A goto statement cannot be used to transfer control into an if, case or loop statement nor between the arms of an if or case statement.

7.5   Statement classification

The statements in Ada can be classified as shown in Figure 7.1.

Further detail on the assignment statement is in the next chapter when we discuss composite types. Procedure calls and return statements are discussed in Chapter 9 and the raise statement which is concerned with exceptions is discussed in Chapter 14. The code statement is mentioned in Chapter 21. The remaining statements (entry call, requeue, delay, abort, accept and select) concern tasking and are dealt with in Chapter 18.

All statements can have one or more labels. The simple statements cannot be decomposed lexically into other statements whereas the compound statements can be so decomposed and can therefore be nested. Statements are obeyed sequentially unless one of them is a control statement (or an exception is implicitly raised).

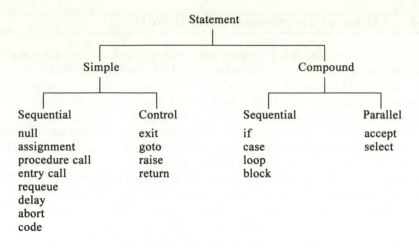

Figure 7.1 Classification of statements.

CHECKLIST 7

Statement brackets must match correctly.

Use **elsif** where appropriate.

The choices in a case statement must be static.

All possibilities in a case statement must be catered for.

If **others** is used it must be last and on its own.

The expression after **case** can be qualified in order to reduce the alternatives.

A loop parameter behaves as a constant.

A named loop must have the name at both ends.

Avoid gotos.

Use the recommended layout.

Changes from Ada 83

The special rules for loops were different in Ada 83 and –1 was not allowed as the bound of a range without an explicit type name.

8 Arrays and Records

In this chapter we describe the main composite types which are arrays and records. (Tasks and protected types which are also classed as composite are discussed in Chapter 18.) We also complete our discussion of enumeration types by introducing characters and strings. At this stage we discuss arrays fairly completely but consider only the simplest forms of records. Tagged records which permit extension and polymorphism are discussed in Chapter 13 and discriminated records which include variant records are deferred until Chapter 16.

8.1 Arrays

An array is a composite object consisting of a number of components all of the same type (strictly, subtype). An array can be of one, two or more dimensions. A typical array declaration might be

A: **array** (Integer **range** 1 .. 6) **of** Float;

This declares A to be a variable object which has six components, each of which is of type Float. The individual components are referred to by following the array name with an expression in brackets giving an integer value in the discrete range 1 .. 6. If this expression, known as the index value, has a value outside the range, then the exception Constraint_Error will be raised. We could set zero in each component of A by writing

```
for I in 1 .. 6 loop
   A(I) := 0.0;
end loop;
```

An array can be of several dimensions, in which case a separate range is given for each dimension. So

```
AA: array (Integer range 0 .. 2, Integer range 0 .. 3) of Float;
```

is an array of 12 components in total, each of which is referred to by two integer index values, the first in the range 0 .. 2 and the second in the range 0 .. 3. Each component of this two-dimensional array could be set to zero by a nested loop thus

```
for I in 0 .. 2 loop
   for J in 0 .. 3 loop
      AA(I, J) := 0.0;
   end loop;
end loop;
```

The discrete ranges do not have to be static; one could have

```
N: Integer := ... ;
B: array (Integer range 1 .. N) of Boolean;
```

and the value of N at the point when the declaration of B is elaborated would determine the number of components in B. Of course, the declaration of B might be elaborated many times during the course of a program – it might be inside a loop for example – and each elaboration will give rise to a new life of a new array and the value of N could be different each time. Like other declared objects, the array B ceases to exist once we pass the end of the block containing its declaration. Because of 'linear elaboration of declarations' both N and B could be declared in the same declarative part but the declaration of N would have to precede that of B.

The discrete range in an array index follows similar rules to that in a for statement. An important one is that a range such as 1 .. 6 implies type Integer so we could have written

```
A: array (1 .. 6) of Float;
```

However, an array index could be of any discrete type. We could for example have

```
Hours_Worked: array (Day) of Float;
```

This array has seven components denoted by Hours_Worked(Mon), ... Hours_Worked(Sun). We could set suitable values in these variables by

```
for D in Weekday loop
   Hours_Worked(D) := 8.0;
end loop;
Hours_Worked(Sat) := 0.0;
Hours_Worked(Sun) := 0.0;
```

If we only wanted to declare the array Hours_Worked to have components corresponding to Mon .. Fri then we could write

```
Hours_Worked: array (Day range Mon .. Fri) of Float;
```

or (better)

```
Hours_Worked: array (Weekday) of Float;
```

Arrays have various attributes relating to their indexes. A'First and A'Last give the lower and upper bound of the first (or only) index of A. So using our last declaration of Hours_Worked

```
Hours_Worked'First = Mon
Hours_Worked'Last = Fri
```

A'Length gives the number of values of the first (or only) index.

```
Hours_Worked'Length = 5
```

A'Range is short for A'First .. A'Last. So

```
Hours_Worked'Range   is   Mon .. Fri
```

The same attributes can be applied to the various dimensions of a multidimensional array by adding the dimension number in brackets. It has to be a static expression. So, in the case of our two-dimensional array AA we have

```
AA'First(1)   = 0
AA'First(2)   = 0
AA'Last(1)    = 2
AA'Last(2)    = 3
AA'Length(1)  = 3
AA'Length(2)  = 4
```

and

```
AA'Range(1)   is   0 .. 2
AA'Range(2)   is   0 .. 3
```

The first dimension is assumed if (1) is omitted. It is perhaps better practice to specifically state (1) for multidimensional arrays and omit it for one-dimensional arrays.

It is always best to use the attributes where possible in order to reflect relationships among entities in a program because it generally means that if the program is modified, the modifications are localized.

The Range attribute is particularly useful with loops. Our earlier examples are better written as

```
for I in A'Range loop
   A(I) := 0.0;
end loop;

for I in AA'Range(1) loop
   for J in AA'Range(2) loop
      AA(I, J) := 0.0;
   end loop;
end loop;
```

The Range attribute can also be used in a declaration. Thus

```
J: Integer range A'Range;
```

is equivalent to

```
J: Integer range 1 .. 6;
```

If a variable is to be used to index an array as in A(J) it is usually best if the variable has the same constraints as the discrete range in the array declaration. This will usually minimize the run-time checks necessary. It has been found that in such circumstances it is usually the case that the index variable J is assigned less frequently than the array component A(J) is accessed. We will return to this topic in Section 14.3.

The array components we have seen are just variables in the ordinary way. They can therefore be assigned to and used in expressions.

Like other variable objects, arrays can be given an initial value. This will often be denoted by an aggregate which is the literal form for an array value. The simplest form of aggregate consists of a list of expressions giving the values of the components in order, separated by commas and enclosed in brackets. So we could initialize the array A by

```
A: array (1 .. 6) of Float := (0.0, 0.0, 0.0, 0.0, 0.0, 0.0);
```

In the case of a multidimensional array the aggregate is written in a nested form

```
AA: array (0 .. 2, 0 .. 3) of Float := ((0.0, 0.0, 0.0, 0.0),
                                        (0.0, 0.0, 0.0, 0.0),
                                        (0.0, 0.0, 0.0, 0.0));
```

and this illustrates that the first index is the 'outer' one. Or thinking in terms of rows and columns, the first index is the row number.

An aggregate must be complete. If we initialize any component of an array, we must initialize them all.

The initial values for the individual components need not be literals, they can be any expressions. These expressions are evaluated when the declaration is elaborated but the order of evaluation of the expressions in the aggregate is not specified.

An array can be declared as constant in which case an initial value is mandatory as explained in Section 6.1. Constant arrays are of frequent value as look-up tables. The following array can be used to determine whether a particular day is a working day or not

> Work_Day: **constant array** (Day) **of** Boolean :=
> (True, True, True, True, True, False, False);

An interesting example would be an array enabling tomorrow to be determined without worrying about the end of the week.

> Tomorrow: **constant array** (Day) **of** Day :=
> (Tue, Wed, Thu, Fri, Sat, Sun, Mon);

For any day D, Tomorrow (D) is the following day.

Finally, it should be noted that the array components can be of any definite type or subtype. Also the dimensions of a multidimensional array can be of different discrete types. An extreme example would be

> Strange: **array** (Colour, 2 .. 7, Weekday **range** Tue .. Thu)
> **of** Planet **range** Mars .. Saturn;

Note we said that the component type must be definite; the distinction between definite and indefinite types is explained in the next section.

EXERCISE 8.1

1   Declare an array F of integers with index running from 0 to N. Write statements to set the components of F equal to the Fibonacci numbers given by

$$F_0 = 0, \ F_1 = 1, \ F_i = F_{i-1} + F_{i-2} \qquad i > 1$$

2   Write statements to find the index values I, J of the maximum component of

  A: **array** (1 .. N, 1 .. M) **of** Float;

3   Declare an array Days_In_Month giving the number of days in each month. See Exercise 7.1(**1**). Use it to rewrite that example. See also Exercise 7.2(**1**).

4   Declare an array Yesterday analogous to the example Tomorrow above.

5 Declare a constant array Bor such that

Bor(P, Q) = P or Q

6 Declare a constant unit matrix Unit of order 3. A unit matrix is one for which all components are zero except those whose indexes are equal which have value one.

8.2 Array types

The arrays we introduced in the last section did not have an explicit type name. They were in fact of anonymous type. This is one of the few cases in Ada where an object can be declared without naming the type – the other cases are tasks and protected objects.

Reconsidering the first example in the previous section, we could write

type Vector_6 **is array** (1 .. 6) **of** Float;

and then declare A using the type name in the usual way

A: Vector_6;

An advantage of using a type name is that it enables us to assign whole arrays that have been declared separately. If we also have

B: Vector_6;

then we can write

B := A;

which has the effect of

B(1) := A(1); B(2) := A(2); ... B(6) := A(6);

although the order of assigning the components is not relevant.

On the other hand if we had written

C: **array** (1 .. 6) **of** Float;
D: **array** (1 .. 6) **of** Float;

then D := C; is illegal because C and D are not of the same type. They are of different types both of which are anonymous. The underlying rule is that every type definition introduces a new type and in this case the syntax tells us that an array type definition is the piece of text from **array** up to (but not including) the semicolon.

Moreover, even if we had written

C, D: **array** (1 .. 6) **of** Float;

then D := C; would still have been illegal. This is because of the rule mentioned in Section 6.1 that such a multiple declaration is only a shorthand for the two declarations above. There are therefore still two distinct type definitions even though they are not explicit.

Whether or not we introduce a type name for particular arrays depends very much on the abstract view of each situation. If we are thinking of the array as a complete object in its own right then we should use a type name. If, on the other hand, we are thinking of the array as merely an indexable conglomerate not related as a whole to other arrays then it should probably be of an anonymous type.

Arrays like Tomorrow and Work_Day of the last section are good examples of arrays which are of the anonymous category. To be forced to introduce a type name for such arrays would introduce unnecessary clutter and a possibly false sense of abstraction.

On the other hand, if we are manipulating lots of arrays of type Float of length 6 then there is a common underlying abstract type and so it should be named. The reader might also like to reconsider the example of Pascal's triangle in Section 2.5.

The model for array types introduced so far is still not satisfactory. It does not allow us to represent an abstract view that embraces the commonality between arrays which have different bounds but are otherwise of the same type. In particular, it would not allow the writing of subprograms which could take an array of arbitrary bounds as an actual parameter. This is generally recognized as a major difficulty with the original design of Pascal. So the concept of an unconstrained array type is introduced in which the constraints for the indexes are not given. Consider

```
type Vector is array (Integer range <>) of Float;
```

(The compound symbol <> is read as 'box'.)

This says that Vector is the name of a type which is a one-dimensional array of Float components with an Integer index. But the lower and upper bounds are not given; **range** <> is meant to convey the notion of information to be added later.

When we declare objects of type Vector we must supply the bounds. We can do this in various ways. We can introduce an intermediate subtype and then declare the objects.

```
subtype Vector_5 is Vector(1 .. 5);
V: Vector_5;
```

Or we can declare the objects directly

```
V: Vector(1 .. 5);
```

In either case the bounds are given by an index constraint which takes the form of a discrete range in brackets. All the usual forms of discrete range can be used.

The index can also be given by a subtype name, thus

type P **is array** (Positive **range** <>) **of** Float;

in which case the actual bounds of any declared object must lie within the range implied by the index subtype Positive. Note that the index subtype must be given by a subtype mark and not by a subtype indication; this avoids the horrid double use of **range** which could otherwise occur as in

type Nasty **is array** (Integer **range** 1 .. 100 **range** <>) **of** ... ;

We can now see that when we wrote

type Vector_6 **is array** (1 .. 6) **of** Float;

this was effectively a shorthand for

subtype index **is** Integer **range** 1 .. 6;
type anon **is array** (index **range** <>) **of** Float;
subtype Vector_6 **is** anon(1 .. 6);

Another useful array type declaration is

type Matrix **is array** (Integer **range** <>, Integer **range** <>) **of** Float;

And again we could introduce subtypes thus

subtype Matrix_3 **is** Matrix(1 .. 3, 1 .. 3);
M: Matrix_3;

or the objects directly

M: Matrix(1 .. 3, 1 .. 3);

An important point to notice is that an array subtype must give all the bounds or none at all. It would be perfectly legal to introduce an alternative name for Matrix by

subtype Mat **is** Matrix;

in which no bounds are given, but we could not have a subtype that just gave the bounds for one dimension but not the other.

In all of the cases we have been discussing, the ranges need not have static bounds. The bounds could be any expressions and are evaluated when the index constraint is encountered. We could have

M: Matrix(1 .. N, 1 .. N);

and then the upper bounds of M would be the value of N when M is declared. A range could even be null as would happen in the above case if N turned out to be zero. In this case the matrix M would have no components at all.

There is a further way in which the bounds of an array can be supplied; they can be taken from an initial value. Remember that all constants must have an initial value and variables may have one. The bounds can then be taken from the initial value if they are not supplied directly. The initial value can be any expression of the appropriate type but will often be an aggregate as shown in the previous section. The form of aggregate shown there consisted of a list of expressions in brackets. Such an aggregate is known as a positional aggregate since the values are given in position order. In the case of a positional aggregate used as an initial value and supplying the bounds, the lower bound is S'First where S is the subtype of the index. The upper bound is deduced from the number of components. (The bounds of positional aggregates in other contexts will be discussed in the next section.)

Suppose we had

> **type** W **is array** (Weekday **range** <>) **of** Day;
> Next_Work_Day: **constant** W := (Tue, Wed, Thu, Fri, Mon);

then the lower bound of the array is Weekday'First = Mon and the upper bound is Fri. It would not have mattered whether we had written Day or Weekday in the declaration of W because Day'First and Weekday'First are the same.

Note that we can also use the box notation with anonymous array types. So we can also write

> Next_Work_Day: **array** (Weekday range <>) **of** Day :=
>   (Tue, Wed, Thu, Fri, Mon);

and there is no need to declare the intermediate type W. Again the bounds are deduced from the aggregate and we have also chosen not to make the array a constant.

Using initial values to supply the bounds needs care. Consider

> Unit_2: **constant** Matrix := ((1.0, 0.0), (0.0, 1.0));

intended to declare a 2 × 2 unit matrix with Unit_2(1, 1) = Unit_2(2, 2) = 1.0 and Unit_2(1, 2) = Unit_2(2, 1) = 0.0.

But disaster! We have actually declared an array whose lower bounds are Integer'First which might be −32768 or some such number, but is most certainly not 1.

If we declared the type Matrix as

> **type** Matrix **is array** (Positive **range** <>, Positive **range** <>) **of** Float;

then all would have been well since Positive'First = 1.

So array bounds deduced from an initial value may lead to surprises.

We continue by returning to the topic of whole array assignment. In order to perform such assignment it is necessary that the array value and the array being assigned to have the same type and that the components can be matched. This does not mean that the bounds have to be equal, but merely that the number of components in corresponding dimensions is the same. In other words so that one array can be slid onto the other, giving rise to the term 'sliding semantics'. So we can write

```
V: Vector(1 .. 5);
W: Vector(0 .. 4);
...
V := W;
```

Both V and W are of type Vector and both have five components.

It is also valid to have

```
P: Matrix(0 .. 1, 0 .. 1);
Q: Matrix(6 .. 7, N .. N+1);
...
P := Q;
```

Equality and inequality of arrays follow similar sliding rules to assignment. Two arrays may only be compared if they are of the same type. They are equal if corresponding dimensions have the same number of components and the matching components are themselves equal. Note, however, that if the dimensions of the two arrays are not of the same length then equality will return False whereas an attempt to assign one array to the other will naturally cause Constraint_Error.

Although assignment and equality can only occur if the arrays are of the same type, nevertheless an array value of one type can be converted to another type if the component subtypes and index types are the same. The usual notation for type conversion is used. So if we have

```
type Vector is array (Integer range <>) of Float;
type Row is array (Integer range <>) of Float;

V: Vector(1 .. 5);
R: Row(0 .. 4);
```

then

```
R := Row(V);
```

is valid. In fact, since Row is an unconstrained type, the bounds of Row(V) are those of V. The normal assignment rules then apply. However, if the conversion uses a constrained type or subtype then the bounds are those of the type or subtype and the number of components in corresponding dimensions must be the same. Array type conversion is of particular value when subprograms from different libraries are used together as we shall see later.

Note that the component subtypes in a conversion must be statically the same. Remember that the component subtype could be constrained as in the array Strange at the end of the previous section. The check that such constraints match is done at compile time.

This is a good moment to mention the distinction between a definite and indefinite type or subtype. A definite subtype is one for which we can declare an object without an explicit constraint or initial value. Thus the subtype Vector_5 is definite. A type such as Vector on the other hand is indefinite since we cannot declare an object of the type without supplying the bounds either from an explicit constraint or from an initial value. Scalar types such as Integer are also definite. Other forms of indefinite type will be encountered in due course.

We conclude this section by observing that the attributes First, Last, Length and Range, as well as applying to array objects, may also be applied to array types and subtypes provided they are constrained and so are definite. Hence

Vector_6'Length = 6

but

Vector'Length

is illegal.

EXERCISE 8.2

1   Declare an array type Bbb corresponding to the array Bor of Exercise 8.1(**5**).

2   Declare a two-dimensional array type suitable for declaring operator tables on values of

subtype Ring5 **is** Integer **range** 0 .. 4;

Then declare addition and multiplication tables for modulo 5 arithmetic. Use the tables to formulate the expression (A + B) * C using modulo 5 arithmetic and assign the result to D where A, B, C and D have been appropriately declared. See Section 6.5.

8.3 Array aggregates

In the previous sections we introduced the idea of a positional aggregate. There is another form of aggregate known as a named aggregate in which the component values are preceded by the corresponding index value and =>. (The symbol => is akin to the 'pointing hand' sign encountered in old railway timetables and used for indicating directions.) A simple example would be

(1 => 0.0, 2 => 0.0, 3 => 0.0, 4 => 0.0, 5 => 0.0, 6 => 0.0)

with the expected extension to several dimensions. The bounds of such an aggregate are self-evident and so our problem with the unit 2 × 2 matrix of the previous section could be overcome by writing

Unit_2: **constant** Matrix := (1 => (1 => 1.0, 2 => 0.0),
2 => (1 => 0.0, 2 => 1.0));

The rules for named aggregates are very similar to the rules for the alternatives in a case statement.

Each choice can be given as a series of alternatives each of which can be a single value or a discrete range. We could therefore rewrite some previous examples as follows

A: **array** (1 .. 6) **of** Float := (1 .. 6 => 0.0);

Work_Day: **constant array** (Day) **of** Boolean :=
(Mon .. Fri => True, Sat | Sun => False);

In contrast to a positional aggregate, the index values need not appear in order. We could equally have written

(Sat | Sun => False, Mon .. Fri => True)

We can also use **others** but then as for the case statement it must be last and on its own (and there do not have to be any more values).

Array aggregates may not mix positional and named notation except that **others** may be used at the end of a positional aggregate.

It should also be realized that although we have been showing aggregates as initial values, they can be used quite generally in any place where an expression of an array type is required. They can also be the argument of type conversion and qualification.

The rules for deducing the bounds of an aggregate depend upon the form of the aggregate and its context. There are quite a lot of cases to consider and this makes the rules seem complicated although they are quite natural. We will first give the rules and then some examples of the consequences of the rules.

There are three kinds of aggregates to be considered

- Named without **others**, these have self-evident bounds.
- Positional without **others**, the number of elements is known but the actual bounds are not.
- Named or positional with **others**, neither the bounds nor the number of elements is known.

There are two main contexts to be considered according to whether the target type is constrained or unconstrained. In addition, the rules for qualification are special. So we have

- Unconstrained, gives no bounds.
- Constrained generally, gives the bounds, sliding usually permitted.
- Constrained qualification, gives the bounds, sliding never permitted.

Table 8.1   Array aggregates and contexts.

	Named	*Positional*	*With* **others**
Unconstrained	OK bounds from aggregate	lower bound is S'First	illegal
Constrained like assignment	length must be same, could slide	length same, bounds from target	bounds from target
Constrained qualification	bounds must exactly match	length same, bounds from target	bounds from target

The philosophy regarding sliding is that it is generally useful and so should be allowed and that aggregates should be no different to other array values in this respect; we saw some examples of sliding in the context of assignment in the last section. Other contexts that behave like assignment will be met in due course when we discuss subprogram parameters and results in Chapter 9 and generic parameters in Chapter 17.

However, qualification is more in the nature of an assertion and so sliding is forbidden since it would be wrong to change the value in any way. If the bounds are not exactly the same then Constraint_Error is raised.

We will now consider the three kinds of aggregates in turn; the various combinations are summarized in Table 8.1.

A named aggregate without **others** has known bounds and will slide if permitted and necessary.

If a positional aggregate without **others** is used in a context which does not give the bounds then the lower bound is by default taken to be S'First where S is the index subtype and the upper bound is then deduced from the number of components. They never need to slide.

Aggregates with **others** are particularly awkward since we can deduce neither the bounds nor the number of elements. They can therefore only be used in a context that gives the bounds and consequently can never slide. Given the bounds, the components covered by **others** follow on from those given explicitly in the positional case and are simply those not given explicitly in the named case.

One way of supplying the bounds for an aggregate with **others** is to use qualification as we did to distinguish between overloaded enumeration literals. In order to do this we must have an appropriate (constrained) type or subtype name. So we might introduce

type Schedule **is array** (Day) **of** Boolean;

and can then write an expression such as

Schedule'(Mon .. Fri => True, **others** => False)

Note that when qualifying an aggregate we do not, as for an expression, need to put it in brackets because it already has brackets.

We have already considered the use of an aggregate as an initial value and providing the bounds in the example of Unit_2; this of course was an unconstrained context. An aggregate with **others** is thus not allowed. In the last section we saw the effect of using a positional aggregate in such a context since it gave surprising bounds. In this section we saw how a named aggregate was more appropriate.

We will now consider the context of assignment which behaves the same as a declaration with an initial value where the initial value is not being used to supply the bounds. These are constrained contexts and can therefore supply the bounds of an aggregate if necessary.

So we can write

```
Work_Day: constant array (Day) of Boolean :=
            (Mon .. Fri => True, others => False);
```

or indeed

```
Work_Day: constant array (Day) of Boolean :=
            (True, True, True, True, True, others => False);
```

Further insight might be obtained by another example. Consider

```
type Vector is array (Integer range <>) of Float;
V: Vector(1 .. 5) := (3 .. 5 => 1.0, 6 | 7 => 2.0);
```

which shows a named aggregate being assigned to V. The bounds of the named aggregate are self-evident being 3 and 7 and the assignment causes the aggregate to slide so that the net result is that components V(1) .. V(3) have the value 1.0 and V(4) and V(5) have the value 2.0.

On the other hand, writing

```
V := (3 .. 5 => 1.0, others => 2.0);
```

has the rather different effect of setting V(3) .. V(5) to 1.0 and V(1) and V(2) to 2.0. The point is that the bounds of the aggregate are taken from the context and there is no sliding. Aggregates with **others** never slide.

Similarly, no sliding occurs in

```
V := (1.0, 1.0, 1.0, others => 2.0);
```

and this results in setting V(1) .. V(3) to 1.0 and V(4) and V(5) to 2.0. It is clear that care is necessary when using **others**.

Array aggregates really are rather complicated and we still have a few points to make. The first is that in a named aggregate all the ranges and values before => must be static (as in a case statement) except for one special situation. This is where there is only one alternative consisting of a single

choice – it could then be a dynamic range or (unlikely) a single dynamic value.
An example might be

> A: **array** (1 .. N) **of** Integer := (1 .. N **=>** 0);

This is valid even if N is zero (or negative) and then gives a null array and a
null aggregate. The following example illustrates a general rule that the
expression after => is evaluated once for each corresponding index value; of
course it usually makes no difference but consider

> A: **array** (1 .. N) **of** Integer := (1 .. N => 1/N);

If N is zero then there are no values and so 1/N is not evaluated and
Constraint_Error cannot occur. The reader will recall from Section 6.1 that a
similar multiple evaluation also occurs when several objects are declared and
initialized together.

In order to avoid awkward problems with null aggregates, a null choice is
only allowed if it is the only choice. Foolish aggregates such as

> (7 .. 6 | 1 .. 0 => 0)

are thus forbidden, and there is no question of the lower bound of such an
aggregate.

Another point is that although we cannot mix named and positional
notation within an aggregate, we can, however, use different forms for the
different components and levels of a multidimensional aggregate. So the initial
value of our matrix Unit_2 could also be written as

> (1 => (1.0, 0.0),   or   ((1 => 1.0, 2 => 0.0),
> 2 => (0.0, 1.0))   (1 => 0.0, 2 => 1.0))

or even as

> (1 => (1 => 1.0, 2 => 0.0),
> 2 => (0.0,   1.0))

and so on.

Note also that the Range attribute stands for a range and therefore can be
used as one of the choices in a named aggregate. However, we cannot use the
range attribute of an object in its own initial value. Thus

> A: **array** (1 .. N) **of** Integer := (A'Range => 0);   -- illegal

is not allowed. This is because an object is not visible until the end of its
declaration. However, we could write

> A: **array** (1 .. N) **of** Integer := (**others** => 0);

and this is probably better than repeating 1 .. N because it localizes the dependency on N.

A final point is that a positional aggregate cannot contain just one component because otherwise it would be ambiguous. We could not distinguish an aggregate of one component from a scalar value which happened to be in brackets. An aggregate of one component must therefore use the named notation. So instead of

       A: **array** (1 .. 1) **of** Integer := (99);   -- illegal

we must write

       A: **array** (1 .. 1) **of** Integer := (1 => 99);

or even

       A: **array** (N .. N) **of** Integer := (N => 99);

which illustrates the obscure case of an aggregate with a single choice and a single dynamic value being that choice.

The reader will by now have concluded that arrays in Ada are somewhat complicated. That is a fair judgement, but in practice there should be few difficulties. There is always the safeguard that if we do something wrong, the compiler will inevitably tell us. In cases of ambiguity, qualification solves the problems provided we have an appropriate type or subtype name to use. Much of the complexity with aggregates is similar to that in the case statement.

We conclude this section by pointing out that the named aggregate notation can greatly increase program legibility. It is especially valuable in initializing large constant arrays and guards against the accidental misplacement of individual values. Consider

```
type Event is (Birth, Accession, Death);
type Monarch is (William_I, William_II, Henry_I, ... ,
                 Victoria, Edward_VII, George_V, ... );
...
Royal_Events: constant array (Monarch, Event) of Integer :=
    (William_I    => (1027, 1066, 1087),
     William_II   => (1056, 1087, 1100),
     Henry_I      => (1068, 1100, 1135),
     ...
     Victoria     => (1819, 1837, 1901),
     Edward_VII   => (1841, 1901, 1910),
     George_V     => (1865, 1910, 1936),
     ...
                                              );
```

The accidental interchange of two lines of the aggregate causes no problems, whereas if we had just used the positional notation then an error would have been introduced and this might have been tricky to detect.

EXERCISE 8.3

1   Rewrite the declaration of the array Days_In_Month in Exercise 8.1(3) using a named aggregate for an initial value.

2   Declare a constant Matrix whose bounds are both 1 .. N where N is dynamic and whose components are all zero.

3   Declare a constant Matrix as in 2 but make it a unit matrix.

4   Declare a constant two-dimensional array which gives the numbers of each atom in a molecule of the various aliphatic alcohols. Declare appropriate enumeration types for both the atoms and the molecules. Consider methanol CH_3OH, ethanol C_2H_5OH, propanol C_3H_7OH and butanol C_4H_9OH.

8.4   Characters and strings

We now complete our discussion of enumeration types by introducing character types. In the enumeration types seen so far such as

    type Colour **is** (Red, Amber, Green);

the values have been represented by identifiers. It is also possible to have an enumeration type in which some or all of the values are represented by character literals.

A character literal is a further form of lexical element. It consists of a single character within a pair of single quotes. The character must be one of the graphic characters; this might be a space but it must not be a control character such as horizontal tabulate or newline.

This is a situation where there is a distinction between upper and lower case letters. The character literals

    'A', 'a'

are different.

So we could declare an enumeration type

    type Roman_Digit **is** ('I', 'V', 'X', 'L', 'C', 'D', 'M');

and then

    Dig: Roman_Digit := 'D';

All the usual properties of enumeration types apply.

    Roman_Digit'First = 'I'
    Roman_Digit'Succ('X') = 'L'

Roman_Digit'Pos'('M') = 6

Dig < 'L' = False

There is a predefined enumeration type Character which is (naturally) a character type. We can think of its declaration as being of the form

type Character **is** (*nul*, ... , '0', '1', '2', ... , 'A', 'B', 'C',

... , 'a', 'b', 'c', ... , ÿ);

where the literals which are not graphic character literals (such as *nul*) are not really identifiers either (which is why they are represented here in italics). This predefined type Character represents the standard ISO 8-bit set, ISO 8859-1 commonly known as Latin-1. It describes the set of characters normally used for input and output and includes the various accented characters used in European languages, for example the last character is lower case y diaeresis; for the full declaration of type Character see Section 20.1.

It is possible to refer to the non-graphic characters as Ada.Characters. Latin_1.Nul and so on (or with a suitable use clause as Latin_1.Nul or simply Nul). We can also refer to the graphic characters (other than digits and the normal 26 upper case letters) by name; this is useful for displaying program text on output devices which do not support all the graphic characters. Finally, we can refer to those characters also in the ASCII set as ASCII.Nul and so on but this feature is obsolescent.

There is also a predefined type Wide_Character corresponding to the ISO 16-bit Basic Multilingual Plane (BMP) set, ISO 10646. The first 256 literals of this set correspond to those of the type Character. The type Wide_Character is used for dealing with Eastern character sets.

It should be noted that the existence of both the predefined type Character and Wide_Character results in overloading of some of the literals. An expression such as

'X' < 'L'

is ambiguous. We do not know whether we are comparing characters of the type Character or Wide_Character (or even Roman_Digit). In order to resolve the ambiguity we must qualify one or both literals.

Character'('X') < 'L' = False
Roman_Digit'('X') < 'L' = True

As well as the predefined type Character there is also the predefined type String

type String **is array** (Positive **range** <>) **of** Character;

This is a perfectly normal array type and obeys all the rules of the previous section. So we can write

S: String (1 .. 7);

to declare an array of range 1 .. 7. The bounds can also be deduced from the initial value thus

> G: **constant** String := ('P', 'I', 'G');

where the initial value takes the form of a normal positional aggregate. The lower bound of G (that is, G'First) is 1 since the index subtype of String is Positive and Positive'First is 1.

An alternative notation is provided for a positional aggregate each of whose components is a character literal. This is the string. So we could more conveniently write

> G: **constant** String := "PIG";

The string is the last lexical element to be introduced. It consists of a sequence of printable characters and spaces enclosed in double quotes. A double quote may be represented in a string by two double quotes so that

> ('A', '"', 'B') = "A""B"

The string may also have just one character or may be null. The equivalent aggregates using character literals have to be written in named notation.

> (1 => 'A') = "A"
> (1 .. 0 => 'A') = ""

Note how we have to introduce an arbitrary character in the null named form. Ada has some strange quirks!

Another rule about a lexical string is that it must fit onto a single line. Moreover it cannot contain control characters such as *soh*. And, of course, as with character literals, the two cases of alphabet are distinct in strings

> "pig" /= "PIG"

In Section 8.6 we will see how to overcome the limitations that a string must fit onto a single line and yet cannot contain control characters.

A major use for strings is, of course, for creating text to be output. A simple sequence of characters can be output by a call of the (overloaded) subprogram Put. Thus

> Put("The Countess of Lovelace");

will output the text

> The Countess of Lovelace

onto some appropriate file.

Note that there is also an array type Wide_String defined as an array of the type Wide_Character. One consequence is that comparisons between literal strings are also ambiguous like comparisons between individual literals and so also have to be qualified as illustrated in Section 8.6.

However, the lexical string is not reserved just for use with the predefined types String and Wide_String. It can be used to represent an array of any character type. We can write

type Roman_Number **is array** (Positive **range** <>) **of** Roman_Digit;

and then

Nineteen_Eighty_Four: **constant** Roman_Number := "MCMLXXXIV";

or indeed

Four: **array** (1 .. 2) **of** Roman_Digit := "IV";

EXERCISE 8.4

1 Declare a constant array Roman_To_Integer which can be used for table look-up to convert a Roman_Digit to its normal integer equivalent (e.g. converts 'C' to 100).

2 Given an object R of type Roman_Number write statements to compute the equivalent integer value V. It may be assumed that R obeys the normal rules of construction of Roman numbers.

8.5   Arrays of arrays and slices

The components of an array can be of any definite subtype. Remember that a definite subtype is one for which we can declare an object (without an explicit constraint or initial value). Thus we can declare arrays of any scalar type; we can also declare arrays of arrays. So we can have

type Matrix_3_6 **is array** (1 .. 3) **of** Vector_6;

where, as in Section 8.2

type Vector_6 **is array** (1 .. 6) **of** Float;

However, we cannot declare an array of an indefinite type such as an unconstrained array (just as we cannot declare an object which is an unconstrained array). So we cannot write

type Matrix_3_N **is array** (1 .. 3) **of** Vector;   -- illegal

On the other hand, there is nothing to prevent us declaring an unconstrained array of constrained arrays thus

type Matrix_N_6 **is array** (Integer **range** <>) **of** Vector_6;

It is instructive to compare the practical differences between declaring an array of arrays

> AOA: Matrix_3_6;   or   AOA: Matrix_N_6(1 .. 3);

and the similar multidimensional array

> MDA: Matrix(1 .. 3, 1 .. 6);

Aggregates for both are completely identical, for example

> ((1.0, 2.0, 3.0, 4.0, 5.0, 6.0),
> (4.0, 4.0, 4.0, 4.0, 4.0, 4.0),
> (6.0, 5.0, 4.0, 3.0, 2.0, 1.0))

but component access is quite different, thus

> AOA(I)(J)
> MDA(I, J)

where in the case of AOA the internal structure is naturally revealed. The individual rows of AOA can be manipulated as arrays in their own right, but the structure of MDA cannot be decomposed. So we could change the middle row of AOA to zero by

> AOA(2) := (1 .. 6 => 0.0);

but a similar technique cannot be applied to MDA.

Arrays of arrays are not restricted to one dimension, we can have a multidimensional array of arrays or an array of multidimensional arrays; the notation extends in an obvious way.

Arrays of strings are revealing. Consider

> **type** String_Array **is array** (Positive **range** <>,
>   Positive **range** <>) **of** Character;

which is an unconstrained two-dimensional array type. We can then declare

> Farmyard: **constant** String_Array := ("pig", "cat", "dog",
>   "cow", "rat", "ass");

where the bounds are conveniently deduced from the aggregate. But note that we cannot have a ragged array where the individual strings are of different lengths such as

> Zoo: **constant** String_Array := ("aardvark", "baboon",
>   "camel", "dolphin", "elephant", ..., "zebra");   -- illegal

This is a real nuisance and means we have to pad the strings to be the same length

```
Zoo: constant String_Array := ("aardvark    ",
                               "baboon      ",
                               "camel       ",
                               "dolphin     ",
                               "elephant    ",
                               ...
                               "zebra       ");
```

The next problem is that we cannot select an individual one of the strings. We might want to output one and so attempt

```
Put(Farmyard(5));
```

hoping to print the text

```
rat
```

but this is not allowed since we can only select an individual component of an array which in this case is just one character.

An alternative approach is to use an array of arrays. A problem here is that the component in the array type declaration has to be constrained and so we have to decide on the length of our strings right from the beginning thus

```
type String_3_Array is array (Positive range <>) of String(1 .. 3);
```

and then

```
Farmyard: constant String_3_Array := ("pig", "cat", "dog",
                                      "cow", "rat", "ass");
```

With this formulation we can indeed select an individual string as a whole and so the statement Put(Farmyard(5)); now works. However, we still cannot declare our Zoo as a ragged array; we will return to this topic in Section 10.3 when another approach will be discussed.

We thus see that arrays of arrays and multidimensional arrays each have their own advantages and disadvantages. Neither is ideal; Ada arrays are rather restrictive and do not offer the flexibility of Algol 68.

A special feature of one-dimensional arrays is the ability to denote a slice of an array object. A slice is written as the name of the object (variable or constant) followed by a discrete range in brackets.

So given

```
S: String(1 .. 10);
```

then we can write S(3 .. 8) to denote the middle six characters of S. The bounds of the slice are the bounds of the range and not those of the index subtype. We could write

    T: **constant** String := S(3 .. 8);

and then T'First = 3, T'Last = 8.

The bounds of the slice need not be static but can be any expressions. A slice would be null if the range turned out to be null.

The use of slices emphasizes the nature of array assignment. The value of the expression to be assigned is completely evaluated before any components are assigned. No problems arise with overlapping slices. So

    S(1 .. 4) := "BARA";
    S(4 .. 7) := S(1 .. 4);

results in S(1 .. 7) = "BARBARA". S(4) is only updated after the expression S(1 .. 4) is safely evaluated. There is no risk of setting S(4) to 'B' and then consequently making the expression "BARB" with the final result of

    "BARBARB"

The ability to use slices is another consideration in deciding between arrays of arrays and multidimensional arrays. With our second Farmyard we can write

    Pets: String_3_Array(1 .. 2) := Farmyard(2 .. 3);

which uses sliding assignment so that the two components of Pets are "cat" and "dog". Moreover, if we had declared the Farmyard as a variable rather than a constant then we could also write

    Farmyard(1)(1 .. 2) := "ho";

which turns the "pig" into a "hog"! We can do none of these things with the old Farmyard.

EXERCISE 8.5

1   Write a single assignment statement to swap the first and second rows of AOA.

2   Declare the second Farmyard as a variable. Then change the cow into a sow.

3   Assume that R contains a Roman number. Write statements to see if the last digit of the corresponding decimal Arabic value is a 4 and change it to a 6 if it is.

8.6 One-dimensional array operations

Many of the operators that we met in Chapter 6 may also be applied to one-dimensional arrays.

The Boolean operators **and, or, xor** and **not** may be applied to one-dimensional Boolean arrays. In the case of the binary operators, the two operands must have the same number of components and be of the same type. The underlying scalar operation is applied component by component and the resulting array is again of the same type. The bounds of the result are the same as the bounds of the left or only operand.

Consider

> **type** Bit_Row **is array** (Positive **range** <>) **of** Boolean;
> A, B: Bit_Row(1 .. 4);
> C, D: **array** (1 .. 4) **of** Boolean;
> T: **constant** Boolean := True;
> F: **constant** Boolean := False;

then we can write

> A := (T, T, F, F);
> B := (T, F, T, F);
>
> A := A **and** B;
> B := **not** B;

and A now equals (T, F, F, F), and B equals (F, T, F, T). Similarly for **or** and **xor**. But note that C **and** D would not be allowed because they are of different (and anonymous) types because of the rule regarding multiple declarations (Section 6.1). This is clearly a case where it is appropriate to give a name to the array type because we are manipulating the arrays as complete objects.

Note that these operators also use sliding semantics, like assignment as explained in Section 8.2, and so only demand that the types and the number of components are the same. The bounds themselves do not have to be equal. However, if the number of components are not the same then, naturally, Constraint_Error will be raised.

Boolean arrays can be used to represent sets. Consider

> **type** Primary **is** (R, Y, B);
> **type** Colour **is array** (Primary) **of** Boolean;
> C: Colour;

then there are $8 = 2 \times 2 \times 2$ values that C can take. C is, of course, an array with three components and each of these has value True or False; the three components are

> C(R),   C(Y)   and   C(B)

The 8 possible values of the type Colour can be represented by suitably named constants as follows

White:	**constant** Colour := (F, F, F);
Red:	**constant** Colour := (T, F, F);
Yellow:	**constant** Colour := (F, T, F);
Blue:	**constant** Colour := (F, F, T);
Green:	**constant** Colour := (F, T, T);
Purple:	**constant** Colour := (T, F, T);
Orange:	**constant** Colour := (T, T, F);
Black:	**constant** Colour := (T, T, T);

and then we can write expressions such as

Red **or** Yellow

which is equal to Orange and

not Black

which is White.

So the values of our type Colour are effectively the set of colours obtained by taking all combinations of the primary colours represented by R, Y and B. The empty set is the value of White and the full set is the value of Black. We are using the paint pot mixing colour model rather than light mixing. A value of True for a component means that the primary colour concerned is mixed in our pot. The murky mess we got at school from mixing too many colours together is our black!

The operations **or, and** and **xor** may be interpreted as set union, set intersection and symmetric difference. A test for set membership can be made by inspecting the value of the appropriate component of the set. Thus

C(R)

is True if R is in the set represented by C. We cannot use the predefined operation **in** for this. A literal value can be represented using the named aggregate notation, so

(R | Y => T, **others** => F)

has the same value as Orange. A more elegant way of doing this will appear in the next chapter.

We now consider the equality and relational operators. The operators = and /= apply to all types anyway and we gave the rules for arrays when we discussed assignment in Section 8.2.

The relational operators <, <=, > and >= may be applied to one-dimensional arrays of a discrete type. (Note discrete.) The result of the comparison is based upon the lexicographic (that is, dictionary) order using the defined order relation for the components. Remembering that the upper and lower case letters are distinct and the upper case ones are lower, then for the type String the following strings are in lexicographic order

"" , "A" , "AZZ" , "CAT" , "CATERPILLAR" , "DOG" , "cat"

Strings are compared component by component until they differ in some position. The string with the lower component is then lower. If one string runs out of components as in CAT *versus* CATERPILLAR then the shorter one is lower. The null string is lowest of all.

Because of the existence of the type Wide_String we cannot actually write comparisons such as

```
"CAT" < "DOG"          -- illegal
"CCL" < "CCXC"         -- illegal
```

because they are ambiguous since we do not know whether we are comparing type String, Wide_String or even Roman_Number. We must qualify one or both of the strings. This is done in the usual way but a string, unlike the bracketed form of aggregates, has to be placed in brackets otherwise we would get an ugly juxtaposition of a single and double quote. So

```
Wide_String'("CAT") < "DOG"          -- True
String'("CCL") < "CCXC"              -- True
Roman_Number'("CCL") < "CCXC"        -- False
```

Note that our compiler is too stupid to know about the interpretation of Roman numbers in our minds and has said that 250 < 290 is false. The only thing that matters is the order relation of the characters 'L' and 'X' in the type definition. In the next chapter we will show how we can redefine < so that it works 'properly' for Roman numbers.

Of course, the relational operators also apply to general expressions and not just to literal strings

```
Nineteen_Eighty_Four < "MM"          -- True
```

The relational operators can be applied to arrays of any discrete types. So

```
(1, 2, 3) < (2, 3)
(Jan, Jan) < (1 => Feb)
```

The predefined operators <=, > and >= are defined by analogy with <.

We finally introduce a new binary operator & which denotes concatenation of one-dimensional arrays. It has the same precedence as binary plus and minus. The two operands must be of the same type and the result is an array of the same type whose value is obtained by juxtaposing the two operands. The length of the result is thus the sum of the lengths of the operands.

The lower bound of the result depends upon whether the underlying array type is constrained or not. If it is unconstrained (considered the usual case) then the lower bound is that of the left operand as for other operators.

However, if it is constrained then the lower bound is that of the array index subtype. (If the left operand is null the result is simply the right operand.)

So

```
"CAT" & "ERPILLAR" = "CATERPILLAR"
```

String concatenation can be used to construct a string which is too long to fit on one line

```
"This string goes" &
"on and on"
```

One or both operands of & can also be a single value of the component type. If the left operand is such a single value then the lower bound of the result is always the lower bound of the array index subtype.

```
"CAT" & 'S' = "CATS"
'S' & "CAT" = "SCAT"
'S' & 'S' = "SS"
```

This is useful for representing the control characters such as CR and LF in strings. So, using an abbreviated form rather than Ada.Characters.Latin_1.CR, we can write

```
"First line" & Latin_1.CR & Latin_1.LF & "Next line"
```

Of course, it might be neater to declare

```
CRLF: constant String := (Latin_1.CR, Latin_1.LF);
```

and then write

```
"First line" & CRLF & "Next line"
```

The operation & can be applied to any one-dimensional array type and so we can apply it to our Roman numbers. Consider

```
R: Roman_Number(1 .. 5);
S: String(1 .. 5);

R := "CCL" & "IV";
S := "CCL" & "IV";
```

This is valid. The context tells us that in the first case we apply & to two Roman numbers whereas in the second we apply it to two values of type String. There is no ambiguity as in

```
B: Boolean := "CCL" < "IV";            -- illegal
```

which arises because the context demands the type Boolean which does not distinguish the various string types.

EXERCISE 8.6

1 Write the eight possible constants White ... Black of the type Colour in ascending order as determined by the operator < applied to one-dimensional arrays.

2 Evaluate

   (a) Red **or** Green
   (b) Black **xor** Red
   (c) **not** Green

3 Show that **not** (Black **xor** C) = C is true for all values of C.

4 Why did we not write

   (Jan, Jan) < (Feb)

5 Put in ascending order the following values of type String: "ABC", "123", "abc", "Abc", "abC", "aBc".

6 Given

   C: Character;
   S: String(5 .. 10);

   What are the lower bounds of

   (a) C & S   (b) S & C   (c) "" & S

7 Given

   type TC **is array** (1 .. 10) **of** Integer;
   type TU **is array** (Natural **range** <>) **of** Integer;
   AC: TC;
   AU: TU(1 .. 10);

   What are the bounds of

   (a) AC(6 .. 10) & AC(1 .. 5)   (c) AU(6 .. 10) & AU(1 .. 5)
   (b) AC(6) & AC(7 .. 10) & AC(1 .. 5) (d) AU(6) & AU(7 .. 10) & AU(1 .. 5)

8.7 Records

As stated at the beginning of this chapter we are only going to consider the simplest form of record at this point. A discussion of tagged and discriminated records will be found in Chapters 13 and 16 respectively.

A record is a composite object consisting of named components which may be of different types. In contrast to arrays, we cannot have anonymous record types – they all have to be named. Consider

   type Month_Name **is** (Jan, Feb, Mar, Apr, May, Jun,
                    Jul, Aug, Sep, Oct, Nov, Dec);

```
type Date is
  record
      Day: Integer range 1 .. 31;
      Month: Month_Name;
      Year: Integer;
  end record;
```

This declares the type Date to be a record containing three named components: Day, Month and Year.

We can declare variables and constants of record types in the usual way.

```
D: Date;
```

declares an object D which is a date. The individual components of D can be denoted by following D with a dot and the component name. Thus we could write

```
D.Day := 4;
D.Month := Jul;
D.Year := 1776;
```

in order to assign new values to the individual components.

Records can be manipulated as whole objects. Literal values can be written as aggregates much like arrays; both positional and named forms can be used. So we could write

```
D: Date := (4, Jul, 1776);
E: Date;
```

and then

```
E := D;
```

or

```
E := (Month => Jul, Day => 4, Year => 1776);
```

The reader will be relieved to know that much of the complexity of array aggregates does not apply to records. This is because the number of components is always known.

In a positional aggregate the components come in order. In a named aggregate they may be in any order. In the particular example shown the use of a named aggregate avoids the necessity to know on which side of the Atlantic the record type was declared.

A named aggregate cannot use a range because the components are not considered to be closely related and the vertical bar can only be used with components which have the same (base) type. The choice **others** can be used but again only when the remaining components are of the same type – and there must be some.

There is one extra possibility for records and that is that the positional and named notations can be mixed in one aggregate. But if this is done then the positional components must come first and in order (without holes) as usual. So in other words, we can change to the named notation at any point in the aggregate but must then stick to it. The above date could therefore also be expressed as

```
(4, Jul, Year => 1776)
(4, Year => 1776, Month => Jul)
```

and so on.

It is possible to give default expressions for some or all of the components in the type declaration. Thus

```
type Complex is
   record
      RI: Float := 0.0;
      Im: Float := 0.0;
   end record;
```

or more succinctly

```
type Complex is
   record
      RI, Im: Float := 0.0;
   end record;
```

declares a record type containing two components of type Float and gives a default expression of 0.0 for each. This record type represents a complex number $x + iy$ where RI and Im are the values of x and y. The default value is thus $(0, 0)$, the origin of the Argand plane. We can now declare

```
C1: Complex;
C2: Complex := (1.0, 0.0);
```

The object C1 will now have the values 0.0 for its components by default. In the case of C2 we have overridden the default values. Note that, irritatingly, even if there are default expressions, an aggregate must be complete even if it supplies the same values as the default expressions for some of the components.

In this case both components are the same type and so the following named forms are possible

```
(RI | Im => 1.0)
(others => 1.0)
```

The only operations predefined on record types are = and /= as well as assignment of course. Other operations must be performed at the component level or be explicitly defined by a subprogram as we shall see in the next chapter.

A record type may have any number of components. It may pathologically have none in which case its declaration takes the form

```
type Hole is
    record
        null;
    end record;
```

The reserved word **null** confirms that we meant to declare a null record type. Null records have their uses and can occur quite frequently and so an abbreviated form is provided

```
type Hole is null record;
```

The components of a record type can be of any definite type; they can be other records or arrays. However, if a component is an array then it must be fully constrained and moreover it must be of a named type and not an anonymous type. And obviously a record cannot contain an instance of itself.

The components cannot be constants but the record as a whole can be. Thus

```
I: constant Complex := (0.0, 1.0);
```

is allowed and represents the square root of -1.

A more elaborate example of a record is

```
type Person is
    record
        Birth: Date;
        Name: String(1 .. 20) := (1 .. 20 => ' ');
    end record;
```

The record Person has two components, the first is another record, a Date, the second an array. The array which is a string of length 20 has a default value of all spaces.

We can now write

```
John: Person;
John.Birth := (19, Aug, 1937);
John.Name(1 .. 4) := "John";
```

and we would then have

```
John = ((19, Aug, 1937), "John            ")
```

The notation is as expected. The aggregates nest and for objects we proceed from left to right using the dot notation to select components of a record and indexes in brackets to select components of an array and ranges in brackets to slice arrays. There is no limit. We could have an array of persons

> People: **array** (1 .. N) **of** Person;

and then have

> People(6).Birth.Day := 19;
> People(8).Name(3) := 'h';

and so on.

A final point concerns the evaluation of expressions in a record declaration. An expression in a constraint applied to a component is evaluated when the record type is elaborated. So our type Person could have

> Name: String(1 .. N) := (**others** => ' ');

and the length of the component Name will be the value of N when the type Person is elaborated. Of course, N need not be static and so if the type declaration is in a loop, for example, then each execution of the loop might give rise to a type with a different size component. However, for each elaboration of the record type declaration all objects of the type will have the same component size.

On the other hand, a default expression in a record type is only evaluated when an object of the type is declared and only then if no explicit initial value is provided. Of course, in simple cases, like our type Complex, it makes no difference but it could bring surprises. For example suppose we write the component Name as

> Name: String(1 .. N) := (1 .. N => ' ');

then the length of the component Name is the value of N when the record type is declared whereas when a Person is subsequently declared without an initial value, the aggregate will be evaluated using the value of N which then applies. Of course, N may by then be different and so Constraint_Error will be raised. This is rather surprising; we do seem to have strayed into an odd backwater of Ada!

EXERCISE 8.7

1   Declare three variables C1, C2 and C3 of type Complex. Write one or more statements to assign (a) the sum, (b) the product, of C1 and C2 to C3.

2   Write statements to find the index of the first person of the array People born on or after 1 January 1950.

CHECKLIST 8

Array types can be anonymous, but record types cannot.

Aggregates must always be complete.

Distinguish constrained array types (definite types) from unconstrained array types (those with <>).

The component subtype of an array must be definite.

Named and positional notations cannot be mixed for array aggregates – they can for records.

An array aggregate with others must have a context giving its bounds. It never slides.

A choice in an array aggregate can only be dynamic or null if it is the only choice.

The attributes First, Last, Length and Range apply to array objects and constrained array types and subtypes but not to unconstrained types and subtypes.

For array assignment to be valid, the number of components must be equal for each dimension – not the bounds.

The cases of alphabet are distinct in character literals and strings.

An aggregate with one component must use the named notation. This applies to records as well as to arrays.

A record component cannot be of an anonymous array type.

A default component expression is only evaluated when an uninitialized object is declared.

Changes from Ada 83

Only a constant and not a variable could obtain its bounds from the initial value in Ada 83.

A named aggregate with **others** was not allowed after := in Ada 83.

The type Character was the 7-bit ISO set in Ada 83.

The types Wide_Character and Wide_String did not exist in Ada 83.

The rules for concatenation of constrained array types were different in Ada 83. The lower bound was that of the left operand and always resulted in Constraint_Error unless the left operand was a single component.

The package Ada.Characters.Latin_1 did not exist in Ada 83; it effectively replaces ASCII which is obsolete in Ada 95.

The abbreviated form for a null record type did not exist in Ada 83.

Subprograms

Subprograms are the conventional parameterized unit of programming. In Ada, subprograms fall into two categories: functions and procedures. Functions are called as components of expressions and return a value as part of the expression, whereas procedures are called as statements standing alone.

As we shall see, the actions to be performed when a subprogram is called are described by a subprogram body. Subprogram bodies are declared in the usual way in a declarative part which may for instance be in a block or indeed in another subprogram.

9.1   Functions

A function is a form of subprogram that can be called as part of an expression. In Chapter 6 we met examples of calls of functions such as Day'Succ, Sqrt and so on.

We now consider the form of a function body which describes the statements to be executed when the function is called. For example the body of the function Sqrt might have the form

```
function Sqrt(X: Float) return Float is
    R: Float;
```

```
begin
   -- compute value of Sqrt(X) in R
   return R;
end Sqrt;
```

All function bodies start with the reserved word **function** and the designator of the function being defined. If the function has parameters the designator is followed by a list of parameter specifications in brackets. If there are several specifications then they are separated by semicolons. Each specification gives the identifiers of one or more parameters followed by a colon and its type or subtype. The parameter list, if any, is then followed by the reserved word **return** and the type or subtype of the result of the function. In the case of both parameters and result the type or subtype must be given by a subtype mark and not by a subtype indication. This is an important example of a situation where an explicit constraint is not allowed; the reason will be mentioned later in this chapter.

The part of the body we have described so far is called the function specification. It specifies the function to the outside world in the sense of providing all the information needed to call the function.

After the specification comes **is** and then the body proper which is just like a block – it has a declarative part, **begin**, a sequence of statements, and then **end**. As for a block the declarative part can be empty, but there must be at least one statement in the sequence of statements. Between **end** and the terminating semicolon we may repeat the designator of the function. This is optional but, if present, must correctly match the designator after **function**.

It is often necessary or just convenient to give the specification on its own but without the rest of the body. In such a case it is immediately followed by a semicolon thus

```
function Sqrt(X: Float) return Float;
```

and is then correctly known as a function declaration – although often still informally referred to as a specification. The uses of such declarations will be discussed later.

The formal parameters of a function act as local constants whose values are provided by the corresponding actual parameters. When the function is called the declarative part is elaborated in the usual way and then the statements are executed. A return statement is used to indicate the value of the function call and to return control back to the calling expression.

Thus considering our example suppose we had

```
S := Sqrt(T + 0.5);
```

then first T + 0.5 is evaluated and then Sqrt is called. Within the body the parameter X behaves as a constant with the initial value given by T + 0.5. It is rather as if we had

```
X: constant Float := T + 0.5;
```

The declaration of R is then elaborated. We then obey the sequence of statements and assume they compute the square root of X and assign it to R. The last statement is **return** R; this passes control back to the calling expression with the result of the function being the value of R. This value is then assigned to S.

The expression in a return statement can be of arbitrary complexity and must be of the same type as and satisfy any constraints implied by the subtype mark given in the function specification. If the constraints are violated then, of course, the exception Constraint_Error is raised. (A result of an array type can slide as mentioned later in this section.)

A function body may have several return statements. The execution of any of them will terminate the function. Thus the function Sign which takes an integer value and returns +1, 0 or –1 according to whether the parameter is positive, zero or negative could be written as

```
function Sign(X: Integer) return Integer is
begin
  if X > 0 then
    return +1;
  elsif X < 0 then
    return –1;
  else
    return 0;
  end if;
end Sign;
```

So we see that the last lexical statement of the body need not be a return statement since there is one in each branch of the statement. Any attempt to 'run' into the final end will raise the exception Program_Error. This is our first example of a situation giving rise to Program_Error; this exception is generally used for situations which would violate the run-time control structure.

It should be noted that each call of a function produces a new instance of any objects declared within it (including parameters of course) and these disappear when we leave the function. It is therefore possible for a function to be called recursively without any problems. So the factorial function could be declared as

```
function Factorial(N: Positive) return Positive is
begin
  if N = 1 then
    return 1;
  else
    return N * Factorial(N–1);
  end if;
end Factorial;
```

If we write

```
F := Factorial(4);
```

then the function calls itself until, on the fourth call (with the other three calls all partly executed and waiting for the result of the call they did before doing the multiply) we find that N is 1 and the calls then all unwind and all the multiplications are performed.

Note that there is no need to check that the parameter N is positive since the parameter is of subtype Positive. So calling Factorial(–2) will result in Constraint_Error. Of course, Factorial(10_000) could result in the computer running out of space in which case Storage_Error would be raised. The more moderate call Factorial(20) would undoubtedly cause overflow and thus raise Constraint_Error.

A formal parameter may be of any type but in general the type must have a name. The one exception is access parameters which are discussed in Chapter 10. So a parameter cannot be of an anonymous type such as

> **array** (1 .. 6) **of** Float

In any event no actual parameter (other than an aggregate) could match such a formal parameter even if it were allowed since the actual and formal parameters must have the same type. Again access parameters are slightly different.

A formal parameter can, however, be of an unconstrained array type such as

> **type** Vector **is array** (Integer **range** <>) **of** Float;

In such a case the bounds of the formal parameter are taken from those of the actual parameter.

Consider

```
function Sum(A: Vector) return Float is
   Result: Float := 0.0;
begin
   for I in A'Range loop
      Result := Result + A(I);
   end loop;
   return Result;
end Sum;
```

then we can write

```
V: Vector(1 .. 4) := (1.0, 2.0, 3.0, 4.0);
S: Float;
...
S := Sum(V);
```

The formal parameter A then takes the bounds of the actual parameter V. So for this call we have

> A'Range   is   1 .. 4

and the effect of the loop is to compute the sum of A(1), A(2), A(3) and A(4). The final value of Result which is returned and assigned to S is therefore 10.0.

The function Sum can be used to sum the components of a vector with any bounds. Ada thus overcomes one of the problems of original Pascal which insists that array parameters have static bounds.

Of course, an Ada function could have a constrained array type as a formal parameter. However, remember that we cannot apply the constraint in the parameter list using a subtype indication as in

> **function** Sum_5(A: Vector(1 .. 5)) **return** Float   -- illegal

but must use the name of a constrained array type or subtype such as

> **subtype** Vector_5 **is** Vector(1 .. 5);

as a subtype mark as in

> **function** Sum_5(A: Vector_5) **return** Float

An actual parameter corresponding to such a constrained formal array must have the same number of components; sliding is allowed as for assignment. So we could have

> W: Vector(0 .. 4);
> ...
> S := Sum_5(W);

The actual parameter of a function can also be an aggregate. In fact the behaviour is exactly as for an initial value and assignment described in Section 8.3. If the formal parameter is unconstrained then the aggregate must supply its bounds and so cannot contain **others**. If the formal parameter is constrained then it provides the bounds; an aggregate without **others** could slide. But remember that an aggregate with **others** never slides.

As another example consider

```
function Inner(A, B: Vector) return Float is
   Result: Float := 0.0;
begin
   for I in A'Range loop
      Result := Result + A(I)*B(I);
   end loop;
   return Result;
end Inner;
```

This computes the inner product of the two vectors A and B by adding together the sum of the products of corresponding components. This is our first example of a function with more than one parameter. Such a function is called by following the function name by a list of the expressions giving the values of the actual parameters separated by commas and in brackets. The order of evaluation of the actual parameters is not defined.

So

```
V: Vector(1 .. 3) := (1.0, 2.0, 3.0);
W: Vector(1 .. 3) := (2.0, 3.0, 4.0);
X: Float;
...
X := Inner(V, W);
```

results in X being assigned the value

1.0 * 2.0 + 2.0 * 3.0 + 3.0 * 4.0 = 20.0

Note that the function Inner is not written well since it does not check that the bounds of A and B are the same. It is not symmetric with respect to A and B since I takes (or tries to take) the values of the range A'Range irrespective of B'Range. So if the array W had bounds of 0 and 2, Constraint_Error would be raised on the third time round the loop. If the array W had bounds of 1 and 4 then no exception would be raised but the result might not be what we expected.

It would be nice to ensure the equality of the bounds by placing a constraint on B at the time of call but this cannot be done. The best we can do is simply check the bounds for equality inside the function body and perhaps explicitly raise Constraint_Error if they are not equal

```
if A'First /= B'First or A'Last /= B'Last then
   raise Constraint_Error;
end if;
```

(The use of the raise statement is described in detail in Chapter 14.)

We saw above that a formal parameter can be of an unconstrained array type. In a similar way the result of a function can be an array whose bounds are not known until the function is called. The result type can be an unconstrained array and the bounds are then obtained from the expression in the appropriate return statement.

As an example the following function returns a vector which has the same bounds as the parameter but whose component values are in the reverse order

```
function Rev(A: Vector) return Vector is
   R: Vector(A'Range);
begin
   for I in A'Range loop
      R(I) := A(A'First+A'Last−I);
   end loop;
   return R;
end Rev;
```

The variable R is declared to be of type Vector with the same bounds as A. Note how the loop reverses the value. The result takes the bounds of the expression R. Note that we have called the function Rev rather than Reverse; this is because **reverse** is a reserved word.

The matching rules for function results of both constrained and unconstrained arrays are the same as for parameters. Sliding is allowed and so on.

If a function returns a record or array value then a component can be immediately selected, indexed or sliced as appropriate without assigning the value to a variable. Indeed the result is treated as a (constant) object in its own right. So we could write

    Rev(Y)(I)

which denotes the component indexed by I of the array returned by the call of Rev.

It should be noted that a parameterless function call, like a parameterless procedure call, has no brackets. There is thus a possible ambiguity between calling a function with one parameter and indexing the result of a parameterless call; such an ambiguity could be resolved by, for example, renaming the functions as will be described in Section 12.6.

EXERCISE 9.1

1   Write a function Even which returns True or False according to whether its Integer parameter is even or odd.

2   Rewrite the factorial function so that the parameter may be positive or zero but not negative. Remember that the value of Factorial(0) is to be 1. Use the subtype Natural introduced in Section 6.5.

3   Write a function Outer that forms the outer product of two vectors. The outer product C of two vectors A and B is a matrix such that $C_{ij} = A_i \cdot B_j$.

4   Write a function Make_Colour which takes an array of values of type Primary and returns the corresponding value of type Colour. See Section 8.6. Check that Make_Colour((R, Y)) = Orange.

5   Rewrite the function Inner to use sliding semantics so that it works providing the arrays have the same length. Raise Constraint_Error (as outlined above) if the arrays do not match.

6   Write a function Make_Unit that takes a single parameter N and returns a unit $N \times N$ real matrix. Use the function to declare a constant unit $N \times N$ matrix. See Exercise 8.3(**3**).

7   Write a function GCD to return the greatest common divisor of two nonnegative integers. Use Euclid's algorithm that

$$\gcd(x, y) = \gcd(y, x \bmod y) \quad y \neq 0$$
$$\gcd(x, 0) = x$$

Write the function using recursion and then rewrite it using a loop statement.

9.2   Operators

In the last section we carefully stated that a function body commenced with the reserved word **function** followed by the designator of the function. In all the examples of the last section the designator was in fact an identifier. However, it can also be a character string provided that the string is one of the language operators in double quotes. These are

abs	**and**	**mod**	**not**	**or**	**rem**	**xor**
=	/=	<	<=	>	>=	
+	–	*	/	**	&	

In such a case the function defines a new meaning of the operator concerned. As an example we can rewrite the function Inner of the last section as an operator.

```
function "*" (A, B: Vector) return Float is
    Result: Float := 0.0;
begin
    for I in A'Range loop
        Result := Result + A(I)*B(I);
    end loop;
    return Result;
end "*";
```

We call this new function by the normal syntax of uses of the operator "*". Thus instead of

```
X := Inner(V, W);
```

we now write

```
X := V * W;
```

This meaning of "*" is distinguished from the existing meanings of integer and floating point multiplication by the context provided by the types of the actual parameters V and W and the type required by X.

The giving of several meanings to an operator is another instance of overloading which we have already met with enumeration literals. The rules for the overloading of subprograms in general are discussed later in this chapter. It suffices to say at this point that any ambiguity can usually be resolved by qualification. Overloading of predefined operators is not new. It has existed in most programming languages for the past thirty years. What is relatively new is the ability to define additional overloadings.

We can now see that the predefined meanings of all operators are as if there were a series of functions with declarations such as

```
function "+" (Left, Right: Float) return Float;
function "<" (Left, Right: Float) return Boolean;
function "<" (Left, Right: Boolean) return Boolean;
```

Moreover, every time we declare a new type, new overloadings of predefined operators such as "=" and "<" may be created.

Observe that the predefined operators always have Left and Right as formal parameter names (real mathematicians would prefer X and Y which has served the community well since the days of Newton; but Ada had to be awkward!).

Although we can add new meanings to operators we cannot change the syntax of the call. Thus the number of parameters of "*" must always be two and the precedence cannot be changed and so on. The operators "+" and "−" are unusual in that a new definition can have either one parameter or two parameters according to whether it is to be called as a unary or binary operator. Thus the function Sum could be rewritten as

```
function "+" (A: Vector) return Float is
   Result: Float := 0.0;
begin
   for I in A'Range loop
      Result := Result + A(I);
   end loop;
   return Result;
end "+";
```

and we would then write

```
S := +V;
```

rather than

```
S := Sum(V);
```

Function bodies whose designators are operators often contain interesting examples of uses of the operator being overloaded. Thus the body of "*" contains a use of "*" in A(I)*B(I). There is, of course, no ambiguity since the expressions A(I) and B(I) are of type Float whereas our new overloading is for type Vector. Sometimes there is the risk of accidental recursion. This particularly applies if we try to replace an existing meaning rather than add a new one.

Apart from the operator "/=" there are no special rules regarding the types of the operands and results of new overloadings. Thus a new overloading of "=" need not return a Boolean result. On the other hand, if it is Boolean then a corresponding new overloading of "/=" is implicitly created. Moreover, explicit new overloadings of "/=" are also allowed provided only that the result type is not Boolean.

The membership tests **in** and **not in** and the short circuit forms **and then** and **or else** cannot be given new meanings. That is why we said in Section 6.9 that they were not technically classed as operators.

Finally note that in the case of operators represented by reserved words, the characters in the string can be in either case. Thus a new overloading of **or** can be declared as "or" or "OR" or even "Or".

EXERCISE 9.2

1 Write a function "<" that operates on two Roman numbers and compares them according to their corresponding numeric values. That is, so that "CCL" <"CCXC". See Exercise 8.4(**2**).

2 Write functions "+" and "*" to add and multiply two values of type Complex. See Exercise 8.7(**1**).

3 Write a function "<" to test whether a value of type Primary is in a set represented by a value of type Colour. See Section 8.6.

4 Write a function "<=" to test whether one value of type Colour is a subset of another.

5 Write a function "<" to compare two values of the type Date of Section 8.7.

9.3 Procedures

The other form of subprogram is a procedure; a procedure is called as a statement. We have seen many examples of procedure calls where there are no parameters such as Work; Party; Action; and so on.

The body of a procedure is very similar to that of a function. The differences are

- a procedure starts with **procedure**,
- its name must be an identifier,
- it does not return a result,
- the parameters may be of three different modes **in**, **out** or **in out**.

The mode of a parameter is indicated by following the colon in the parameter specification by **in** or by **out** or by **in out**. If the mode is omitted then it is taken to be **in**. The form of parameter known as an access parameter is actually an **in** parameter. Access parameters are discussed with access types in Chapter 10.

In the case of functions the only allowed mode is **in**; the examples earlier in this chapter omitted **in** but could have been written, for instance, as

> **function** Sqrt(X: **in** Float) **return** Float;
> **function** "*" (A, B: **in** Vector) **return** Float;

The general effect of the three modes can be summarized as follows.

> **in**   The formal parameter is a constant initialized by the value of the associated actual parameter.

in out The formal parameter is a variable initialized by the actual parameter; it permits both reading and updating of the value of the associated actual parameter.

out The formal parameter is an uninitialized variable; it permits updating of the value of the associated actual parameter.

Note that both **in out** and **out** parameters behave as normal variables within the subprogram but the key difference is that an **in out** parameter is always initialized by the actual parameter whereas an **out** parameter is not.

The fine detail of the behaviour depends upon whether a parameter is passed by copy or by reference. Parameters of scalar types (and access types, see Chapter 10) are always passed by copy and we will consider them first.

As a simple example of the modes **in** and **out** consider

```
procedure Add(A, B: in Integer; C: out Integer) is
begin
   C := A + B;
end Add;
```

with

```
P, Q: Integer;
...
Add(2+P, 37, Q);
```

On calling Add, the expressions 2+P and 37 are evaluated (in any order) and assigned to the formals A and B which behave as constants. The value of A+B is then assigned to the formal variable C. On return the value of C is assigned to the variable Q. Thus it is (more or less) as if we had written

```
declare
   A: constant Integer := 2+P;      -- in
   B: constant Integer := 37;       -- in
   C: Integer;                      -- out
begin
   C := A + B;                      -- body
   Q := C;                          -- out
end;
```

As an example of the mode **in out** consider

```
procedure Increment(X: in out Integer) is
begin
   X := X + 1;
end;
```

with

```
I: Integer;
...
Increment(I);
```

On calling Increment, the value of I is assigned to the formal variable X. The value of X is then incremented. On return, the final value of X is assigned to the actual parameter I. So it is rather as if we had written

```
declare
   X: Integer := I;
begin
   X := X + 1;
   I := X;
end;
```

For any scalar type (such as Integer) the modes thus correspond simply to copying the value **in** at the call or **out** upon return or both in the case of **in out**.

If the mode is **in** then the actual parameter may be any expression of the appropriate type or subtype. If the mode is **out** or **in out** then the actual parameter must be a variable. The identity of such a variable is determined when the procedure is called and cannot change during the call.

Suppose we had

```
I: Integer;
A: array (1 .. 10) of Integer;

procedure Silly(X: in out Integer) is
begin
   I := I + 1;
   X := X + 1;
end;
```

then the statements

```
A(5) := 1;
I := 5;
Silly(A(I));
```

result in A(5) becoming 2, I becoming 6, but A(6) is not affected.

If a parameter is an array or record then the mechanism of copying, described above may generally be used but alternatively an implementation may use a reference mechanism in which the formal parameter provides direct access to the actual parameter. A program which depends on the particular mechanism is not portable. An example of such a program is given in the exercises at the end of this section.

Parameters of certain types (and arrays and records with any components of those types) are always passed by reference. It so happens that we have not yet dealt with any of these types which are: task and protected types (Chapter 18), tagged record types (Chapter 13) and explicitly limited types (Chapter 11). Private types behave as the corresponding full type (Chapter 11).

Note that because a formal array parameter takes its bounds from the actual parameter, the bounds are always copied in at the start even in the case of an **out** parameter. Of course, for simplicity, an implementation could always copy in the whole array anyway. Indeed, when **out** parameters are passed by copy certain types are always copied in so that dangerous undefined values do not arise. This applies to access types (Chapter 10), discriminated record types (Chapter 16) and record types which have components with default initial values such as the type Complex in Section 8.7.

We now discuss the question of constraints on parameters and the results of functions.

In the case of scalar parameters the situation is as expected from the copying model. For an **in** or **in out** parameter any constraint on the formal must be satisfied by the value of the actual at the beginning of the call. Conversely for an **in out** or **out** parameter any constraint on the variable which is the actual parameter must be satisfied by the value of the formal parameter upon return from the subprogram. Any constraint imposed by the result of a function must also be satisfied.

In the case of arrays the situation is somewhat different. If the formal parameter is a constrained array type, the association is just as for assignment, the number of components in each dimension must be the same but sliding is permitted. If, on the other hand, the formal parameter is an unconstrained array type, then, as we have seen, it takes its bounds from those of the actual. The foregoing applies irrespective of the mode of the array parameter. Similar rules apply to function results; if the result is a constrained array type then the expression in the result can slide.

In the case of the simple records we have discussed so far there are no constraints and so there is nothing to say. The parameter mechanism for other types will be discussed in detail when they are introduced.

We stated above that an actual parameter corresponding to a formal **out** or **in out** parameter must be a variable. This includes the possibility of the actual parameter in turn being an **out** or **in out** formal parameter of some outer subprogram.

A further possibility is that an actual parameter can also be a type conversion of a variable provided, of course, that the conversion is allowed. As an example, since conversion is allowed between any numeric types, we can write

```
F: Float;
...
Increment(Integer(F));
```

If F initially had the value 2.3, it would be converted to the integer value 2, incremented to give 3 and then on return converted back to 3.0 and assigned to F.

This conversion (technically known as a view conversion) of **in out** or **out** parameters is particularly useful with arrays. Suppose we write a library of subprograms applying to our type Vector and then acquire from someone else some subprograms written to apply to the type Row of Section 8.2. The types Row and Vector are essentially the same; it just so happened that the authors used different names. Array type conversion allows us to use both sets of subprograms without having to change the type names systematically.

As a final example consider the following

```
procedure Quadratic(A, B, C: in Float;
                        Root_1, Root_2: out Float; OK: out Boolean) is
    D: constant Float := B**2 – 4.0*A*C;
begin
    if D < 0.0 or A = 0.0 then
        OK := False;
        return;
    end if;
    Root_1 := (–B+Sqrt(D)) / (2.0*A);
    Root_2 := (–B–Sqrt(D)) / (2.0*A);
    OK := True;
end Quadratic;
```

The procedure Quadratic attempts to solve the equation

$$ax^2 + bx + c = 0$$

If the roots are real they are returned via the parameters Root_1 and Root_2 and OK is set to True. If the roots are complex (D < 0.0) or the equation degenerates (A = 0.0) then OK is set to False.

Note the use of the return statement. Since this is a procedure there is no result to be returned and so the word **return** is not followed by an expression. It just updates the **out** or **in out** parameters as necessary and returns control back to where the procedure was called. Note also that unlike a function we can 'run' into the **end**; this is equivalent to obeying **return**.

The reader will note that if OK is set to False then no value is assigned to the **out** parameters Root_1 and Root_2. The copy rule for scalars then implies that the corresponding actual parameters become undefined. In practice, junk values are presumably assigned to the actual parameters and this could possibly raise Constraint_Error if an actual parameter were constrained. This is probably bad practice and so it might be better to assign safe values such as 0.0 to the roots just in case. (In examples like this, the **out** mechanism does not seem so satisfactory as the simple reference mechanism of Algol 68 or Pascal.)

The procedure could be used in a sequence such as

```
declare
    L, M, N: Float;
    P, Q: Float;
    Status: Boolean;
begin
    –– sets values into L, M and N
    Quadratic(L, M, N, P, Q, Status);
    if Status then
        –– roots are in P and Q
    else
```

```
          -- fails
       end if;
     end;
```

This is a good moment to emphasize the point made in Section 6.7 that it is often better to introduce our own two-valued enumeration type rather than use the predefined type Boolean. The above example would be clearer if we had declared

```
     type Roots is (Real_Roots, Complex_Roots);
```

with other appropriate alterations.

We conclude this section by emphasizing that an **out** parameter passed by copy behaves as an ordinary variable that happens not to be initialized. Thus the statements of the above example could be recast in the form

```
     begin
       OK := D >= 0.0 and A /= 0.0;
       if not OK then
          return;
       end if;
       Root_1 := ... ;
       Root_2 := ... ;
     end Quadratic;
```

where the Boolean expression **not** OK reads the **out** parameter OK.

EXERCISE 9.3

1   Write a procedure Swap to interchange the values of the two parameters of type Float.

2   Rewrite the function Rev of Section 9.1 as a procedure with a single parameter. Use it to reverse an array R of type Row.

3   Why is the following not portable?

```
     A: Vector(1 .. 1);

     procedure P(V: Vector) is
     begin
       A(1) := V(1)+V(1);
       A(1) := V(1)+V(1);
     end;
     ...
     A(1) := 1.0;
     P(A);
```

9.4 Named and default parameters

The forms of subprogram call we have been using so far have given the actual parameters in positional order. As with aggregates we can also use the named notation in which the formal parameter name is also supplied; the parameters do not then have to be in order.

So we could write

```
Quadratic(A => L, B => M, C => N,
                         Root_1 => P, Root_2 => Q, OK => Status);
Increment(X => I);
Add(C => Q, A => 2+P, B => 37);
```

We could even write

```
Increment(X => X);
```

as we will see in the next section.

This notation can also be used with functions

```
F := Factorial(N => 4);
S := Sqrt(X => T+0.5);
X := Inner(B => W, A => V);
```

The named notation cannot, however, be used with operators called with the usual infixed syntax (such as V*W) because there is clearly no convenient place to put the names of the formal parameters.

As with record aggregates, the named and positional notations can be mixed and any positional parameters must come first and in their correct order. However, unlike record aggregates, each parameter must be given individually and **others** may not be used. So we could write

```
Quadratic(L, M, N, Root_1 => P, Root_2 => Q, OK => Status);
```

The named notation leads into the topic of default parameters. It sometimes happens that one or more **in** parameters usually take the same value on each call; we can give a default expression in the subprogram specification and then omit it from the call.

Consider the problem of ordering a dry martini in the United States. One is faced with choices described by the following enumeration types

```
type Spirit is (Gin, Vodka);
type Style is (On_The_Rocks, Straight_Up);
type Trimming is (Olive, Twist);
```

The default expressions can then be given in a procedure specification thus

```
procedure Dry_Martini(Base: Spirit := Gin;
                      How: Style := On_The_Rocks;
                      Plus: Trimming := Olive);
```

Typical calls might be

```
Dry_Martini(How => Straight_Up);
Dry_Martini(Vodka, Plus => Twist);
Dry_Martini;
Dry_Martini(Gin, On_The_Rocks);
```

The first call uses the named notation; we get gin, straight up plus olive. The second call mixes the positional and named notations; as soon as a parameter is omitted the named notation must be used. The third call illustrates that all parameters can be omitted. The final call shows that a parameter can, of course, be supplied even if it happens to take the same value as the default expression; in this case it avoids using the named form for the second parameter.

Note that default expressions can only be given for **in** parameters. They cannot be given for operators but they can be given for functions designated by identifiers. Such a default expression (like a default expression for an initial value in a record type declaration) is only evaluated when required; that is, it is evaluated each time the subprogram is called and no corresponding actual parameter is supplied. Hence the default value need not be the same on each call although it usually will be. Default expressions are widely used in the standard input–output package to provide default formats.

Default expressions illustrate the subtle rule that a parameter specification of the form

```
P, Q: in Integer := E
```

is strictly equivalent to

```
P: in Integer := E;  Q: in Integer := E
```

(The reader will recall a similar rule for object declarations; it also applies to record components.) As a consequence, the default expression is evaluated for each omitted parameter in a call. This does not usually matter but would be significant if the expression E included a function call with side effects.

EXERCISE 9.4

1   Write a function Add which returns the sum of the two integer parameters and takes a default value of 1 for the second parameter. How many different ways can it be called to return N+1 where N is the first actual parameter?

2   Rewrite the specification of Dry_Martini to reflect that you prefer Vodka at weekends. Hint: declare a function to return your favourite spirit according to the global variable Today.

9.5 Overloading

We saw in Section 9.2 how new meanings could be given to existing language operators. This overloading applies to subprograms in general.

A subprogram will overload an existing meaning rather than hide it, provided that its specification is sufficiently different. Hiding will occur if the number, order and base types of the parameters and result (if any) are the same; this level of matching is known as type conformance. A procedure cannot hide a function and vice versa. Note that the names of the parameters, their mode and the presence or absence of constraints or default expressions do not matter. Two or more overloaded subprograms may be declared in the same declarative part.

Subprograms and enumeration literals can overload each other. In fact an enumeration literal is formally thought of as a parameterless function with a result of the enumeration type. There are two kinds of uses of identifiers – the overloadable ones and the non-overloadable ones. At any point an identifier either refers to a single entity of the non-overloadable kind or to one or many of the overloadable kind. A declaration of one kind hides the other kind and cannot occur in the same declaration list.

As we have seen, ambiguities arising from overloading can be resolved by qualification. This was necessary when the operator "<" was used with the strings in Section 8.4. As a further example consider the British Channel Islands; the larger three are Guernsey, Jersey and Alderney. There are woollen garments named after each island

    type Garment **is** (Guernsey, Jersey, Alderney);

and breeds of cattle named after two of them (the Alderney breed became extinct as a consequence of the Second World War)

    type Cow **is** (Guernsey, Jersey);

and we can imagine (just) shops that sell both garments and cows according to

    procedure Sell(G: Garment);
    procedure Sell(C: Cow);

Although

    Sell(Alderney);

is not ambiguous

    Sell(Jersey);

is, since we cannot tell which subprogram is being called. We must write for example

    Sell(Cow'(Jersey));

We conclude by noting that ambiguities typically arise only when there are several overloadings. In the case here both Sell and Jersey are overloaded; in the example in Section 8.4 both the operator "<" and the literals 'X' and 'L' were overloaded.

EXERCISE 9.5

1   How else could Sell(Jersey); be made unambiguous?

9.6   Declarations, scopes and visibility

We said earlier that it is sometimes necessary or just convenient to give a subprogram specification on its own without the body. The specification is then followed by a semicolon and is known as a subprogram declaration. A complete subprogram, which always includes the full specification, is known as a subprogram body.

Subprogram declarations and bodies must, like other declarations, occur in a declarative part and a subprogram declaration must be followed by the corresponding body in the same declarative part.

An example of where it is necessary to use a subprogram declaration occurs with mutually recursive procedures. Suppose we wish to declare two procedures F and G which call each other. Because of the rule regarding linear elaboration of declarations we cannot write the call of F in the body of G until after F has been declared and vice versa. Clearly this is impossible if we just write the bodies because one must come second. However, we can write

```
procedure F( ... );          -- declaration of F

procedure G( ... ) is        -- body of G
begin
   F( ... );
end G;

procedure F( ... ) is        -- body of F repeats
begin                        -- its specification
   G( ... );
end F;
```

and then all is well.

If the specification is repeated then it must be given in full and the two must be the same. Technically we say that the two profiles in the specification must have full conformance. The profile is the formal parameter list plus result type if any. Some slight variation is allowed provided the static meaning is the same. For example: a numeric literal can be replaced by another numeric literal with the same value; an identifier can be replaced by a dotted name as described later in this section; an explicit mode **in** can be omitted; a list of parameters of the same subtype can be given distinctly; and of course the lexical spacing can be different. Thus the following two profiles are fully conformant

> (X: **in** Integer := 1000; Y, Z: **out** Integer)
> (X: Integer := 1e3; Y: **out** Integer; Z: **out** Integer)

It is worth noting that one reason for not allowing subtype indications in parameter specifications is to remove any problem regarding conformance since there is then no question of evaluating constraint expressions twice and possibly having different results because of side effects. No corresponding question arises with default expressions (which are of course written out twice) since they are only evaluated when the subprogram is called.

There are other, less rigorous, levels of conformance which we will meet when we discuss access to subprogram types in Section 10.7 and renaming in Section 12.6. We have already met the weakest level of conformance which is called type conformance and controls the hiding of one subprogram declaration by another. As we saw in the last section, hiding occurs provided just the types in the profiles are the same.

Another important situation where we have to write a subprogram declaration as well as a body, occurs in Chapter 11 when we discuss packages. Even if not always necessary, it is sometimes clearer to write subprogram declarations as well as bodies. An example might be in the case where many subprogram bodies occur together. The subprogram declarations could then be placed together at the head of the declarative part in order to act as a summary of the bodies to come.

Since subprograms occur in declarative parts and themselves contain declarative parts, they may be textually nested without limit. The normal hiding rules applicable to blocks described in Section 6.2 also apply to declarations in subprograms. (The only complication concerns overloading as discussed in the previous section.) We are also now in a position to describe the difference between visibility and direct visibility as illustrated by the nested procedures in Figure 9.1.

Just as for the example in Section 6.2, the inner I hides the outer one and so the outer I is not directly visible inside the procedure Q after the start of the declaration of the inner I.

However, we say that it is still visible even though not directly visible because we can refer to the outer I by the so-called dotted notation; in this the identifier I is prefixed by the name of the unit immediately containing its declaration followed by a dot. So within Q we can refer to the outer I as P.I as illustrated by the initialization of J.

If the prefix is itself hidden then it can always be written the same way. Thus the inner I could be referred to as P.Q.I.

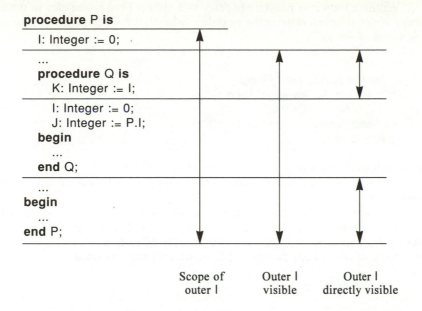

Scope of   Outer I   Outer I
outer I   visible   directly visible

Figure 9.1　Scope and visibility.

An object declared in a block cannot usually be referred to in this way since a block does not normally have a name. However, a block can be named in a similar way to a loop as shown in the following

```
Outer:
declare
   I: Integer := 0;
begin
   ...
   declare
      K: Integer := I;
      I: Integer;
      J: Integer := Outer.I;
   begin
      ...
   end;
end Outer;
```

Here the outer block has the identifier Outer. Unlike subprograms, but like loops, the identifier has to be repeated after the matching **end**. Naming the block enables us to initialize the inner declaration of J with the value of the outer I.

Within a loop it is possible to refer to a hidden loop parameter in the same way. We could even rewrite the example in Section 8.1 of assigning zero to the elements of AA as

```
L:
for I in AA'Range(1) loop
   for I in AA'Range(2) loop
      AA(L.I, I) := 0.0;
   end loop;
end loop L;
```

although one would be a little crazy to do so!

It should be noted that the dotted form can always be used even if it is not necessary.

This notation can also be applied to operators. Thus the variable Result declared inside "*" can be referred to as "*".Result. And equally if "*" were declared inside a block B then it could be referred to as B."*". If it is called with this form of name then the normal function call must be used

```
X := B."*"(V, W);
```

Indeed, the functional form can always be used as in

```
X := "*"(V, W);
```

and we could then also use the named notation

```
X := "*"(A => V, B => W);
```

The named notation also permits the formal parameter name to be used even if it is not directly visible. Thus we can write

```
X: Integer;
...
Increment(X => X);
```

even though the formal parameter X is not directly visible because it has been hidden by the newly declared X used as the actual parameter.

As we have seen, subprograms can alter global variables and therefore have side effects. (A side effect is one brought about other than via the parameter mechanism.) It is generally considered rather undesirable to write subprograms, especially functions, which have side effects. However, some side effects are beneficial. Any subprogram which performs input–output has a side effect on the file; a function delivering successive members of a sequence of random numbers only works because of its side effects; if we need to count how many times a function is called then we use a side effect; and so on. However, care must be taken when using functions with side effects that the program is correct since there are various circumstances in which the order of evaluation is not defined.

We conclude this section with a brief discussion of the hierarchy of **exit**, **return** and **goto** and the scopes of block and loop identifiers and labels.

A **return** statement terminates the execution of the immediately embracing subprogram. It can occur inside an inner block or inside a loop in the subprogram and therefore also terminate the loop. On the other hand an **exit** statement terminates the named or immediately embracing loop. It can also occur inside an inner block but cannot occur inside a subprogram declared in the loop and thereby also terminate the subprogram. A **goto** statement can transfer control out of a loop or block but not out of a subprogram.

As far as scope is concerned, identifiers of labels, blocks and loops behave as if they are declared at the end of the declarative part of the immediately embracing subprogram or block (or package or task body). Moreover, distinct identifiers must be used for all blocks, loops and labels inside the same subprogram (or package or task body) even if some are in inner blocks. Thus two labels in the same subprogram cannot have the same identifier even if they are inside different inner blocks. This rule reduces the risk of goto statements going to the wrong label particularly when a program is amended.

CHECKLIST 9

Parameter and result subtypes must be given by a subtype mark and not by a subtype indication.

Formal parameter specifications are separated by semicolons not commas.

A function must return a result and should not run into its final end although a procedure can.

"/=" can only be explicitly defined if the result is not Boolean.

The order of evaluation of parameters is not defined.

The parameter and result mechanism is like assignment and so an array can slide.

Scalar parameters are passed by copy. Arrays and simple records may be passed by copy or by reference.

A default parameter expression is only evaluated when the subprogram is called and the corresponding parameter is omitted.

Changes from Ada 83

There were severe restrictions on new overloadings of "=" in Ada 83. They were only allowed for private types and the result had to be of type Boolean.

Parameters of mode **out** could not be read in Ada 83.

Array parameters and results were different in Ada 83. Actual and formal bounds had to match and sliding was not allowed.

Ada 83 had methodological rules concerning the order of declarations. For example a body could not be followed by an object or type declaration.

The full conformance rules in Ada 83 were stricter since they were based on syntactic equivalence. This gave odd effects.

The terminology regarding visibility was somewhat different in Ada 83 although the effect was the same.

Access Types

This last chapter concerning the small-scale aspects of Ada is about access types. These are often known as pointer types or reference types in other languages and provide indirect access to other entities.

Playing with pointers is like playing with fire. Fire is perhaps the most important tool known to man. Carefully used, fire brings enormous benefits; but when fire gets out of control, disaster strikes. Pointers have similar characteristics but are well tamed in the form of access types in Ada.

This taming is done through the notion of accessibility which is discussed in some detail in Sections 10.5 and 10.6. Parts of these sections might be found hard to digest and could well be mostly skipped at a first reading.

There are two forms of access types, those which access other objects and those which access subprograms. In this chapter we deal with both forms and also with access parameters which are parameters of an anonymous access type. The related access discriminants are discussed in Chapter 16.

10.1   Flexibility versus integrity

The manipulation of objects by referring to them indirectly through values of other objects is a common feature of most programming languages. It is also a contentious topic since, although the technique provides considerable flexibility, it is also the cause of many programming errors and moreover, used incautiously, can make programs very hard to understand and maintain.

Algol 68 was an early language to use indirection and used the term references. Indeed the whole basis of definition of Algol 68 revolved around references to such an extent that it must have been an ingredient in creating the general impression that the language was academically elaborate. There were also technical difficulties of dangling references, that is variables pointing to objects that no longer exist.

BCPL, from which C is derived, used references or pointers as the foundation of its storage model. Indeed arrays were seen as simply objects that could be referred to dynamically by adding an index to a base reference. Thus the quite natural implementation model was made visible in the language itself. This almost negative abstraction could be considered a great mistake and a step backwards in the evolution of abstraction as being the driving force in language design.

C has inherited the BCPL model and it is considered quite normal practice in C to add integers to pointers thereby creating implementation dependencies and complete freedom to do silly things.

Pascal is an example of austerity in the use of pointers. No doubt a reaction against the excesses of Algol 68, Pascal only allows pointers to objects created in a distinct storage area commonly called the heap. The rules in Pascal are such that it is not possible to create a pointer to an object declared in the normal way on the stack. There is thus no risk of leaving the scope of the referenced object while still within the scope of the referring object and thereby leaving the latter pointing nowhere.

Ada 83 followed the Pascal model and so although secure was inflexible. This inflexibility was particularly noticeable when attempting to interface to programs written in other languages such as C and especially for interaction with Graphical User Interfaces.

The objective of the design of Ada 95 was thus to add flexibility while keeping the security inherent in the strongly typed model. As we will see, this has been achieved through the introduction of accessibility rules whose general objective is to prevent dangling references. Most accessibility rules are applied statically and thus incur no run-time overhead. However, this is sometimes not flexible enough and so more dynamic techniques are also provided plus complete escape routes from all checks when really necessary.

We start our discussion by considering those access types which can only refer to objects in a storage pool (the Ada term for heap). These are naturally called pool specific access types. We then consider the extension to more general access types which can refer to objects declared anywhere. We finish by considering those access types which can refer to subprograms.

10.2   Pool specific access types

In the case of the types we have met so far, the name of an object has been bound irretrievably to the object itself, and the lifetime of an object has been from its declaration until control leaves the unit containing the declaration. This is too restrictive for many applications where a more fluid control of the allocation of objects is desired. In Ada this can be done by using an access type. Objects of an access type, as the name implies, provide access to other objects and these other objects can be allocated in a manner independent of the block structure.

One of the simplest uses of an access type is for list processing. Consider

```
type Cell;
type Cell_Ptr is access Cell;

type Cell is
   record
      Value: Integer;
      Next: Cell_Ptr;
   end record;

L: Cell_Ptr;
```

These declarations introduce type Cell_Ptr which accesses Cell. The variable L can be thought of as a reference variable which can only point at objects of type Cell; these are records with two components, Value of type Integer and Next which is also a Cell_Ptr and can therefore access (point to or reference) other objects of type Cell. The records can therefore be formed into a linked list. Initially there are no record objects, only the single pointer L which by default takes the value **null** which points nowhere. We could have explicitly given L this default value thus

```
L: Cell_Ptr := null;
```

Note the circularity in the definitions of Cell_Ptr and Cell. Because of this circularity and the rule of linear elaboration it is necessary first to give an incomplete declaration of Cell. Having done this we can declare Cell_Ptr and then complete the declaration of Cell. Between the incomplete and complete declarations, the type name Cell can only be used in the definition of an access type. Moreover, the incomplete and complete declarations must be in the same list of declarations except for one case which we will mention in the next chapter when we deal with private types; see Section 11.2.

The accessed objects are created by the execution of an allocator which can (but need not) provide an initial value. An allocator consists of the reserved word **new** followed by either just the type of the new object or a qualified expression providing also the initial value of the object. The result of an allocator is an access value which can then be assigned to a variable of the access type.

So

```
L := new Cell;
```

creates a record of type Cell and then assigns to L a designation of (reference to or pointer to) the object. We can picture the result as in Figure 10.1.

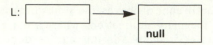

Figure 10.1 An access object.

Note that the Next component of the record takes the default value **null** whereas the Value component is undefined.

The components of the object referred to by L can be accessed using the normal dotted notation. So we could assign 37 to the Value component by

>   L.Value := 37;

Alternatively we could have provided an initial value with the allocator

>   L := **new** Cell'(37, **null**);

The initial value here takes the form of a qualified aggregate, and as usual has to provide values for all the components irrespective of whether some have default initial expressions.

Of course, the allocator could have been used to initialize L when it was declared

>   L: Cell_Ptr := **new** Cell'(37, **null**);

Distinguish carefully the types Cell_Ptr and Cell. L is of type Cell_Ptr which accesses Cell and it is the accessed type which follows **new**.

Suppose we now want to create a further record and link it to our existing record. We can do this by declaring a further variable

>   N: Cell_Ptr;

and then executing

>   N := **new** Cell'(10, L);
>   L := N;

The effect of these three steps is illustrated in Figure 10.2. Note how the assignment statement

>   L := N;

copies the access values (that is, the pointers) and not the objects. If we wanted to copy the objects we could do it component by component

>   L.Value := N.Value;
>   L.Next := N.Next;

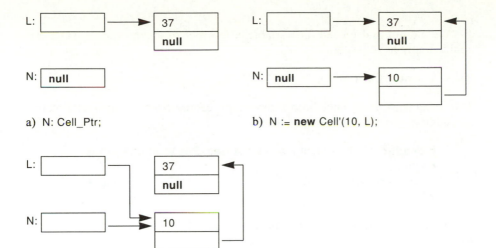

a) N: Cell_Ptr;   b) N := **new** Cell'(10, L);

c) L := N;

Figure 10.2   Extending a list.

or by using **all**

>   L.**all** := N.**all**;

L.**all** refers to the whole object accessed by L. In fact we can think of L.Value as short for L.**all**.Value. Unlike Pascal, dereferencing is automatic.
Similarly

>   L = N

will be true if L and N refer to the same object, whereas

>   L.**all** = N.**all**

will be true if the objects referred to happen to have the same value.
We could declare a constant of an access type but, of course, since it is a constant we must supply an initial value

>   C: **constant** Cell_Ptr := **new** Cell'(0, **null**);

The fact that C is constant means that it must always refer to the same object. However, the value of the object could itself be changed. So

>   C.**all** := L.**all**;

is allowed but

>   C := L;

is not.

We did not really need the variable N in order to extend the list since we could simply have written

```
L := new Cell'(10, L);
```

This statement can be made into a general procedure for creating a new record and adding it to the beginning of a list

```
procedure Add_To_List(List: in out Cell_Ptr; V: in Integer) is
begin
    List := new Cell'(V, List);
end;
```

The new record containing the value 10 can now be added to the list accessed by L by

```
Add_To_List (L, 10);
```

The parameter passing mechanism for access types is defined to be by copy like that for scalar types. However, in order to prevent an access value from becoming undefined an **out** parameter is always copied in at the start. Remember also that an uninitialized access object takes the specific default value **null**. These two facts prevent undefined access values which could cause a program to go berserk.

The value **null** is useful for determining when a list is empty. The following function returns the sum of the Value components of the records in a list

```
function Sum(List: Cell_Ptr) return Integer is
    Local: Cell_Ptr := List;
    S: Integer := 0;
begin
    while Local /= null loop
        S := S + Local.Value;
        Local := Local.Next;
    end loop;
    return S;
end Sum;
```

Observe that we have to make a copy of List because formal parameters of mode **in** are constants. The variable Local is then used to work down the list until we reach the end. The function works even if the list is empty.

A more elaborate data structure is the binary tree. This can be represented by nodes each of which has a value plus pointers to two subnodes (subtrees) one or both of which could be null. Appropriate declarations are

```
type Node;
type Node_Ptr is access Node;
```

```
type Node is
  record
    Value: Float;
    Left, Right: Node_Ptr;
  end record;
```

As an interesting example of the use of trees consider the following procedure Sort which sorts the values in an array into ascending order

```
procedure Sort(A: in out Vector) is
  I: Integer;
  Tree: Node_Ptr := null;

  procedure Insert(T: in out Node_Ptr; V: Float) is
  begin
    if T = null then
      T := new Node'(V, null, null);
    else
      if V < T.Value then
        Insert(T.Left, V);
      else
        Insert(T.Right, V);
      end if;
    end if;
  end Insert;

  procedure Output(T: Node_Ptr) is
  begin
    if T /= null then
      Output(T.Left);
      A(I) := T.Value;
      I := I + 1;
      Output(T.Right);
    end if;
  end Output;

begin                         -- body of Sort
  for J in A'Range loop
    Insert(Tree, A(J));
  end loop;
  I := A'First;
  Output(Tree);
end Sort;
```

The recursive procedure Insert adds a new node containing the value V to the tree in such a way that the values in the left subtree of a node are always less than the value at the node and the values in the right subtree are always greater than (or equal to) the value at the node. The recursive procedure Output copies the values at all the nodes of the tree into the array A by first outputting the left subtree (which has the smaller values), then copying the value at the node and finally outputting the right subtree.

The procedure Sort simply builds up the tree by calling Insert with each of the components of the array in turn and then calls Output to copy the ordered values back into the array.

The access types we have met so far have referred to records. This will often be the case but an access type can refer to any type, even another access type. So we could have

```
type Ref_Int is access Integer;
R: Ref_Int := new Integer'(46);
```

Note that the value of the integer referred to by R is, perhaps inappropriately, denoted by R.**all**. So we can write

```
R.all := 13;
```

to change the value from 46 to 13.

It is most important to understand that all objects referred to by pool specific access types must be acquired through an allocator. We cannot write

```
C: Cell;
...
List: Cell_Ptr := C;        -- illegal
```

This restriction does not apply to general access types which we will discuss in the next section.

The accessed objects are allocated in a space called a storage pool associated with the access type. This pool will typically cease to exist when the scope of the access type is finally left but, of course, by then all the access variables will also have ceased to exist; so no dangling reference problems can arise.

If an object becomes inaccessible because no variables refer to it directly or indirectly then the storage it occupies may be reclaimed so that it can be reused by other objects. An implementation may (but need not) provide a garbage collector to do this.

Alternatively, there is a mechanism whereby a program can indicate that an object is no longer required; if, mistakenly, there are still references to such objects then the use of such references is erroneous. For details see Sections 21.2 and 21.3 which also outline how a user may create and control individual storage pools. In this chapter we will assume the use of default storage pools and ignore the problems associated with the reclamation of storage.

A few final points of detail. Allocators illustrate the importance of the rules regarding the number of times and when an expression is evaluated in certain contexts. For example, an expression in an aggregate is evaluated for each index value concerned and so

```
A: array (1 .. 10) of Cell_Ptr := (1 .. 10 => new Cell);
```

creates an array of ten components and initializes each of them to access a different new cell.

As a further example

A, B: Cell_Ptr := **new** Cell;

creates two new cells (see Section 6.1), whereas

A: Cell_Ptr := **new** Cell;
B: Cell_Ptr := A;

naturally creates only one. Remember also that default expressions for record components and subprogram parameters are re-evaluated each time they are required; if such an expression contains an allocator then a new object will be created each time.

If an allocator provides an initial value then this can take the form of any qualified expression. So we could have

L: Cell_Ptr := **new** Cell'(N.**all**);

in which case the object is given the same value as the object referred to by N. We could have

I: Integer := 46;
R: Ref_Int := **new** Integer'(I);

in which case the new object takes the value of I; it does not matter that I is not an allocated object since only its value concerns us.

It is important to realize that each declaration of an access type introduces a new logically distinct set of accessed objects. Such sets might be in different storage pools. Two access types can refer to objects of the same type but the access objects must not refer to objects in the wrong set. So we could have

type Ref_Int_A **is access** Integer;
type Ref_Int_B **is access** Integer;
RA: Ref_Int_A := **new** Integer'(10);
RB: Ref_Int_B := **new** Integer'(20);

The objects created by the two allocators are both of the same type but the access values are of different types determined by the context of the allocator and the objects might be in different pools.

So, although we can write

RA.**all** := RB.**all**;

we cannot write

RA := RB;   -- illegal

Note moreover that it is not possible to convert one pool specific access type into another pool specific access type even when they have the same accessed type as in the case of Ref_Int_A and Ref_Int_B. It is thus not possible for a value of one type to refer to an object in the wrong pool.

EXERCISE 10.2

1   Write a

    procedure Append(First: **in out** Cell_Ptr; Second: **in** Cell_Ptr);

which appends the list Second (without copying) to the end of the list First. Take care of any special cases.

2   Write a function Size which returns the number of nodes in a tree.

3   Write a function Copy which makes a complete copy of a tree.

10.3   Access types and constraints

We now consider the question of constraints which can be applied to both the type being accessed and to the access type itself.

Considering first the type being accessed, we could have

    type Ref_Pos **is access** Positive;

or equivalently

    type Ref_Pos **is access** Integer **range** 1 .. Integer'Last;

The values in the objects referred to are all constrained to be positive. We can write

    RP: Ref_Pos := **new** Positive'(10);

or even

    RP: Ref_Pos := **new** Integer'(10);

Note that if we wrote **new** Positive'(0) then Constraint_Error would be raised because 0 is not of subtype Positive. However, if we wrote **new** Integer'(0) then Constraint_Error is only raised because of the context of the allocator.

Access types can also refer to constrained and unconstrained arrays. We could have

    type Ref_Matrix **is access** Matrix;
    R: Ref_Matrix;

and then obtain new matrices with an allocator where the bounds must be provided either through an explicit initial value thus

R := **new** Matrix'(1 .. 10 => (1 .. 10 => 0.0));

or by applying constraints

R := **new** Matrix(1 .. 10, 1 .. 10);

Note the subtle distinction whereby a quote is needed in the case of the full initial value but not when we just give the constraints. This is because the first takes the form of a qualified expression whereas the second is just a subtype indication.

We could not write just

R := **new** Matrix;

because all array objects must have bounds (must be definite). Moreover once allocated the bounds of a particular matrix cannot be changed. However, since R itself is unconstrained it can refer to matrices of different bounds from time to time.

The access type can also be constrained. We can do this by introducing a subtype

subtype Ref_Matrix_3 **is** Ref_Matrix(1 .. 3, 1 .. 3);
R_3: Ref_Matrix_3;

and R_3 can then only reference matrices with corresponding bounds. Alternatively we could have directly written

R_3: Ref_Matrix(1 .. 3, 1 .. 3);

Using

subtype Matrix_3 **is** Matrix(1 .. 3, 1 .. 3);

we can then write

R_3 := **new** Matrix_3;

This is allowed because the subtype supplies the array bounds.

This introduces another example of an array aggregate with **others**. Because the subtype Matrix_3 supplies the array bounds and qualifies the aggregate, we could initialize the new object as follows

R_3 := **new** Matrix_3'(**others** => (**others** => 0.0));

The components of an accessed array can be referred to by the usual mechanism, so

R(1, 1) := 0.0;

would set component (1, 1) of the matrix accessed by R to zero. The whole matrix can be referred to by **all**. So

R_3.**all** := (1 .. 3 => (1 .. 3 => 0.0));

would set all the components of the matrix accessed by R_3 to zero. We can therefore think of R(1, 1) as an abbreviation for R.**all**(1, 1). As with records, dereferencing is automatic. We can also write attributes R'First(1) or alternatively R.**all**'First(1). In the case of a one-dimensional array slicing is also allowed.

We conclude this section by considering the problem of variable length strings. In Section 8.5 we noted, when declaring the Zoo, that the animals (or rather their names) all had to be the same length. The strong type model of Ada means that the type String does not have the flexibility found in cruder languages such as BASIC. However, with a bit of ingenuity, we can build our own flexibility by using access types. Consider

type A_String **is access** String;

which enables us to declare a-string variables which can access strings of any size. So we can write

A: A_String := **new** String'("Hello");

We see that although we no longer have to pad the strings to a fixed length, we now have the burden of the allocation. However, we can craftily write

```
function "+" (S: String) return A_String is
begin
   return new String'(S);
end "+";
```

and then

type A_String_Array **is array** (Positive **range** <>) **of** A_String;

Zoo: **constant** A_String_Array :=
         (+"aardvark", +"baboon", ..., +"very long animal... ", ..., +"zebra");

Remember from Section 8.5 that we can declare an array of any definite subtype; all access types are definite even if they designate objects with different constraints and so we can declare arrays of a-strings. (This flexibility of access types is especially crucial for object oriented programming as we saw in our brief overview in Section 3.3.)

With this formulation there is no limit on the length of the strings and we have more or less created a ragged array. But of course there is the overhead of the access value which is significant if the strings are short. We will return to the topic of ragged arrays in the next section and also in Section 16.2.

EXERCISE 10.3

1   Write the converse unary function "+" which takes an A_String as parameter and returns the corresponding String. Use this function to output the camel.

2   Write a function "&" to concatenate two a-strings.

10.4   General access types

We have just seen how access types provide a means of manipulating objects created by allocators. Access types can also be used to provide indirect access to declared objects.

We can declare a general access type such as

```
type Int_Ptr is access all Integer;
```

and we can then assign the 'address' of any variable of type Integer to a variable of type Int_Ptr provided that the designated variable is marked as aliased. So we can write

```
IP: Int_Ptr;
I: aliased Integer;
...
IP := I'Access;
```

and we can then read and update the variable I through the access variable IP. Observe how the access value (the pointer) is created by the use of the Access attribute; this contrasts with the pool specific types where it was created by the allocator.

Note the use of **all** in the general access type declaration which distinguishes it from pool specific types. Note also that we can only apply the Access attribute to objects declared as aliased (or those considered by default to be aliased such as tagged type parameters, see Section 13.2). There are two reasons for specifically requiring that an object is marked as aliased; one is simply as a warning to the programmer that this object might be manipulated indirectly and the other is for the compiler so that it does not allocate space for the object in some non-standard way (such as in a register) which could not then be accessed in the normal manner.

As mentioned earlier there are accessibility rules which ensure that dangling references cannot arise. They are dealt with in detail in the next section but the general principle is that we can only apply the Access attribute to an object whose lifetime is at least that of the access type.

A variation is that we can restrict the access to be read-only by replacing **all** in the type definition by **constant**. This allows read-only access to any variable and also to a constant thus

```
type Const_Int_Ptr is access constant Integer;
CIP: Const_Int_Ptr;
I: aliased Integer;
C: aliased constant Integer := 1815;
```

followed by

```
CIP := I'Access;          -- access to a variable, or
CIP := C'Access;          -- access to a constant
```

The type accessed by a general access type can of course be any type such as an array or record. We can thus build chains from records statically declared. Note that we can also use an allocator to generate general access values. Our chain could thus include a mixture of records from both storage mechanisms although this would be unusual.

The components of an array can also be aliased as in

```
AI: array (1 .. 100) of aliased Integer;
...
IP := AI(I)'Access;
```

Finally note that the accessed value could be a component of any composite type. Thus we could point into the middle of a record (provided the component is marked as aliased). In a fast implementation of Conway's Game of Life a cell might contain access values directly referencing the component of its eight neighbours containing the counter indicating whether the cell is alive or dead.

```
type Ref_Count is access constant Integer range 0 .. 1;
type Ref_Count_Array is array (Integer range <>) of Ref_Count;

type Cell is
   record
      Life_Count: aliased Integer range 0 .. 1;
      Total_Neighbour_Count: Integer range 0 .. 8;
      Neighbour_Count: Ref_Count_Array(1 .. 8);
   end record;
```

We can now link the cells together according to our model by statements such as

```
This_Cell.Neighbour_Count(1) :=
      Cell_To_The_North.Life_Count'Access;
```

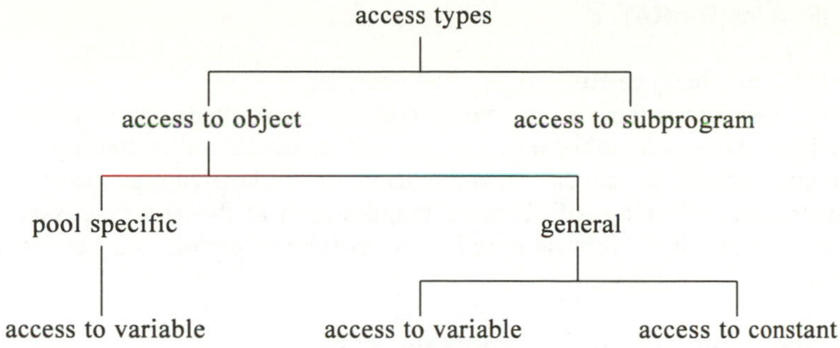

Figure 10.3   Categories of access types.

and then the heart of the computation which computes the sum of the life counts in the neighbours might be

```
C.Total_Neighbour_Count := 0;
for I in C.Neighbour_Count'Range loop
   C.Total_Neighbour_Count :=
        C.Total_Neighbour_Count + C.Neighbour_Count(I).all;
end loop;
```

Note that we have given the type Ref_Count and the component Life_Count the same static subtypes so that they can be checked against each other at compile time. This is not necessary but avoids a run-time check that would otherwise be required if the subtypes did not statically match. We also made the type Ref_Count an **access constant** type since we only need read access to the counter; this prevents us accidentally updating it indirectly. Such details are important for creating confidence in the program and give the compiler further opportunities for spotting errors.

We noted in Section 10.2 that conversion between different pool specific access types was not allowed. However conversion between general access types is permitted with obvious restrictions. The accessed type must be the same and any constraints must statically match (but see Section 13.2 for the case where the accessed type is tagged). Furthermore an access to constant type cannot be converted to an access to variable type since otherwise we might obtain write access to a constant. So we can write

```
CIP := Const_Int_Ptr(IP);
```

but not

```
IP := Int_Ptr(CIP);          -- illegal
```

We can also convert a pool specific type to a general access type but not vice versa. Thus we can write

```
IP := Int_Ptr(RA);
```

where RA is of the type Ref_Int_A of Section 10.2.

For convenience the various categories of access types are summarized in Figure 10.3. Access to subprogram types will be discussed in Section 10.7.

General access types can also be used to declare ragged arrays as for example a table of strings of different lengths such as the Zoo discussed in the previous section. We might declare an access type referring to a general string as

type G_String **is access constant** String;

and the strings can then be declared in the normal way. Without general access types we would have to allocate all the strings dynamically using an allocator. Nevertheless this technique is not very convenient because all the individual strings have to be named objects.

EXERCISE 10.4

1 Using the type G_String declare the Zoo with declared strings (that is without the use of allocators).

2 Declare a world of N by M cells for the Game of Life. Link them together in an appropriate manner. Use a dummy dead cell for the boundary so that the heart of the computation remains unchanged.

3 Reformulate the cells by making the access type refer to the cell as a whole rather than the internal component; how would this change the heart of the computation and the answer to the previous exercise?

4 List all permitted conversions between the types Int_Ptr, Const_Int_Ptr, Ref_Int_A and Ref_Int_B (see Section 10.2).

10.5 Accessibility

The accessibility rules are designed to provide reasonable flexibility with complete security. A simple static strategy applies in most circumstances and ensures that no run-time checks are required.

The basic rule is that the lifetime of an accessed object must be at least as long as that of the access type. Lifetime is a bit like scope except that it refers to the dynamic existence of the entity whereas scope refers to its (potential) static visibility.

As an illustration of the problem consider

```
procedure Main is
   type AI is access all Integer;
   Ref1: AI;
begin
   declare
      Ref2: AI;
      I: aliased Integer;
   begin
      Ref2 := I'Access;
         ...
      Ref1 := Ref2;
   end;
      ...
   declare
      -- some other variables
   begin
      Ref1.all := 0;
   end;
end Main;
```

This is illegal because we have applied Access to a variable I with a lesser
lifetime than the access type AI. The problem is not so much with the
assignment to Ref2 which has the same lifetime as I but the fact that we can
later assign Ref2 to Ref1 and Ref1 has a lifetime longer than I. The eventual
assignment of 0 to Ref1.all could in principle overwrite almost anything
because the value in Ref1 now refers to where I was and this space could now
be used by some other variable of a different type (maybe another access type).

   Other rules would have been possible. For example it might have been
decreed that the assignment to Ref1 be forbidden or that the final assignment
to Ref1.all was the real culprit. For a number of reasons these alternatives are
not sensible because they require extensive run-time checks or violate the idea
that values can be assigned freely between variables of the same subtype.

   So the actual rule is simply that the access value cannot be created in the
first place if there is a risk that it might outlive the object that it refers to. In
principle this is a dynamic rule but in most situations the check can be
performed statically. Thus in

```
procedure Main is
   type T is ...
   X: aliased T;
begin
   declare
      type A is access all T;
      Ptr: A;
   begin
      Ptr := X'Access;
         ...
   end;
end Main;
```

the object X outlives the access type A and so the assignment of X'Access to Ptr is permitted. In this example the dynamic lifetime follows from the simple static structure. However, because of the existence of procedure calls and recursion and so on we know that the dynamic structure at any time can include more active levels than just those in the static structure visible from the point concerned. It might thus be thought that static checks would not be satisfactory at all. However, because we can only write X'Access at points where both X and the access type A are in scope, it can in fact be shown that static checks based on the scope are exactly equivalent to dynamic checks based on the lifetime in examples such as this.

Of course some particular programs might be quite safe even though they violate the rules. If the programmer is absolutely convinced that the program is safe and that the check is simply a hindrance then the alternative attribute Unchecked_Access can be applied by writing

```
Ref2 := I'Unchecked_Access;
```

and the compiler will then simply shrug its shoulders at the situation. The first program above would then execute and be erroneous; anything could happen.

As mentioned in the last section, it is possible to convert one access type to another. In order to ensure that the lifetime of the accessed object is at least that of the target access type, conversion is only allowed if the target access type has a lifetime not greater then the source access type. Consider

```
declare
   type AI is access all Integer;
   I: aliased Integer;
   RefI: AI := I'Access;
begin
   ...
   declare
      type AJ is access all Integer;
      J: aliased Integer;
      RefJ: AJ := J'Access;
   begin
      ...
      RefI := AI(RefJ);        -- illegal
      ...
   end;
   ...
end;
```

The conversion to the outer type is not permitted since this would mean that RefI would have a dangling reference on exit from the inner block. On the other hand a conversion from RefI to RefJ is perfectly safe and is thus permitted. Note once more that the check can always be performed statically when converting from one named access type to another.

10.6   Access parameters

In the simple cases considered in the previous section, static checks always
suffice. Many applications will use access types at the outermost level only and
then everything will have the same lifetime. But sometimes the static structure
is too severe and fails even though nothing could go wrong. Consider

```
procedure Main is
   type T is ...
   procedure P is
      type A is access all T;
      Ptr: A := X'Access;
   begin
      ...
   end P;
begin
   declare
      X: aliased T;
   begin
      P;
   end;
end Main;
```

This is actually illegal because X is out of scope at the point where we have
written X'Access. However, if we could have assigned the 'address' of X to Ptr
then nothing could have gone wrong because the dynamic lifetime of the type
A is less than that of the variable X. This is such a common requirement that a
new form of parameter is introduced which enables us to pass an access value
safely and flexibly. This parameter is known as an access parameter and is
classed as an in parameter although the word **in** never appears. We can now
recast the above example as

```
procedure Main is
   type T is ...
   procedure P(Ptr: access T) is
   begin
      ...
   end P;
begin
   declare
      X: aliased T;
   begin
      P(X'Access);
   end;
end Main;
```

The parameter Ptr is initialized with the value of X'Access and all is well.
Within the body of P we can dereference Ptr and manipulate the components

of X as expected. The parameter Ptr is of course a constant and cannot be changed although the object it refers to can naturally be changed by assignment.

It is very important to observe that an access parameter is of an anonymous type. This has a number of important consequences. We cannot declare any other objects of the type and so assignment and equality are not defined for access parameters. Another important property is that an access parameter can never have a null value since we are not allowed to pass null as an actual parameter (this is checked on the call). As a consequence there is never any need when using an access parameter to check for a null value. This simplifies the code both for the programmer and for the compiler.

Type conversion between an access parameter and a named access type is possible. Just allowing conversion to an inner type (this can be checked statically) would be too restrictive and so conversion to an outer type is also permitted and in this case an accessibility check is carried out at run time to ensure that the lifetime of the object referred to is not less than the target access type. The following is therefore allowed

```
procedure Main is
   type T is ...
   type A is access all T;
   Ref: A;
   procedure P(Ptr: access T) is
   begin
      ...
      Ref := A(Ptr);          -- dynamic check on conversion
   end P;
   X: aliased T;
begin
   P(X'Access);
   ...        -- can now manipulate X via Ref
end Main;
```

Here we have converted the access parameter to the outer type A and assigned it to the variable Ref. For the call of P with X'Access this is quite safe because the lifetime of X is not less than the type A. But of course it might not be safe for all calls of P (such as in the previous example where X was declared in a local block). So the check has to be dynamic. If it fails then Program_Error is raised.

In order for this check to be possible all access parameters carry with them an indication of the accessibility of the actual parameter. Typically all that is necessary is to pass the static depth of the original object and this is then checked against the depth of the target type on the conversion.

Perhaps surprisingly this simple model with its combination of static checks in most circumstances and dynamic checks on some conversions of access parameters gives exactly the correct degree of flexibility combined with complete security.

The full benefit of access parameters cannot be illustrated at the moment but will become clear when we discuss object oriented programming in Chapter 13 and access discriminants in Chapter 16.

We conclude by summarizing the operations allowed on access parameters and a brief comparison with in out parameters.

The actual parameter corresponding to an access parameter can be (i) an access to an aliased object such as X'Access, (ii) another access parameter with the same accessed type, (iii) a value of a named access type again with the same accessed type, or (iv) an allocator. In each case an appropriate indication of accessibility is passed.

An access parameter can be (i) used to provide access to the accessed object by dereferencing, (ii) passed as an actual parameter to another access parameter, or (iii) converted to a named access type.

Dynamic accessibility checks only occur on conversion to a named access type such as

```
Ref := A(Ptr);
```

or (which is really equivalent) if we write

```
Ref := Ptr.all'Access;
```

which first dereferences to give the accessed object and then creates a reference to it once more.

Note that an access parameter can be passed on to another access parameter; typically the accessibility indication is passed on unchanged but in the unusual circumstance where the called subprogram is internal to the calling subprogram, the accessibility level is replaced by that of the (statically known) formal calling parameter if less than the original actual parameter.

Access parameters are often an alternative to in out parameters. They both provide read and write access to the data concerned. And indeed, in the case of a record the components are referred to in the same way because of automatic dereferencing. On the other hand, the form of the actual parameter is different. Given

```
type T is ...
type A is access T;
X: T;
Ref: A := new T'( ... );

procedure PIO(P: in out T);
procedure PA(Ptr: access T);
```

then calls of PIO take the form

```
PIO(X);  PIO(Ref.all);
```

whereas calls of PA require that variables be aliased so we have

```
X: aliased T;
PA(X'Access);  PA(Ref);
```

An important difference between access and in out parameters is that a function can have an access parameter but not an in out parameter. This is particularly useful with tagged types as we will see in Chapter 13. Another point is that access parameters are never null which simplifies the code as illustrated by the exercises in Section 19.3. And of course access parameters overcome accessibility problems.

The reader will probably have found the whole topic of accessibility and access parameters rather tedious. Accessibility is a bit like visibility; if we do something silly the compiler will tell us and we need not bother with the details of the rules most of the time. In any case, practical programs usually have a quite flat structure and problems will rarely arise. It is, however, very comforting to know that provided we avoid Unchecked_Access then dangling references will not arise and our program will not crash in a heap.

EXERCISE 10.6

1   Analyse the checks on the type conversions in the following indicating whether they are dynamic or static and whether they pass or fail.

```
procedure Main is
  type T is ...
  type A1 is access all T;
  Ref1: A1;
  procedure P(Ptr: access T) is
    type A2 is access all T;
    Ref2: A2;
  begin
    Ref1 := A1(Ptr);
    Ref2 := A2(Ptr);
    ...
  end P;
  X1: aliased T
begin
  declare
    X2: aliased T;
  begin
    P(X1'Access);
    P(X2'Access);
  end;
end Main;
```

2   Similarly analyse the following. Note that the chained call of P2 from P1 is the interesting situation where the accessibility level has to be adjusted if the level of the original object is deeper than that of the formal parameter Ptr2. For convenience the level of the identifiers is indicated by their name. Note that the level of a formal parameter is one deeper than the subprogram itself.

```
procedure Main is
  type T is ...
  type A1 is access all T;
  Ref1: A1;
  procedure P1(Ptr2: access T) is
    type A2 is access all T;
    Ref2: A2;
    procedure P2(Ptr3: access T) is
      type A3 is access all T;
      Ref3: A3;
    begin
      Ref1 := A1(Ptr3);
      Ref2 := A2(Ptr3);
      Ref3 := A3(Ptr3);
    end P2;
  begin
    P2(Ptr2);        -- chained call
  end P1;
  X1: aliased T;
begin
  declare
    X2: aliased T;
  begin
    declare
      X3: aliased T;
    begin
      P1(X1'Access);
      P1(X2'Access);
      P1(X3'Access);
    end;
  end;
end Main;
```

10.7   Access to subprograms

The ability to pass subprograms as parameters of other subprograms has been a feature of most languages since Fortran and Algol 60. A notable exception was Ada 83 in which all binding of subprogram calls to the actual subprogram was determined statically.

There were a number of reasons for taking such a static approach in Ada 83. There was concern for the implementation cost of dynamic binding, it was also clear that the presence of dynamic binding would reduce the provability of programs and moreover it was felt that the introduction of generics where subprograms could be passed as parameters would cater for practical situations where formal procedure parameters were used in other languages.

However, it is now realized that implementation costs are trivial and not pervasive; provability is not a relevant argument because we now know that in any safety-critical software where mathematical provability is a real issue, we only use a small subset of the language. And furthermore, the generic mechanism had not proved to be a sufficiently flexible alternative anyway.

In Ada 95 an access type can refer to a subprogram; such an access to subprogram value can be created by the Access attribute and a subprogram can be called indirectly by dereferencing such an access value. Thus we can write

```
type Trig_Function is access function (F: Float) return Float;
T: Trig_Function;
X, Theta: Float;
```

and T can then 'point to' functions such as Sin, Cos and Tan which we will assume have specifications such as

```
function Sin(X: Float) return Float
```

We can then assign an appropriate access to subprogram value to T by for example

```
T := Sin'Access;
```

and later indirectly call the subprogram currently referred to by T as expected

```
X := T(Theta);
```

which is really an abbreviation for

```
X := T.all(Theta);
```

Just as with many other uses of access types the .**all** is not usually required but it would be necessary if there were no parameters.

The access to subprogram mechanism can be used to program general dynamic selection and to pass subprograms as parameters. It allows program call-back to be implemented in a natural and efficient manner.

There are a number of rules which ensure that access to subprogram values cannot be misused. Subtype conformance matching between the profiles ensures that the subprogram always has the correct number and type of parameters and that any constraints statically match. Subtype conformance is weaker than the full conformance required between the body and specification of the same subprogram as described in Section 9.6. Subtype conformance ignores the formal parameter names and also the presence, absence or value of default initial expressions.

Accessibility rules also apply to access to subprogram types and ensure that a subprogram is not called out of context. Thus we can only apply the Access attribute if the subprogram has a lifetime at least that of the access type. One consequence is that we cannot use an access to a local procedure as a parameter of a more globally declared procedure; this might be a nuisance for some applications and the alternative of using a generic parameter should be considered as discussed in Sections 17.3 and 19.6. There is no Unchecked_ Access for access to subprogram types (far too dodgy).

Simple classic numerical codes can be implemented in the traditional way. Thus an integration routine might have the following specification

> **type** Integrand **is access function** (X: Float) **return** Float;

> **function** Integrate(F: Integrand; A, B: Float) **return** Float;

for the evaluation of

$$\int_a^b f(x)dx$$

and we might then write

> Area := Integrate(Log'Access, 1.0, 2.0);

which will compute the area under the curve for $\log(x)$ from 1.0 to 2.0. Within the body of the function Integrate there will be calls of the actual subprogram passed as parameter; this is a simple form of call-back.

A common paradigm within the process control industry is to implement sequencing control through successive calls of a number of interpreter actions. A sequence compiler might interactively build an array of such actions which are then obeyed. Thus we might have

> **type** Action **is access procedure**;
> Action_Sequence: **array** (1 .. N) **of** Action;
>
> ...   -- build the array
>
>   -- and then obey it
> **for** I **in** Action_Sequence'Range **loop**
>   Action_Sequence(I).**all**;
> **end loop**;

where we note the need for **.all** because there are no parameters.

It is of course possible for a record to contain components whose types are access to subprogram types. We will now consider a possible fragment of the system which drives the controls in the cockpit of some mythical Ada Airlines. There are a number of physical buttons on the console and we wish to associate different actions corresponding to pushing the various buttons.

> **type** Button;

> **type** Response_Ptr **is access procedure** (B: **in out** Button);

> **type** Button **is**
>   **record**
>   Response: Response_Ptr;
>   ...   -- other aspects of the button
>   **end record**;

```
procedure Associate(B: in out Button; ... );
procedure Push(B: in out Button);
procedure Set_Response(B: in out Button; R: in Response_Ptr);
```

A button is represented as a record containing a number of components describing properties of the button (position of message on the display for example). The component Response is an access to a procedure which is the action to be executed when the button is pushed. Note carefully that the button value is passed to this procedure as a parameter so that the procedure can obtain access to the other components of the record describing the button. Incidentally, observe that the incomplete type Button is allowed to be used for a parameter or result of the access to subprogram type Response_Ptr before its full type declaration; this is necessary in order to break the otherwise inevitable circularity just as for Cell and Cell_Ptr in Section 10.2.

The procedure Set_Response assigns an appropriate access value to the component Response and the procedure Associate makes the connection between the physical button and the software button and fills in the other components. Other functions (not shown) provide access to them. The procedure Push is called when any physical button is pushed, the parameter indicating its identity. The bodies of the subprograms might be as follows

```
procedure Push(B: in out Button) is
begin
   B.Response(B);          -- indirect call
end Push;

procedure Set_Response(B: in out Button; R: in Response_Ptr) is
begin
   B.Response := R;        -- set procedure value in record
end Set_Response;
```

We can now set the specific actions we want when a button is pushed. Thus we might want some emergency action to take place when a big red button is pushed.

```
Big_Red_Button: Button;

procedure Emergency(B: in out Button) is
begin
   Broadcast("mayday");
   ...
   Eject(Pilot);
end Emergency;
...

Associate(Big_Red_Button, ... );
Set_Response(Big_Red_Button, Emergency'Access);
...

Push(Big_Red_Button);
```

An important use of access to subprogram types is for interfacing to subprograms written in other languages; see Section 21.4.

Finally we should mention that certain subprograms are considered intrinsic which means that they are essentially built in to the compiler. The **Access** attribute cannot be applied to intrinsic subprograms. Important examples of intrinsic subprograms are the predefined operations in **Standard** such as "+", the enumeration literals (which as mentioned in Section 9.5 are thought of as parameterless functions), an implicitly declared "/=" as a companion to "=" (see Section 9.2), and attributes that are subprograms such as Pred and Succ.

EXERCISE 10.7

1 Using the function **Integrate** show how to evaluate

$$\int_0^P e^t \sin t \, dt$$

2 Declare the specification of an appropriate function for finding a root of the equation $f(x) = 0$, and then show how you would find the root of

$$e^x + x = 7$$

3 Write two parameterless procedures This and That and declare an access to subprogram variable P that can refer to them. Arrange matters so that calls via the variable automatically ensure that the other procedure is called next time with This being called the first time.

CHECKLIST 10

An incomplete declaration can only be used in an access type.

The scope of an allocated object is that of the access type.

Access objects have a default initial value of **null**.

An allocator in an aggregate is evaluated for each index value.

An allocator with a complete initial value uses a quote.

A general access type has **all** or **constant** in its definition.

Access can only be applied to aliased objects.

Beware Unchecked_Access.

An access parameter can never be **null**.

Conversion to a pool specific access type is not allowed.

Changes from Ada 83

Ada 83 did not have general access types, only pool specific access types.

Access to subprogram types did not exist in Ada 83.

Access parameters did not exist in Ada 83.

Part 3

The Big Picture

This third part is the core of the book and is largely about abstraction. As mentioned in Chapter 1, the evolution of programming languages is essentially about understanding various aspects of abstraction and here we look in depth at the facilities for data abstraction and especially Object Oriented Programming.

Chapter 11 shows how packages and private types are the keystone of Ada and can be used to control visibility by giving a client and server different views of an object. This chapter also introduces the simplest ideas of type derivation and inheritance and the very important notion of a limited type which is a type (strictly a view of a type) for which assignment is not permitted. Limited types are important for modelling those real-world objects for which copying is inappropriate. Chapter 12 then discusses the hierarchical library structure and the facilities for separate compilation. As mentioned earlier, these enable a program to be compiled in distinct units without any loss of strong typing between units.

The basic facilities for Object Oriented Programming are then introduced in Chapter 13. This covers type extension and inheritance, dynamic polymorphism, dispatching and class wide types. This chapter concentrates very much on the basic nuts and bolts and a further discussion of OOP and especially techniques for multiple inheritance are deferred until Chapter 19 when other aspects of the language have been introduced.

Chapters 14 and 15 are slightly different in that they are not related to data abstraction. Chapter 14 covers exceptions and Chapter 15 is a detailed discussion of numeric types including modular types and the rather specialized fixed point types which were not discussed in Chapter 6.

Chapters 16 and 17 return to the theme of abstraction by considering two forms of parameterization. Chapter 16 discusses the parameterization of types by discriminants. Some aspects of discriminants are of lesser importance in Ada 95 since the use of variants in Ada 83 is largely superseded by type extension in Ada 95. But access discriminants are very important for parameterizing one type with another type. Chapter 17 discusses genericity which enables subprograms and packages to be parameterized in various ways. Genericity provides static polymorphism checked at compile time in contrast to the dynamic polymorphism of type extension.

Chapter 18 completes the main discussion of new features by describing the concepts relating to tasking; these includes tasks which are units which execute in parallel and protected objects which provide shared access to common data without risk of interference.

At this point all the important features of the language have been described and the purpose of the final Chapter 19 is to illustrate how the various facilities work together within an OOP framework.

11 Packages and Private Types

11.1 Packages	11.4 Equality
11.2 Private types	11.5 Limited types
11.3 Primitive operations and derived types	11.6 Resource management

The previous chapters have described the small-scale features of Ada in considerable detail. The language presented so far corresponds to the areas addressed by languages of the 1960s and early 1970s, although Ada provides more functionality in those areas. However, we now come to the new areas which broadly speaking correspond to the concepts of abstraction and programming in the large which were discussed in Chapter 3.

In this chapter we discuss packages (which is what Ada is all about) and the important concept of a private type. The topic of library units and especially library packages is discussed in the next chapter.

11.1 Packages

One of the major problems with the traditional block structured languages, such as Algol and Pascal, is that they do not offer enough control of visibility. For example, suppose we have a stack represented by an array and a variable which indexes the current top element, a procedure Push to add an item and a function Pop to remove an item. We might write

```
Max: constant := 100;
S: array (1 .. Max) of Integer;
Top: Integer range 0 .. Max;
```

to represent the stack and then declare

```
procedure Push(X: Integer) is
begin
   Top := Top + 1;
   S(Top) := X;
end Push;

function Pop return Integer is
begin
   Top := Top - 1;
   return S(Top + 1);
end Pop;
```

In a simple block structured language there is no way in which we can be given access to the subprograms Push and Pop without also being given direct access to the variables S and Top. As a consequence we cannot be forced to use the correct protocol and so be prevented from making use of knowledge of how the stack is implemented.

The Ada package overcomes this by allowing us to place a wall around a group of declarations and only permit access to those which we intend to be visible. A package actually comes in two parts: the specification which gives the interface to the outside world, and the body which gives the hidden details.

The above example should be written as

```
package Stack is                       -- specification
   procedure Push(X: Integer);
   function Pop return Integer;
end Stack;

package body Stack is                  -- body
   Max: constant := 100;
   S: array (1 .. Max) of Integer;
   Top: Integer range 0 .. Max;

   procedure Push(X: Integer) is
   begin
      Top := Top + 1;
      S(Top) := X;
   end Push;

   function Pop return Integer is
   begin
      Top := Top - 1;
      return S(Top + 1);
   end Pop;

begin                                  -- initialization
   Top := 0;
end Stack;
```

The package specification (strictly declaration) starts with the reserved word **package**, the identifier of the package and **is**. This is then followed by declarations of the entities which are to be visible. It finishes with **end**, the identifier (optionally) and the terminating semicolon. In the example we just have the declarations of the two subprograms Push and Pop.

The package body also starts with **package** but this is then followed by **body**, the identifier and **is**. We then have a normal declarative part, **begin**, sequence of statements, **end**, optional identifier and terminating semicolon just as in a block or subprogram body.

In the example the declarative part contains the variables which represent the stack and the bodies of Push and Pop. The sequence of statements between **begin** and **end** is executed when the package is declared and can be used for initialization. If there is no need for an initialization sequence, the **begin** can be omitted. Indeed in this example we could equally and perhaps more naturally have performed the initialization by writing

```
Top: Integer range 0 .. Max := 0;
```

Note that a package is itself declared and so is just one of the items in an outer declarative part (unless it is a library unit which is the outermost layer anyway).

The package illustrates another case where we need distinct subprogram declarations and bodies. Indeed we cannot put a body into a package specification. And moreover, if a package specification contains the specification of a subprogram, then the package body must contain the corresponding subprogram body. We can think of the package specification and body as being just one large declarative part with only some items visible. But, of course, a subprogram body can be declared in a package body without its specification having to be given in the package specification. Such a subprogram would be internal to the package and could only be called from within, either from other subprograms, some of which would presumably be visible, or perhaps from the initialization sequence.

The elaboration of a package body consists simply of the elaboration of the declarations inside it followed by the execution of the initialization sequence if there is one. The package continues to exist until the end of the scope in which it is declared. Entities declared inside the package have the same lifetime as the package itself. Thus the variables S and Top can be thought of as 'own' variables in the Algol 60 sense; their values are retained between successive calls of Push and Pop.

Packages may be declared in any declarative part such as that in a block, subprogram or indeed another package. If a package specification is declared inside another package specification then, as for subprograms, the body of one must be declared in the body of the other. But again both specification and body could be in a package body.

Apart from the rule that a package specification cannot contain bodies, it can contain any of the other kinds of declarations we have met.

Now to return to the use of our package. The package itself has a name and the entities in its visible part (the specification) can be thought of as components of the package in some sense. It is entirely natural therefore that, in order to call Push, we must also mention Stack. In fact the dotted notation is used. So we could write

```
declare
   package Stack is          -- specification
      ...                    -- and
      ...                    -- body
   end Stack;
begin
   ...
   Stack.Push(M);
   ...
   N := Stack.Pop;
   ...
end;
```

Inside the package we would call Push as just Push, but we could still write Stack.Push just as in Chapter 9 we saw how we could refer to a local variable X of procedure P as P.X. Inside the package we can refer to S or Stack.S, but outside the package, Max, S and Top are not accessible in any way.

It would in general be painful always to have to write Stack.Push to call Push from outside. Instead we can write

```
use Stack;
```

as a sort of declaration and we may then refer to Push and Pop directly. The use clause could follow the declaration of the specification of Stack in the same declarative part or could be in another declarative part where the package is visible. So we could write

```
declare
   use Stack;
begin
   ...
   Push(M);
   ...
   N := Pop;
   ...
end;
```

The use clause is like a declaration and similarly has a scope to the end of the block. Outside we would have to revert to the dotted notation. We could have an inner use clause referring to the same package – it would do no harm.

Two or more packages could be declared in the same declarative part. Generally, we could arrange all the specifications together and then all the bodies, or alternatively the corresponding specifications and bodies, could be together. Thus we could have spec A, spec B, body A, body B, or spec A, body A, spec B, body B.

The rules governing the order are simply

- linear elaboration of declarations,
- specification must precede body for same package (or subprogram).

Of course, the specification of a package may contain things other than subprograms. Indeed an important case is where it does not contain subprograms at all but merely a group of related variables, constants and types. In such a case the package needs no body. It does not provide any hiding properties but merely gives commonality of naming. (A body could be provided; its only purpose would be for initialization.)

However, a package declared at the library level is only allowed to have a body if it requires one for some reason such as providing the body for a subprogram declared in the specification. This avoids some awkward surprises which could otherwise occur as will be explained in Section 23.4.

As an example we could provide a package containing our type Day and some useful related constants.

```
package Diurnal is
    type Day is (Mon, Tue, Wed, Thu, Fri, Sat, Sun);
    subtype Weekday is Day range Mon .. Fri;
    Tomorrow: constant array (Day) of Day :=
                                (Tue, Wed, Thu, Fri, Sat, Sun, Mon);
    Next_Work_Day: constant array (Weekday) of Weekday :=
                                (Tue, Wed, Thu, Fri, Mon);
end Diurnal;
```

A final point. A subprogram cannot be called successfully during the elaboration of a declarative part if its body appears later. This did not prevent the mutual recursion of the procedures F and G in Section 9.6 because in that case the call of F actually only occurred when we executed the sequence of statements of the body of G. But it can prevent the use of a function in an initial value. So

```
function A return Integer;
I: Integer := A;
```

is illegal, and would result in Program_Error being raised.

A similar rule applies to subprograms in packages. If we call a subprogram from outside a package but before the package body has been elaborated, then Program_Error will be raised.

EXERCISE 11.1

1 The sequence defined by

$$X_{n+1} = X_n.5^5 \bmod 2^{13}$$

provides a crude source of pseudo random numbers. The initial value X_0 should be an odd integer in the range 0 to 2^{13}.

Write a package Random containing a procedure Init to initialize the sequence and a function Next to deliver the next value in the sequence.

2 Write a package Complex_Numbers which makes visible the type Complex, a constant $I = \sqrt{-1}$, and functions +, –, *, / acting on values of type Complex. See Exercise 9.2(**2**).

11.2 Private types

We have seen how packages enable us to hide internal objects from the user of a package. Private types enable us to hide the details of the construction of a type from a user.

In Exercise 11.1(**2**) we wrote a package Complex_Numbers providing a type Complex, a constant I and some operations on the type. The specification of the package was

```
package Complex_Numbers is
   type Complex is
      record
         RI, Im: Float;
      end record;

   I: constant Complex := (0.0, 1.0);

   function "+" (X: Complex) return Complex;      -- unary +
   function "–" (X: Complex) return Complex;      -- unary –

   function "+" (X, Y: Complex) return Complex;
   function "–" (X, Y: Complex) return Complex;
   function "*" (X, Y: Complex) return Complex;
   function "/" (X, Y: Complex) return Complex;
end;
```

The trouble with this formulation is that the user can make use of the fact that the complex numbers are held in cartesian representation. Rather than always using the complex operator "+", the user could also write things like

```
C.Im := C.Im + 1.0;
```

rather than the more abstract

```
C := C + I;
```

In fact, with the above package, the user has to make use of the representation in order to construct values of the type.

We might wish to prevent use of knowledge of the representation so that we could change the representation to perhaps polar form at a later date and know that the user's program would still be correct. We can do this with a private type. Consider

```
package Complex_Numbers is
  type Complex is private;
  I: constant Complex;
  function "+" (X: Complex) return Complex;
  function "-" (X: Complex) return Complex;
  function "+" (X, Y: Complex) return Complex;
  function "-" (X, Y: Complex) return Complex;
  function "*" (X, Y: Complex) return Complex;
  function "/" (X, Y: Complex) return Complex;
  function Cons(R, I: Float) return Complex;
  function Rl_Part(X: Complex) return Float;
  function Im_Part(X: Complex) return Float;

private
  type Complex is
    record
      Rl, Im: Float;
    end record;
  I: constant Complex := (0.0, 1.0);
end;
```

The part of the package specification before the reserved word **private** is the visible part and gives the information available externally to the package. The type Complex is declared to be private. This means that outside the package nothing is known of the details of the type. The only operations available are assignment, = and /= plus those added by the writer of the package as subprograms specified in the visible part.

We may also declare constants of a private type such as I in the visible part. The initial value cannot be given in the visible part because the details of the type are not yet known. Hence we just state that I is a constant; we call it a deferred constant.

After **private** we have to give the details of types declared as private and give the initial values of corresponding deferred constants.

A private type can be implemented in any way consistent with the operations visible to the user. It can be a record as we have shown; equally it could be an array, an enumeration type and so on; it could even be declared in terms of another private type. In our case it is fairly obvious that the type Complex is naturally implemented as a record; but we could equally have used an array of two components such as

```
type Complex is array (1 .. 2) of Float;
```

Having declared the details of the private type we can use them and so declare the constants properly and give their initial values.

It should be noted that as well as the functions +, -, * and / we have also provided Cons to create a complex number from its real and imaginary components and RI_Part and Im_Part to return the components. Some such functions are necessary because the user no longer has direct access to the internal structure of the type. Of course, the fact that Cons, RI_Part and Im_Part correspond to our thinking externally of the complex numbers in cartesian form does not prevent us from implementing them internally in some other form as we shall see in a moment.

The body of the package is as shown in the answer to Exercise 11.1(**2**) plus the additional functions which are trivial. It is therefore

```
package body Complex_Numbers is

   -- unary + -

   function "+" (X, Y: Complex) return Complex is
   begin
      return (X.RI + Y.RI, X.Im + Y.Im);
   end "+";

   -- plus - * / similarly

   function Cons(R, I: Float) return Complex is
   begin
      return (R, I);
   end Cons;

   function RI_Part(X: Complex) return Float is
   begin
      return X.RI;
   end RI_Part;

   -- Im_Part similarly

end Complex_Numbers;
```

The package Complex_Numbers could be used in a fragment such as

```
declare
   use Complex_Numbers;
   C, D: Complex;
   F: Float;
begin
   C := Cons(1.5, -6.0);
   D := C + I;              -- Complex +
   F := RI_Part(D) + 6.0;   -- Float +
   ...
end;
```

Outside the package we can declare variables and constants of type Complex in the usual way. Note the use of Cons to create a complex literal. We cannot, of course, do mixed operations between our complex and real (type Float) numbers. Thus we cannot write

```
C := 2.0 * C;
```

but instead must write

        C := Cons(2.0, 0.0) * C;

If this is felt to be tedious we could add further overloadings of the operators to allow mixed operations.

Let us suppose that for some reason we now decide to represent the complex numbers in polar form. The visible part of the package will be unchanged but the private part could now become

```
private
   Pi: constant := 3.14159_26536;
   type Complex is
      record
         R: Float;
         Theta: Float range 0.0 .. 2.0*Pi;
      end record;
   I: constant Complex := (1.0, 0.5*Pi);
end;
```

Note how the constant Pi is for convenience declared in the private part; anything other than a body can be declared in a private part if it suits us – we are not restricted to just declaring the types and constants in full. Things declared in the private part are also available in the body. An alternative to declaring our own constant Pi is to use the value in the package Ada.Numerics or at least to initialize our own constant with that value; see Section 12.6.

The body of our package Complex_Numbers will now need completely rewriting. Some functions will become simpler and others will be more intricate. In particular it will be convenient to provide a function to normalize the angle θ so that it lies in the range 0 to 2π. The details are left for the reader.

However, since the visible part has not been changed the user's program will not need changing; we are assured of this since there is no way in which the user could have written anything depending on the details of the private type. Nevertheless, as we will see in the next chapter, the user's program will need recompiling because of the general dependency rules. This may seem slightly contradictory but remember that the compiler needs the information in the private part in order to be able to allocate storage for objects of the private type declared in the user's program. If we change the private part the size of the objects could change and then the object code of the user's program would change even though the source was the same and compiled separately.

An interesting point is that rather than declare a deferred constant we could provide a parameterless function

        function I **return** Complex;

This has the slight advantage that we can change the value returned without changing the package specification and so having to recompile the user's program. Of course in the case of I we are unlikely to need to change the value anyway! Another advantage is mentioned in the next section.

Between a private type declaration and the later full type declaration, the type is in a curiously half-defined state (technically it is not frozen which means that we do not yet know all about it). Because of this there are severe restrictions on its use, the main ones being that it cannot be used to declare variables or allocate objects. But it can be used to declare deferred constants, other types and subtypes and subprogram specifications (also entries of tasks and protected types).

Thus we could write

type Complex_Array **is array** (Integer **range** <>) **of** Complex;

and then

C: **constant** Complex_Array;

But until the full declaration is given we cannot declare variables of the type Complex or Complex_Array.

However, we can declare the specifications of subprograms with parameters of the types Complex and Complex_Array and can even supply default expressions. Such default expressions can use deferred constants and functions; this is allowed because of course a default expression is only evaluated when a subprogram is called and this cannot occur until the body of the package has been declared and this is bound to be after the full type declaration.

An interesting point with regard to deferred constants is that they are another example of a situation where information has to be repeated and thus be consistent. Both deferred and full declarations must have the same type; if they both supply constraints (directly or using a subtype) then they must statically match. However, it is possible for the deferred declaration just to give the type and then for the full declaration to impose a constraint. Similarly if the deferred constant is marked as aliased then the full one must also be so marked.

So in the case of the array C above the full declaration might be

C: **constant** Complex_Array(1 .. 10) := ... ;

or even

C: **constant** Complex_Array := ... ;

where in the latter case the bounds are taken from the initial value.

Two final points on deferred constants: one is that any constant in a package specification can be deferred to the private part; it does not have to be of a private type. The other is that a deferred constant can also be used to import a constant from an external system; see Section 21.4.

There are various other subtle points which need not concern the normal user but which are described in the *ARM*. However, the general rule is that you can only use what you can see. Outside the package we know only that the type is private; inside the package and after the full type declaration we know all the properties implied by the declaration. Thus we see that we have two different views of the type according to where we are and hence which declaration we can see; these are referred to as the partial view and the full view.

As an example consider the type Complex_Array and the operator "<". (Remember that "<" only applies to arrays if the component type is discrete.) Outside the package we cannot use "<" since we do not know whether or not the type Complex is discrete. Inside the package we find that it is not discrete and so still cannot use "<". If it had been discrete we could have used "<" after the full type declaration but of course we still could not use it outside. On the other hand slicing is applicable to all one-dimensional arrays and so can be used both inside and outside the package.

EXERCISE 11.2

1   Write additional functions "*" to enable mixed multiplication of real and complex numbers.

2   Rewrite the fragment of user program for complex numbers omitting the use clause.

3   Complete the package Rational_Numbers whose visible part is

    package Rational_Numbers **is**

      type Rational **is private**;
      function "+" (X: Rational) **return** Rational;   -- unary +
      function "–" (X: Rational) **return** Rational;   -- unary –
      function "+" (X, Y: Rational) **return** Rational;
      function "–" (X, Y: Rational) **return** Rational;
      function "*" (X, Y: Rational) **return** Rational;
      function "/" (X, Y: Rational) **return** Rational;

      function "/" (X: Integer; Y: Positive) **return** Rational;
      function Numerator(R: Rational) **return** Integer;
      function Denominator(R: Rational) **return** Positive;

    private
      ...
    end;

A rational number is a number of the form N/D where N is an integer and D is a positive integer. For predefined equality to work it is essential that rational numbers are always reduced by cancelling out common factors. This may be done using the function GCD of Exercise 9.1(7). Ensure that an object of type Rational has an appropriate default value of zero.

4   Why does

    function "/" (X: Integer; Y: Positive) **return** Rational;

    not hide the predefined integer division?

11.3 Primitive operations and derived types

This seems a good moment to discuss the question of which operations really belong to a type. In Section 6.3 we noted that 'A type is characterized by a set of values and a set of primitive operations ...'. The set of values is pretty obvious but the set of primitive operations is not intuitively obvious nor is it obvious why the definition of such a set should be important.

The key to why we need to define the set of primitive operations of a type lies in the concept of a class which we mentioned in Chapter 3. We noted that a class was characterized by a group of types with common properties. Classes play two roles in Ada, as the basis for type derivation and extension and also as the basis for formal parameter types of generics. We will introduce the ideas by first considering the simplest form of derived types; the more flexible tagged types which can be extended will be discussed in Chapter 13 and generic parameters will be discussed in Chapter 17.

Sometimes it is useful to introduce a new type which is similar in most respects to an existing type but which is nevertheless a distinct type. If T is a type we can write

   type S **is new** T;

and then S is said to be a derived type and T is the parent type of S.

A derived type belongs to the same class as its parent. If T is a record type then S will be a record type and its components will have the same names and so on.

The set of values of a derived type is a copy of the set of values of the parent. An important instance of this is that if the parent type is an access type then the derived type is also an access type and they share the same storage pool. Note that we say that the set of values is a copy; this reflects that they are truly different types and values of one type cannot be assigned to objects of the other type; however, as we shall see in a moment, conversion between the two types is possible. The notation for literals and aggregates (if any) is the same and any default initial expressions for the type or its components are the same.

The primitive operations of a type are

- intrinsic predefined operations such as assignment, predefined equality, appropriate attributes and so on, and

- for a derived type, primitive operations inherited from its parent (these can be overridden), and

- for a type (immediately) declared in a package specification, subprograms with a parameter or result of the type also declared in the package specification.

The predefined types follow the same rules, for example the primitive operations of Integer include the operators such as "+", "−" and "<" which are notionally declared in Standard along with Integer.

Enumeration literals are also primitive operations of a type since they are considered to be parameterless functions returning a value of the type. So in the case of the type Boolean, True and False are primitive operations. It is as if there were functions such as

```
function True return Boolean is
begin
   return Boolean'Val(1);
end;
```

So the general idea is that a type has certain intrinsic primitive operations, it inherits some from its parent (if any) and more can be added.

Note especially that any operations inherited from a parent can be overridden provided the overriding occurs in the same declarative region (which is a list of declarations such as in a block or subprogram or a package specification and body taken together).

A subtle point is that inherited primitive operations are also intrinsic so that the Access attribute cannot be applied to them whereas of course it can be applied to explicitly declared operations.

There are a couple of minor rules which arise from consideration of the freezing of the type (see Section 21.1). We cannot derive from a private type until after its full type declaration. Also if we derive from a type in the same package specification as it is declared then the derived type will inherit all the primitive operations of the parent but we cannot add any more primitive operations to the parent type after the derivation.

Although derived types are distinct, nevertheless because they are really the same type underneath, a value of one type can be directly converted to another type if they have a common ancestor. Consider

```
type Light is new Colour;
type Signal is new Colour;
type Flare is new Signal;
```

These types form a hierarchy rooted at Colour. We can convert from any one type to another and do not have to give the individual steps. So we can write

```
L: Light;
F: Flare;
...
F := Flare(L);
```

and we do not need to laboriously write

```
F := Flare(Signal(Colour(L)));
```

The introduction of derived types extends the possibility of conversion between array types discussed in Section 8.2. In fact a value of one array type can be converted to another array type if the component subtypes statically match and the index types are the same or convertible to each other.

The reader might wonder at the benefit of derived types and why we might wish to have one type very like another.

One use for derived types is when we want to use an existing type, but wish to avoid the accidental mixing of objects of conceptually different types. Suppose we wish to count apples and oranges. Then we could declare

```
type Apples is new Integer;
type Oranges is new Integer;
No_Of_Apples: Apples;
No_Of_Oranges: Oranges;
```

Since Apples and Oranges are derived from the type Integer they both inherit "+". So we can write

```
No_Of_Apples := No_Of_Apples + 1;
No_Of_Oranges := No_Of_Oranges + 1;
```

but we cannot inadvertently write

```
No_Of_Apples := No_Of_Oranges;
```

If we did want to convert the oranges to apples we would have to write

```
No_Of_Apples := Apples(No_Of_Oranges);
```

The numeric types will be considered in Chapter 15 in more detail but it is worth mentioning here that strictly speaking a type such as Integer has no literals. Literals such as 1 and integer named numbers are of a type known as universal integer and implicit conversion to any integer type occurs if the context so demands. Thus we can use 1 with Apples and Oranges because of this implicit conversion and not because the literal is inherited.

Now suppose that we have overloaded procedures to sell the apples and oranges

```
procedure Sell(N: Apples);
procedure Sell(N: Oranges);
```

Then we can write

```
Sell(No_Of_Apples);
```

but

```
Sell(6);
```

is ambiguous because we do not know which fruit we are selling. We can resolve the ambiguity by qualification thus

```
Sell(Apples'(6));
```

When a subprogram is derived a new subprogram is not actually created. A call of the derived subprogram is really a call of the parent subprogram; **in** and

in out parameters are implicitly converted just before the call; **in out** and **out** parameters or a function result are implicitly converted just after the call.

So

    My_Apples + Your_Apples

is effectively

    Apples(Integer(My_Apples) + Integer(Your_Apples))

An important use of derived types is with private types when we wish to express the fact that a private type is to be implemented as an existing type such as Integer. We will see an example of this in Section 11.6.

Looking back at the type Complex of the last section we can see that the primitive operations are assignment, predefined equality and inequality and the subprograms "+", ... Im_Part.

In Exercise 11.2(**2**) we noted that it was tedious to use the operators of the type Complex without a use clause since we had to write

    C := Complex_Numbers."+"(A, B);

which is painful to say the least. However, there is a strong school of thought that use clauses are bad for you since they obscure the origin of entities. In order to alleviate this dilemma there is also another form of use clause, the so-called use type clause. This allows us to make just the primitive operators of a type directly visible. So writing

    use type Complex_Numbers.Complex;

provides visibility of the operators of the type Complex but not other entities in the package. We can then simply write

    C := A + B;

and yet the full dotted notation is still required for referring to other entities in the package.

If we wished to introduce a distinct type derived from Complex for an electromagnetic application (much as we had distinct types to count apples and oranges) then we could perhaps write

    type Field **is new** Complex;

and we could then ensure that values of the field would not inadvertently get mixed up with other complex numbers. However, it is important to note that although the type Field inherits all the operations of Complex, it does not inherent the constant I. In order to preserve the inheritance abstraction it is clearly necessary to make I into a function.

A few words on constraints; we can derive from a subtype using either a subtype mark or the more general subtype indication. So we could have

    type Chance **is new** Float **range** 0.0 .. 1.0;

in which case the underlying derived type is derived from the underlying base type. It is as if we had written

    type anon **is new** Float;
    subtype Chance **is** anon **range** 0.0 .. 1.0;

and so Chance denotes a constrained subtype of the (anonymous) derived type. The set of values of the new derived type is actually (a copy of) the full set of values of the type Float. The derived operations "+", ">" and so on also work on the full set of values. So given

    C: Chance;

we can legally write

    C > 1.0

even though 1.0 could never be successfully assigned to C. The Boolean expression is, of course, always false (unless C was uninitialized and by chance had a silly value).

As a further example of constraints it is instructive to consider the specification of a derived subprogram in more detail. It is obtained from that of the parent by simply replacing all instances of the parent base type in the original specification by the new derived type. Subtypes are replaced by equivalent subtypes with corresponding constraints and default initial expressions are converted by adding a type conversion. Any parameters or result of a different type are left unchanged. As an abstract example consider

    type T **is** ... ;
    subtype S **is** T **range** L .. R;

    function F(X: T; Y: T := E; Z: Q) **return** S;

where E is an expression of type T and the type Q is quite unrelated. If we write

    type TT **is new** T;

then it is as if we had also written

    subtype SS **is** TT **range** TT(L) .. TT(R);

and the specification of the derived function F will then be

    function F(X: TT; Y: TT := TT(E); Z: Q) **return** SS;

in which we have replaced T by TT, S by SS, added the conversion to the expression E but left the unrelated type Q unchanged. Note that the parameter names are naturally the same.

Derived types are in some ways an alternative to private types. Derived types have the advantage of inheriting literals but they often have the disadvantage of inheriting too much. For instance, we could derive types Length and Area from Float.

> **type** Length **is new** Float;
> **type** Area **is new** Float;

We would then be prevented from mixing lengths and areas but we would also have inherited the ability to multiply two lengths to give a length and to multiply two areas to give an area as well as hosts of irrelevant operations such as exponentiation. Of course, it is possible to redefine these operations to be useful or to raise exceptions but it is often simpler to use private types and just define the operations we need.

We finish this section by mentioning a curious anomaly concerning the type Boolean which really does not matter so far as the normal user is concerned. If we derive a type from Boolean then the predefined relational operators =, < and so on continue to deliver a result of the predefined type Boolean whereas the logical operators **and**, **or**, **xor** and **not** are inherited normally and deliver a result of the derived type. We cannot go into the reason here other than to say that it is because of the fundamental nature of the type Boolean. However, it does mean that the theorem of Exercise 6.7(**3**) that **xor** and /= are equivalent only applies to the type Boolean and not to a type derived from it.

EXERCISE 11.3

1   Declare a package containing types Length and Area with appropriate redeclarations of the incorrect operations "*".

11.4   Equality

In the previous section we saw that predefined equality was an operation of most types; however, it is sometimes inappropriate and needs to be overridden. Remember from Section 9.2 that if we do redefine "=" and it returns the type Boolean then a corresponding function "/=" is automatically implied.

Consider

> **package** Stacks **is**
>   **type** Stack **is private**;
>   **procedure** Push(S: **in out** Stack; X: **in** Integer);
>   **procedure** Pop(S: **in out** Stack; X: **out** Integer);
>   **function** "=" (S, T: Stack) **return** Boolean;
> **private**

```
Max: constant := 100;
type Integer_Vector is array (Integer range <>) of Integer;
type Stack is
  record
    S: Integer_Vector(1 .. Max);
    Top: Integer range 0 .. Max := 0;
  end record;
end;
```

Each object of type Stack is a record containing an array S and integer Top. Note that Top has a default initial value of zero. This ensures that when we declare a stack object, it is correctly initialized to be empty. Note also the introduction of the type Integer_Vector because a record component may not be of an anonymous array type.

The body of the package could be

```
package body Stacks is

  procedure Push(S: in out Stack; X: in Integer) is
  begin
    S.Top := S.Top + 1;
    S.S(S.Top) := X;
  end Push;

  procedure Pop(S: in out Stack; X: out Integer) is
  begin
    X := S.S(S.Top);
    S.Top := S.Top - 1;
  end Pop;

  function "=" (S, T: Stack) return Boolean is
  begin
    if S.Top /= T.Top then
      return False;
    end if;
    for I in 1 .. S.Top loop
      if S.S(I) /= T.S(I) then
        return False;
      end if;
    end loop;
    return True;
  end "=";

end Stacks;
```

This example illustrates many points. The parameter S of Push has mode **in out** because we need both to read from and to write to the stack. Further note that Pop cannot be a function since S has to be **in out** and functions can only have **in** parameters. (But it could be an access parameter, see Section 10.6.) However, "=" can be a function because we only need to read the values of the two stacks and not to update them.

The function "=" has the interpretation that two stacks are equal only if they have the same number of items and the corresponding items have the same value. It would obviously be quite wrong to compare the whole records because the unused components of the arrays would also be compared.

This is a typical example of a data structure where the value of the whole is more than just the sum of the parts; the interpretation of the array S depends on the value of Top. Cases where there is such a relationship usually need redefinition of equality.

A minor point is that we are using the identifier S in two ways: as the name of the formal parameter denoting the stack and as the array inside the record. There is no conflict because, although the scopes overlap, the regions of visibility do not as is explained in Section 12.5. Of course, it is rather confusing to the reader and not good practice but it illustrates the freedom of choice of record component names.

The package could be used in a fragment such as

```
declare
   use Stacks;
   St: Stack;
   Empty: Stack;
   ...
begin
   Push(St, N);
   ...
   Pop(St, M);
   ...
   if St = Empty then
      ...
   end if;
   ...
end;
```

Here we have declared two stacks St and Empty. Both are originally empty because their internal component Top has an initial value of zero. Assuming that we do not manipulate Empty then it can be used to see whether the stack St is empty or not by calling the function "=". This seems a rather dubious way of testing for an empty stack since there is no guarantee that Empty has not been manipulated. It would be better if Empty were a constant but we have no easy way of giving it an initial value. We could however declare a constant Empty in the visible part of the package. A much better technique for testing the state of a stack would, of course, be to provide a function Is_Empty and possibly a corresponding function Is_Full.

Having declared our own equality for the type Stack we might decide to declare a type such as

```
type Stack_Array is array (Integer range <>) of Stack;
```

This array type has predefined equals (see Section 8.2) but it is important to note that it works in terms of the original predefined equals for the type Stack and not our redefined version. We thus probably need to redefine equality for such an array type (this will also apply to slices of that type). We might even choose to define equality to return a Boolean array with each element indicating the equality of the matching components. Remember that if we do define equality to return a type other than just Boolean then a new version of "/=" will not automatically be provided and so we might need to redefine that as well.

So the general principle is always to go back to the predefined equality unless we specifically declare otherwise. (But this does not apply to tagged types which have a different philosophy as discussed in Chapter 13.)

Situations where equality will need redefinition usually only arise with composite types where, as we have mentioned, there is the possibility for the meaning of the whole to be more than just the sum of the parts. Nevertheless we can redefine equality for elementary types. If we do then the meaning of certain intrinsic structures effectively involving predefined equality is not changed. Thus the case statement always uses predefined equality in choosing the sequence to be obeyed.

Another interesting example is provided by a type such as Rational of Exercise 11.2(**3**); it would be quite reasonable to allow manipulation – including assignment – of values which were not reduced provided that equality is suitably redefined. If we wish to use predefined equality then we must reduce all values to a canonical form in which component by component equality is satisfactory. In the case of the type Stack implemented as an array, a suitable form would be one in which all unused elements of the array had a standard dummy value such as zero.

EXERCISE 11.4

1   Rewrite the specification of Stacks to include a constant Empty in the visible part.

2   Write functions Is_Empty and Is_Full for Stacks. Comment on their usefulness.

3   Rewrite the **function** "=" (S, T: Stack) using slices.

4   Write a suitable body for

       function "=" (A, B; Stack_Array) **return** Boolean;

Make it conform to the normal rules for array equality which we mentioned towards the end of Section 8.2. Also write appropriate equality functions returning an array of Boolean values.

5   Rewrite Stacks so that predefined equality is satisfactory.

6   Redefine "=" for the type Rational of Exercise 11.2(**3**) assuming that the package Rational_Numbers does not reduce values to a canonical form using GCD. Would this be sensible?

11.5   Limited types

The primitive operations of a private type can be completely restricted to just those specified in the visible part of the package. This is done by declaring the type as limited as well as private thus

   type T **is limited private**;

In such a case assignment and predefined = and **/**= are not available outside the package. Of course we can redefine equality for any type anyway and so the important issue in deciding whether a type should be limited private or just private is whether we wish to prevent assignment.

An important consequence of the absence of assignment for limited types is that the declaration of an object cannot include an initial value; this in turn implies that a constant cannot be declared outside the defining package. Similarly a record component of a limited type cannot have a default initial expression. However, the procedure parameter mechanism is not formally assignment and in fact we can declare our own subprograms with limited types as parameters of any mode outside the defining package and we can even supply default expressions for **in** parameters.

The advantage of making a private type limited is that the package writer has complete control over the objects of the type – the copying of resources can be monitored and so on. It also gives more freedom of implementation for the full type as we will see in a moment.

We now consider an alternative formulation of the type **Stack** and suppose that we wish to impose no maximum stack size other than that imposed by the overall size of the computer. This can be done by representing the stack as an access type referring to a list

```
package Stacks is
   type Stack is limited private;
   procedure Push(S: in out Stack; X: in Integer);
   procedure Pop(S: in out Stack; X: out Integer);
   function "=" (S, T: Stack) return Boolean;
private
   type Cell;
   type Stack is access Cell;
   type Cell is
      record
         Value: Integer;
         Next: Stack;
      end record;
end;

package body Stacks is

   procedure Push(S: in out Stack; X: in Integer) is
   begin
      S := new Cell'(X, S);
   end;
```

```
        procedure Pop(S: in out Stack; X: out Integer) is
        begin
          X := S.Value;
          S := S.Next;
        end;

        function "=" (S, T: Stack) return Boolean is ...

      end Stacks;
```

When the user declares a stack

```
      S: Stack;
```

it automatically takes the default initial value **null** which denotes that the stack is empty. If we call Pop when the stack is empty then this will result in attempting to evaluate

```
      null.Value
```

and this will raise Constraint_Error. The only way in which Push can fail is by running out of storage; an attempt to evaluate

```
      new Cell'(X, S)
```

could raise Storage_Error.

This formulation of stacks is one in which we have made the type limited private. Assignment would, of course, copy only the pointer to the stack rather than the stack itself and would have resulted in a complete mess. The writing of an appropriate function "=" needs some care. We could attempt

```
        function "=" (S, T: Stack) return Boolean is
          SS: Stack := S;
          TT: Stack := T;
        begin
          while SS /= null and TT /= null loop
            SS := SS.Next;
            TT := TT.Next;
            if SS.Value /= TT.Value then
              return False;
            end if;
          end loop;
          return SS = TT;            -- True if both null
        end;
```

but this does not work because we have hidden the predefined equality (and hence inequality) which we wish to use inside the body of "=" by the new definition itself. So this function will recurse indefinitely. The solution is to distinguish between the type Stack and its representation in some way. One possibility would be to make the type Stack a record of one component thus

```
type Cell;
type Cell_Ptr is access Cell;

type Cell is
   record
      Value: Integer;
      Next: Cell_Ptr;
   end record;

type Stack is
   record
      List: Cell_Ptr;
   end record;
```

so that we can distinguish between S, the Stack, and S.List, its internal representation. A much better approach however is to use a derived type and write

```
type Stack is new Cell_Ptr;
```

The type Stack now has all the operations of the type Cell_Ptr but we can replace the inherited equality by our own definition without difficulty.

In Section 10.2 we stated that if we had to write an incomplete declaration first because of circularity (as in the type Cell) then there was an exception to the general rule that the complete declaration had to occur in the same list of declarations. The exception is that a private part and the corresponding package body are treated as a single list of declarations as far as this rule is concerned.

Thus, the complete declaration of the type Cell could be moved from the private part to the body of the package Stacks. This might be an advantage since (as we will see in Section 12.1), it then follows from the dependency rules that a user program would not need recompiling just because the details of the type Cell are changed. In implementation terms it is possible to do this because it is assumed that values of all access types occupy the same space – typically a single word.

Observe that an access type could itself refer to a private type. So we could have

```
type Ref_Stack is access Stack;
```

The only special point of interest is that if the accessed type is limited private then an allocator cannot provide an initial value since this would be equivalent to assignment and assignment is not allowed for limited types.

We can write subprograms with limited private types as parameters outside the defining package despite the absence of assignment. As a simple example, the following procedure enables us to determine the top value on the stack without permanently removing it.

```
procedure Top_Of(S: in out Stack; X: out Integer) is
begin
   Pop(S, X);
```

```
        Push(S, X);
    end;
```

It is worth emphasizing that a private type such as Stack presents two views known as the partial view and the full view. Remember that within the private part (after the full type declaration) and within the body, any private type (limited or not) is treated in terms of how it is represented using the full view. On the other hand, outside the defining package and in the visible part we can only see the partial view as defined by the private declaration and the visible operations.

The parameter mechanism for a private type is simply that corresponding to how the type is represented. This applies both inside and outside the package. Of course, outside the package, we know nothing of how the type is represented and therefore should make no assumption about the mechanism used.

Note also that the primitive operations of the type are those declared in the package specification including the private part. Thus some may be private and only known to the full view. We will return to the topic of primitive operation and views of a type when we consider tagged types in Chapter 13. Some rules for tagged types and derivation are somewhat different (such as conversion) and it is important to remember that in this chapter we have only been discussing the properties of nontagged types.

We have seen that there are occasions when it is an advantage to make a type limited private since this prevents the user from using assignment. This is typically a sensible thing to do when the implementation might involve access types or the object represents a resource as illustrated in the next section. However, it is also possible to redefine assignment using controlled types which will be discussed in Section 13.7.

We have discussed limited types in the context of private types, nevertheless they are distinct concepts; they both relate to properties of views of the type.

A limited type is just one for which assignment and predefined equality are not available; we can always define equality but can never add assignment. A record type can be explicitly declared as limited by placing **limited** before **record** in its type declaration. A composite type containing a limited component is itself limited. Some types are inherently limited as we will see when we discuss task and protected types in Section 18.7.

A simple example of a limited composite type is given by an array of a limited type and we might reconsider the type Stack_Array of the previous section. In the case where the component is limited the array is also limited and so does not have predefined equality; but it could be defined and indeed the definition given as the answer to Exercise 11.4(**4**) would be satisfactory.

Limited types are very important in object oriented programming since there are many situations where an object represents a real-world entity and where making a copy would be quite inappropriate. Furthermore, there are a number of techniques that only apply to limited types such as the use of access discriminants as we will see later. There are therefore good reasons for always making a type explicitly limited if assignment is not appropriate.

EXERCISE 11.5

1   Write functions Is_Empty and Is_Full for the type Stack using the formulation where Stack is derived from Cell_Ptr.

2   Write "=" for the type Stack. Ignore the possibility of exceptions.

3   Complete the package whose visible part is

```
package Queues is
   Empty: exception;
   type Queue is limited private;
   procedure Join(Q: in out Queue; X: in Item);
   procedure Remove(Q: in out Queue; X: out Item);
   function Length(Q: Queue) return Integer;
private
```

Items join a queue at one end and are removed from the other so that a normal first-come–first-served protocol is enforced. An attempt to remove an item from an empty queue raises the exception Empty. Implement the queue as a singly linked list but maintain pointers to both ends of the list so that scanning of the list is avoided. The function Length returns the number of items in the queue; again, avoid scanning the list.

11.6   Resource management

An important example of the use of a limited private type is in providing controlled resource management. Consider the simple human model where each resource has a corresponding unique key. This key is then issued to the user when the resource is allocated and then has to be shown whenever the resource is accessed. So long as there is only one key and copying and stealing are prevented we know that the system is foolproof. A mechanism for handing in keys and reissuing them is usually necessary if resources are not to be permanently locked up. Typical human examples are the use of metal keys with safe deposit boxes, credit cards and so on.

Now consider the following

```
package Key_Manager is
   type Key is limited private;
   procedure Get_Key(K: in out Key);
   procedure Return_Key(K: in out Key);
   function Valid(K: Key) return Boolean;
   ...
   procedure Action(K: in Key; ... );
   ...
private
   Max: constant := 100;              -- number of keys
```

```
            subtype Key_Code is Integer range 0 .. Max;
            type Key is
              record
                 Code: Key_Code := 0;
              end record;
         end;

         package body Key_Manager is
            Free: array (Key_Code range 1 .. Key_Code'Last) of
                                              Boolean := (others => True);

            function Valid(K: Key) return Boolean is
            begin
               return K.Code /= 0;
            end Valid;

            procedure Get_Key(K: in out Key) is
            begin
               if K.Code = 0 then
                  for I in Free'Range loop
                     if Free(I) then
                        Free(I) := False;
                        K.Code := I;
                        return;
                     end if;
                  end loop;
                                    -- all keys in use
               end if;
            end Get_Key;

            procedure Return_Key(K: in out Key) is
            begin
               if K.Code /= 0 then
                  Free(K.Code) := True;
                  K.Code := 0;
               end if;
            end Return_Key;
            ...
            procedure Action(K: in Key; ... ) is
            begin
               if Valid(K) then
                 ...
            end Action;

         end Key_Manager;
```

The type Key is represented by a record with a single component Code. This has a default value of 0 which represents an unused key. Values from 1 .. Max represent the allocation of the corresponding resource. When we declare a variable of type Key it automatically takes an internal code value of zero. In order to use the key we must first call the procedure Get_Key; this allocates the first free key number to the variable. The key may then be used with various procedures such as Action which represents a typical request for some access to the resource guarded by the key.

Finally, the key may be relinquished by calling Return_Key. So a typical fragment of user program might be

```
declare
  use Key_Manager;
  My_Key: Key;
begin
  ...
  Get_Key(My_Key);
  ...
  Action(My_Key, ... );
  ...
  Return_Key(My_Key);
  ...
end;
```

A variable of type Key can be thought of as a container for a key. When initially declared the default value can be thought of as representing that the container is empty; the type Key has to be a record because only record components can take default initial values. Note how the various possible misuses of keys are overcome.

- If we call Get_Key with a variable already containing a valid key then no new key is allocated. It is important not to overwrite an old valid key otherwise that key would be lost.

- A call of Return_Key resets the variable to the default state so that the variable cannot be used as a key until a new one is issued by a call of Get_Key. Note that the user is unable to retain a copy of the key because assignment is not valid since the type Key is limited.

The function Valid is provided so that the user can see whether a key variable contains the default value or an allocated value. It is obviously useful to call Valid after Get_Key to ensure that the key manager was able to provide a new key value; note that once all keys are issued, a call of Get_Key does nothing.

One apparent flaw is that there is no compulsion to call Return_Key before the scope containing the declaration of My_Key is left. The key would then be lost. This corresponds to the real life situation of losing a key (although in our model no one else can find it again – it is as if it were thrown into a black hole). We can overcome this by using a controlled type as described in Section 13.6.

Observe that we could have made the component Code of a type derived from Integer such as

```
type Key_Code is new Integer range 0 .. Max;
```

and this would have the advantage of preventing confusion between codes and any other integers in the program.

EXERCISE 11.6

1 Complete the package whose visible part is

```
package Bank is
   type Money is new Natural;
   type Key is limited private;
   procedure Open_Account(K: in out Key; M: in Money);
      -- open account with initial deposit M
   procedure Close_Account(K: in out Key; M: out Money);
      -- close account and return balance
   procedure Deposit(K: in Key; M: in Money);
      -- deposit amount M
   procedure Withdraw(K: in out Key; M in out Money);
      -- withdraw amount M; if account does not contain M
      -- then return what is there and close account
   function Statement(K: Key) return Money;
      -- returns a statement of current balance
   function Valid(K: Key) return Boolean;
      -- checks the key is valid
private
   ...
```

2 Assuming that your solution to the previous question allowed the bank the use of the deposited money, reformulate the private type to represent a home savings box or safe deposit box where the money is in a box kept by the user.

3 A thief writes the following

```
declare
   use Key_Manager;
   My_Key: Key;
   procedure Cheat(Copy: in out Key) is
   begin
      Return_Key(My_Key);
      Action(Copy, ... );
      ...
   end;
begin
   Get_Key(My_Key);
   Cheat(My_Key);
   ...
end;
```

He attempts to return his key and then use the copy. Why is he thwarted?

4 A vandal writes the following

```
declare
   use Key_Manager;
   My_Key: Key;
```

```
      procedure Destroy(K: out Key) is
      begin
         null;
      end;
   begin
      Get_Key(My_Key);
      Destroy(My_Key);
      ...
   end;
```

He attempts to destroy the value in his key by calling a procedure which does not update the **out** parameter; he anticipates that the copy back rule will result in a junk value being assigned to the key. Why is he thwarted?

CHECKLIST 11

Variables inside a package exist between calls of subprograms of the package.

For predefined equality to be sensible, the values should be in a canonical form.

Predefined equality for a composite type uses predefined equality of its components.

A nonlimited private type can be implemented in terms of another private type provided it is also nonlimited.

A limited private type can be implemented in terms of any private type limited or not.

Assignment and predefined equality are not available for limited types.

Changes from Ada 83

The rules for deferred constants were stricter.

A subprogram (declared outside the defining package) could not have limited private parameters of mode **out**.

The concept of limited was bound to private in Ada 83.

Only a limited private type could have equality redefined in Ada 83.

The use type clause did not exist in Ada 83.

12 Overall Structure

In this chapter we discuss the hierarchical library structure and other mechanisms for separate compilation which were outlined in Chapter 4.

Many languages ignore the simple fact that programs are written in pieces, compiled separately and then joined together. Indeed large programs should be thought of as being composed out of a number of subsystems which themselves have internal structure. There are in fact two distinct requirements.

There is a requirement for decomposing a large coherent program into a number of internal subcomponents. Such a decomposition has particular advantages when a large program is being developed by a team.

There is a also a requirement for the creation of a program library where subsystems are written for general use and consequently are written before the programs that use them. Within this structure it is convenient to decompose the interface presented to future clients so that they may select only those parts of a system that are required.

This chapter also contains a further discussion on scope and visibility and summarizes the curious topic of renaming.

12.1   Library units

We will start by considering which units of Ada can be compiled separately and the general idea of dependency.

The most common units of compilation are subprogram or package specifications and bodies. Such units may be compiled individually or for convenience several could be submitted to the compiler together. Thus we could compile the specification and body of a package together but, as we shall see, it may be more convenient to compile them individually. As usual a subprogram body alone is sufficient to define the subprogram fully.

A library unit can also be a generic package or subprogram or an instantiation of one as discussed further in Section 23.4.

Compilation units are kept in a program library in some form. We will describe the behaviour in general terms but an implementation may use any model that satisfies two major requirements: a program cannot be built out of units that are not consistent, and a unit cannot be compiled until all units it depends upon are present in the library.

There are two obvious compilation models depending upon the form in which the compiler needs the information regarding dependency. In one, the source model, the compiler might only need access to the source text of the other units; in the other, the object model, the compiler requires the other units to be compiled as well. Note that the latter object model was the one presumed in Ada 83. In order to cover such variation we use phrases such as 'entered into the library'.

So, once entered into the library, a unit can be used by any subsequently compiled unit but the using unit must indicate the dependency by a with clause.

As a simple example suppose we compile the package **Stack** of Section 11.1. This package depends on no other unit and so it needs no with clause. We will compile both specification and body together so the text submitted will be

```
package Stack is
    ...
end Stack;

package body Stack is
    ...
end Stack;
```

As well as producing the object code corresponding to the package, the compiler has to ensure that the program library has all the information required in order to compile subsequent dependent units. In the case of the source model nothing extra will be needed, whereas for the object model some encoded form of the information in the specification will need to be inserted.

We now suppose that we write a procedure **Main** which will use the package **Stack**. Our procedure **Main** is going to be the main subprogram in the usual sense. It will have no parameters and we can imagine that it is called by some magic outside the language itself. The Ada definition does not prescribe that the main subprogram should have the identifier **Main**; it is merely a convention which we are adopting here because it has to be called something.

The text we submit to the compiler could be

```
with Stack;
procedure Main is
```

```
        use Stack;
        M, N: Integer;
     begin
        ...
        Push(M);
        ...
        N := Pop;
        ...
     end Main;
```

The with clause goes before the unit so that the dependency of the unit on other units is clear at a glance. A with clause may not be embedded in an inner scope.

On encountering a with clause the compiler retrieves from the program library the information describing the interface presented by the withed unit (in source or encoded form) so that it can check that the unit being compiled uses the interface correctly. Thus if procedure Main tried to call Push with the wrong number or type of parameters then this will be detected during compilation. This thorough checking between separately compiled units is a major factor in the increased productivity obtained through using Ada.

If a unit is dependent on several other units then they can go in the one with clause, or it might be a convenience to use distinct with clauses. Thus we could write

```
     with Stack, Diurnal;
     procedure Main is
        ...
```

or equally

```
     with Stack;
     with Diurnal;
     procedure Main is
        ...
```

For convenience we can place a use clause after a with clause. Thus

```
     with Stack; use Stack;
     procedure Main is
        ...
```

and then Push and Pop are directly visible without more ado. A use clause in such a position can only refer to packages mentioned in the with clause.

Only direct dependencies need be given in a with clause. Thus if package P uses the facilities of package Q which in turn uses the facilities of package R, then, unless P also directly uses R, the with clause for P should mention only Q. The user of Q does not care about R and should not need to know since otherwise the hierarchy of development would be made more complicated.

Another point is that the with clause in front of a package or subprogram declaration will also apply to the body. It can but need not be repeated. Of course, the body may have additional dependencies which will need indicating

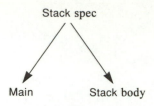

Figure 12.1 Dependencies between units.

with a with clause anyway. Dependencies which apply only to the body should not be given with the specification since otherwise the independence of the body and the specification would be reduced.

If a package specification and body are compiled separately then the body must be compiled after the specification has been entered into the library. We say that the body is dependent on the specification. However, any unit using the package is dependent only on the specification and not the body. If the body is changed in a manner consistent with not changing the specification, any unit using the package will not need recompiling. The ability to compile specification and body separately simplifies program maintenance and clearly distinguishes the logical interface from the physical implementation.

The dependencies between the specification and body of the package Stack and the procedure Main are illustrated by the graph in Figure 12.1.

The general rule regarding the order of compilation is simply that a unit must be compiled after all units on which it depends are entered into the library. Consequently, if a unit is changed and so has to be recompiled then all dependent units must also be recompiled before they can be linked into a total program.

There is one package that need not (and indeed cannot) be mentioned in a with clause. This is the package Standard which effectively contains the declarations of all the predefined types such as Integer and Boolean and their predefined operations. The package Standard is described in more detail in Section 20.1.

Finally there are two important rules regarding library units. They must have distinct names; they cannot be overloaded. Moreover they cannot be operators. These rules simplify the implementation of an Ada program library on top of a conventional file system or database.

EXERCISE 12.1

1 The package D and subprograms P and Q and Main have with clauses as follows

specification of D	no with clause
body of D	**with** P, Q;
subprogram P	no with clause
subprogram Q	no with clause
subprogram Main	**with** D;

Draw a graph showing the dependencies between the units. How many different orders of compilation are possible (a) if the library uses the source model, (b) if it uses the object model?

12.2   Subunits

In this section we introduce a further form of compilation unit known as a subunit. The body of a package, subprogram (or task or protected object, see Chapter 18) can be 'taken out' of an immediately embracing library unit or secondary unit and itself compiled separately. The body in the embracing unit is then replaced by a body stub. As an example suppose we remove the bodies of the subprograms Push and Pop from the package Stack. The body of Stack would then become

```
package body Stack is
   Max: constant := 100;
   S: array (1 .. Max) of Integer;
   Top: Integer range 0 .. Max;
   procedure Push(X: Integer) is separate;      -- stub
   function Pop return Integer is separate;     -- stub
begin
   Top := 0;
end Stack;
```

The removed units are termed subunits; they may then be compiled separately. They have to be preceded by **separate** followed by the name of the parent unit in brackets. Thus the subunit Push becomes

```
separate (Stack)
procedure Push(X: Integer) is
begin
   Top := Top + 1;
   S(Top) := X;
end Push;
```

and similarly for Pop.

In the above example the parent unit is (the body of) a library unit. The parent body could itself be a subunit; in such a case its name must be given in full using the dotted notation starting with the ancestor library unit. Thus if R is a subunit of Q which is a subunit of P which is a library unit, then the text of R must start

```
separate (P.Q)
```

As with library units and for similar reasons, the subunits of a library unit must have distinct identifiers. But note that we could have a subunit P.S.R as well as P.Q.R and indeed P.R. And again subunits cannot be operators.

A subunit is dependent on its parent body (and any library units explicitly mentioned) and so must be compiled after they are entered into the library.

Visibility within a subunit is as at the corresponding body stub – it is exactly as if the subunit were plucked out with its environment intact and full type checking is maintained. As a consequence any with clause applying to the parent body need not be repeated just because the subunit is compiled separately. However, it is possible to give the subunit access to additional library units by preceding it with its own with clauses (and possibly use clauses). Such clauses precede **separate**. So the text of R might commence

> **with** X; **use** X;
> **separate** (P.Q)
> ...

A possible reason for doing this might be if we can then remove any reference to library unit X from the parent P.Q and so reduce the dependencies. This would give us greater freedom with recompilation; if X were recompiled for some reason then only R would need recompiling as a consequence and not also Q.

Note that a with clause only refers to library units and never to subunits. Finally observe that several subunits or a mixture of library units, library unit bodies and subunits can be compiled together.

EXERCISE 12.2

1   Suppose that the package Stack is written with separate subunits Push and Pop. Draw a graph showing the dependencies between the five units: procedure Main, procedure Push, function Pop, package specification Stack, package body Stack. How many different orders of compilation are possible (a) if the library uses the source model, (b) if it uses the object model?

12.3   Child library units

One of the great strengths of Ada is the library package where the distinct specification and body decouple the user interface to a package (the specification) from its implementation (the body). This enables the details of the implementation and the clients to be recompiled separately without interference provided the specification remains stable.

However, although the simple structure we have seen so far works well for smallish programs it is not satisfactory when programs become large or complex. There are two aspects of the problem: the coarse control of visibility of private types and the inability to extend without recompilation.

There are occasions when we wish to write two distinct packages which nevertheless share a private type. We cannot do this with unrelated packages. We either have to make the type not private so that both packages can see it with the unfortunate consequence that all the client packages can also see the type; this breaks the abstraction. Or, on the other hand, if we wish to keep the abstraction, then we have to merge the two packages together and this results in a large monolithic package with increased recompilation costs.

The other aspect of the difficulty arises when we wish to extend an existing system by adding more facilities to it. If we add to a package specification then naturally we have to recompile it but moreover we also have to recompile all existing clients even if the additions have no impact upon them.

Another similar problem with a simple flat structure is the potential clash of names between library units in different parts of the system.

These problems are solved by the introduction of a hierarchical library structure containing child packages and child subprograms. There are two kinds of children: public children and private children. We will first consider public children; private children will be discussed later.

Consider the familiar example of a package for the manipulation of complex numbers as described in Section 11.2. It contains the private type itself plus the arithmetic operations and also subprograms to construct and decompose a complex number taking a cartesian view.

```
package Complex_Numbers is
    type Complex is private;
    ...
    function "+" (X, Y: Complex) return Complex;
    ...
    function Cons(R, I: Float) return Complex;
    function Rl_Part(X: Complex) return Float;
    function Im_Part(X: Complex) return Float;

private
    ...
end Complex_Numbers;
```

We have deliberately not shown the completion of the private type since it is immaterial how it is implemented. Although this package gives the user a cartesian view of the type, nevertheless it certainly does not have to be implemented that way as we saw in Chapter 11.

Some time later we might need to additionally provide a polar view by the provision of subprograms which construct and decompose a complex number from and to its polar coordinates. We can do this without disturbing the existing package and its clients by adding a child package as follows

```
package Complex_Numbers.Polar is

    function Cons_Polar(R, Theta: Float) return Complex;
    function "abs" (X: Complex) return Float;
    function Arg(X: Complex) return Float

end Complex_Numbers.Polar;
```

and within the body of this package we can access the full details of the private type **Complex**.

Note the notation, a package having the name P.Q is a child package of its parent package P. We can think of the child package as being declared inside the declarative region of its parent but after the end of the specification of its parent; most of the visibility rules stem from this model. In other words the declarative region defined by the parent (which is primarily the specification and body of the parent, see Section 12.5) also includes the space occupied by the text of the children; but it is important to realize that the children are inside that region and do not just extend it. The rules are worded this way to make it clear that a child subprogram is not a primitive operation of a type declared in its parent's specification because the child is not declared in the specification but after it. (Primitive operations were introduced in Section 11.3.)

In just the same way, root library packages can be thought of as being declared in the declarative region of the package **Standard** and after the end of its specification. So library units are children of **Standard**.

The important special visibility rule is that the private part (if any) and the body of the child have visibility of the private part of their parent. (They naturally also have visibility of the visible part.) However, the visible part of a (public) child package does not have visibility of the private part of its parent; if it did it would allow renaming (discussed later in this chapter) and hence the export of the hidden private details to any client; this would break the abstraction of the private type (this rule does not apply to private children).

The body of the child package for our complex number example could simply be

```
package body Complex_Numbers.Polar is

  -- bodies of Cons_Polar etc

end Complex_Numbers.Polar;
```

In order to access the procedures of the child package the client must have a with clause for the child package. However this also implicitly provides a with clause for the parent as well thereby saving us the burden of having to write one separately. Thus we might have

```
with Complex_Numbers.Polar;
package Client is
  ...
```

and then within Client we can access the various subprograms in the usual way by writing Complex_Numbers.Rl_Part or Complex_Numbers.Polar.Arg and so on.

Direct visibility can be obtained by use clauses as expected. However, a use clause for the child does not imply one for the parent; but, because of the model that the child is in the declarative region of the parent, a use clause for the parent makes the child name itself directly visible. So writing

```
with Complex_Numbers.Polar; use Complex_Numbers;
```

now allows us to refer to the subprograms as RI_Part and Polar.Arg respectively.

We could of course have added

    use Complex_Numbers.Polar;

and we would then be able to refer to the subprogram in Polar just as Arg.

As stated in Section 12.1 a use clause in a context clause can only mention the packages in the with clause. So we could not abbreviate this last use clause to just **use** Polar; on the grounds that we already have direct visibility of the parent but we could do so if the use clause were in a declarative part.

Child packages thus neatly solve both the problem of sharing a private type over several compilation units and the problem of extending a package without recompiling the clients. They thus provide a form of programming by extension.

A package may of course have several children. In fact with hindsight it might have been more logical to have developed our complex number package as three packages: a parent containing the private type and the four arithmetic operations and then two child packages, one giving the cartesian view and the other giving the polar view of the type. At a later date we could add yet another package providing perhaps the trigonometric functions on complex numbers and again this can be done without modifying what has already been written and thus without the risk of introducing errors.

Finally, it is very important to realize that the child mechanism is hierarchical. Children may have children to any level so we can build a complete tree providing decomposition of facilities in a natural manner. A child may have a private part and this is then visible from its children but not its parent.

With regard to siblings a child can obviously only have visibility of a sibling previously entered into the library anyway. And then the normal rules apply: a child can only see the visible part of its siblings.

A parent body may access (via with clauses) and thus depend upon its children and grandchildren. A child (specification and body) automatically depends upon its parent (and grandparent) and needs no with clause for them. A child body can depend upon its siblings (again via with clauses).

One very important use of the hierarchical structure was discussed in Chapter 4 where we saw that the predefined library is structured as packages System, Interfaces and Ada each of which have numerous child packages.

We have already superficially met the package Ada.Characters.Latin_1 which is a grandchild of Ada when discussing the type Character in Section 8.4. This package contains constants for the various control characters and so we now see why we can refer to them as Ada.Characters.Latin_1.Nul and so on. Writing

    use Ada.Characters.Latin_1; .

allows this to be abbreviated to simply Nul.

Note the distinction between child packages and lexically nested packages such as the (obsolete) package ASCII in Standard. Lexically nested packages cannot be separately compiled (although their bodies could be subunits) and just have single identifiers as their name. But externally they are both referred to using the same notation and as a consequence it is illegal to have a nested package and a child package with the same identifier because it would be ambiguous. Nested packages are of infrequent use in Ada 95.

EXERCISE 12.3

1 Rewrite the package Complex_Numbers as a parent and two children as suggested above.

2 Draw the dependency graph for the hierarchy of the previous exercise.

3 If we derive the type Field (see Section 11.3) from Complex as now structured, then which operations are inherited?

12.4   Private child units

In the previous section we introduced the concept of hierarchical child units and showed how these allowed extension and continued privacy of private types without recompilation. However, the whole idea was based around the provision of additional facilities for the client. The specifications of the additional units were all visible to the client.

In the development of large subsystems it often happens that we would like to decompose the system for implementation reasons but without giving any additional visibility to clients.

In Section 12.2 we saw how a body could be separately compiled as a subunit. However, although a subunit can be recompiled without affecting other subunits at the same level, any change to its specification requires its parent body and hence all sibling subunits to be recompiled.

Greater flexibility is provided by a form of child unit that is totally private to its parent. In order to illustrate this idea consider the following outline of an operating system.

```
package OS is
   -- parent package defines types used throughout the system
   type File_Descriptor is private;
      ...
private
   type File_Descriptor is new Integer;
end OS;
```

```
package OS.Exceptions is
  -- exceptions used throughout the system
  File_Descriptor_Error,
  File_Name_Error,
  Permission_Error: exception;
end OS.Exceptions;

with OS.Exceptions;
package OS.File_Manager is
  type File_Mode is (Read_Only, Write_Only, Read_Write);
  function Open(File_Name: String; Mode: File_Mode)
                                            return File_Descriptor;

  procedure Close(File: in File_Descriptor);
  ...
end OS.File_Manager;

procedure OS.Interpret(Command: String);

private package OS.Internals is
  ...
end OS.Internals;

private package OS.Internals_Debug is
  ...
end OS.Internals_Debug;
```

In this example the parent package contains the types used throughout the system. There are then three child units, the package OS.Exceptions containing various exceptions, the package OS.File_Manager which provides file open/close routines (note the explicit with clause for its sibling OS.Exceptions) and a procedure OS.Interpret which interprets a command line passed as a parameter. (Incidentally this illustrates that a child unit can be a subprogram as well as a package. It can actually be any library unit and that includes a generic declaration and a generic instantiation.) Finally we have two private child packages called OS.Internals and OS.Internals_Debug.

A private child (distinguished by starting with the word **private**) can be declared at any point in the child hierarchy. The visibility rules for private children are similar to those for public children but there are two extra rules.

The first extra rule is that a private child is only visible within the subtree of the hierarchy whose root is its parent. And moreover within that tree it is not visible to the specifications of any public siblings (although it is visible to their bodies). In our example, since the private child is a direct child of the package OS, the package OS.Internals is visible to the bodies of OS itself, of OS.File_Manager and of OS.Interpret (OS.Exceptions only has a null body anyway) and it is also visible to both body and specification of OS.Internals_Debug. But it is not visible outside OS and a client package certainly cannot access OS.Internals at all.

The other extra rule is that the visible part of the private child can access the private part of its parent. This is quite safe because it cannot export information about a private type to a client because it is not itself visible. Nor can it export information indirectly via its public siblings because, as we have seen, it is not visible to their specifications but only to their bodies.

We can now safely implement our system in the package OS.Internals and we can create a subtree for the convenience of development and extensibility. We would then have a third level in the hierarchy containing packages such as OS.Internals.Devices, OS.Internals.Access_Rights and so on.

We conclude this section by summarizing the various visibility rules which are actually quite simple and mostly follow from the model of the child being located after the end of the specification of its parent but inside the parent's declarative region.

- A specification never needs to with its parent; it may with a sibling except that a visible child specification may not with a private sibling; it may not with its own child.

- A body never needs to with its parent; it may with a sibling (private or not); it may with its own child.

- A context clause on a specification applies to the body and any children (and transitively to subunits and grandchildren ...).

- The entities of the parent are directly visible within a child; a use clause is not required.

- A private child is never visible outside the tree rooted at its parent. And within that tree it is not visible to the specifications of public siblings.

- The private part and body of any child can access the private part of its parent (and grandparent...).

- In addition the visible part of a private child can also access the private part of its parent (and grandparent...).

- A with clause for a child automatically implies with clauses for all its ancestors.

- A use clause for a unit makes the child units accessible by simple name (this only applies to child units for which there is also a with clause).

These rules may seem a bit complex but actually stem from just a few considerations of consistency. Questions regarding access to children of sibling units and other remote relatives follow by analogy with an external client viewing the appropriate subtree.

EXERCISE 12.4

1   Rewrite the body of the package Rational_Numbers of Exercise 11.2(**3**) so that the functions Normal and GCD are in a private child package Rational_Numbers.Slave.

2   Declare (in outline) an additional child package Complex_Numbers.Trig for computing the trigonometric functions Sin, Cos, etc. of complex numbers. Use a private child function Sin_Cos for the common part of the calculation. Ensure that with and use clauses are correct.

12.5   Scope, visibility and accessibility

Having just introduced the concepts of library and child units it seems appropriate to summarize the major points regarding scope and visibility which will be relevant to the everyday use of Ada. For some of the fine detail, the reader is referred to the *ARM*. We have already mentioned the term declarative region. Blocks and subprograms are examples of declarative regions and the scope rules associated with them were described in Sections 6.2 and 9.6. We now have to consider the broad effect of the introduction of packages and library units.

A package specification and body together constitute a single declarative region. Thus if we declare a variable X in the specification then we cannot redeclare X in the body (except of course in an inner region such as a local subprogram).

In the case of a declaration in the visible part of a package, its scope extends from the declaration to the end of the scope of the package itself. Note that if the package is inside the visible part of another package then this means that, applying the rule again, the scope extends to the end of that of the outer package and so on.

In the case of a declaration in a package body or in the private part of a package, its scope extends to the end of the package body.

If a unit is a library unit then its scope includes just those units which depend upon it; these are its children, body and subunits as appropriate plus those mentioning the unit in a with clause.

The rules for child units follow largely from the model of the child being in the declarative region of the parent and just after the specification of the parent. So the scope of a declaration in the specification of the parent extends through all child units. There is one important variation in the case of a declaration in the private part of a library unit: its scope does not include the visible part of any public children.

We recall from Section 9.6 say that a declaration is directly visible if we can refer to it by just its direct name such as X. If not directly visible then it may still be visible and can be referred to by the dotted notation such as P.X.

Moreover, a declaration is not visible (as opposed to directly visible) throughout all its scope. For example, a scalar, array or record object is not visible in its own declaration at all and a package is not visible until the reserved word **is** of its declaration.

In the case of the simple nesting of blocks and subprograms a declaration is otherwise directly visible throughout its scope and so can be referred to by its direct name except where hidden by another declaration. Where not directly visible it can be referred to by using the dotted notation where the prefixed name is that of the unit embracing the declaration.

In the case of a declaration in a package the same rules apply inside the package. Outside the package, a declaration in the visible part is visible but not directly visible unless we write a use clause.

The declarations directly visible at a given point are those directly visible before considering any use clauses plus those made directly visible by use clauses.

The basic rule is that an identifier declared in a package is made directly visible by a use clause provided the same identifier is not also in another package with a use clause and also provided that the identifier is not already directly visible anyway. If these conditions are not met then the identifier is not made directly visible and we have to continue to use the dotted notation.

A slightly different rule applies if all the identifiers are subprograms or enumeration literals. In this case they all overload each other and all become directly visible. If the specifications have type conformance (and so would normally hide each other) then the identifiers are still directly visible although things like formal parameter names may be needed to identify a particular call.

The general purpose of these rules is to ensure that adding a use clause cannot silently change the meaning of an existing piece of text. We have only given a brief sketch here and the reader is probably confused. In practice there should be no problems since the Ada compiler will, we hope, indicate any ambiguities or other difficulties and things can always be put right by adding a qualifier or using a dotted name.

There are other rules regarding record component names, subprogram parameters and so on which are as expected. For example there is no conflict between an identifier of a record component and another use of the identifier outside the type definition itself. Consider

```
declare
  type R is
    record
        I: Integer;
    end record;
  type S is
    record
        I: Integer;
    end record;
  AR: R;
  AS: S;
  I: Integer;
begin
  ...
  I := AR.I + AS.I;      -- legal
  ...
end;
```

The visibility of the I in the type R extends from its declaration until the end of the block and so it can be referred to using the dotted notation. However, its direct visibility is confined to within the declaration of R. Another example is the use of S both as the stack and as the internal array in Section 11.4.

Similar considerations prevent conflict in named aggregates and in named parameters in subprogram calls where the name before => is not directly visible.

Observe that a use clause can mention several packages and that it may be necessary for a package name to be given using dotted notation as well. A use clause does not take effect until the semicolon. Suppose we have nested packages

```
package P1 is
  package P2 is
    ...
  end P2;
  ...
end P1;
```

then outside P1 we could write

```
use P1; use P2;
```

or

```
use P1, P1.P2;
```

but not

```
use P1, P2;      -- illegal
```

We could even write **use** P1.P2; to gain direct visibility of the entities in P2 but not those in P1 – however, this seems an odd thing to do. Similar rules apply in the case of child rather than nested packages. So assuming

```
package P1 is
  ...
end P1;

package P1.P2 is
  ...
end P1.P2;
```

then we can again write exactly the same use clauses as for the nested packages.

Remember that a use clause following a with clause can only refer to packages mentioned in the with clause; moreover a use clause in a context clause does not take effect until the end of the context clause. So we cannot write something like

```
with P1.P2; use P1; use P2;      -- illegal
```

but have to spell it out in detail as

```
with P1.P2; use P1; use P1.P2;
```

Note that writing **with** P1.P2; implies **with** P1; but **use** P1.P2; does not imply **use** P1; as well. The reason is that dependency on the child implies dependency on the parent but there is no reason why we should not choose to have direct visibility of internal declarations as we wish.

As mentioned is Section 11.3, there is also the use type clause which makes directly visible just the primitive operators of a type. This avoids making all declarations directly visible but allows the convenience of infixed notation.

Finally, there is the package Standard. This contains all the predefined entities and moreover every library unit should be thought of as being declared as a child of Standard. This explains why an explicit use clause for Standard is not required. Another important consequence is that, provided we do not hide the name Standard by redefining it, a library unit P can always be referred to as Standard.P. Hence, in the absence of anonymous blocks, loops and overloading, every identifier in the program has a unique name commencing with Standard. Thus we could even pedantically refer to the predefined operators in this way

```
Four: Integer := Standard."+" (2, 2);
```

It is probably good advice not to redefine Standard; indeed declaring a package Standard simply results in Standard.Standard which is very confusing.

We conclude this section by remarking that the existence of packages plays no part in the accessibility rules. Packages are static scope walls whereas accessibility concerns dynamic lifetimes; packages can therefore be ignored in considering levels of accessibility.

12.6   Renaming

Certain entities can be renamed. As an example we can write

```
declare
    procedure S_Push(X: Integer) renames Stack.Push;
    function S_Pop return Integer renames Stack.Pop;
begin
    ...
    S_Push(M);
    ...
    N := S_Pop;
    ...
end;
```

A possible reason for doing this is to resolve ambiguities and yet avoid the use of the full dotted notation. Thus if we had two packages with a procedure Push (with an Integer parameter) then the use clause would be of no benefit since the full name would still be needed to resolve the ambiguity.

There is also a strong school of thought that use clauses are bad for you. Consider the case of a large program with many library units and suppose that the unit we are in has withed several packages. If we have use clauses for all

these packages then it is not clear from which package an arbitrary identifier
has been imported. In the absence of use clauses we have to use the full dotted
notation and the origin of everything is then obvious. However, it is also
commonly accepted that long meaningful identifiers should be generally used.
A long meaningful package name followed by the long meaningful name of an
entity in the package is often too much. However, we can introduce an
abbreviation by renaming such as

> V: Float **renames** Aeroplane_Data.Current_Velocity;

and then compactly use V in local computation and yet still have the full
identification available in the text of the current unit.

As another example suppose we wish to use both the function Inner and the
equivalent operator "*" of Chapter 9 without declaring two distinct
subprograms. We can write

> **function** "*" (X, Y: Vector) **return** Float **renames** Inner;

or

> **function** Inner(X, Y: Vector) **return** Float **renames** "*";

according to which we declare first.

Renaming of operators can also be used to avoid the use of prefixed
notation in the absence of a use clause (which, as we mentioned, many consider
to be evil); the alternative of a use type clause should be considered as
described in Section 11.3.

Renaming is also useful in the case of library units. Thus we might wish to
have two or more overloaded subprograms and yet compile them separately.
This cannot be done directly since library units must have distinct names.
However, differently named library units could be renamed so that the user
sees the required effect. The restriction that a library unit cannot be an operator
can similarly be overcome. The same tricks can be done with subunits.

Note in particular that a library unit can be renamed as another library unit.
We saw an example of this in Chapter 4 when we noted that Ada.Text_IO was
renamed as Text_IO for compatibility with Ada 83.

If a subprogram is renamed, the number, base types and modes of the
parameters (and result if a function) must be the same. This information can be
used to resolve overloadings (as in the example of "*") and, of course, this
matching of the profiles occurs during compilation; we call this mode
conformance. Rather strangely, any constraints on the parameters or result in
the new subprogram are ignored; those on the original still apply.

On the other hand, the presence, absence or value of default parameters do
not have to match. Renaming can be used to introduce, change or delete default
expressions; the default parameters associated with the new name are those
shown in the renaming declaration. Hence renaming cannot be used as a trick
to give an operator default values. Similarly, parameter names do not have to
match but naturally the new names must be used for named parameters of calls
of the new subprogram.

Table 12.1 Conformance matching of profiles.

Level	Matches	Used for
type	base types	hiding (see Section 9.5)
mode	+ modes	renaming as spec generic subprograms (17.3)
subtype	+ subtypes statically	renaming as body access to subprograms (10.7)
full	+ names + defaults	distinct specs and bodies (9.6) repeated discriminants (16.1)

We can also provide the body of a subprogram as simply a renaming of another subprogram. There is, however, an extra rule on the matching of profiles when renaming is used for this purpose. All constraints must statically match; this is called subtype conformance and is the same as that required for access to subprogram types. The reason for requiring subtype conformance is so that a simple jump to the old subprogram can be compiled as the call to the new one.

The reader may be baffled by all the various levels of conformance we have mentioned from time to time. For convenience they are summarized in Table 12.1 which gives them in increasing order of strength.

The unification of subprograms and enumeration literals is further illustrated by the fact that an enumeration literal can be renamed as a parameterless function with the appropriate result. For example

```
function Ten return Roman_Digit renames 'X';
```

Renaming can also be used to partially evaluate the name of an object. Suppose we have an array of records such as the array People in Section 8.7 and that we wish to scan the array and print out the dates of birth in numerical form. We could write

```
for I in People'Range loop
   Put(People(I).Birth.Day); Put(":");
   Put(Month_Name'Pos(People(I).Birth.Month)+1);
   Put(":");
   Put(People(I).Birth.Year);
end loop;
```

It is clearly painful to repeat People(I).Birth each time. We could declare a variable D of type Date and copy People(I).Birth into it, but this would be very wasteful if the record were at all large. We could also use an access variable to refer to it but this would mean making the variable aliased as well as introducing an access type which might otherwise not be necessary. A better technique is to use renaming thus

```
for I in People'Range loop
   declare
      D: Date renames People(I).Birth;
   begin
      Put(D.Day); Put(":");
      Put(Month_Name'Pos(D.Month)+1);
      Put(":");
      Put(D.Year);
   end;
end loop;
```

Beware that renaming does not correspond to text substitution – the identity of the object is determined when the renaming occurs. If any variable in the name subsequently changes then the identity of the object does not change. Any constraints implied by the subtype mark in the renaming declaration are ignored; those of the original object still apply.

Renaming can be applied to objects (variables and constants), components of composite objects (including slices of arrays), exceptions (see Chapter 14), subprograms and packages. In the case of a package it takes the simple form

```
package P renames Stack;
```

Although renaming does not directly apply to types an almost identical effect can be achieved by the use of a subtype

```
subtype S is T;
```

or in order to overcome a lack of standardization even

```
subtype Color is Colour;
```

Note also that renaming cannot be applied to a named number. This is partly because renaming requires a type name and named numbers do not have an explicit type name (we will see in Chapter 15 that they are of so-called universal types which cannot be explicitly named). Thus the constant e (the base of natural logarithms) in the package Ada.Numerics cannot be given a local renaming for brevity (not that it is exactly long anyway!). However, there is no need, we can just declare another named number

```
E: constant := Ada.Numerics.e;
```

which is no disadvantage because the named numbers are not run-time objects anyway and so there is no duplication.

Finally note that renaming does not hide the old name nor does it ever introduce a new entity; it just provides another way of referring to an existing entity or, in other words, another view of it (that is why new constraints in a renaming declaration are ignored). Renaming can be very useful at times but the indiscriminate use of renaming should be avoided since the aliases introduced make program proving much more difficult.

EXERCISE 12.6

1 Declare a renaming of the literal Mon of type Day from the package Diurnal of Section 11.1.

2 Declare a renaming of Diurnal.Next_Work_Day.

3 Declare Pets as a renaming of the relevant part of the second Farmyard of Section 8.5.

4 Rename the operator "+" from the package Complex_Numbers of Section 11.2 so that it can be used in infix notation without a use or use type clause.

5 Declare a renaming to avoid the repeated evaluation of World(I, J) in the answer to Exercise 10.4(**2**).

12.7 Programs, partitions and elaboration

We have mentioned the idea that an overall program starts execution by some external magic calling the main subprogram which has to be a library unit. In fact in the general case a program can comprise a number of partitions each of which can have its own main subprogram. Partitions typically have their own address space and communication between partitions is restricted although the typing rules are enforced across the whole program. The details of this topic are outside the core language and are covered by the Distributed Systems annex discussed very briefly in Section 22.3. We will restrict ourselves here to programs consisting of just one partition.

The first thing that happens when a program starts is that the library units have to be elaborated. This has to be done before the main subprogram is called because it might depend upon the library units.

Elaboration of some library units may be trivial, but in the case of a package the initial values of top level objects must be evaluated and if the body has an initialization part then that must be executed.

The order of these elaborations is not precisely specified but it must be consistent with the dependencies between the units. In addition, the pragma Elaborate (or Elaborate_All) can be used to ensure that a body is elaborated before a unit that calls it; this may be necessary to prevent Program_Error. Consider the situation mentioned at the end of Section 11.1 thus

```
package P is
   function A return Integer;
end P;

package body P is
   function A return Integer is
   begin
      return 0;
```

```
      end A;
   end P;

   with P;
   package Q is
      I: Integer := P.A;
   end Q;
```

The three units can be compiled separately and the dependency requirements are that the body of P and the specification of Q must both be compiled after the specification of P is entered into the library. But there is no need for the body of P to be compiled before the specification of Q. However, when we come to elaborate the three units it is important that the body of P be elaborated before the specification of Q otherwise Program_Error will be raised.

The key point is that the dependency rules only partially constrain the order in which the units are elaborated and so we need some way to impose order at the library level much as the linear text imposes elaboration order within a unit. This can be done by various pragmas. Thus writing

```
   with P;
   pragma Elaborate(P);
   package Q is
      I: Integer := P.A;
   end Q;
```

ensures that the body of P is elaborated before the specification of Q. The pragma goes in the context clause and can refer to one or more of the library units mentioned earlier in the context clause.

The pragma Elaborate_All specifies that all library units needed by the named units are elaborated before the current unit (and is thus transitive). The pragma Elaborate_Body specifies that the body of the named unit must be elaborated immediately after its specification; it is placed in or after the specification.

We mentioned in Section 11.1 that a package at the library level could only have a body if it needed one in order to satisfy language rules. Thus a package such as Diurnal just containing types and objects could not have a body. If for some reason we wanted to provide one in order to have an initialization part, then we can use the pragma Elaborate_Body to force a body to be required, thus

```
   pragma Elaborate_Body(Diurnal);
```

If the dependencies and any elaboration pragmas are such that no consistent order of elaboration exists then the program is illegal; if there are several possible orders and the behaviour of the program depends on the particular order then it will not be portable.

There are two other pragmas relating to elaboration. The first is Preelaborate and appears inside the unit concerned. It essentially states that the unit can be elaborated before the program executes; generally this means that it is all static and has no code. It doesn't mean that it necessarily will be elaborated before the program runs but simply that it could be if the implementation were up to it; but certainly all such preelaborated units will be elaborated before other units which are not marked as preelaborated. This concept is important for certain real-time and distributed systems.

The other pragma is Pure and this indicates that the unit is not only preelaborated but also has no state. As noted in Chapter 4, this applies to the package Ada

```
package Ada is
   pragma Pure(Ada);
end Ada;
```

Pure units can only depend upon other pure units and preelaborated units can only depend upon other preelaborated units including pure units. Many other examples of pure and preelaborated units will be found in the predefined library discussed in Chapter 20.

CHECKLIST 12

A library unit cannot be compiled until other library units mentioned in its with clause are entered into the library.

A subunit cannot be compiled until its parent body is entered into the library.

A body cannot be compiled until the corresponding specification is entered into the library.

A child cannot be compiled until the specification of its parent is entered into the library.

A package specification and body form a single declarative region.

A library package can only have a body if it needs one to satisfy other language rules.

Do not attempt to redefine Standard.

Renaming is not text substitution.

Changes from Ada 83

The program library in Ada 83 always presumed the object model.

Ada 83 had rules about the order of declarations.

Library packages could have an optional body in Ada 83.

Child units did not exist in Ada 83.

A library unit could not be renamed as another library unit in Ada 83.

A subprogram body could not be provided by renaming in Ada 83.

13 Object Oriented Programming

13.1 Type extension	13.5 Views and redispatching
13.2 Polymorphism	13.6 Private types and extensions
13.3 Abstract types and subprograms	13.7 Controlled types
13.4 Operations and dispatching	13.8 Multiple implementations

We now come to a discussion of the basic features of Ada which support what is generally known as Object Oriented Programming or OOP. As mentioned earlier it is not entirely clear what constitutes OOP but ingredients include the ability to extend a type with new components and operations, to identify a specific type at run time and to select a particular operation depending on the specific type. A major goal is the reuse of existing reliable software without the need for recompilation and retesting.

This chapter concentrates on the fundamental ideas of type extension and polymorphism. Other topics relevant to OOP are type parameterization (using discriminants) and genericity; these are discussed in Chapters 16 and 17 respectively. Finally, Chapter 19 considers how these various aspects of OOP all fit together especially with regard to multiple inheritance.

The reader might find it helpful to reread Chapter 3 before considering this chapter in detail.

13.1 Type extension

In Section 11.3 we saw how it was possible to declare a new type as derived from an existing type. We saw how this enabled us to use strong typing to prevent inadvertent mixing of different uses of similar types although they were really the same type underneath. We also noted that primitive operations were inherited by the derived type and that they could be replaced and, moreover, that further primitive operations could be added if the derivation was in a package specification.

We now introduce a more flexible form of derivation where it is possible to add additional components to a record type as well as additional operations. This gives rise to a possible tree of types where each type contains the components of its parent plus other components as well. Since the types are clearly different, although with common properties, it is convenient to be able to deal with an object of any type in the tree and to determine the type of the object at run time. It is clear therefore that each object has to have some additional information indicating its type. This additional information is provided by a hidden component called the tag.

The word tag will be familiar to Pascal programmers where it is used to denote a component of a record distinguishing different variants of the type and so the term is very appropriate. (In Chapter 16 we will see that the tag is effectively a hidden discriminant.)

Accordingly, we allow record types to be extended on derivation provided they are marked as tagged. Private types implemented as records can also be tagged.

We saw a simple example of a hierarchy of tagged types plus associated primitive operations in Chapter 3 where we declared the types Object, Circle and so on. These could be declared in one or several packages as illustrated in the answer to Exercise 3.2(**1**).

```
package Objects is

   type Object is tagged
      record
         X_Coord: Float;
         Y_Coord: Float;
      end record;

   function Distance(O: Object) return Float;
   function Area(O: Object) return Float;

end Objects;

with Objects; use Objects;
package Shapes is

   type Point is new Object with null record;

   type Circle is new Object with
      record
         Radius: Float;
      end record;

   function Area(C: Circle) return Float;

   type Triangle is new Object with
      record
         A, B, C: Float;
      end record;
```

```
        function Area(T: Triangle) return Float;

    end Shapes;
```

where we have omitted the details of the bodies.

In this example the type Object is the root of a tree of types and Circle, Point and Triangle are derived from it. Note how the extra components are indicated and that in the case of the type Point where no extra components are added we have to indicate this explicitly by **with null record**; this makes it clear to the reader that it is a tagged type since every tagged type has **tagged** or **with** in its declaration.

The primitive operations of Object are Area and Distance and these are inherited by Circle, Point and Triangle. Although Distance is appropriate for all the types, the function Area is redefined for Circle and Triangle.

Type conversion is always allowed towards the root of the tree, so we can write

```
    O: Object := (1.0, 0.5);
    C: Circle := (0.0, 0.0, 34.7);
    T: Triangle;
    P: Point;
    ...
    O := Object(C);
```

and the conversion effectively ignores the third component. Conversion in the other direction is not technically allowed since additional components may be required. However, a value of a descendant type can be created by an extension aggregate thus

```
    C := (O with 41.2);
    T := (O with 3.0, 4.0, 5.0);
    P := (O with null record);
```

where the expression O is extended after **with** by the values of the extra components written just as in a normal aggregate. Note that even when there are no extra components we still have to use an extension aggregate and write the familiar **with null record**. We could have used named notation

```
    C := (O with Radius => 41.2);
    T := (O with A => 3.0, B => 4.0, C => 5.0);
```

The expression before **with** can be any expression of an ancestor type, it does not have to be the immediate parent. So moving into another dimension we might have

```
    type Cylinder is new Circle with
        record
            Height: Float;
        end record;
```

```
Cyl: Cylinder;
```

and then we could write any of

```
Cyl := (O with Radius => 41.2, Height => 231.6);
Cyl := (C with Height => 231.6);
Cyl := (Object(T) with 41.2, 231.6);
```

In the last case we first converted the triangle T to an object and then extended it to give a cylinder.

When we come to Section 13.6 we will find that it is sometimes not possible to give an expression of an ancestor type; as an alternative we can simply provide a subtype mark instead. In fact we can always do this and then the components corresponding to the ancestor type are initialized by default (if at all) as for any object of the type. So writing

```
C := (Object with Radius => 41.2);
```

will result in the circle having components as if we had written

```
Obj: Object;        -- no initial value
C: Circle := (Obj with Radius => 41.2);
```

and so the coordinates of C are not defined.

This is clearly not very sensible in this case but we might have chosen to declare the type Object so that it was by default at the origin thus

```
type Object is tagged
   record
      X_Coord: Float := 0.0;
      Y_Coord: Float := 0.0;
   end record;
```

and then the circle would also by default be at the origin.

At this point we pause to consider the main commonalities and differences between type derivation with tagged types which we have just been discussing and the type derivation with other types discussed in Section 11.3.

The common points are

- existing components are inherited,
- inheritance, overriding and addition of primitive operations are allowed in the same places, additional operations are only allowed if the derivation occurs in a package specification,
- derivation can occur in the same package specification as the parent and inherits all its primitive operations but no further primitive operations can then be added to the parent.

The differences are

- only a record type can be tagged and only a tagged type can have additional components,
- type conversion is only allowed towards the ancestor for a tagged type, both ways for untagged types,
- inherited operations of tagged types are not intrinsic and so the **Access** attribute can be applied to them,
- if an inherited operation is overridden then the conformance requirements are different; in the case of a tagged type it must have subtype conformance, whereas for an untagged type it only has to have type conformance,
- a derived type must be at the same accessibility level as the parent type in the case of a tagged type, whereas it can be anywhere in the scope of the parent for untagged types.

The reason for the last two differences will become apparent later. The last one means that we cannot do type extension in an inner block or subprogram. In practice it is not a restriction. Remember that packages do not enter into considerations of accessibility anyway as noted in Section 12.5.

We now consider a more extensive example which illustrates the use of tagged types to build a system as a hierarchy of types and packages. We will see how this allows the system to be extended without recompilation of its central part.

Our system concerns the processing of reservation requests for Ada Airlines. We can imagine that there are a number of aspects to this; the creation of a reservation request by interaction with an operator; the processing of the request by some central system; and then reporting back to the operator indicating success or failure. There are three categories of travel, Basic, Nice and Posh. The better categories have options which can be requested when making the reservation. Nice passengers are given a choice of seat (Aisle or Window) and a choice of meal which can be Green (vegetarian), White (fish or fowl) or Red (for the carnivores). Posh passengers are also given onward personal ground transport (or Personal Onward Surface Help).

We concentrate on the part of the system that processes the requests and first decide upon the hierarchy of types required. The package specification might be

```
package Reservation_System is

   type Position is (Aisle, Window);
   type Meal_Type is (Green, White, Red);

   type Reservation is tagged
      record
         Flight_Number: Integer;
         Date_Of_Travel: Date;
         Seat_Number: String(1 .. 3) := "   ";
      end record;

   procedure Make(R: in out Reservation);
   procedure Select_Seat(R: in out Reservation);
```

```
type Basic_Reservation is new Reservation with null record;

type Nice_Reservation is new Reservation with
   record
      Seat_Sort: Position;
      Food: Meal_Type;
   end record;

procedure Make(NR: in out Nice_Reservation);        -- overrides
procedure Order_Meal(NR: in Nice_Reservation);

type Posh_Reservation is new Nice_Reservation with
   record
      Destination: Address;
   end record;

procedure Make(PR: in out Posh_Reservation);        -- overrides
procedure Arrange_Limo(PR: in Posh_Reservation);

end Reservation_System;
```

We start with the root type Reservation which contains the components common to all reservations. It also has a procedure Make which performs all those actions common to making a reservation of any category. The type Basic_Reservation is simply a copy of Reservation (note **with null record**;) and could be dispensed with; Basic_Reservation inherits the procedure Make from Reservation. The type Nice_Reservation extends Reservation and provides its own procedure Make thus overriding the inherited version. The type Posh_Reservation further extends Nice_Reservation and similarly provides its own procedure Make. The procedures Select_Seat, Order_Meal and Arrange_Limo are called by the various procedures Make as required. Note that the main purpose of Select_Seat is to fill in the seat number with a string such as "56A"; hence the parameter has in out mode.

The package body might be as follows

```
package body Reservation_System is

   procedure Make(R: in out Reservation) is
   begin
      Select_Seat(R);
   end Make;

   procedure Make(NR: in out Nice_Reservation) is
   begin
      Make(Reservation(NR));            -- make as plain reservation
      Order_Meal(NR);
   end Make;

   procedure Make(PR: in out Posh_Reservation) is
   begin
      Make(Nice_Reservation(PR));       -- make as nice reservation
      Arrange_Limo(PR);
   end Make;
```

```
    procedure Select_Seat(R: in out Reservation) is separate;
    procedure Order_Meal(NR: in Nice_Reservation) is separate;
    procedure Arrange_Limo(PR: in Posh_Reservation) is separate;
end Reservation_System;
```

Each distinct body for **Make** contains just the code immediately relevant to the type and delegates other processing back to its parent using an explicit type conversion. This avoids repetition of code and simplifies maintenance. Note carefully that all type checking is static; the choice of **Make** is done with simple overload resolution based on the known type of the parameter. (The reader may be concerned that **Select_Seat** does not have enough information to work for nice and posh passengers; do not worry – all will be revealed in Section 13.5.)

If at a later date the growing Ada Airlines purchases some second hand Concordes then a new reservation type such as **Supersonic_Reservation** will be required. This can be added without recompiling (and perhaps more importantly, without retesting) the existing code.

```
    with Reservation_System;
    package Supersonic_Reservation_System is

        type Supersonic_Reservation is
                                new Reservation_System.Reservation with
            record
                Champagne: Vintage;
                -- other supersonic components
            end record;

        procedure Make(SR: in out Supersonic_Reservation);
        ...
    end Supersonic_Reservation_System;
```

We could have made this package a child of **Reservation_System**. This would have avoided the need for a with clause and emphasized that it was all really part of the same system. The entities in the parent package would also be immediately visible and use clauses or dotted names would be avoided. Furthermore, as we will see later, the fact that the child package can see the private part of its parent can be of value.

EXERCISE 13.1

1 Declare a point P with the same coordinates as a given circle C.

2 Declare an object R of the type **Reservation** and assign an appropriate flight number and date to it. Then declare an object NR of the type **Nice_Reservation** with common components the same as R and a window seat and vegetarian meal.

3 Rewrite the package **Supersonic_Reservation_System** as a child of **Reservation_System**.

13.2 Polymorphism

The facilities we have seen so far have allowed us to define a new type as an extension of an existing one. We have introduced the different categories of Reservation as distinct but related types. What we also need is a means to manipulate any kind of Reservation and to process it accordingly. We do this through the introduction of the notion of class wide types which provide dynamic polymorphism.

Each tagged type T has an associated type denoted by T'Class. This type comprises the union of all the types in the tree of derived types rooted at T. The values of T'Class are thus the values of T and all its derived types. Moreover a value of any type derived from T can be implicitly converted to the type T'Class.

So, for example, in the case of the type Reservation the tree of types can be pictured as in Figure 13.1. A value of any of the reservation types can be implicitly converted to Reservation'Class. Note carefully that Nice_Reservation'Class is not the same as Reservation'Class; the former consists just of Nice_Reservation and Posh_Reservation.

Each value of a class wide type has a tag which identifies its particular type from other types in the tree of types at run time. Thus the tag acts as a hidden component as mentioned earlier.

The type T'Class is treated as an indefinite type (like an unconstrained array type); this is because we cannot possibly know how much space could be required by any value of a class wide type because the type might be extended. As a consequence, although we can declare an object of a class wide type we must initialize it with a value of a specific type and it is then constrained by the tag of that type. So we could write

    NR: Nice_Reservation;
    ...
    RC: Reservation'Class := NR;

although this is not very helpful. Of more importance is the fact that a formal parameter can be of a class wide type and the actual parameter can then be of any specific type in the class. (Note again the analogy with arrays; a formal can be of an unconstrained array type and the actual can then be constrained.)

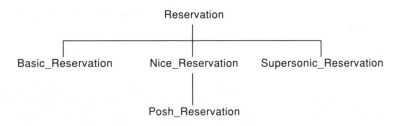

Figure 13.1 A tree of types.

We now continue our example by considering how we might queue a series of reservation requests and process them in sequence by some central routine. The whole essence of the problem is that such a routine cannot assume knowledge of the individual types because we need it to work (without recompilation) even if we extend the system by adding a new reservation type to it.

The central routine could thus take a class wide value as its parameter so we might have

```
procedure Process_Reservation(RC: in out Reservation'Class) is
   ...
begin
   ...
   Make(RC);     -- dispatch according to tag
   ...
end Process_Reservation;
```

In this case we do not know which procedure Make to call until run time because we do not know which specific type the reservation belongs to. However, RC is of a class wide type and so its value includes a tag indicating the specific type of the value. The choice of Make is then determined by the value of this tag; the parameter is then implicitly converted to the appropriate specific reservation type before being passed to the appropriate procedure Make.

This run-time choice of procedure is called dispatching and is key to the flexibility of class wide programming. It is important to realize that dispatching can be implemented very efficiently. A possible implementation is to make the tag point to a dispatch table each entry of which in turn points to the code of the body of a primitive operation. Each value of a tagged type will have the tag at a standard place such as at the beginning of the value. This model is illustrated in Figure 13.2 which shows how the various operations are inherited, replaced or added. (For simplicity, we have omitted the predefined primitive operations such as equality.)

The reason that dispatching is efficient is that there is never any need to check anything at run time. The dispatch table is arranged so that the displacements are the same for all types in the class. Also we know that every operation in the class is present because operations cannot be removed on derivation; only replaced or added.

We can now see the importance of the distinction between Reservation'Class and Nice_Reservation'Class. We can only dispatch to Order_Meal from the latter class wide type since only the latter has Order_Meal as a primitive operation of every type in the class.

The reasons for the restrictions on tagged type derivation mentioned in the previous section can now be explained. An overridden operation has to have subtype conformance so that the call always works dynamically. And extension has to be at the same accessibility level so that all the dispatching operations are at the same level; this avoids potential problems with nonlocal variables.

We continue by considering how the various requests might be held on a heterogeneous list awaiting processing. We can declare an access type

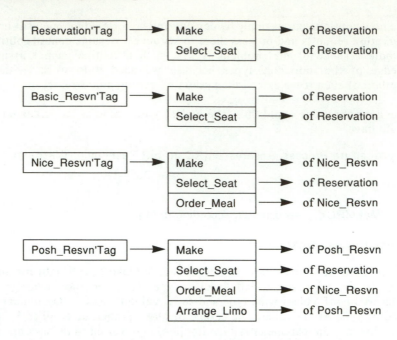

Figure 13.2 Tags and dispatch tables.

referring to a class wide type. So we can write

       type Reservation_Ptr **is access all** Reservation'Class;

in which case an access variable of this type could designate any value of the class wide type. We cannot change the specific type of the object referred to at any time into another type but we can from time to time refer to objects of different specific types. (This is much as the access variable R of Section 10.3 can refer to matrices of different sizes since the type Matrix is unconstrained; we cannot change the size of a particular matrix but R can refer to different sized matrices at different times.) The flexibility of access types is a key factor in class wide programming.

A heterogeneous list can be made in the obvious way using

```
type Cell;
type Cell_Ptr is access Cell;

type Cell is
  record
     Element: Reservation_Ptr;
     Next: Cell_Ptr;
  end record;
```

and the central routine can then manipulate the reservations using an access value as parameter

```
procedure Process_Reservation (RP: in Reservation_Ptr) is
   ...
begin
   ...
   Make(RP.all);              -- dispatch to appropriate Make
   ...
end Process_Reservation;
...
List: Cell_Ptr;              -- list of reservations
...
while List /= null loop      -- process the list
   Process_Reservation(List.Element);
   List := List.Next;
end loop;
```

In this case, the value of the object referred to by RP is of a class wide type and so includes a tag indicating the specific type. The parameter RP.**all** is thus dereferenced, the value of the tag gives the choice of Make and the parameter is then implicitly converted before being passed to the chosen procedure Make as before.

It is fundamental in class wide programming to manipulate objects via references; this is largely because the objects may be of different sizes. As a consequence references to the objects will almost inevitably be on a list of some kind and will move from list to list as they are processed within the system. (The objects themselves typically will not move and as mentioned in Section 10.4 can therefore be limited.) If, as is likely, each object is only on one list at a time, then we can adopt a rather neater approach to chaining the objects together.

The general idea is that we first declare some root type which contains the pointer to the next item in the list and then extend the types to be placed on the list from the root type. Consider

```
type Element;
type Element_Ptr is access all Element'Class;

type Element is tagged
   record
      Next: Element_Ptr;
   end record;
```

Objects of any type in the class Element'Class can be linked together through the one common element. We can now modify the reservation system so that the type Reservation is

```
type Reservation is new Element with
   record
      Flight_Number: Integer;
      Date_Of_Travel: Date;
      Seat_Number: String(1 .. 3) := "   ";
   end record;
```

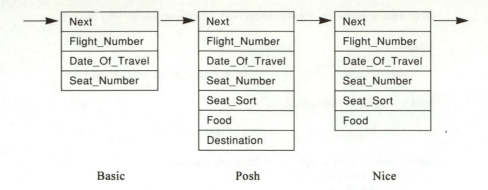

Figure 13.3 A heterogeneous list.

with the rest of the system as before. The various reservations can now be joined together to form a list as illustrated in Figure 13.3.

The manipulation of such lists or queues is very common in object oriented programming and it is convenient to have a package providing appropriate standard operations. So, somewhat like Exercise 11.5(**3**), we might have

```
package Queues is
   Queue_Error: exception;
   type Queue is limited private;
   type Element is tagged private;
   type Element_Ptr is access all Element'Class;
   procedure Join(Q: access Queue; E: in Element_Ptr);
   function Remove(Q: access Queue) return Element_Ptr;
   function Length(Q: Queue) return Integer;
private
   type Element is tagged
     record
        Next: Element_Ptr;
     end record;
   type Queue is limited
     record
        Count: Integer := 0;
        First, Last: Element_Ptr;
     end record;
end Queues;
```

This package illustrates many points. We have hidden away the inner workings from the user by making both the type Queue and the type Element private. The type Queue is also limited since assignment must not be allowed (it would mess up the internal pointers); we have also made the full type explicitly limited just to ensure that the implementation of the body does not inadvertently attempt to assign a Queue either. (This is a useful safeguard because remember that we might later write a child package and that could see

the private part also.) The type Element is given as tagged private. This means
that the full type must also be tagged and permits the user to extend from the
type without knowing its details.

The subprograms Join and Remove take an access parameter rather than an
in out parameter. One advantage is that Remove can then be a function which
is perhaps more convenient to use. A possible disadvantage is that we have to
specifically create a reference to the queue and this means marking it as aliased
or creating the queue with an allocator.

Using this package we can now declare the root type Reservation and so on

```
with Queues;
package Reservation_System is
   ...
   type Reservation is new Queues.Element with
      record
         ...
      end record;
   ...
end Reservation_System;
```

and then create and place reservations on a queue by statements such as

```
type Queue_Ptr is access Queue;
The_Queue: Queue_Ptr := new Queue;
...
New_Resvn: Reservation_Ptr := new Nice_Reservation;
...
Join(The_Queue, New_Resvn);
...
```

Removing a reservation from the queue can later be done by

```
Next_Resvn: Reservation_Ptr;
...
Next_Resvn := Reservation_Ptr(Remove(The_Queue));
Process_Reservation(Next_Resvn);
```

Note very carefully that we have to explicitly convert the result of Remove to
the type Reservation_Ptr. This is because Remove returns a result of the type
Element_Ptr. Nothing would have prevented us from putting any type derived
from Element on the queue and so there is no guarantee that it is indeed a
reservation. The conversion performs a check that the type referred to is indeed
a member of Reservation'Class and Constraint_Error is raised if the check fails.

In Section 19.3 we will see how we can ensure that only reservations are
placed on such a queue.

Having introduced class wide types and access types to tagged types this
seems a good moment to summarize the rules concerning type conversions and
tagged types. The general principle is that we can only convert towards the root
and run-time checks may be needed to ensure this if the source is a class wide
type; if the check fails then Constraint_Error is raised. In detail

- Conversion between two specific types is only permitted if towards the root.
- Conversion between a specific type and a class wide type of any ancestor type is implicitly allowed (no conversion need be stated). Conversion to a class wide type which is not of an ancestor is of course not allowed.
- Conversion between a class wide type and a specific type is allowed provided the type of the actual value is a descendant of the specific type. A dynamic check is required.
- Conversion between two class wide types is allowed provided the actual value is in the target class. A dynamic check is required if the source class is not a subclass of the target class.

Conversion between access types is allowed provided the designated types can be converted in the same direction; this may cause a check at run time. Of course all that happens when we convert between access types is that we get a different view of the same object and so the new view must be an allowed interpretation. So we can convert between the types Element_Ptr and Reservation_Ptr as in the example above and a check is required to ensure that the designated object does indeed have a specific type within the class rooted at Reservation. We will come back to the topic of views and conversions in more detail in Section 13.5.

We conclude this section by noting that tagged type parameters are always passed by reference and considered aliased. The similarities and differences between in out and access parameters were discussed in Section 10.6. Note that dispatching occurs with all modes of formal parameters including access parameters but does not occur with a parameter of a named access type. The use of access parameters for dispatching is important as we will see later when we consider the use of access discriminants in Chapter 19.

EXERCISE 13.2

1   Declare a procedure that will print the area of any geometrical object of a type derived from the type Object.

2   In a traditional world women do not have beards and men do not bear children. However all persons have a date of birth. Declare a type Person with the common component Birth and then derived types Man and Woman that have additional components as appropriate indicating whether they have a beard or not and how many children they have borne respectively.

3   Declare procedures Print_Details for Person, Man and Woman which output information regarding the current values of their components. Then declare a procedure Analyse_Person which takes a parameter of the class wide type Person'Class and calls the appropriate procedure Print_Details.

4   Write the body of the package Queues.

13.3   Abstract types and subprograms

It is sometimes convenient to declare a type solely to act as the foundation upon which other types can be built by derivation and not in order to declare objects of the type itself. We can do this by marking a tagged type as abstract; objects of the type may then not be declared. An abstract type can have abstract primitive subprograms; these cannot be called directly and have no body and act as sort of placeholders for operations to be added later.

Upon derivation from an abstract type we can provide actual subprograms for all the abstract subprograms (if any) of the parent type (and it is in this sense that they are placeholders). If all the abstract subprograms are replaced by concrete subprograms then the derived type need not be declared as abstract and we can then declare objects of the type in the usual way. (The various rules ensure that dispatching always works.)

We can now reformulate our example of processing reservations so that the root type Reservation is just an abstract type and then build the specific types upon it. This enables us to program and compile all the infrastructure routines, such as Process_Reservation in the previous section, that deal with reservations in general without any concern at all for the individual reservation types and indeed before deciding what they should contain.

The baseline package can then simply become

```
package Reservation_System is
   type Reservation is abstract tagged null record;
   type Reservation_Ptr is access all Reservation'Class;
   procedure Make(R: in out Reservation) is abstract;
end Reservation_System;
```

in which we have declared the type Reservation as a tagged null record with just the procedure Make as an abstract subprogram; remember that it does not have a body and hence the package also has no body. (Note also that we have used the abbreviated form for a null record mentioned in Section 8.7.)

We can now develop our reservation infrastructure and then later add the normal reservation system containing the three types of reservations. We introduce a child package as follows

```
package Reservation_System.Subsonic is

   type Position is (Aisle, Window);
   type Meal_Type is (Green, White, Red);

   type Basic_Reservation is new Reservation with
      record
         Flight_Number: Integer;
         Date_Of_Travel: Date;
         Seat_Number: String(1 .. 3) := "   ";
      end record;

   -- now provide actual subprogram for abstract Make
   procedure Make(BR: in out Basic_Reservation);
```

```
        procedure Select_Seat(BR: in out Basic_Reservation);

        type Nice_Reservation is new Basic_Reservation with
          record
            Seat_Sort: Position;
            Food: Meal_Type;
          end record;

        procedure Make(NR: in out Nice_Reservation);
        procedure Order_Meal(NR: in Nice_Reservation);

        type Posh_Reservation is new Nice_Reservation with
          record
            Destination: Address;
          end record;

        procedure Make(PR: in out Posh_Reservation);
        procedure Arrange_Limo(PR: in Posh_Reservation);

    end Reservation_System.Subsonic;
```

In this revised formulation we must provide a procedure Make for the concrete type Basic_Reservation to meet the promise of the abstract type Reservation. The procedure Select_Seat now takes a parameter of type Basic_Reservation and the type Nice_Reservation is more naturally derived from Basic_Reservation.

Note carefully that we did not make Select_Seat an abstract subprogram in the package Reservation_System. There was no need; it is only Make that is required by the general infrastructure such as the procedure Process_ Reservation and to add anything else would weaken the abstraction and clutter the base level.

We also have to make corresponding changes to the package body. This is left as an exercise for the reader.

When we now add our Supersonic_Reservation we can choose to derive this from the baseline Reservation as before or perhaps from some other point in the tree picking up the existing facilities of one of the other levels.

As a further example of the use of an abstract type consider the types Person, Man and Woman of Exercise 13.2(**2**). We really do not want to be able to declare objects of the type Person because they are incomplete; we want all real persons to be either of the type Man or Woman and the type Person is merely a convenience for the common properties. We can prevent the declaration of objects of the type Person by making it abstract

```
    type Person is abstract tagged
      record
        Birth: Date;
      end record;
```

and then the types Man and Woman can be derived as before.

Despite the type Person being abstract there is no reason why we should not continue to declare the nonabstract procedure Print_Details of Exercise 13.2(**3**)

```
procedure Print_Details(P : in Person) is
begin
   Print_Date(P.Birth);
end Print_Details;
```

Although we will never dispatch to this procedure because there can never be an object of the type Person itself, nevertheless it can be used to print the common information of the types derived from Person. We will return to this topic in Section 13.5.

For completeness, we mention a few further minor points about abstract types. When we derive from an abstract type we do not have to provide a concrete subprogram for every abstract one. However, if we do not, then the newly derived type will also be abstract and must be so declared. On the other hand when we derive from a nonabstract type we can provide abstract operations (either additional ones or to replace inherited ones) and as a consequence the derived type must be declared as abstract.

Although we can declare a nonabstract subprogram with parameters of an abstract type such as Print_Details above, a function returning an abstract type must always be abstract. A related situation occurs in the case of a function which returns a nonabstract type when the type is extended. Clearly the function cannot return a value of the extended type (since it does not know how to provide values for the new components) and so in order for the extended type to use that function it must be overridden with a new definition providing an appropriate result. If we do not provide such a function then it becomes abstract for the derived type and so the type itself must be declared as abstract. This applies even if the extension is in fact null.

EXERCISE 13.3

1   Reformulate the type Object as an abstract type containing no components and where the function Area is abstract but Distance is not abstract. Then declare types Point and Circle etc. from the type Object.

2   Declare a function Further that takes two parameters of type Object and returns the one further from the origin by comparing their distances. Can this be inherited and thus applied to objects of the type Point and Circle?

3   Declare a function Further that takes two parameters of type Object'Class and returns the further one by comparing their areas.

4   Repeat the previous two exercises for a function Bigger that bases the comparison on the areas of the objects.

5   Write the body of the package Reservation_System.Subsonic.

13.4 Operations and dispatching

In this section we consider in a little more detail some of the fundamental properties of tagged types and their operations. We have mentioned the existence of the tag of an object as being effectively a hidden component and we have seen how the value of the tag of a class wide object is used for dispatching. An object thus has the property of being self-identifying; it carries an indication of the identity of its type with it.

In the last section we considered the formulation of the type Person as

```
type Person is abstract tagged
   record
      Birth: Date;
   end record;

type Man is new Person with
   record
      Bearded: Boolean;
   end record;

type Woman is new Person with
   record
      Children: Integer;
   end record;
```

Note that, perhaps worryingly, there is no explicit component indicating the sex of a person; it might appear as if there was no way to find out one's sex! But luckily this information is not lost since it is implicit in the tag. The tag can be implicitly tested by membership tests such as

```
if P in Woman then
   -- special processing for Women
end if;
```

where P is of the class wide type Person'Class.

Indeed, it is also possible to test the tag explicitly using the attribute Tag which can be applied to a value of a class wide type and to a tagged type itself. So we could alternatively have written

```
if P'Tag = Woman'Tag then
```

The value of the attribute Tag is of the private (but nonlimited) type Tag declared in the package Ada.Tags. We can declare variables of the type Tag in the usual way. It is important to note that the attribute Tag cannot be applied to a value of a specific type. The reason will be explained later.

We could also write

```
if P in Woman'Class then ...
```

and this would then cover any types derived from Woman as well. Note that there is no corresponding test involving the explicit use of tags because we cannot talk about possible future extensions in terms of tags. It is thus generally better to use membership tests wherever possible in order to ensure that a program is extensible.

It is important to understand exactly when dispatching is used as opposed to the static resolution of binding familiar with calls with untagged parameters. The basic principle is that dispatching is only used when a controlling operand is of a class wide type. Thus the call

```
Make(RC);      -- RC of type Reservation'Class
```

in the procedure Process_Reservation in Section 13.2 is a dispatching call. The value of the tag of RC is used to determine which procedure Make to call and this is determined at run time.

On the other hand a call such as

```
Make(Reservation(NR));      -- NR of type Nice_Reservation
```

in the package body of Reservation_System in Section 13.1 is not a dispatching call because the type of the operand is the specific type Reservation as a result of the explicit type conversion.

It is also possible to dispatch on the result of a function when the context of the call determines the specific type. In order to illustrate this we need to remember that an operation may have several controlling operands. Consider for example

```
package Example is
   type T is tagged ... ;
   procedure P(X: T; Y: T);
   function F return T;
   function G(Z: T) return T;
   procedure Q(U: T; V: T := F);
   type TT is new T with ... ;      -- inherits the operations
   ...
end Example;
```

so that P, Q, F and G are dispatching operations of T. Actual parameters corresponding to U, V, X, Y and Z are controlling operands and the results of calls of F and G are controlling results. Note that the parameter V of Q has a default initial expression consisting of a call of F.

It is an important principle that all controlling operands and results of a call must be of the same type. If they are statically determined then, of course, this is checked at compile time. If they are dynamically determined (for example, variables of a class wide type) then again the actual values must all be of the same specific type and of course this check has to be made at run time (the tags are compared) and Constraint_Error is raised if the check fails. In order to avoid confusion a mixed situation whereby some operands are static and some are dynamic is not allowed.

Now let us suppose that we have variables whose types are as follows

```
A, B: T;
AA, BB: TT;
C: T'Class := ... ;        -- must be initialized
D: T'Class := ... ;        -- because a class wide type
```

then we can write calls such as

```
P(A, B);           -- non-dispatching, type T
P(AA, BB);         -- non-dispatching, type TT
P(C, D);           -- dispatching
```

and in the last case a check is made before the call that C'Tag equals D'Tag. On the other hand the following are illegal for the reasons stated

```
P(A, BB);          -- illegal - mixed specific types
P(A, C);           -- illegal - mixed static and dynamic
```

and both these situations are detected at compile time.

We can now look at the use of the functions F and G which have controlling results. Consider

```
P(A, F);           -- non-dispatching, type T
P(C, F);           -- dispatching
```

In the first case, the controlling operand A is static and determines that the call of F is also static; the call of F is thus chosen at compile time to be the F with result of type T. In the second case the controlling operand C is dynamic and determines the type at run time; in this case the call of F dispatches to the particular F with the same type as C; there is no run-time check because only one controlling operand is used to determine the type. The call of F is thus like a chameleon and adapts to the circumstances; we say that it is tag indeterminate.

The situation can be nested, for example

```
P(C, G(D));        -- dispatching
```

in which case the tags of C and D are checked to ensure that they are the same; Constraint_Error is raised if they are not. A more elaborate expression such as G(F) is also indeterminate so we can have

```
P(A, G(F));        -- non-dispatching
P(C, G(F));        -- dispatching
```

In the second case the call of G is then determined by the specific type of C and this in turn determines the call of F.

We can also use a call of a function such as F to determine a default value. Thus we can have

```
Q(A);              -- non-dispatching
Q(C);              -- dispatching
```

and in the first case the default call of F is statically determined to be that of type T whereas in the second case the call of F is dynamically determined by the specific type of the value of C.

It is interesting to note that a default expression for a controlling operand has to be tag indeterminate and so has to be a call of a function such as F or an expression such as G(F). The reason is that we need to be able to use the default expression in both dispatching and non-dispatching contexts.

Another use for an indeterminate expression is as the initial value for a class wide object or as a class wide actual parameter. For example

```
C: T'Class := F;      -- non-dispatching
```

In this case the type of F is *statically* determined to be T.

Finally note that

```
P(F, F);       -- illegal
```

is ambiguous and thus illegal. Because of inheritance we do not know whether we are dealing with the P and F of the type T or TT. In other words the overload resolution fails. Dispatching is not involved because there are no class wide operands.

The above discussion may have seemed a bit tedious but it is important to grasp the essential ideas which are really quite simple and are aimed to make things as explicit as possible so that surprises are minimized or at least show up at compile time.

Another rule designed to avoid confusion is that it is not possible for a subprogram to have controlling operands or results of different tagged types. Although we can of course declare two tagged types in the same package we cannot in that package declare a subprogram that has operands or result of both types. We can naturally do this outside the package but then in that case the subprogram is not inherited and does not dispatch anyway.

Equality is a primitive operation and so dispatches in the general case. However, the rules are slightly different. If we compare two class wide values and they have different tags then the result False is returned rather than raising Constraint_Error which would occur with other operations with two controlling operands. On the other hand if we assign a class wide value to an object of a class wide type then Constraint_Error will be raised if the tags are not the same. Remember that a class wide object is constrained by its initial value. There is a strong analogy with operations on arrays. We can only assign one array to another if the lengths are the same but equality never raises Constraint_Error but simply returns False if the lengths are different. But operations such as **and** and **or** on one-dimensional arrays raise Constraint_Error if the lengths are different.

Equality is also different with regard to inheritance; this is because it is normally predefined and so is always expected to be available and have sensible properties. On the other hand we might wish to redefine equality; directly inheriting a redefined version could bring surprises. Suppose we decided that two values of the type Object of Section 13.1 are to be considered equal if they are located within some small distance, delta, of the same point. We might declare

```
function "=" (A, B: Object) return Boolean is
begin
  return (A.X_Coord – B.X_Coord)**2
        + (A.Y_Coord – B.Y_Coord)**2 < Delta**2;
end "=";
```

The normal rules for inheritance would mean that this would be inherited unchanged by Point and Circle. This would be very surprising for the type Circle since it would ignore the Radius component completely. On the other hand, without redefinition of "=" for the type Object, the predefined equality for Circle would have applied predefined equality to all its components including the Radius. Because this drastic change of behaviour would be so surprising, what actually happens is that the equality for Object is not inherited for Circle but simply incorporated into the predefined equality for Circle. So two circles would be equal if their centres were within delta and their radii exactly equal.

The full rule for predefined equality of a type extension is that the primitive operation (possibly redefined) is used for the parent part and for any tagged components in the extension whereas predefined equality is always used for non-tagged components in the extension (much as predefined equality is always used for slice comparison).

EXERCISE 13.4

1   Define "=" for the type Circle so that two circles are equal if they are within delta of the same location and their radii are within delta of each other. Assume that "=" for Object has been appropriately redefined.

2   Now define "=" for the type Circle so that they have to be at the same location but their radii are within delta of each other.

3   Consider the effect of the following

```
procedure Swap(X, Y: in out Object) is
  T: Object := X;
begin
  X := Y;  Y := T;
end Swap;
```

when inherited by a Circle. Assume Object is not abstract. Make it work properly.

13.5   Views and redispatching

We now consider the rules for type conversion once more. Recall that the basic
rule is that type conversion is only allowed towards the root of a tree of tagged
types and so, as we have seen, we can convert a Nice_Reservation into a
Reservation as in the call

      Make(Reservation(NR));

On the other hand we cannot convert a specific type away from the root; we
have to use an extension aggregate even if there are no extra components.
      We can however convert a value of a class wide type to a specific type as
in

      NR := Nice_Reservation(RC);

where RC is of the type Reservation'Class. In such a case there is a run-time
check that the current value of the class wide parameter RC is of a specific type
for which the conversion is possible. Hence it must be of the type
Nice_Reservation or derived from it so that the conversion is not away from the
root of the tree. In other words we check that the value of RC is actually in
Nice_Reservation'Class. Constraint_Error is raised if the check fails.
      Some conversions are what is known as view conversions. This means that
the underlying object is not changed but we merely get a different view of it.
(Much as the private view and full view of a type are just different views; the
type is still the same.) We met an example of a view conversion in Section 9.3
when we called the procedure Increment with the view conversion Integer(R)
as parameter.
      Most conversions of tagged types are view conversions. For example the
conversion in

      Make(Reservation(NR));

is a view conversion. The value passed to the call of Make (with parameter of
type Reservation) is in fact the same value as held in NR (tagged types are
always passed by reference) but we can no longer see the components relating
to the type Nice_Reservation. And in fact the tag still relates to the underlying
value and this might even be the tag for Posh_Reservation because it could
have been view converted all the way down the tree.
      Moreover, if we did an assignment as in

      NR := Nice_Reservation(PR);

then the tag of NR is of course not changed. All that happens is that the
components appropriate to the type of NR are copied from the object PR. We
can also have a view conversion as the destination of an assignment

      Nice_Reservation(PR) := NR;

and the components copied are then just those appropriate to the type of the
view. Other components, and in particular the tag, are not changed.

It is indeed an important principle that the tag of an object (both specific and class wide) is never changed. In particular, the fact that a view conversion does not change the tag is very important for what is called redispatching.

It often happens that after one dispatching operation we apply a further common (and inherited) operation and so need to dispatch once more to an operation of the original type. If the original tag is lost then this is not possible. An example of the seeds of this difficulty already lies in our reservation system for Ada Airlines.

Consider again

```
procedure Make(NR: in out Nice_Reservation) is
begin
   Make(Reservation(NR));      -- make as plain reservation
   Order_Meal(NR);
end Make;
```

in which there is a call of the procedure Order_Meal. This call is not a dispatching call because the parameter is of a specific type and indeed there is only one procedure Order_Meal. Inside the body of Order_Meal we would expect to deal just with an order from a nice reservation and would not anticipate having to take account of the fact that the order might have originated from a posh passenger. (Although one would hope that posh meals are indeed better than nice meals.)

Actually we *could* write

```
procedure Order_Meal(NR: Nice_Reservation) is
   NRC: Nice_Reservation'Class := NR;
begin
   if NRC in Posh_Reservation then
      -- order a posh meal
   else
      -- order a nice meal
   end if;
end Order_Meal;
```

where we have regained the original type by converting to the class wide type Nice_Reservation'Class. We could actually avoid the burden of the assignment by writing

```
NRC: Nice_Reservation'Class renames Nice_Reservation'Class(NR);
```

although this is rather a mouthful.

Note also that we could alternatively have written the test as

```
if NRC'Tag = Posh_Reservation'Tag then
```

but remember that we cannot apply the attribute Tag to an object of a specific type. So we could not have avoided the introduction of the class wide variable by writing

```
if NR'Tag = Posh_Reservation'Tag then
```

This is disallowed because it would be very confusing to allow NR'Tag because we would naturally expect this always to be Nice_Reservation'Tag and to find that it had some other value would be strange.

It is of course against the spirit of the game to mess about inside Order_Meal to see if it was ordered by a posh passenger. The whole idea of programming by extension is that one should be able to write the body for Order_Meal without considering how the type system might be extended later. Indeed the type Posh_Reservation (like Supersonic_Reservation) might be in a later package in which case we could not here refer to the type Posh_Reservation at all.

The proper approach is to use redispatching. We write a distinct procedure

```
    procedure Order_Meal(PR: in Posh_Reservation);
```

for posh passengers and redispatch in the body of Make as follows

```
    procedure Make(NR: in out Nice_Reservation) is
    begin
        Make(Reservation(NR));        -- make as plain reservation
        Order_Meal(Nice_Reservation'Class(NR));        -- redispatch
    end Make;
```

Redispatching occurs because we have converted the parameter to the class wide type Nice_Reservation'Class; remember that dispatching occurs if and only if the actual parameter is class wide and the formal parameter is of a specific type. So it works properly and our posh passenger will now get a posh meal instead of just a nice one.

We will now leave our reservation system noting that there is an analogous possible difficulty with Select_Seat; it seems likely that the requests of nice and posh passengers for an aisle or window seat might be overlooked. We leave the consideration of this as an exercise.

The fact that view conversion does not change the tag explains why we can safely and usefully declare a nonabstract procedure for an abstract type such as the procedure Print_Details for the type Person. We can never declare an object of the type Person and so a dispatching call of this procedure is not possible. A static call is however possible with a view conversion as in

```
    procedure Print_Details(W: in Woman) is
    begin
        Print_Details(Person(W));        -- view conversion
        Print_Integer(W.Children);
    end;
```

but since the tag never changes no harm can arise.

It is hoped that the discussion in this and the previous section has not seemed overly complex and detailed. Object oriented programming may be very flexible but it has its pitfalls and it is important that the reader be aware of these. Ada strives for clarity. The basic rule is that dispatching is only used if the actual parameter is of a class wide type and this is clear at the point of the call. This simple rule coupled with the fact that the original tag is never lost should cause fewer surprises than the more obscure rules of some languages.

We conclude this section with a brief summary of the main points regarding tagged types.

- Record (and private) types can be tagged. Values of tagged types carry a tag with them. The tag indicates the specific type. A tagged type can be extended on derivation with additional components. The tag of an object can never be changed.

- The primitive operations of a type are those implicitly declared, plus, in the case of a type declared in a package specification, all subprograms with a parameter or result of that type also declared in the package specification.

- Primitive operations are inherited on derivation and can be overridden. If the derivation occurs in a package specification then further primitive operations can be added.

- Types and subprograms can be declared as abstract. An abstract subprogram does not have a body but one can be provided on derivation. Only an abstract tagged type can have abstract primitive subprograms.

- T'Class denotes the class wide type rooted at T. It is an indefinite type. An appropriate access type can designate any value of T'Class.

- Type conversion must always be towards the root. Implicit conversion from a specific type to an ancestor class wide type is allowed.

- Parameters of tagged types are always passed by reference. They are also considered aliased so that the Access attribute can be applied.

- Calling a primitive operation with an actual parameter of a class wide type results in dispatching: that is the run-time selection of the operation according to the tag.

The above summary and our discussion in general has used the model that the tag is part of the value of an object. Strictly speaking this is an implementation detail. It is not necessary for the compiler to attach the tag to an object of a specific type in all circumstances; the tag value can be made up on the spot when a class wide value is created. But it is a very convenient and efficient model for the purpose of both discussion and implementation.

EXERCISE 13.5

1   In the revised procedure Make for Nice_Reservation why could we not write

    Order_Meal(Reservation'Class(NR));   -- redispatch

2   Add a procedure Select_Seat appropriate for nice passengers (and better) and rewrite the procedure Make for the type Reservation to dispatch on Select_Seat.

13.6   Private types and extensions

We now come to a detailed consideration of the interaction between type extension, private types and child packages.

In Section 13.2 we saw that the type Element in the package Queue was declared as

> **type** Element **is tagged private**;

The full type then also has to be tagged. The partial view could in fact be declared as abstract thus

> **type** Element **is abstract tagged private**;

and this would be an advantage in this case since there is no point in the user being able to declare objects of the type Element.

The rules regarding matching of full and partial views are as expected from the general principle that the full view must deliver the properties promised by the partial view. If the partial (external) view is tagged then the full view must also be tagged but the reverse is not the case. The partial view can be untagged and the full view can be tagged. Of course the external client cannot use any of the properties of type extension in such a situation. A similar pattern applies to the property of being abstract. If the partial view is abstract then the full view need not be but clearly the reverse is not the case; if the partial view is not abstract then the full view cannot be abstract either.

Abstract and private types pose small problems with aggregates. We can only give a normal aggregate if all the components are visible. However, we can always use an extension aggregate if the ancestor part is private

> Some_Element: Element;
> ...
> (Some_Element **with** ...)

or, if the type is abstract so that the object Some_Element cannot be declared, then we can simply use the subtype name as explained in Section 13.1 thus

> (Element **with** ...)

and any components corresponding to the type Element will be default initialized.

The type Element illustrates that we can extend from a private tagged type with additional components visible to the user even though the original components are hidden from the user. The reverse is also possible; we can extend an existing type with additional components and keep these additional components hidden from the external user. We could declare a private type Shape and might wish to make visible the fact that the type Shape is derived from Object and yet keep the additional components hidden. In this case we would write

```
package Hidden_Shape is
   type Shape is new Object with private;      -- client view
   ...
private
   type Shape is new Object with              -- server view
      record
         -- the private components
      end record;
   function Area(S: Shape) return Float;
end Hidden_Shape;
```

In this case it is not necessary for the full declaration of **Shape** to be derived directly from the type **Object**. There might be a chain of intermediate derived types (it could be derived from Circle); all that matters is that **Shape** is ultimately derived from **Object**. If there are no extra components then we write **with null record**; as expected.

Of course the type **Shape** could never be an existing type. Writing

```
type Shape is new Circle with null record;
```

in the private part does not make the type **Shape** the same as Circle but merely derived from it.

We can declare and override primitive operations (such as **Area**) in the private part or in the visible part. New and overridden operations in the visible part behave as expected; they are visible to both client and server. But operations in the private part bring interesting possibilities.

A new operation in the private part will have a new slot in the dispatch table even though it is not visible for all views of the type. It is an important principle that there is only one dispatch table for a type and it may be that some operations are not visible for some views.

A minor point is that an abstract type is not allowed to have private abstract operations because it would not be possible to override them and so it would be impossible to extend the type. This would be a serious violation of the abstraction because the poor external user should be totally unaware of the private operation. A similar restriction is that a function with a controlling result cannot be a private operation because again it could not be overridden.

The final case is where we override an inherited operation such as **Area** for **Shape** in the private part. Despite not being directly visible, nevertheless the overridden operation will be used whether called directly or indirectly through dispatching. It is an important principle that the same operation is called both directly and indirectly for the same tag – this allows a fragment to be tested with static binding and then we know we will still get the same effect if the final program does dispatching.

One curiosity is that a renaming in the package before the overriding always refers to the old operation whether the overriding is private or not

```
function Old_Area(S: Shape) return Float renames Area;
   ...
function Area(S: Shape) return Float;
```

Of course a renaming after the overriding will refer to the new operation. All renamings in the package specification are genuine primitive operations and have their own slots in the dispatch table which are initialized with the operation that is current at the point of the renaming. These new names thus denote primitive operations in their own right and can themselves be overridden on later inheritance. This might seem peculiar because the principle of renaming is that no new entity is ever created. But of course this is still true, the new slots just give further ways of referring to existing entities.

A good example of the use of private extensions is provided by reconsidering the reservation system. For the purposes of the general processing, full visibility of the individual types is not necessary. Consider

```
package Reservation_System is
  type Reservation is abstract tagged private;
  procedure Make(R: in out Reservation);
  type Basic_Reservation is new Reservation with private;
  type Nice_Reservation is new Reservation with private;
  type Posh_Reservation is new Reservation with private;
private
  type Reservation is tagged
    record
      Flight_Number: Integer;
      Date_Of_Travel: Date;
      Seat_Number: String(1 .. 3) := "   ";
    end record;

  procedure Select_Seat(R: in out Reservation);

  type Basic_Reservation is new Reservation with null record;

  type Position is (Aisle, Window);
  type Meal_Type is (Green, White, Red);

  type Nice_Reservation is new Reservation with
    record
      Seat_Sort: Position;
      Food: Meal_Type;
    end record;

  procedure Make(NR: in out Nice_Reservation);        -- overrides
  procedure Select_Seat(R: in out Nice_Reservation);  -- ditto
  procedure Order_Meal(NR: in Nice_Reservation);      -- new

  type Posh_Reservation is new Nice_Reservation with
    record
      Destination: Address;
    end record;

  procedure Make(PR: in out Posh_Reservation);        -- overrides
  procedure Order_Meal(NR: in Posh_Reservation);      -- ditto
  procedure Arrange_Limo(PR: in Posh_Reservation);    -- new
end Reservation_System;
```

Externally all that is visible is that there are the various types and there is a procedure **Make**. The relationships between the types is not visible since they are just shown as deriving from **Reservation**; this is a good illustration of the fact that the full declaration of a private type need not be directly derived from the ancestor type given in the private extension.

Note also that **Select_Seat** and **Order_Meal** are private primitive operations (we have properly provided the various versions so that passengers get their appropriate choices of seat and meal).

In Section 11.1 we mentioned that we cannot add further primitive operations to a type after a type has been derived from it. This is a consequence of the freezing rules which are discussed in Chapter 21; these rules concern when the representation of a type is determined or frozen and the effect of it being frozen. The two rules that concern us here are that first, we cannot add more primitive operations to a type once its representation is frozen (since this determines the dispatch table) and secondly, deriving a type freezes its parent (if not already frozen). Luckily this second rule applies only to the full type declaration and not to a private extension. Otherwise we could not declare the private dispatching operations such as **Select_Seat**. The full declaration of say **Basic_Reservation** then freezes the type **Reservation** and prevents us from adding further primitive operations to it. The other point is that we cannot derive from a private type until after its full declaration. It is therefore important that the various types and operations are declared in the proper order.

We can now add the supersonic package

```
package Reservation_System.Supersonic is
   type Supersonic_Reservation is new Reservation with private;
private
   type Supersonic_Reservation is new ... with
      record
         ...
      end record;

   procedure Make(SR: in out Supersonic_Reservation);
   procedure Select_Seat(SR: in out Supersonic_Reservation);
   ...
end Reservation_System.Supersonic;
```

The type **Supersonic_Reservation** can now be an extension of any member of the tree as appropriate. Moreover by making the package a child it can see the full details of the various types and call their operations. Note that **Select_Seat** overrides properly despite being a private primitive operation of **Reservation**.

EXERCISE 13.6

1   Could we declare the functions **Further** of Exercise 13.3(**2**) and 13.3(**3**) for the type **Shape** in the private part of the package **Hidden_Shape**?

13.7   Controlled types

A very interesting example of the use of type extension is provided by considering the facilities for controlled types. These allow a user complete control over the initialization and finalization of objects and also provide the capability for user defined assignment.

The general principle is that there are three distinct primitive activities concerning the control of objects

- initialization after creation,
- finalization before destruction,
- adjustment after assignment.

and the user is given the ability to provide appropriate procedures which are called to perform whatever is necessary at various points in the life of an object. These procedures are Initialize, Finalize and Adjust and they take the object as a parameter.

To see how this works, consider

```
declare
   A: T;                    -- create A, Initialize(A)
begin
   A := E;                  -- Finalize(A), copy value, Adjust(A)
   ...
end;                        -- Finalize(A)
```

After A is declared and any normal default initialization carried out, the Initialize procedure is called. On the assignment, Finalize is first called to tidy up the old object about to be overwritten and thus destroyed, the physical copy is then made and finally Adjust is called to do whatever might be required for the new copy. At the end of the block Finalize is called once more before the object is destroyed. Note, of course, that the user does not have to physically write the calls of the three control procedures, they are called automatically by the compiled code.

In the case of a nested structure where inner components might themselves be controlled, the rules are that components are initialized and adjusted before the object as a whole and on finalization everything is done in the reverse order.

There are many other situations where the control procedures are invoked such as when calling allocators, evaluating aggregates and so on; the details are omitted but the principles will be clear.

In order for a type to be controlled it has to be extended from one of two tagged types declared in the library package Ada.Finalization whose specification is as follows

```
package Ada.Finalization is
   type Controlled is abstract tagged private;
```

```
      procedure Initialize(Object: in out Controlled);
      procedure Adjust(Object: in out Controlled);
      procedure Finalize(Object: in out Controlled);

      type Limited_Controlled is abstract tagged limited private;

      procedure Initialize(Object: in out Limited_Controlled);
      procedure Finalize(Object: in out Limited_Controlled);
   private
      ...
   end Ada.Finalization;
```

We see that there are distinct abstract types for nonlimited and limited
types. Naturally enough the Adjust procedure does not exist in the case of
limited types because they cannot be copied.

As a simple example, suppose we wish to declare a type and keep track of
how many objects (values) of the type are in existence and also record the
identity number of each object in the object itself. We could declare

```
with Ada.Finalization; use Ada.Finalization;
package Tracked_Things is

   type Thing is new Controlled with
      record
         Identity_Number: Integer;
         ...   -- other data;
      end record;

   procedure Initialize(Object: in out Thing);
   procedure Adjust(Object: in out Thing);
   procedure Finalize(Object: in out Thing);

end Tracked_Things;

package body Tracked_Things is

   The_Count: Integer := 0;
   Next_One: Integer := 1;

   procedure Initialize(Object: in out Thing) is
   begin
      The_Count := The_Count + 1;
      Object.Identity_Number := Next_One;
      Next_One := Next_One + 1;
   end Initialize;

   procedure Adjust(Object: in out Thing)
      renames Initialize;

   procedure Finalize(Object: in out Thing) is
   begin
      The_Count := The_Count - 1;
   end Finalize;

end Tracked_Things;
```

In this example we have considered each value of a thing to be a new one and so Adjust is the same as Initialize and we can conveniently use a renaming declaration to provide the body as was mentioned in Section 12.6. An alternative approach might be to consider new things to be created only when an object is first declared (or allocated). This variation is left as an exercise.

The observant reader will note that the identity number is visible to users of the package and thus liable to abuse. We can overcome this by using a child package in which we extend the type. This enables us to provide different views of a type and effectively allows us to create a type with some components visible to the user and some components hidden.

Consider

```
package Tracked_Things is

  type Identity_Controlled is abstract tagged private;

private
  type Identity_Controlled is abstract new Controlled with
    record
      Identity_Number: Integer;
    end record;

  procedure Initialize...
  -- etc.
end Tracked Things;

package Tracked_Things.User_View is

  type Thing is new Identity_Controlled with
    record
      ...   -- visible data
    end record;

end Tracked_Things.User_View;
```

In this arrangement we first declare a private type Identity_Controlled just containing the component Identity_Number (this component being hidden from the user) and then in the child package we further extend the type with the visible data which we wish the user to see. Note carefully that the type Identity_ Controlled is abstract so objects of this type cannot be declared and moreover the user cannot even see that it is actually a controlled type. We also declare Initialize, Adjust and Finalize in the private part and so they are also hidden from the user.

The child package is not really necessary in this situation since nothing is shared although the commonality of naming is helpful. Note also that several different types could be derived from Identity_Controlled all sharing the same control mechanism.

Another possible arrangement would be to declare the visible data first and then extend with the hidden identity number.

We finish this section with a few observations on the package Ada.Finalization. The procedures Initialize, Adjust and Finalize are not abstract although they do nothing and this will often be an appropriate default. The types Controlled and Limited_Controlled are of course abstract.

A key reason for making the default procedures null is because it will often be the case that the Finalize procedure for a type will naturally include a call of the Finalize procedure for the parent type. We might write

```
type T is new Parent with
  record
    -- additional components
  end record;
...
procedure Finalize(Object: in out T) is
begin
  -- operations to finalize additional components
  Finalize(Parent(Object));
end Finalize;
```

This is particularly relevant where the parent is a generic formal parameter (see Section 19.2). In such a case all we might know is that the parent type is some controlled type; since the default Finalize is null it can always be called with impunity.

Controlled types provide a good example of the use of the form of extension aggregate where the ancestor part is just given by a subtype mark. We can typically write

```
X: T := (Controlled with ... );
```

Note that we cannot easily give an expression for the ancestor part since it is abstract.

EXERCISE 13.7

1 Rewrite Initialize, Adjust and Finalize as necessary for the situation where we only consider new things to be created when an object is declared or allocated.

2 Rearrange the declarations of the types in the second version of the package Tracked_Things so that the intermediate type has the visible components and the identity number is then declared in the type extension in the child package.

3 Show how to modify the key manager of Section 11.6 so that Return_Key is automatically called on scope exit.

13.8   Multiple implementations

We conclude this chapter on the fundamentals of OOP in Ada with a discussion on an important characteristic of object oriented programming – the ability to provide different implementations of a single abstraction. Of course one can do this statically by writing a package with alternative bodies but only one body can appear in one program.

Tagged types and inheritance enable different types to be treated as different realizations of a common abstraction. The tag of an object indicates its implementation and allows a dynamic binding between the client and the appropriate implementation.

We can thus develop different implementations of a single abstraction, such as a family of set types, as in the next example. We naturally start with an abstract type

```ada
package Abstract_Sets is

    type Set is abstract tagged null record;

    function Empty return Set is abstract;
    function Unit(E: Element) return Set is abstract;
    function Union(S, T: Set) return Set is abstract;
    function Intersection(S, T: Set) return Set is abstract;
    procedure Take(From: in out Set; E: out Element) is abstract;
end Abstract_Sets;
```

This package provides an abstract specification of sets where we assume that the type Element is some discrete subtype such as Integer or Colour. The type Set is an abstract tagged null record. The package also defines a set of abstract primitive operations for the type Set. Implementations of the abstraction can then be created by extending the root type Set with appropriate components and can then override the primitive operations for that implementation.

The primitive operations are Empty which returns the null set, Unit which builds a set of one element, Union and Intersection as expected, and Take which removes one (arbitrary) element from the set.

One possible implementation would be to use a Boolean array as in Section 8.6 where each element represents the presence or absence of a member in the set.

```ada
with Abstract_Sets;
package Bit_Vector_Sets is

    type Bit_Set is new Abstract_Sets.Set with private;

    function Empty return Bit_Set;
    function Unit(E: Element) return Bit_Set;
    function Union(S, T: Bit_Set) return Bit_Set;
    function Intersection(S, T: Bit_Set) return Bit_Set;
    procedure Take(From: in out Bit_Set; E: out Element);

private
```

```
            type Bit_Vector is array (Element) of Boolean;

            type Bit_Set is new Abstract_Sets.Set with
               record
                  Data: Bit_Vector;
               end record;
         end Bit_Vector_Sets;

         package body Bit_Vector_Sets is

            function Empty return Bit_Set is
            begin
               return (Data => (others => False));
            end;

            function Unit(E: Element) return Bit_Set is
               S: Bit_Set := Empty;
            begin
               S.Data(E) := True;
               return S;
            end;

            function Union(X, Y: Bit_Set) return Bit_Set is
            begin
               return (X.Data or Y.Data);
            end;

               ...
         end Bit_Vector_Sets;
```

Such an implementation is only appropriate if the number of values in the subtype Element is not too large (note that we would typically pack the array anyway using the pragma Pack described in Chapter 21).

An alternative implementation more appropriate to sparse sets might be based on using a linked list containing the elements present in a set. For such an implementation we would have to redefine equality and assignment as well as the abstract operations; we will return to this in a moment.

But the really interesting thing is that we could then write a program which contained both forms of sets; we could convert from one representation to any other by using

```
         procedure Convert(From: in Set'Class; To: out Set'Class) is
            Temp: Set'Class := From;
            E: Element;
         begin
            -- build target set, element by element
            To := Empty;
            while Temp /= Empty loop
               Take(Temp, E);
               To := Union(To, Unit(E));
            end loop;
         end Convert;
```

This works by extracting the elements one at a time from the source set From and then building them up into the target set To. It is instructive to consider the fine details of how it dispatches onto the appropriate operations according to the specific type of its parameters using the rules described in Section 13.4.

The first action is to copy the original set into the class wide variable Temp. This avoids damaging the original set. Remember that all variables of class wide types such as Temp have to be initialized since class wide types are indefinite.

We then have

    To := Empty;

which illustrates the case of a tag being indeterminate. The function Empty has a controlling result but no controlling operands to determine the tag; the choice of function to call has to be determined by the tag of the class wide parameter To which is the destination of the assignment.

We then come to

    while Temp /= Empty **loop**

where the dispatching equality operator has two controlling operands. These are not static and so there would normally be a dynamic check to ensure that the tags are equal. But as we have seen Empty is tag indeterminate so all that happens is that the tag of Temp is used to determine which Empty and then which equality operator to call.

The statement

    Take(Temp, E);

has the single controlling operand Temp and so dispatches according to the tag of Temp which is that of From.

Finally the statement

    To := Union(To, Unit(E));

also causes dispatching to Unit and Union according to the tag of To.

An interesting property of the procedure Convert is that nothing can go wrong; it is not possible for two controlling operands to have different tags and thus raise Constraint_Error. Indeed there are no checks but just enough information to do the dispatching correctly.

We mentioned above that assignment is also a dispatching operation although this is not often apparent. In this example, however, if the type of From were a linked list then a deep copy would be required otherwise the original value could be damaged when the copy is decomposed. Such a deep copy can be performed by using a controlled type as described in the last section.

The general idea is that the set is implemented as a record containing one inner component which is controlled; this controlled component is an access to a linked list containing the various elements. Whenever the controlled component is assigned it makes a new copy of the complete linked list. Note that the type Linked_Set as a whole cannot be controlled because it is derived directly from Abstract_Sets.Set. However, assigning a value of the Linked_Set causes the inner component to be assigned and then invokes the procedure Adjust on the inner component. The implementation might be as follows

```ada
with Abstract_Sets;
with Ada.Finalization; use Ada.Finalization;
package Linked_Sets is

   type Linked_Set is new Abstract_Sets.Set with private;

   ...   -- the various operations on Linked_Set

private
   type Cell;
   type Cell_Ptr is access Cell;
   type Cell is
      record
         E: Element;
         Next: Cell_Ptr;
      end record;

   function Copy(P: Cell_Ptr) return Cell_Ptr;       -- deep copy

   type Inner is new Controlled with
      record
         The_Set: Cell_Ptr;
      end record;

   procedure Adjust(Object: in out Inner);

   type Linked_Set is new Abstract_Sets.Set with
      record
         Component: Inner;
      end record;

end Linked_Sets;

package body Linked_Sets is

   function Copy(P: Cell_Ptr) return Cell_Ptr is
   begin
      if P = null then
         return null;
      else
         return new Cell'(P.E, Copy(P.Next));
      end if;
   end Copy;
```

```
      procedure Adjust(Object: in out Inner) is
      begin
         Object.The_Set := Copy(Object.The_Set);
      end Adjust;
      ...
   end Linked_Sets;
```

The types Cell and Cell_Ptr form the usual linked list containing the elements; Cell is of course not tagged or controlled. The function Copy performs a deep copy of the list passed as parameter. The type Inner is controlled and contains a single component referring to the linked list. The procedure Adjust for Inner performs a deep copy on this single component. The visible type Linked_Set is then simply a record containing a component of the controlled type Inner. As mentioned above, performing an assignment on the type Linked_Set causes Adjust to be called on its inner component thereby making the deep copy. But none of this is visible to the user of the package Linked_Sets. Observe that we do not need to provide a procedure Initialize and that we have not bothered to provide Finalize although it would be appropriate to do so in order to discard unused space.

The details of the remaining subprograms are left to the imagination of the reader. Some thought is necessary in order to avoid excessive manipulation. It is probably best to arrange that elements are not duplicated. It might also be advisable to keep the elements on the list in some canonical order otherwise the equality operation will be tedious.

EXERCISE 13.8

1 Given

```
    B1: Bit_Set;
    B2: Bit_Set;
    L1: Linked_Set;
    C1: Set'Class := ... ;
    C2: Set'Class := ... ;
```

then which of the following are legal and which involve a run-time check?

(a) Union(B1, B2)   (c) Union(B1, C1)
(b) Union(B1, L1)   (d) Union(C1, C2)

2 The procedure Convert will convert between any two sets but is somewhat inefficient if the two sets happen to have the same representation. Modify it to overcome this inefficiency.

3 Declare an abstract type Stack with operations Push, Pop and Empty (returns an empty stack). Declare a procedure Convert that will convert between stacks of different representations. Sketch two representations of a stack using an array and linked lists much as in Sections 11.4 and 11.5.

CHECKLIST 13

Additional primitive operations can only be added if derivation is in a package specification.

Additional primitive operations cannot be added to the parent type after a type is derived from it.

Conversion of tagged types can only be towards the root.

Type extension must be at the same accessibility level as the parent.

Objects of a class wide type must be initialized.

Dispatching only occurs with a class wide actual parameter and a specific formal parameter.

It is not possible to derive from a class wide type.

Tagged type parameters are always passed by reference.

Tagged formal parameters are considered aliased.

Objects of an abstract type are not allowed.

Functions returning an abstract type must themselves be abstract.

Functions returning a tagged type become abstract on extension.

The attribute Tag cannot be applied to an object of a specific type.

Equality has special rules on extension.

The tag of an object can never be changed.

An abstract type cannot have private abstract operations.

Changes from Ada 83

Tagged types and related concepts such as class wide and abstract types did not exist in Ada 83.

Exceptions

At various times in the preceding chapters we have said that if something goes wrong when the program is executed, then an exception, often Constraint_ Error, will be raised. In this chapter we describe the exception mechanism and show how remedial action can be taken when an exception occurs. We also show how we may define and use our own exceptions. Exceptions concerned with interacting tasks are dealt with when we come to Chapter 18.

14.1   Handling exceptions

We have seen that if we break various language rules then an exception may be raised when we execute the program.

There are four predefined exceptions (declared in the package Standard) of which we have met three so far

Constraint_Error   This generally corresponds to something going out of range; this includes when something goes wrong with arithmetic such as an attempt to divide by zero.

Program_Error   This will occur if we attempt to violate the control structure in some way such as running into the **end** of a function, breaking the accessibility rules or calling a subprogram whose body has not yet been elaborated – see Sections 9.1, 10.6 and 11.1.

Storage_Error   This will occur if we run out of storage space as for example if we called the recursive function Factorial with a large parameter – see Section 9.1.

The other predefined exception is Tasking_Error. This is concerned with tasking and so is dealt with in Chapter 18.

Note that for historical reasons the exception Constraint_Error is also renamed as Numeric_Error in the package Standard. Numeric_Error is considered obsolete and should be avoided.

If we anticipate that an exception may occur in a part of our program then we can write an exception handler to deal with it. For example, suppose we write

```
begin
  -- sequence of statements
exception
  when Constraint_Error =>
    -- do something
end;
```

If Constraint_Error is raised while we are executing the sequence of statements between **begin** and **exception** then the flow of control is interrupted and immediately transferred to the sequence of statements following the =>. The clause starting **when** is known as an exception handler.

As a trivial example we could compute Tomorrow from Today by writing

```
begin
  Tomorrow := Day'Succ(Today);
exception
  when Constraint_Error =>
    Tomorrow := Day'First;
end;
```

If Today is Day'Last (that is, Sun) then when we attempt to evaluate Day'Succ(Today), the exception Constraint_Error is raised. Control is then transferred to the handler for Constraint_Error and the statement Tomorrow := Day'First; is executed. Control then passes to the end of the block.

This is really a bad example. Exceptions should be used for rarely occurring cases or those which are inconvenient to test for at their point of occurrence. By no stretch of the imagination is Sunday a rare day. Over 14% of all days are Sundays. Nor is it difficult to test for the condition at the point of occurrence. So we should really have written

```
if Today = Day'Last then
  Tomorrow := Day'First;
else
  Tomorrow := Day'Succ(Today);
end if;
```

However, it is a simple example with which to illustrate the mechanism.

Several handlers can be written between **exception** and **end**. Consider

```
begin
   -- sequence of statements
exception
   when Constraint_Error | Program_Error =>
      Put("Constraint or Program Error occurred");
      ...
   when Storage_Error =>
      Put("Ran out of space");
      ...
   when others =>
      Put("Something else went wrong");
      ...
end;
```

In this example a message is output according to the exception. Note the similarity to the case statement. Each **when** is followed by one or more exception names separated by vertical bars. As usual we can write **others** but it must be last and on its own; it handles any exception not listed in the previous handlers.

Note that we can mention the same exception twice in the same handler; this is useful when exceptions are renamed such as in the case of historic programs which might have a common handler for Constraint_Error and its renaming Numeric_Error.

Exception handlers can appear at the end of a block, subprogram body, package body (also task body and accept statement, see Chapter 18) and have access to all entities declared in that unit. The examples have shown a degenerate block in which there is no **declare** and declarative part; the block was introduced just for the purpose of providing somewhere to hang the handlers. We could rewrite our bad example to determine tomorrow as a function thus

```
function Tomorrow(Today: Day) return Day is
begin
   return Day'Succ(Today);
exception
   when Constraint_Error =>
      return Day'First;
end Tomorrow;
```

It is important to realize that control can never be returned directly to the unit where the exception was raised. The sequence of statements following => replaces the remainder of the unit containing the handler and thereby completes execution of the unit. Hence a handler for a function must generally contain a return statement in order to provide the 'emergency' result.

In particular, a goto statement cannot transfer control from a unit into one of its handlers or vice versa or from one handler to another. However, the statements of a handler can otherwise be of arbitrary complexity. They can include blocks, calls of subprograms and so on. A handler of a block could contain a goto statement which transferred control to a label outside the block and it could contain an exit statement if the block were inside a loop.

A handler at the end of a package body applies only to the initialization sequence of the package and not to subprograms in the package. Such subprograms must have individual handlers if they are to deal with exceptions.

We now consider the question of what happens if a unit does not provide a handler for a particular exception. The answer is that the exception is propagated dynamically. This simply means that the unit is terminated and the exception is raised at the point where the unit was executed. In the case of a block we therefore look for a handler in the unit containing the block.

In the case of a subprogram, the call is terminated and we look for a handler in the unit which called the subprogram. This unwinding process is repeated until either we reach a unit containing a handler for the particular exception or come to the top level. If we find a unit containing a relevant handler then the exception is handled at that point. Alternatively we have reached the main subprogram and have still found no handler – the main subprogram is then abandoned and we can expect the run-time environment to provide us with a suitable diagnostic message. (Unhandled exceptions in tasks are dealt with in Chapter 18.)

It is most important to understand that exceptions are propagated dynamically and not statically. That is, an exception not handled by a subprogram is propagated to the unit calling the subprogram and not to the unit containing the declaration of the subprogram – these may or may not be the same.

If the statements in a handler themselves raise an exception then the unit is terminated and the exception propagated to the calling unit; the handler does not loop.

EXERCISE 14.1

Note: these are exercises to check your understanding of exceptions. They do not necessarily reflect good Ada programming techniques.

1 Assuming that calling Sqrt with a negative parameter and attempting to divide by zero both raise Constraint_Error, rewrite the procedure Quadratic of Section 9.3 without explicitly testing D and A.

2 Rewrite the function Factorial of Section 9.1 so that if it is called with a negative parameter (which would normally raise Constraint_Error) or a large parameter (which would normally raise Storage_Error or Constraint_Error) then a standard result of say −1 is returned. Hint: declare an inner function Slave which actually does the work.

14.2   Declaring and raising exceptions

Relying on the predefined exceptions to detect unusual but anticipated situations is usually bad practice because they do not provide a guarantee that the exception has in fact been raised because of the anticipated situation. Something else may have gone wrong instead.

As an illustration consider the package Stack of Section 11.1. If we call Push when the stack is full then the statement Top := Top + 1; will raise Constraint_Error and similarly if we call Pop when the stack is empty then Top := Top − 1; will also raise Constraint_Error. Since Push and Pop do not themselves have exception handlers, the exception will be propagated to the unit calling them. So we could write

```
declare
   use Stack;
begin
   ...
   Push(M);
   ...
   N := Pop;
   ...
exception
   when Constraint_Error =>
      -- stack manipulation incorrect?
end;
```

and misuse of the stack would then result in control being transferred to the handler for Constraint_Error. However, there would be no guarantee that the exception had arisen because of misuse of the stack; something else could have gone wrong in the block.

A better solution is to raise an exception specifically declared to indicate misuse of the stack. Thus the package could be rewritten

```
package Stack is
   Error: exception;
   procedure Push(X: Integer);
   function Pop return Integer;
end Stack;

package body Stack is
   Max: constant := 100;
   S: array (1 .. Max) of Integer;
   Top: Integer range 0 .. Max;

   procedure Push(X: Integer) is
   begin
      if Top = Max then
         raise Error;
      end if;
      Top := Top + 1;
```

```
        S(Top) := X;
     end Push;

     function Pop return Integer is
     begin
        if Top = 0 then
           raise Error;
        end if;
        Top := Top – 1;
        return S(Top + 1);
     end Pop;

begin
   Top := 0;
end Stack;
```

An exception is declared in a similar way to a variable and is raised by an explicit raise statement naming the exception. The handling and propagation rules are just as for the predefined exceptions. We can now write

```
declare
   use Stack;
begin
   ...
   Push(M);
   ...
   N := Pop;
   ...
exception
   when Error =>
      -- stack manipulation incorrect
   when others =>
      -- something else went wrong
end;
```

We have now successfully separated the handler for misusing the stack from the handler for other exceptions.

Note that if we had not provided a use clause then we would have had to refer to the exception in the handler as Stack.Error; the usual dotted notation applies.

What could we expect to do in the handler in the above case? Apart from reporting that the stack manipulation has gone wrong, we might also expect to reset the stack to an acceptable state although we have not provided a convenient means of doing so. A procedure Reset in the package Stack would be useful. A further thing we might do is relinquish any resources that were acquired in the block and might otherwise be inadvertently retained. Suppose for instance that we had also been using the package Key_Manager of Section 11.6. We might then call Return_Key to ensure that a key declared and acquired in the block had been returned. Remember that Return_Key does no harm if called unnecessarily.

We would probably also want to reset the stack and return the key in the case of any other exception as well; so it would be as well to declare a procedure Clean_Up to do all the actions required. So our block might look like

```
declare
  use Stack, Key_Manager;
  My_Key: Key;

  procedure Clean_Up is
  begin
    Reset;
    Return_Key(My_Key);
  end;

begin
  Get_Key(My_Key);
  ...
  Push(M);
  ...
  Action(My_Key, ... );
  ...
  N := Pop;
  ...
  Return_Key(My_Key);
exception
  when Error =>
    Put("Stack used incorrectly");
    Clean_Up;
  when others =>
    Put("Something else went wrong");
    Clean_Up;
end;
```

Note that we could make the return of the key automatic by using a controlled type for the key as in Exercise 13.7(**3**). Leaving a unit via a handler will invoke any Finalize procedures properly.

We have rather assumed that Reset is a further procedure declared in the package Stack but note that we could write our own procedure externally thus

```
procedure Reset is
  Junk: Integer;
  use Stack;
begin
  loop
    Junk := Pop;
  end loop;
exception
  when Error =>
    null;
end Reset;
```

This works by repeatedly calling Pop until Error is raised. We then know that the stack is empty. The handler needs to do nothing other than prevent the exception from being propagated; so we merely write **null**. This procedure seems a bit like trickery; it would be far better to have a reset procedure in the package.

Sometimes the actions that require to be taken as a consequence of an exception need to be performed on a layered basis. In the above example we returned the key and then reset the stack but it is probably the case that the block as a whole cannot be assumed to have done its job correctly. We can indicate this by raising an exception as the last action of the handler

```
exception
  when Error =>
    Put("Stack used incorrectly");
    Clean_Up;
    raise Another_Error;
  when others =>
    ...
end;
```

The exception Another_Error will then be propagated to the unit containing the block. We could put the statement

```
raise Another_Error;
```

in the procedure Clean_Up.

Sometimes it is convenient to handle an exception and then propagate the same exception. This can be done by just writing

```
raise;
```

This is particularly useful when we handle several exceptions with the one handler. So we might have

```
  when others =>
    Put("Something else went wrong");
    Clean_Up;
    raise;
end;
```

The current exception will be remembered even if the action of the handler raises and handles its own exceptions such as occurred in our trick procedure Reset. However, note that there is a rule that we can only write **raise**; directly in a handler and not for instance in a procedure called by the handler such as Clean_Up.

The stack example illustrates a legitimate use of exceptions. The exception Error should rarely, if ever, occur and it would also be inconvenient to test for the condition at each possible point of occurrence. To do that we would presumably have to provide an additional parameter to Push of type Boolean and mode **out** to indicate that all was not well, and then test it after each call.

In the case of Pop we would also have to recast it as a procedure since a function cannot take a parameter of mode **out**.

The package specification would then become

```
package Stack is
    procedure Push(X: in Integer; B: out Boolean);
    procedure Pop(X: out Integer; B: out Boolean);
end;
```

and we would have to write

```
declare
    use Stack;
    OK: Boolean;
begin
    ...
    Push(M, OK);
    if not OK then ...      end if;
    ...
    Pop(N, OK);
    if not OK then ...      end if;
end;
```

It is clear that the use of an exception provides a better structured program.

Note finally that nothing prevents us from explicitly raising one of the predefined exceptions. We recall that in Section 9.1 when discussing the function Inner we stated that probably the best way of coping with parameters whose bounds were unequal was to explicitly raise Constraint_Error.

EXERCISE 14.2

1 Rewrite the package Random of Exercise 11.1(**1**) so that it declares and raises an exception Bad if the initial value is not odd.

2 Rewrite your answer to Exercise 14.1(**2**) so that the function Factorial always raises Constraint_Error if the parameter is negative or too large.

3 Declare a function "+" which takes two parameters of type Vector and returns their sum using sliding semantics by analogy with the predefined one-dimensional array operations described in Section 8.6. Use type Vector from Section 8.2. Raise Constraint_Error if the arrays do not match.

4 Are we completely justified in asserting that Stack.Error could only be raised by the stack going wrong?

5 Assuming that the exception Error is declared in the specification of Stacks, rewrite procedures Push and Pop of Section 11.5 so that they raise Error rather than Storage_Error and Constraint_Error.

14.3   Checking and exceptions

In the previous section we came to the conclusion that it was logically better to check for the stack overflow condition ourselves rather than rely upon the built-in check associated with the violation of the subtype of Top. At first sight the reader may well feel that this would reduce the execution efficiency of the program. However this is not necessarily so, assuming a reasonably intelligent compiler, and this example can be used to illustrate the advantages of the use of appropriate subtypes.

We will concentrate on the procedure Push, similar arguments apply to the function Pop.

First consider the original package Stack of Section 11.1. In that we had

```
S: array (1 .. Max) of Integer;
Top: Integer range 0 .. Max;

procedure Push(X: Integer) is
begin
   Top := Top + 1;
   S(Top) := X;
end Push;
```

If the stack is full (that is Top = Max) and we call Push then it is the assignment to Top that raises Constraint_Error. This is because Top has a range constraint. However, the only run-time check that needs to be compiled is that associated with checking the upper bound of Top. There is no need to check for violation of the lower bound since the expression Top + 1 could not be less than 1 (assuming that the value in Top is always in range). Note moreover that no checks need be compiled with respect to the assignment to S(Top). This is because the value of Top at this stage must lie in the range 1 .. Max (which is the index range of S) – it cannot exceed Max because this has just been checked by the previous assignment and it cannot be less than 1 since 1 has just been added to its previous value which could not have been less than 0. So just one check needs to be compiled in the procedure Push.

On the other hand, if the variable Top had not been given a range constraint but just declared as

```
Top: Integer;
```

then although no checks would have been applied to the assignment to Top, nevertheless checks would have had to be compiled for the assignment to S(Top) instead in order to ensure that Top lay within the index range of S. Two checks would be necessary – one for each end of the index range.

So applying the range constraint to Top actually reduces the number of checks required. This is typical behaviour given a compiler with a moderate degree of flow analysis. The more you tell the compiler about the properties of the variables (and assuming the constraints on the variables match their usage), the better the object code.

Now consider what happens when we add our own test as in the previous section (and we assume that Top now has its range constraint)

```
procedure Push(X: Integer) is
begin
  if Top = Max then
    raise Error;
  end if;
  Top := Top + 1;
  S(Top) := X;
end Push;
```

Clearly we have added a check of our own. However, there is now no need for the compiler to insert the check on the upper bound of Top in the assignment statement

```
Top := Top + 1;
```

because our own check will have caused control to be transferred away via the raising of the Error exception for the one original value of Top that would have caused trouble. So the net effect of adding our own check is simply to replace a compiler check by our own; the object code is not less efficient.

There are two morals to this tale. The first is that we should tell the compiler the whole truth about our program; the more it knows about the properties of our variables, the more likely it is to be able to keep the checks to the appropriate minimum. In fact this is just an extension of the advantage of strong typing discussed in Section 6.3 where we saw how arbitrary run-time errors can be replaced by easily understood compile-time errors.

The second moral is that introducing our own exceptions rather than relying upon the predefined ones need not reduce the efficiency of our program. In fact it is generally considered bad practice to rely upon the predefined exceptions for steering our program and especially bad to raise the predefined exceptions explicitly ourselves. It is all too easy to mask an unexpected genuine error that needs fixing.

It should also be noted that we can always ask the compiler to omit the run-time checks by using the pragma Suppress. This is described in more detail in Section 21.1.

Finally, an important warning. Our analysis of when checks can be omitted depends upon all variables satisfying their constraints at all times. Provided checks are not suppressed we can be reasonably assured of this apart from one nasty loophole. This is that we are not obliged to supply initial values in the declarations of variables in the first place. So they can start with a junk value which does not satisfy any constraints and may not even be a value of the base type. If such a variable is read before being updated then our program has a bounded error and all our analysis is worthless. It is thus a good idea to initialize all variables unless it is perfectly obvious that updating will occur first.

EXERCISE 14.3

1 Consider the case of the procedure Push with explicit raising of Error but suppose
   that there is no range constraint on Top. How many checks would then be required?

14.4 Exception occurrences

We now consider a number of auxiliary facilities which enable a more detailed
analysis of exceptions and their cause. In the general clean-up clause in Section
14.2 we wrote

```
when others =>
    Put("Something else went wrong");
    Clean_Up;
    raise;
end;
```

This is not very helpful since we would really like to record what actually
happened. We can do this using an exception occurrence which identifies both
the exception and the instance of its being raised (that is, the circumstances
associated with the particular error condition).

The limited type Exception_Occurrence is declared in the package
Ada.Exceptions together with various subprograms including functions
Exception_Name, Exception_Message and Exception_Information. These
functions take an exception occurrence as their single parameter and return a
string.

As their names suggest Exception_Name returns the name of the exception
(the full dotted name in upper case) and Exception_Message and Exception_
Information return two levels of more detailed information which identify the
cause and location. The result of Exception_Message should be a one line
message and not contain the exception name whereas Exception_Information
will include both the name and the message and might provide full details of a
trace back as well. Although the details are dependent upon the implementation
the general intent is that the messages are suitable for output and analysis on
the system concerned.

To get hold of the occurrence we write a 'choice parameter' in the handler
and this behaves as a constant of the type Exception_Occurrence. We can now
more usefully write

```
when Event: others =>
    Put("Unexpected exception: ");
    Put(Exception_Name(Event));
    New_Line;
    Put(Exception_Message(Event));
```

```
            Clean_Up;
            raise;
    end;
```

The object Event of the type Exception_Occurrence acts as a sort of marker which enables us to identify the current occurrence; its scope is the handler. Such a choice parameter can be placed in any handler.

The package Ada.Exceptions contains other types and subprograms which provide further facilities. Its specification is

```
    package Ada.Exceptions is
        type Exception_Id is private;
        Null_Id: constant Exception_Id;
        function Exception_Name(Id: Exception_Id) return String;

        type Exception_Occurrence is limited private;
        type Exception_Occurrence_Access is
                                    access all Exception_Occurrence;
        Null_Occurrence: constant Exception_Occurrence;

        procedure Raise_Exception(E: in Exception_Id;
                                  Message: in String := "");
        function Exception_Message(X: Exception_Occurrence)
                                                    return String;
        procedure Reraise_Occurrence(X: in  Exception_Occurrence);

        function Exception_Identity(X: Exception_Occurrence)
                                                    return Exception_Id;
        function Exception_Name(X: Exception_Occurrence) return String;
        function Exception_Information(X: Exception_Occurrence)
                                                    return String;

        procedure Save_Occurrence(Target: out Exception_Occurrence;
                                  Source: in Exception_Occurrence);
        function Save_Occurrence(Source: Exception_Occurrence)
                                  return Exception_Occurrence_Access;
    private;
        ...
    end Ada.Exceptions;
```

The two subprograms Save_Occurrence enable exception occurrences to be saved for detailed later analysis. Note that the type Exception_Occurrence is limited; using subprograms rather than allowing the user to save values through assignment gives better control over the use of storage for saved exception occurrences (which could be large since they may contain extensive trace back information).

The procedure Save_Occurrence copies the occurrence from the Source to the Target. It may truncate the message associated with the occurrence to 200 characters; this corresponds to the minimum size of line length required to be supported as mentioned in Section 5.3. On the other hand the function

Save_Occurrence copies the occurrence to a newly created object and returns an access value to the new object. It is not permitted to truncate the message.

So we might have some debugging package containing an array in which perhaps up to 100 exception occurrences might be stored. A fragment of the body of a crude implementation might be

```
Dump: array(1 .. 100) of Exception_Occurrence;
Dump_Index: Integer := 0;
...
procedure Dump_Ex(E: Exception_Occurrence) is
begin
   Dump_Index := Dump_Index + 1;
   Save_Occurrence(Dump(Dump_Index), E);
end Dump_Ex;

procedure Analyse_Ex is
begin
   Put("Analysis of saved occurrences:");
   New_Line;
   for I in 1 .. Dump_Index loop
      Put(Exception_Information(Dump(I)));
      New_Line;
   end loop;
   Dump_Index := 0;        -- reset dump
end Analyse_Ex;
```

and then a handler could save an occurrence for later analysis by writing

```
   when Event: others =>
      Dump_Ex(Event);
      Clean_Up;
      raise;
end;
```

Care is clearly needed to ensure that the dumping package does not itself raise exceptions and thereby get the system into a mess.

An occurrence may be reraised by calling the procedure Reraise_ Occurrence. This is precisely equivalent to reraising an exception by a raise statement without an exception name and does not create a new occurrence (this ensures that the original cause is not lost). An important advantage of Reraise_Occurrence is that it can be used to reraise an occurrence that was stored by one of the subprograms Save_Occurrence.

It is possible to attach our own specific message to the raising of an exception by the procedure Raise_Exception. In order to do this we need some way of referring to the exception. However, exceptions are not proper types and cannot be passed as parameters in the normal way. So instead we pass a value of the type Exception_Id which can be thought of as a global enumeration type whose literals represent the individual exceptions. The identity of an exception is provided by the attribute Identity.

So in order to attach a message using Raise_Occurrence we pass the identity of the exception as the first parameter and the message (a string) as the second parameter. The message can then be retrieved by calling Exception_ Message. This provides a convenient means of identifying the cause of an exception during program debugging. Consider

```
declare
    Trouble: exception;
begin
    ...
    Raise_Exception(Trouble'Identity, "Doom");
    ...
    Raise_Exception(Trouble'Identity, "Gloom");
    ...
exception
    when Event: Trouble =>
        Put(Exception_Message(Event));
end;
```

Calling Raise_Exception raises the exception Trouble with the string attached as the message. The call of Put in the handler will output "Doom" or "Gloom" according to which occurrence of Trouble was raised. Note that our own messages work consistently with the predefined messages; for example Exception_Information will include our message if we have supplied one.

We mentioned above that the exceptions can be thought of as representing the literals of some type Exception_Id and that the Identity attribute enabled conversion from an exception to its identity. We can sort of go in the reverse direction by calling the function Exception_Name applied to an exception identity; this returns the full dotted name of the exception as a string. So

```
Exception_Name(Error'Identity);
```

might return the string "STACK.ERROR". The identity of an exception associated with an occurrence can be obtained by calling the function Exception_Identity. Note that the following two calls are thus equivalent

```
Exception_Name(Event);
Exception_Name(Exception_Identity(Event));
```

and that there are two overloadings of Exception_Name.

EXERCISE 14.4

---

1   Revise the package Stack of Section 14.2 so that appropriate messages are attached to the raising of the exception Error. Change the handler to output the specific message.

14.5   Scope of exceptions

To a large extent exceptions follow the same scope rules as other entities. An exception can hide and be hidden by another declaration; it can be referred to by the dotted notation and so on. An exception can be renamed

> Help: **exception renames** Bank.Alarm;

Exceptions are, however, different in many ways. We cannot declare arrays of exceptions, and they cannot be components of records, parameters of subprograms and so on. In short, exceptions are not objects and so cannot be manipulated. They behave a bit like literals of some globally defined enumeration type Exception_Id as mentioned in the last section.

A very important characteristic of exceptions is that they are not created dynamically as a program executes but should be thought of as existing throughout the life of the program. Indeed the full set of exceptions in a program is only known when the program is bound and so the representation of the type Exception_Id can be thought of as occurring at bind time. This aspect of exceptions relates to the way in which they are propagated dynamically up the chain of execution rather than statically up the chain of scope. An exception can be propagated outside its scope although of course it can then only be handled anonymously by **others**. This is illustrated by the following

```
procedure Main is
  procedure P is
    X: exception;
  begin
    raise X;
  end P;
begin
  P;
exception
  when others =>
          -- X handled here
end Main;
```

The procedure P declares and raises the exception X but does not handle it. When we call P, the exception X is propagated to the block calling P where it is handled anonymously.

We could of course rediscover the textual form of the exception by writing

> **when** Event: **others** =>

and then Exception_Name(Event) would return the string "MAIN.P.X".

It is even possible to propagate an exception out of its scope, where it becomes anonymous, and then back in again where it can once more be handled by its proper name. Consider (and this is really a crazy example)

```
procedure Main is
  package P is
    procedure F;
    procedure H;
  end P;

  procedure G is
  begin
    P.H;
  exception
    when others =>
      raise;
  end G;

  package body P is
    X: exception;

    procedure F is
    begin
      G;
    exception
      when X =>
        Put("Got it!");
    end F;

    procedure H is
    begin
      raise X;
    end H;

  end P;

begin
  P.F;
end Main;
```

The procedure Main declares a package P containing procedures F and H
and also a procedure G. The procedure Main calls F in P which calls G outside
P which in turn calls H back in P. The procedure H raises the exception X
whose scope is the body of P. The procedure H does not handle X, so it is
propagated to G which called H. The procedure G is outside the package P, so
the exception X is now outside its scope; nevertheless G handles the exception
anonymously and propagates it further by reraising it. G was called by F so X
is now propagated back into the package and so can be handled by F by its
proper name.

   A further illustration of the nature of exceptions is afforded by a recursive
procedure containing an exception declaration. Unlike variables declared in a
procedure we do not get a new exception for each recursive call. Each recursive
activation refers to the same exception – they have the same Exception_Id.
Consider the following artificial example

```
procedure F(N: Integer) is
   X: exception;
begin
   if N = 0 then
      raise X;
   else
      F(N – 1);
   end if;
exception
   when X =>
      Put("Got it!");
      raise;
   when others =>
      null;
end F;
```

Suppose we execute F(4); we get recursive calls F(3), F(2), F(1) and finally F(0). When F is called with parameter zero, it raises the exception X, handles it, prints out a confirmatory message and then reraises it. The calling instance of F (which itself had N = 1) receives the exception and again handles it as X and so on. The message is therefore printed out five times in all and the exception is finally propagated anonymously. Observe that if each recursive activation had created a different exception then the message would only be printed out once.

In all the examples we have seen so far exceptions have been raised in statements. An exception can however also be raised in a declaration. Thus

```
N: Positive := 0;
```

would raise Constraint_Error because the initial value of N does not satisfy the range constraint 1 .. Integer'Last of the subtype Positive. An exception raised in a declaration is not handled by a handler (if any) of the unit containing the declaration but is immediately propagated up a level. This means that in any handler we are assured that all declarations of the unit were successfully elaborated and so there is no risk of referring to something that does not exist.

Finally, a warning regarding parameters of mode **out** or **in out**. If a subprogram is terminated by an exception then any actual parameter of a scalar type will not have been updated since such updating occurs on a normal return. On the other hand, a parameter of a tagged record type is always passed by reference and so will always have been updated. For an array or other record type the parameter mechanism is not so closely specified and the actual parameter may or may not have its original value. A program assuming a particular mechanism may have a bounded error. As an example consider the procedure Withdraw of the package Bank in Exercise 11.6(1). It would be incorrect to attempt to take the key away and raise an alarm as in

```
procedure Withdraw (K: in out Key; M: in out Money) is
begin
   if Valid (K) then
```

```
        if M > amount remaining then
            M := amount remaining;
            Free(K.Code) := True;
            K.Code := 0;
            raise Alarm;
        else
            ...
        end if;
    end if;
end Withdraw;
```

If the parameter mechanism were implemented by copy then the bank would think that the key were now free but would have left the greedy customer with a copy. However, if the key were a tagged type as in Exercise 13.7(**3**) then this problem would not arise.

EXERCISE 14.5

1   Rewrite the package Bank of Exercise 11.6(**1**) to declare an exception Alarm and raise it when any illegal banking activity is attempted. Avoid problems with the parameters.

2   Consider the following pathological procedure

```
procedure P is
begin
    P;
exception
    when Storage_Error =>
        P;
end P;
```

What happens when P is called? To be explicit suppose that there is enough stack space for only N simultaneous recursive calls of P but that on the $N+1$th call the exception Storage_Error is raised. How many times will P be called in all and what eventually happens?

CHECKLIST 14

Do not use exceptions unnecessarily.

Use specific user declared exceptions rather than predefined exceptions where relevant.

Ensure that handlers return resources correctly.

Match the constraints on index variables to the arrays concerned.

Beware of uninitialized variables.

Out and in out parameters may not be updated correctly if a procedure is terminated by an exception.

Numeric_Error is obsolete.

Changes from Ada 83

The same exception was not allowed twice in a handler in Ada 83.

Numeric_Error and Constraint_Error were distinct exceptions in Ada 83.

Exception occurrences were not available in Ada 83.

15 Numeric Types

We now come at last to a more detailed discussion of numeric types. There are two categories of numeric types in Ada: integer types and real types. The integer types are subdivided into signed integer types and modular types. The real types are subdivided into floating point types and fixed point types; the latter include decimal types.

There are two problems concerning the representation of numeric types in a computer. First, the range may be restricted and indeed many machines have hardware operations for various ranges so that we can choose our own compromise between range of values and space occupied by values. Secondly, it may not be possible to represent accurately all the possible values of a type. These difficulties cause problems with program portability because the constraints vary from machine to machine.

Getting the right balance between portability and performance is not easy. The best performance is achieved by using types that correspond exactly to the hardware. Perfect portability requires using types with precisely identical range and accuracy and identical operations.

Ada recognizes these difficulties and provides numeric types in ways that allow a programmer to choose the correct balance for the application. High performance can thus be achieved while keeping portability problems to a minimum.

We start by discussing integer types because these suffer only from range problems but not from accuracy problems.

15.1   Signed integer types

All implementations of Ada have the predefined type Integer. In addition there may be other predefined types such as Long_Integer, Short_Integer and so on with a respectively longer or shorter range than Integer (could actually be the same). The range of values of these predefined types will be symmetric about zero except for an extra negative value in two's complement machines (which now seem to dominate over one's complement machines). All predefined integer types have the same predefined operations that were described in Chapter 6 as applicable to the type Integer (except that the second operand of "**" is always just type Integer).

Thus we might find that on machine A we have types Integer and Long_Integer with

> range of Integer:
>   –32768 .. +32767   (i.e. 16 bits)
>
> range of Long_Integer:
>   –21474_83648 .. +21474_83647   (i.e. 32 bits)

whereas on machine B we might have types Short_Integer, Integer and Long_Integer with

> range of Short_Integer:
>   –2048 .. +2047   (i.e. 12 bits)
>
> range of Integer:
>   –83_88608 .. +83_88607   (i.e. 24 bits)
>
> range of Long_Integer:
>   –14073_74883_55328 .. +14073_74883_55327   (i.e. 48 bits)

For most purposes the type Integer will suffice on either machine and that is why we have simply used Integer in examples in this book so far. However, suppose we have an application where we need to manipulate signed values up to a million. The type Integer is inadequate on machine A and to use Long_Integer on machine B would be extravagant. We *could* overcome our problem by using derived types and writing (for machine A)

> **type** My_Integer **is new** Long_Integer;

and then using My_Integer throughout the program. To move the program to machine B we would just replace this one declaration by

> **type** My_Integer **is new** Integer;

However, Ada enables the choice to be made automatically; if we write

> **type** My_Integer **is range** –1E6 .. 1E6;

then the implementation will implicitly choose the smallest appropriate
hardware type and it will be somewhat as if we had written

   type My_Integer **is new** hardware_type **range** –1E6 .. 1E6;

where the anonymous hardware type is chosen appropriately. So in effect
My_Integer will be a subtype of an anonymous type based on one of the
predefined types and so objects of type My_Integer will be constrained to take
only the values in the range –1E6 .. 1E6 and not the full range of the
anonymous type. Note that the range must have static bounds since the choice
of machine type is made at compile time.

   To really understand what is going on we need to distinguish between the
range of a type and the *base range* of a type. The range of a type is the
requested range whereas the base range is the actual implemented range. So in
the case of My_Integer, the range is –1E6 .. 1E6 whereas the base range is the
full range of the underlying machine type.

   The base type can be indicated by applying the attribute **Base** to the type.
Thus My_Integer'Base is the base type (strictly the base subtype) and
My_Integer'Base'Range is the base range; we could declare variables of this
subtype by writing

   Var: My_Integer'Base;

Note that the attribute **Base** always denotes an unconstrained subtype whereas
My_Integer is constrained.

   It is an important rule that range checks are applied to constrained subtypes
but not to unconstrained subtypes. If a range check fails then of course
Constraint_Error is raised. Although range checks do not apply to
unconstrained subtypes nevertheless overflow checks always apply and so we
either get the correct mathematical result or Constraint_Error is raised. Using a
constrained subtype is more portable whereas an unconstrained subtype is
likely to be more efficient.

   Another point regarding unconstrained types is that the compiler is
permitted to optimize intermediate expressions and storage for variables by
using a larger range if helpful. For example all registers might be of 32 bits and
all arithmetic be performed using 32 bits on machine A even though the type
Integer itself was only 16 bits. An unconstrained variable could be held in a
register and thus although the base range is only 16 bits nevertheless values
outside this range can be held in the variable since it is unconstrained.

   We can illustrate these points by considering

   type Index **is range** 0 .. 20000;
   I, J, K: Index;
   IB, JB: Index'Base;

on machine A. The range of Index is as given whereas the base range is –32768
.. +32767. Suppose furthermore that IB is held in a 16-bit store whereas JB is
optimized and held in a 32-bit register. Now consider

```
I := 17000;
J := 16000;
...
K := I + J;              -- range check fails, Constraint_Error
IB := I + J;             -- overflows, Constraint_Error
JB := I + J;             -- OK
```

The addition of I and J is successfully performed in a 32-bit register. The assignment to the constrained variable K fails because the result is outside the range of Index. The assignment to IB fails because the value is outside the base range and IB is implemented using the base range. The assignment to JB succeeds because JB is in a 32-bit register.

The fact that the addition can be performed using registers with a larger range than the base range is reflected by the fact that the specification of "+" can be thought of as

    function "+" (Left, Right: Index'Base) **return** Index'Base;

so that there are no range checks on evaluating the parameters and returning the results.

Similar considerations apply to the predefined named types such as Integer. The subtype Integer is constrained whereas Integer'Base is unconstrained. The range and base range happen to be the same. The predefined operations take the form

    function "+" (Left, Right: Integer'Base) **return** Integer'Base;

as shown in Section 20.1.

Not all the implemented base ranges need correspond to a predefined type such as Integer or Long_Integer declared in Standard. There could be others. Indeed the *ARM* recommends that only Integer and Long_Integer be given such names. The type Integer will always exist and have at least a 16-bit range; if Long_Integer does exist then it will have at least a 32-bit range.

In addition to the types Integer and Long_Integer an implementation should provide types directly corresponding to the hardware in the package Interfaces. These will have names such as Integer_8, Integer_16, ..., Integer_128 according to the supported ranges.

We can convert between one integer type and another by using the normal notation for type conversion. Given

```
type My_Integer is range –1E6 .. 1E6;
type Index is range 0 .. 20000;
M: My_Integer;
I: Index;
```

then we can write

```
M := My_Integer(I);
I := Index(M);
```

On machine A a genuine hardware conversion is necessary but on machine B both types will have the same representation as Integer and the conversion will be null.

The derivation model should not be taken too literally as we will see when we discuss generic parameters in Section 17.2. However, all the integer types can be thought of as being ultimately derived from an anonymous type known as *root_integer*. The range of root integer is System.Min_Int .. System.Max_Int where Min_Int and Max_Int are constants declared in the package System. These are the minimum and maximum signed integer values supported by the executing program. Root integer has all the usual integer operations.

The integer literals are considered to belong to another anonymous type known as *universal_integer*. The range of this type is essentially infinite. Integer numbers declared in a number declaration (see Section 6.1) such as

>   Ten: **constant** := 10;

are also of type universal integer. However, there are no universal integer variables and no universal integer operations.

Conversion between universal integer and all other integer types is implicit and does not require an explicit type conversion. In fact the type universal integer behaves very much like the class wide type for the integers; that is like *root_integer*'Class. (But of course there is no tag and so the analogy cannot be taken too far.)

It should be noted that certain attributes such as Pos in fact deliver a universal integer value and since Pos can take a dynamic argument it follows that certain universal integer expressions may actually be dynamic (but they immediately get converted to some other integer type).

The initial value in a number declaration has to be static; it can be of any integer type. So

>   M: **constant** := 10;
>   MM: **constant** := M * M;
>   N: **constant** Integer := 10;
>   NN: **constant** := N * N;

are all allowed.

Sometimes an expression involving literals is ambiguous. In such a case there is a preference for the root type if that overcomes the ambiguity. For example

>   MM: **constant** := M * M;

is apparently ambiguous since the operator "*" is defined for all the specific integer types (not universal). It is then taken to be root integer by this preference rule.

Of course since these expressions are all static and thus evaluated at compile time the distinction is somewhat theoretical especially since static expressions are always evaluated exactly and may exceed the base range of the type concerned. A fuller description of static expressions will be found in

Section 23.1 but the general rule for scalar types is that if it looks static then it is static. Thus 2 + 3 is always static and not just in a context demanding a static expression.

The reader may recall that a range such as 1 .. 10 occurring in a for statement or in an array type definition is considered to be of type Integer. This is a consequence of the preference rule and a special rule which says that a range of type root integer in such contexts is taken to be Integer. Note incidentally that specifying that the range is type Integer rather than any other integer type means that the predefined type Integer does have rather special properties.

We now see why we could write

> **for** I **in** –1 .. 10 **loop**

in Section 7.3. This is ambiguous but by preference taken to be root integer and then the special rule considers it to be of type Integer.

The use of integer type declarations which reflect the need of the program rather than the arbitrary use of Integer and Long_Integer is good practice because it not only encourages portability but also enables us to distinguish between different classes of objects as, for example, when we were counting apples and oranges in Section 11.3.

Consideration of separation of concerns is the key to deciding whether to use numeric constants (of a specific type) or named numbers (of type universal integer). If a literal value is a pure mathematical number then it should be declared as a named number. If, however, it is a value related naturally to just one of the program types then it should be declared as a constant of that type. Thus if we are counting oranges and are checking against a limit of 100 it is better to write

> Max_Oranges: **constant** Oranges := 100;

rather than

> Max_Oranges: **constant** := 100;

so that the accidental mixing of types as in

> **if** No_Of_Apples = Max_Oranges **then**

will be detected by the compiler.

Returning to the question of portability it should be realized that complete portability is not easily obtained. We have seen that although we can specify the ranges for our types and thus ensure that variables are constrained and can never have values outside their range, nevertheless intermediate expressions are typically computed with a wider range that is not prescribed exactly. For example, assume

> **type** My_Integer **is range** –1E6 .. +1E6;
> I, J: My_Integer;

and consider

```
I := 10_000;
J := (I * I) / 5_000;
```

We saw that the operations actually applied to My_Integer'Base. And even then
might have values outside the base range. Ignoring this last possibility for the
moment, on machine A the intermediate product and final result are computed
with no problem and the final result lies within the range of J. But on machine
B we get Constraint_Error because the intermediate product 1E8 is outside the
base range. So the program is not fully portable.

We could declare

```
function Old_Multiply(Left, Right: My_Integer) return My_Integer
                                                    renames "*";

function "*"(Left, Right: My_Integer) return My_Integer is
begin
   return Old_Multiply(Left, Right);
end "*";
```

and then this new function "*" will hide the old one; in the new one the
operands and result have range checks and so our program will be portable
although slow (and this example will fail on both machines!). Note that the
hiding and renaming work because the constraints do not matter for the
conformance rules involved (see Section 12.6). Remember that My_Integer and
My_Integer'Base are both really subtypes of some anonymous type.

In conclusion, portability can be achieved at various levels. Using Integer
is acceptable if we know that the values are always within 16 bits. Using
Long_Integer is less wise. It is far better to use our own types such as
My_Integer. If we are confident about the hardware we are using then we can
use types such as Integer_32 in the package Interfaces.

EXERCISE 15.1

1   What types on machines A and B are used to represent

```
type P is range 1 .. 1000;
type Q is range 0 .. +32768;
type R is range -1E14 .. +1E14;
```

2   Would it make any difference if A and B were one's complement machines with the
same number of bits in the representations?

3   Given

```
N: Integer := 6;
P: constant := 3;
R: My_Integer := 4;
```

what are the types of

(a) N + P   (c) P + R   (e) P ∗ P
(b) N + R   (d) N ∗ N   (f) R ∗ R

4   Declare a type Longest_Integer which is the maximum supported by the implementation.

15.2   Modular types

The modular types are unsigned integer types and exhibit cyclic arithmetic. Suppose for example that we wish to perform unsigned 8-bit arithmetic (that is byte arithmetic). We can declare

type Unsigned_Byte **is mod** 256;

and then the range of values supported by Unsigned_Byte is 0 .. 255. The normal arithmetic operations apply but all arithmetic is performed modulo 256 and overflow cannot occur.

The modulus of a modular type has to be static. It need not be a power of two although it often will be. It might, however, be convenient to use some obscure prime number as the modulus in the implementation of hash tables.

The logical operations **and**, **or**, **xor** and **not** are also available on modular types; the binary operations treat the values as bit patterns; the **not** operation subtracts the value from the maximum for the type. No problems arise with mixing these logical operations with arithmetic operations because negative values are not involved.

The logical operations are of most use when the modulus is a power of two; they are well defined for other moduli but do have some curious properties.

In the last section we noted that the package Interfaces contains declarations of types such as Integer_16. Corresponding to each of these there is a modular type such as Unsigned_16. For these modular types (whose modulus will inevitably be a power of two) a number of shift and rotate operations are defined. They are Shift_Left, Shift_Right, Shift_Right_Arithmetic, Rotate_Left and Rotate_Right. They all have an identical profile such as

function Shift_Left(Value: Unsigned_16; Amount: Natural)
                                            return Unsigned_16;

These subprograms have the expected behaviour. They are intrinsic which means that the Access attribute cannot be applied to them in order to produce an access to subprogram value.

Conversion between modular types and signed integer types is possible provided the value is not out of range of the destination. If it is then Constraint_Error is naturally raised.

Thus suppose we had

```
type Signed_Byte is range –128 .. +127;
X: Unsigned_Byte := 150;
Y: Signed_Byte := Signed_Byte(X);
```

then the type conversion will raise Constraint_Error. Conversion as bit patterns (which would avoid the exception and convert the 150 into –106) can conveniently be performed using unchecked conversion as described in Section 21.2. Beware that literals (which are of type universal integer) are also converted, albeit implicitly, and so

```
X := 256;
```

also raises Constraint_Error. On the other hand, a computation such as

```
X := 128;
X := X + X;
```

which is performed using modulo arithmetic will result in zero being assigned to X.

Note that since modular types are integer types they are also discrete types and so have all the common properties of the class of discrete types. Subtypes can be declared with a reduced range (this would be unusual). Modular types can be sensibly used as array index types and for loop parameters. An example of an array index dealing with a circular buffer will be found in Section 18.4.

The attribute Modulus applies to modular subtypes and naturally returns the modulus; it is of type universal integer.

EXERCISE 15.2

1   Given

```
X: Unsigned_Byte := 16#AB#;
Y: Unsigned_Byte := 16#CD#;
```

what are the values of

(a) X **or** Y   (c) X – Y
(b) X + Y   (d) X * Y

2   Reconsider Exercise 8.2(**2**) using an appropriate modular type.

3   Given

```
type Ring5 is mod 5;
A: Ring5 := 3;
B: Ring5 := 4;
```

what are the values of

(a) **not** (A **and** B)   (b) **not** A **or** **not** B

15.3 Real types

Integer types are exact types. Real types, however, are approximate and introduce problems of accuracy which have subtle effects. This book is not a specialized treatise on errors in numerical analysis and so we do not intend to give all the details of how the features of Ada can be used to minimize errors and maximize portability but will concentrate instead on outlining the basic principles.

Real types are subdivided into floating point types and fixed point types. Apart from the details of representation, the key abstract difference is that floating point values have a relative error whereas fixed point values have an absolute error. Concepts common to both floating and fixed point types are dealt with in this section and further details of the individual types are in subsequent sections.

There are types universal real and root real having similar properties to the types universal integer and root integer. Again the preference rule chooses root real in the case of an ambiguity. Static operations on the type root real are notionally carried out with infinite accuracy during compilation. The real literals (see Section 5.4) are of type universal real. Real numbers declared in a number declaration such as

    Pi: **constant** := 3.14159_26536;

are also of type universal real. (The reader will recall that the difference between an integer literal and a real literal is that a real literal always has a point in it.)

As well as the usual operations on a numeric type, some mixing of root real and root integer operands is also allowed. Specifically, a root real can be multiplied by a root integer and vice versa and division is allowed with the first operand being root real and the second operand being root integer; in all cases the result is root real.

So we can write either

    Two_Pi: **constant** := 2 * Pi;

or

    Two_Pi: **constant** := 2.0 * Pi;

but not

    Pi_Plus_Two: **constant** := Pi + 2;

because mixed addition is not defined. Note that we cannot do an explicit type conversion between root integer and root real although we can always convert the former into the latter by multiplying by 1.0.

EXERCISE 15.3

1 Given

> Two: Integer := 2;
> E: **constant** := 2.71828_18285;
> Max: **constant** := 100;

what are the types of

(a) Two * E   (c) E * Max   (e) E * E
(b) Two * Max   (d) Two * Two   (f) Max * Max

2 Given

> N: **constant** := 100;

declare a real number R having the same value as N.

15.4   Floating point types

In a similar way to integers, all implementations have a predefined type Float
and may also have further predefined types Long_Float, Short_Float and so on
with respectively more and less precision (could be the same). These types all
have the predefined operations that were described in Chapter 6 as applicable
to the type Float.

The type Float will have at least 6 digits of precision (provided the
hardware can cope) and the type Long_Float (if available) will have at least 11
digits of precision. Other named types in Standard are not recommended in the
interests of portability. In a similar way to the integer types, named types
corresponding to the hardware supported floating types may be declared in the
package Interfaces with appropriate names such as IEEE_Float_64. (Note the
contrast between Integer and Float. Integer always has at least 16 bits but, for
awkward hardware, Float is permitted not to have 6 digits.)

However, as mentioned in Section 2.4, it is good practice not to use the
predefined types because of potential portability problems. If we write

> **type** Real **is digits** 7;

then we are asking the implementation to base Real on a predefined floating
point type with at least 7 decimal digits of precision.

The number of decimal digits requested, D, must be static. The actual
precision and range supported will of course depend upon the hardware. The
actual precision is known as the base decimal precision and the implemented
range is the base range. For some awkward hardware, the base decimal
precision might not hold over the whole of the base range and so that part of
the range for which it does hold is called the safe range. We are guaranteed that

the safe range includes $-10.0**(4*D)$ .. $+10.0**(4*D)$. For most applications that is all we need to know.

For specialized applications the Numerics annex contains a description of the minimum guaranteed properties in terms of what are called model numbers. See Section 22.5.

The types Float, Long_Float and Real are unconstrained and so no range checks are imposed on assignments to variables of these types. But overflow checks always apply and raise Constraint_Error if they fail (provided the attribute Machine_Overflows is true).

It is possible to declare a constrained type by for example

type Risk **is digits** 7 **range** 0.0 .. 1.0;

in which case the range constraint must be static. We can impose a (possibly dynamic) range constraint on a floating point subtype or object by

R: Real **range** 0.0 .. 100.0;

or

subtype Positive_Real **is** Real **range** 0.0 .. Real'Last;

and so on. If a range is violated then Constraint_Error is raised.

If we do declare a type with a range such as Risk then the safe range will always include the range given and the 4*D rule does not apply. This might force the use of a higher precision than without the range (not in the case of Risk though which has a relatively small range compared with the precision!)

The attribute Base can be applied so that Risk'Base gives the corresponding unconstrained subtype. Note that in contrast to Integer, the type Float is unconstrained and consequently Float and Float'Base are the same.

As well as a portable type Real, we might declare a more accurate type Long_Real perhaps for the more sensitive parts of our calculation

type Long_Real **is digits** 12;

and then declare variables of the two types

R: Real;
LR: Long_Real;

as required. Conversion between these follows similar rules to integer types

R := Real(LR);
LR := Long_Real(R);

and we need not concern ourselves with whether Real and Long_Real are based on the same or different predefined types.

Again in a similar manner to integer types, conversion of real literals, real numbers and universal real attributes to floating types is automatic.

The detailed workings of floating point types are defined in terms of various attributes based on a canonical model. In this model, nonzero values are represented as

$$sign.mantissa.radix^{exponent}$$

where

sign is +1 or −1,
radix is the hardware radix such as 2 or 16,
mantissa is a fraction in the base *radix* with nonzero leading digit,
exponent is an integer.

For any subtype S of a type T, the attribute S'Machine_Radix gives the *radix* and the three attributes S'Machine_Mantissa, S'Machine_Emin and S'Machine_Emax collectively give the maximum number of digits in the *mantissa* and the range of values of the *exponent* for which every number in the canonical form is exactly represented in the machine. They all have type universal integer.

For example, one possible representation in a 32-bit word might be in binary with 1 sign bit, 8 bits for the exponent and 23 bits for the mantissa. Since the leading mantissa bit is always 1, it need not be stored. The exponent can be held in a biased form with logical values ranging from −128 to +127. For such a type the attributes would be 2, 24, −128 and 127 respectively. This format was used on the PDP-11.

The 32-bit IBM 370 format has a hexadecimal radix, with again 1 sign bit, 7 exponent bits and 24 mantissa bits. The attributes are 16, 6, −64 and 63. Note carefully that the 24 bits only allow for 6 hexadecimal digits.

There are also the closely related model attributes Model_Mantissa, Model_Emin, Model_Epsilon, Model_Small and the function Model. Although they have to be provided by all implementations and are thus in the core language, their full description relates to implementations supporting the Numerics annex; see Section 22.5. Nevertheless, the following relationships always hold where D is the requested decimal precision for the subtype S

$$1 + D.\log_{radix}10 <= Model\_Mantissa <= Machine\_Mantissa$$

$$Model\_Emin >= Machine\_Emin$$

$$Model\_Epsilon = radix^{(1-Model\_Mantissa)}$$

$$Model\_Small = radix^{(Model\_Emin-1)}$$

The requested precision D determines the choice of underlying type. The model attributes relate to the abstract properties of an ideal hardware type whereas the machine attributes relate to what the hardware actually does (which in many cases will be the same, but sometimes has marginal variations). Model_Epsilon is a measure of the accuracy and is typically the difference between one and the next number above one. Model_Small is typically the smallest positive number. These two attributes are of type universal real.

Various other attributes enable the specialized programmer to manipulate the internals of floating point numbers. For example S'Exponent returns the exponent and S'Fraction returns the fraction part. These and other similar attributes are described in a little more detail in Appendix 1.

An interesting possibility is that the hardware may distinguish between positive and negative zero. The attribute S'Signed_Zeros is then true. A negative zero would arise for example if a small negative number were divided by a large positive one such that the result underflowed to zero. The distinction can be useful in certain boundary situations; for example the function Arctan behaves differently as mentioned in Section 20.3. Note that negative zero can also be distinguished by copying its sign to a nonzero number using S'Copy_Sign and then testing the result. But otherwise a negative zero behaves as positive zero and for example X = 0.0 is true if X is a negative zero.

The attribute S'Digits gives the number of decimal digits requested, and S'Base'Digits gives the number of decimal digits provided.

There are also the usual attributes S'First and S'Last which are the bounds of the subtype. The base range is S'Base'First .. S'Base'Last and the safe range is S'Safe_First .. S'Safe_Last.

Digits and Base'Digits are of type universal integer; Safe_First and Safe_Last are of type universal real; First and Last are of type T.

We do not intend to say more about floating point here but hope that the reader will have understood the principles involved. In general one can simply specify the precision required and all will work. But care is sometimes needed and the advice of a professional numerical analyst should be sought when in doubt. For further details the reader should consult Section 22.5 and the *ARM*.

EXERCISE 15.4

1 Rewrite the function Inner of Section 9.1 using the type Real for parameters and result and a local type Long_Real with 14 digits accuracy to perform the calculation in the loop.

15.5   Fixed point types

The fixed point types come in two forms, the normal fixed point which is based on a binary representation and decimal fixed point which is based on a decimal representation. Normal fixed point is typically used only in specialized applications or for doing approximate arithmetic on machines without floating point hardware. Decimal fixed point is typically used for accountancy and is discussed in the next section.

A fixed point type declaration specifies an absolute error and also a mandatory range. It takes the form

    type F **is delta** D **range** L .. R;

In effect this is asking for values in the range L to R with an accuracy of D which must be positive. D, L and R must be real and static.

The implemented values of a fixed point type are the multiples of a positive real number *small*. The actual value of *small* chosen by the implementation can be any power of 2 less than or equal to D. The base range includes all multiples of small within the requested range.

As an example, if we have

> **type** T **is delta** 0.1 **range** −1.0 .. +1.0;

then *small* could be $^1/_{16}$. So the implemented values of T will always include

$$-^{15}/_{16}, -^{14}/_{16}, ..., -^1/_{16}, 0, +^1/_{16}, ..., +^{14}/_{16}, +^{15}/_{16}$$

Note carefully that L and R might actually be outside the base range by as much as *small*; the definition just allows this.

If we have a typical 16-bit implementation then there will be a wide choice of values of *small*. At one extreme *small* could be 2^{-15} which would give us a much greater accuracy but just the required range (the base range would include −1.0 but not +1.0 on a two's complement machine). At the other extreme *small* could be $^1/_{16}$ in which case we would have a much greater base range but just the required accuracy.

The type T is of course constrained and range checks will apply; the corresponding unconstrained base subtype is given by T'**Base**. So the base range as usual is T'**Base'Range**.

Of course, a different implementation might use just eight bits for T. Moreover, using representation clauses (which will be discussed in more detail in Chapter 21) it is possible to give the compiler more precise instructions. We can say

> **for** T'Size **use** 5;

which will force the implementation to use the minimum five bits. Of course, it might be ridiculous for a particular architecture and in fact the compiler is allowed to refuse unreasonable representation clauses.

We can also override the rule that *small* is a power of 2 by using a representation clause. Writing

> **for** T'Small **use** 0.1;

will result in the implemented numbers being multiples of 0.1. On an 8-bit implementation the base range would then be from −12.8 to +12.7. Note that if we explicitly specify *small* then any spare bits give extra range and not extra accuracy. This is yet another win for the accountants at the expense of the engineers!

The advantage of using the default standard whereby *small* is a power of 2 is that conversion between fixed point and other numeric types can be based on shifting. The use of other values of *small* will in general mean that conversion requires implicit multiplication and division.

A standard simple example is given by

```
Del: constant := 2.0**(-15);
type Frac is delta Del range -1.0 .. 1.0;
```

which will be represented as a pure fraction on a 16-bit two's complement machine. Note that it does not really matter whether the upper bound is written as 1.0 or 1.0–Del; the largest implemented number will be 1.0–Del in either case.

A good example of the use of a specified value for *small* is given by a type representing an angle and which uses the whole of a 16-bit word

```
type Angle is delta 0.1 range -Pi .. Pi;
for Angle'Small use Pi * 2**(-15);
```

Note that the value given for the representation clause for Angle'Small must not exceed the value for delta which it overrides.

The arithmetic operations +, −, *, / and **abs** can be applied to fixed point values. Addition and subtraction can only be applied to values of the same type and, of course, return that type. Addition and subtraction are of course exact.

Multiplication and division are explained in terms of the type universal fixed; the parameters and result are of this type which is matched by any fixed point type. As a consequence, multiplication and division are allowed between different fixed point types and the result is then of the type expected by the context. However, if the result is a parameter of a further multiplication or division then the result must first be explicitly converted to a particular type; this ensures that the scale of the intermediate value is properly determined. Multiplication and division by type Integer are also allowed and these return a value of the fixed point type. If the result of a multiplication or division is not an exact multiple of *small* then either adjacent multiple of *small* is permitted.

Conversion of real literals, real numbers and universal real attributes to fixed point types (including universal fixed) is again automatic.

So given

```
F, G, H: Frac;
```

we can write

```
F := F + G;
F := F * G;
F := 0.5 * F;
F := F + 0.5;
```

but not

```
F := F * G * H;              -- illegal
```

but must explicitly state the intermediate type such as

```
F := Frac(F * G) * H;
```

As expected, we cannot write

```
F := 2 + F;                   -- illegal
```

but we can write

```
F := 2 * F;
```

because multiplication is defined between fixed point types and Integer.

As a more detailed example we return to the package Complex_Numbers of Section 11.2 and consider how we might implement the package body using a polar representation. Any reader who gave thought to the problem will have realized that writing a function to normalize an angle expressed in radians to lie in the range 0 to 2π using floating point raises problems of accuracy since 2π is not a representable number.

An alternative approach is to use a fixed point type. We can then arrange for π to be exactly represented. Another natural advantage is that fixed point types have uniform absolute error which matches the physical behaviour. The type Angle declared above is not quite appropriate because, as we shall see, it will be convenient to allow for angles of up to 2π.

The private part of the package could be

```
private
   Pi: constant := Ada.Numerics.Pi;
   type Angle is delta 0.1 range -4*Pi .. 4*Pi;
   for Angle'Small use Pi * 2**(-13);
   type Complex is
      record
         R: Real;
         Theta: Angle range -Pi .. Pi;
      end record;
   I: constant Complex := (1.0, 0.5*Pi);
end;
```

where we have taken the opportunity to use the portable floating point type Real which seems more appropriate for this example.

The function for normalizing an angle to lie in the range of the component Theta (which is neater if symmetric about zero) could now be

```
function Normal(A: Angle) return Angle is
begin
   if A >= Pi then
      return A - 2*Pi;
   elsif A < -Pi then
      return A + 2*Pi;
   else
      return A;
   end if;
end Normal;
```

Another interesting point is that the values for Theta that we are using do not include the upper bound of the range +Pi; the function Normal converts this into the equivalent –Pi. Unfortunately we cannot express the idea of an open bound in Ada although it would be perfectly straightforward to implement the corresponding checks.

The range for the type Angle has been chosen so that it will accommodate the sum of any two values of Theta. This includes –2*Pi; however, making the lower bound of the range for Angle equal to –2*Pi is not adequate since there is no guarantee that the lower bound will be a represented number – it will not be on a one's complement implementation. So to be on the safe side we squander a bit on doubling the range.

The various functions in the package body can now be written; we assume that we have access to appropriate trigonometric functions applying to the fixed point type Angle and returning results of type Real. So we might have

```
package body Complex_Numbers is
    function Normal ...    –– as above

    ...
    function "*" (X, Y: Complex) return Complex is
    begin
        return (X.R * Y.R, Normal(X.Theta + Y.Theta));
    end "*";
    ...
    function Rl_Part(X: Complex) return Real is
    begin
        return X.R * Cos(X.Theta);
    end Rl_Part;
    ...
end Complex_Numbers;
```

where we have left the more complicated functions for the enthusiastic reader.

The attributes of a fixed point subtype S of a type T include S'Delta which is the requested delta, *D*, and S'Small which is the smallest positive represented number, *small*. Machine_Radix, Machine_Rounds and Machine Overflows also apply to all fixed point types. There are also the usual attributes S'First and S'Last which give the actual upper and lower bounds of the subtype.

Delta and Small are of type universal real; First and Last are of type T.

EXERCISE 15.5

1   Given F of type Frac explain why we could write

   F := 0.5 * F;

2   Write the following further function for the package Complex_Numbers implemented as in this section

   function "**" (X: Complex; N: Integer) **return** Complex;

Remember that if a complex number z is represented in polar form (r, θ), then

$$z^n \equiv (r, \theta)^n = (r^n, n\theta).$$

3   An alternative approach to the representation of angles in fixed point would be to hold the values in degrees. Rewrite the private part and the function Normal using a canonical range of 0.0 .. 360.0 for Theta. Make the most of a 16-bit word but use a power of 2 for *small*.

15.6   Decimal types

Decimal types are used in specialized commercial applications and are dealt with in depth in the Information Systems annex which is outside the scope of this book. However, the basic syntax of decimal types is in the core language and it is therefore appropriate to give a very brief overview.

A decimal type is a form of fixed point type. The declaration provides a value of delta as for an ordinary fixed point type (except that in this case it must be a power of 10) and also prescribes the number of significant decimal digits. So we can write

> **type** Money **is delta** 0.01 **digits** 14;

which will cope with values of some currency such as Eurodollars up to one trillion (billion for older Europeans) in units of one Eurocent. This allows 2 digits for the cents and 12 for the dollars so that the maximum allowed value is

> $999,999,999,999.99

The usual operations apply to decimal types as to other fixed point types; they are more exactly prescribed than for ordinary fixed point types since accountants abhor rounding errors. For example, type conversion always rounds towards zero and if the result of a multiplication or division lies midway between two multiples of *small* then again it rounds towards zero. Furthermore, the Information Systems annex describes a number of special packages for decimal types including conversion to external format using picture strings. See Section 22.4.

The attributes Digits, Scale and Round apply to decimal types; see Appendix 1. The attributes which apply to ordinary fixed point types also apply to decimal types. For most machines, Machine_Radix will always be 2 but some machines support packed decimal types and for them Machine_Radix will be 10.

CHECKLIST 15

Declare explicit types for increased portability.

Beware of overflow in intermediate expressions.

Use named numbers or typed constants as appropriate.

The type Integer is constrained but Float is not.

If in doubt consult a numerical analyst.

Changes from Ada 83

Modular and decimal types did not exist in Ada 83.

The models of floating and fixed point types were different in Ada 83 and there were different attributes.

The attribute Base could only be used with other attributes in Ada 83.

Small was always the highest power of two less than delta in Ada 83.

Explicit type conversion was required for all fixed point multiplication and division in Ada 83.

There was no preference rule in Ada 83. The loop range −1 .. 100 was not allowed.

The initial value of a named number had to be of universal type in Ada 83.

16 Parameterized Types

In this chapter we describe the parameterization of types by what are known as discriminants. Discriminants are components of types which have special properties. All composite types other than arrays can have discriminants. In this chapter we deal with the properties of discriminants in general and their use with record types (both tagged and untagged); their use with task and protected types is discussed in Chapter 18.

Discriminants can be of a discrete type or an access type. In the latter case the access type can be a named access type or it can be anonymous. A discriminant of an anonymous access type is called an access discriminant by analogy with an access parameter.

We start by dealing with discrete discriminants of untagged types.

16.1   Discriminated record types

In the record types we have seen so far there was no formal language dependency between the components. Any dependency was purely in the mind of the programmer as for example in the case of the private type Stack in Section 11.4 where the interpretation of the array S depended on the value of the integer Top.

In the case of a discriminated record type, some of the components are known as discriminants and the remaining components can depend upon these.

The discriminants can be thought of as parameterizing the type and the syntax reveals this analogy.

As a simple example, suppose we wish to write a package providing various operations on square matrices and that in particular we wish to write a function Trace which sums the diagonal elements of a square matrix. We could contemplate using the type Matrix of Section 8.2

```
type Matrix is array (Integer range <>, Integer range <>) of Float;
```

but our function would then have to check that the matrix passed as an actual parameter was indeed square. We would have to write something like

```
function Trace(M: Matrix) return Float is
   Sum: Float := 0.0;
begin
   if M'First(1) /= M'First(2) or M'Last(1) /= M'Last(2) then
      raise Non_Square;
   end if;
   for I in M'Range loop
      Sum := Sum + M(I, I);
   end loop;
   return Sum;
end Trace;
```

This is somewhat unsatisfactory; we would prefer to use a formulation which ensured that the matrix was always square and had a lower bound of 1. We can do this using a discriminated type. Consider

```
type Square(Order: Positive) is
   record
      Mat: Matrix(1 .. Order, 1 .. Order);
   end record;
```

This is a record type having two components: the first, Order, is a discriminant of the discrete subtype Positive and the second, Mat, is an array whose bounds depend upon the value of Order.

Variables and constants of type Square can be declared in the usual way but (like array bounds) a value of the discriminant must be given either explicitly as a constraint or from an initial value. Thus the following are permitted

```
M: Square(3);
M: Square(Order => 3);
M: Square := (3, (1 .. 3 => (1 .. 3 => 0.0)));
```

The value provided for the discriminant could be any dynamic expression but once the variable is declared its constraint cannot be changed. The initial value for M could be provided by an aggregate as shown; note that the number of components in the subaggregate depends upon the first component of the aggregate. This can also be dynamic so that we could declare a Square of order

N and initialize it to zero by

```
M: Square := (N, (1 .. N => (1 .. N => 0.0)));
```

We could avoid repeating N by giving the initial value separately (remember that we cannot refer to an object in its own declaration). So we could also write

```
M: Square(N);
...
M := (M.Order, (M.Mat'Range(1) =>
                (M.Mat'Range(2) => 0.0)));
```

If we attempt to assign a value to M which does not have the correct discriminant value then Constraint_Error will be raised.

We can, of course, introduce subtypes

```
subtype Square_3 is Square(3);
M: Square_3;
```

We can now rewrite our function Trace as follows

```
function Trace(M: Square) return Float is
  Sum: Float := 0.0;
begin
  for I in M.Mat'Range loop
    Sum := Sum + M.Mat(I, I);
  end loop;
  return Sum;
end Trace;
```

There is now no way in which a call of Trace can be supplied with a non-square matrix. Note that the discriminant of the formal parameter is taken from that of the actual parameter in a similar way to the bounds of an array. Discriminants of parameters have much in common with array bounds. Thus, like arrays, the formal parameter could be constrained as in

```
function Trace_3(M: Square_3) return Float;
```

but then the actual parameter would have to have a discriminant value of 3; otherwise Constraint_Error would be raised.

The result of a function could be of a discriminated type and, like arrays, the result could be a value whose discriminant is not known until the function is called. Thus we could write a function to return the transpose of a square matrix

```
function Transpose(M: Square) return Square is
  R: Square(M.Order);
begin
  for I in 1 .. M.Order loop
    for J in 1 .. M.Order loop
      R.Mat(I, J) := M.Mat(J, I);
```

```
            end loop;
          end loop;
          return R;
        end Transpose;
```

A private type can have discriminants in the partial view and it must then be implemented as a type with corresponding discriminants (this will usually be a record but it could be a task or protected type, see Section 18.10). A good example is provided by reconsidering the type Stack in Section 11.4. We can overcome the problem that all the stacks had the same maximum length of 100 by making Max a discriminant. Thus we can write

```
package Stacks is
   type Stack(Max: Natural) is private;
   procedure Push(S: in out Stack; X: in Integer);
   procedure Pop(S: in out Stack; X out Integer);
   function "=" (S, T: Stack) return Boolean;
private
   type Integer_Vector is array (Integer range <>) of Integer;
   type Stack(Max: Natural) is
      record
         S: Integer_Vector(1 .. Max);
         Top: Integer := 0;
      end record;
end;
```

Each variable of type Stack now includes a discriminant component giving the maximum stack size. When we declare a stack we must supply the value thus

```
ST: Stack(100);
```

and as for the type Square the value of the discriminant cannot later be changed. Of course, the discriminant is visible and can be referred to as ST.Max although the remaining components are private.

The body of the package Stacks remains as before (see Section 11.4). Observe in particular that the function "=" can be used to compare stacks with different values of Max since it only compares those components of the internal array which are in use.

This is a good point to mention that discriminants bear a resemblance to subprogram parameters in several respects. The subtype of a discriminant must be given by a subtype mark and not by a subtype indication. This is so that the same full conformance rules can be used when a discriminant specification has to be repeated in the case of a private type with discriminants, as illustrated by the type Stack above.

We can also have deferred constants of a discriminated type and they follow similar rules to array types as discussed in Section 11.2. The deferred constant need not provide a discriminant but if it does then it must statically match that in the full constant declaration.

Suppose we wish to declare a constant Stack with a discriminant of 3. We can omit the discriminant in the visible part and merely write

    C: **constant** Stack;

and then give the discriminant in the private part either as a constraint or through the mandatory initial value (or both)

    C: **constant** Stack(3) := (3, (1, 2, 3), 3);

It is possible to declare a type with several discriminants. We may for instance wish to manipulate matrices which although not constrained to be square nevertheless have both lower bounds of 1. This could be done by

    type Rectangle(Rows, Columns: Positive) **is**
      record
        Mat: Matrix(1 .. Rows, 1 .. Columns);
      end record;

and we could then declare either of

    R: Rectangle(2, 3);
    R: Rectangle(Rows => 2, Columns => 3);

The usual rules apply: positional values must be given in order, named ones may be in any order, mixed notation can be used but the positional ones must come first.

    Similarly to multidimensional arrays, a subtype must supply all the constraints or none at all. We could not declare

    subtype Row_3 **is** Rectangle(Rows => 3);

in order to get the equivalent of

    type Row_3(Columns: Positive) **is**
      record
        Mat: Matrix(1 .. 3, 1 .. Columns);
      end record;

although a similar effect can be achieved using derived types as explained in Section 16.4.

    The above examples have shown discriminants used in index constraints as the upper bounds of arrays; they can also be used as the lower bounds of arrays. In Section 16.3 we will describe how a discriminant can also be used to introduce a variant part. In all these cases a discriminant must be used directly and not as part of a larger expression. So we could not declare

    type Symmetric_Array(N: Positive) **is**
      record
        A: Vector(–N .. N);   -- illegal
      end record;

where the discriminant N is part of the expression –N.

EXERCISE 16.1

1 Suppose that M is an object of the type Matrix. Write a call of the function Trace whose parameter is an aggregate of type Square in order to determine the trace of M. What would happen if the two dimensions of M were not equal?

2 Rewrite the specification of Stacks to include a constant Empty in the visible part. See also Exercise 11.4(**1**).

3 Write a function Is_Full for Stacks. See also Exercise 11.4(**2**).

4 Declare a constant Square of order N and initialize it to a unit matrix. Use the function Make_Unit of Exercise 9.1(**6**).

16.2 Default discriminants

The discriminant types we have encountered so far have been such that once a variable is declared, its discriminant cannot be changed just as the bound of an array cannot be changed. It is possible, however, to provide a default expression for a discriminant and the situation is then quite different. A variable can then be declared with or without a discriminant constraint. If one is supplied then that value overrides the default and as before the discriminant cannot be changed. If, on the other hand, a variable is declared without a value for the discriminant, then the value of the default expression is taken but it can then be changed by a complete record assignment (unless the variable is marked as aliased, see Section 16.5).

A record type with default discriminants is an example of a definite type whereas one without defaults is an indefinite type. Remember that we can declare (uninitialized) objects and arrays of a definite type but not of an indefinite type, see Section 8.5.

Suppose we wish to manipulate polynomials of the form

$$P(x) = a_0 + a_1x + a_2x^2 + \ldots a_nx^n$$

where $a_n \neq 0$ if $n \neq 0$.

Such a polynomial could be represented by

```
type Poly(N: Index) is
   record
      A: Integer_Vector(0 .. N);
   end record;
```

where

```
        subtype Index is Integer range 0 .. Max;
```

but then a variable of type Poly would have to be declared with a constraint and would thereafter be a polynomial of that fixed size. This would be most inconvenient because the sizes of the polynomials may be determined as the consequences of elaborate calculations. For example, if we subtract two polynomials which have $n = 3$, then the result will only have $n = 3$ if the coefficients of x^3 are different.

However, if we declare

```
type Polynomial(N: Index := 0) is
   record
      A: Integer_Vector(0 .. N);
   end record;
```

then we can declare variables

```
P, Q: Polynomial;
```

which do not have constraints. The initial value of their discriminants would be zero because the default value of N is zero but the discriminants could later be changed by assignment. Note however that a discriminant can only be changed by a complete record assignment. So

```
P.N := 6;
```

would be illegal. This is quite natural since we cannot expect the array P.A to adjust its bounds by magic.

Variables of the type Polynomial could be declared with constraints

```
R: Polynomial(5);
```

but R would thereafter be constrained forever to be a polynomial with $n = 5$.

Initial values can be given in declarations in the usual way

```
P: Polynomial := (3, (5, 0, 4, 2));
```

which represents $5 + 4x^2 + 2x^3$. Note that despite the initial value, P is not constrained.

In practice we might make the type Polynomial a private type so that we could enforce the rule that $a_n \neq 0$. Observe that predefined equality is satisfactory. We can give the discriminant in the partial view and then both the private type declaration and the full type declaration must give the default expression for N.

Note once more the similarity to subprogram parameters; the default expression is only evaluated when required and so need not produce the same value each time. Moreover, the same conformance rules apply when it has to be written out again in the case of a private type.

We can alternatively choose that the partial view does not show the discriminant at all. We might write

```
package Polynomials is
  type Polynomial is private;
  ...
private
  type Polynomial(N: Index := 0) is ...
  ...
end;
```

and then of course we can only declare unconstrained polynomials outside the package. Of course it is vital that the full type has defaults so that the type is definite.

If we declare functions such as

```
function "–" (P, Q: Polynomial) return Polynomial;
```

then it will be necessary to ensure that the result is normalized so that a_n is not zero. This could be done by the following function

```
function Normal(P: Polynomial) return Polynomial is
  Size: Integer := P.N;
begin
  while Size > 0 and P.A(Size) = 0 loop
    Size := Size – 1;
  end loop;
  return (Size, P.A(0 .. Size));
end Normal;
```

This is a further illustration of a function returning a value whose discriminant is not known until it is called. Note the use of the array slice.

If default expressions are supplied then they must be supplied for all discriminants of the type. Moreover an object must be fully constrained or not at all; we cannot supply constraints for some discriminants and use the defaults for others.

The attribute Constrained can be applied to an object of a discriminated type and gives a Boolean value indicating whether the object is constrained or not. For any object of types such as Square and Stack which do not have default values for the discriminants this attribute will, of course, be True. But in the case of objects of a type such as Polynomial which does have a default value, the attribute may be True or False. So

```
P'Constrained = False
R'Constrained = True
```

We mentioned above that an unconstrained formal parameter will take the value of the discriminant of the actual parameter. In the case of an **out** or **in out** parameter, the formal parameter will be constrained if the actual parameter is constrained (an **in** parameter is constant anyway). Suppose we declare a procedure to truncate a polynomial by removing its highest order term

```
procedure Truncate(P: in out Polynomial) is
begin
   P := (P.N–1, P.A(0 .. P.N–1));
end Truncate;
```

Then given

```
Q: Polynomial;
R: Polynomial(5);
```

the statement

```
Truncate(Q);
```

will be successful, but

```
Truncate(R);
```

will result in Constraint_Error being raised. (We will also get Constraint_Error if we try to remove the only term of an unconstrained polynomial.)

We have seen that a discriminant can be used as the bound of an array. It can also be used as the discriminant constraint of an inner component. We could declare a type representing rational polynomials (that is one polynomial divided by another) by

```
type Rational_Polynomial(N, D: Index := 0) is
   record
      Num: Polynomial(N);
      Den: Polynomial(D);
   end record;
```

The relationship between constraints on the rational polynomial as a whole and its component polynomials is interesting. If we declare

```
R: Rational_Polynomial(2, 3);
```

then R is constrained for ever and the components R.Num and R.Den are also permanently constrained with constraints 2 and 3 respectively. However

```
P: Rational_Polynomial := (2, 3, Num => (2, (–1, 0, 1)),
                                 Den => (3, (–1, 0, 0, 1)));
```

is not constrained. This means that we can assign complete new values to P with different values of N and D. The fact that the components Num and Den are declared as constrained does not mean that P.Num and P.Den must always have a fixed length but simply that for given N and D they are constrained to have the appropriate length. So we could not write

```
P.Num => (1, (1, 1));
```

because this would violate the constraint on P.Num. However, we can write

P := (1, 2, Num => (1, (1, 1)), Den => (2, (1, 1, 1)));

because this changes everything together. Of course we can always make a direct assignment to P.Num that does not change the current value of its own discriminant.

The original value of P represented $(x^2 - 1)/(x^3 - 1)$ and the final value represents $(x + 1)/(x^2 + x + 1)$ which is, in fact, the same with the common factor $(x - 1)$ cancelled. The reader will note the strong analogy between the type Rational_Polynomial and the type Rational of Exercise 11.2(**3**). We could write an equivalent function Normal to cancel common factors of our rational polynomials and the whole package of operations would then follow.

Another possible use of a discriminant is as part of the expression giving a default initial value for one of the other record components (but not another discriminant). Although the discriminant value may not be known until an object is declared, this is not a problem since the default initial expression is of course only evaluated when the object is declared and no other initial value is supplied. A discriminant can also be used to introduce a variant part as described in the next section.

However, we cannot use a discriminant for any other purpose. This unfortunately meant that when we declared the type Stack in the previous section we could not continue to apply the constraint to Top by writing

```
type Stack(Max: Natural) is
   record
      S: Integer_Vector(1 .. Max);
      Top: Integer range 0 .. Max := 0;      -- illegal
   end record;
```

since the use of Max in the range constraint is not allowed.

We conclude this section by reconsidering the problem of variable length strings and ragged arrays previously discussed in Sections 8.5, 10.3 and 10.4. Yet another approach is to use discriminated records. There are a number of possibilities such as

```
subtype String_Size is Integer range 0 .. 80;
```

```
type V_String(N: String_Size := 0) is
   record
      S: String(1 .. N);
   end record;
```

The type V_String is very similar to the type Polynomial (the lower bound is different). We have chosen a maximum string size corresponding to a typical page width (or historic punched card).

We can now declare fixed or varying v-strings and make appropriate assignments

V: V_String := (5, "Hello");

We can overcome the burden of having to specify the length by writing

```
function "+" (S: String) return V_String is
begin
   return (S'Length, S);
end "+";
```

and then

```
type V_String_Array is array (Positive range <>) of V_String;

Zoo: constant V_String_Array := (+"aardvark", +"baboon",
                        +"camel", +"dolphin", +"elephant", ..., +"zebra");
```

Since v-strings have default discriminants they are definite and so we can declare unconstrained v-strings and also arrays of them.

With this formulation there is a limit of 80 on our strings and, moreover, the storage space for the maximum size string is likely to be allocated irrespective of the actual string.

The reader might feel bemused by the number of different ways in which variable length strings can be handled. There are indeed many conflicting requirements and in order to promote portability a number of predefined packages for manipulating strings are provided; see Section 20.2.

EXERCISE 16.2

1   Declare a Polynomial representing zero (that is, $0x^0$).

2   Write a function "*" to multiply two polynomials.

3   Write a function "−" to subtract two polynomials. Use the function Normal.

4   Rewrite the procedure Truncate to raise Truncate_Error if we attempt to truncate a constrained polynomial.

5   What would be the effect of replacing the discriminant of the type Polynomial by (N: Integer := 0)?

6   Rewrite the declaration of the type Polynomial so that the default initial value of a polynomial of degree n represents x^n. Hint: declare an auxiliary function returning an appropriate array value.

7   Write the specification of a package Rational_Polynomials. Make the type Rational_Polynomial private with visible discriminants. The functions should correspond to those of the package Rational_Numbers of Exercise 11.2(**3**).

8   Write a function "&" to concatenate two v-strings.

16.3 Variant parts

It is sometimes convenient to have a record type in which part of the structure is fixed for all objects of the type but the remainder can take one of several different forms. This can be done using a variant part and the choice between the alternatives is governed by the value of a discriminant.

In many ways the use of a variant is an alternative to a tagged type where the hidden tag plays the role of the discriminant. For example in Section 13.4 we had an abstract type Person and derived types Man and Woman; we can reformulate this using a variant part as follows

```
type Gender is (Male, Female);

type Person(Sex: Gender) is
  record
    Birth: Date;
    case Sex is
      when Male =>
        Bearded: Boolean;
      when Female =>
        Children: Integer;
    end case;
  end record;
```

This declares a record type Person with a discriminant Sex. The component Birth of type Date (see Section 8.7) is common to all objects of the type. However, the remaining components depend upon Sex and are declared as a variant part. If the value of Sex is Male then there is a further component Bearded whereas if Sex is Female then there is a component Children.

Since no default expression is given for the discriminant all objects of the type must be constrained either explicitly or from an initial value. We can therefore declare

```
John: Person(Male);
Barbara: Person(Female);
```

or we can introduce subtypes and so write

```
subtype Man is Person(Sex => Male);
subtype Woman is Person(Sex => Female);
John: Man;
Barbara: Woman;
```

Aggregates take the usual form but, of course, give only the components for the corresponding alternative in the variant. The value for a discriminant governing a variant must be static so that the compiler can check the consistency of the aggregate. We can therefore write

```
John := (Male, (19, Aug, 1937), False);
Barbara := (Female, (13, May, 1943), 2);
```

but not

>   S: Gender := Female;
>   ...
>   Barbara := (S, (13, May, 1943), 2);

because S is not static but a variable.

The components of a variant can be accessed and changed in the usual way. We could write

>   John.Bearded := True;
>   Barbara.Children := Barbara.Children + 1;

but an attempt to access a component of the wrong alternative such as John.Children would raise Constraint_Error.

Note that although the sex of objects of type Person cannot be changed, it need not be known at compile time. We could have

>   S: Gender := ...
>   ...
>   Chris: Person(S);

where the sex of Chris is not determined until he or she is declared. The rule that a discriminant must be static applies only to aggregates.

The variables of type Person are necessarily constrained because the type has no default expression for the discriminant. It is therefore not possible to assign a value which would change the sex; an attempt to do so would raise Constraint_Error. However, as with the type Polynomial, we could declare a default initial expression for the discriminant and consequently declare unconstrained variables. Such unconstrained variables could then be assigned values with different discriminants but only by a complete record assignment.

We could therefore have

```
type Gender is (Male, Female, Neuter);

type Mutant(Sex: Gender := Neuter) is
   record
      Birth: Date;
      case Sex is
        when Male =>
           Bearded: Boolean;
        when Female =>
           Children: Integer;
        when Neuter =>
           null;
      end case;
   end record;
```

Note that we have to write **null**; as the alternative in the case of Neuter where we did not want any components. In a similar way to the use of a null statement in a case statement this indicates that we really meant to have no components and did not omit them by accident.

We can now declare

    M: Mutant;

The sex of this unconstrained mutant is neuter by default but can be changed by a whole record assignment.

Note the difference between

    M: Mutant := (Neuter, (1, Jan, 1984));

and

    N: Mutant(Neuter) := (Neuter, (1, Jan, 1984));

In the first case the mutant is not constrained but just happens to be initially neuter. In the second case the mutant is permanently neuter. This example also illustrates the form of the aggregate when there are no components in the alternative; there are none so we write none – we do not write **null**.

The rules regarding the alternatives closely follow those regarding the case statement described in Section 7.2. Each **when** is followed by one or more choices separated by vertical bars and each choice is either a simple expression or a discrete range. The choice **others** can also be used but must be last and on its own. All values and ranges must be static and all possible values of the discriminant must be covered once and once only. The possible values of the discriminant are those of its static subtype (if there is one) or type. Each alternative can contain several component declarations and as we have seen could also be null.

A record can only contain one variant part and it must follow other components. However, variants can be nested; the component lists in a variant part could themselves contain one variant part but again it must follow other components.

Also observe that it is unfortunately not possible to use the same identifier for components in different alternatives of a variant – all components of a record must have distinct identifiers.

It is perhaps worth emphasizing the rules regarding the changing of discriminants. If an object is declared with a discriminant constraint then it cannot be changed – after all it is a constraint just like a range constraint and so the discriminant must always satisfy the constraint. Because the constraint allows only a single value this naturally means that the discriminant can only take that single value and so cannot be changed.

The other basic consideration is that, for implementation reasons, all objects must have values for discriminant components. Hence if the type does not provide a default initial expression, the object declaration must and since it is expressed as a constraint the object is then consequently constrained.

There is a restriction on renaming components of a variable of a discriminated type. If the existence of the component depends upon the value of a discriminant then it cannot be renamed if the variable is unconstrained. (This only applies to variables and not to constants and it does not apply if the variable is marked as aliased because it is then considered to be constrained.) So we cannot write

    C: Integer **renames** M.Children;

because there is no guarantee that the component M.Children of the mutant M will continue to exist after the renaming even if it does exist at the moment of renaming. A similar restriction prevents the application of the Access attribute to such a component. However,

    C: Integer **renames** Barbara.Children;

is valid because Barbara is a person and cannot change sex.
    Note, amazingly, that we can write

    Bobby: Man **renames** Barbara;

because the constraint in the renaming declaration is ignored (see Section 12.6). Barbara has not had a sex change – she is merely in disguise!
    Observe that Person is indefinite but Man, Woman and Mutant are definite. So we can declare arrays of Mutant, Man and Woman, but not of Person.
    It is very instructive to consider how the above might be rewritten using tagged types. The differences stem from the fact that tagged type derivation gives rise to distinct types whereas variants are simply different subtypes of the same type. The key differences using tagged types are

- An aggregate for a tagged type would not give the sex since it is inherent in the tag.
- Attempting to access the wrong component John.Children is a compile-time error with tagged types whereas it raises Constraint_Error with variants.
- The secretive Chris of unknown sex could be of a class wide type and then the sex would be dynamically determined by the mandatory initial value; this is not quite so flexible because the sex has to be copied from another person.
- The Mutant has no corresponding formulation using tagged types because a mutation would correspond to changing the tag and this can never happen.
- The restriction on renaming does not apply to tagged types because the tag of an object never changes and it is the tag which determines which components are present.

    In deciding whether it is appropriate to use a variant or a tagged type, the key consideration is mutability. If an object must change its shape at run time then a variant must be used. If an individual object can never change its shape then a tagged type would be more appropriate especially if the categories might be extended.

EXERCISE 16.3

1 Write a procedure Shave which takes an object of type Person and removes any beard if the object is male and raises the exception Shaving_Error if the object is female.

2 Write a procedure Sterilize which takes an object of type Mutant and ensures that its sex is Neuter by changing it if necessary and possible and otherwise raises an appropriate exception.

3 Declare a discriminated type Object which describes geometrical objects which are either a circle, a triangle or just a point. Use the same properties as for the corresponding tagged types of Section 13.1.

4 Write a function Area which returns the area of an Object.

5 Declare a discriminated type Reservation corresponding to the types of the subsonic reservation system of Section 13.3.

16.4   Discriminants and derived types

We now consider the interaction of discriminants with derived types. This is rather different according to whether the type is tagged or not and so in order to avoid confusion we consider the two situations separately starting with untagged types.

We can of course derive from a discriminated record such as Rectangle in Section 16.1 in the usual way by

type Another_Rectangle **is new** Rectangle;

and then the discriminants become inherited so that Another_Rectangle also has the two discriminants Rows and Columns.

We could also derive from a constrained subtype

type Square_4 **is new** Rectangle(Rows => 4, Columns => 4);

in which case Square_4 is a constrained subtype of some anonymous type with the two discriminants.

Of more interest are situations where the new type has its own discriminants. In such a case the parent must be constrained and the new discriminants replace the old ones which are therefore not inherited. Moreover each new discriminant must be used to constrain one or more discriminants of the parent. So the new type may have fewer discriminants than its parent but cannot have more. Remember that extension cannot occur with untagged types and so the implementation model is that each apparent new discriminant has to use the space of one of the discriminants of the parent. There are a number of interesting possibilities

```
type Row_3(Columns: Positive) is
    new Rectangle(Rows => 3, Columns => Columns);
type Square(N: Positive) is
    new Rectangle(Rows => N, Columns => N);
type Transpose(Rows, Columns: Positive) is
    new Rectangle(Rows => Columns, Columns => Rows);
```

where we have used named notation for clarity. In all these cases the names of
the old discriminants are no longer available in the new view.

The type Row_3 has lost one degree of freedom since it no longer has a
visible discriminant called Rows; we could of course convert to type Rectangle
and then look at the Rows and find it was 3.

In the case of the type Square (and we are essentially back to the type
Square we started with in Section 16.1), the one new discriminant is used to
constrain both old ones. As a consequence a conversion of a value of type
Rectangle to type Square will check that the two discriminants of the rectangle
are equal and raise Constraint_Error if they are not.

The type Transpose has the discriminants mapped in the reverse order. So
if R is a rectangle then R.Rows = Transpose(R).Columns; we can use the result
of the conversion as a name and then select the discriminant. But of course the
internal array is still the same and so this is not a very interesting example.

We now turn to a consideration of tagged types. Tagged record types can
also have discriminants but they cannot have defaults (and so all objects must
be constrained). Again there is the basic rule that if the derived type has its own
discriminants then these replace any old ones and so the parent type must be
constrained. The new discriminants may be used to constrain the parent, but
they need not. So in the tagged case, extension is allowed and the derived type
may have more discriminants than its parent.

Thus an alternative implementation for the type Person might be based
upon

```
type Gender is (Male, Female);

type Person(Sex: Gender) is tagged
    record
        Birth: Date;
    end record;
```

and we can then extend with, for example

```
type Man is new Person(Male) with
    record
        Bearded: Boolean;
    end record;
```

The type Man naturally inherits the discriminant from Person in the sense that
a man still has a component called Sex although of course it is constrained to
be Male.

We could also extend from the unconstrained type and then the new type
would inherit the old discriminant just as any other component

```
type Old_Person is new Person with
  record
     Pension: Money;
  end record;
```

and the Old_Person also has a component Sex (although it is not visible in the declaration but then neither is the Birth component). We cannot declare an object of type Old_Person without a constraint.

As an example of providing new discriminants (in which case the parent type must be constrained) we might declare a type Boxer who must be male (females don't box in this model of the world) and then add a discriminant giving his weight

```
type Weight is (Light, Middle, Heavy);
```

```
type Boxer(W: Weight) is new Person(Male) with
  record
     -- information according to weight
  end record;
```

In this case the Boxer does not have a sex component at all since the discriminant has been replaced.

Other examples are provided by the type Object and its descendants. A useful guide is that discriminants make sense for controlling structure but not other attributes. We might have

```
type Regular_Polygon(No_Of_Sides: Natural) is new Object with
  record
     Side: Float;
  end record;
```

and then

```
type Pentagon is new Regular_Polygon(5) with null record;
```

There is a limit to the amount of specialization that can be performed through syntactic structures. For example, one might think it would be nice to write

```
type Polygon(No_Of_Sides: Natural) is new Object with
  record
     Sides: Float_Array(1 .. No_Of_Sides);
  end record;
```

but of course this is no good because we also need the values of the angles in order to pin the polygon down. So it is probably better to write

```
type Polygon(No_Of_Sides: Natural) is new Object with private;
```

and hide all the details from the user. Of course we could still have

> **type** Quadrilateral **is new** Polygon(4) **with private**;
> **type** Parallelogram **is new** Quadrilateral **with private**;
> **type** Rhombus **is new** Parallelogram **with private**;
> **type** Square **is new** Rhombus **with private**;

so that the hierarchy is revealed. This would allow operations that apply to all parallelograms to also apply to rhombi and squares. But objects now have to be made through constructor functions that can ensure that the required properties hold.

EXERCISE 16.4

1   Declare the type Boxer so that it can be of either sex.

16.5   Access types and discriminants

Access types can refer to discriminated record types in much the same way that they can refer to array types. In both cases they can be constrained or not.

Consider the problem of representing a family tree. We could declare

> **type** Person;
> **type** Person_Name **is access** Person;
>
> **type** Person **is**
>   **record**
>   Sex: Gender;
>   Birth: Date;
>   Spouse: Person_Name;
>   Father: Person_Name;
>   First_Child: Person_Name;
>   Next_Sibling: Person_Name;
>   **end record**;

This model assumes a monogamous and legitimate system. The children are linked together through the component Next_Sibling and a person's mother is identified as the spouse of the father. (We leave the reader to consider how the model should be altered to accomodate the complexity of more flexible social systems.)

Although the above type Person is adequate for the model, it is more interesting to use a discriminated type so that different components can exist for the different sexes and more particularly so that appropriate constraints can be applied. Consider

```
type Person(Sex: Gender);
type Person_Name is access Person;

type Person(Sex: Gender) is
  record
    Birth: Date;
    Father: Person_Name(Male);
    Next_Sibling: Person_Name;
    case Sex is
      when Male =>
        Wife: Person_Name(Female);
      when Female =>
        Husband: Person_Name(Male);
        First_Child: Person_Name;
    end case;
  end record;
```

The incomplete declaration of Person also gives the discriminants (and any default initial expressions); these must, of course, conform to those in the subsequent complete declaration. The component Father is now constrained always to access a person whose sex is male (or **null** of course). Similarly the components Wife and Husband are constrained; note that these had to have distinct identifiers and so could not both be Spouse. However, the components First_Child and Next_Sibling are not constrained and so could access a person of either sex. We have also taken the opportunity to save on storage by making the children belong to the mother only.

When the object of type Person is created by an allocator a value must be provided for the discriminant either through an explicit initial value as in

```
Janet: Person_Name;
...
Janet := new Person'(Female, (22, Feb, 1967), John, others => null);
```

or by supplying a discriminant constraint thus

```
Janet := new Person(Female);
```

Note that as in the case of arrays (see Section 10.3) a quote is needed in the case of the full initial value but not when we just give the constraint. Note also the use of **others** in the aggregate; this is allowed because the last three components all have the same base type.

We could not write

```
Janet := new Person;
```

because the type Person does not have a default discriminant. However we could declare

```
subtype Woman is Person(Female);
...
Janet := new Woman;
```

Such an object cannot later have its discriminant changed. This rule applies even if the discriminant has a default initial expression; objects created by an allocator are in this respect different to objects created by a normal declaration where a default initial expression allows unconstrained objects to be declared and later to have their discriminant changed.

On the other hand, we see that despite the absence of a default initial expression for the discriminant, we can nevertheless declare unconstrained objects of type Person_Name; such objects, of course, take the default initial value **null** and so no problem arises. Thus although an allocated object cannot have its discriminant changed, nevertheless an unconstrained access variable could refer from time to time to objects with different discriminants.

The reason for not allowing an allocated object to have its discriminant changed is that it could be accessed from several constrained objects such as the components Father and it would be difficult to ensure that such constraints were not violated. Incidentally, declared objects marked as aliased are treated in the same way; they cannot have their discriminants changed either for the same reason.

For convenience we can define subtypes

```
subtype Mans_Name is Person_Name(Male);
subtype Womans_Name is Person_Name(Female);
```

We can now write a procedure to marry two people.

```
procedure Marry(Bride: Womans_Name; Groom: Mans_Name) is
begin
  if Bride.Husband /= null or Groom.Wife /= null then
    raise Bigamy;
  end if;
  Bride.Husband := Groom;
  Groom.Wife := Bride;
end Marry;
```

The constraints on the parameters are checked when the parameters are passed (remember that access parameters are always implemented by copy). An attempt to marry people of the wrong sex will raise Constraint_Error at the point of call. On the other hand an attempt to marry a nonexistent person will result in Constraint_Error being raised inside the body of the procedure. Remember that although **in** parameters are constants we can change the components of the accessed objects – we are not changing the values of Bride and Groom to access different objects. The procedure could then be used as in the sequence

```
David: Person_Name;
...
David := new Person'(Male, (24, May, 1965), Ian, others => null);
...
Marry(Janet, David);
```

A function could return an access value as for example

```
function Spouse(P: Person_Name) return Person_Name is
begin
  case P.Sex is
    when Male =>
      return P.Wife;
    when Female =>
      return P.Husband;
  end case;
end Spouse;
```

The result of such a function call is treated as a constant and can be directly used as part of a name so we can write

```
Spouse(P).Birth
```

to give the birthday of the spouse of P. (See the end of Section 9.1.) We could even write

```
Spouse(P).Birth := Newdate;
```

but this is only possible because the function delivers an access value. It could not be done if the function actually delivered a value of type **Person** rather than **Person_Name**. Moreover, we cannot write

```
Spouse(P) := Q;
```

in an attempt to replace our spouse by someone else, whereas

```
Spouse(P).all := Q.all;
```

is valid and would change all the components of our spouse to be the same as those of Q.

The following function gives birth to a new child. We need the mother, the sex of the child and the date as parameters.

```
function New_Child(Mother: Womans_Name;
                   Boy_Or_Girl: Gender;
                   Birthday: Date) return Person_Name is
  Child: Person_Name;
begin
  if Mother.Husband = null then
    raise Out_Of_Wedlock;
  end if;
  Child := new Person(Boy_Or_Girl);
  Child.Birth := Birthday;
  Child.Father := Mother.Husband;
  declare
    Last: Person_Name := Mother.First_Child;
```

```
      begin
        if Last = null then
           Mother.First_Child := Child;
        else
           while Last.Next_Sibling /= null loop
             Last := Last.Next_Sibling;
           end loop;
           Last.Next_Sibling := Child;
        end if;
      end;
      return Child;
   end New_Child;
```

Observe that a discriminant constraint need not be static – the value of Boy_Or_Girl is not known until the function is called. As a consequence we cannot give the complete initial value with the allocator because we do not know which components to provide. Hence we allocate the child with just the value of the discriminant and then separately assign the date of birth and the father. The remaining components take the default value **null**. We can now write

```
   Helen: Person_Name := New_Child(Barbara, Female, (28, Sep, 1969));
```

It is interesting to consider how our family saga could be rewritten using type extension and inheritance rather than discriminants. Clearly we can use an abstract root type Person and derived types Man and Woman. We also need three distinct access types. So

```
   type Person;
   type Man;
   type Woman;

   type Person_Name is access all Person'Class;
   type Mans_Name is access all Man;
   type Womans_Name is access all Woman;

   type Person is abstract tagged
      record
        Birth: Date;
        Father: Mans_Name;
        Next_Sibling: Person_Name;
      end record;

   type Man is new Person with
      record
        Wife: Womans_Name;
      end record;

   type Woman is new Person with
      record
        Husband: Mans_Name;
        First_Child: Person_Name;
      end record;
```

Note the various incomplete type declarations required because of the recursive nature of the types.

In practice we would undoubtedly declare the various types (in either formulation) as private although keeping the relationships between the types visible. In the tagged case we would have

```
package People is

    type Person is abstract tagged private;
    type Man is new Person with private;
    type Woman is new Person with private;

    type Person_Name is access all Person'Class;
    type Mans_Name is access all Man;
    type Womans_Name is access all Woman;

private
```

We could then declare all the various subprograms Marry, Spouse and so on inside this package or maybe in a child package which of course would have full visibility of the details of the types. We need to take care in starting the system because we cannot assign to the various components externally. The function New_Child cannot be used initially because it needs married parents. However, a sequence such as

```
Adam := new Man;
Eve := new Woman;
Marry(Eve, Adam);
Cain := New_Child(Eve, Male, Long_Ago);
```

seems to work although it leaves some components of Adam and Eve not set properly.

We leave to the reader the task of writing the various subprograms using this new formulation. One advantage is that more checking is done at compile time because Man and Woman are distinct types rather than just subtypes of Person. Observe that we made the access types general (with **all**); this is so that we can convert between them and conversion is not allowed between pool specific access types.

EXERCISE 16.5

1   Write a function to return a person's heir (use the variant formulation). Follow the historical rules of primogeniture applicable to monarchies – the heir is the eldest son if there is one and otherwise is the eldest daughter. Return **null** if there is no heir.

2   Write a procedure to divorce a woman. Divorce is only permitted if there are no children.

3   Modify the procedure Marry in order to prevent incest. A person may not marry their sibling, parent or child.

4   Rewrite Marry using the tagged type formulation; this is trivial.

5   Rewrite Spouse using the tagged type formulation. Hint: consider dispatching.

6   Rewrite New_Child using the tagged type formulation.

16.6   Private types and discriminants

In this section we bring together a number of matters relating to the control of resources through private types and discriminants.

In earlier sections we have seen how private types provide general control by ensuring that all operations on a type are through defined subprograms. Making a type also limited prevents assignment.

The introduction of discriminants adds other possibilities. We have seen that a partial view might show the discriminants as in the type Stack of Section 16.1

```
package Stacks is
  type Stack(Max: Natural) is private;
  ...
private
  type Stack(Max: Natural) is ...
```

and also that the partial view might hide them as with

```
package Polynomials is
  type Polynomial is private;
  ...
private
  type Polynomial(N: Index := 0) is ...
```

of Section 16.2 even though the full type has a discriminant; we noted that the full type has to be definite and so the discriminant has to have a default in this case.

Another possibility is that the partial view might have discriminants and then the full type could be implemented in terms of an existing type with discriminants thus

```
package Squares is
  type Square(N: Positive) is private;
  ...
private
  type Square(N: Positive) is new Rectangle(N, N);
```

using the examples of Section 16.4.

The final possibility is that the partial view might have unknown discriminants written

type T(<>) **is private**;

This view is considered indefinite and prevents the user from declaring uninitialized objects of the type. Making the partial view also limited by writing

type T(<>) **is limited private**;

prevents the user from declaring any objects at all. This enables the provider of the package to have complete control over all objects of the type; typically the user would be given access to objects of the type through an access type which is then often called a handle. We will consider some examples of controlling the privacy of abstractions in this way in Section 19.8.

If the partial view has unknown discriminants then the full view may or may not have discriminants; none were promised and so none need be provided. The full type can also be another type with unknown discriminants (such as being derived from one).

A class wide type is also treated as having unknown discriminants (the tag is a hidden discriminant). Remember that a class wide type is another example of an indefinite type so that uninitialized objects are not allowed.

We conclude this section with a curious example of discriminants by reconsidering the type Key of Section 11.6. We could change this to

type Key(Code: Natural := 0) **is limited private**;

with

type Key(Code: Natural := 0) **is null record**;

With this formulation the user can read the code number of the key, but cannot change it. There is, however, a small flaw whose detection and cure is left as an exercise. Note also that we have declared Code as subtype Natural rather than subtype Key_Code; this is because Key_Code is not visible to the user. Of course we could make Key_Code visible but this would make Max visible as well and we might not want the user to know how many keys there are.

However, as observed in Exercise 13.7(**3**), it is far better to make the type tagged and controlled so that it can be initialized and finalized properly. The inquisitive user can always be given read access to the value of the code through a function.

EXERCISE 16.6

1 What is the flaw in the suggested new formulation for the type Key? Hint: remember that the user declares keys explicitly. Show how it can be overcome.

16.7   Access discriminants

A discriminant may also be of an access type. This enables a record (or task or protected object) to be parameterized with some other structure with which it is associated. The access type can be a named access type or it can be anonymous when the discriminant is then known as an access discriminant.

Discriminants of a named access type are not particularly interesting; they behave much as other components of the record except that they can be visible while the rest of the record might be private; but they have no controlling function in the way that discrete discriminants can control array bounds and variants.

Access discriminants have similar accessibility properties to access parameters; they contain an indication of the accessibility of the object referred to. This gives extra flexibility and so most discriminants of access types are in fact access discriminants. A typical structure might be

```
type Data is ...

type R(D: access Data) is limited
   record

      ...

   end record;
```

and then a declaration of an object of type R must include an access value to an associated object of type Data. Thus

```
My_Data: aliased Data := ...
My_Record: R := (My_Data'Access, ... );
```

or we could have

```
My_Record: R(My_Data'Access);
```

and assign the other components to My_Record separately.

Access discriminants, like other discriminants, are constant. Moreover a record can only have an access discriminant if it is explicitly marked as limited. Thus the two objects are bound together permanently.

An interesting special case is where the object having the discriminant is actually a component of the type the discriminant refers to! This can be used to enable a component of a record to obtain the identity of the record in which it is embedded. Consider

```
type Inner(Ptr: access Outer) is limited...

type Outer is limited
   record

      ...

      Component: Inner(Outer'Access);

      ...

   end record;
```

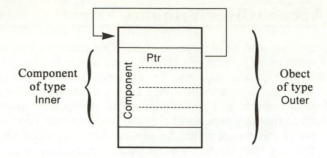

Figure 16.1 A self-referential structure.

The Component of type Inner has an access discriminant Ptr which refers back to the instance of the record Outer. This is because the attribute Access applied to the name of a record type inside its declaration refers to the current instance. (When we deal with tasks we will see that a similar situation arises when the name of a task type is used inside its own body; see Section 18.10.) If we now declare an object of the type Outer

```
Obj: Outer;
```

then the structure created is as shown in Figure 16.1. We call it a self-referential structure for obvious reasons. Note that it becomes self-referential automatically which is not the same as the effect that would be obtained with a record of a type such as Cell in which an instance might happen to have a component referring to itself. All instances of the type Outer will refer to themselves.

We will return to this topic in Sections 19.6 and 19.7 when we will see how the types Inner and Outer could be extensions of other types and thereby enable complex chained structures to be created – this allows us to have several different views of the same object.

Access discriminants work together with access parameters and thereby avoid accessibility problems. Suppose we had some general procedure to manipulate the type Data

```
procedure P(A: access Data);
```

then we can make calls such as in

```
declare
    My_Data: aliased Data := ...
    My_Record: R := (My_Data'Access, ... );
begin
    P(R.D);                    -- legal
    ...
end;
```

and the accessibility of the data is passed via the discriminant to the procedure P. On the other hand using a named access type as the parameter of P thus

```
type Data_Ptr is access all Data;
procedure P(A: Data_Ptr);
```

fails because the type conversion required in the corresponding call

```
P(Data_Ptr(R.D));          -- illegal
```

breaks the static accessibility rules. Examples of the use of access parameters with access discriminants will be found in Sections 19.4 and 19.7.

EXERCISE 16.7

1 Analyse the following and explain why the various attempts to assign the reference to the local data to the more global variable or component are thwarted.

```
procedure Main is
  type Data is ...
  type Data_Ptr is access all Data;
  type R(D: access Data) is limited
    record
      ...
    end record;
  Global_Ptr: Data_Ptr;
  Global_Data: aliased Data;
  Global_Record: R(Global_Data'Access);
begin
  declare
    Local_Data: aliased Data;
    Local_Record: R(Local_Data'Access);
  begin
    Global_Ptr := Local_Record.D;              -- illegal
    Global_Ptr := Data_Ptr(Local_Record.D);    -- illegal
    Global_Record := Local_Record;             -- illegal
  end;
end Main;
```

CHECKLIST 16

If a discriminant does not have a default expression then all objects must be constrained.

The discriminant of an unconstrained object can only be changed by a complete record assignment.

Discriminants can only be used as array bounds or to govern variants or as nested discriminants or in default initial expressions for components.

A discriminant in an aggregate and governing a variant must be static.

Any variant must appear last in a component list.

If an accessed object has a discriminant then it is always constrained.

Discriminants of tagged types must not have defaults.

On derivation, discriminants are all inherited or completely replaced with a new set.

A record type with access discriminants must be explicitly limited.

Access discriminants have dynamic accessibility.

Changes from Ada 83

Discriminants could not be of an access type in Ada 83.

Unknown discriminants were not in Ada 83.

Both partial and full view had to show any discriminants in Ada 83.

Derived types could not have their own discriminants in Ada 83.

17 Generics

In this chapter we describe the generic mechanism which allows a special form of parameterization at compile time which can be applied to subprograms and packages. The generic parameters can be types, subprograms and packages as well as values and objects.

Genericity is important for reuse. It provides static polymorphism as opposed to the dynamic polymorphism provided by type extension and class wide types. Being static it is intrinsically more reliable but usually less flexible. However, in the case of subprogram parameters it does not have the accessibility restrictions imposed by access to subprogram types and thus is particularly useful for certain applications where subprograms need to be at different levels.

Package parameters enable the composition of generic packages while ensuring that their instantiations are compatible. They can also be used to group together the parameters of other generic units.

17.1   Declarations and instantiations

We often get the situation that the logic of a piece of program is independent of the types involved and it therefore seems unnecessary to repeat it for all the different types to which we might wish it to apply. A simple example is provided by the procedure Swap of Exercise 9.3(**1**)

```
procedure Swap(X, Y: in out Float) is
   T: Float;
begin
   T := X;  X := Y;  Y := T;
end;
```

It is clear that the logic is independent of the type Float. If we also wanted to swap integers or Booleans we could of course write other procedures but this would be tedious. The generic mechanism allows us to overcome this. We can declare

```
generic
   type Item is private;
procedure Exchange(X, Y: in out Item);

procedure Exchange(X, Y: in out Item) is
   T: Item;
begin
   T := X;  X := Y;  Y := T;
end;
```

The subprogram Exchange is a generic subprogram and acts as a kind of template. The subprogram specification is preceded by the generic formal part consisting of the reserved word **generic** followed by a (possibly empty) list of generic formal parameters. The subprogram body is written exactly as normal but note that, in the case of a generic subprogram, we have to give both the specification and the body separately.

The generic procedure cannot be called directly but from it we can create an actual procedure by a mechanism known as generic instantiation. For example, we may write

```
procedure Swap is new Exchange(Float);
```

This is a declaration and states that Swap is to be obtained from the template described by Exchange. Actual generic parameters are provided in a parameter list in the usual way. The actual parameter in this case is the type Float which corresponds to the formal parameter Item. We could also use the named notation

```
procedure Swap is new Exchange(Item => Float);
```

So we have now created the procedure Swap acting on type Float and can henceforth call it in the usual way. We can make further instantiations

```
procedure Swap is new Exchange(Integer);
procedure Swap is new Exchange(Date);
```

and so on. We are here creating further overloadings of Swap which can be distinguished by their parameter types just as if we had laboriously written them out in detail.

Superficially, it may look as if the generic mechanism is merely one of text substitution and indeed in this simple case the behaviour would be the same. However, the important difference relates to the meaning of identifiers in the generic body but which are neither parameters nor local to the body. Such nonlocal identifiers have meanings appropriate to where the generic body is declared and not to where it is instantiated. If text substitution were used then nonlocal identifiers would of course take their meaning at the point of instantiation and this could give very surprising results.

As well as generic subprograms we may also have generic packages. A simple example is provided by the package Stack in Section 11.1. The trouble with that package is that it only works on type Integer although of course the same logic applies irrespective of the type of the values manipulated. We can also take the opportunity to make Max a parameter as well so that we are not tied to an arbitrary limit of 100. We write

```
generic
   Max: Positive;
   type Item is private;
package Stack is
   procedure Push(X: Item);
   function Pop return Item;
end Stack;

package body Stack is
   S: array (1 .. Max) of Item;
   Top: Integer range 0 .. Max;
   -- etc. as before but with Integer
   -- replaced by Item
end Stack;
```

We can now create and use a stack of a particular size and type by instantiating the generic package as in the following

```
declare
   package My_Stack is new Stack(100, Float);
   use My_Stack;
begin
   ...
   Push(X);
   ...
   Y := Pop;
   ...
end;
```

The package My_Stack which results from the instantiation behaves just as a normal directly written out package. The use clause allows us to refer to Push and Pop directly. If we did a further instantiation

```
package Another_Stack is new Stack(50, Integer);
use Another_Stack;
```

then Push and Pop are further overloadings and can be distinguished by the type provided by the context. Of course, if Another_Stack was also declared with the actual generic parameter being Float, then we would have to use the dotted notation to distinguish the instances of Push and Pop despite the use clauses.

Both generic units and generic instantiations may be library units. Thus, having compiled the generic package Stack, an instantiation could itself be separately compiled just on its own thus

```
with Stack;
package Boolean_Stack is new Stack(200, Boolean);
```

If we added an exception Error to the package as in Section 14.2 so that the generic package declaration was

```
generic
   Max: Positive;
   type Item is private;
package Stack is
   Error: exception;
   procedure Push(X: Item);
   function Pop return Item;
end Stack;
```

then each instantiation would give rise to a distinct exception and because exceptions cannot be overloaded we would naturally have to use the dotted notation to distinguish them.

We could, of course, make the exception Error common to all instantiations by making it global to the generic package. It and the generic package could perhaps be declared inside a further package

```
package All_Stacks is
   Error: exception;
   generic
      Max: Positive;
      type Item is private;
   package Stack is
      procedure Push(X: Item);
      function Pop return Item;
   end Stack;
end All_Stacks;

package body All_Stacks is
   package body Stack is
      ...
   end Stack;
end All_Stacks;
```

This illustrates the binding of identifiers global to generic units. The meaning of Error is determined at the point of the generic declaration irrespective of the meaning at the point of instantiation.

The above examples have illustrated formal parameters which were types and also integers. In fact generic formal parameters can be values and objects much as the parameters applicable to subprograms; they can also be types, subprograms and packages. As we shall see in the next sections, we can express the formal types, subprograms and packages so that we can assume in the generic body that the actual parameters have the properties we require.

Object parameters can be of mode **in** or **in out** but not **out** (nor are there access parameters). As with subprograms, **in** is taken by default as illustrated by Max in the example above.

An **in** generic parameter acts as a constant whose value is provided by the corresponding actual parameter. A default expression is allowed as in the case of parameters of subprograms; such a default expression is evaluated at instantiation if no actual parameter is supplied in the same way that a default expression for a subprogram parameter is evaluated when the subprogram is called if no actual parameter is supplied. Observe that an **in** generic parameter cannot be of a limited type; this is because assignment is not allowed for limited types and the mechanism of giving the value to the parameter is treated as assignment. Note that this is a different mechanism to that used for **in** subprogram parameters where limited types are allowed.

An **in out** parameter, however, acts as a variable renaming the corresponding actual parameter. The actual parameter must therefore be the name of a variable and its identification occurs at the point of instantiation using the same rules as for renaming described in Section 12.6. One such rule is that any constraints on the actual parameter apply to the formal parameter and any constraints implied by the formal subtype mark are, perhaps surprisingly, completely ignored. Another rule is that if any identifier in the name subsequently changes then the identity of the object referred to by the generic formal parameter does not change. Because of this there is a restriction, like that on renaming, that the actual parameter cannot be a component of an unconstrained discriminated record if the very existence of the component depends on the value of the discriminant. Thus if M is a Mutant as in Section 16.3, M.Children could not be an actual generic parameter because M could have its Sex changed. However, M.Birth would be valid.

It will now be realized that although the notation **in** and **in out** is identical to subprogram parameters the meaning is somewhat different. Thus there is no question of copying in and out and indeed no such thing as **out** parameters.

Inside the generic body, the formal generic parameters can generally be used quite freely – but there is one important restriction. This arises because generic parameters (and their attributes) are not considered to be static. There are various places where an expression has to be static such as in the alternatives in a case statement or variant, and in the range in an integer type definition, or the number of digits in a floating point type definition and so on. In all these situations a generic formal parameter cannot be used because the expression would not then be static.

However, the type of the expression in a case statement and similarly the type of the discriminant in a variant may be a generic formal type provided there is an others clause – this ensures that all values are covered.

Our final example in this section illustrates the nesting of generics. The following generic procedure performs a cyclic interchange of three values and for amusement is written in terms of the generic procedure Exchange

```
generic
   type Thing is private;
procedure Cab(A, B, C: in out Thing);

procedure Cab(A, B, C: in out Thing) is
   procedure Swap is new Exchange(Item => Thing);
begin
   Swap(A, B);
   Swap(A, C);
end Cab;
```

Although nesting is allowed, it must not be recursive.

Finally, note that a generic unit can be renamed. So we could write

```
generic procedure Taxi renames Cab;
```

although perhaps confusing for this example.

EXERCISE 17.1

---

1   Write a generic package declaration based on the package Stacks in Section 16.1 so that stacks of arbitrary type may be declared. Declare a stack S of length 30 and type Boolean. Use named notation.

2   Write a generic package containing both Swap and Cab.

17.2   Type parameters

In the previous section we introduced types as generic parameters. The examples showed the formal parameter taking the form

```
type T is private;
```

In this case, inside the generic subprogram or package, we may assume that assignment and equality are defined for T and that T is definite so that we may declare uninitialized objects of type T. We can assume nothing else unless we specifically provide other parameters as we shall see in a moment. Hence T behaves in the generic unit much as a private type outside the package defining it; this analogy explains the notation for the formal parameter. The corresponding actual parameter must, of course, provide assignment and equality and so it can be any definite type except one that is limited. Note carefully that it cannot be an indefinite type such as String.

A formal generic type parameter can take other forms. It can be

> **type** T **is limited private**;

and in this case assignment and predefined equality are not available. The corresponding actual parameter can be any definite type, limited or nonlimited, tagged or nontagged.

Either of the above forms could have unknown discriminants such as

> **type** T(<>) **is private**;

in which case the type is considered indefinite within the generic unit and so uninitialized objects cannot be declared. The actual type could then be any nonlimited indefinite type such as String as well as any nonlimited definite type. It could also be a class wide type since these are considered as indefinite.

Another possibility is that the formal type could have known discriminants

> **type** T(X: U; Y: V; ...) **is private**;

and the actual type must then have discriminants with statically matching subtypes. The formal type must not have default expressions for the discriminants but the actual type can. This means that the formal type is indefinite.

We can also require that the actual type is tagged by

> **type** T **is tagged private**;

in which case the actual type must be tagged but not abstract. Writing

> **type** T **is abstract tagged private**;

allows the actual type to be abstract as well.

All the above forms can be put together in the obvious way, so an extreme example might be

> **type** T(I: Index) **is abstract tagged limited private**;

in which case the actual type must have one discriminant of subtype Index, it must be tagged, it might be abstract, it might be limited.

The matching rules are expressed simply in terms of classes as outlined in Section 3.4. A class of types in the general sense is simply a set of types with common properties. The formal parameter defines the class and the actual can then be any type in that class.

Derivation classes are important kinds of classes and the forms

```
type T is new S;
type T is new S with private;
```

indicate that the actual type must be derived from S. The first form applies if S is not tagged and the second if S is tagged. We can also insert **abstract** in the second case. Within the generic unit all the properties of the derivation class may be assumed. Unknown discriminants and limited can also be added to these two forms.

The formal parameter could also be one of

```
type T is (<>);
type T is range <>;
type T is mod <>;
type T is digits <>;
type T is delta <>;
type T is delta <> digits <>;
```

In the first case the actual parameter must be a discrete type – an enumeration type or integer type. In the other cases the actual parameter must be a signed integer type, modular type, floating point type, ordinary fixed point type or decimal type respectively. Within the generic unit the appropriate predefined operations and attributes are available.

As a simple example consider

```
generic
   type T is (<>);
function Next(X: T) return T;

function Next(X: T) return T is
begin
   if X=T'Last then
      return T'First;
   else
      return T'Succ(X);
   end if;
end Next;
```

The formal parameter T requires that the actual parameter must be a discrete type. Since all discrete types have attributes First, Last and Succ we can use these attributes in the body in the knowledge that the actual parameter will supply them.

We could now write

```
function Tomorrow is new Next(Day);
```

so that Tomorrow(Sun) = Mon.

An actual generic parameter can also be a subtype but an explicit constraint is not allowed; in other words the actual parameter must be just a subtype mark

and not a subtype indication. The formal generic parameter then denotes the
subtype. Thus we can have

>   **function** Next_Work_Day **is new** Next(Weekday);

so that Next_Work_Day(Fri) = Mon. Note how the behaviour depends on the
fact that the Last attribute applies to the subtype and not to the base type so that
Day'Last is Sun and Weekday'Last is Fri.

The actual parameter could also be an integer type so we could have

>   **subtype** Digit **is** Integer **range** 0 .. 9;
>   **function** Next_Digit **is new** Next(Digit);

and then Next_Digit(9) = 0.

Now consider the package Complex_Numbers of Section 11.2; this could
be made generic so that the particular floating point type upon which the type
Complex is based can be a parameter. It would then take the form

>   **generic**
>   **type** Floating **is digits** <>;
>   **package** Generic_Complex_Numbers **is**
>   **type** Complex **is private**;
>   ... -- as before with Float replaced by Floating
>   I: **constant** Complex := (0.0, 1.0);
>   **end**;

Note that we can use the literals 0.0 and 1.0 because they are of the universal
real type which can be converted to whichever type is passed as actual
parameter. The package could then be instantiated by for instance

>   **package** My_Complex_Numbers **is**
>   **new** Generic_Complex_Numbers(My_Float);

A formal generic parameter can also be an array type. The actual parameter
must then also be an array type with the same number of dimensions, the same
component subtypes and the same index subtypes. Either both must be
unconstrained arrays or both must be constrained arrays. If they are constrained
then the index ranges must be the same for corresponding indexes. All
constraints must statically match.

It is possible for one generic formal parameter to depend upon a previous
formal parameter which is a type. This will often be the case with arrays. As
an example consider the function Sum in Section 9.1. This added together the
elements of an array of type Float with Integer index. We can generalize this to
add together the elements of any floating point array with any index type

>   **generic**
>   **type** Index **is** (<>);
>   **type** Floating **is digits** <>;
>   **type** Vec **is array** (Index **range** <>) **of** Floating;
>   **function** Sum(A: Vec) **return** Floating;

```
function Sum(A: Vec) return Floating is
   Result: Floating := 0.0;
begin
   for I in A'Range loop
      Result := Result+A(I);
   end loop;
   return Result;
end Sum;
```

Note that although Index is a formal parameter it does not explicitly appear in the generic body; nevertheless it is implicitly used since the loop parameter I is of type Index.

We could instantiate this by

```
function Sum_Vector is new Sum(Integer, Float, Vector);
```

and this will give the function Sum of Section 9.1.

The matching of actual and formal arrays takes place after any formal types have been replaced in the formal array by the corresponding actual types. As an example of matching index subtypes note that if we had

```
type Vector is array (Positive range <>) of Float;
```

then we would have to use Positive (or an equivalent subtype) as the actual parameter for the Index.

The final possibility for formal type parameters is the case of an access type. The formal can be

```
type A is access T;
type A is access constant T;
type A is access all T;
```

where T may but need not be a previous formal parameter. The actual parameter corresponding to A must then access T. In the first case the actual type can be any such access type other than an access to constant type. In the second case it must be an access to constant type and in the third it must be a general access to variable type. Constraints on the accessed type must statically match.

A formal access to subprogram type takes one of the forms

```
type P is access procedure ...
type F is access function ...
```

and the profiles of actual and formal subprograms must have mode conformance. This is the same conformance as applies to the renaming of subprogram specifications and so follows the model that generic parameter matching is like renaming.

Observe that there is no concept of a formal record type; the effect can be achieved by the use of a formal derived type.

Incidentally, we have noted that a numeric type such as

type My_Integer **is range** –1E6 .. 1E6;

is implemented as a hardware type that might correspond to one of the predefined types such as Integer or Long_Integer. However, it is not actually derived from one of these although ultimately all are conceptually derived from root integer. So if we had

> **generic**
>   **type** T **is new** Integer;
>   ...

then this could never be matched by My_Integer. Another thought is that **type** T **is range** <>; can be considered as equivalent to **type** T **is new** *root_integer,* which we cannot write.

As a final example in this section, we return to the question of sets. We saw in Section 8.6 how a Boolean array could be used to represent a set. Exercises 9.1(**4**), 9.2(**3**) and 9.2(**4**) also showed how we could write suitable functions to operate upon sets of the type Colour. The generic mechanism allows us to write a package to enable the manipulation of sets of an arbitrary type.

Consider

```
generic
   type Element is (<>);
package Set_Of is
   type Set is private;
   type List is array (Positive range <>) of Element;

   Empty, Full: constant Set;

   function Make_Set(L: List) return Set;
   function Make_Set(E: Element) return Set;
   function Decompose(S: Set) return List;

   function "+" (S, T: Set) return Set;        -- union
   function "*" (S, T: Set) return Set;        -- intersection
   function "-" (S, T: Set) return Set;        -- symmetric difference
   function "<" (E: Element; S: Set) return Boolean;    -- inclusion
   function "<=" (S, T: Set) return Boolean;            -- contains
   function Size(S: Set) return Natural;       -- no of elements

private
   type Set is array (Element) of Boolean;

   Empty: constant Set := (Set'Range => False);
   Full: constant Set := (Set'Range => True);
end;
```

The single generic parameter is the element type which must be discrete. The type Set is made private so that the Boolean operations cannot be directly applied (inadvertently or malevolently). Aggregates of the type List are used to represent literal sets. The constants Empty and Full denote the empty and full set respectively. The functions Make_Set enable the creation of a set from a list of the element values or a single element value. Decompose turns a set back into a list of elements.

The operators +, * and − represent union, intersection and symmetric difference; they are chosen as more natural than the underlying **or, and** and **xor**. The operator < tests to see whether an element value is in a set. The operator <= tests to see whether one set is a subset of another. Finally, the function Size returns the number of element values present in a particular set.

In the private part the type Set is declared as a Boolean array indexed by the element type (which is why the element type had to be discrete). The constants Empty and Full are declared as arrays whose elements are all False and all True respectively. The body of the package is left as an exercise.

Turning back to Section 8.6, we can instantiate the package to work on our type Primary by

```
package Primary_Sets is new Set_Of(Primary);
use Primary_Sets;
```

For comparison we could then write

```
subtype Colour is Set;
White: Colour renames Empty;
Black: Colour renames Full;
```

and so on.

We can use this example to explore the creation and composition of types. Our attempt to give the type Set the name Colour through a subtype is poor. We would really like to pass the name Colour in some way to the generic package as the type to be used. We cannot do this and retain the private nature of the type. But we can use the derived type mechanism to create a proper type Colour from the type Set

```
type Colour is new Set;
```

Recalling the rules for inheriting primitive subprograms from Section 11.3, we note that the new type Colour automatically inherits all the functions in the specification of Set_Of (strictly the instantiation Primary_Sets) because they all have the type Set as a parameter or result type.

However, this is a bit untidy; the constants Empty and Full will not have been inherited and the type List will still be as before.

One improvement therefore is to replace the constants Empty and Full by equivalent parameterless functions so that they will also be inherited. A better approach to the type List is to make it and its index type into further generic parameters. The visible part of the package will then just consist of the type Set and its subprograms

```
generic
   type Element is (<>);
   type Index is (<>);
   type List is array (Index range <>) of Element;
package Nice_Set_Of is
   type Set is private;
   function Empty return Set;
   function Full return Set;
   ...
private
```

We can now write

```
type Primary_List is array (Positive range <>) of Primary;
```

```
package Primary_Sets is new Nice_Set_Of(Element => Primary,
                                        Index => Positive,
                                        List => Primary_List);
```

```
type Colour is new Primary_Sets.Set;
```

The type Colour now has all the functions we want and the array type has a name of our choosing. We might still want to rename Empty and Full thus

```
function White return Colour renames Empty;
```

or we can still declare White as a constant by

```
White: constant Colour := Empty;
```

As a general rule it is better to use derived types rather than subtypes because of the greater type checking provided during compilation; sometimes, however, derived types introduce a need for lots of explicit type conversions which clutter the program, in which case the formal distinction is probably a mistake and one might as well use subtypes.

We conclude by summarizing the general principle regarding the matching of actual to formal generic types which should now be clear. The formal type represents a class of types which have certain common properties and these properties can be assumed in the generic unit. The corresponding actual type must then supply these properties. The matching rules are designed so that this is assured by reference to the parameters only and without considering the details of the generic body. As a consequence the user of the generic unit need not see the body for debugging purposes. This notion of matching guaranteed by the parameters is termed the contract model.

Some properties cannot be passed via the parameters and have to be checked upon instantiation. The general principle is to assume the best in the specification and then check it at instantiation but to assume the worst in the body so that it cannot go wrong. An example is type extension. The reader may recall that we cannot extend from a type at an inner accessibility level, see Section 13.1. Because a generic unit might be instantiated at any level this means that there is a restriction that extension is not allowed in a generic body at all. Extension is allowed in a generic specification and is checked at instantiation. The restriction disallowing extension in a body should not be found irksome; one possible alternative is to move the extension to the private part.

Another example of different behaviour in a generic body is that the accessibility checks are dynamic; this is again because a unit might be instantiated at any level. Apart from these and a few other minor cases which need not concern the normal user, the general principle that any unit can be made generic holds true.

The attribute Definite can be applied to an indefinite formal type T(<>) and gives a Boolean value indicating whether the actual type is definite or not. Thus considering the types of Section 16.3, T'Definite would be True if the actual parameter were Man or Mutant but False if the actual parameter were Person.

Finally we recall that our use of generic formal parameters within the body is restricted by the rule that they are not static.

EXERCISE 17.2

1   Instantiate Next to give a function behaving like **not**.

2   Rewrite the specification of the package Rational_Numbers so that it is a generic package taking the integer type as a parameter. See Exercise 11.2(**3**).

3   Rewrite the function Outer of Exercise 9.1(**3**) so that it is a generic function with appropriate parameters. Instantiate it to give the original function.

4   Write the body of the package Set_Of.

5   Rewrite the private part of Set_Of so that an object of the type Set is by default given the initial value Empty when declared.

17.3   Subprogram parameters

As mentioned earlier a generic parameter can also be a subprogram. There are a number of characteristic applications of this facility and we introduce the topic by considering the classical problem of sorting.

Suppose we wish to sort an array into ascending order. There are a number of general algorithms that can be used but they do not depend on the type of the values being sorted. All we need is some comparison operation such as "<" which is defined for the type.

We might start by considering the specification

```
generic
   type Index is (<>);
   type Item is (<>);
   type Collection is array (Index range <>) of Item;
procedure Sort(C: in out Collection);
```

Although the body is largely irrelevant it might help to illustrate the problem to consider the following crude possibility

```
procedure Sort(C: in out Collection) is
   Min: Index;
   Temp: Item;
begin
   for I in C'First .. Index'Pred(C'Last) loop
      Min := I;
      for J in Index'Succ(I) .. C'Last loop
         if C(J) < C(Min) then Min := J; end if;        -- use of <
      end loop;
      Temp := C(I); C(I) := C(Min); C(Min) := Temp;
   end loop;
end Sort;
```

This trivial algorithm repeatedly scans the part of the array not sorted, finds the least component (which because of the previous scans will be not less than any component of the already sorted part) and then swaps it so that it is then the last element of the now sorted part. Note that because of the generality we have imposed upon ourselves, we cannot write

```
   for I in C'First .. C'Last-1 loop
```

because we cannot rely upon the array index being an integer type. We only know that it is a discrete type and therefore have to use the attributes Index'Pred and Index'Succ which we know to be available since they are common to all discrete types.

However, the main point to note is the call of "<" in the body of Sort. This calls the predefined function corresponding to the type Item. We know that there is such a function because we have specified Item to be discrete and all discrete types have such a function. Unfortunately the net result is that our generic sort can only sort arrays of discrete types. It cannot sort arrays of floating types. Of course we could write a version for floating types by replacing the generic parameter for Item by

```
   type Item is digits <>;
```

but then it would not work for discrete types. What we really need to do is specify the comparison function to be used in a general manner. We can do this by adding a fourth parameter which is a formal subprogram so that the specification becomes

```
generic
   type Index is (<>);
   type Item is private;
   type Collection is array (Index range <>) of Item;
   with function "<" (X, Y: Item) return Boolean;
procedure Sort(C: in out Collection);
```

The formal subprogram parameter is like a subprogram declaration preceded by **with**. (The leading **with** is necessary to avoid a syntactic ambiguity and has no other subtle purpose.)

We have also made the type Item private since the only common property now required (other than supplied through the parameters) is that the type Item can be assigned. The body remains as before.

We can now sort an array of any (nonlimited) type provided that we have an appropriate comparison to supply as parameter. So in order to sort an array of our type Vector, we first instantiate thus

```
procedure Sort_Vector is
   new Sort(Integer, Float, Vector, "<");
```

and we can then apply the procedure to the array concerned

```
An_Array: Vector( ... );
...
Sort_Vector(An_Array);
```

Note carefully that our call of "<" inside Sort is actually a call of the function passed as actual parameter; in this case it is indeed the predefined function "<" anyway.

Passing the comparison rule gives our generic sort procedure amazing flexibility. We can, for example, sort in the reverse direction by

```
procedure Reverse_Sort_Vector is
   new Sort(Integer, Float, Vector, ">");
...
Reverse_Sort_Vector(An_Array);
```

This may come as a slight surprise but it is a natural consequence of the call of the formal "<" in

```
if C(J) < C(Min) then ...
```

being, after instantiation, a call of the actual ">". No confusion should arise because the internal call is hidden but the use of the named notation for instantiation would look curious

```
procedure Reverse_Sort_Vector is
         new Sort(Index => Integer,
                  Item => Float,
                  Collection => Vector,
                     "<" => ">");
```

We could also sort our second **Farmyard** of Section 8.5 assuming it to be a variable so that the animals are in alphabetical order

> **subtype** String_3 **is** String(1 .. 3);
>
> **procedure** Sort_String_3_Array **is**
>   **new** Sort(Positive, String_3, String_3_Array, "<");
> ...
> Sort_String_3_Array(Farmyard);

The "<" operator passed as parameter is the predefined operation applicable to one-dimensional arrays described in Section 8.6.

The correspondence between formal and actual subprograms is such that the formal subprogram just renames the actual subprogram. Thus the matching rules regarding parameters, results and so on are as described in Section 12.6. In particular the constraints on the parameters are those of the actual subprogram and any implied by the formal subprogram are ignored. A parameterless formal function can also be matched by an enumeration literal of the result type just as for renaming.

Generic subprogram parameters (like generic object parameters) can have default values. These are given in the generic formal part and take two forms. In the above example we could write

> **with function** "<" (X, Y: Item) **return** Boolean **is** <>;

This means that we can omit the corresponding actual parameter if there is visible at the point of *instantiation* a unique subprogram with the same designator and matching specification. With this alteration to Sort we could have omitted the last parameter in the instantiation giving Sort_Vector.

The other form of default value is where we give an explicit name for the default parameter. The usual rules for defaults apply; the default name is only evaluated if required by the instantiation but the binding of identifiers in the expression which is the name occurs at the point of *declaration* of the generic unit. In our example

> **with function** "<" (X, Y: Item) **return** Boolean **is** Less_Than;

could never be valid because the specification of **Less_Than** must match that of "<" and yet the parameter **Item** is not known until instantiation. The only valid possibilities are where the formal subprogram has no parameters depending on formal types or the default subprogram is itself another formal parameter or an attribute. Thus we might have

> **with function** Next(X: T) **return** T **is** T'Succ;

The same rules for mixing named and positional notation apply to generic instantiation as to subprogram calls. Hence if a parameter is omitted, subsequent parameters must be given using named notation. Of course, a generic unit need have no parameters in which case the instantiation takes the same form as for a subprogram call – the brackets are omitted.

As a final example of the use of our generic Sort (which we will assume now has a default parameter <> for "<"), we show how any type can be sorted provided we supply an appropriate rule.

Thus consider sorting an array of the type Date from Section 8.7. We write

```
type Date_Array is array (Positive range <>) of Date;

function "<" (X, Y: Date) return Boolean is
begin
   if X.Year /= Y.Year then
      return X.Year < Y.Year;
   elsif X.Month /= Y.Month then
      return X.Month < Y.Month;
   else
      return X.Day < Y.Day;
   end if;
end "<";

procedure Sort_Date_Array is
   new Sort(Positive, Date, Date_Array);
```

where the function "<" is passed through the default mechanism.

It might have been nicer to give our comparison rule a more appropriate name such as

```
function Earlier(X, Y: Date) return Boolean;
```

but we would then have to pass it as an explicit parameter; this might be considered better style anyway.

Formal subprograms can be used to supply further properties of type parameters in a quite general way. Consider the generic function Sum of the last section. We can generalize this even further by passing the adding operator itself as a generic parameter

```
generic
   type Index is (<>);
   type Item is private;
   type Vec is array (Index range <>) of Item;
   with function "+" (X, Y: Item) return Item;
function Apply(A: Vec) return Item;

function Apply(A: Vec) return Item is
   Result: Item := A(A'First);
begin
   for I in Index'Succ(A'First) .. A'Last loop
      Result := Result+A(I);
   end loop;
   return Result;
end Apply;
```

The operator "+" has been added as a parameter and Item is now just private and no longer floating. This means that we can apply the generic function to any binary operation on any type. However, we no longer have a zero value and so have to initialize Result with the first component of the array A and then iterate through the remainder. In doing this, remember that we cannot write

```
for I in A'First+1 .. A'Last loop
```

because the type Index may not be an integer type.

Our original function Sum of Section 9.1 is now given by

```
function Sum is new Apply(Integer, Float, Vector, "+");
```

We could equally have

```
function Prod is new Apply(Integer, Float, Vector, "*");
```

A very important use of formal subprograms is in mathematical applications such as integration. As we saw in Section 10.7, subprograms can be passed as parameters to other subprograms and so simple applications can thus be programmed as in traditional languages such as Algol and Pascal. However, for serious reuse we would need to make the unit generic so that any floating type can be used. We can then pass the function to be integrated as a further generic parameter and this has advantages because there are then no accessibility restrictions on the actual function.

We could have a generic function

```
generic
    type Floating is digits <>;
    with function F(X: Floating) return Floating;
function Integrate(A, B: Floating) return Floating;
```

and then in order to integrate a particular function we must instantiate Integrate with our function as actual generic parameter. Thus suppose we needed to evaluate

$$\int_0^P e^t \sin t \; dt$$

using the type Long_Real. We would write

```
function G(T: Long_Real) return Long_Real is
begin
    return Exp(T)*Sin(T);
end;

function Integrate_G is new Integrate(Long_Real, G);
```

and then the result is given by the expression

```
Integrate_G(0.0, P)
```

In practice the function Integrate would have other parameters indicating the accuracy required and so on.

Examples such as this are often found confusing at first sight. The key point to remember is that there are two distinct levels of parameterization. First we fix the function to be integrated at instantiation and then we fix the bounds when we call the integration function thus declared. The sorting examples were similar; first we fixed the parameters defining the type of array to be sorted and the rule to be used at instantiation, and then we fixed the actual array to be sorted when we called the procedure.

We conclude with an important remark concerning the identification of primitive operations. A primitive operation such as "<" which applies to all discrete types (as in our first example of sorting) and occurring inside the generic unit always refers to the predefined operation even if it has been redefined for the actual type concerned. The general principle is that since the generic unit applies to the class of discrete types as a whole then the primitive operations ought to refer to those guaranteed for all members of the class. Of course if the operation is passed as a distinct parameter (explicitly or by default) then the redefined operation will apply.

On the other hand, if the formal parameter is tagged, so that the actual type is an extension of the formal, then primitive operations refer to overridden ones. The reason for the different approach is that the whole essence of tagged types is to override operations and so within the generic it is natural to refer to the operation of the actual type. For example if we wrote

```
generic
   type T is new Object with private;
package P ...
```

so that the actual type must be derived from Object then inside P we expect the function Area to refer to that of the actual type supplied such as Circle and not to that of Object. Indeed in the formulation of Exercise 13.3(**1**) it would be a disaster if it referred to the Area of Object since it is abstract.

EXERCISE 17.3

1 Instantiate Sort to apply to

   type Poly_Array **is array** (Integer **range** <>) **of** Polynomial;

   See Section 16.2. Define a sensible ordering for polynomials.

2 Instantiate Sort to apply to an array of the type Mutant of Section 16.3. Put neuter things first, then females, then males and within each class the younger first. Could we sort an array of the type Person from the same section?

3 Sort the array People of Section 8.7.

4 What happens if we attempt to sort an array of less than two components?

5   Describe how to make a generic sort procedure based on the procedure Sort of Section 10.2. It should have an identical specification to the procedure Sort of this section.

6   Instantiate Apply to give a function to "and" together all the components of a Boolean array.

7   Rewrite Apply so that a null array can be a parameter without raising an exception. Use this new version to redo the previous exercise.

8   Write a generic function Equals to define the equality of one-dimensional arrays of a private type. See Exercise 11.4(**4**). Instantiate it to give the function "=" applying to the type Stack_Array.

9   Reconsider Exercise 10.7(**2**) using generics.

17.4   Package parameters

The last kind of formal generic parameter is the formal package. This greatly simplifies the composition of generic packages by allowing one package to be used as a parameter to another so that a hierarchy of consistently related packages can be created.

There are two possible forms of formal package parameters. The simplest is

        with package P **is new** Q(<>);

which indicates that the actual parameter corresponding to P must be a package which has been obtained by instantiating Q which must itself be a generic package. We can also explicitly indicate the actual parameters required by the instantiation of Q thus

        with package R **is new** Q(P1, P2, ...);

and then the actual package corresponding to R must have been instantiated with the given parameters.

As a simple example suppose we wish to develop a package for the manipulation of complex vectors; we want to make it generic with respect to the underlying floating type. Naturally enough we will build on our simple package for complex numbers in its generic form outlined in Section 17.2

```
generic
   type Floating is digits <>;
package Generic_Complex_Numbers is
   type Complex is private;
   ...
   function "+" (X, Y: Complex) return Complex;
   ...
end;
```

Our new generic package will need to use the various arithmetic operations exported from some instantiation of Generic_Complex_Numbers. These could all be imported as individual subprogram parameters but this would give a very long formal parameter list. Instead we can import the instantiated package as a whole. All we have to write is

```
generic
    type Index is (<>);
    with package Complex_Numbers is
        new Generic_Complex_Numbers (<>);
package Generic_Complex_Vectors is
    use Complex_Numbers;
    type Vector is array (Index range <>) of Complex;
    -- other types and operations on vectors
end;
```

and then we can instantiate the two packages by a sequence such as

```
package Long_Complex is
    new Generic_Complex_Numbers(Long_Float);
use Long_Complex;
package Long_Complex_Vectors is
    new Generic_Complex_Vectors(Integer, Long_Complex);
```

Note the use clause in the specification of Generic_Complex_Vectors. Without this the component subtype of the type Vector would have to be written as Complex_Numbers.Complex. Note also that within Generic_Complex_Vectors not only do we have visibility of all the operations exported by the instantiation of Generic_Complex_Numbers but we can also refer to the formal parameter Floating. This is a special rule for formal packages with the default form (<>).

We now consider a more elaborate example where the new package builds on the properties of two other packages. One is the toy package Generic_Complex_Numbers and the other is the predefined library package for computing elementary functions. This is described in detail in Section 20.3 but for this chapter all we need is the following outline sketch

```
generic
    type Float_Type is digits <>;
package Ada.Numerics.Generic_Elementary_Functions is
    ...
    function Sqrt(X: Float_Type'Base) return Float_Type'Base;
    -- similarly other functions such as
    -- Log, Exp, Sin, Cos, Sinh, Cosh, plus
    function Arctan(Y, X: Float_Type'Base) return Float_Type'Base;
    ...
end;
```

Although the following example is of a rather mathematical nature it is hoped that the general principles will be appreciated. It follows on from the above elementary functions package and concerns the provision of similar functions but working on complex arguments. Suppose we want to provide the ability to compute Sqrt, Log, Exp, Sin and Cos with functions such as

function Sqrt(X: Complex) **return** Complex;

Many readers will have forgotten that this can be done or perhaps never knew. It is not necessary to dwell on the details of how such calculations are performed or their use; the main point is to concentrate on the principles involved. These computations use various operations on the real numbers out of which the complex numbers are formed. Our goal is to write a generic package which works however the complex numbers are implemented (cartesian or polar) and also allows any floating point type as the basis for the underlying real numbers.

Here are the formulæ which we will need to compute.

Taking $z \equiv x + iy \equiv r(\cos \theta + i \sin \theta)$ as the argument:

$\text{sqrt } z = r^{1/2} (\cos \theta/2 + i \sin \theta/2)$
$\log z = \log r + i\, \theta$
$\exp z = e^x(\cos y + i \sin y)$
$\sin z = \sin x \cosh y + i \cos x \sinh y$
$\cos z = \cos x \cosh y - i \sin x \sinh y$

We thus see that we will need the functions Sqrt, Cos, Sin, Log, Exp, Cosh and Sinh applying to the underlying floating type. We also need to be able to decompose and reconstruct a complex number using both cartesian and polar forms; we will assume that the package Generic_Complex_Numbers has been extended to do this (we will consider the question of child packages in the next section).

We can now write

```
with Ada.Numerics.Generic_Elementary_Functions;
use Ada.Numerics;
with Generic_Complex_Numbers;
generic
   with package Elementary_Functions is
        new Generic_Elementary_Functions(<>);
   with package Complex_Numbers is
        new Generic_Complex_Numbers
                              (Elementary_Functions.Float_Type);
package Generic_Complex_Functions is
   use Complex_Numbers;

   function Sqrt(X: Complex) return Complex;

   ...

end Generic_Complex_Functions;
```

where the actual packages must be instantiations of Generic_Elementary_
Functions and Generic_Complex_Numbers. Note that both forms of formal
package are used. Any instantiation of Generic_Elementary_Functions is
allowed but the instantiation of Generic_Complex_Numbers must have
Elementary_Functions.Float_Type as its actual parameter. This ensures that
both packages are instantiated with the same floating type.

Note carefully that we are using the formal exported from the first
instantiation as the required parameter for the second instantiation. As noted
above, the formal parameters are only accessible in this way when the default
form (<>) is used. In order to reduce verbosity it is permitted to have a use
clause in the generic formal list, so we could have written

```
with package Elementary_Functions is
     new Generic_Elementary_Functions(<>);
use Elementary_Functions;
with package Complex_Numbers is
     new Generic_Complex_Numbers(Float_Type);
```

although this is perhaps not so clear.

Finally our instantiations are

```
type My_Float is digits 9;

package My_Elementary_Functions is
     new Generic_Elementary_Functions(My_Float);

package My_Complex_Numbers is
     new Generic_Complex_Numbers(My_Float);

package My_Complex_Functions is
     new Generic_Complex_Functions
                  (My_Elementary_Functions, My_Complex_Numbers);
```

and *Hey presto!* it all works. Note that, irritatingly, the complex type is just
Complex and not My_Complex. However we could use a subtype or derived
type as we did for the type Colour and the package Set_Of in Section 17.2.

The reader might wonder why we could not simply instantiate the various
packages inside the body of Generic_Complex_Functions and thereby avoid the
package parameters. This works but could result in wasteful and unnecessary
multiple instantiations especially since we may well need them at the user level
anyway.

It is hoped that the general principles have been understood and that the
mathematics has not clouded the issues. The principles are important but not
easily illustrated with short examples. It should also be noted that although the
package Generic_Elementary_Functions described above is exactly as in the
predefined library, the complex number packages are just an illustration of how
generics can be used. The Numerics annex does indeed provide packages for
complex numbers and complex functions but they use a rather different
approach as outlined in Section 22.5.

Another application of formal packages is where we wish to bundle
together a number of related types and operations and treat them as a whole.

We make them parameters of an otherwise null generic package. In essence, the successful instantiation of the generic package is an assertion that the entities have the required relationship and the group can then be referred to using the instantiated package (sometimes known as a signature).

As a very trivial example we will have noticed that the group of parameters

```
type Index is (<>);
type Item is private;
type Vector is (Index range <>) of Item;
```

has occurred from time to time; see Sort and Apply in the last section. For a successful instantiation of a generic unit having these as parameters it is necessary that the actual types have the required relationship. We could write

```
generic
   type Index is (<>);
   type Item is private;
   type Vector is (Index range <>) of Item;
package General_Vector is end;
```

(note the ugly juxtaposition of **is end**) and then rewrite Sort and Apply as

```
generic
   with package P is new General_Vector(<>);
   with function "<" (X, Y: P.Item) return Boolean is <>;
procedure Sort (V: in out P.Vector);

generic
   with package P is new General_Vector(<>);
   use P;
   with function "+" (X, Y: Item) return Item;
function Apply(A: Vector) return Item;
```

Note that the use clause in the formal list for Apply simplifies the text with some risk of obscurity. We can now perform instantiations as follows. First we might write

```
package Float_Vector is new General_Vector(Integer, Float, Vector);
```

which ensures that Integer, Float and Vector have the required relationship. Then we can write

```
procedure Sort_Vector is new Sort(Float_Vector, "<");

function Sum is new Apply(Float_Vector, "+");
```

which should be compared with the corresponding instantiations in the previous section. Clearly this example is rather trivial and the gain obtained by simplifying the parameter lists for Sort and Apply is barely worth the effort of the extra layer of abstraction. Practical uses will inevitably have longer parameter lists.

EXERCISE 17.4

1 Write a body for the package Generic_Complex_Functions using the formulae defined above. Ignore exceptions.

2 Reconsider Exercises 17.3(**1**) and 17.3(**6**) using the package General_Vector.

3 A mathematical group is defined by an operation over a set of elements thus

```
generic
    type Element is private;
    Identity: in Element;
    with function Op(X, Y: Element) return Element;
    with function Inverse(X: Element) return Element;
package Group is end;
```

Declare a generic function Power which takes an element E and a signed integer N as parameters and delivers the Nth power of the element using the group operation. Then define the addition group over the type Integer and finally instantiate the power function.

4 Any finite group can be represented as a discrete type. Adapt the definition of Group of the previous exercise accordingly and then define a (generic) function Is_Group that checks whether a signature conforms to the semantic requirements of a group.

17.5 Generic library units

We now consider the interaction between generics and hierarchical libraries. Both are important tools in the construction of subsystems and it is essential that genericity be usable with the child concept.

The children of a nongeneric parent may be generic or not but children of a generic unit must always be generic.

If the parent unit is not generic then a generic child may be instantiated in the usual way at any point where it is visible. On the other hand, if the parent unit is itself generic, then the rules regarding the instantiation of the children are somewhat different. A generic child of a generic parent can be instantiated inside the parent and its hierarchy as normal but it can only be instantiated externally provided its parent is first instantiated.

In effect the instantiation of the parent creates an actual unit with a generic child inside it; we can then instantiate this child provided we have a with clause for the original generic child. Note that these instantiations do not have to be as library units although they might be.

As a simple example, we will consider the complex numbers once more and assume that the package takes the hierarchical form of Exercise 12.3(**1**). We can now make the hierarchy generic with respect to the underlying floating point type. We write

```
      generic
         type Floating is digits <>;
      package Generic_Complex_Numbers is
         ...
      end Generic_Complex_Numbers;

      generic
      package Generic_Complex_Numbers.Cartesian is
         ...
      end Generic_Complex_Numbers.Cartesian;

      generic
      package Generic_Complex_Numbers.Polar is
         ...
      end Generic_Complex_Numbers.Polar;
```

and then instantiations internally might be

```
      with Generic_Complex_Numbers;
      with Generic_Complex_Numbers.Cartesian;
      with Generic_Complex_Numbers.Polar;
      package P is
         package My_Complex_Numbers is
            new Generic_Complex_Numbers(My_Float);
         package My_Complex_Cartesian is
            new My_Complex_Numbers.Cartesian;
         package My_Complex_Polar is
            new My_Complex_Numbers.Polar;
         ...
      end P;
```

whereas instantiations at the library level might be

```
      with Generic_Complex_Numbers;
      package My_Complex_Numbers is
         new Generic_Complex_Numbers(My_Float);

      with Generic_Complex_Numbers.Cartesian;
      package My_Complex_Numbers.My_Cartesian is
         new My_Complex_Numbers.Cartesian;

      with Generic_Complex_Numbers.Polar;
      package My_Complex_Numbers.My_Polar is
         new My_Complex_Numbers.Polar;
```

We thus have to instantiate the generic hierarchy (or as much of it as we want) unit by unit. The main reason for requiring all children of a generic unit to be generic is to provide a handle to do this; as a consequence it is often the case, as here, that the child units have no formal generic parameters.

If the instantiations are internal then of course the instantiated units simply have different names. If we instantiate at the library level then we can (but need not) make the new units into a similar child hierarchy – but the names of the child units have to be different otherwise there would be a name clash with the notional generic units in the instance of the parent.

Of course, we need not instantiate the whole hierarchy for a particular application; indeed, one of the reasons for the unit by unit approach is to eliminate problems concerning the impact of the addition of new children to the generic hierarchy on existing instantiations.

EXERCISE 17.5

1   Rewrite the specification of Generic_Complex_Functions of the previous section using the hierarchical form for the package Generic_Complex_Numbers.

2   Write the body of Generic_Complex_Numbers.Polar. See Section 12.3 for its specification. Use the elementary functions from the predefined library outlined in the previous section.

CHECKLIST 17

The generic mechanism is not text replacement; nonlocal name binding would be different.

Object **in out** parameters are bound by renaming.

Object **in** parameters are always copied unlike parameters of subprograms.

Subprogram generic parameters are bound by renaming.

Generic subprograms may not overload – only the instantiations can.

Generic subprograms always have a separate specification and body.

Formal parameters (and defaults) may depend upon preceding parameters.

Generic formal parameters and their attributes are not static.

Type extension is not allowed in a generic body.

Changes from Ada 83

Ada 83 did not distinguish between indefinite and definite formal parameters. The form **type** T(<>) **is private**; did not exist. This resulted in violations of the contract model.

The parameter forms for modular, decimal and derived types did not exist in Ada 83.

Package parameters did not exist in Ada 83.

18 Tasking

The final major topic to be introduced is tasking. This has been left to the end, not because it is unimportant or particularly difficult, but because, apart from the interaction with exceptions, it is a fairly self-contained part of the language.

Ada is fairly unusual in having tasking constructions as an intrinsic part of the language. Some might argue that such matters are the concern of the operating system and are better done by calls from an otherwise sequential program. However, built-in constructions provide greater reliability, general operating systems do not provide the control and timing needed by many applications, and every operating system is different.

Building tasking into the language also makes it easier to benefit from any inherent parallelism in the machine and increases the potential for optimization.

18.1 Parallelism

So far we have only considered sequential programs in which statements are obeyed in order. In many applications it is convenient to write a program as several parallel activities which cooperate as necessary. This is particularly true of programs which interact in real time with physical processes in the real world, simulation programs (which mimic parallel activities in the real world), and programs which wish to exploit multiprocessor architectures directly.

In Ada, parallel activities are described by means of tasks. In simple cases a task is lexically described by a form very similar to a package. This consists of a specification describing the interface presented to other tasks and a body describing the dynamic behaviour of the task.

```
task T is                    -- specification
  ...
end T;
task body T is              -- body
  ...
end T;
```

In some cases a task presents no interface to other tasks in which case the specification reduces to just

```
task T;
```

As a simple example of parallelism, consider a family going shopping to buy ingredients for a meal. Suppose they need meat, salad and wine and that the purchase of these items can be done by calling procedures Buy_Meat, Buy_Salad and Buy_Wine respectively. The whole expedition could be represented by

```
procedure Shopping is
begin
  Buy_Meat;
  Buy_Salad;
  Buy_Wine;
end;
```

However, this solution corresponds to the family buying each item in sequence. It would be far more efficient for them to split up so that, for example, mother buys the meat, the children buy the salad and father buys the wine. They agree to meet again perhaps in the car park. This parallel solution is represented by

```
procedure Shopping is
  task Get_Salad;

  task body Get_Salad is
  begin
    Buy_Salad;
  end Get_Salad;

  task Get_Wine;

  task body Get_Wine is
  begin
    Buy_Wine;
  end Get_Wine;
```

```
begin
   Buy_Meat;
end Shopping;
```

In this formulation, mother is represented as the main processor and calls Buy_Meat directly from the procedure Shopping. The children and father are considered as subservient processors and perform the locally declared tasks Get_Salad and Get_Wine which respectively call the procedures Buy_Salad and Buy_Wine.

The example illustrates the declaration, activation and termination of tasks. A task is a program component like a package and is declared in a similar way inside a subprogram, block, package or indeed another task body. A task specification can also be declared in a package specification in which case the task body must be declared in the corresponding package body. However, a task specification cannot be declared in the specification of another task but only in the body.

The activation of a task is automatic. In the above example the local tasks become active when the parent unit reaches the **begin** following the task declaration. Such a task will terminate when it reaches its final **end**. Thus the task Get_Salad calls the procedure Buy_Salad and then promptly terminates.

A task declared in the declarative part of a subprogram, block or task body is said to depend on that unit. It is an important rule that a unit cannot be left until all dependent tasks have terminated. This termination rule ensures that objects declared in the unit and therefore potentially visible to local tasks cannot disappear while there exists a task which could access them. (Note that a task cannot depend on a package – we will return to this later.)

It is important to realize that the main subprogram is itself considered to be called by a hypothetical main task. We can now trace the sequence of actions when this main task calls the procedure Shopping. First the tasks Get_Salad and Get_Wine are declared and then when the main task reaches the **begin** these dependent tasks are set active in parallel with the main task. The dependent tasks call their respective procedures and terminate. Meanwhile the main task calls Buy_Meat and then reaches the **end** of Shopping. The main task then waits until the dependent tasks have terminated if they have not already done so. This corresponds to mother waiting for father and children to return with their purchases.

In the general case termination therefore occurs in two stages. We say that a unit is completed when it reaches its final **end**. It will subsequently become terminated only when all dependent tasks, if any, are also terminated. Of course, if a unit has no dependent tasks then it effectively becomes completed and terminated at the same time (but see Section 18.7).

EXERCISE 18.1

1   Rewrite procedure Shopping to contain three local tasks so that the symmetry of the situation is revealed.

18.2 The rendezvous

In the Shopping example the various tasks did not interact with each other once they had been set active except that their parent unit had to wait for them to terminate. Generally, however, tasks will interact with each other during their lifetime.

There are two main ways in which tasks can interact: directly, by sending messages to each other, and indirectly, by common access to shared data. We consider direct message communication in this section and indirect communication through shared data in Section 18.4.

Messages are directly passed between tasks in Ada by a mechanism known as the rendezvous. This is similar to the human situation where two people meet, perform a transaction and then go on independently.

A rendezvous between two tasks occurs as a consequence of one task calling an entry declared in another. An entry is declared in a task specification in a similar way to a procedure in a package specification

```
task T is
   entry E( ... );
end;
```

An entry can have **in, out** and **in out** parameters in the same way as a procedure. It cannot however have a result like a function. An entry is called in a similar way to a procedure

```
T.E( ... );
```

A task name cannot appear in a use clause and so the dotted notation is necessary to call the entry from outside the task. Of course, a local task could call an entry of its parent directly – the usual scope and visibility rules apply.

A task can also have a private part containing the declaration of entries which are not visible to the external user; they could be called by local tasks.

The statements to be obeyed during a rendezvous are described by corresponding accept statements in the body of the task containing the declaration of the entry. An accept statement usually takes the form

```
accept E( ... ) do
   -- sequence of statements
end E;
```

The formal parameters of the entry E are repeated in the same way that a procedure body repeats the formal parameters of a corresponding procedure declaration. The **end** is optionally followed by the name of the entry. A significant difference is that the body of the accept statement is just a sequence of statements plus optional exception handlers. Any local declarations must be provided by writing a local block.

The most important difference between an entry call and a procedure call is that in the case of a procedure, the task that calls the procedure also immediately executes the procedure body whereas in the case of an entry, one task calls the entry but the corresponding accept statement is executed by the task owning the entry. Moreover, the accept statement cannot be executed until a task calls the entry and the task owning the entry reaches the accept statement. Naturally one of these will occur first and the task concerned will then be suspended until the other reaches its corresponding statement. When this occurs the sequence of statements of the accept statement is executed by the called task while the calling task remains suspended. This interaction is called a rendezvous. When the end of the accept statement is reached the rendezvous is completed and both tasks then proceed independently. The parameter mechanism is exactly as for a subprogram call; note that expressions in the actual parameter list are evaluated before the call is issued.

We can elaborate our shopping example by giving the task Get_Salad two entries, one for mother to hand the children the money for the salad and one to collect the salad from them afterwards. We do the same for Get_Wine (although perhaps father has his own funds in which case he might keep the wine to himself anyway).

We can also replace the procedures Buy_Salad, Buy_Wine and Buy_Meat by functions which take money as a parameter and return the appropriate ingredient. Our shopping procedure might now become

```
procedure Shopping is
  task Get_Salad is
    entry Pay(M: in Money);
    entry Collect(S: out Salad);
  end Get_Salad;

  task body Get_Salad is
    Cash: Money;
    Food: Salad;
  begin
    accept Pay(M: in Money) do
      Cash := M;
    end Pay;

    Food := Buy_Salad(Cash);

    accept Collect(S: out Salad) do
      S := Food;
    end Collect;
  end Get_Salad;

  -- Get_Wine similarly

begin
  Get_Salad.Pay(50);
  Get_Wine.Pay(100);
  MM := Buy_Meat(200);
  Get_Salad.Collect(SS);
  Get_Wine.Collect(WW);
end Shopping;
```

The final outcome is that the various ingredients end up in the variables MM, SS and WW whose declarations are left to the imagination.

The logical behaviour should be noted. As soon as the tasks Get_Salad and Get_Wine become active they encounter accept statements and wait until the main task calls the entries Pay in each of them. After calling the function Buy_Meat, the main task calls the Collect entries. Curiously, mother is unable to collect the wine until after she has collected the salad from the children.

As a more abstract example consider the problem of providing a task to act as a single buffer between one or more tasks producing items and one or more tasks consuming them. Our intermediate task can hold just one item.

```
task Buffer is
   entry Put(X: in Item);
   entry Get(X: out Item);
end;

task body Buffer is
   V: Item;
begin
   loop
      accept Put(X: in Item) do
         V := X;
      end Put;
      accept Get(X: out Item) do
         X := V;
      end Get;
   end loop;
end Buffer;
```

Other tasks may then dispose of or acquire items by calling

```
Buffer.Put( ... );
Buffer.Get( ... );
```

Intermediate storage for the item is the variable V. The body of the task is an endless loop which contains an accept statement for Put followed by one for Get. Thus the task alternately accepts calls of Put and Get which fill and empty the variable V.

Several different tasks may call Put and Get and consequently may have to be queued. Every entry has a queue of tasks waiting to call the entry – this queue is normally processed in a first-in–first-out manner (but see Section 22.2). It may, of course, be empty at a particular moment. The number of tasks on the queue of entry E is given by E'Count but this attribute may only be used inside the body of the task owning the entry.

This example was for illustration only; as we will see in a moment such data manager tasks which effectively decouple the producer and consumer are usually not necessary – this is really a shared data application and is more efficiently programmed using protected objects which are described in Section 18.4.

An entry may have several corresponding accept statements (usually only one). Each execution of an accept statement removes one task from the queue.

Note the asymmetric naming in a rendezvous. The calling task must name the called task but not vice versa. Moreover, several tasks may call an entry and be queued but a task can only be on one queue at a time.

Entries may be overloaded both with each other and with subprograms and obey the same rules. An entry may be renamed as a procedure

>   **procedure** Write(X: **in** Item) **renames** Buffer.Put;

This mechanism may be useful in avoiding excessive use of the dotted notation. An entry, renamed or not, may be an actual or default generic parameter corresponding to a formal subprogram.

An entry may have no parameters, such as

>   **entry** Signal;

and it could then be called by

>   T.Signal;

An accept statement need have no body as in

>   **accept** Signal;

In such a case the purpose of the call is merely to effect a synchronization and not to pass information. However, an entry without parameters can have an accept statement with a body and vice versa. There is nothing to prevent us writing

>   **accept** Signal **do**
>   Fire;
>   **end**;

in which case the task calling Signal is only allowed to continue after the call of Fire is completed. We could also have

>   **accept** Put(X: Item);

although clearly the parameter value is not used.

There are few constraints on the statements in an accept statement. They may include entry calls, subprogram calls, blocks and further accept statements. However an accept statement may not contain an asynchronous select (Section 18.8), nor an accept statement for the same entry or one of the same family (Section 18.9). On the other hand an accept statement may not itself appear in a subprogram body but must be in the sequence of statements of the task although it could be in a block or other accept statement. The execution of a **return** statement in an accept statement corresponds to reaching the final end and therefore terminates the rendezvous. Similarly to a subprogram body, a **goto** or **exit** statement cannot transfer control out of an accept statement.

A task may call one of its own entries but, of course, will promptly deadlock. This may seem foolish but programming languages allow lots of silly things such as endless loops and so on. We could expect a good compiler to warn us of obvious potential deadlocks.

EXERCISE 18.2

Note: this is simply an exercise on using the rendezvous. A better solution is to use a protected object as described in Section 18.4.

1   Write the body of a task whose specification is

```
task Char_To_Line is
   entry Put(C: in Character);
   entry Get(L: out Line);
end;
```

where

```
type Line is array (1 .. 80) of Character;
```

The task acts as a buffer which alternately builds up a line by accepting successive calls of Put and then delivers a complete line on a call of Get.

18.3   Timing and scheduling

As we have seen, an Ada program may contain several tasks. Conceptually, it is best to think of these tasks as each having its own personal processor so that, provided a task is not waiting for something to happen, it will actually be executing.

In practice, of course, most implementations will not be able to allocate a unique processor to each task and indeed, in many cases, there will be only one physical processor. It will then be necessary to allocate the processor(s) to the tasks that are logically able to execute by some scheduling algorithm. This can be done in many ways.

One of the simplest mechanisms is to use time slicing. This means giving the processor to each task in turn for some fixed time interval such as 10 milliseconds. Of course, if a task cannot use its turn (perhaps because it is held up awaiting a partner in a rendezvous), then a sensible scheduler would allocate its turn to the next task. Similarly, if a task cannot use all of its turn then the remaining time could be allocated to another task.

Time slicing is somewhat rudimentary since it treats all tasks equally. It is often the case that some tasks are more urgent than others and in the face of a shortage of processing power this equality is wasteful. The idea of a task having a priority is therefore introduced. A simple scheduling system would be one where each task had a distinct priority and the processor would then be given to the highest priority task which could actually run. Combinations of time slicing and priority scheduling are also possible. A system might permit several tasks to have the same priority and time slice between them.

The core of the Ada language remains silent about scheduling and leaves the details of the techniques supported to the Real-Time Systems annex. In this chapter we will therefore generally take the abstract view that each task has its own notional processor. A brief discussion of priorities will be found in Section 22.2.

A task may be held up for various reasons; it might be waiting for a partner in a rendezvous or for a dependent task to terminate. It can also be held up by executing a delay statement such as

> **delay** 3.0;

This suspends the task (or main subprogram) executing the statement for three seconds. The expression after the reserved word **delay** is of a predefined fixed point type Duration and gives the period in seconds. At the expiry of the delay the task will be ready again. (Note, however, that there might not be a processor immediately available to execute the task since in the meantime a higher priority task might have obtained control. On a single processor system, if it has a higher priority than a task running when the interval expires then it will preempt.)

The type Duration is a fixed point type so that the addition of durations can be done without systematic loss of accuracy. If we add together two fixed point numbers of the same type then we always get the exact mathematical answer; this does not apply to floating point. On the other hand, we need to express fractions of a second in a convenient way and so the use of a real type rather than an integer type is much more satisfactory.

Delays can be more easily expressed by using suitable constant declarations, thus

> Seconds: **constant** Duration := 1.0;
> Minutes: **constant** Duration := 60.0;
> Hours: **constant** Duration := 3600.0;

We can then write for example

> **delay** 2*Hours+40*Minutes;

in which the expression uses the rule that a fixed point value can be multiplied by an integer giving a result of the same fixed point type.

A delay statement with a zero or negative argument has no effect (other than possibly causing rescheduling).

Although the type Duration is implementation defined, we are guaranteed that it will allow durations (both positive and negative) of up to at least one day (86400 seconds). Delays of more than a day (which are unusual) would have to be programmed with a loop. At the other end of the scale, the smallest value of Duration, that is Duration'Small, is guaranteed to be not greater than 20 milliseconds.

More general timing operations can be performed by using the predefined package Ada.Calendar whose specification is

```ada
package Ada.Calendar is

   type Time is private;

   subtype Year_Number is Integer range 1901 .. 2099;
   subtype Month_Number is Integer range 1 .. 12;
   subtype Day_Number is Integer range 1 .. 31;
   subtype Day_Duration is Duration range 0.0 .. 86_400.0;

   function Clock return Time;

   function Year(Date: Time) return Year_Number;
   function Month(Date: Time) return Month_Number;
   function Day(Date: Time) return Day_Number;
   function Seconds(Date: Time) return Day_Duration;

   procedure Split(Date: in Time;
                   Year: out Year_Number;
                   Month: out Month_Number;
                   Day: out Day_Number;
                   Seconds: out Day_Duration);

   function Time_Of(Year: Year_Number;
                    Month: Month_Number;
                    Day: Day_Number;
                    Seconds: Day_Duration := 0.0) return Time;

   function "+" (Left: Time; Right: Duration) return Time;
   function "+" (Left: Duration; Right: Time) return Time;
   function "–" (Left: Time; Right: Duration) return Time;
   function "–" (Left: Time; Right: Time) return Duration;
   function "<" (Left, Right: Time) return Boolean;
   function "<=" (Left, Right: Time) return Boolean;
   function ">" (Left, Right: Time) return Boolean;
   function ">=" (Left, Right: Time) return Boolean;

   Time_Error: exception;
                   -- can be raised by Time_Of, Year, Split, +, and –

private
   -- implementation dependent
end Ada.Calendar;
```

A value of the private type Time is a combined time and date; it can be decomposed into the year, month, day and the duration since midnight of the day concerned by the procedure Split. Alternatively, the functions Year, Month, Day and Seconds may be used to obtain the individual values. On the other hand, the function Time_Of can be used to build a value of Time from the four constituents; the seconds parameter has a default of zero. Note the subtypes Year_Number, Month_Number and Day_Number; the range of Year_Number is such that the leap year calculation is simplified. The exception Time_Error is raised if the parameters of Time_Of satisfy the constraints but nevertheless do not form a proper date. A careful distinction must be made between Time and Duration. Time is absolute but Duration is relative.

The current Time is returned by a call of the function Clock. The result is, of course, returned in an indivisible way and there is no risk of getting the time of day and the date inconsistent around midnight as there would be if there were separate functions delivering the individual components of the current time and date.

The various overloadings of "+", "-" and the relational operators allow us to add, subtract and compare times and durations as appropriate. Attempts to create a time or duration outside the implemented range will result in Time_Error being raised. Note the strange formal parameter names Left and Right; these are the normal names for the parameters of the predefined operators in the package Standard.

As well as the relative delay statement mentioned above there is also an absolute delay statement; this takes a time rather than a duration as parameter. Thus to delay until a given time we write

```
    delay until Some_Time;
```

where Some_Time is of type Time.

As an example of the use of the package Calendar suppose we wish a task to call a procedure Action at regular intervals, every five minutes perhaps. Our first attempt might be to write

```
    loop
       delay 5*Minutes;
       Action;
    end loop;
```

However, this is unsatisfactory for various reasons. First, we have not taken account of the time of execution of the procedure Action and the overhead of the loop itself, and secondly, we have seen that a delay statement sets a minimum delay only (since a higher priority task may retain the processor on the expiry of the delay). Furthermore, we might get preempted by a higher priority task at any time anyway. So we will inevitably get a cumulative timing drift. This can be overcome by writing for example

```
    declare
       use Calendar;
       Interval: constant Duration := 5*Minutes;
       Next_Time: Time := First_Time;
    begin
       loop
          delay until Next_Time;
```

```
            Action;
            Next_Time := Next_Time + Interval;
        end loop;
    end;
```

In this formulation Next_Time contains the time when Action is next to be called; its initial value is in First_Time and it is updated exactly on each iteration by adding Interval. This solution will have no cumulative drift provided the mean duration of Action plus the overheads of the loop and updating Next_Time and so on do not exceed Interval. Of course, there may be a local drift if a particular call of Action takes a long time or other tasks temporarily use the processors. Finally, there is one other condition that must be satisfied for the required timing to be obtained: the interval has to be a multiple of small for the type Duration.

EXERCISE 18.3

1 Write a generic procedure to call a procedure regularly. The generic parameters should be the procedure to be called, the time of the first call, the interval and the number of calls. If the time of the first call passed as parameter is in the past use the current time as the first time.

2 What is the least number of bits required to implement the type Duration?

3 Is there any difference between

   delay until Next_Time;
   delay Next_Time – Clock;

4 Declare a variable High_Noon of type Time and assign to it the time of the next noon.

18.4 Protected objects

Consider the problem of protecting a variable V from uncontrolled access. We might consider using a package and two procedures Read and Write

```
package Protected_Variable is
    procedure Read(X: out Item);
    procedure Write(X: in Item);
end;

package body Protected_Variable is
    V: Item := initial value;
```

```
procedure Read(X: out Item) is
begin
   X := V;
end;

procedure Write(X: in Item) is
begin
   V := X;
end;

end Protected_Variable;
```

However this is very unsatisfactory. Nothing prevents different tasks in our system from calling Read and Write simultaneously and thereby causing interference. As a more specific example, suppose that the type Item is a record giving the coordinates of an aircraft or ship

```
type Item is
   record
      X_Coord: Float;
      Y_Coord: Float;
   end record;
```

Suppose that a task A acquires pairs of values and uses a call of Write to store them into V and that another task B calls Read whenever it needs the latest position. Now assume that A is halfway through executing Write when it is interrupted by task B which promptly calls Read. It is clear that B could get a value consisting of the new *x*-coordinate and the old *y*-coordinate which would no doubt represent a location where the vessel had never been. The use of such inconsistent data for calculating the heading of the vessel from regularly read pairs of readings would obviously lead to inaccuracies.

The reader may wonder how the task A could be interrupted by task B anyway. In a single processor system with time slicing it may merely have been that B's turn came at an unfortunate moment. Alternatively B might have a higher priority than A; if B had been waiting for time to elapse before taking the next reading by obeying a delay statement, then A might be allowed to execute and B's delay might expire just at the wrong moment. In practical real-time situations things are always happening at the wrong moment!

The proper solution is to use a protected object rather than a package. A protected object has a distinct specification and body in a similar style to a package or task. The specification provides the access protocol and the body provides the implementation details.

The specification of a protected object is also split into a visible part and a private part. The visible part contains the specifications of subprograms and entries providing the protocol. The private part contains the hidden shared data and also the specifications of any other subprograms and entries which are private to the object.

Unlike packages and tasks, the body of a protected object is not allowed to declare any data. It can only contain the bodies of subprograms and entries; all data must be in the private part.

Now consider the following

```
protected Variable is
   procedure Read(X: out Item);
   procedure Write(X: in Item);
private
   V: Item := initial value;
end Variable;

protected body Variable is

   procedure Read(X: out Item) is
   begin
     X := V;
   end Read;

   procedure Write(X: in Item) is
   begin
     V := X;
   end Write;

end Variable;
```

The protected object Variable provides controlled access to the private variable V. The procedure Read enables us to read the current value whereas the procedure Write enables us to update the value. Calls are written in the usual way using the familiar dotted notation

```
Variable.Read(Current_Value);
...
Variable.Write(New_Value);
```

Within a protected body we can have a number of subprograms and the implementation is such that (like a monitor) calls of the subprograms are mutually exclusive and thus cannot interfere with each other. This exclusivity is an intrinsic part of the implementation typically performed using a lock. A lock can be likened to a token such as used on 19th century railways to ensure unique access to a section of track; only the train with the token could proceed. Here only the task with the lock can proceed.

We could alternatively have used a function for the reading

```
function Read return Item is
begin
   return V;
end Read;
```

An important difference between a procedure and function in the protected body is that a procedure can access the private data in an arbitrary manner whereas a function is only allowed read access to the private data. The implementation is consequently permitted to perform the useful optimization of allowing multiple calls of functions at the same time thus automatically solving the basic classic readers and writers problem.

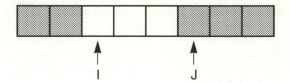

Figure 18.1   The bounded buffer.

In the above example, the subprograms can always be executed as soon as the lock is available. Sometimes however, a system is such that certain calls cannot always be processed but must await some condition. A good example is provided by the classic bounded buffer. This allows up to N items to be buffered between the producer and the consumer. Just for fun we use a modular type as promised in Section 15.2. Consider the following

```
N: constant := 8;              -- for instance
type Index is mod N;
type Item_Array is array (Index) of Item;

protected type Buffering is
   entry Put(X: in Item);
   entry Get(X: out Item);
private
   A: Item_Array;
   I, J: Index := 0;
   Count: Integer range 0 .. N := 0;
end Buffering;

protected body Buffering is

   entry Put(X: in Item) when Count < N is
   begin
     A(I) := X;
     I := I + 1;  Count := Count + 1;
   end Put;

   entry Get(X: out Item) when Count > 0 is
   begin
     X := A(J);
     J := J + 1;  Count := Count - 1;
   end Get;

end Buffering;
```

The buffer is the array A of length N which is a number set to 8 in this example. Note that the index type of the array is the modular type Index. The variables I and J index the next free and last used locations of the buffer respectively and Count is the number of locations of the buffer which are full. The buffer is used cyclically so I need not be greater than J. The situation in Figure 18.1 shows a partly filled buffer with Count = 5, I = 2 and J = 5. The portion of the buffer in use is shaded. The variables I, J and Count are all initialized to 0 so that the buffer is initially empty.

The objective is to allow items to be added to and removed from the buffer in a first-in–first-out manner but to prevent the buffer from being overfilled or under-emptied. This is done by the introduction of protected entries which always have barrier conditions.

The syntax of an entry body is similar to that of a procedure body except that it always has a mandatory barrier. An entry body can have a declarative part in contrast to an accept statement which cannot.

We have also taken the opportunity to show how the general notion of a protected object is generalized into a protected type by the addition of the reserved word **type** after **protected**. The type then acts as a template for protected objects and individual objects are then declared in the usual way. The various subprograms and entries of a particular protected object can then be called using the dotted notation. We thus write

```
My_Buffer: Buffering;
...
My_Buffer.Put(X);
```

As an aside, note that we have had to declare the constant N, the type Index and the array type Item_Array external to the protected type; this is because we are only allowed components inside the protected type. There is a general rule that we cannot declare a type inside a type; a similar problem occurred with the type Stack in Section 11.4. These restrictions do not really matter since in practice the protected type is likely to be declared inside a (possibly generic) package.

The behaviour of the protected object is controlled by the barriers. When an entry is called its barrier is evaluated; if the barrier is false then the calling task is queued until circumstances are such that the barrier is true and the lock is released so that some other task can call the object meanwhile. When My_Buffer is declared, the buffer is empty, and so the barrier for Put (the condition Count < N) is true whereas the barrier for Get is false. So initially only a call of Put can be executed and a task issuing a call of Get will be queued.

The statements of the entry bodies copy the item to or from the buffer and then update I or J and Count to reflect the new state. Since I and J are of the modular type Index, the addition wraps around automatically as required.

At the end of the execution of an entry body (or a procedure body) of the protected object, all barriers which have queued tasks are re-evaluated thus possibly permitting the processing of an entry call which had been queued on a false barrier. So at the end of the first call of Put, if a call of Get had been queued, then the barrier is re-evaluated thus permitting a waiting call of Get to be serviced at once.

It is important to realize that there is no task associated with the buffer itself; the evaluation of barriers is effectively performed by the run-time system. Barriers are evaluated when an entry is first called and when something happens which could sensibly change the state of a barrier with a waiting task.

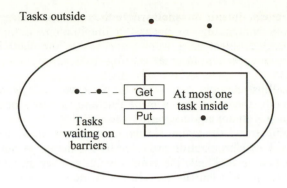

Figure 18.2   The eggshell model.

Thus barriers are only re-evaluated at the end of an entry or procedure body and not at the end of a protected function call because a function call cannot change the state of the protected object and so is not expected to change the values of barriers. These rules ensure that a protected object can be implemented efficiently.

It may happen that two or more entries with queued tasks have true barriers as a result of re-evaluation. In such a case the core language does not specify which queue is serviced. Moreover, within a queue the core language by default specifies that the calls are serviced in order of arrival. The Real-Time Systems annex enables other policies to be specified; see Section 22.2.

Note that a barrier *could* refer to a global variable; such a variable might get changed other than through a call of a protected procedure or entry – it could be changed by another task or even by a call of a protected function; such changes will thus not be acted upon promptly. The programmer needs to be aware of this and should not use global variables in barriers without due consideration.

It must be understood that the barrier protection mechanism is superimposed upon the natural mutual exclusion of the protected construct thus giving two distinct levels of protection. At the end of a protected call, already queued entries (whose barriers have now become true) take precedence over other calls contending for the protected object. On the other hand, a new entry call cannot even evaluate its barrier if the protected object is busy with another call until that call (and any processible queued calls) have finished.

This has the following important consequence: if the state of a protected resource changes and there is a task waiting for the new state, then this task will gain access to the resource and be guaranteed that the state of the resource when it gets it is the same as when the decision to release the task was made. Unsatisfactory polling and race conditions are completely avoided.

The two level model has been termed the eggshell model. We can envisage the protected object with its entry queues as surrounded by a shell as illustrated in Figure 18.2. The shell can only be penetrated by a new task trying to call a subprogram or entry when the protected object is quiescent. Tasks can thus be waiting at two levels, outside the shell where they are just milling around in an unstructured way contending for access to the implementation lock which guards the protected object as a whole, and inside the shell in an orderly manner on entry queues. The internal waiting tasks always take priority over the external tasks.

Figure 18.2 illustrates the state when the first two calls were of Get (and thus were queued), the third call was of Put and is being obeyed and two subsequent calls of Put are contending for the lock.

Protected objects are somewhat similar to monitors; they are both passive constructions with synchronization provided by the language run-time system. However, protected objects have the great advantage over monitors in that the protocols are described by barrier conditions (which are fairly easy to prove correct) rather than the low level and unstructured signals internal to monitors as found in Modula.

Protected types enable very efficient implementations of various semaphore and similar paradigms. For example a general semaphore might be implemented as follows

```
protected type Semaphore(Start_Count: Integer := 1) is
  entry Secure;
  procedure Release;
private
  Count: Integer := Start_Count;
end Semaphore;

protected body Semaphore is

  entry Secure when Count > 0 is
  begin
    Count := Count - 1;
  end Secure;

  procedure Release is
  begin
    Count := Count + 1;
  end Release;

end Semaphore;
```

The entry Secure and the procedure Release correspond to Dijkstra's classic P and V operations (from the Dutch *Passeren* and *Vrijmaken*). This example also illustrates that a protected type can have a discriminant which is here used to provide the initial value of the semaphore or in other words the number of items of the resource being guarded by the semaphore. The discriminant has a default value of one which corresponds to the usual binary semaphore. So we can write

```
S: Semaphore;
...
S.Secure;
...      -- protected statements
S.Release;
```

Observe that we have used the default value for the discriminant. However, this does not mean that S is mutable in the sense that we can change its discriminant as we did with the Mutant in Section 16.3. Protected objects are inherently limited and cannot be changed in any way.

The number of tasks on an entry queue is given by the attribute Count. This is often useful as part of a barrier condition; we will see some examples later.

We conclude by observing that the general principle of a protected operation is that it should be of a short duration; this is of course left up to the programmer. Moreover certain so-called potentially blocking operations are considered bounded errors if invoked during a protected action; these include: attempting a rendezvous, an entry call, a delay, an abort (see Section 18.8), and creating a task. Note that although we cannot call an entry from within a protected operation, we can call a protected subprogram of the same or another protected object; however if we call a subprogram of the same protected object then we must do it directly (and not for example by calling some external subprogram that in turn calls back in). Finally we can call an entry using the requeue statement as described in Section 18.9.

EXERCISE 18.4

1   Modify the protected object Variable so that a call of Write will be obeyed first.

2   Encapsulate the protected type Buffering inside a generic package with the type Item as a parameter and make the size of the buffer a discriminant of the type.

3   Declare a protected object with similar semantics to the task Buffer of Section 18.2.

4   Reconsider Exercise 18.2(**1**) using a protected object.

18.5   Simple select statements

A protected object in effect passively provides a number of possible services. Sometimes, the passive nature of a protected object is somewhat restrictive and we can then use a task to dynamically provide a number of alternative services. This can be done by the select statement which allows a task to select from one of several possible rendezvous. In order to illustrate the ideas we will now show alternative solutions to the problems of the previous section using a task to manage the protected data. Consider

```
task Protected_Variable is
   entry Read(X: out Item);
   entry Write(X: in Item);
end;
```

```
task body Protected_Variable is
   V: Item := initial value;
begin
   loop
      select
         accept Read(X: out Item) do
            X := V;
         end;
      or
         accept Write(X: in Item) do
            V := X;
         end;
      end select;
   end loop;
end Protected_Variable;
```

The task body consists of an endless loop containing a single select statement. A select statement starts with the reserved word **select** and finishes with **end select**; it contains two or more alternatives separated by **or**. In this example each alternative consists of an accept statement – one for Read and one for Write.

When we encounter the select statement various possibilities have to be considered according to whether calls of Read or Write or both or neither have been made.

- If neither Read nor Write has been called then the task is suspended until one or the other is called and then the corresponding accept statement is obeyed.
- If calls of Read are queued but none of Write are queued then a call of Read is accepted and vice versa with Read and Write reversed.
- If calls of both Read and Write are queued then an arbitrary choice is made.

Thus each execution of the select statement results in one of its branches being obeyed and one call of Read or Write being dealt with. We can think of the task as corresponding to a person serving two queues of customers waiting for two different services. If only one queue has customers then the server deals with it; if there are no customers then the server waits for the first irrespective of the service required; if both queues exist, the server rather capriciously serves either and makes an arbitrary choice each time.

As with protected entry queues, the core language specifies that task entry queues are serviced in order of arrival by default but remains silent about which queue is serviced when more than one is possible. Again the Real-Time Systems annex allows other policies to be specified; see Section 22.2.

So each time round the loop the task Protected_Variable accepts a call of Read or Write according to the demands upon it. It thus prevents multiple access to the variable V since it can only deal with one call at a time but does not impose any order upon the calls. Compare this with the task Buffer in Section 18.2 where an order was imposed upon the calls of Put and Get.

A more complex form of select statement is illustrated by the tasking equivalent of the classic problem of the bounded buffer implemented by the protected type Buffering of the previous section. Consider

```
task type Buffering is
   entry Put(X: in Item);
   entry Get(X: out Item);
end;

task body Buffering is
   A: Item_Array;
   I, J: Index := 0;
   Count: Integer range 0 .. N := 0;
begin
   loop
      select
         when Count < N =>
         accept Put(X: in Item) do
            A(I) := X;
         end;
         I := I + 1;  Count := Count + 1;
      or
         when Count > 0 =>
         accept Get(X: out Item) do
            X := A(J);
         end;
         J := J + 1;  Count := Count - 1;
      end select;
   end loop;
end Buffering;
```

The various data structures are as before. Control is exercised by a more general form of select statement which includes the use of guarding conditions which correspond to the barriers of the protected object.

Each branch of the select statement commences with

```
when condition =>
```

and is then followed by an accept statement and then some further statements. Each time the select statement is encountered all the guarding conditions are evaluated. The behaviour is then as for a select statement without guards but containing only those branches for which the conditions were true. So a branch will be taken and the corresponding rendezvous performed. After the accept statement a branch may contain further statements. These are executed by the server task as part of the select statement but outside the rendezvous.

So the guarding conditions are conditions which have to be true before a service can be offered. The accept statement represents the rendezvous with the customer and the giving of the service. The statements after the accept statement represent bookkeeping actions performed as a consequence of giving the service and which can be done after the customer has left but, of course, need to be done before the next customer is served.

In our example the guarding conditions for being able to accept the calls of Put and Get are exactly the same as the barrier conditions in the case of the corresponding protected object.

A few points need emphasis. The guards are re-evaluated at the beginning of each execution of the select statement (but their order of evaluation is not defined). An absent guard is taken as true. If all guards turn out to be false then the exception Program_Error is raised. It should be realized that a guard need not still be true when the corresponding rendezvous is performed because it might use global variables and therefore be changed by another task. In the example here, of course, nothing can go wrong. One guard is always true, so Program_Error can never be raised and they both only involve the local variable Count and so cannot be changed between their evaluation and the rendezvous.

The simple example of the protected object Variable of Section 18.4 solved the classic reader writer problem of allowing multiple readers and a single writer. However, as observed in the answer to Exercise 18.4(1), the multiple reading optimization is destroyed if barrier conditions are involved.

For our final example in this section, we show an alternative approach to the reader writer problem using a control task encapsulated within a package. Consider

```
package Reader_Writer is
  procedure Read(X: out Item);
  procedure Write(X: in Item);
end;

package body Reader_Writer is
  V: Item;

  task Control is
    entry Start;
    entry Stop;
    entry Write(X: in Item);
  end;

  task body Control is
    Readers: Integer := 0;
  begin
    accept Write(X: in Item) do
      V := X;
    end;
    loop
      select
        accept Start;
        Readers := Readers + 1;
      or
        accept Stop;
        Readers := Readers - 1;
```

```
        or
          when Readers = 0 =>
          accept Write(X: in Item) do
            V := X;
          end;
        end select;
      end loop;
    end Control;

    procedure Read(X: out Item) is
    begin
      Control.Start;
      X := V;
      Control.Stop;
    end Read;

    procedure Write(X: in Item) is
    begin
      Control.Write(X);
    end Write;

  end Reader_Writer;
```

The task Control has three entries: Write to do the writing and Start and Stop associated with reading. A call of Start indicates a wish to start reading and a call of Stop indicates that reading has finished. The task is wrapped up in a package because we wish to provide multiple reading access. This can be done by providing a procedure Read which can then be called reentrantly; it also enforces the protocol of calling Start and then Stop.

So the whole thing is a package containing the variable V, the task Control and the access procedures Read and Write. As stated, Read enforces the desired calls of Start and Stop around the statement X := V; the procedure Write merely calls the entry Write.

The task Control declares a variable Readers which indicates how many readers are present. It begins with an accept statement for Write to ensure that the variable is initialized and then enters a loop containing a select statement. This has three branches, one for each entry. On a call of Start or Stop the count of number of readers is incremented or decremented. A call of Write can only be accepted if the condition Readers = 0 is true. Hence writing when readers are present is forbidden. Of course, since the task Control actually does the writing, multiple writing is prevented and, moreover, it cannot at the same time accept calls of Start and so reading is not possible when writing is in progress. However, multiple reading is allowed as we have seen.

Although the above solution does fulfil the general conditions it is not really satisfactory. A steady stream of readers will completely block out a writer. Since writing is probably rather important, this is not acceptable. An obvious improvement would be to disallow further reading if one or more writers are waiting. We can do this by using the attribute Write'Count in a guard so that the select statement now becomes

```
select
   when Write'Count = 0 =>
   accept Start;
   Readers := Readers + 1;
or
   accept Stop;
   Readers := Readers - 1;
or
   when Readers = 0 =>
   accept Write(X: in Item) do
      V := X;
   end;
end select;
```

The attribute Write'Count is the number of tasks currently on the queue for the entry Write. The use of the count attribute in guards needs care. It gives the value when the guard is evaluated and can well change before a rendezvous is accepted. It could increase because another task joins the queue – that would not matter in this example. But, as we shall see in a moment, it could also decrease unexpectedly and this would indeed give problems.

18.6   Timed and conditional calls

There are also various other forms of select statement. It is possible for one or more of the branches to start with a delay statement rather than an accept statement. Consider

```
select
   accept Read( ... ) do
      ...
   end;
or
   accept Write( ... ) do
      ...
   end;
or
   delay 10*Minutes;
   -- time out statements
end select;
```

If neither a call of Read nor Write is received within ten minutes, then the third branch is taken and the statements following the delay are executed. The task might decide that since its services are no longer apparently required it can do something else or maybe it can be interpreted as an emergency. In a process

control system we might be awaiting an acknowledgement from the operator
that some action has been taken and after a suitable interval take our own
emergency action

```
Operator.Call("Put out fire");

select
   accept Acknowledge;
or
   delay 1*Minutes;
   Fire_Brigade.Call;
end select;
```

A delay alternative can be guarded and indeed there could be several in a
select statement although clearly only the shortest one with a true guard can be
taken. It should be realized that if one of the accept statements is obeyed then
any delay is cancelled – we can think of a delay alternative as waiting for a
rendezvous with the clock. A delay is, of course, set from the start of the select
statement and reset each time the select statement is encountered. Finally, note
that it is the start of the rendezvous that matters rather than its completion as
far as the time out is concerned.

Another form of select statement is one with an else part. Consider

```
select
   accept Read( ... ) do
   ...
   end;
or
   accept Write( ... ) do
   ...
   end;
else
   -- alternative statements
end select;
```

In this case the final branch is preceded by **else** rather than **or** and consists of
just a sequence of statements. The else branch is taken at once if none of the
other branches can be immediately accepted. A select statement with an else
part is rather like one with a branch starting **delay** 0.0; it times out at once if
there are no customers to be dealt with. A select statement cannot have both an
else part and delay alternatives.

There is a subtle distinction between an accept statement starting a branch
of a select and an accept statement anywhere else. In the first case the accept
statement is bound up with the workings of the select statement and is to some
extent conditional. In the second case, once encountered, it will be obeyed
come what may. The same distinction applies to a delay statement starting a
branch of a select statement and one elsewhere. Thus if we change the **or** to
else in our emergency action to give

```
select
   accept Acknowledge;
else
   delay 1*Minutes;
   Fire_Brigade.Call;
end select;
```

then the status of the delay is quite different. It just happens to be one of a sequence of statements and will be obeyed in the usual way. So if we cannot accept a call of Acknowledge at once, we immediately take the else part. The fact that the first statement is a delay is fortuitous – we immediately delay for one minute and then call the fire brigade. There is no time out. We see therefore that the simple change from **or** to **else** causes a dramatic difference in meaning which may not be immediately obvious; so take care!

If a select statement has an else part then Program_Error can never be raised. The else part cannot be guarded and so will always be taken if all branches have guards and they all turn out to be false.

There are two other forms of select statement which are rather different; they concern a single entry call rather than one or more accept statements. The timed entry call allows a sequence of statements to be taken as an alternative to an entry call if it is not accepted within the specified duration. Thus

```
select
   Operator.Call("Put out fire");
or
   delay 1*Minutes;
   Fire_Brigade.Call;
end select;
```

will call the fire brigade if the operator does not accept the call within one minute. The entry call can be to a task or to a protected object and it is the acceptance of the call that matters rather than its completion. Finally there is the conditional entry call. Thus

```
select
   Operator.Call("Put out fire");
else
   Fire_Brigade.Call;
end select;
```

will call the fire brigade if the operator cannot immediately accept the call.

Timed and conditional entry calls are quite different to the general select statement. They concern only a single unguarded call and so these select statements always have exactly two branches – one with the entry call and the other with the alternative sequence of statements. Timed and conditional calls apply only to entries. They do not apply to procedures or even to entries renamed as procedures.

Timed and conditional calls are useful if a task does not want to be unduly delayed when a server task or protected object is busy. They correspond to a customer in a shop giving up and leaving the queue after waiting for a time or, in the conditional case, a highly impatient customer leaving at once if not immediately served.

Timed calls on task entries need some care particularly if the Count attribute is used. A decision based on the value of that attribute may be invalidated because of a timed call unexpectedly removing a task from an entry queue. Note however, that the analogous problem cannot arise with protected objects; the removal of a task from the queue of a protected entry is itself a protected action and causes the re-evaluation of barriers.

The final form of select statement is the asynchronous select statement; this is discussed in Section 18.8.

18.7   Concurrent types and activation

We observed in Section 18.4 how a protected type declaration acted as a template from which a number of similar protected objects could be declared. In the same way, it is sometimes useful to have several similar but distinct tasks. Moreover, it is often not possible to predict the number of such tasks required. For example, we might wish to create distinct tasks to follow each aircraft within the zone of control of an air traffic control system. Clearly, such tasks need to be created and disposed of in a dynamic way not related to the static structure of the program. Protected types and task types (which we can collectively refer to as concurrent types) follow similar rules which we now look at in more detail. We will concentrate on task types because they have additional properties resulting from their active nature.

A template for similar tasks is provided by a task type declaration. This is identical to the simple task declarations we have seen so far except that the reserved word **type** follows **task** in the specification. Thus we may write

```
task type T is
   entry E( ... );
end T;

task body T is
   ...
end T;
```

The task body follows the same rules as before.

To create an actual task we use the normal form of object declaration. So we can write

```
X: T;
```

and this declares a task X of type T.

Task objects and protected objects can be used in structures in the usual way. Thus we can declare arrays of tasks and protected objects

```
AOT: array (1 .. 10) of T;
```

records containing tasks and protected objects

```
type Rec is
  record
    CT: T;
    ...
  end record;
R: Rec;
```

and so on.

The entries of such tasks and protected objects are called using the object name; thus we write

```
X.E( ... );
AOT(I).E( ... );
R.CT.E( ... );
```

A most important consideration is that concurrent objects are not variables but behave as constants. Thus a task object declaration creates a task which is permanently represented by the object. Hence assignment is not allowed for task and protected types and nor are the comparisons for equality and inequality. Task types and protected types are therefore forms of limited types and so could be used as the actual type corresponding to a formal generic parameter specified as limited private and as the actual type in a private part corresponding to a limited private type.

Subprogram parameters may be of concurrent types; they are always passed by reference and so the formal and actual parameters always refer to the same object. All modes have the same effect for task types. For a protected type, the mode **in** allows calls of protected functions only whereas modes **in out** and **out** also allow calls of protected entries and procedures.

In Section 18.1 we briefly introduced the idea of dependency. Each task is dependent on some unit and there is a general rule that a unit cannot be left until all tasks dependent upon it have terminated.

A task declared as a task object (or using the abbreviated singleton form) is dependent upon the enclosing block, subprogram or task body in which it is declared. Inner packages do not count in this rule – this is because a package is merely a passive scope wall and has no dynamic life. If a task is declared in a package (or nested packages) then the task is dependent upon the block, subprogram or task body in which the package or packages are themselves declared. For completeness, a task declared in a library package is said to depend on that package and we refer to it as a library task. After termination of the main subprogram, the main environment task (which calls the main subprogram) must wait for all library tasks to terminate. Only then does the program as a whole terminate.

We saw earlier that a task becomes active only when the declaring unit reaches the **begin** following the declaration. The execution of a task can be thought of as a two-stage process. The first stage, known as activation, consists of the elaboration of the declarations of the task body whereas the second stage

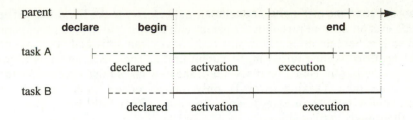

Figure 18.3   Task activation.

consists, of course, of the execution of its statements. During the activation stage the parent unit is not allowed to proceed. If several tasks are declared in a unit then their activations and the subsequent execution of their statements occur independently and in parallel. But it is only when the activation of all the tasks is complete that the parent unit can continue with the execution of the statements following the **begin** in parallel with the new tasks.

The activation process is depicted in Figure 18.3 which illustrates the behaviour of a block containing the declarations of two tasks A and B

```
declare
    ...
    A: T;
    B: T;
    ...
begin
    ...
end;
```

Time flows from left to right and a solid line indicates that a unit is actively doing something whereas a dashed line indicates that it exists but is suspended. Points of synchronization are indicated by vertical dots between the lines.

For the sake of illustration, we show task A finishing its activation after task B so that the parent resumes execution when task A enters its execution stage. We also show task A finishing its execution and therefore becoming completed and terminated before task B. The parent is shown reaching its **end** and therefore completing execution of the block after task A has terminated but before task B has terminated. The parent is therefore suspended until task B is terminated when it can then resume execution with the statements following the block.

One reason for treating task activation in this way concerns exceptions. The reader may recall that an exception raised during the elaboration of declarations is not handled at that level but immediately propagated. So an exception raised in the declarations in a new task could not be handled by that task at all. However, since it is clearly desirable that some means be provided for detecting such an exception, it is obvious that an exception has to be raised in the parent unit. In fact the predefined exception Tasking_Error is raised irrespective of the original exception. It would clearly make life rather difficult if this exception were raised in the parent unit after it had moved on in parallel and so it is held up until all the new tasks have been activated. The exception Tasking_Error is then raised in the parent unit as soon as it attempts to move on from the **begin**. Note that if several of the new tasks raise exceptions during activation then Tasking_Error is only raised once. Such tasks become completed (not terminated) and do not affect sibling tasks being simultaneously activated.

The other thing that can go wrong is that an exception can occur in the declarations of the parent unit itself. In this case any new tasks which have been declared (but of course will not have been activated because the parent unit has not yet reached its **begin**) will automatically become terminated and are never activated at all.

Task objects can be declared in a package and although not dependent upon the package are nevertheless set active at the **begin** of the package body. If the package body has no initialization statements and therefore no **begin**, then a null initialization statement is assumed; if a package has no body, then a body with just a null initialization statement is assumed. So the task Control in the package Reader_Writer of Section 18.5 is set active at the end of the declaration of the package body.

Tasks and protected objects can also be created through access types. We can write

   type Ref_T **is access** T;

and then we can create a task using an allocator in the usual way

   RX: Ref_T := **new** T;

The type Ref_T is a normal access type and so assignment and equality comparisons of objects of the type are allowed. The entry E of the task accessed by RX can be called as expected by

   RX.E(...);

Tasks created through access types obey slightly different rules for activation and dependency. They commence activation immediately upon evaluation of the allocator whether it occurs in a sequence of statements or in an initial value – we do not wait until the ensuing **begin**. Moreover, activation is completed before the allocator returns with the access value. Furthermore, such tasks are not dependent upon the unit where they are created but are dependent upon the block, subprogram body or task body containing the declaration of the access type itself.

If tasks are components of a composite object and such an object is created using an allocator, then all the tasks in the object are created and activated before the allocator returns. There are rules that parallel those for declaring several tasks described above. Elaboration and intialization of the components occurs before activation of the tasks and the allocator only returns when all

activations are completed. Similarly Tasking_Error can only be raised once and
so on.

The reader will probably feel that the activation mechanism is somewhat
elaborate. However, in practice, the details will rarely need to be considered.
They are mentioned in order to show that the mechanism is well defined rather
than because of their everyday importance.

Note that entries in a task can be called as soon as it is declared and even
before activation commences – the call will just be queued. However,
situations in which this is sensibly possible are rare.

An interesting use of task types is for the creation of agents. An agent is a
task that does something on behalf of another task. As an example suppose a
task Server provides some service that is asked for by calling an entry Request.
Suppose also that it may take Server some time to provide the service so that
it is reasonable for the calling task User to go away and do something else
while waiting for the answer to be prepared. There are various ways in which
the User could expect to collect the answer. It could call another entry Enquire;
the Server task would need some means of recognizing the caller – it could do
this by issuing a key on the call of Request and insisting that it be presented
again when calling Enquire (or, if the Real-Time Systems annex is supported,
the mechanism of task identification could be used; see Section 22.2). This
protocol corresponds to taking something to be repaired, being given a ticket
and then having to exchange it when the repaired item is collected later. An
alternative approach which avoids the issue of keys, is to create an agent. This
corresponds to leaving your address and having the repaired item mailed back
to you. We will now illustrate this approach.

First of all we declare a task type as follows

```
task type Mailbox is
   entry Deposit(X: in Item);
   entry Collect(X: out Item);
end;

task body Mailbox is
   Local: Item;
begin
   accept Deposit(X: in Item) do
     Local := X;
   end;
   accept Collect(X: out Item) do
     X := Local;
   end;
end Mailbox;
```

A task of this type acts as a simple mailbox. An item can be deposited and
collected later. What we are going to do is to give the identity of the mailbox
to the server so that the server can deposit the item in the mailbox from which
the user can collect it later. We need an access type

```
type Address is access Mailbox;
```

The tasks Server and User now take the following form

```
task Server is
  entry Request(A: Address; X: Item);
end;

task body Server is
  Reply: Address;
  Job: Item;
begin
  loop
    accept Request(A: Address; X: Item) do
      Reply := A;
      Job := X;
    end;

    -- work on job

    Reply.Deposit(Job);
  end loop;
end Server;

task User;

task body User is
  My_Box: Address := new Mailbox;
  My_Item: Item;
begin
  Server.Request(My_Box, My_Item);

  -- do something while waiting

  My_Box.Collect(My_Item);
end User;
```

In practice the user might poll the mailbox from time to time to see if the item is ready. This is easily done using a conditional entry call.

```
select
  My_Box.Collect(My_Item);
  -- item collected successfully
else
  -- not ready yet
end select;
```

It is important to realize that the agent serves several purposes. It enables the deposit and collect to be decoupled so that the server can get on with the next job. Moreover, and perhaps of more importance, it means that the server need know nothing about the user; to call the user directly would mean that the user would have to be of a particular task type and this would be most unreasonable. The agent enables us to factor off the only property required of the user, namely the existence of the entry Deposit.

If the decoupling property were not required then the body of the agent could be written as

```
task body Mailbox is
begin
   accept Deposit(X: in Item) do
      accept Collect(X: out Item) do
         Collect.X := Deposit.X;
      end;
   end;
end Mailbox;
```

The agent does not need a local variable in this case since the agent now only exists in order to aid closely coupled communication. Note also the use of the dotted notation in the nested accept statements in order to distinguish the two uses of X; we could equally have written X := Deposit.X; but the use of Collect is more symmetric.

EXERCISE 18.7

1   Rewrite the agent task as a protected object. What are the advantages and disadvantages of doing this?

18.8   Termination, exceptions and ATC

A task can become completed and then terminate in various ways as well as running into its final end. It will have been noticed that in some of our earlier examples, the body of a task was an endless loop and clearly never terminated. (This is typical of server tasks although they are less common in Ada 95 since typical servers are implemented as protected objects.) This means that it would never be possible to leave the unit on which the task was dependent. Suppose, for example, that we chose to use a task implementation of the protected variable type. If we then declared

```
PV: Protected_Variable
```

we could not leave the unit on which PV depends without terminating the task in some way. We could, of course, add a special entry Stop and call it just before leaving the unit, but this might be inconvenient. Instead it is possible to make a task automatically terminate itself when it is of no further use by a special form of select alternative. We thus rewrite the main loop as

```
loop
  select
    accept Read(X: out Item) do
      X := V;
    end;
  or
    accept Write(X: in Item) do
      V := X;
    end;
  or
    terminate;
  end select;
end loop;
```

The terminate alternative is taken if the unit on which the task depends has reached its end and so is completed and all sibling tasks and dependent tasks are terminated or are similarly able to select a terminate alternative. In such circumstances all the tasks are of no use since they are the only tasks that could call their entries and they are all dormant. Thus the whole set automatically terminates. In practice, this merely means that all service tasks should have a terminate alternative and will then terminate themselves without more ado.

A terminate alternative may be guarded. However, it cannot appear in a select statement with a delay alternative or an else part.

Selection of a terminate alternative is classified as normal termination – the task is under control of the situation and terminates voluntarily.

However, as mentioned above, the terminate alternative will rarely be needed in Ada 95 since most applications of servers will use protected objects and they cause no dependency problems because they are passive. In other cases it is possible to use finalization to cause some Stop entry to be called. This has other advantages, since it can cause any cleanup actions to be performed whereas terminate cannot be followed by any other statements.

At the other extreme, the abort statement unconditionally terminates one or more tasks. It consists of the reserved word **abort** followed by a list of task names as for example

    abort X, AOT(3), RX.**all**;

If a task is aborted then all tasks dependent upon it or a subprogram or block currently called by it are also aborted. If the task is suspended for some reason, then it immediately becomes completed; any delay is cancelled; if the task is on an entry queue, it is removed; other possibilities are that it has not yet even commenced activation or it is at an accept or select statement awaiting a partner. If the task is not suspended, then completion will occur as soon as convenient and certainly no new communication with the task will be possible.

Complications arise if the task is engaged in a rendezvous when it is aborted, since we then also have to consider the effect on the partner. This depends on the situation. If the called task is aborted, then the calling task receives the exception Tasking_Error. On the other hand, if the calling task is aborted, then the called task is not affected; the rendezvous carries on to

completion with the caller in a somewhat abnormal state and it is only when
the rendezvous is complete that the caller becomes properly completed. The
rationale is simple; if a task asks for a service and the server dies so that it
cannot be provided then the customer should be told. On the other hand, if the
customer dies, too bad – but we must avoid upsetting the server who might
have the database in a critical state.

The rendezvous is thus an example of an abort deferred region for the
caller. Similarly the operations of a protected object are abort deferred regions
since it would be far too disruptive to abort a task while inside such a region.
Thus we are assured that a task will not be aborted while 'inside' a protected
object. Other abort deferred regions concern controlled types; the Initialize and
Finalize operations and assignment of a controlled type are all abort deferred.

Note that the rules for abort are formulated in terms of completing the tasks
rather than terminating them. This is because a parent task cannot be
terminated until its dependent tasks are terminated and if one of those is the
caller in a rendezvous with a third party then its termination will be delayed.
Thus completion of the tasks is the best that can be individually enforced and
their termination will then automatically occur in the usual way.

The abort statement is very disruptive and should only be used in extreme
situations. It might be appropriate for a command task to abort a complete
subsystem in response to an operator command.

Another possible use for the abort statement might be in an exception
handler. Remember that we cannot leave a unit until all dependent tasks are
terminated. Hence, if an exception is raised in a unit, then we cannot tidy up
that unit and propagate the exception on a layered basis while dependent tasks
are still alive and so one of the actions of tidying up might be to abort all such
tasks. Thus the procedure Clean_Up of Section 14.2 might do just this.

However, it is probably always best to attempt a controlled shutdown and
only resort to the abort statement as a desperate measure. Statements in the
command task might be as follows

```
select
   T.Closedown;
or
   delay 60*Seconds;
   abort T;
end select;
```

If the slave task does not accept the Closedown call within a minute, then it is
ruthlessly aborted. We are assuming, of course, that the slave task polls the
Closedown entry at least every minute using a conditional accept statement
such as

```
select
   accept Closedown;
   -- tidy up and die
else
   -- carry on normally
end select;
```

If we cannot trust the slave to close down properly even after accepting the entry call, then the command task can always issue an abort after a due interval just in case. Aborting a task which has already terminated has no effect. So the command task might read

```
select
    T.Closedown;
    delay 10*Seconds;
or
    delay 60*Seconds;
end select;
abort T;
```

Of course, even this is not foolproof since the malevolent slave might continue for ever in the rendezvous itself

```
accept Closedown do
  loop
      Put("Can't catch me");
  end loop;
end;
```

Some minimal degree of cooperation is obviously needed!

The status of task T can be ascertained by the use of two attributes. Thus T'Terminated is true if a task is terminated. The other attribute, T'Callable, is true unless the task is completed or terminated or in the abnormal state pending final abortion. The use of these attributes needs care. For example, between discovering that a task has not terminated and taking some action based on that information, the task could become terminated. However, the reverse is not possible since a task cannot be restarted and so it is quite safe to take an action based on the information that a task has terminated.

In Section 18.1 we mentioned that if a task has no dependents then completion and termination effectively occur together. However, completion and termination might not be exactly simultaneous and so it is possible for both T'Terminated and T'Callable to be false even though T has no dependents.

We continue by discussing a few remaining points on exceptions. The exception Tasking_Error is concerned with general communication failure. As we have seen, it is raised if a failure occurs during task activation and it is also raised in the caller of a rendezvous if the server is aborted. In addition, no matter how a task is completed, all tasks still queued on its entries receive Tasking_Error. Similarly calling an entry of a task that is already completed also raises Tasking_Error in the caller.

If an exception is raised during a rendezvous (as a consequence of an action by the called task) and is not handled by the accept statement, then it is propagated into both tasks as the same exception on the grounds that both need to know. Of course, if the accept statement handles the exception internally, then that is the end of the matter anyway.

It might be convenient for the called task, the server, to inform the calling task, the user, of some event by the explicit raising of an exception. In such a case it is likely that the server task will not wish to take any action and so a null handler will be required. So in outline we might write

```
begin
  select
    accept E( ... ) do
      ...
      raise Error;          -- tell user
      ...
    end E;
    ...
  end select;
exception
  when Error =>
    null;                   -- server forgets
end;
```

If an exception is not handled by a task at all, then, like the main subprogram, the task is abandoned and the exception is lost; it is not propagated to the parent unit because it would be too disruptive to do so. However, we might expect the run-time environment to provide a diagnostic message. If it does not, it might be good practice for all significant tasks to have a general handler at the outermost level in order to guard against the loss of exceptions and consequential silent death of the task.

Finally, in the case of a protected object, an exception raised during a protected operation and not handled locally is propagated to the calling task.

We conclude this section by considering the final form of select statement which is used for asynchronous transfer of control (or ATC for short). ATC enables an activity to be abandoned if some condition arises (such as running out of time) so that an alternative sequence of statements can be executed instead. This gives the capability of performing mode changes.

The general effect can of course be programmed by the introduction of an agent task and the use of the abort statement but this is a heavy solution not at all appropriate for most applications needing a mode change.

Asynchronous transfer of control is achieved by a form of select statement which comprises two parts: an abortable part and a triggering alternative. As a simple example consider

```
select
  delay 5.0;                          -- triggering alternative
  Put_Line("Calculation did not complete");
then abort
  Invert_Giant_Matrix(M);            -- abortable part
end select;
```

The general idea is that if the statements between **then abort** and **end select** do not complete before the expiry of the delay then they are abandoned and the statements following the delay executed instead. Thus if we cannot invert our giant matrix in five seconds we give up and print a message.

The statement that triggers the abandonment can alternatively be an entry call instead of a delay statement. If the call returns before the computation is complete then again the computation is abandoned and any statements following the entry call are executed instead. On the other hand if the computation completes before the entry call, then the entry call is itself abandoned. The entry call can, of course, be to a task or to a protected object.

One possible scenario is where an iterative calculation is allowed to proceed until the answer is required. Two tasks are involved, a slave task to do the calculation and a controlling task which uses the answer and morever decides when it wants the answer. The best estimate is to be used irrespective of whether the computation has completely converged.

The best estimate to date can be kept in a protected object such as

```
protected Result is
   procedure Set_Estimate(X: in Data);
   function Get_Estimate return Data;
private
   The_Estimate: Data;
end;
```

The slave task calls the protected procedure Set_Estimate each time it produces a better estimate. The current best estimate can then be retrieved at any time by the controlling task by calling the protected function Get_Estimate.

The slave task performs its iterative calculation in the abortable part of an asynchronous select statement. The triggering event of this asynchronous select statement is used to indicate that the slave task is to stop; it can be a call on an entry Wait of yet another protected object which also has a protected procedure Signal. Thus

```
protected Trigger is
   entry Wait;
   procedure Signal;
private
   Flag: Boolean := False;
end;
```

The use of such protected objects for signalling is discussed in more detail in the next section.

The controlling task might then execute

```
Trigger.Signal;
Final_Answer := Result.Get_Estimate;
```

where the call Trigger.Signal causes the entry Wait to be accepted and this in turn stops the slave task.

An important advantage of this approach is that the slave task is decoupled from the controlling task and is able to perform its computation without having to poll some shared variable to see whether it should stop.

EXERCISE 18.8

1   Rewrite the task Buffering of Section 18.4 so that it has the following specification

```
task Buffering is
  entry Put(X: in Item);
  entry Finish;
  entry Get(X: out Item);
end;
```

The writing task calls Put as before and finally calls Finish. The reading task calls Get as before; a call of Get when there are no further items raises the global exception Done.

2   What happens in the following bizarre situation

```
task body Server is
begin
  accept E do
    abort Caller;
    raise Havoc;
  end E;
end Server;
```

```
task body Caller is
begin
  Server.E;
exception
  when Havoc =>
    Put("What a mess");
end Caller;
```

3   Sketch the asynchronous select statement containing the iterative calculation performed by the slave task.

18.9   Signalling and scheduling

In this section we consider a few standard paradigms concerning signalling of events between tasks and the scheduling of tasks.

The simplest form of signal is the persistent signal where the signalling of the event allows one waiting task to proceed. This can done by the following

```
protected Event is
  entry Wait;
  procedure Signal;
private
  Occurred: Boolean := False;
end Event;
```

```
protected body Event is

   entry Wait when Occurred is
   begin
      Occurred := False;
   end Wait;

   procedure Signal is
   begin
      Occurred := True;
   end Signal;

end Event;
```

Events of this kind are called persistent since, even if no task is waiting when the event occurs, it is remembered until some task issues a wait. Such events are very similar to binary semaphores with the wait operation corresponding to P and the signal to V. See Section 18.4.

Another form of signal is the broadcast signal; this allows all the currently waiting tasks to proceed and is then forgotten. So if there are no waiting tasks then the signal has no effect. This can be programmed in many ways and can be used to illustrate the requeue statement.

It sometimes happens that a service needs to be provided in two parts and that the calling task has to be suspended after the first part until conditions are such that the second part can be done.

In the example of the broadcast signal, the difficulty is to prevent tasks that call the wait operation after the event has occurred, but before the signal can be reset, from getting through. In other words, we must reset the signal in preference to letting new tasks through. The requeue statement allows us to program such preference control. An implementation is

```
protected Event is
   entry Wait;
   entry Signal;
private
   entry Reset;
   Occurred: Boolean := False;
end Event;

protected body Event is

   entry Wait when Occurred is
   begin
      null;                          -- note null body
   end Wait;

   entry Signal when True is         -- barrier is always true
   begin
      if Wait'Count > 0 then
         Occurred := True;
         requeue Reset;
      end if;
   end Signal;
```

```
    entry Reset when Wait'Count = 0 is
    begin
       Occurred := False;
    end Reset;

  end Event;
```

In contrast to the persistent signal, the Boolean variable Occurred is normally false and is only true while tasks are being released. The entry Wait has a null body and just exists so that calling tasks can suspend themselves on its queue while waiting for Occurred to become true.

The entry Signal has a permanently true barrier and so is always processed. If there are no tasks on the queue of Wait (that is no tasks are waiting), then there is nothing to do and so it exits. On the other hand, if there are tasks waiting then it must release them in such a way that no further tasks can get on the queue and, moreover, it must then regain control so that it can reset the flag. It does this by requeuing itself on the entry Reset after setting Occurred to true to indicate that the event has occurred.

The semantics of requeue are such that this completes the action of Signal. However, remember that at the end of the body of a protected entry or procedure the barriers are re-evaluated for those entries which have tasks queued. In this case there are indeed tasks on the queue for Wait and there is also a task on the queue for Reset (the task that called Signal in the first place); the barrier for Wait is now true but of course the barrier for Reset is false since there are still tasks on the queue for Wait. A waiting task is thus allowed to execute the body of Wait (being null this does nothing) and the task thus proceeds and then the barrier evaluation repeats. The process continues until all the waiting tasks have gone when finally the barrier of Reset also becomes true. The original task which called signal now executes the body of Reset thus resetting Occurred to false so that the system is once more in its initial state. The protected object as a whole is now finally left since there are no waiting tasks on any of the barriers.

Note carefully that if any tasks had tried to call Wait or Signal while the whole process was in progress then they would not have been able to do so because the protected object as a whole was busy. This illustrates the two levels of protection and is the underlying reason why a race condition does not arise.

Another consequence of the two levels is that it still all works properly even in the face of such difficulties as timed and conditional calls and aborts. The reader may recall, for example, that by contrast, the Count attribute for entries in tasks cannot be relied upon in the face of timed entry calls.

In the case of a protected object a queued entry call can still disappear from the queue as a consequence of abort or a timed call but such removal is treated as a protected operation of the protected object and can only be performed when the object is quiescent. (Remember that protected operations are abort deferred.) After such removal any barrier using the Count attribute for that queue will be immediately re-evaluated so that consistency is maintained. Removing a task from a queue might thus allow a task queued on a different queue to proceed.

A minor point to note is that the entry **Reset** is declared in the private part of the protected type and thus cannot be called from outside.

The above example has been used for illustration only. The astute reader will have observed that the condition is not strictly needed inside Signal; without it the caller will simply always requeue and then immediately be processed if there are no waiting tasks. But the condition clarifies the description. Indeed, we can actually program this example without using requeue at all; this is left as an exercise.

We now illustrate a quite general technique which effectively allows the requests in a single entry queue to be handled in an arbitrary order. Consider the problem of allocating a group of resources from a set. We do not wish to hold up a later request that can be satisfied just because an earlier request must wait for the release of some of the resources it wants. One essence of the problem is that requests typically have to be handled in stages; the first stage is to say what is wanted and indeed it might be possible to satisfy the request at that stage but typically the task will then have to wait until conditions are appropriate. A practical difficulty is that guards and barriers cannot use the parameters of the call. This inevitably leads to several entry calls and introduces the requeue statement.

We suppose that the resources are represented by a discrete type **Resource**. We can conveniently use the generic package Set_Of from Section 17.2

```
package Resource_Sets is new Set_Of(Resource);
use Resource_Sets;
```

and then

```
protected Resource_Allocator is
   entry Request(S: Set);
   procedure Release(S: Set);
private
   entry Again(S: Set);
   function Allocated(S: Set) return Boolean;
   Free: Set := Full;
   Waiters: Integer := 0;
end Resource_Allocator;

protected body Resource_Allocator is

   function Allocated(S: Set) return Boolean is
   begin
      if S <= Free then
         Free := Free - S;    -- allocation successful
         return True;
      else
         return False;        -- no good, try later
      end if;
   end Allocated;
```

```
        procedure Release(S: Set) is
        begin
           Free := Free + S;
           Waiters := Again'Count;
        end Release;

        entry Request(S: Set) when True is
        begin
           if not Allocated(S) then
              requeue Again;
           end if;
        end Request;

        entry Again(S: Set) when Waiters > 0 is
        begin
           Waiters := Waiters - 1;
           if not Allocated(S) then
              requeue Again;
           end if;
        end Again;

     end Resource_Allocator;
```

This protected object has an entry Request and a procedure Release which have as parameters the set S of resources to be acquired or returned; the type Set is from the instantiation of Set_Of.

There is also a private entry Again which is very similar to the entry Request and both call a common function Allocated. This checks the set S against the set Free of available resources using the inclusion operator "<=" from (the instantiation of) Set_Of. If all the resources are available, Free is altered correspondingly using the symmetric difference operator "-" from Set_Of and True is returned; if they are not all available, then False is returned. The entry Release returns the resources passed as the parameter S by updating Free using the union operator "+" from Set_Of. Note that the declaration of Free gives it the initial value Full which is also from Set_Of.

A first attempt at acquiring the resources is made by calling the entry Request. If it fails then it is requeued on the entry Again. We have to make Request an entry because only an entry can do a requeue; the guard of Request is permanently true since a new call is always allowed an immediate attempt. A call of Release allows all those tasks waiting on Again to have another try. The variable Waiters is set to the number of tasks waiting on the entry Again and is decremented by Again thus allowing each waiting task just one further attempt. The entry Again is similar to Request and requeues on itself if the request still fails.

Readers of the earlier book *Programming in Ada* describing Ada 83 might contrast the solution shown there (which uses a controlling task) with that shown here. The solution using a protected object works exactly; the Count attribute is always correct and no race conditions arise (a task is requeued at once and cannot get out of order and new tasks cannot even enter the system). It is also proof against aborting tasks (except that resources might get lost but that can be remedied by using a controlled type for the resources); timed and conditional calls cause no problems and so on. This is all because of the two level nature of the protected object which provides preference control (existing queued or requeued calls take preference over new ones) and thereby enables race conditions to be avoided.

Our examples of requeue have shown an entry in a protected object requeuing on another or the same entry of the same protected object. In fact requeue can be from any entry to any other entry including to and from and between entries of tasks.

A requeue can either pass on all the parameters of the original call (implicitly) or none. For implementation reasons no other possibilities are allowed. Thus the destination entry must either have a parameter profile with the same types as the original call in which case all the parameters are passed on or no parameters at all. In either case the requeue statement has no explicit parameters.

Abort raises issues with regard to requeue. Because a requeue is normally seen as continuing the same service as was asked for by the original call, a requeued call is normally treated specially and is not allowed to be aborted because this might mess up the internal structures of the protected object. If this special treatment is not required then we can requeue with abort thus

```
requeue Again with abort;
```

and in this example no problem will arise.

We conclude this section by introducing the concept of families of entries. There are occasions when we might want to compute in some way which of various entries to call. Of course we could write a case statement or use an access to procedure variable to refer to an entry. But it is simpler to use an entry family which is rather like a one-dimensional array of entries.

For example, requests with priorities can be handled by a family of entries. Suppose we have three levels of priority given by

```
type Priority is (Urgent, Normal, Low);
```

and that we have a task Controller providing access to some action on a type Data but with requests for the action on three queues according to their priority. We could do this with three distinct entries but it is neater to use a family of entries. Consider

```
task Controller is
    entry Request(Priority) (D: Data);
end;

task body Controller is
begin
    loop
        select
            accept Request(Urgent) (D: Data) do
                Action(D);
            end;
```

```
      or
        when Request(Urgent)'Count = 0 =>
        accept Request(Normal) (D: Data) do
          Action(D);
        end;
      or
        when Request(Urgent)'Count = 0 and
                    Request(Normal)'Count = 0 =>
        accept Request(Low) (D: Data) do
          Action(D);
        end;
      end select;
    end loop;
  end Controller;
```

Request is a family of entries, indexed by a discrete range which in this case is the type Priority.

A protected object can also have entry families but in this case there is just one body for the whole family which takes the form

```
    entry Request (for P in Priority) (D: Data) when Barrier_Condition(P) is
    begin
      Action(D);
    end Request;
```

where the barrier condition can depend upon the entry index. It might thus even be the function

```
    function Barrier_Condition(P: Priority) return Boolean is
      Result: Boolean;
    begin
      case P is
        when Urgent =>
          Result := True;
        when Normal =>
          Result := Request(Urgent)'Count = 0;
        when Low =>
          Result := Request(Urgent)'Count = 0 and
                        Request(Normal)'Count = 0;
      end case;
      return Result;
    end Barrier_Condition;
```

which would be declared within the protected object.

Clearly the approach shown here is only feasible if the number of priority values is small. In the case of the protected object, the case statement can easily be replaced by a loop but in the case of the task we would have to write out the various entry bodies which would be irksome.

As an alternative, we could try checking each queue in turn thus

```
task body Controller is
begin
  loop
    for P in Priority loop
      select
        accept Request(P) (D: Data) do
          Action(D);
        end;
        exit;
      else
        null;
      end select;
    end loop;
  end loop;
end Controller;
```

Unfortunately this is not satisfactory since it results in the task Controller continuously polling when all the queues are empty. We need a mechanism whereby the task can wait for the first of any requests. This can be done by a two-stage process; the calling task must first 'sign in' by calling a common entry and then requeue on the appropriate entry of the family. The details are left as an exercise for the reader.

EXERCISE 18.9

1   In the protected object Event for the broadcast signal would it be sensible for the requeue on Reset to be **with abort**?

2   Write the protected object Event without the use of requeue. Hint: the last task out switches off the light.

3   Rewrite the task Controller in a way which avoids continuous polling. The specification should be

```
task Controller is
  entry Sign_In(P: Priority; D: Data);
private
    ...
end;
```

where the private part contains the entry family.

4   Show how a protected object could be used as the interface to a task which performs some laborious operation and can be used to monitor the time of calls on the task. Use a requeue from the protected object to the task.

18.10   Examples of tasks

In this final section on tasking we briefly summarize the main differences between packages, tasks and protected objects and then give a number of further examples.

Tasks, protected objects and packages have a superficial lexical similarity – they all have specifications (with private parts) and bodies. However, there are many differences

- A task is an active construction whereas a package or protected object is passive.
- A task can only have entries in its specification and representation clauses associated with the entries. A package can have anything except entries. A protected object can have entries and subprograms.
- A package can be generic but a task or protected object cannot.
- A package can appear in a use clause but a task or protected object cannot.
- A package can be a library unit but a task or protected object cannot. However, a task or protected body can be a subunit.

The overall distinction is that the package should be considered to be the main tool for structuring purposes whereas the task and protected object provide concurrency. Thus typical subsystems will consist of a (possibly generic) package containing one or more tasks interacting through protected objects.

Incidentally, as noted above, a task can have a private part but like the visible part this can only contain entries; such entries can only be called by local tasks.

Our first example illustrates the use of protected types as private types by the following generic package which provides a general type Buffer

```
generic
   type Item is private;
package Buffers is
   type Buffer(N: Positive) is limited private;
   procedure Put(B: in out Buffer; X: in Item);
   procedure Get(B: in out Buffer; X: out Item);
private
   type Item_Array is array (Integer range <>) of Item;

   protected type Buffer(N: Positive) is
      entry Put(X: in Item);
      entry Get(X: out Item);
   private
      A: Item_Array(1 .. N);
      I, J: Integer := 1;
      Count: Integer := 0;
   end Buffer;

end;
```

```
package body Buffers is
    protected body Buffer is
        entry body Put(X: in Item) when Count < N is
        begin
            A(I) := X;
            I := I mod N + 1;  Count := Count + 1;
        end Put;

        entry body Get(X: out Item) when Count > 0 is
        begin
            X := A(J);
            J := J mod N + 1;  Count := Count - 1;
        end Get;

    end Buffer;

    procedure Put(B: in out Buffer; X: in Item) is
    begin
        B.Put(X);
    end Put;

    procedure Get(B: in out Buffer; X: out Item) is
    begin
        B.Get(X);
    end Get;

end Buffers;
```

The buffer is implemented as a protected object which contains the storage for the buffer. (Remember that a protected type is limited and can thus be the full type corresponding to a limited private type.) Calls of the procedures Put and Get access the buffer by calling the entries of the protected object.

The length of the buffer has been passed as a discriminant rather than as a generic parameter to avoid unnecessary instantiations. In any event we can no longer use a modular type for the indexing because N is not static (nor would it be if a generic parameter). Also, the bounds of the array have to be 1 and N because a discriminant used as a bound must be used directly and not as part of a larger expression. And moreover, we cannot use the discriminant to give range constraints for I, J and Count (see Section 16.2).

Other arrangements are possible. For example the data could be outside the protected object itself and the protected object could then access the data by using a self-referential access discriminant.

We now come to an interesting demonstration example which illustrates the dynamic creation of task objects. The objective is to find and display the first few prime numbers using the Sieve of Eratosthenes.

This ancient algorithm works using the observation that if we have a list of all the primes below N so far, then N is also prime if none of these divide exactly into it. So we try the existing primes in turn and as soon as one divides N we discard N and try again with N set to $N+1$. On the other hand, if we get to the end of our list of primes without dividing N, then N must be prime, so we add it to our list and also start again with $N+1$.

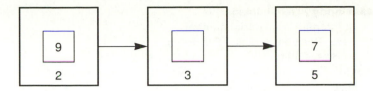

Figure 18.4   The Sieve of Eratosthenes.

Our implementation (reproduced by permission of Alsys) uses a separate task for each prime P which is linked (via an access value) to the previous prime task and next prime task as shown in Figure 18.4. Its duty is to take a trial number N from the previous task and to check whether it is divisible by its prime P. If it is, the number is discarded; if it is not, the number is passed to the next prime task. If there is no next prime task then P was the largest prime so far and N is a newly found prime; the P task then creates a new task whose duty is to check for divisibility by N and links itself to it. Each task thus acts as a filter removing multiples of its own prime value.

On the screen each task displays a frame containing its own prime and an inner box which displays the trial value currently being tested, if any. Figure 18.4 shows the situation when the primes 2, 3 and 5 have been found. The 5 task is testing 7 (which will prove to be a new prime), the 3 task is resting and waiting to receive another number from the 2 task, the 2 task (having just discarded 8) is testing 9 (which it will pass to the 3 task in a moment).

The program comprises a package Frame containing subprograms which manipulate the display (the body of this package is not shown), a task type Filter which describes the activities of the prime tasks and a main procedure Sieve.

```
package Frame is
   type Position is private;
   function Make_Frame(Divisor: Integer) return Position;
   procedure Write_To_Frame(Value: Integer; Where: Position);
   procedure Clear_Frame(Where: Position);
private
   ...
end Frame;

use Frame;

task type Filter(P: Integer) is
   entry Input(Number: Integer);
end Filter;

type A_Filter is access Filter;

function Make_Filter(N: Integer) return A_Filter is
begin
   return new Filter(N);
end Make_Filter;
```

```
task body Filter(P: Integer) is
  N: Integer;      -- trial number
  Here: Position := Make_Frame(P);
  Next: A_Filter;
begin
  loop
    accept Input(Number: Integer) do
      N := Number;
    end;
    Write_To_Frame(N, Here);
    if N mod P /= 0 then
      if Next = null then
        Next := Make_Filter(N);
      else
        Next.Input(N);
      end if;
    end if;
    Clear_Frame(Here);
  end loop;
end Filter;

procedure Sieve is
  First: A_Filter := new Filter(2);
  N: Integer := 3;
begin
  loop
    First.Input(N);
    N := N+1;
  end loop;
end Sieve;
```

The subprograms in the package Frame behave as follows. The function Make_Frame draws a new frame on the screen and permanently writes the divisor number (that is P for the task calling it) into the frame; the inner box is left empty. The function returns a value of the private type Position which identifies the position of the frame; this value is later passed as a parameter to the two other procedures which manipulate the inner box in order to identify the frame concerned. The procedure Write_To_Frame has a further parameter giving the value to be written in the inner box; the procedure Clear_Frame wipes the inner box clean.

The task type Filter is fairly straightforward. It has a discriminant P which is its prime number and a single entry Input which is called by the preceding task to give it the next trial divisor. It starts by creating its frame (noting the position in Here) and then enters the loop and awaits a number N to test. Having collected N it displays it in the inner box and then tests for divisibility by P. If it is divisible, it clears the inner box and goes to the beginning of the loop for a new value of N. If N is not divisible by P, it makes a successor task if necessary with discriminant N and otherwise passes the value of N to it by calling its entry Input. Only after the successor task has taken the value does it clear the inner box and go back to the beginning.

The driving procedure Sieve makes the first task with discriminant 2, sets N to 3 and then enters an endless loop giving the task successive integer values until the end of time (or some other limitation is reached).

The reader may wonder why we declared the function Make_Filter rather than simply writing

```
Next := new Filter(N);
```

within the body of the task Filter. The reason is that within a task body the name of the task refers to the current execution of the task and cannot be used as a subtype mark. Thus we could abort the current task or pass it as a parameter to a procedure by using the name Filter and this would refer to the task object currently executing the body.

Our final example illustrates in outline a typical application using several processors. In recent years the cost of processors has fallen dramatically and for many applications it is now more sensible to use several individual processors rather than one very high performance processor. Indeed the finite value of the velocity of light coupled with the nonzero value of Planck's constant places physical limits to the performance that one can get from a single processor. We are then faced with the software organizational problem of how to use several processors effectively. For many applications this is hard, but for those where there is a replication of some sort it is often feasible. The processing of algorithms on arrays in graphics, signal processing and so on are good examples.

In Ada the task type gives us a natural means of describing a process which can be run in parallel on several processors simultaneously. For the moment we will suppose that we have a computer comprising several processors with a common address space. Thus when several tasks are active they really will be active and we assume that there are enough processors for all the tasks in the program to truly run in parallel.

Suppose we wish to solve the differential equation

$$\partial^2 P/\partial x^2 + \partial^2 P/\partial y^2 = F(x, y)$$

over a square region. The value of P is given on the boundary and the value of F is given throughout. The problem is to find the value of P at internal points of the region. This equation arises in many physical situations. One example might concern the flow of heat in a thin sheet of material; $P(x, y)$ would be the temperature of point (x, y) in the sheet and $F(x, y)$ would be the external heat flux applied at that point. However, the physics doesn't really matter.

The standard approach is to consider the region as a grid and to replace the differential equation by a corresponding set of difference equations. For simplicity we consider a square region of side N with unit grid. We end up with something like having to solve

$$4P(i, j) = P(i{-}1, j) + P(i{+}1, j) + P(i, j{-}1) \\ + P(i, j{+}1) - F(i, j) \qquad 0 < i, j < N$$

This equation gives a value for each point in terms of its four neighbours. Remember that the values on the boundary are known and fixed. We use an iterative approach (Gauss-Seidel) and allocate a task to each point (i, j). The tasks then repeatedly compute the value of their point from the neighbouring points until the values cease to change. The function F could be of arbitrary complexity. A possible program is as follows

```
procedure Gauss_Seidel is
   N: constant := 5;
   subtype Full_Grid is Integer range 0 .. N;
   subtype Grid is Full_Grid range 1 .. N-1;
   type Real is digits 7;           -- declare our own type
   type Matrix is (Integer range <>, Integer range <>) of Real;
   pragma Atomic_Components(Matrix);

   P: Matrix(Full_Grid, Full_Grid);
   Delta_P: Matrix(Grid, Grid);

   Tolerance: constant Real := 0.0001;
   Error_Limit: constant Real := Tolerance * (N-1)**2;
   Converged: Boolean := False;
   Error_Sum: Real;
   pragma Atomic(Converged);

   function F(I, J: Grid) return Real is separate;

   task type Iterator is
      entry Start(I, J: in Grid);
   end;

   Process: array (Grid, Grid) of Iterator;

   task body Iterator is
      I, J: Grid;
      New_P: Real;
   begin

      accept Start(I, J: in Grid) do
         Iterator.I := Start.I;
         Iterator.J := Start.J;
      end Start;

      loop
         New_P := 0.25 * (P(I-1, J) + P(I+1, J) + P(I, J-1)
                                        + P(I, J+1) - F(I, J));
         Delta_P(I, J) := New_P - P(I, J);
         P(I, J) := New_P;
         exit when Converged;
      end loop;

   end Iterator;

begin                -- main subprogram, Iterator tasks now active
```

```
...                        -- initialize P and Delta_P
for I in Grid loop
  for J in Grid loop
    Process(I, J).Start(I, J);        -- tell them who they are
  end loop;
end loop;

loop
  Error_Sum := 0.0;
  for I in Grid loop
    for J in Grid loop
      Error_Sum := Error_Sum + Delta_P(I, J)**2;
    end loop;
  end loop;

  Converged := Error_Sum < Error_Limit;
  exit when Converged;
end loop;

...                                -- output results

end Gauss_Seidel;
```

The main task starts by telling the Iterator tasks who they are through the call of the entry Start. Thereafter the individual tasks execute independently and communicate through shared variables. The Iterator tasks continue until the Boolean Converged is set by the main task; they then exit their loop and terminate. The main task repeatedly computes the sum of squares of the errors from Delta_P (set by the Iterator tasks) and sets Converged accordingly. When stability is reached the main task outputs the results.

This example illustrates the use of shared objects; they are the Boolean Converged and the two arrays P and Delta_P. The pragma Atomic applied to the variable Converged ensures that all accesses to the variable are done atomically and cannot interfere. In the case of the arrays all we need is to ensure that the individual components are treated atomically and this is ensured by applying the pragma Atomic_Components to the array type.

It is somewhat irritating to have to tell the tasks who they are. An alternative approach is to use discriminants. If we simply write

```
task type Iterator(I, J: Grid);
```

then we have to laboriously declare all the tasks as follows

```
Process_11: Iterator(1 ,1);
Process_12: Iterator(1, 2);
...
```

An interesting alternative is to write

```
task type Iterator(I: Grid := Next_I; J: Grid := Next_J);
Process: array (Grid, Grid) of Iterator;
```

where the functions Next_I and Next_J are designed to deliver all the required pairs of values; they might be in some initializing package as follows

```
package Start_Up is
  function Next_I return Grid;
  function Next_J return Grid;
end;

package body Start_Up is
  I: Integer := 1;
  II, J: Integer := 0;

  function Next_I return Grid is
  begin
    if II = N-1 then
      II := 0;  I := I + 1;
    end if;
    II := II + 1;
    return I;
  end;

  function Next_J return Grid is
  begin
    if J = N-1 then J := 0; end if;
    J := J + 1;
    return J;
  end;

end Start_Up;
```

(Observe that the pairs for the discriminants might not match the index pairs because the order of evaluation of the components of an array is not defined by the language; that does not matter since we are guaranteed that they will all be distinct. Note moreover that each pair of calls of Next_I and Next_J might also be in any order. But frankly this is all a nasty trick.)

The program as shown (with $N = 5$) requires 17 tasks and thus 17 processors. This is not unreasonable and of course the program is based on the assumption of one asynchronous processor per task. Nevertheless, the reader will observe a number of flaws. The convergence criterion is a bit suspect. It might be possible for waves of divergence to slurp around the grid in a manner which escapes the attention of the asynchronous main task – but this is unlikely. Another point is that the Iterator tasks might still be computing one last iteration while the main task is printing the results. It would be better to add a Stop entry so that the main task can wait until the Iterator tasks have finished their loops. Alternatively, the array of tasks could be declared in an inner block and the main task could do the printing outside that block where it would know that the other tasks must have terminated. Thus

```
begin                          -- main subprogram
  ...                          -- initialize arrays
  declare
    Process: array (Grid, Grid) of Iterator;
```

```
    begin                    -- Iterator tasks active
      ...
    end;                     -- wait for Iterator tasks to terminate
      ...                    -- output results
end Gauss_Seidel;
```

Many multiprocessor systems will not have a shared memory in which case a different approach is necessary. A naive first attempt might be to give each Iterator an entry which when called delivers the current value of the corresponding point of the grid. Direct *ad hoc* calls from one task to another in a casual design will quickly lead to deadlock. A better approach is to have a task and a protected object at each point; the task does the computation and the protected object provides controlled access to the point.

It is hoped that our simple example has given the reader some glimpse of how tasking may be distributed over a multiprocessor system. It is a complex subject which is only now being addressed seriously. Of course our example has a ludicrously trivial computation in each task and the system (especially without shared memory) will spend much of its time on communication rather than computation. Nevertheless the principles should be clear. Note that we have not discussed how the different tasks become associated with the different processors; this lies outside the domain of the language itself. See also Section 22.3 on Distributed Systems.

EXERCISE 18.10

1   A boot repair shop has one man taking orders and three others actually repairing the boots. The shop has storage for 100 boots awaiting repair. The person taking the orders notes the address of the owner and this is attached to the boots; he then puts the boots in the store. Each repairman takes boots from the store when he is free, repairs them and then mails them.

   Write a package Cobblers whose specification is

```
package Cobblers is
    procedure Mend(A: Address; B: Boots);
end;
```

   The package body should contain four tasks representing the various men. Use an instantiation of the package Buffers to provide a store for the boots and agent objects as mailboxes to deliver them.

2   Sketch a solution of the differential equations using a task and a protected object for each point and no shared variables. Evaluate and store Delta_P in the protected object. The main subprogram should use the same convergence rule as before. You will not need arrays (other than for the tasks and protected objects) since the data will be distributed in the protected objects.

CHECKLIST 18

A task is active whereas a package or protected object is passive.

A task specification can contain only entries.

A protected body cannot contain data.

A task or protected object cannot be generic.

A task or protected object name cannot appear in a use clause.

Entries may be overloaded and renamed as procedures.

The Count attribute can only be used inside the task or protected object owning the entry.

An accept statement must not appear in a subprogram.

The order of evaluation of guards is not defined.

A select statement can have just one of an else part, a single terminate alternative, one or more delay alternatives.

A terminate or delay alternative can be guarded.

Several alternatives can refer to the same entry.

Beware of the Count attribute in guards; it is quite safe in barriers.

Task and protected types are limited.

A task declared as an object is dependent on a block, subprogram or task body but not an inner package.

A task created by an allocator is dependent on the block, subprogram or task body containing the access type definition.

A task declared as an object is made active at the following (possibly notional) **begin**.

A task created by an allocator is made active at once.

Do not use **abort** without good reason.

A requeue statement can only occur in an entry body or accept statement.

Requeue must be to a parameterless entry or an entry with the same parameter profile.

Changes from Ada 83

Accept statements could not have exception handlers in Ada 83.

Protected objects did not exist in Ada 83.

Tasks did not have private parts in Ada 83.

Tasks did not have discriminants in Ada 83.

The requeue statement and ATC did not exist in Ada 83.

19 Object Oriented Techniques

We have now introduced all the main features of Ada 95 and illustrated them with many examples. An important topic which has arisen in various forms is object oriented programming. Chapter 13 introduced type extension and dynamic polymorphism using tagged types. Chapter 16 discussed type parameterization by discriminants. Chapter 17 covered static polymorphism through genericity. And finally Chapter 18 on tasking discussed concurrent objects which some might feel are the only true objects anyway.

However, the linear exposition has prevented us from exploring a number of important interactions between these features. Accordingly this chapter addresses a number of examples which further illustrate the various techniques and show how they fit together.

19.1   Inheritance and composition

We start this chapter on object oriented techniques with some general remarks about type composition.

There are a number of ways in which types can be put together. An array type is composed of two other types, the index type and the component type. A record type is composed of the several types of its components. Type extension is a special form of composition in which a record type has the same components as another type plus additional components at the same level.

449

So we distinguish

```
type Circle is new Object with
   record
      Radius: Float;
   end record;
```

and

```
type Circle is
   record
      Obj: Object;
      Radius: Float;
   end record;
```

since although both have three eventual components, the structure and naming is quite different. The fundamental difference is between 'X is a Y' and 'X has a Y'. The circle *is* an object and so the type extension is the appropriate form.

It is interesting to contrast this with

```
type Cylinder is new Circle with
   record
      Height: Float;
   end record;
```

briefly introduced in Section 13.1. This type Cylinder is foolish; a cylinder is *not* a circle although it does have a circle as part of its structure. One obvious problem is that it will inherit Distance which is certainly curious because the distance to the centre of the cylinder will depend upon whether we are thinking of the cylinder as standing on the plane or not. It also inherits Area which is obviously wrong since it is a rather different concept in three dimensions. Even if we do provide a definition of Area that is sensible (the area of the surface), the application of the class wide function Moment of Section 3.3 will give a silly answer. The general point is that we have extended out of the domain in which we were originally thinking. A typical pitfall of OOP if misused. Clearly we should write

```
type Cylinder is tagged
   record
      Base: Circle;
      Height: Float;
   end record;
```

which reflects that a cylinder *has* a circle.

Language philosophers get very excited about multiple inheritance. At the linguistic level, Ada has single inheritance and the set of derived types forms a simple tree. This is both easy to understand and easy to implement. Multiple inheritance at the linguistic level raises various issues. The general idea would be to require that one type can have two (or more) parents of equal status. This

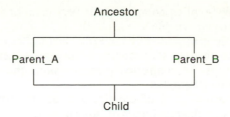

Figure 19.1   The problems of multiple inheritance.

gets into trouble once the parents have a common ancestor as illustrated in Figure 19.1.

The awkward issues to be resolved are whether the type Child has two copies of the components of the type Ancestor and what happens if the same operation is inherited from both parents and possibly derived from Ancestor and overridden differently on the way.

Clearly the symmetry causes ambiguity and this has to be resolved in some way. Different languages have different ways of solving this problem but all too often they cause surprises for the user.

The Ada solution is simply not to get into the problem in the first place and to force the user to break the symmetry (an echo of Quantum Mechanics) by only allowing single inheritance.

It is almost always the case that one parent is dominant so the extension can be from that parent and then the other properties simply added as an inner component. In other words we have single direct inheritance plus indirect secondary inheritance. Consider

```
type Tried_And_Trusted is tagged ...

type Wizard_Stuff is ...
procedure Magic(W: Wizard_Stuff);

type Adventure is new Tried_And_Trusted with
   record
      Spice: Wizard_Stuff;
   end record;
```

where the new type has all the operations of Tried_And_Trusted but none of those of Wizard_Stuff. However, we can effectively give it the magic operation by simply writing

```
procedure Magic(A: Adventure) is
begin
   Magic(A.Spice);
end Magic;
```

This may seem tedious but in fact often both relationships are 'has a' relationships in which case type extension is probably not appropriate anyway.

Composition through explicit components is very clear and the operations then have an explicit ancestry visible at each call.

Another example is provided by the type Linked_Set of Section 13.8. This directly inherits the abstract set property by being derived from the type Set and indirectly inherits the controlled property since the component Inner is derived from the type Controlled.

We will see further ways of creating composite structures and explicit multiple inheritance in the remainder of this chapter.

EXERCISE 19.1

---

1   Declare appropriate functions Area and Volume for the second type Cylinder. What happens if we attempt to apply the function Moment of Section 3.3 to an object of type Cylinder?

19.2   Mixin inheritance

Genericity adds static polymorphism to the dynamic polymorphism provided by type extension and class wide types.

In the previous section we mentioned that linguistic multiple inheritance creates complexity and that Ada takes the approach of giving the user various techniques for explicit composition. Genericity plays an important role in providing what is known as mixin inheritance.

Consider the generic package

```
generic
   type S is tagged private;
package P is
   type T is new S with private;
   ...   -- operations on T
private
   type T is new S with
      record
         ...   -- additional components
      end record;
end P;
```

where the specification exports the extended type T plus various operations on T which are implemented in the body.

We can then use an instantiation of P to add the operations of T to any existing tagged type and the resulting type will of course still be in the class of the type passed as actual parameter. There is also some merit in marking both S and T as abstract.

This approach allows us to extend a type with generic operations that might or might not be made visible to the client. For example, we recall from Section 13.6 that the full type corresponding to

type Shape **is new** Object **with private**;

need not be directly derived from Object. We can therefore write

```
private
   package Q is new P(Object);
   type Shape is new Q.T with null record;
   ...
end;
```

and then the type Shape will also have all the components and properties of the type T in the generic package. As written, these are, of course, not visible to the client but subprograms in the visible part of the package in which Shape is declared could provide access to them. Note that even if we had marked T as abstract then Shape would not be abstract.

A variation is where the extension is only valid for types in a certain class presumably because certain properties of that class are required for the extension. Thus

```
generic
   type S is new Object with private;
package Colour_Mixin is
   type Coloured_Object is new S with private;
   ...
end;
```

can only be applied to types in Object'Class. Some existing inherited operations could be replaced and others added.

A whole series of such extensions could be made

```
package Amazing is
   type Special_Object is new Object with private;
   ...    -- operations
private
   package A is new Colour_Mixin(Object);
   package B is new Strange_Mixin(A.Coloured_Object);
   package C is new Charge_Mixin(B.Strange_Object);
   type Special_Object is new C.Charged_Object with null record;
end Amazing;
```

and then the final type Special_Object will have colour, strangeness and charge and these properties will be available through the exported operations. It is important to note that such operations of the final exported type can often be provided by renamings (in the package body) of operations inherited from an ancestor as illustrated in one of the exercises below.

EXERCISE 19.2

1   Complete the package Colour_Mixin and provide subprograms to set and read the colour of a coloured object. Coloured objects cannot be set Red if their area is less than 10.0.

2   Write a generic package whose visible part is

```
generic
   type Raw_Type is tagged private;
package Tracking is
   type Tracked_Type is new Raw_Type with private;
   function Identity(TT: Tracked_Type) return Integer;
private ...
```

The purpose is to extend the Raw_Type so that objects of the resulting type Tracked_Type contain an identity number as in the controlled type Thing of Section 13.7. Although Tracked_Type will not be controlled in the sense that it is directly descended from the type Controlled, it will have a component of a controlled type and this will give the effect of controlling objects of Tracked_Type. The function Identity returns the identity number of the object TT.

3   Using the generic package Tracking of the previous example, write a package whose visible part is

```
package Hush_Hush is
   type Secret_Shape is new Object with private;
   function Shape_Identity(SS: Secret_Shape) return Integer;
   ...   -- other operations on a secret shape
private ...
```

The intent is that objects of the type Secret_Shape should be controlled and have an identity number which is returned by a call of Shape_Identity plus other hidden components which can be manipulated by the other operations in the visible part of the package.

19.3   Containers

Types such as queues which can hold values of other types are called container types. Such types are often implemented in terms of linked data structures.

We have encountered a number of such structures from time to time. The simplest is the pair Cell and Cell_Ptr which provide a simple list. The pair Node and Node_Ptr from Section 10.2 provide a binary tree. In Chapter 3 we showed an example where the elements of a list were access to class wide values thereby allowing the list to be indirectly heterogeneous.

An interesting variation was shown in Section 13.2 where various reservations were chained together using a pointer in a root type from which they were all derived; the main advantage of this approach is that the number of pointers is reduced. This mechanism was then encapsulated in the package Queues which we then used to create a queue containing reservations.

However, we observed that it was not possible to prevent any type being placed on the queue of reservations since the queue was completely heterogeneous. We can overcome this by making the package **Queues** generic thus

```
generic
   type Data is abstract tagged private;
package Queues is
   Queue_Error: exception;
   type Queue is limited private;
   type Element is abstract new Data with private;
   type Element_Ptr is access all Element'Class;
   procedure Join(Q: access Queue; E: in Element_Ptr);
   function Remove(Q: access Queue) return Element_Ptr;
   function Length(Q: Queue) return Integer;
private
   type Element is abstract new Data with
      record
         Next: Element_Ptr;
      end record;
   type Queue is limited
      record
         Count: Integer := 0;
         First, Last: Element_Ptr;
      end record;
end Queues;
```

The generic parameter **Data** is used as a token to identify the type of queue as we shall see in a moment. It is made abstract so that the actual type can also be abstract. The type **Element** is now an extension of **Data**; it is also abstract.

The base of the reservation system can now become (using the formulation of Section 13.3)

```
with Queues;
package Reservation_System is
   type Root_Resvn is abstract tagged null record;
   procedure Make(R: in out Root_Resvn) is abstract;
   package Resvn_Queues is new Queues(Root_Resvn);
   subtype R_Queue is Resvn_Queues.Queue;
   subtype Reservation is Resvn_Queues.Element;
   subtype Reservation_Ptr is Resvn_Queues.Element_Ptr;
end Reservation_System;
```

with the rest of the system as before. Note the use of subtypes to give relevant names to the types exported from the instantiated package. The actual reservation types are then all derived from Reservation (that is Resvn_Queues.Element). We can then write

```
type R_Queue_Ptr is access R_Queue;
The_Queue: R_Queue_Ptr := new R_Queue;
...
Join(The_Queue, New_Resvn);
```

and then only reservations can be placed on the queue. (Strictly only types in the class Resvn_Queues.Element'Class.) So although the queue is still heterogeneous it is constrained to accept only objects of the appropriate class and there is no risk of placing the wrong type on the queue. And moreover, no conversion is required when removing an object from the queue

```
Next_Resvn: Reservation_Ptr := Remove(The_Queue);
...
```

because Reservation_Ptr is correctly an access to the queue element class.

This example also illustrates the use of a series of abstract types. We start with Root_Resvn which is abstract and only exists in order to characterize the queues; we then add the queue element property and so export Element which is also abstract. Using a subtype we rename that exported type as Reservation and only then do we develop the specific types for the various reservations. Observe that Make is a primitive operation of Root_Resvn; we could not make it a primitive operation of Reservation since that is really Queues.Element and a primitive operation cannot be declared outside the package Resvn_Queues where it is declared.

This is really another example of mixin inheritance. The reservations have the properties of Root_Resvn (such as Make) and also the queuing properties of the type Element.

But of course although we have got rid of the conversion problem and ensured that the queue can only have elements of the correct class, nevertheless this approach of extension from a root type is somewhat inflexible. If we really want a reservation to be on two different queues at the same time or perhaps on a tree structure then we are in difficulties. However, for limited types, this can be overcome by using access discriminants as we will see in Section 19.6.

The most flexible and simplest technique of all is that of Chapter 3 where we simply put the pointers in the queue. We can use the original package Queues of Exercise 11.5(3) but make it generic so it starts

```
generic
    type Data is private;
package Queues is ...
```

which can then be instantiated with Reservation_Ptr which is a definite type. Of course, we cannot put the reservations themselves on the queue because that would require a class wide actual parameter and hence an indefinite formal and the implementation would then require another level of indirection. But frankly we wouldn't want to put the reservations themselves on a queue anyway.

Although we have just dismissed the extension approach as restrictive, nevertheless it does have advantages. One is that the packages do not have to worry about storage control since all the storage is provided by the user; one might argue that this is simply passing the buck but it might be that the user is in a better position to know how to deal with unwanted objects. For example, the user might declare special storage pools for the objects (see Section 21.3) whereas it would be surprising for a common routine to use other than the default pool (one could pass a pool as a generic parameter but that seems overkill). We will now briefly look at some other structures.

The type Queue was actually implemented in terms of a singly linked list. For some applications it is convenient to use a lower level of abstraction where the individual cells are directly accessible; this allows items to be added or removed from any point of the list. Thus consider

```
package Lists is
   List_Error: exception;
   type Cell is tagged limited private;
   type Cell_Ptr is access all Cell'Class;
   procedure Insert(After: Cell_Ptr; Item: Cell_Ptr);
   function Remove(After: Cell_Ptr) return Cell_Ptr;
   function Next(After: Cell_Ptr) return Cell_Ptr;
private
   type Cell is tagged limited
      record
         Next: Cell_Ptr;
      end record;
end;
```

In this example we designate a list as a whole, a place in it, an item to be added and an item removed all by values of type Cell_Ptr. Iteration over a list can be performed by the function Next. Singly linked lists are a bit awkward because we cannot go backwards without scanning the list. Thus we designate the place to insert an item by pointing to the cell one before where it is to go; similarly for removing an item. This makes things difficult for the head since there is not one before it and so we cannot use this technique to add an item at the beginning or remove the first one. There are various solutions to this such as having extra procedures, or an extra parameter designating the head of the list, or always having a dummy cell at the start, or using a doubly linked list. We leave these details to the reader. However, the key point is that the type Cell can be extended with the data to be put on the list just as we did for the queue elements.

Note that we have made the type Cell a limited type. This is in anticipation of using a Cell in conjunction with access discriminants to be described in Section 19.6. It is not really a restriction because, as mentioned in Section 13.2, we don't usually want to move the data itself but only the pointer values and the data is held inside (an extension of) the type Cell.

Another common structure is the binary tree and a doubly linked form of this might be built around

```
type Node;
type Node_Ptr is access all Node'Class;
```

```
type Node is limited tagged
record
        Parent: Node_Ptr;
        Left, Right: Node_Ptr;
end record;
```

These list and tree structures can of course be made generic with respect to some abstract root data type just as for the package Queues.

EXERCISE 19.3

1   Write an appropriate body for the package Lists. Keep a dummy item at the head.

2   Reconsider the previous example using access parameters for Insert, Remove and Next.

19.4   Iterators

A common requirement is to apply an action to all the objects in some sort of structure, for example all the nodes in a tree or all the items in a list.

This can be approached in a number of ways and in order not to confuse with complex actions we will consider two very simple ones. We will suppose that the elements of the list or tree are simply values of an enumeration type such as Colour; we might consider our structures as representing a list or tree of coloured balls. The two actions will be a function which simply counts the number of entities in the structure and a procedure which turns all Green ones into Red ones.

We first consider the approach of a so-called active iterator applied to the simple case of a list. Consider

```
package Lists is
    type List is limited private;
    ...
    type Iterator(L: access List) is limited private;
    procedure Start(I: Iterator);
    function Done(I: Iterator) return Boolean;
    procedure Next(I: in out Iterator);
    function Get_Colour(I: Iterator) return Colour;
    procedure Set_Colour(I: in out Iterator; C: Colour);
private

    type Cell;
    type Cell_Ptr is access Cell;
```

```
        type Cell is
          record
            C: Colour;
            Next: Cell_Ptr;
          end record;
        type List is new Cell_Ptr;

        type Iterator(L: access List) is
          record
            This: Cell_Ptr;
          end record;

  end;

  package body Lists is
    ...

    procedure Start(I: in out iterator) is
    begin
      I.This := Cell_Ptr(I.L.all);
    end Start;

    function Done(I: Iterator) return Boolean is
    begin
      return I.This = null;
    end Done;

    procedure Next(I: in out Iterator) is
    begin
      I.This := I.This.Next;
    end Next;

    function Get_Colour(I: Iterator) return Colour is
    begin
      return I.This.C;
    end Get_Colour;

    procedure Set_Colour(I: Iterator; C: Colour) is
    begin
      I.This.C := C;
    end Set_Colour;

  end Lists;
```

We have not shown the various operations required to construct and otherwise manipulate the list in the ordinary way. Note that we have distinguished the type List from its representation Cell_Ptr as a point of clarification.

The general idea is that Start, Done and Next enable us to move over the structure and the component This of the type Iterator gives access to the current item at each stage.

The subprograms to count the number of items and change the green ones to red are

```
function Count(L: access List) return Natural is
  I: Iterator(L);
  Result: Natural:
begin
  Start(I);
  while not Done(I) loop
    Result := Result + 1;
    Next(I);
  end loop;
  return Result;
end Count;

procedure Green_To_Red(L: access List) is
  I: Iterator(L);
  C: Colour;
begin
  Start(I);
  while not Done(I) loop
    C := Get_Colour(I);
    if C = Green then
      Put_Colour(I, Red);
    end if;
    Next(I);
  end loop;
end Green_To_Red;
```

Observe how the objects of type Iterator are declared inside Count and Green_To_Red with an access discriminant identifying the List. Using access discriminants is not really necessary for this simple structure since we could have declared Iterator and Start as

```
type Iterator is
  record
    This: Cell_Ptr;
  end record;

procedure Start(L: List; I: in out Iterator) is
begin
  I.This := Cell_Ptr(L);
end Start;
```

However, for more complex structures the access discriminant enables the iterator to hold on to a pointer to the structure as a whole although this is not necessary for simply traversing a list.

It should also be noted that the procedure Start could be omitted by declaring the type Iterator as

```
type Iterator(L: access List) is
  record
    This: Cell_Ptr := Cell_Ptr(L.all);
  end record;
```

so that initialization occurs automatically.

It is clear that the actions Count and Green_To_Red are quite independent of the structure over which they are being applied. Moreover, we should arrange that the iteration mechanism is itself distinct from other aspects of the structure.

One approach is to put the type List and its other operations in a parent package and then put the iterator operations in a child (which would of course have access to the private part of the parent)

```
package Lists is
   type List is limited private;
   ...
private
   ...
end;

package Lists.Iterators is
   type Iterator(L: access List) is limited private;
   procedure Start(I: in out Iterator);
   ...   -- and Done, Next, Get_Colour
   procedure Set_Colour(I: Iterator; C: Colour);
private
   ...
end;
```

If we had several such structures then we could make the subprograms such as Count generic with respect to the various entities. If we had several subprograms to parameterize then we could put them all together in a single generic package. Alternatively, we could keep them distinct and use the package parameter technique to bundle the parameters together

```
generic
   type Structure is limited private;
   type Iterator(S: access Structure) is limited private;
   with procedure Start(I: in out Iterator) is <>;
   ...   -- and Done, Next, Get_Colour
   with procedure Set_Colour(I: Iterator; C: Colour) is <>;
package Iteration_Stuff is end;

generic
   with package I_S is new Iteration_Stuff(<>);
   use I_S;
procedure Generic_Green_To_Red(S: access Structure) is
   I: Iterator(S);
   C: Colour;
begin
   Start(I);
   while not Done(I) loop
      C := Get_Colour(I);
      if C = Green then
         Put_Colour(I, Red);
```

```
            end if;
            Next(I);
         end loop;
      end Generic_Green_To_Red;
```

And now all we have to do is instantiate Iteration_Stuff with the items from Lists.Iterators and then in turn instantiate Generic_Green_To_Red with the resulting package. Note the default parameters in Iteration_Stuff.

We now turn to a different approach which in a sense is a complete inversion of what we have done so far. The idea here is to hide the iteration loop once and for all inside a fixed procedure and then for that procedure to call by dispatching from within the loop to do whatever is required. This perhaps safer approach is known as a passive iterator.

Assuming the parent package Lists as before we can write

```
      package Lists.Iterators is
         type Iterator is abstract tagged null record;
         procedure Iterate(L: List; IC: Iterator'Class);
         procedure Action(C: in out Colour; I: in out Iterator) is abstract;
      end;

      package body Lists.Iterators is

         procedure Iterate(L: List; IC: Iterator'Class) is
            This: Cell_Ptr := Cell_Ptr(L);
         begin
            while This /= null loop
               Action(This.C, IC);             -- dispatches
               This := This.Next;
            end loop;
         end Iterate;

      end Lists.Iterators;
```

and the subprograms to perform the specific operations can now be declared in a package as follows

```
      package Lists.Iterators.Ops is
         function Count(L: List) return Natural;
         procedure Green_To_Red(L: in out List);
      end;

      package body Lists.Iterators.Ops is

         type Count_Iterator is new Iterator with
            record
               Result: Natural;
            end record;

         procedure Action(C: in out Colour; I: in out Count_Iterator) is
         begin
            I.Result := I.Result + 1;
         end Action;
```

```
        function Count(L: List) return Natural is
            I: Count_Iterator;
        begin
            I.Result := 0;
            Iterate(L, I);
            return I.Result;
        end Count;

        type GTR_Iterator is new Iterator with null record;

        procedure Action(C: in out Colour; I: in out GTR_Iterator) is
        begin
            if C = Green then C := Red; end if;
        end Action;

        procedure Green_To_Red(L: List) is
            I: GTR_Iterator;
        begin
            Iterate(L, I);
        end Green_To_Red;

    end Lists.Iterators.Ops;
```

The workings should be noted carefully. The subprograms call Iterate and pass a particular iterator as parameter. The tag of this identifies the associated Action which is then called from within the loop of Iterate. Each iterator is an extension of the abstract type Iterator and acts as a call-back handle.

Observe that the extensions are not within a package specification and so no new primitive operations can be added but nevertheless the existing operation Action can be overridden. Another vital point is that the extension cannot be done inside the subprograms such as Count because that would be at an inner level and violate the accessibility rules; remember that an extension must be at the same level as the parent type.

As well as providing the tag to identify the action, the iterator types also provide any working space required (such as Result) and a means of passing any general parameters into Iterate. For example, if we wanted to change all balls of a given colour to another given colour then we would write

```
    type Change_Iterator is new Iterator with
        record
            Old_Colour: Colour;
            New_Colour: Colour:
        end record;

    procedure Action(C: in out Colour; I: in out Change_Iterator) is
    begin
        if C = I.Old_Colour then
            C := I.New_Colour;
        end if;
    end Action;
```

```
procedure Change_Colour(L: List: From: Colour; To: Colour) is
   I: Change_Iterator;
begin
   I.Old_Colour := From;
   I.New_Colour := To;
   Iterate(L, I);
end Change_Colour;
```

Clearly the same technique can be used with any data structure and we leave the reader to explore how it might be generalized as an exercise.

We conclude this discussion by considering how we might like to have solved this problem using access to subprogram values. Consider (and this is illegal)

```
procedure Iterate(L: List;
               Action: access procedure(C: in out Colour)) is    -- illegal
   This: Cell_Ptr := Cell_Ptr(L);
begin
   while This /= null loop
      Action(This.C);           -- indirect call
      This := This.Next;
   end loop;
end Iterate;

function Count(L: List) return Natural is
   Result: Natural := 0;

   procedure Count_Action(C: in out Colour) is
   begin
      Result := Result + 1;
   end Count_Action;

begin
   Iterate(L, Count_Action'Access);
   return Result;
end Count;
```

This is illegal because we cannot have anonymous access to subprogram types. Nor can we write

```
type Action_Type is access procedure(C: in out Colour);
   ...
procedure Iterate(L: List; Action: Action_Type) is ...
```

because then Count_Action'Access in the call of Iterate is illegal because it violates the accessibility rules (the application of Access must not be at an inner level to the access type). Of course we could flatten the structure and make the variable Result and Count_Action external to Count but this would break the proper abstraction and would not work in a multitasking program. But perhaps that does not matter for many applications. This point also arises in typical numerical problems which are considered in the next section.

EXERCISE 19.4

1   Make the appropriate instantiations of the generic package Iteration_Stuff and
        generic procedure Green_To_Red for the type List.

2   Consider how to generalize the passive iterator approach to work on any structure by
        declaring a package containing abstract types Structure and Iterator plus primitive
        operations Iterate and Action. Apply the generalization to a binary tree by declaring a
        type Tree as an extension of Structure. Then declare a function that counts the
        number of balls of a given colour in any structure and apply it to determine how
        many Green balls are in a tree. Hint: use double dispatching.

19.5   Numerical applications

In the previous section we noted that we could not pass an access to
subprogram value from an inner level to an outer level. This was a traditional
technique for many numerical applications written in languages such as Algol
and Pascal. We will now consider the issues in a little more detail.

Suppose we have to find the best values of some parameters to fit certain
data. To be explicit, given some function f of n variables x_i

$$f = f(x_i) \qquad i = 1 .. n$$

we need to find those values of the x_i which make f a minimum. Suppose
further that the value of f for given x_i is obtained by integrating some other
function g over time t between certain limits and where the function g is
parameterized by the values x_i thus

$$f(x_i) = \int_0^T g(x_i, t)\, dt \qquad i = 1 .. n$$

This may seem a bit intricate but is typical of numerical analysis. We need
two standard routines, one for integration and one for minimization. They
might be

```
generic
   type Floating is digits <>;
   type Vector is array (Positive range <>) of Floating;
package Generic_Minimize is
   type Argument is access function (V: Vector) return Floating;
   procedure Minimize(N: Positive; V: in out Vector; A: Argument;
                 Accuracy: Floating := 10.0 * Floating'Model_Epsilon);
end Generic_Minimize;
```

```
generic
   type Floating is digits <>;
package Generic_Integrate is
   type Integrand is access function(X: Floating) return Floating;
   function Integrate(F: Integrand; From, To: Floating;
                   Accuracy: Floating := 10.0 * Floating'Model_Epsilon);
end Generic_Integrate;
```

The general idea is that the procedure Minimize adjusts the values of the vector V until the result of calling A with V as parameter is a minimum within the relative accuracy specified – this accuracy is by default set to ten times the Model_Epsilon of the floating type. Similarly the function Integrate evaluates the integral of the Integrand between the given limits.

The problem is solved by writing

```
with Generic_Minimize;
with Generic_Integrate;
procedure Main is
   N: Integer := 10;                        -- number of variables
   type My_Float is digits 12;              -- an accurate type
   type Vector is array (Integer range <>) of My_Float;
   X: Vector(1 .. N);
   T_Final: My_Float;

   function F(X: Vector) return My_Float is

      function G(T: My_Float) return My_Float is
      begin
         -- compute the function G using the nonlocal array X
         -- and the parameter T
      end G;

      package My_Integrate is new Generic_Integrate(My_Float);
      use My_Integrate;

   begin
      return Integrate(G'Access, 0.0, T_Final);
   end F;

   package My_Minimize is new Generic_Minimize(My_Float, Vector);
   use My_Minimize;

begin
   -- read initial estimates for the array X
   -- read upper limit T_Final
   Minimize(N, X, F'Access);
   -- write final values of the array X;
end Main;
```

The key point to notice is that the instantiations are done at the same level as the corresponding slave subprograms – this ensures that there are no accessibility problems.

Genericity can always be used for this purpose and, as in this example, is not a burden since typically the routines will be generic anyway because they are naturally parameterized by the floating type concerned. Furthermore, the slave subprograms could also be generic parameters as illustrated in Section 17.3.

EXERCISE 19.5

1 Consider whether the accessibility problem which arises with access to subprogram values – and so forced us to do the instantiation at an inner level – could be overcome by the use of dispatching for the example of this section as it was for the iterator of the previous section.

19.6   Multiple views

As mentioned in Section 19.1, multiple inheritance can often be avoided by simply adding one property as a component as in the case of the type Adventure. Sometimes this is not enough and a closer relationship is required in which the new type can truly be used in either context. This can be done by an interesting use of access discriminants. In Section 16.7 we showed how an inner component of a record can refer to the record as a whole thus

    type Inner(Ptr: **access** Outer) **is limited** ...

    type Outer **is limited**
      record
        ...
        Component: Inner(Outer'Access);
        ...
      end record;

The point is that types Inner and Outer can both be extensions of other types. For example the type Inner might be an extension of some type Node (such as in Section 10.2) containing components which access other objects of the type Node in order to create a tree (Node would have to be limited). Note in particular that the access discriminant of Inner could be class wide thus

    type Inner(Ptr: **access** Outer'Class) **is new** Node **with** ...

so that heterogeneous chains can be constructed. The important point is that we can navigate over the tree which consists of the components of type Inner linked together but at any point in the tree we can reach to the enclosing Outer record as a whole by the access discriminant Ptr as illustrated in Figure 19.2.

In a very real sense we have two quite different views of such an object and we can move from one view to another. Thus given the outer view from an

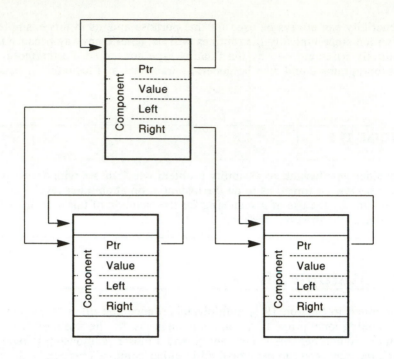

Figure 19.2 Navigation over a tree.

object O, the inner view is provided by selecting the component of type Inner thus

O.Component

whereas starting from a view I of the inner part we can regain the view of the outer by

I.Ptr.**all**

Observe the lack of symmetry since the outer view is dominant. (Of course we can create a symmetrical situation where the outer type is simply a container for two or more inner views.)

It should be noted that an access discriminant is only allowed for a limited type. This avoids copying problems with the self-referring components.

As a simple example suppose we have a linked list of coloured things much as in the packages Lists and Lists.Iterators of Section 19.4. So the essence is

```
type Cell is tagged limited
   record
      Next: Cell_Ptr;
   end record;
```

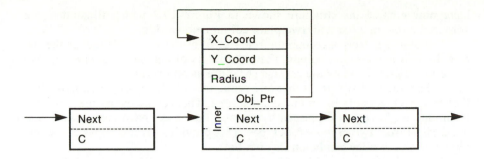

Figure 19.3   The coloured circle in the list of colours.

```
type Coloured is new Cell with
   record
      C: Colour;
   end record;

procedure Set_Colour(This: Coloured; To: Colour);
```

where Set_Colour is a primitive operation of Coloured. Note that the type Cell is a limited type because an extension of it is going to have a limited component and only a limited record type can have limited components.

On the other hand we also have our type Object and its descendants, Circle, Point, Polygon and so on. Now suppose we want to create a type which can act (like a chameleon) as either a coloured thing on a list or as a geometrical object according to our point of view. This is not quite the same as simply extending an Object with a colour as we will see. We assume for this application that Object is limited.

We do this in two stages. First we create a sort of gluon which can stick the types together

```
type Coloured_Gluon(Obj_Ptr: access Object'Class) is
                              new Coloured with null record;
```

This is of course directly derived from Coloured and will inherit Set_Colour; we could redefine this operation to use the properties of the Object available through the access discriminant.

Now we make the second step by extending say a Circle by

```
type Coloured_Circle is new Circle with
   record
      Inner: Coloured_Gluon(Coloured_Circle'Access);
   end record;
```

This is of course a circle and will inherit the properties of the type Circle, its Radius and functions such as Area; we could redefine this operation to take account of the associated colour available through the internal component. We have now created the structure shown in Figure 19.3 which illustrates one coloured circle in a list with two plain colours either side.

The object is truly a coloured circle but from the point of view of the list of colours it is a circular colour. The situation is of course not symmetric; we leave the reader to create the reverse structure as an exercise.

In Section 19.3 we stated that one problem with the extension approach is that an object can only be on one list at a time. This can be overcome using the technique we have just discussed by making the object have components that are derived from two or more root types. This provides several views of the one object and each view can be on its own list.

As a whimsical example, suppose we have a collection of objects such as garments. They will have various properties such as style (long, short, French), pattern (spotted, striped, plain), and of course they will come in different colours and different sizes. We need to search the stock for various combinations. To make this easier, we might decide to keep them on lists according to colour and also according to size. So each garment will be on two lists, its size list and its colour list. Of course several garments may have the same combination of colour and size.

This can be done by using the type Coloured and also introducing

```
type Sized is new Cell with
  record
    S: Size;
  end record;
```

and then two gluons for a type Garment

```
type Coloured_Gluon(CG_Ptr: access Garment) is
                              new Coloured with null record;

type Sized_Gluon(SG_Ptr: access Garment) is
                              new Sized with null record;
```

We can now write the type Garment as

```
type Garment is limited
  record
    Style: ... ;              -- components defining style and so on
    Pattern: ... ;
    Inner_Colour: Coloured_Gluon(Garment'Access);
    Inner_Size: Sized_Gluon(Garment'Access);
    ...
  end record;
```

and then garments can be placed on the various lists defined as

```
Red_List: Cell_Ptr;
Large_List: Cell_Ptr;
```

and this will result in cross linked chains as shown in Figure 19.4.

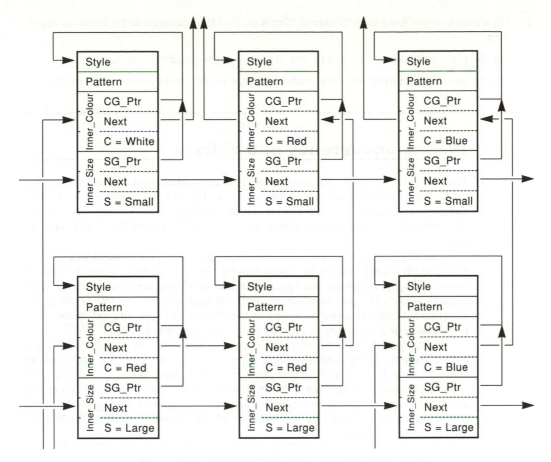

Figure 19.4   Double chains of garments.

The figure shows six garments, two large red ones and one each of large blue, small white, small red and small blue, threaded on various lists. Note that the components giving the size and colour could be direct components of the type Garment and not on the lists at all. The lists would then simply be chains of pointers that happen to thread through the records. This would perhaps be a better approach. Of course the components Next are actually Inner_Colour.Next and Inner_Size.Next and so are distinguished.

EXERCISE 19.6

1   For the example of the coloured circle redefine Set_Colour so that it will not update an object with area less than 10.0. Then do it with the condition that the Radius must not be less than 2.0.

2   Now redefine the **Area** of a Coloured_Circle so that it is deemed to be twice as big if Red.

3   Do the gluing the other way round and draw the corresponding diagram.

4   Do the garment example with the colour and size being direct components of the type Garment.

19.7   Concurrency and objects

This section considers the interaction between concurrent objects (tasks and protected objects) and type extension. A key to the interaction is that concurrent objects can have discriminants and in particular may have access discriminants which can reference the data being controlled by a task or protected object.

Ada does not allow tasks and protected objects to be extended since it was felt that efficiency would be compromised. In this context, extension might mean adding more protected operations and more private data to a protected object. However, the interaction with access discriminants enables the concurrency aspects to be provided by the concurrent type and extension to be provided by the tagged type pointed to by the discriminant.

In many systems it is often the case that a number of activities follow a cyclic pattern. Each activity might have a start time, an end time and an interval as well as auxiliary activities to be executed when it finishes or if something goes wrong. We can write a task type which acts as a general template with the details provided by dispatching calls or through data in the discriminant (this should be compared with the iterator example in Section 19.4). We might have

```
task type Control(Activity: access Descriptor'Class);

task body Control is
   Next_Time: Calendar.Time := Activity.Start_Time;
begin
   loop
     delay until Next_Time;
     Action(Activity);                      -- dispatches
     Next_Time := Next_Time + Activity.Interval;
     exit when Next_Time > Activity.End_Time;
   end loop;
   Last_Wishes(Activity);                   -- dispatches
exception
   when Event: others =>
     Handle(Activity, Event);              -- dispatches
end Control;
```

It is very important to note that the access discriminant is class wide. This is essential so that dispatching to the various operations can occur. The root type would be abstract and contain the timing information thus

```
package Root_Activity is
  type Descriptor is abstract tagged
    record
      Start_Time, End_Time: Calendar.Time;
      Interval: Duration;
    end record;
  procedure Action(D: access Descriptor) is abstract;
  procedure Last_Wishes(D: access Descriptor);
  procedure Handle(D: access Descriptor;
                      E: Exception_Occurrence);
end;

package body Root_Activity is
  procedure Last_Wishes(D: access Descriptor) is
  begin
    null;
  end Last_Wishes;

  procedure Handle(D: access Descriptor;
                      E: Exception_Occurrence) is
  begin
    Put_Line("Unhandled exception");
    Put_Line(Exception_Information(E));
  end Handle;
end Root_Activity;
```

where we have provided a null procedure for last wishes and a default handle
for exceptions but of course the central procedure Action is abstract and thus
has to be provided on extension.

A cyclic activity such as one to fire a cannon at noon each day could then
be created as follows

```
use Root_Activity;

type Cannon_Data is new Descriptor with
  record
    Pounds_Of_Powder: Integer;
  end record;

procedure Action(CD: access Cannon_Data) is
begin
  Load_Cannon(CD.Pounds_Of_Powder);
  Fire_Cannon;
end Action;

The_Data: Cannon_Data :=
    (Start_Time => High_Noon;
     End_Time => When_The_Stars_Fade_And_Fall;
     Interval => 24*Hours;
     Pounds_Of_Powder => 100);

Cannon_Task: Control(The_Data'Access);
```

Note how the specific data is passed to the procedure Action through the type extension. The timing data itself could have been provided by dispatching functions but it seems best to put such standard information in the root type. The control task could conveniently be declared in the package Root_Activity; private information not available to the cyclic activities but available to the control task could be held in a private ancestor type of the root type.

As another example consider the package Buffers of Section 18.10. The protected data was actually inside the protected objects. But we could have placed the data outside and referred to it though an access discriminant

```
type Buffer(N: Positive) is
  record
    A: Item_Array(1 .. N);
    I, J: Integer := 1;
    Count: Integer := 0;
  end record;

protected type Guardian(B: access Buffer) is
  entry Put(X: in Item);
  entry Get(X: out Item);
end;

protected body Guardian is

  entry body Put(X: in Item) when B.Count < B.N is
  begin
    B.A(B.I) := X;
    B.I := B.I + 1;  B.Count := B.Count + 1;
  end Put;
  ...
end Guardian;
```

and now we can declare the buffer and the protected object separately

```
A_Buffer: aliased Buffer(10);
Guard_A_Buffer: Guardian(A_Buffer'Access);
```

although they are permanently bound together. Of course this does not provide a type suitable as the full type corresponding to the private type Buffer but for that we could use the self-referential technique discussed in the previous section and put the protected object into the buffer alongside the data thus

```
type Buffer(N: Positive) is limited
  record
    A: Item_Array(1 .. N);
    I, J: Integer := 1;
    Count: Integer := 0;
    The_Guardian(Buffer'Access);
  end record;
```

This curious structure might have some merit if we wanted to bypass the protected object in some circumstances and access the data directly. It is especially curious that the Guardian has access to itself through the buffer.

A better technique might be to use type extension so that the Guardian only sees the root part of the buffer

```
type Buffer(N: Positive) is tagged limited
   record
      A: Item_Array(1 .. N);
      I, J: Integer := 1;
      Count: Integer := 0;
   end record;

protected type Guardian(B: access Buffer'Class) is
   entry Put(X: in Item);
   entry Get(X: out Item);
end;

type Guarded_Buffer is new Buffer with
   record
      The_Guardian(Guarded_Buffer'Access);
   end record;
```

Note that the discriminant is now class wide so that it can refer to the Guarded_Buffer. However, from within the Guardian, only the root part can be accessed.

EXERCISE 19.7

1   Provide a procedure Handle which takes some appropriate action if the cannon should explode and thereby raise the exception Bang from within Fire_Cannon.

2   Could we do the cannon example without dispatching by placing access to subprogram values in the type Descriptor and using indirect calls?

19.8   Controlling abstraction

We conclude this chapter by considering how we might control access to an abstract model of a system using various techniques. An interesting example is provided by the family saga of Section 16.5. Two formulations were considered, one using discriminants where the discriminant indicated the sex, and the other using tagged types where the tag indicated the sex. That section concluded by observing that the types should be private so that the correct interrelationships are always maintained.

However, as presented, both formulations suffer from the flaw that we can declare persons (objects of **Man** or **Woman**) which are not properly initialized and indeed we can copy persons and thereby create incorrectly linked clones. In fact there is no need for the user to declare persons at all; they can all be allocated inside the package and all the user need do is declare names.

As far as names are concerned it would be desirable if all names were initialized. At the moment they are null by default and indeed unset name components are also null by default. As a consequence any misuse of the system gives rise to Constraint_Error inside the various subprograms. Clearly we can arrange that all internal subprograms check properly and raise a specific exception. However, we still need some way of designating nobody when a function such as **Spouse** is applied to an unmarried person. We could use null for this but it would be better practice to use a **Nobody** value. It probably does no harm to copy names provided they are always complete (this gives rise to aliasing of course).

In conclusion we want to be able to declare initialized names but not persons. We would also like to be able to distinguish sex at compile time if possible (so that, for example, any attempt at a wrong marriage is caught by the compiler).

We can prevent objects from being declared by making them abstract or by making them limited with unknown discriminants.

Consider first the case of the variant formulation. If we give the type **Person** unknown discriminants then we cannot see the discriminants in the visible part and so cannot declare **Mans_Name** and **Womans_Name** in the visible part either. The best we can do is

```
package People is

   type Person(<>) is limited private;
   type Person_Name is access Person;
   ...   -- the subprograms
private
```

but this is silly since we might as well hide **Person** anyway. So we have

```
package People is

   type Person_Name(<>) is private;

   procedure Marry(Bride, Groom: Person_Name);
   function Spouse(P: Person_Name) return Person_Name;

      ...
private
```

All declarations of objects of the type **Person_Name** now have to be initialized by for example

```
Helen: Person_Name := New_Child( ... );
```

or we could get a new handle on someone else's spouse by

```
Friend: Person_Name := Spouse( ... );
```

Sadly we have lost the ability to distinguish externally between the sexes when calling Marry. We will of course now need many other subprograms and the type Gender will need to be visible.

We now turn to the tagged type formulation. The first thing to note is that it could match the visible part we have just shown. However another approach is

```ada
package People is

   type Person is abstract tagged private;
   type Man is abstract new Person with private;
   type Woman is abstract new Person with private;

   type Person_Name is access all Person'Class;
   type Mans_Name is access all Man;
   type Womans_Name is access all Woman;
   ...
private
```

This has the merit of preventing the external declaration of objects of the types Man and Woman by making them abstract while still retaining the external relationship between the access types. Of course we can no longer prevent uninitialized names from being declared. Also we have to use explicit conversion between the name types.

If we wanted to ensure that all names were initialized then we could try

```ada
package People is

   type Person_Name(<>) is private;
   type Mans_Name(<>) is private;
   type Womans_Name(<>) is private;
   ...
private
```

but now we have lost the external relationship between the types and so have to provide conversion functions between them. We leave further consideration of this to an exercise.

As the reader will appreciate, there is a limit to how much support the language can give in defining the relationships between structures. When the requirements reach a certain level it is necessary to program it ourselves even though that might mean extra complexity in the implementation or that the detection of errors is deferred to run time.

We now turn to consider some possible internal details of how our model could be controlled and monitored. For simplicity we will suppose that the external view just provides the type Person_Name and that the internal formulation uses the tagged mechanism.

We might want to iterate over the population so they ought to be linked together in some simple way – other than the family relationship which is complex and easily leads to double accounting.

So using a list model we might have

```
type Person is abstract new Cell with
record
    Birth: Date;
    ...
end record;
```

and then every time a new person is created they are linked onto one unique list. So

```
Everbody: Cell_Ptr;

function New_Child( ... ) return Person_Name is
    ...
    Insert(Everybody, Child);
    return Child;
end New_Child;
```

The total population could be counted using an iterator exactly as in the package Lists.Iterators.Ops of Section 19.4. Other queries could be handled in the same way. Indeed the external user might want to be able to perform such computations and so sufficient mechanism must be available externally for relevant queries to be formulated. So we might provide

```
package People.Iterators is
    type Iterator is abstract tagged private;
    procedure Iterate(IC: Iterator'Class);
    procedure Action(P: Person_Name; I: Iterator) is abstract;
end;
```

Note that there is no parameter designating which list to iterate over since there is only one. To count the number of single persons the associated Action might be

```
procedure Action(P: Person_Name; I: in out Single_Count_Iterator) is
begin
    if Spouse(P) = null then              -- or Nobody perhaps
        I.Result := I.Result + 1;
    end if;
end Action;
```

A final touch might be to animate the system. Each person could contain a task which outputs a message at regular intervals giving their name and indicating that they were alive. Other important events might also be announced. The task would have an access discriminant so

```
type Person;

task Monitor(My: access Person'Class);
```

```
type Person is abstract new Cell with
  record
    ...
    Name: String_Ptr;
    Ego: Monitor(Person'Access);
  end record;

task body Monitor is
  ...
begin
  loop
    delay ...
    Put_Line("Hello world. It is I, " & My.Name.all & " .");
    Today := Clock;
    if Month_Name'Val(Month_Number(Today)–1) = My.Birth.Month
      and Day_Number(Today) = My.Birth.Day then
        Put_Line("And today is my Birthday.");
    end if;
  end loop;
end Monitor;
```

The internal task automatically becomes active when the object in which it is embedded is created. Quite clearly some sort of queuing system is required for the messages otherwise the inane chatter could become garbled with interleaved messages. We leave the reader to contemplate other possibilities in this world simulation.

This example has shown how all objects of the type Person are created within the system but nevertheless the user has been able to create and manipulate them through the type Person_Name. It is possible to be even more restrictive. For example the coloured balls of Section 19.4 might be kept hidden from the user within a bag; the user might be able to command that another ball of a given colour be created and to institute searches using an iterator. Thus

```
package Balls is
  type Ball(<>) is limited private;
  procedure Create_Ball(C: Colour);
  function Colour_Of(B: Ball) return Colour;
  procedure Set_Colour(B: in out Ball; C: Colour);
  procedure Remove_Ball(B: in out Ball);
private
  ...
end;

package Balls.Iterators is
  type Iterator is abstract tagged private;
  procedure Iterate(IC: Iterator'Class);
  procedure Action(B: in out Ball; I: Iterator);
end;
```

This is quite fascinating. We cannot externally declare or get hold of a ball at all. We can command that a ball be created but it is then hidden from us. The subprograms that take a ball as a parameter can only be called from within an iterator.

EXERCISE 19.8

1 Explore the possibility of providing the three external types

   type Person_Name(<>) **is private**;
   type Mans_Name(<>) **is private**;
   type Womans_Name(<>) **is private**;

   together with appropriate conversion functions for both formulations.

2 Consider how a restricted view of the world simulation might be created in which some external viewer could only interrogate the system though an iterator but not create new persons or their names.

Part 4

Completing the Story

This final part completes the story and largely describes the predefined library and other material which enable the Ada program to communicate with various aspects of its environment.

In essence the predefined environment comprises the four packages Standard, Ada, System and Interfaces. Chapter 20 covers Standard and Ada which are independent of the underlying system whereas Chapter 21 covers System and Interfaces which very much depend upon the underlying system. The discussion in Chapter 20 is reasonably comprehensive and covers all the points necessary for normal use. The discussion in Chapter 21 is rather less thorough because it depends upon the implementation.

Chapter 22 is a very brief overview of the scope of the six specialized annexes. Although this book does not attempt serious coverage of these annexes nevertheless a brief overview of their scope seems appropriate. In particular enough information is given to use the complex number facilities of the Numerics annex.

The final Chapter 23 pulls together a small number of loose threads, considers the problems of portability and concludes with some thoughts on design.

There are then three appendices. Appendix 1 lists the reserved words, attributes and pragmas; Appendix 2 contains a brief glossary; and Appendix 3 gives the complete syntax plus index.

The book concludes with comprehensive answers to all the exercises; the reader is encouraged to study these and especially any discussion which often covers minor but nevertheless important points.

20 Predefined Library

The previous chapters have covered the intrinsic aspects of the Ada language; that is all the various syntactic forms. In this chapter and the next chapter we describe the predefined library which comes with every implementation of Ada. As outlined in Chapter 4, the predefined library is structured as three packages, Ada, System and Interfaces with numerous child packages. These three packages are themselves (like all root library units) considered to be child units of Standard. This chapter is largely about the packages Standard and Ada whereas System and Interfaces are discussed in the next chapter.

The predefined library is quite extensive and an exhaustive discussion would be very long. We therefore concentrate on a general overview and refer the reader to the *ARM* for some of the fine detail.

20.1 The package Standard

As mentioned earlier, certain entities are predefined through their declaration in the special package Standard. It should not be thought that this package necessarily actually exists; it is just that the compiler behaves as if it does. Indeed, as we shall see, some entities notionally declared in Standard cannot be truly declared in Ada at all. The general effect of Standard is indicated by the outline specification below.

The operators that are predefined for the types declared in the package Standard are given in comments since they are implicitly declared. Italics are used for identifiers that are not available to users (such as the identifier *universal_real*) and for undefined information (such as *implementation-defined*).

```
package Standard is
  pragma Pure(Standard);

  type Boolean is (False, True);

  -- function "=" (Left, Right: Boolean) return Boolean;
  -- similarly "/=", "<", "<=", ">", ">="
  -- "and", "or", "xor"

  function "not" (Right: Boolean) return Boolean;

  -- The types root_integer and universal_integer are
  -- predefined.

  type Integer is range implementation-defined;

  subtype Natural is Integer range 0 .. Integer'Last;
  subtype Positive is Integer range 1 .. Integer'Last;

  -- function "=" (Left, Right: Integer'Base) return Boolean;
  -- similarly "/=", "<", "<=", ">", ">="

  -- function "+" (Right: Integer'Base) return Integer'Base;
  -- similarly "-", "abs"

  -- function "+" (Left, Right: Integer'Base) return Integer'Base;
  -- similarly "-", "*", "/", "rem", "mod"

  -- function "**" (Left: Integer'Base; Right: Natural) return
                                              Integer'Base;

  -- And similarly for root_integer and any other predefined integer
  -- types with Integer replaced by the name of the type.
  -- The right operand of "**" remains as Natural.

  -- The types root_real and universal_real are predefined.

  type Float is digits implementation-defined;

  -- function "=" (Left, Right: Float) return Boolean;
  -- similarly "/=", "<", "<=", ">", ">="

  -- function "+" (Right: Float) return Float;
  -- similarly "-", "abs"

  -- function "+" (Left, Right: Float) return Float;
  -- similarly "-", "*", "/"

  -- function "**" (Left: Float; Right: Integer'Base) return Float;

  -- And similarly for root_real and any other predefined floating
  -- point types with Float replaced by the name of the type.
```

-- The following also apply to *root_integer* and *root_real*

-- **function** "*" (Left: *root_integer*; Right: *root_real*) **return** *root_real*;
-- **function** "*" (Left: *root_real*; Right: *root_integer*) **return** *root_real*;
-- **function** "/" (Left: *root_real*; Right: *root_integer*) **return** *root_real*;

-- The type *universal_fixed* is predefined.

-- **function** "*" (Left, Right: *universal_fixed*) **return** *universal_fixed*;
-- **function** "/" (Left, Right: *universal_fixed*) **return** *universal_fixed*;

-- The type Character is based on ISO 8859-1. There are
-- no literals for control characters shown in italics.

type Character **is**

(*nul*,	*soh*,	*stx*,	*etx*,	*eot*,	*enq*,	*ack*,	*bel*,	--	0	..	7
bs,	*ht*,	*lf*,	*vt*,	*ff*,	*cr*,	*so*,	*si*,	--	8	..	15
dle,	*dc1*,	*dc2*,	*dc3*,	*dc4*,	*nak*,	*syn*,	*etb*,	--	16	..	23
can,	*em*,	*sub*,	*esc*,	*fs*,	*gs*,	*rs*,	*us*,	--	24	..	31
' ',	'!',	'"',	'#',	'$',	'%',	'&',	''',	--	32	..	39
'(',	')',	'*',	'+',	',',	'-',	'.',	'/',	--	40	..	47
'0',	'1',	'2',	'3',	'4',	'5',	'6',	'7',	--	48	..	55
'8',	'9',	':',	';',	'<',	'=',	'>',	'?',	--	56	..	63
'@',	'A',	'B',	'C',	'D',	'E',	'F',	'G',	--	64	..	71
'H',	'I',	'J',	'K',	'L',	'M',	'N',	'O',	--	72	..	79
'P',	'Q',	'R',	'S',	'T',	'U',	'V',	'W',	--	80	..	87
'X',	'Y',	'Z',	'[',	'\',	']',	'^',	'_',	--	88	..	95
'`',	'a',	'b',	'c',	'd',	'e',	'f',	'g',	--	96	..	103
'h',	'i',	'j',	'k',	'l',	'm',	'n',	'o',	--	104	..	111
'p',	'q',	'r',	's',	't',	'u',	'v',	'w',	--	112	..	119
'x',	'y',	'z',	'{',	'|',	'}',	'~',	*del*,	--	120	..	127
128,	*129*,	*bph*,	*nbh*,	*132*,	*nel*,	*ssa*,	*esa*,	--	128	..	135
hts,	*htj*,	*vts*,	*pld*,	*plu*,	*ri*,	*ss2*,	*ss3*,	--	136	..	143
dcs,	*pu1*,	*pu2*,	*sts*,	*cch*,	*mw*,	*spa*,	*epa*,	--	144	..	151
sos,	*153*,	*sci*,	*csi*,	*st*,	*osc*,	*pm*,	*apc*,	--	152	..	159
' ',	'¡',	'¢',	'£',	'¤',	'¥',	'¦',	'§',	--	160	..	167
'¨',	'©',	'ª',	'«',	'¬',	'',	'®',	'¯',	--	168	..	175
'°',	'±',	'²',	'³',	'´',	'µ',	'¶',	'·',	--	176	..	183
'¸',	'¹',	'º',	'»',	'¼',	'½',	'¾',	'¿',	--	184	..	191
'À',	'Á',	'Â',	'Ã',	'Ä',	'Å',	'Æ',	'Ç',	--	192	..	199
'È',	'É',	'Ê',	'Ë',	'Ì',	'Í',	'Î',	'Ï',	--	200	..	207
'Ð',	'Ñ',	'Ò',	'Ó',	'Ô',	'Õ',	'Ö',	'×',	--	208	..	215
'Ø',	'Ù',	'Ú',	'Û',	'Ü',	'Ý',	'Þ',	'ß',	--	216	..	223
'à',	'á',	'â',	'ã',	'ä',	'å',	'æ',	'ç',	--	224	..	231
'è',	'é',	'ê',	'ë',	'ì',	'í',	'î',	'ï',	--	232	..	239
'ð',	'ñ',	'ò',	'ó',	'ô',	'õ',	'ö',	'÷',	--	240	..	247
'ø',	'ù',	'ú',	'û',	'ü',	'ý',	'þ',	'ÿ');	--	248	..	255

-- The operators for Character are as any enumeration type.

-- The type Wide_Character is based on ISO 10646. The
-- first 256 positions are as for Character.

> **type** Wide_Character **is** (*nul, soh, ... FFFE, FFFF*);
>
> **package** ASCII **is**
>   — this is obsolescent, see Ada.Characters.Latin_1
> **end** ASCII;
>
> — Predefined string type:
>
> **type** String **is array** (Positive **range** <>) **of** Character;
> **pragma** Pack(String);
>
> — **function** "=" (Left, Right: String) **return** Boolean;
> — similarly "**/**=", "<", "<=", ">", ">="
>
> — **function** "&" (Left: String; Right: String) **return** String;
> — **function** "&" (Left: Character; Right: String) **return** String;
> — **function** "&" (Left: String; Right: Character) **return** String;
> — **function** "&" (Left: Character; Right: Character) **return** String;
>
> **type** Wide_String **is array** (Positive **range** <>) **of** Wide_Character;
> **pragma** Pack(Wide_String);
>
> — The operators correspond to those for String.
>
> **type** Duration **is delta** *implementation–defined*
>   **range** *implementation–defined*;
>
> — The operators for Duration are as any fixed point type.
>
> Constraint_Error, Program_Error, Storage_Error,
>   Tasking_Error: **exception**;
>
>   **end** Standard;

The above specification is not complete. For example, although the type Boolean can be written showing the literals False and True, the short circuit control forms cannot be expressed explicitly. Moreover, each further type definition implicitly introduces new declarations of some operators. All types, except limited types, introduce new declarations of = and **/**=. All scalar types and discrete one-dimensional array types introduce new declarations of & and those with Boolean components also introduce new declarations of **and, or, xor** and **not**. All fixed point types introduce new declarations of +, –, *, **/** and **abs**.

Note carefully that parameters and results for integers use the unconstrained subtype Integer'Base as explained in Section 15.1. On the other hand, the subtype Float is already unconstrained and so is used directly.

20.2   Character and string handling

The packages for character handling are

    Ada.Characters.Handling
    Ada.Characters.Latin_1

Table 20.1   Classification of characters.

Classification	Values in set
Is_Control	0..31, 127..159
Is_Graphic	**not** Is_Control
Is_Letter	Is_Lower **or** Is_Upper
Is_Lower	97..122, 223..246, 248..255
Is_Upper	65..90, 192..214, 216..222
Is_Basic	65..90, 97..122, 198, 208, 222, 223, 230, 240, 254
Is_Digit	48..57
Is_Decimal_Digit	48..57
Is_Hexadecimal_Digit	48..57, 65..70, 97..102
Is_Alphanumeric	Is_Letter **or** Is_Digit
Is_Special	Is_Graphic **and not** Is_Alphanumeric
Is_ISO_646	0..127

where Ada.Characters itself is empty.

Characters.Handling contains a number of functions for the classification and conversion of characters and strings. To a large extent their identifiers indicate their meaning. Thus

> **function** Is_Control(Item: **in** Character) **return** Boolean;

indicates whether the parameter is a control character (that is, in the ranges 0..31 or 127..159). Other similar functions are Is_Graphic, Is_Letter, Is_Lower, Is_Upper, Is_Basic, Is_Digit, Is_Decimal_Digit, Is_Hexadecimal_Digit, Is_Alphanumeric, Is_Special and Is_ISO_646.

Remember that the type Character covers the full Latin-1 set and thus includes many accented letters and other less familiar characters. The upper case letters are A to Z and those in 192..222 (excluding 215 which is multiplication); the lower case are a to z and those in 223..255 (excluding 247 which is division). The basic letters are A to Z plus AE Diphthong (198), Icelandic Eth (208), Icelandic Thorn (222) and their lower case versions (a to z, 230, 240, 254) plus German Sharp S which only has a lower case form (223). The general rule is that the lower case letter is 32 more than the upper case one. An oddity is lower case y Diaeresis (255) which does not have an upper case form. The various categories are summarized in Table 20.1.

The functions

> **function** To_Lower(Item: **in** Character) **return** Character;
> **function** To_Lower(Item: **in** String) **return** String;

convert an individual character or a whole string to lower case (characters not originally upper case are unchanged). There are also functions To_Upper and To_Basic. The last converts to characters without diacritical marks.

There are also functions to check for and convert to the 7-bit set ISO 646

```
function Is_ISO_646(Item: in String) return Boolean;
function To_ISO_646(Item: in String;
                            Substitute: in ISO_646 := ' ') return String;
```

where ISO_646 is a subtype of Character covering 0..127. The conversion function replaces all characters not in ISO 646 by the substitute character. There are similar functions with the same identifiers for individual characters.

Finally there are functions to check for and convert to and from the 16-bit set Wide_Character

```
function Is_String(Item: in Wide_String) return Boolean;
function To_String(Item: in Wide_String:
                        Substitute: in Character := ' ') return String;
function To_Wide_String(Item: in String) return Wide_String;
```

with again similar functions for individual characters obtained by replacing String by Character in both the identifiers and profiles.

The package Characters.Latin_1 consists of the declaration of constants giving names to most of the characters so that they can be referred to as, for example, Characters.Latin_1.Exclamation or simply Exclamation given an appropriate use clause. The names are listed in Table 20.2.

There are also a number of alternative names (introduced by renamings). They include: Minus_Sign for Hyphen, NBSP for No_Break_Space, Ring_Above for Degree_Sign and Paragraph_Sign for Pilcrow_Sign.

The obsolete package ASCII internal to Standard also defines names for some characters in the 7-bit set. The names of all the control characters and many of the others are the same as for Latin_1.

String handling is provided by an extensive range of packages

```
Ada.Strings
Ada.Strings.Maps
Ada.Strings.Maps.Constants
Ada.Strings.Fixed
Ada.Strings.Bounded
Ada.Strings.Unbounded
```

The reason for so many packages is that different applications have rather different needs which could not be met by just one approach. There are thus three main packages.

The package Strings.Fixed deals with objects of the type String which of course all individually have a fixed length.

The package Strings.Bounded deals with a string type which has a maximum length but of which only part is in use at any time; since the maximum length will depend upon the application everything is in an inner generic package which takes this length as its sole parameter. The type Bounded_String is private although clearly it will typically be implemented using a discriminated record. The current length of a bounded string is given by a function Length (the lower bound is considered to be one).

Table 20.2   The Latin-1 names.

0.. 15	NUL, SOH, STX, ETX,	EOT, ENQ, ACK, BEL,	BS, HT, LF, VT, FF, CR, SO, SI
16.. 31	DLE, DC1, DC2, DC3,	DC4, NAK, SYN, ETB,	CAN, EM, SUB, ESC, FS, GS, RS, US
32.. 35	Space,	Exclamation,	Quotation, Number_Sign
36.. 39	Dollar_Sign,	Percent_Sign,	Ampersand, Apostrophe
40.. 43	Left_Parenthesis,	Right_Parenthesis,	Asterisk, Plus_Sign
44.. 47	Comma,	Hyphen,	Full_Stop, Solidus
48.. 57	(the digits 0 to 9 are not named)		
58.. 61	Colon,	Semicolon,	Less_Than_Sign, Equals_Sign
62.. 64	Greater_Than_Sign,	Question,	Commercial_At
65.. 90	(the upper case letters A to Z are not named)		
91.. 94	Left_Square_Bracket,	Reverse_Solidus,	Right_Square_Bracket, Circumflex
95..122	Low_Line,	Grave,	LC_A, LC_B, ... LC_Z
123..126	Left_Curly_Bracket,	Vertical_Line,	Right_Curly_Bracket, Tilde
127..130	DEL,	Reserved_128,	Reserved_129, BPH
131..140	NBH,	Reserved_132,	NEL, SSA, ESA, HTS, HTJ, VTS, PLD, PLU
141..153	RI, SS2, SS3, DCS,	PU1, PU2, STS, CCH,	MW, SPA, EPA, SOS, Reserved_153
154..161	SCI, CSI, ST, OSC,	PM, APC,	No_Break_Space, Inverted_Exclamation
162..165	Cent_Sign,	Pound_Sign,	Currency_Sign, Yen_Sign
166..169	Broken_Bar,	Section_Sign,	Diaeresis, Copyright_Sign
170..173	Feminine_Ordinal_Indicator,	Left_Angle_Quotation,	Not_Sign, Soft_Hyphen
174..177	Registered_Trade_Mark_Sign,	Macron,	Degree_Sign, Ring_Above
178..181	Superscript_Two,	Superscript_Three,	Acute, Micro_Sign
182..185	Pilcrow_Sign,	Middle_Dot,	Cedilla, Superscript_One
186..188	Masculine_Ordinal_Indicator,		Right_Angle_Quotation, Fraction_One_Quarter
189..191	Fraction_One_Half,	Fraction_Three_Quarters,	Inverted_Question
192..195	UC_A_Grave,	UC_A_Acute,	UC_A_Circumflex, UC_A_Tilde
196..199	UC_A_Diaeresis,	UC_A_Ring,	UC_AE_Diphthong, UC_C_Cedilla
200..203	UC_E_Grave,	UC_E_Acute,	UC_E_Circumflex, UC_E_Diaeresis
204..207	UC_I_Grave,	UC_I_Acute,	UC_I_Circumflex, UC_I_Diaeresis
208..211	UC_Icelandic_Eth,	UC_N_Tilde,	UC_O_Grave, UC_O_Acute
212..215	UC_O_Circumflex,	UC_O_Tilde,	UC_O_Diaeresis, Multiplication_Sign
216..219	UC_O_Oblique_Strike,	UC_U_Grave,	UC_U_Acute, UC_U_Circumflex
220..223	UC_U_Diaeresis,	UC_Y_Acute,	UC_Icelandic_Thorn, LC_German_Sharp_S
224..227	LC_A_Grave,	LC_A_Acute,	LC_A_Circumflex, LC_A_Tilde
228..231	LC_A_Diaeresis,	LC_A_Ring,	LC_AE_Diphthong, LC_C_Cedilla
232..235	LC_E_Grave,	LC_E_Acute,	LC_E_Circumflex, LC_E_Diaeresis
236..239	LC_I_Grave,	LC_I_Acute,	LC_I_Circumflex, LC_I_Diaeresis
240..243	LC_Icelandic_Eth,	LC_N_Tilde,	LC_O_Grave, LC_O_Acute
244..247	LC_O_Circumflex,	LC_O_Tilde,	LC_O_Diaeresis, Division_Sign
248..251	LC_O_Oblique_Strike,	LC_U_Grave,	LC_U_Acute, LC_U_Circumflex
252..255	LC_U_Diaeresis,	LC_Y_Acute,	LC_Icelandic_Thorn, LC_Y_Diaeresis

The package Strings.Unbounded deals with completely unbounded strings (actually bounded by Integer'Last). The type Unbounded_String is private and clearly has to be implemented using dynamic allocation. Again there is a function Length and the lower bound is one.

The packages Strings.Maps and Strings.Maps.Constants concern mappings between sets of characters; these enable various operations to be performed as modified or qualified by a mapping. We will come back to these later but first consider examples without such complications.

The parent package is as follows

```
package Ada.Strings is
   pragma Pure(Strings);

   Space: constant Character := ' ';
   Wide_Space: constant Wide_Character := ' ';

   Length_Error, Pattern_Error,
                        Index_Error, Translation_Error: exception;

   type Alignment is (Left, Right, Center);
   type Truncation is (Left, Right, Error);
   type Membership is (Inside, Outside);
   type Direction is (Forward, Backward);
   type Trim_End is (Left, Right, Both);
end Ada.Strings;
```

The enumeration types relate to the control of various options and the exceptions naturally get raised when something goes wrong.

We will illustrate all three packages together by considering various common operations. The general idea is that the three styles of strings should be handled in much the same way as far as possible. The main difference is of course the problem of varying size. The unbounded strings cause no problems; the bounded strings only have a problem with the limit on the size. Thus, provided the length is not exceeded, the corresponding operations do the same on both and, in particular, the Length function will return the same value.

But the fixed length strings are fixed and there is no Length function (there is the attribute Length of course). In order to enable much of the functionality to correspond for fixed strings the concept of justification and padding is introduced. The default behaviour is that fixed strings are left justified and any unused space is filled with space characters. So provided the strings being manipulated do not have significant trailing spaces then they will behave much the same as for bounded and unbounded strings.

A related point is that bounded and unbounded strings have a notional lower bound of 1 whereas a fixed string need not; but we will use fixed strings with a lower bound of 1 in our examples.

We will suppose that the bounded package has been instantiated and various objects declared thus

```
use Ada.Strings.Fixed;
use Ada.Strings.Bounded;
use Ada.Strings.Unbounded;
package Bounded_80 is new Generic_Bounded_Length(80);
use Bounded_80;
C: Character;
S: String := ... ;
S5: String(1 .. 5);
```

```
S10: String(1 .. 10);
S15: String(1 .. 15);
BS: Bounded_String;          -- from Bounded_80
US: Unbounded_String;
```

String literals provide values of fixed strings and there are conversion functions for bounded and unbounded strings thus

```
BS := To_Bounded("A Bounded String");
US := To_Unbounded("An Unbounded String");
```

There are also constants Null_Bounded_String and Null_Unbounded_String. Bounded and unbounded strings can be converted to a string by the function To_String. Conversion between bounded and unbounded strings has to be via an intermediate string.

```
US := To_Unbounded(To_String(BS));
```

Assignment for bounded and unbounded strings is performed in the usual way using :=. Bounded strings always fit and unbounded strings will be properly copied using controlled types so that the old and new values do not interfere. Copying of fixed strings of the same length can also be done by assignment. The procedure Move can deal with fixed strings of different lengths; it uses padding characters and justification as mentioned above. The default behaviour is for all operations to be left justified with space used as a right padding character; strings can then be copied naturally with extra spaces added on the right or removed from the right as necessary; if the destination is too short so that nonpadding characters would be lost then an exception is raised (Length_Error). The justification and padding/trimming options are controlled by various parameters with defaults.

```
procedure Move(Source: in String;
               Target: out String;
               Drop: in Truncation := Error;
               Justify: in Alignment := Left;
               Pad: in Character := Space);
```

Justification on padding can be to the right or even to the centre (with any odd extra padding character on the right). For trimming, if Drop is Left or Right, then an exception is not raised and characters simply lost from the end specified; otherwise if Drop is Error then only padding characters can be removed (from the opposite end to that given by Justify) and Length_Error raised if necessary as mentioned above. So

```
Move("Barbara", S10);              -- "Barbara "
Move(S10, S5, Drop => Right);      -- "Barba"
```

where there are three spaces at the end of the first string.

Bounded strings can be built up using "&" which is overloaded for a bounded string with a character, string or another bounded string; similarly for unbounded strings. (Other combinations would cause irritating ambiguities at times.)

The mechanism of dropping characters is also relevant for some operations on bounded strings. For example, since "&" will always raise Length_Error if an attempt is made to create an oversize bounded string, alternative subprograms Append are provided which give greater control. They have a third optional parameter Drop which causes extra characters to be lost if its value is Left or Right, or Length_Error to be raised if it is Error (the default). The functions Append return the required result, whereas procedures Append update the first parameter. So assuming BS has the value "Barbara", the following assignments are equivalent

```
BS := BS & ' ' & "Barnes";
BS := Append(BS, ' ' & "Barnes");
Append(BS, " Barnes");
```

and all give Barbara her surname. For convenience Append procedures also exist for unbounded strings but of course need no third parameter.

Extracting or replacing a single character or part of a string at a known position is easy for fixed strings since normal indexing and slice operations can be used. For bounded and unbounded strings, subprograms are provided. We can write

```
C := Element(US, I);                -- extract Ith element
Replace_Element(US, I, C);          -- replace Ith element
S(I .. J) := Slice(US, I, J);       -- extract elements I to J
Replace_Slice(US, I, J, S(I .. J)); -- replace elements I to J
```

with appropriate sliding as necessary.

The procedures Replace_Slice (there is also a version for fixed strings) can actually insert either a greater or lesser number of elements than those removed. An unbounded string can always adjust to the required size. A bounded string is limited by Max_Length and the behaviour is then controlled by an additional parameter Drop with default Error. In the case of fixed strings there are two further parameters, Justify and Pad, as for the subprogram Move. Finally, there are equivalent functions Replace_Slice which just return the appropriate result and do not alter the original string; in the case of fixed strings no parameters for padding and trimming are required. So we can elevate Barbara by

```
Lady: Bounded_String;
...
Lady := Replace_Slice(BS, 4, 7, "oness");   -- "Baroness Barnes"
```

Searching for patterns is performed by Index which returns the index of the start of the pattern or 0 if no match is found. The direction of search is given by the optional parameter Going which can be Forward from the beginning (by default) or Backward. Thus, continuing the theme, but reverting to a commoner

```
BS := To_Bounded("Barbara Barnes");
Index(BS, "bar")                        -- is 4
Index(BS, "Bar")                        -- is 1
Index(BS, "Bar", Backward)              -- is 9
```

There are versions of Index for fixed, bounded and unbounded strings.

This is possibly a good moment to introduce the idea of character mappings. These enable searches and other operations to be generalized. The private type Character_Mapping is defined in the package Strings.Maps; a value of the type defines a mapping between characters, and the mapped character is given by the function

```
function Value(Map: Character_Mapping;
               Element: Character) return Character;
```

Some standard mappings are defined in Strings.Maps.Constants. An example is the mapping Lower_Case_Map which maps upper case characters onto the corresponding lower case character and leaves others unchanged. So Value(Lower_Case_Map, 'B') is 'b'. The other predefined maps are Upper_Case_Map and Basic_Map where the latter corresponds to Characters. Handling.To_Basic.

We can now search a string without concern for case by

```
Index(BS, "bar", Forward, Lower_Case_Map)     -- is 1
```

Another version of Index looks for the first of a set of characters. This uses the type Character_Set also defined in Strings.Maps. Again this type is private and a number of constants are defined in Strings.Maps.Constants with names such as Control_Set, Graphic_Set, Letter_Set, Lower_Set corresponding exactly to the functions Is_Control, Is_Graphic and so on. (Oddly there is no Digit_Set and we have to use the equivalent Decimal_Digit_Set.) Thus we can search for the first lower case letter by

```
Index(BS, Set => Lower_Set)                   -- is 2
```

Additional optional parameters (Test and Going) enable us to search for the first character outside the set and also specify the direction of search. Thus

```
Index(BS, Lower_Set, Outside, Forward)        -- is 1
```

because the first character not in the lower case set has index one.

Other forms of search enable us to count the number of matches so

```
Count(BS, "Bar")                        -- is 2
Count(BS, "BAR", Upper_Case_Map)        -- is 3
Count(BS, Lower_Set)                     -- is 11
```

and we can also look for a sequence all of whose characters satisfy some condition. Thus

    Find_Token(BS, Lower_Set, Inside, I, J)

sets I to 2 and J to 7 because the slice BS(2) .. BS(7) is the first slice whose characters are all inside the lower case set. The largest such slice which is first is chosen. If there were no such slice then I would be set to 1 and J to 0. (Find_Token for a fixed string S would return S'First which might not be 1.)

Although Replace_Slice is very flexible, some other subprograms are provided for convenience, thus a string can be inserted before a given location by Insert

    Insert(BS, 9, "W ");   -- "Barbara W Barnes"
    -- same as Replace_Slice(BS, 9, 8, "W ");

and removed by Delete

    Delete(BS, 2, 7);   -- "B W Barnes"
    -- same as Replace_Slice(BS, 2, 7, "");

A part can be overwritten by Overwrite

    Overwrite(BS, 2, "ob");   -- "Bob Barnes"
    -- same as Replace_Slice(BS, 2, 3, "ob");

and the new section extends the string if necessary with all the usual options. Functional forms of Insert, Delete and Overwrite are also provided.

The subprograms Trim enable space characters to removed from one or both ends. Thus

    Trim(BS, Side => Left);   -- deletes leading spaces
    Trim(BS, Side => Both);   -- deletes leading and trailing spaces

Another version of Trim gives the character sets which are to be removed for both ends. Thus

    Trim(BS, Left => Decimal_Digit_Set, Right => Null_Set);

deletes leading digits but deletes no trailing characters. For fixed strings the procedure Trim has the odd effect of typically having to add padding characters after doing any trimming. Functional forms of Trim also exist.

Subprograms Head and Tail produce a string comprising a given number of characters from the head or tail respectively. So

    Head(BS, 3)   -- "Bob"
    Tail(BS, 6)   -- "Barnes"

If the original string is not long enough then additional padding characters are added at the end for Head and at the beginning for Tail (this is the one case where padding is required for bounded and unbounded strings; it is normally only needed for fixed strings of course). A final optional parameter Drop exists for bounded strings; if the requested number of characters exceeds Max_Length then superfluous characters are dropped as for Replace_Slice; any such dropping is performed after any padding spaces are added. A curiosity is that the procedural form for fixed strings does not have this optional parameter but always raises Length_Error if nonpadding characters would have to be dropped. So

```
S5 := "ABCDE";
Head(S5, 6, Justify => Left);            -- "ABCDE"
Head(S5, 6, Justify => Right);           -- Length_Error
```

where in the second case the attempt to right justify the string "ABCDE " would require the nonpadding character 'A' to be dropped. However, the bizarre statement

```
Head(S5, 6, Justify := Right; Pad := 'A');     -- "BCDE "
```

would succeed.

Appropriate overloadings of "*" create strings which are replications of characters or strings. The first parameter is the number of replications and the second is a character or string. So

```
BS := 2 * "Bar";          -- "BarBar"
US := 3 * 'A';            -- "AAA"
S15 := 5 * "SOS";         -- "SOSSOSSOSSOSSOS"
```

There are also similar functions Replicate for bounded strings with an optional parameter Drop in the same way that Append relates to "&".

The various relational operators are defined between two bounded strings and between a string and a bounded string. And similarly for unbounded strings but they are not defined between a bounded string and an unbounded string; such a comparison can be performed after first converting both to strings.

Finally, the subprograms Translate enable a string to be converted using a translation defined by a character mapping. As usual there are both functional and procedural forms for the three kinds of strings. So using functions

```
Translate("Barbara", Lower_Case_Map)     -- "barbara"
Translate("Café", Basic_Map)             -- "Cafe"
```

where in the last case the sophisticated café is degraded into a mundane cafe.

The user will often want to use mappings other than those provided as standard. This can be done by writing a character mapping function whose profile corresponds to

```
type Character_Mapping_Function is
     access function (From: in Character) return Character;
```

For example suppose we want to remove the accents from all upper case letters but not the lower case letters (this is a common style in French literature). We would declare

```
function Upper_Basic(C: in Character) return Character is
begin
  if Is_Upper(C) then
    return To_Basic(C);
  else
    return C;
  end if;
end Upper_Basic;
```

and then we can use a version of Translate which takes a parameter of the type Character_Mapping_Function rather than the type Character_Mapping as in the previous examples. So

```
Translate("Été", Upper_Basic'Access)      -- "Eté"
```

Character mapping functions can also be used with the subprograms Index and Count.

Another approach is to create our own values of the private type Character_Mapping. This is done by calling the function

```
function To_Mapping(From, To: Character_Sequence)
                              return Character_Mapping;
```

where the subtype Character_Sequence is simply a renaming of String for readability. The two parameters must be sequences of the same length and there must be no repetition in the first. Characters in the first sequence map to characters in the corresponding position in the second sequence and other characters remain unchanged. Thus if we wanted a map that just made all square brackets and curly brackets into round brackets then we would write

```
Bracket_Map: Character_Mapping := To_Mapping("{}[]", "()()");
Translate(US, Bracket_Map);
```

which would apply the mapping to the unbounded string US. Reverse functions To_Domain and To_Range return the domain and range of a mapping if desired. There is also a constant Identity giving the identity map which is used as a default parameter.

As noted earlier, the subprograms Count, Find_Token and Trim can take parameters of the type Character_Set and again we will want to define our own values. Although this type is also private, various subprograms are provided in the package Strings.Maps to enable the general manipulation of objects of this type. (Remember that this type defines a set of characters in the mathematical sense and not a complete set such as Latin-1 in the standard sense.)

A character set can be created by various functions To_Set which can take
a single character, a string (a character sequence), a single character range, or
finally an array of character ranges. The last are defined by

```
type Character_Range is
   record
      Low, High: Character;
   end record;

type Character_Ranges is
      array (Positive range <>) of Character_Range;
```

and so possible calls of functions To_Set are

```
S: Character_Set;
...
S := To_Set('?');                     -- a single character
S := To_Set("AEIOU");                 -- a string
S := To_Set(('0', '9'));              -- a range
S := To_Set((('A', 'Z'), ('a', 'z')));   -- an array of two ranges
```

Note that any duplicate characters are ignored.

Operations on character sets are "=", "not", "and", "or", "xor" with obvious
meanings; "–" is such that X – Y is the same as X **and not** Y; Is_Subset and its
renaming "<=" are such that X <= Y returns true if X is a subset of Y. The
function Is_In(C, S) returns true if the character C is in the set S. Finally, there
is a constant Null_Set, a function To_Ranges that turns a set back into the
ordered minimal array of ranges and a function To_Sequence that turns a set
back into an ordered sequence.

As a trivial example, suppose we wish to find the index of the last non-
blank character in a string. The character set consisting of just the space
character is given by To_Set(Space) and so all we need is

```
Index(BS, To_Set(Space), Outside, Backward)
```

and in fact, since this is a common requirement, the function Index_Non_Blank
does this directly

```
Index_Non_Blank(BS, Backward)
```

A more realistic example might be

```
Index(BS, To_Set(('0', '7')))
```

which finds the first octal digit.

We conclude our survey of the string handling facilities by noting that the
various exceptions are raised as follows

Length_Error	Result will not fit (fixed or bounded).
Pattern_Error	Pattern is null for Index or Count.

Table 20.3 Auxiliary parameters for string subprograms.

Name	Second and other parameters	Notes
Index	Pattern: String; Going: Direction := Forward; Mapping: Character_Mapping := Identity	
Index	Pattern: String; Going: Direction := Forward; Mapping: Character_Mapping_Function	
Index	Set: Character_Set; Test: Membership := Inside; Going: Direction := Forward	
Index_Non_Blank	Going: Direction := Forward	
Count	Pattern: String; Mapping: Character_Mapping := Identity	
Count	Pattern: String; Mapping: Character_Mapping_Function	
Count	Set: Character_Set	
Find_Token	Set: Character_Set; Test: Membership; First: **out** Positive; Last: **out** Natural	
Translate	Mapping: Character_Mapping	
Translate	Mapping: Character_Mapping_Function	
Replace_Slice	Low: Positive; High: Natural; By: String	1, 2
Insert	Before: Positive; New_Item: String	1
Overwrite	Position: Positive; New_Item: String	1
Delete	From: Positive; Through: Natural	2
Trim	Side: Trim_End	2
Trim	Left, Right: Character_Set	2
Head	Count: Natural; Pad: Character := Space	3, 4
Tail	Count: Natural; Pad: Character := Space	3, 4
Notes	Extra parameters for fixed functions and bounded subprograms	Types
1	Drop: Truncation := Error	bnd/fixed
2	Justify: Alignment := Left; Pad: Character := Space	fixed
3	Drop: Truncation := Error (after Pad)	bounded
4	Justify: Alignment := Left (between Count and Pad)	fixed

Index_Error   Index(es) outside string for Element, Replace_Element, Slice or Replace_Slice.

Translation_Error Parameters of To_Mapping are incorrect.

Although the survey has been brief it has covered all the topics and the reader ought to be able to use the packages to the full from the description given here. For convenience the main subprograms (which all apply to fixed, bounded and unbounded strings) are listed in Table 20.3. This shows the second and other parameters. The first parameter is always called Source and it and the result are of the type String, Bounded_String or Unbounded_String where appropriate. Find_Token only exists as a procedure. Count and Index only exist as functions with result Natural. Some procedures for fixed strings and procedures and functions for bounded strings have additional parameters for padding and trimming as shown.

There is also a hierarchy of packages Ada.Wide_Strings for manipulating wide strings with a similar structure to Ada.Strings.

EXERCISE 20.2

1   Search the string S for the first character which is either a decimal digit or decimal point.

2   Evaluate

    To_Sequence(To_Set(To_Upper("O Sodom seems doomed!")));

3   A simple encryption algorithm is based on a keyword K ignoring any repeating letters. These letters are placed in lexicographic order followed by the remaining letters of the alphabet in lexicographic order. This sequence then defines the result of mapping the alphabet. Define such a mapping which works on either case of the usual alphabet and leaves other characters unchanged. Use the mapping to encrypt a string S using the keyword "Byron".

4   Given a mapping M write a function Decode which returns the reverse mapping. Raise Translation_Error if the original mapping was not (1, 1). Use this function to decode the message of the previous exercise.

20.3   Numerics

The numeric library was introduced in Section 4.3 where we observed that the package Ada.Numerics contained the constants Pi and e plus the exception Argument_Error. The child packages of Numerics provided by the core language are

    Numerics.Discrete_Random
    Numerics.Float_Random
    Numerics.Generic_Elementary_Functions

plus nongeneric forms of the last for the predefined types with the names

    Numerics.Elementary_Functions   -- for Float
    Numerics.Long_Elementary_Functions   -- for Long_Float

and so on.

The Numerics annex defines additional packages for dealing with complex numbers; see Section 22.5.

Although numerical applications are in a minority, we will nevertheless consider the elementary functions package in some detail because it provides a good illustration of the use of generics and other key features of Ada.

As we will see, the package provides ease of casual use for simple calculations, the ability to provide the ultimate in accuracy for serious numerical work, as well as portability across different implementations.

The package specification is as follows

```
generic
  type Float_Type is digits <>;
package Ada.Numerics.Generic_Elementary_Functions is
  pragma Pure(Generic_Elementary_Functions);

  -- subtype FTB is Float_Type'Base;

  function Sqrt(X: FTB) return FTB;
  function Log(X: FTB) return FTB;
  function Log(X, Base: FTB) return FTB;
  function Exp(X: FTB) return FTB;
  function "**" (Left, Right: FTB) return FTB;

  function Sin(X: FTB) return FTB;
  function Sin(X, Cycle: FTB) return FTB;
  -- similarly Cos, Tan, Cot, Arcsin, Arccos

  function Arctan(Y: FTB; X: FTB := 1.0) return FTB;
  function Arctan(Y: FTB; X: FTB := 1.0; Cycle: FTB) return FTB;
  function Arccot(X: FTB; Y: FTB := 1.0) return FTB;
  function Arccot(X: FTB; Y: FTB := 1.0; Cycle: FTB) return FTB;

  function Sinh(X: FTB) return FTB;
  function Arcsinh(X: FTB) return FTB;
  -- similarly Cosh, Tanh, Coth, Arccosh, Arctanh, Arccoth

end Ada.Numerics.Generic_Elementary_Functions;
```

where we have written FTB as an abbreviation for Float_Type'Base.

The single generic parameter is the floating type. The package might be instantiated with a user's own type such as My_Float

```
package My_Elementary_Functions is
  new Generic_Elementary_Functions(My_Float);
```

The body could then choose an implementation appropriate to the accuracy of the user's type through the attribute Float_Type'Digits rather than necessarily using the accuracy of the predefined type from which the user's type has been derived. This could have significant timing advantages.

The package can also be instantiated with a constrained subtype such as

```
subtype Normal is Float range –1.0 .. +1.0;
```

which might occur if the user was dealing with data which was known to be in such a range. Note however, that the parameters and results of the various functions use Float_Type'Base and so there are no constraint checks on passing the parameters or on returning results.

Moreover, the body of the package will undoubtedly declare working variables for use in the algorithms and these can similarly be declared

```
Local: Float_Type'Base;
```

so that any constraints on the actual subtype do not apply to the internal calculations.

We continue by considering the individual functions in the package. The functions Sqrt and Exp need little comment except perhaps concerning exceptions. Calling Sqrt with a negative parameter will raise Argument_Error whereas calling Exp with a large parameter will raise Constraint_Error.

The general principle is that intrinsic mathematical restrictions raise Argument_Error whereas implementation range restrictions raise Constraint_Error.

There are two overloadings of Log. That with a single parameter gives the natural logarithm to base e, whereas that with two parameters allows us to choose any base at all. Thus to find $log_{10}2$, we write

    Log(2.0, 10.0)   -- 0.3010 ...

The reader may wonder why there is not just a single function with a default parameter thus

        function Log(X: Float_Type'Base; Base: Float_Type'Base := e)
                                        return Float_Type'Base;

which would seem to give the desired result with less fuss. The reason concerns obtaining the ultimate in precision. Passing a default parameter means that the accuracy of the value of e used can only be that of the Float_Type. Using a separate function enables the function body to obtain the benefit of the full accuracy of the universal real named number Numerics.e.

The restrictions on the parameters of Log are X > 0.0, Base > 0.0 and also Base /= 1.0. So Base could be 0.5 which is an amusing thought.

The function "**" effectively extends the predefined operator to allow non-integral exponents. Consequently the formal parameters are Left and Right to match (the other functions follow mathematical convention and use X and Y). The parameter Left must not be negative.

The trigonometric functions Sin, Cos, Tan and Cot also come in pairs like Log and for a similar reason. The single parameter versions assume the parameter is in radians whereas the second parameter allows the use of any unit by giving the number of units in a whole cycle. Thus to find the sine of 30 degrees, we write

    Sin(30.0, 360.0)   -- 0.5

because there are 360 degrees in a cycle.

In these functions the single parameter versions enable the highly accurate number Numerics.Pi to be used directly rather than being passed with less accuracy as a parameter.

The inverse functions, Arcsin and Arccos, are straightforward; the result of Arcsin is in the range $-\pi/2$ to $+\pi/2$, and that of Arccos is in the range 0 to π. However, Arctan has a default value of 1.0 for a second parameter (the Cycle then being third). This enables us to call Arctan with two parameters giving the classical x- and y-coordinates (thus fully identifying the quadrant). So

```
Arctan(Y => –1.0, X => +1.0)          -- –Pi/4
Arctan(Y => +1.0, X => –1.0)          -- +3*Pi/4
```

Note carefully that the first parameter of Arctan is Y since it is the *x*-coordinate that is taken to be 1.0 by default. Arccot is very similar except that the parameters are naturally in the other order.

Arctan and Arccot are examples where the question of signed zeros may make a difference. If Float_Type'Signed_Zeros is true then Arctan(Y, X) and Arccot(X, Y) where X is negative and Y is zero return $+\pi$ if Y is a positive zero and $-\pi$ if Y is a negative zero; if Signed_Zeros is false then the result is always $+\pi$.

There are no obvious comments to make on the hyperbolic functions or their inverses.

The random number packages were briefly introduced in Chapter 4. The full specification of the floating point package is

```
package Ada.Numerics.Float_Random is

    type Generator is limited private;
    subtype Uniformly_Distributed is Float range 0.0 .. 1.0;
    function Random(Gen: Generator) return Uniformly_Distributed;

    procedure Reset(Gen: in Generator; Initiator: in Integer);
    procedure Reset(Gen: in Generator);

    type State is private;
    procedure Save(Gen: in Generator; To_State: out State);
    procedure Reset(Gen: in Generator; From_State; in State);
    Max_Image_Width: constant := implementation–defined;
    function Image(Of_State: State) return String;
    function Value(Coded_State: String) return State;
private
    ...
end Ada.Numerics.Float_Random;
```

A pseudo-random sequence of values of the type Float uniformly distributed in the range 0.0 .. 1.0 is obtained by declaring an object of the type Generator and then calling the function Random with that object as parameter much as in the example in Chapter 4 for the generic package Discrete_Random.

Other distributions can be obtained by transforming the uniform distribution with a suitable function. Note that the end values 0.0 and 1.0 might or might not be produced. Thus an exponential distribution with mean and variance 1.0 can be obtained by the transformation

```
–Log(Random(G) + Float'Model_Small)
```

where the addition of the smallest possible number ensures that Log never has the parameter zero and thus never raises an exception.

Different sequences can be obtained by calling Reset. The version with just the generator as parameter initiates a sequence whose starting state depends upon the time and so will not be reproducible. The version with the additional integer parameter initiates a reproducible sequence corresponding to the value of the integer. Reproducible sequences are often important for debugging purposes. (Note that if we do not call Reset at all then we always get the same sequence which is boring and statistically unhelpful but useful for trivial programs.)

The internal state of the generator can be preserved and then restored by calling Save and Reset with the parameter of the type State. A sequence can thus be stopped, analysed and we can then carry on from where it was stopped. The saved value could even be written to a file and used in a different execution of the program. Finally, the functions Image and Value enable such a state to be converted to and from a string for the ultimate in external representation; the maximum length of string required is given by Max_Image_Width.

The mechanisms for resetting and saving the state of the generators for the package Discrete_Random are just the same.

EXERCISE 20.3

1   Write a body for the package Simple_Maths of Exercise 2.2(**1**) using the package Elementary_Functions. Raise Constraint_Error for all exceptional circumstances.

2   Simulate a game of paper, stone and scissors between Jack and Jill. Paper wraps the · stone, the stone blunts the scissors, and the scissors cut the paper. Give each player their own generator.

20.4   Input and output

Unlike many other languages, Ada does not have any intrinsic features for input–output. Instead existing general features such as subprogram overloading and generic instantiation are used. This has the merit of enabling different input–output packages to be developed for different application areas without affecting the language itself. On the other hand this approach can lead to a consequential risk of anarchy in this area; the (older) reader may recall that this was one of the reasons for the downfall of Algol 60. In order to prevent such anarchy the *ARM* defines standard packages for input–output.

Two categories of input–output are recognized and we can refer to these as binary and text respectively. As an example consider

    I: Integer := 75;

We can output the binary image of I onto file F by

    Write(F, I);

and the pattern transmitted might be (on a 16-bit machine)

```
0000 0000 0100 1011
```

In fact the file can be thought of as essentially an array of the type Integer. On the other hand we can output the text form of I by

```
Put(F, I);
```

and the pattern transmitted might then be

```
0011 0111 0011 0101
```

which is the representation of the characters '7' and '5'. In this case the file can be thought of as an array of the type Character.

Input–output of the binary category is in turn subdivided into sequential and direct access and is provided by distinct generic packages Ada.Sequential_IO and Ada.Direct_IO respectively. Text input–output (which is always sequential) is provided by the non-generic package Ada.Text_IO.

These forms of input–output result in uniform files containing objects all of the same type. This is often too restrictive and accordingly a general stream mechanism is defined which allows files of arbitrary types; these are implemented using the facilities of the package Ada.Streams.

There is also a package Ada.IO_Exceptions which contains the declarations of the exceptions used by the other packages. We will deal here first with Sequential_IO and then with Direct_IO and consider Text_IO and Streams in subsequent sections.

The specification of the package Sequential_IO is as follows

```
with Ada.IO_Exceptions;
generic
   type Element_Type(<>) is private;
package Ada.Sequential_IO is
   type File_Type is limited private;
   type File_Mode is (In_File, Out_File, Append_File);

   -- File management

   procedure Create(File: in out File_Type;
                    Mode: in File_Mode := Out_File;
                    Name: in String := "";
                    Form: in String := "");
   procedure Open(File: in out File_Type;
                  Mode: in File_Mode;
                  Name: in String;
                  Form: in String := "");
   procedure Close(File: in out File_Type);
   procedure Delete(File: in out File_Type);
   procedure Reset(File: in out File_Type;
                   Mode: in File_Mode);
```

```
procedure Reset(File: in out File_Type);
function Mode(File: in File_Type) return File_Mode;
function Name(File: in File_Type) return String;
function Form(File: in File_Type) return String;
function Is_Open(File: in File_Type) return Boolean;

-- Input and output operations

procedure Read(File: in File_Type; Item: out Element_Type);
procedure Write(File: in File_Type; Item: in Element_Type);
function End_Of_File(File: in File_Type) return Boolean;

-- Exceptions

Status_Error: exception renames IO_Exceptions.Status_Error;
...
Data_Error: exception renames IO_Exceptions.Data_Error;
private
-- implementation dependent
end Ada.Sequential_IO;
```

The package has a single generic parameter giving the type of element to be manipulated. Note that limited types cannot be handled since the generic formal parameter is private rather than limited private. However, the formal parameter is indefinite and so the actual type can be an indefinite type such as String or a class wide type.

Externally a file has a name which is a string but internally we refer to a file by using objects of type File_Type. An open file also has an associated value of the enumeration type File_Mode; there are three possible values, In_File provides read-only access, Out_File provides write-only access starting at the beginning of the file and Append_File provides write-only access starting at the end of the file. Read-write access is not allowed for sequential files. The mode of a file is originally set when the file is opened or created but can be changed later by a call of the procedure Reset. Manipulation of sequential files is done using various subprograms whose behaviour is generally as expected.

As an example, suppose we have a file containing measurements of various populations and that we wish to compute the sum of these measurements. The populations are recorded as values of type Integer and the name of the file is "Census 47". (The actual conventions for the external file name are dependent upon the implementation.) The computed sum is to be written onto a new file to be called "Total 47". This could be done by the following program

```
with Ada.Sequential_IO; use Ada;
procedure Compute_Total_Population is
   package Integer_IO is new Sequential_IO(Integer);
   use Integer_IO;

   Data_File: File_Type;
   Result_File: File_Type;
   Value: Integer;
   Total: Integer := 0;
```

```
      begin
        Open(Data_File, In_File, "Census 47");

        while not End_Of_File(Data_File) loop
          Read(Data_File, Value);
          Total := Total+Value;
        end loop;
        Close(Data_File);

        -- now write the result

        Create(Result_File, Name => "Total 47");
        Write(Result_File, Total);
        Close(Result_File);
      end Compute_Total_Population;
```

We start by instantiating the generic package Sequential_IO with the actual parameter Integer. It is convenient to add a use clause.

The file with the data to be read is referred to via the object Data_File and the output file is referred to via the object Result_File of the type File_Type. Note that this type is limited private; this enables the implementation to use techniques similar to those described in Section 11.6 where we discussed the example of the key manager.

The call of Open establishes the object Data_File as referring to the external file "Census 47" and sets its mode as read-only. The external file is then opened for reading and positioned at the beginning.

We then obey the loop statement until the function End_Of_File indicates that the end of the file has been reached. On each iteration the call of Read copies the item into Value and positions the file at the next item. Total is then updated. When all the values on the file have been read, it is closed by a call of Close.

The call of Create creates a new external file named "Total 47" and establishes Result_File as referring to it and sets its mode by default to write-only. We then write our total onto the file and then close it.

The procedures Create and Open have a further parameter Form; this is provided so that auxiliary implementation dependent information can be specified; the default value is a null string so its use is not mandatory. Note that the Name parameter of Create also has a default null value; such a value corresponds to a temporary file. The procedures Close and Delete both close the file and thereby sever the connection between the file variable and the external file. The variable can then be reused for another file. Delete also destroys the external file if the implementation so allows.

The overloaded procedures Reset cause a file to be repositioned as for Open. Reset can also change the access mode so that, for example, having written a file, we can now read it. Or perhaps having read it, we can now write further items to it starting at the end.

The functions Mode, Name and Form return the corresponding properties of the file. The function Is_Open indicates whether the file is open; that is indicates whether the file variable is associated with an external file or not.

The procedures Read and Write automatically reposition the file ready for a subsequent call so that the file is processed sequentially. The function End_Of_File only applies to an input file and returns true if there are no more elements to be read.

If we do something wrong then one of the exceptions in the package Ada.IO_Exceptions will be raised. This package is as follows

```
package Ada.IO_Exceptions is
   pragma Pure(IO_Exceptions);
   Status_Error, Mode_Error, Name_Error, Use_Error,
         Device_Error, End_Error, Data_Error, Layout_Error: exception;
end Ada.IO_Exceptions;
```

This is an example of a package that does not need a body. The various exceptions are declared in this package rather than in Sequential_IO so that the same exceptions apply to all instantiations of Sequential_IO. If they were inside Sequential_IO then each instantiation would create different exceptions and this would be rather more inconvenient in the case of a program manipulating files of various types since general purpose exception handlers would need to refer to all the instances. The renaming declarations on the other hand enable the exceptions to be referred to without use of the name IO_Exceptions.

The following brief summary gives the general flavour of the circumstances giving rise to each exception

Status_Error	File is open when expected to be closed or vice versa.
Mode_Error	File of wrong mode, for example, In_File when should be Out_File.
Name_Error	Something wrong with Name parameter of Create or Open.
Use_Error	Various such as unacceptable Form parameter or trying to print on card reader.
Device_Error	Physical device broken or not switched on.
End_Error	Malicious attempt to read beyond end of file.
Data_Error	Read or Get (see next section) cannot interpret data as value of desired type.
Layout_Error	Something wrong with layout in Text_IO (see next section) or Put overfills string parameter.

For fuller details of which exception is actually raised in various circumstances the reader is referred to the *ARM* and to the documentation for the implementation concerned.

We continue by considering the package Direct_IO which is very similar to Sequential_IO but gives us more flexibility by enabling us to manipulate the file position directly.

As mentioned earlier a file can be considered as a one-dimensional array. The elements in the file are ordered and each has an associated positive index.

This ranges from 1 to an upper value which can change since elements can be added to the end of the file. Not all elements necessarily have a defined value in the case of a direct file as we shall see.

Associated with a direct file is a current index which indicates the position of the next element to be transferred. When a file is opened or created this index is set to 1 so that the program is ready to read or write the first element. The main difference between sequential and direct input–output is that in the sequential case this index is implicit and can only be altered by calls of Read, Write and Reset whereas in the direct case, the index is explicit and can be directly manipulated. One consequence of this is that the generic parameter takes the definite form

```
generic
   type Element_Type is private;
package Ada.Direct_IO is ...
```

and so the actual parameter must also be definite; this ensures that the values occupy the same space so that indexing is straightforward.

The extra facilities of Direct_IO are as follows. The enumeration type File_Mode has a value Inout_File (and not Append_File) so that read-write access is possible; this is also the default mode when a new file is created (thus the Mode parameter of Create has a different default for direct and sequential files). The type and subtype

```
type Count is range 0 .. implementation–defined;
subtype Positive_Count is Count range 1 .. Count'Last;
```

are introduced so that the current index can be referred to and finally there are various extra subprograms whose specifications are as follows

```
procedure Read(File: in File_Type; Item: out Element_Type;
                    From: in Positive_Count);
procedure Write(File: in File_Type; Item: in Element_Type;
                    To: in Positive_Count);
procedure Set_Index(File: in File_Type;
                        To: in Positive_Count);
function Index(File: in File_Type) return Positive_Count;
function Size(File: in File_Type) return Count;
```

The extra overloadings of Read and Write first position the current index to the value given by the third parameter and then behave as before. A call of Index returns the current index value; Set_Index sets the current index to the given value and a call of Size returns the number of elements in the file. Note that a file cannot have holes in it; all elements from 1 to Size exist although some may not have defined values.

As an illustration of the manipulation of these positions we can alter our example to use Direct_IO and we can then write the total population onto the end of an existing file called "Totals". The last few statements then become

```
         -- now write the result
      Open(Result_File, Out_File, "Totals");
      Set_Index(Result_File, Size(Result_File)+1);
      Write(Result_File, Total);
      Close(Result_File);
   end Compute_Total_Population;
```

Note that if we set the current index well beyond the end of the file and then write to it, the result will be to add several undefined elements to the file and then finally the newly written element.

Note also that the language does not define whether it is possible to write a file with Sequential_IO and then read it with Direct_IO or vice versa. This depends upon the implementation.

EXERCISE 20.4

1   Write a generic library procedure to copy a file to another file but with the elements in reverse order. Pass the external names as parameters.

20.5   Text input–output

Text input–output, which we met in Chapter 4, is the more familiar form and provides two overloaded procedures Put and Get to transmit values as streams of characters as well as various other subprograms such as New_Line for layout control. In addition the concept of current default files is introduced so that every call of the various subprograms need not tiresomely repeat the file name. Thus if F is the current default output file, we can write

```
      Put("Message");
```

rather than

```
      Put(F, "Message");
```

There are two current default files, one of mode Out_File for output, and one of mode In_File for input. Text_IO is like Sequential_IO and also has a mode Append_File but not Inout_File.

When we enter our program these two files are set to standard default files which are automatically open; we can assume that these are attached to convenient external files such as keyboard and screen or (in olden days) a card reader and line printer. If we wish to use other files and want to avoid repeating the file names in the calls of Put and Get then we can change the default files to refer to our other files. We can also set them back to their original values. This is done with subprograms

```
procedure Set_Output(File: File_Type);
function Standard_Output return File_Type;
function Current_Output return File_Type;

type File_Access is access constant File_Type;
function Standard_Output return File_Access;
function Current_Output return File_Access;
```

with similar subprograms for input. The procedure Set_Output enables us to change the current default output file to the file passed as parameter, the two functions Standard_Output return the initial default output file and the two functions Current_Output return the current default output file (directly or indirectly respectively).

Thus we could bracket a fragment of program with

```
New_File: File_Type;
...
Open(New_File, ... );
Set_Output(New_File);
... -- use Put
Set_Output(Standard_Output);
```

so that having used the file New_File, we can reset the default file to its standard value.

The more general case is where we wish to reset the default file to its previous value which may, of course, not be the standard value. The reader may recall that the type File_Type is limited private and therefore values cannot be assigned; hence the version of Current_Output returning an access value is useful. We could write

```
Old_File_Ref: constant File_Access := Current_Output;
...
Set_Output(New_File);
... -- use Put
Set_Output(Old_File_Ref.all);
```

An alternative approach is to note that the result of a function can be renamed

```
Old_File: File_Type renames Currrent_Output;
...
Set_Output(Old_File);
```

although this is less flexible since the value cannot be stored.

For convenience there is also a default error file for the user to output

messages; this has an initial standard value and there are similar subprograms
to manipulate this error file. A typical use might be in an exception handler

```
exception
   when Event: others =>
      Put(Current_Error, Exception_Message(Event));
```

which thereby avoids cluttering whatever file might be used for the current
normal output.

The full specification of Text_IO is rather long and so only the general
form is reproduced here

```
with Ada.IO_Exceptions;
package Ada.Text_IO is
   type File_Type is limited private;
   type File_Mode is (In_File, Out_File, Append_File);

   type Count is range 0 .. implementation-defined;
   subtype Positive_Count is Count range 1 .. Count'Last;
   Unbounded: constant Count := 0;       -- line and page length

   subtype Field is Integer range 0 .. implementation-defined;
   subtype Number_Base is Integer range 2 .. 16;
   type Type_Set is (Lower_Case, Upper_Case);

   -- File management

   -- Create, Open, Close, Delete, Reset, Mode, Name,
   -- Form and Is_Open as for Sequential_IO

   -- Control of default input and output files

   procedure Set_Output(File: in File_Type);
   function Standard_Output return File_Type;
   function Current_Output return File_Type;

   type File_Access is access constant File_Type;
   function Standard_Output return File_Access;
   function Current_Output return File_Access;

   -- Similarly for input and error file

   -- Buffer control

   procedure Flush(File: in out File_Type);
   procedure Flush;

   -- Specification of line and page lengths
   -- also with File parameter

   procedure Set_Line_Length(To: in Count);
   procedure Set_Page_Length(To: in Count);
   function Line_Length return Count;
   function Page_Length return Count;
```

-- Column, line and page control
-- also with File parameter

procedure New_Line(Spacing: **in** Positive_Count := 1);
procedure Skip_Line(Spacing: **in** Positive_Count := 1);
function End_Of_Line **return** Boolean;
procedure New_Page;
procedure Skip_Page;
function End_Of_Page **return** Boolean;
function End_Of_File **return** Boolean;
procedure Set_Col(To: **in** Positive_Count);
procedure Set_Line(To: **in** Positive_Count);
function Col **return** Positive_Count;
function Line **return** Positive_Count;
function Page **return** Positive_Count;

-- Character input-output

procedure Get(File: **in** File_Type; Item: **out** Character);
procedure Get(Item: **out** Character);
procedure Put(File: **in** File_Type; Item: **in** Character);
procedure Put(Item: **in** Character);

procedure Look_Ahead(Item: **out** Character;
                    End_Of_Line: **out** Boolean);
procedure Get_Immediate(Item: **out** Character);
procedure Get_Immediate(Item: **out** Character;
                    Available: **out** Boolean);

-- String input-output

procedure Get(Item: **out** String);
procedure Put(Item: **in** String);
procedure Get_Line(Item: **out** String; Last: **out** Natural);
procedure Put_Line(Item: **in** String);

-- Generic package for input-output of integer types

generic
   type Num **is range** <>;
package Integer_IO **is**
   Default_Width: Field := Num'Width;
   Default_Base: Number_Base := 10;

   procedure Get(Item: **out** Num; Width: **in** Field := 0);
   procedure Put(Item: **in** Num;
                Width: **in** Field := Default_Width;
                Base: **in** Number_Base := Default_Base);
   procedure Get(From: **in** String; Item: **out** Num;
                Last: **out** Positive);
   procedure Put(To: **out** String;
                Item: **in** Num;
                Base: **in** Number_Base := Default_Base);
end Integer_IO;

```
generic
   type Num is mod <>;
package Modular_IO is
   -- then as for Integer_IO
end Modular_IO;

-- Generic packages for input-output of real types

generic
   type Num is digits <>;
package Float_IO is
   Default_Fore: Field := 2;
   Default_Aft: Field := Num'Digits-1;
   Default_Exp: Field := 3;

   procedure Get(Item: out Num; Width: in Field := 0);
   procedure Put(Item: in Num;
                    Fore: in Field := Default_Fore;
                    Aft: in Field := Default_Aft;
                    Exp: in Field := Default_Exp);
   procedure Get(From: in String;
                    Item: out Num;
                    Last: out Positive);
   procedure Put(To: out String;
                    Item: in Num;
                    Aft: in Field := Default_Aft;
                    Exp: in Field := Default_Exp);
end Float_IO;

generic
   type Num is delta <>;
package Fixed_IO is
   Default_Fore: Field := Num'Fore;
   Default_Aft: Field := Num'Aft;
   Default_Exp: Field := 0;
   -- then as for Float_IO
end Fixed_IO;

generic
   type Num is delta <> digits <>;
package Decimal_IO is
   -- then as for Fixed_IO
end Decimal_IO;

-- Generic package for input-output of enumeration types

generic
   type Enum is (<>);
package Enumeration_IO is
   Default_Width: Field := 0;
   Default_Setting: Type_Set := Upper Case;

   procedure Get(Item: out Enum);
```

```
                    procedure Put(Item: in Enum;
                                  Width: in Field := Default_Width;
                                  Set: in Type_Set := Default_Setting);
                    procedure Get(From: in String;
                                  Item: out Enum;
                                  Last: out Positive);
                    procedure Put(To: out String;
                                  Item: out Enum;
                                  Set: in Type_Set := Default_Setting);
                  end Enumeration_IO;

                  -- Exceptions

                  Status_Error: exception renames IO_Exceptions.Status_Error;
                  ...
                  Layout_Error: exception renames IO_Exceptions.Layout_Error;

                private
                  -- implementation dependent
                end Ada.Text_IO;
```

The types File_Type and File_Mode and the various file management procedures are similar to those for Sequential_IO since text files are of course sequential in nature.

Procedures Put and Get occur in two forms for characters and strings, one with the file and one without; both are shown only for type Character.

In the case of type Character, a call of Put just outputs that character; for type String a call of Put outputs the characters of the string.

A problem arises in the case of numeric and enumeration types since there is not a fixed number of such types. This is overcome by the use of internal generic packages for each category. Thus for integer input–output we instantiate the package Integer_IO with the appropriate type thus

```
      type My_Integer is range –1E6 .. +1E6;
      ...
      package My_Integer_IO is new Integer_IO(My_Integer);
      use My_Integer_IO;
```

However, as noted in Chapter 4, there are nongeneric equivalents to Integer_IO and Float_IO corresponding to instantiations with the predefined types Integer, Long_Integer, Float and so on. They have names such as

```
      Ada.Integer_Text_IO          -- for Integer
      Ada.Long_Integer_Text_IO     -- for Long_Integer
      Ada.Float_Text_IO            -- for Float
```

For integer output (both signed and modular), Put occurs in three forms, one with the file, one without and one with a string as the destination; only the last two are shown.

In the case of Put to a file, there are two format parameters Width and Base which have default values provided by the variables Default_Width and Default_Base. The default width is initially Num'Width which gives the smallest field which is adequate for all values of the subtype expressed with base 10 (including a leading space or minus). Base 10 also happens to be the initial default base. These default values can be changed by the user by directly assigning new values to the variables Default_Width and Default_Base (they are directly visible); remember that a default parameter is re-evaluated on each call requiring it and so the default obtained is always the current value of these variables. The integer is output as an integer literal without underlines and leading zeros but with a preceding minus sign if negative. It is padded with leading spaces to fill the field width specified; if the field width is too small, it is expanded as necessary. Thus a default width of 0 results in the field being the minimum to contain the literal. If base 10 is specified explicitly or by default, the value is output using the syntax of decimal literal; if the base is not 10, the syntax of based literal is used.

The attribute Width deserves attention. It is a property of the subtype of the actual generic type parameter and not of the type. Thus the default format is appropriate to the range as the user sees it and not to that of the underlying machine type on which it is based. This is important for portability. So in the case of My_Integer, the attribute has the value 8 (7 digits for one million plus the space or sign).

The general effect is shown by the following sequence of statements where the output is shown in a comment. The quotes delimit the output and s designates a space. We start with the initial default values for the format parameters.

```
X: My_Integer := 1234;
...
Put(X);                    -- "ssss1234"
Put(X, 5);                 -- "s1234"
Put(X, 0);                 -- "1234"
Put(X, Base => 8);         -- "s8#2322#"
Put(X, 11, 8);             -- "ssss8#2322#"
Default_Base := 8;
Put(X);                    -- "s8#2322#"
```

In the case of Put to a string, the field width is taken as the length of the string. If this is too small, then Layout_Error is raised. Put to strings is useful for building up strings containing various bits and pieces and perhaps editing them before actually sending them to a file. It will be found that slices are useful for this sort of manipulation.

Similar techniques are used for real types. A value is output as a decimal literal without underlines and leading zeros but with a preceding minus sign if negative. If Exp is zero, then there is no exponent and the format consists of Fore characters before the decimal point and Aft after the decimal point. If Exp is nonzero, then a signed exponent in a field of Exp characters is output after a letter E with leading zeros if necessary; the exponent value is such that only one significant digit occurs before the decimal point. If the Fore or Exp parts of the field are inadequate, then they are expanded as necessary. Base 10 is always used and the value is rounded to the size of Aft specified.

The initial default format parameters for floating point types are 2, Num'Digits–1 and 3; this gives an exponent form with a space or minus sign plus single digit before the decimal point, Num'Digits–1 digits after the decimal point and a two-digit exponent. The corresponding parameters for fixed point types (including decimal types) are Num'Fore, Num'Aft and 0; this gives a form without an exponent and the attributes give the smallest field such that all values of the type can be expressed with appropriate precision.

Enumeration types use a similar technique. A default field of zero is used. If the field has to be padded then the extra spaces go after the value and not before as with the numeric types. Upper case is normally used, but lower case may be specified. A value of a character type which is a character literal is output in single quotes.

Note the subtle distinction between Put defined directly for the type Character and for enumeration values.

```
Text_IO.Put('X');
```

outputs the single character X, whereas

```
package Char_IO is new Text_IO.Enumeration_IO(Character);
...
Char_IO.Put('X');
```

outputs the character X between single quotes.

Input using Get works in an analogous way; a call of Get always skips line and page terminators. In the case of the type Character the next character is read. In the case of the type String, the procedure Get reads the exact number of characters as determined by the actual parameter. In the case of enumeration types, leading blanks (spaces or horizontal tabs) are also skipped; input is terminated by a character which is not part of the value or by a line terminator. Numeric types normally have the same behaviour but they also have an additional and optional Width parameter and if this has a value other than zero, then reading stops after this number of characters including skipped blanks. In the case of Get where the source is a string rather than a file, the value of Last indexes the last character read; the end of the string behaves as the end of a file.

The allowed form of data for reading an enumeration value is an identifier (case of letters being ignored), or a character literal in single quotes. The allowed form for an integer value is first and optionally a plus or minus sign and then according to the syntax of an integer literal which may be a based literal and possibly have an exponent (see Section 5.4). The allowed form for a real value is similarly an optional sign followed by a real literal (one with a radix point in it); however leading or trailing zeros and the point may be omitted and so an integer literal is also an acceptable form. If the data item is not of the correct form or not a value of the subtype Num then Data_Error is raised. The collector of Ada curiosities will note that Put cannot output integer based forms where the base is 10 such as

10#41#

although Get can read them. Similarly Put cannot output real based forms at all although Get can read them. On the other hand Get can read whatever Put can write.

A text file is considered as a sequence of lines. The characters in a line have a column position starting at 1. The line length on output can be fixed or variable. A fixed line length is appropriate for the output of tables, a variable line length for dialogue. The line length can be changed within a single file. It is initially not fixed. The lines in turn are similarly grouped into pages starting at page 1.

On output a call of Put will result in all the characters going on the current line starting at the current position in the line. If, however, the line length is fixed and the characters cannot fit in the remainder of the line, a new line is started and all the characters are placed on that line starting at the beginning. If they still will not fit, Layout_Error is raised. If the length is not fixed, the characters always go on the end of the current line.

The layout may be controlled by various subprograms. In some cases they apply to both input and output files; in these cases if the file is omitted then it is taken to apply to the output case and the default output file is assumed. In most cases, a subprogram only applies to one direction and then omitting the file naturally gives the default in that direction.

The function Col returns the current position in the line and the procedure Set_Col sets the position to the given value. A call of Set_Col never goes backwards. On output extra spaces are produced and on input characters are skipped. If the parameter of Set_Col equals the current value of Col then there is no effect; if it is less then a call of New_Line or Skip_Line is implied.

The procedure New_Line (output only) outputs the given number of newlines (default 1) and resets the current column to 1. Spare positions at the end of a line are filled with spaces. The procedure Skip_Line (input only) similarly moves on the given number of lines (default 1) and resets the current column. The function End_Of_Line (input only) returns True if we have reached the end of a line.

The function Line_Length (output only) returns the current line length if it is fixed and zero if it is not. The procedure Set_Line_Length (output only) sets the line length fixed to the given value; a value of zero indicates that it is not to be fixed.

There are also similar subprograms for the control of lines within pages. These are Line, Set_Line, New_Page, Skip_Page, End_Of_Page, Page_Length and Set_Page_Length. Finally the function Page returns the current page number from the start of the file. There is no Set_Page.

The procedures Put_Line and Get_Line are particularly appropriate for manipulating whole lines. A call of Put_Line outputs the string and then moves to the next line (by calling New_Line). A call of Get_Line reads successive characters into the string until the end of the string or the end of the line is encountered; in the latter case it then moves to the next line (by calling Skip_Line); Last indexes the last character moved into the string. Successive calls of Put_Line and Get_Line therefore manipulate whole lines. However, the behaviour of Get_Line is curious when the string is exactly the right length to accommodate the remaining characters on the line – it doesn't move to the next line! So, given a series of lines of length 80, successive calls of Get_Line with a string of length 80 (bounds 1 .. 80) return alternately lines of 80 characters and null strings (or in other words the value of Last is alternately 80 and 0). This unhelpful behaviour can be overcome by using a string of length 81 or calling Skip_Line ourselves after each call of Get_Line.

It will be found helpful to use slices with Get_Line and Put_Line; thus to copy a text file (with lines of less than 100 characters) and adding the string "--" to each line we could write

```
S: String(1 .. 100);
N: Natural;
...
while not End_Of_File loop
   Get_Line(S, N);
   Put_Line("--" & S(1 .. N));
end loop;
```

where we have assumed default files throughout.

The subprograms, Flush, Look_Ahead and Get_Immediate are useful for interactive applications. Flush applies to an output file and flushes any internal buffer.

Get_Immediate reads the next character (control or graphic). There are two versions, that with the extra parameter Available returns false if a character is not immediately available, that without the extra parameter waits for a character if necessary. (The current column, line and page number are not affected.)

Look_Ahead gets the next character without consuming it. However, it does not move to the next line and so Item is not defined if it is at the end of the line and End_Of_Line is set true. This procedure will be found vital for writing subprograms with behaviour corresponding to the predefined Get for the integer, real and enumeration types which all look ahead to see if the literal value has finished but do not remove the character which terminates it.

The package Text_IO may seem somewhat elaborate but for simple output all we need is Put and New_Line and these are very straightforward.

There is also a package Wide_Text_IO which is identical to Text_IO except that it works in terms of the types Wide_Character and Wide_String instead of Character and String.

EXERCISE 20.5

1   What do the following calls output? Assume the initial values for the default parameters.

(a) Put("Fred");   (f) Put(120, 8, 8);
(b) Put(120);   (g) Put(-38.0);
(c) Put(120, 8);   (h) Put(0.07, 6, 2, 2);
(d) Put(120, 0);   (i) Put(3.14159, 1, 4);
(e) Put(-120, 0);   (j) Put(9_999_999_999.9, 1, 1, 1);

Assume that the real values are of a type with **digits** = 6 and the integer values are of a type with 16 bits.

2   Write a body for the package Simple_IO of Section 2.2. Ignore exceptions.

20.6   Streams

As we remarked earlier, the packages Sequential_IO and Direct_IO only permit the creation of files whose elements are all of the same type. This is often too restrictive and so additional ·stream facilities are provided which allow the creation of quite arbitrary heterogeneous files.

The stream facilities are quite general and can be used for other purposes as well as creating files. They are provided by the packages

    Ada.Streams
    Ada.Streams.Stream_IO
    Ada.Text_IO.Text_Streams

The parent package Ada.Streams defines an abstract type Root_Stream_ Type from which all streams are derived. There are two abstract primitive procedures Read and Write which enable streams to be manipulated in terms of stream elements. We will not consider the underlying mechanism in detail but simply show how streams can be used with files.

Files declared by the package Streams.Stream_IO may be processed sequentially using the stream mechanism. Such files can be created, opened and closed in the usual manner. Moreover, the package Stream_IO also declares an access type and the function Stream thus

    type Stream_Access **is access all** Root_Stream_Type'Class;
    function Stream(File: **in** File_Type) **return** Stream_Access;

The function Stream takes a stream file and returns an access to the stream associated with the file.

The reading and writing of streams is done with attributes T'Read, T'Write, T'Input and T'Output. These attributes are predefined for all nonlimited types. They can be replaced by using an attribute definition clause (see Section 21.1) and can also be supplied for limited types. We will first consider T'Read and T'Write; T'Input and T'Output (which are especially relevant for arrays and discriminated records) will be considered later.

The attributes Read and Write take parameters denoting the stream and the element of type T thus

    procedure T'Write(Stream: **access** Root_Stream_Type'Class;
                    Item: **in** T);

    procedure T'Read(Stream: **access** Root_Stream_Type'Class;
                    Item: **out** T);

As a simple example, suppose we wish to write a mixture of integers, month names and dates where the type Date is the familiar

```
type Date is
  record
    Day: Integer range 1 .. 31;
    Month: Month_Name;
    Year: Integer;
  end record;
```

Having created a file in the normal way, we then call the Write attributes for the values to be written to the stream. Thus

```
use Streams.Stream_IO;
Mixed_File: File_Type;
S: Stream_Access;
...
Create(Mixed_File);
S := Stream(Mixed_File);
...
Date'Write(S, Some_Date);
Integer'Write(S, Some_Integer);
Month_Name'Write(S, This_Month);
...
```

All files created this way are of the same type. Note also that they are binary files. A file written in this way can be read back in a similar manner, but if we attempt to read things in the wrong order and thus with the inappropriate subprogram then we will get a funny value or Data_Error. The attribute Valid discussed in Section 21.2 is useful in such circumstances.

The predefined Write attribute for a simple record such as Date simply calls the attributes for the components in order. So conceptually it is

```
procedure Date'Write(Stream: access Root_Stream_Type'Class;
                         Item: in Date) is
begin
  Integer'Write(Stream, Item.Day);
  Month_Name'Write(Stream, Item.Month);
  Integer'Write(Stream, Item.Year);
end;
```

However, if we wish to output the month as an integer then we can redefine the attribute as follows

```
procedure Date_Write(Stream: access Root_Stream_Type'Class;
                         Item: in Date) is
begin
  Integer'Write(Stream, Item.Day);
  Integer'Write(Stream, Month_Name'Pos(Item.Month) + 1);
```

```
        Integer'Write(Stream, Item.Year);
    end Date_Write;

    for Date'Write use Date_Write;
```

and then the statement

```
    Date'Write(S, Some_Date);
```

will use the new format for the output of dates. Similar facilities apply to input and so in order to read the file back we would have to declare the corresponding version of Date'Read to read the month as an integer and convert to the corresponding value of Month_Name.

If we wish to change the format of all months and not just those in dates, then we simply redefine Month_Name'Write and this naturally has the indirect effect of also changing the output of dates.

Observe that the attributes T'Read and T'Write can only be overridden in the same package specification or declarative part as that containing the declaration of the type T. As a consequence they cannot be changed for the predefined types. But they can be changed for types derived from them.

The situation is more complex in the case of arrays and records with discriminants since we have to take account of the 'dope' information represented by the bounds and discriminants. (In the case of a record discriminant with defaults, the discriminant is treated as an ordinary component.) This is done with the additional attributes Input and Output. The general idea is that Input and Output process dope information (if any) and then call Read and Write to process the rest of the value. Their profiles are

```
    procedure T'Output(Stream: access Streams.Root_Stream_Type'Class;
                       Item: in T);

    function T'Input(Stream: access Streams.Root_Stream_Type'Class)
                                                          return T;
```

Note that Input is a function since T may be indefinite (such as String) and we may not know the constraints for a particular call.

So for an array the procedure Output outputs the bounds of the value and then calls Write to output the value itself. Thus

```
    S: String := "String";
    ...
    String'Output(S);        -- outputs bounds
    String'Write(S);         -- does not output bounds
```

Note that the attributes Output and Write belong to the types and so it is immaterial whether we write String'Write or use some subtype String_6'Write.

For a record type with discriminants, if it has defaults (is definite) then Output simply calls Write which treats the discriminants as just other components. If there are no defaults then Output first outputs the discriminants and then calls Write to process the remainder of the record.

The above description of T'Input and T'Output applies to the default attributes. They could be redefined to do anything and not necessarily call T'Read and T'Write. Note moreover that Input and Output also exist for elementary types; their defaults just call Read and Write.

There are also attributes T'Class'Output and T'Class'Input for dealing with class wide types. For output, an external representation of the tag is output and then the procedure Output for the specific type is called (by dispatching) in order to output the specific value (which in turn will call Write). Similarly on input, the tag is first read and then, according to its value, the corresponding function Input is called by dispatching. For completeness, T'Class'Read and T'Class'Write are defined to dispatch to the subprogram denoted by the Read or Write attribute of the specific type identified by the tag.

Note that the external representation of a tag mentioned above is a string. The functions

```
function External_Tag(T: Tag) return String;
function Internal_Tag(External: String) return Tag;
```

in the package Ada.Tags perform the required conversions. (There is also an atttribute External_Tag.) If we try to convert a string which does not represent a tag then Tag_Error is raised.

The general principle is, of course, that whatever is written can then be read back in again by the appropriate reverse operation.

It is also possible to treat a text file as a stream and thus to mix binary and text in one file. The child package Text_IO.Text_Streams defines a function Stream which takes a file of the type Text_IO.File_Type and returns an access to the corresponding stream. We could then write binary to the current output file by

```
use Text_IO;
S: Text_Streams.Stream_Access := Stream(Current_Output);
...
Date'Write(S, Today);
```

That concludes a rather brief discussion of streams. They have many other uses. For example, they underly the mechanism for remote procedure calls in distributed systems; this is briefly alluded to in Section 22.3. Another aspect we have not discussed is that streams can also be processed in an indexed rather than a sequential manner using the notion of stream elements rather like Direct_IO works in terms of typed elements. It is also possible to create streams by the declaration and manipulation of such stream elements; thus a stream could be mapped onto storage in main memory rather than to a file. For details the reader is referred to the *ARM*.

EXERCISE 20.6

1   Redefine the attribute Date'Read to read the month name as a number.

20.7　　**Other facilities**

The package Ada.Command_Line enables the Ada program to access the arguments of the command which invoked it and to set its exit status if defined for the execution environment.

The parameterless function Argument_Count returns the number of arguments as an integer. The function Argument takes a positive argument number and returns the argument as a string. The parameterless function Command_Name returns the invoking command as a string.

The program can set its exit status by a call of the procedure Set_Exit_Status. The parameter is of the implementation defined integer type Exit_Status; there are also standard constants Success and Failure of the type Exit_Status.

Changes from Ada 83

The package ASCII is obsolete.

The standard packages for character and string handling did not exist in Ada 83.

The package Numerics did not exist in Ada 83.

The mode Append_File did not exist in Ada 83.

The functions such as Current_Output returning the access value did not exist in Ada 83.

The error file did not exist in Ada 83.

The subprograms Flush, Look_Ahead and Get_Immediate were not in Ada 83.

Get on real values would only accept data in the form of a real literal in Ada 83.

The nongeneric packages for integer and float text input–output were not in Ada 83.

The concept of streams was not in Ada 83.

The package Command_Line did not exist in Ada 83.

---

21 Interfacing

21.1 Representations	21.3 The package System
21.2 Unchecked programming	21.4 Other languages

In this chapter we consider various aspects of how an Ada program interfaces to the outside world. One area is the mapping of our abstract Ada program onto an implementation; how the data structures are represented and so on. (Communication through interrupts is dealt with in Section 22.2.) Another important aspect is communication with programs in other languages. However, the discussion in this chapter cannot be exhaustive because many details of this area will depend upon the implementation. The intent, therefore, is to give the reader a general overview of the facilities available.

21.1   Representations

When compiling a program, the compiler needs to decide how the various data items are to be represented. Certain uses or occurrences of entities require that their representation be known; such occurrences are called freezing points. We can provide explicit information about the representation of aspects of an entity and that of course determines that aspect. If no representation is provided then the compiler has to make some default decision at the first freezing point.

An obvious example is that declaring an object requires that its type be frozen. (In the case of private types the freezing is deferred until the full type declaration.) If we wish to provide our own representation then this must be done before the entity is otherwise frozen. Note that the end of a declarative part freezes all the items declared in it anyway (except for incomplete types) and so any representation information must be in the same declaration part as the entity to which it applies.

In most cases the freezing rules are very much a fringe aspect of the language and intuitively obvious and have little impact on the normal programmer. One important interaction with other rules was however noted in Section 13.6 when we discussed type extension and primitive operations. We noted that we cannot add further primitive operations after a type is frozen and moreover that a type is frozen when a type is derived from it.

In summary, a type must be fully defined, including all representation clauses and dispatching operations, before it is frozen. Declaring an object of a type or extending a type freezes it.

We can provide our own representations using a representation clause which can take various forms.

For example we can specify the amount of storage to be allocated for objects of a type, for the storage pool of an access type and for the working storage of a task type. This is done by an attribute definition clause. Thus

```
type Byte is range 0 .. 255;
for Byte'Size use 8;
```

indicates that objects of the type Byte should occupy only 8 bits. The size of individual objects can also be specified.

The topic of Size is quite complex since it concerns not only single objects but also arrays and records containing components of the type. In addition there is also the pragma Pack which can be applied to a composite type and is a broad hint to the compiler to squeeze things up. An example occurs in Standard where we find

```
pragma Pack(String);
```

The attribute Size may be applied to an object or subtype whether we have supplied a value or not. For a single object it gives the actual size occupied. For a subtype it gives the value that will be used in a packed record. We are assured that

```
Boolean'Size = 1
```

and so in a packed record any Boolean components will be squeezed right up. But individual objects would typically occupy a word or byte for addressability reasons.

There is also an attribute Component_Size which applies to array types and objects and indicates the size for the components. Thus for speed we might want a particular array of Booleans to be packed loosely, thus

```
Loose_Bits: array (1 .. 10) of Boolean;
for Loose_Bits'Component_Size use 4;
```

and the compiler should then pack the bits two to a byte which we assume is easily addressed on the hardware concerned.

The space for storage pools and tasks is indicated using the attribute Storage_Size. In these cases the unit is not bits but storage elements. The number of bits in a storage element is implementation dependent and is given by the constant Storage_Unit in the package System. Thus if we wanted to ensure that the pool for

>   **type** Cell_Ptr **is access** Cell;

will accommodate 500 cells then we can write

>   **for** Cell_Ptr'Storage_Size **use** 500 * Cell'Size / System.Storage_Unit;

which assumes that Cell'Size is an exact multiple of Storage_Unit and that there are no hidden overheads. Alternatively we can write

>   **for** Cell_Ptr'Storage_Size **use** 500 * Cell'Max_Size_In_Storage_Units;

which does any rounding up and is especially appropriate if the accessed type is indefinite (such as the discriminated record Person of Section 16.5) since it allows for the maximum possible size of object. In that example, an object of subtype Woman would typically take more space than one of subtype Man.

The data space for tasks is best set by the pragma Storage_Size which is placed in the task specification and can thus depend upon a discriminant. This enables individual tasks of a task type to have different amounts of storage. Thus we might have

>   **task type** T(Work_Space: Integer) **is**
>   **pragma** Storage_Size(Work_Space);
>   ...
>   **end**;

The value of *small* for a fixed point type can also be indicated as was discussed in Section 15.5.

An enumeration representation clause can be used to specify, as an aggregate, the internal integer codes for the literals of an enumeration type. We might have a status value transmitted into our program as single bit settings, thus

>   **type** Status **is** (Off, Ready, On);
>   **for** Status **use** (Off => 1, Ready => 2, On => 4);

There is a constraint that the ordering of the values must be the same as the logical ordering of the literals. However, despite the holes, the functions Succ, Pred, Pos and Val always work in logical terms.

If these single bit values were autonomously loaded into our machine at location octal 100 then we could conveniently access them in our program by declaring a variable of type Status and placing it at that location using a representation clause

>   S: Status;
>   **for** S'Address **use** 8#100#;

However, if by some hardware mishap a value which is not 1, 2 or 4 turns up then the program will clearly misbehave. We will see how to overcome this difficulty in the next section.

The final form of representation clause is used to indicate the layout of a record type. Thus if we have

```
type Register is range 0 .. 15;
type Opcode is ( ... );

type RR is
   record
      Code: Opcode;
      R1: Register;
      R2: Register;
   end record;
```

which represents a machine instruction of the RR format in the IBM System 370, then we can specify the exact mapping by

```
for RR'Alignment use 2;

for RR use
   record
      Code at 0 range 0 .. 7;
      R1   at 1 range 0 .. 3;
      R2   at 1 range 4 .. 7;
   end record;
```

The first representation clause indicates that the record is to be aligned on a double byte boundary; the alignment is given in terms of the number of storage elements and in the case of the 370 a storage element would naturally be one 8-bit byte.

The position and size of the individual components are given relative to the start of the record. The value after **at** gives a storage element and the range is in terms of bits. The bit number can extend outside the storage element; we could equally have written

```
R1 at 0 range 8 .. 11;
```

If we do not specify the location of every component, the compiler is free to juggle the rest as best it can. However, we must allow enough space for those we do specify and they must not overlap unless they are in different alternatives of a variant. There may also be hidden components (array dope information for example) and this may interfere with our freedom. The position of a component is given by attributes First_Bit, Last_Bit and Position.

The order of numbering of bits in a record type can be specified. Thus

```
for RR'Bit_Order use Low_Order_First;
```

indicates little endian numbering as opposed to big endian using the Gulliverian vernacular (the type Bit_Order is defined in **System**).

It is an important principle that all subtypes of a type have the same representation. Accordingly these attributes can only be specified for the first subtype of a type. Derived types inherit the representation of the parent but can generally override it.

We mentioned the pragma Pack above; other pragmas that relate to setting the balance between speed and time are Inline and Optimize. Inline indicates that all calls of the subprograms mentioned should be expanded inline. Good examples would be the short subprograms for manipulating complex numbers. So we might write

    pragma Inline("+", "–", "*", "**/**");

in the specification of the package Complex_Numbers in Section 11.2.

The pragma Suppress can be used to indicate that the run-time checks associated with detecting conditions which could give rise to exceptions can be omitted if to do so would lead to a more efficient program. However, it should be remembered that such a pragma is merely a recommendation and so there is no guarantee that the exception will not be raised. Indeed it could be propagated from another unit compiled with checks.

The checks corresponding to the exception Constraint_Error are Access_Check (checking that an access value is not null), Discriminant_Check (checking that a discriminant value is consistent with the component being accessed or a constraint), Division_Check (checking the second operand of **/**, **rem** and **mod**), Index_Check (checking that an index is in range), Length_Check (checking that the number of components of an array match), Overflow_Check (checking for numeric overflow), Range_Check (checking that various constraints are satisfied) and Tag_Check (checking that tags are equal when dispatching).

The checks corresponding to Program_Error are Elaboration_Check (checking that the body of a unit has been elaborated) and Accessibility_Check (checking an accessibility level).

The check corresponding to Storage_Error is Storage_Check (checking that space for an access pool or task has not been exceeded).

The pragma takes the form

    pragma Suppress(Range_Check);

in which case it applies to all operations in the unit concerned or it can list the types and objects to which it is to be applied. Thus

    pragma Suppress(Access_Check, Cell_Ptr);

indicates that no checks are to be applied when accessing objects of the access type Cell_Ptr.

We can also write

    pragma Suppress(All_Checks);

which does the obvious thing.

21.2 Unchecked programming

Sometimes the strict integrity of a fully typed language is a nuisance. This particularly applies to system programs where, in different parts of a program, an object is thought of in different terms. This difficulty can be overcome by the use of a generic function called Ada.Unchecked_Conversion. Its specification is

```
generic
    type Source(<>) is limited private;
    type Target(<>) is limited private;
function Ada.Unchecked_Conversion(S: Source) return Target;
```

As an example, we can overcome our problem with possible unexpected values of the type Status of the previous sect. We can receive the values into our program as values of type Byte, check their validity in numeric terms and then convert the values to type Status for the remainder of the program. In order to perform the conversion we first instantiate the generic function thus

```
function Byte_To_Status is
    new Unchecked_Conversion(Byte, Status);
```

and we can then write

```
B: Byte;
for B'Address use 8#100#;
S: Status;
...
case B is
    when 1 | 2 | 4 =>
        null;
    when others =>
        raise Bad_Data;
end case;

S := Byte_To_Status(B);
```

The effect of the unchecked conversion is typically nothing; the bit pattern of the source type is merely passed on unchanged and reinterpreted as the bit pattern of the target type. Clearly, certain conditions must be satisfied for this to be possible; an obvious one which may be imposed by the implementation is that the number of bits in the representations of the two types must be the same. Misuse of unchecked conversion can give rise to an erroneous program.

The Valid attribute is useful for checking that the value of a scalar object is sensible. Thus we can rewrite the above example as

```
B: Byte;
for B'Address use 8#100#;
S: Status;
```

```
...
S := Byte_To_Status(B);
if not S'Valid then raise Bad_Data; end if;
```

Another good example of the use of unchecked conversion is converting between signed integer and modular types. Thus following Section 15.2 we might write

```
function Convert_Byte is
    new Unchecked_Conversion(Signed_Byte, Unsigned_Byte);
function Convert_Byte is
    new Unchecked_Conversion(Unsigned_Byte, Signed_Byte);
```

where we have used the same name in both directions.

Another area where the programmer can be given extra freedom is in the deallocation of access types. As mentioned in Section 10.2, there may or may not be a garbage collector. In any event we may prefer to do our own garbage collection perhaps on the grounds that this gives us better timing control in a real-time program. We can do this with a generic procedure called Ada.Unchecked_Deallocation. Its specification is

```
generic
    type Object is limited private;
    type Name is access Object;
procedure Ada.Unchecked_Deallocation(X: in out Name);
```

If we take our old friend

```
type Cell_Ptr is access Cell;
```

then we can write

```
procedure Free is
    new Unchecked_Deallocation(Cell, Cell_Ptr);
```

and then

```
List: Cell_Ptr;
...
Free(List);
```

After calling Free, the value of List will be **null** and the cell will have been returned to free storage. Of course, if we mistakenly still had another variable referring to the cell then we would be in a mess; the program would be erroneous. If we use unchecked deallocation then the onus is on us to get it right. We should also insert

```
pragma Controlled(Cell_Ptr);
```

to tell the compiler that we are looking after ourselves and that any garbage collector should not be used for this access type.

The use of both these forms of unchecked programming needs care and it would be sensible to restrict the use of these generic subprograms to privileged parts of the program. Note that since both generic functions are library functions then any compilation unit using them must refer to them in a with clause. This makes it fairly straightforward for a tool to check for their use. And also for our manager to peer over our shoulders to see whether we are writing naughty programs!

EXERCISE 21.2

---

1 Reconsider the reading of the value of type Status without the intermediary type Byte.

21.3 The package System

The package System is concerned with the fine details of the control of storage and related issues. Its specification is as follows

```
package System is
    pragma Preelaborate(System);
    type Name is implementation-defined-enumeration-type;
    System_Name: constant Name := implementation-defined;

    -- system-dependent named numbers

    Min_Int: constant := implementation-defined;
    Max_Int: constant := implementation-defined;
    Max_Binary_Modulus: constant := implementation-defined;
    Max_Nonbinary_Modulus: constant := implementation-defined;
    Max_Base_Digits: constant := implementation-defined;
    Max_Digits: constant := implementation-defined;
    Max_Mantissa: constant := implementation-defined;
    Fine_Delta: constant := implementation-defined;
    Tick: constant := implementation-defined;

    -- storage-related declarations

    type Address is implementation-defined;
    Null_Address: constant Address;
    Storage_Unit: constant := implementation-defined;
    Word_Size: constant := implementation-defined * Storage_Unit;
    Memory_Size: constant := implementation-defined;

    function "<" (Left, Right: Address) return Boolean;
    -- similarly "<=", ">", ">=" and "="
```

```
      type Bit_Order is (High_Order_First, Low_Order_First);
      Default_Bit_Order: constant Bit_Order;

      subtype Any_Priority is Integer range implementation-defined;
      subtype Priority is
            Any_Priority range Any_Priority'First .. implementation-defined;
      subtype Interrupt_Priority is
                        Any_Priority range Priority'Last+1 .. Any_Priority'Last;
      Default_Priority: constant Priority := (Priority'First+Priority'Last)/2;

   private

      ...

   end System;
```

Min_Int and Max_Int give the most negative and most positive values of a signed integer type, Max_Binary_Modulus and Max_Modulus give the maximum supported modulus of a modular type, Max_Base_Digits is the largest number of decimal digits of a floating type (Max_Digits if no range given) and Max_Mantissa is the largest number of binary digits of a fixed type; they are all of type universal integer. Fine_Delta is a bit redundant since it always has the value 2.0**(–Max_Mantissa) and Tick is the clock period in seconds; they are both of type universal real.

The type Address is that given by the corresponding attribute; it might be an integer type or possibly a record type. The numbers Storage_Unit, Word_Size and Memory_Size give the number of bits in a storage element, the number of bits in a word and the memory size in storage elements; they are of type universal integer.

There is also a child package System.Storage_Elements for messing about with addresses and offsets thus

```
      package System.Storage_Elements is
         type Storage_Offset is range implementation-defined;
         subtype Storage_Count is Storage_Offset
                                          range 0 .. Storage_Offset'Last;
         type Storage_Element is mod implementation-defined;
         for Storage_Element'Size use Storage_Unit;
         type Storage_Array is array (Storage_Offset range <>)
                                          of aliased Storage_Element;
         for Storage_Array'Component_Size use Storage_Unit;

         function "+" (Left: Address; Right: Storage_Offset) return Address;
         function "+" (Left: Storage_Offset; Right: Address) return Address;
         function "–" (Left: Address; Right: Storage_Offset) return Address;
         function "–" (Left, Right: Address) return Storage_Offset;

         type Integer_Address is implementation-defined;
         function To_Address(Value: Integer_Address) return Address;
         function To_Integer(Value: Address) return Integer_Address;
      end System.Storage_Elements;
```

The type Storage_Element is unsigned and represents a storage element and the type Storage Array represents a contiguous lump of store. The various operations "+" and "−" enable addresses and offsets to be added and subtracted. The functions To_Address and To_Integer enable an Address to be converted to an integer type Integer_Address and vice versa.

The generic package

```
generic
    type Object(<>) is limited private;
package System.Address_To_Access_Conversions is

    ...
    type Object_Pointer is access all Object;
    function To_Pointer(Value: Address) return Object_Pointer;
    function To_Address(Value: Object_Pointer) return Address;

    ...
end;
```

enables naughty peeking and poking to be done.

Another important child package of System concerns the control of storage pools for access types. Its specification is

```
with Ada.Finalization;
with System.Storage_Elements;
package System.Storage_Pools is
    pragma Preelaborate(System.Storage_Pools);

    type Root_Storage_Pool is
        new Ada.Finalization.Limited_Controlled with private;

    procedure Allocate(Pool: in out Root_Storage_Pool;
                    Storage_Address: out Address;
                    Size_In_Storage_Elements, Alignment:
                        in Storage_Elements.Storage_Count) is abstract;

    procedure Deallocate ... ;    -- similar with in for Storage_Address

    function Storage_Size(Pool: Root_Storage_Pool)
                            return Storage_Elements.Storage_Count is abstract;
private
    ...
end;
```

The general idea is that the user defines a type derived from Root_Storage_Pool and provides concrete subprograms for Allocate, Deallocate and Storage_Size. The user then declares an object of the type to be used as the pool and then associates this object with an access type using the attribute Storage_Pool. Thus

```
with System.Storage_Pools;
with System.Storage_Elements;
use System;
```

```
package My_Pool is
  type Pond(Size: Storage_Elements.Storage_Count) is
      new Storage_Pools.Root_Storage_Pool with private;
  procedure Allocate is ... ;
  ...    -- also Deallocate, Storage_Size, Initialize, Finalize
  ...
end My_Pool;
...
Cell_Ptr_Pool: Pond(5000);
for Cell_Ptr'Storage_Pool use Cell_Ptr_Pool;
```

The implementation then automatically calls Allocate and Deallocate whenever storage is required or released for the access type concerned rather than using the default pool. Remember that storage is normally released when the scope of the type is left but can also be released by using unchecked deallocation as described in the previous section. This automatic calling of Allocate and Deallocate is similar to the automatic calling of Initialize and Finalize for controlled types. Note that the storage pool types are controlled anyway and so the user also has to provide procedures Initialize and Finalize as well.

21.4   Other languages

Another possible form of communication between an Ada program and the outside world is via other languages. These could be machine languages or other high level languages such as Fortran or C. In order for such communication to be possible it is clear that the data must conform to appropriate conventions. This can be assured by various pragmas.

As an example suppose we wish to communicate with some mouse handling program written in C. We wish the C program to call our Ada procedure Action when the mouse is clicked. We therefore need to tell the C program which procedure to call. Suppose this is done by calling the C function Set_Click with the address of our Ada procedure as its parameter. We might write

```
type Response is access procedure (D: Data);
pragma Convention(C, Response);

procedure Set_Click(P: Response);
pragma Import(C, Set_Click);

procedure Action(D: Data) is separate;
pragma Convention(C, Action);
...
Set_Click(Action'Access);
```

The pragma Import indicates that the body of Set_Click is external to the Ada program. There is also a corresponding pragma Export that makes one of our subprograms visible externally (we did not need it in this example because the address was passed indirectly via the access value). These pragmas have additional optional parameters for passing the name of the foreign language subprogram and the link name if they are different to the Ada name.

The pragmas Export and Import can also be used with other entities. For example a deferred constant can be completed with a pragma Import.

The package Interfaces was mentioned in Chapter 15 when we noted that it contained the declarations of the various machine integer types plus the shift and rotate functions for modular types.

The package Interfaces also has a number of child packages namely

    Interfaces.C
    Interfaces.C.Strings
    Interfaces.C.Pointers
    Interfaces.COBOL
    Interfaces.Fortran

which contain facilities for communication with the languages concerned. We leave the reader to consult the *ARM* for details.

Finally it may be possible to use machine code. This is done by writing a subprogram all of whose statements are code statements; these take the unlikely form of an aggregate of a type defined in the package System.Machine_Code. Such a subprogram would typically be called inline. For details the reader is referred to the implementation concerned. Another approach is of course simply to call an external subprogram written in assembler.

Changes from Ada 83

Many attributes and pragmas did not exist in Ada 83.

The child packages of System did not exist in Ada 83.

The package Interfaces did not exist in Ada 83.

Ada 83 had different notations for setting the address attribute and record alignment; these are obsolete in Ada 95.

---

22 The Specialized Annexes

This chapter contains a very brief survey of the scope of the six specialized annexes. These annexes are optional and many implementations will not support them in full. Validation of an Ada compiler will state which of the annexes, if any, is supported. A compiler which is not validated for an annex may nevertheless provide partial support for that annex but if it does the material must conform to the annex.

It is a general principle that the annexes contain no new syntax but only additional packages, attributes and pragmas. They are thus not intrinsically hard to understand particularly if the reader is familiar with the application area concerned. We thus briefly catalogue the principles and main facilities with just a few examples and refer the reader to the *ARM* for the full details.

The annexes are generally independent but the Real-Time annex requires that the Systems Programming annex be supported.

22.1   Systems Programming

This annex covers access to machine code, interrupt handling, some extra requirements on representations and preelaboration, a pragma for discarding names at run time, the pragmas for shared variables and packages for general task identification and attributes.

Interrupt handling is important. The general idea is that an interrupt handler is provided by a protected procedure which is called by some mythical external task. The protected procedure can be attached to the interrupt statically by the pragma Attach_Handler or dynamically by a procedure of the same name in the package Ada.Interrupts. This package also defines the type Interrupt_Id which is used to identify the interrupts which are declared as constants in the package Ada.Interrupts.Names. Thus

```
protected Contact_Handler is
   use Ada.Interrupts;
   procedure Response;
   pragma Attach_Handler(Response, Names.Contact_Int);
end;

protected body Contact_Handler is
   procedure Response is
      -- the interrupt handling code
   end Response;
end Contact_Handler;
```

statically attaches the procedure Response to the interrupt identified by the constant Contact_Int. Dynamic attachment is performed by using the pragma Interrupt_Handler to indicate that the protected procedure is to be used as a handler and then calling the procedure Attach_Handler thus

```
protected Contact_Handler is
   use Ada.Interrupts;
   procedure Response;
   pragma Interrupt_Handler(Response);
end;
...
Attach_Handler(Contact_Handler.Response'Access,
Names.Contact_Int);
```

where the first parameter of Attach_Handler is of the access type

```
type Parameterless_Handler is access protected procedure;
```

Other subprograms in Ada.Interrupts allow a handler to be detached or exchanged.

The pragma Discard_Names may be used to indicate that various voluminous tables of names associated with a type or exception need not be retained at run time. Such tables are required by Image and Value, Enumeration_IO, Exception_Name and Tags.Expanded_Name. Omitting these tables might be vital for saving space in an embedded application.

The pragmas Atomic and Atomic_Components were illustrated in Section 18.10. They ensure that all reads and writes to the objects are atomic. The pragmas Volatile and Volatile_Components ensure in addition that the object is always in memory (and not for example optimized into a register). We should really have written

```
pragma Volatile(S);
```

when we were discussing the status value in Section 21.1.

Sometimes it is convenient to be able to refer to a task without it having to be of a specific task type. A server task might wish to keep a record of past callers so that they can be recognized in the future. This can be done using the package Ada.Task_Identification which defines a type Task_ID and a few operations upon tasks in general. The parameterless function Current_Task returns the identity of the currently executing task; the attribute E'Caller may be applied inside an accept statement or entry body and gives the task currently calling the entry E. The task identity of a task T is denoted by T'Identity. Task identities are particularly useful for manipulating priorities as discussed in the next section.

Finally, the generic package Ada.Task_Attributes enables attributes to be identified with tasks on a per-task basis using task identities.

22.2   Real-Time Systems

This annex covers priorities and scheduling, detailed requirements on the immediacy of the abort statement, restrictions enabling simplified run-time systems, a monotonic time package and direct task control.

The core language says little about scheduling and priorities. It does however state that entry queues are serviced in order of arrival.

This annex defines scheduling in terms of priorities. A general problem is the risk of priority inversion; this is where a high priority task is held up by a lower priority task using some resource. In order to define appropriate behaviour a task has a base priority and an active priority. The active priority is the one that is used to decide which tasks get the processors and is never less than the base priority; indeed, unless a task is involved in some interaction with another task or protected object, the active priority is the same as the base priority.

An obvious example of interaction is the rendezvous in which case the called task takes the active priority of the caller if that is higher; this is called priority inheritance. Similarly when a task is being activated, it inherits the active priority of its activator if it is higher.

The base priority of a task can be set by the pragma Priority in its specification

```
task type T(P: Any_Priority) is
    pragma Priority(P);
    ...
```

where we have shown the priority being set by a discriminant; but it could of course be a constant.

The integer subtype Any_Priority is defined in System. The subtypes Priority and Interrupt_Priority together embrace the full range of Any_Priority without overlapping. The range of values of Priority is always at least 30 and there is always at least one value for Interrupt_Priority which is of course higher. The pragma Interrupt_Priority can be used to set the priority level of a protected object used as an interrupt handler.

Base priorities can be manipulated dynamically using subprograms Set_Priority and Get_Priority in the package Ada.Dynamic_Priorities. For example

```
Fred: T(10);                          -- initial base priority 10
...
Set_Priority(15, Fred'Identity);      -- change to 15
```

The second parameter can be omitted and then by default is the result of calling Current_Task.

Protected objects can also be given priorities thus

```
protected Object is
   pragma Priority(20);
   entry E ...
```

and this is then known as the ceiling priority of the object. A task calling the entry E will then inherit the ceiling priority while executing the protected operation. A calling task with higher active priority than the ceiling priority is not permitted to execute the protected operation; it receives Program_Error instead. This ensures a degree of predictability for the other tasks.

Various pragmas enable different scheduling policies to be specified; some are standard and others may be defined by the implementation. The standard ones are

```
pragma Task_Dispatching_Policy(FIFO_Within_Priorities);
pragma Locking_Policy(Ceiling_Locking);
pragma Queuing_Policy(FIFO_Queuing);
pragma Queuing_Policy(Priority_Queuing);
```

FIFO_Within_Priorities specifies that tasks are to be scheduled with the highest active priority taking precedence and then within each level on a queued basis. Ceiling_Locking imposes ceiling priorities as mentioned above. FIFO_Queuing is the default core policy for servicing entry queues which is in order of arrival irrespective of priorities; Priority_Queuing on the other hand indicates that entry queues are to be serviced according to the active priorities of the queued tasks. Incidentally, these pragmas are of a category known as configuration pragmas and they apply throughout a partition.

Another configuration pragma is the pragma Restrictions; this enables the programmer to assert that the program does not use certain features of the language at all or does not exceed some limits. For example

```
pragma Restrictions(No_Task_Hierarchy, Max_Tasks = 100);
```

indicates that all tasks are at the library level and that there are no more than 100. Judicious use of this pragma may enable a program to use a specially small or fast version of the run-time system.

For some applications, the timing facilities of the package Calendar are not adequate. For example the associated clock is likely to be 'political time' and thus subject to daylight saving and time zone changes; in other words it can go backwards. The package Ada.Real_Time defines a type Time and function Clock which is monotonic and thus not subject to such difficulties. Time intervals for this clock are defined in terms of a type Time_Span. There are also appropriate operators for manipulating times and time spans. The functions Nanoseconds, Microseconds and Milliseconds which take an integer parameter and return a time span will be found useful for creating exact regular intervals.

The delay until statement can take a value of the type Calendar.Time or Real_Time.Time. The relative delay statement always takes an interval of the type Duration. This is because durations are intrinsic and not defined by the apparent value of a worldly clock. Boiling an egg takes three minutes and does not suddenly require an extra hour if being cooked when the clocks change!

The package Ada.Synchronous_Task_Control enables tasks to suspend according to the state of suspension objects; these objects can be set true and false and a task can suspend itself until an object is true. The package Ada.Asynchronous_Task_Control enables tasks to be held and then allowed to continue; these essentially work by reducing the priority to an idle level; the task is identified by its task identity.

22.3 Distributed Systems

This annex defines facilities for splitting a program up into a number of partitions and communication between the partitions.

Partitions may be active or passive. A passive partition has no threads of control and thus may only include certain kinds of library units.

The general idea is that the partitions execute independently other than when communicating. Each active partition has its own environment task, copy of the run-time system and so on. However, unlike a set of quite distinct programs, the strong typing is imposed rigorously between the partitions.

Library units are categorized into a hierarchy by a number of pragmas thus

```
pragma Pure( ... );
pragma Shared_Passive( ... );
pragma Remote_Types( ... );
pragma Remote_Call_Interface( ... );
```

Each category imposes restrictions on what the unit can contain. An important rule is that a unit can only depend on (via with clauses) units in the same or higher categories (the bodies of the last two are not restricted).

A pure unit cannot contain any state; since it has no state a distinct copy can be placed in each partition.

A shared passive unit can have visible state but no tasks or protected objects with entries. There are also restrictions on access types. The general idea is to avoid references to active units. It requires no run-time system.

A remote types unit defines types used for communication between partitions.

A remote call interface (RCI) unit cannot have visible state; its main purpose is to define the subprograms to be called remotely from other partitions.

A passive partition can only contain pure and shared passive units. Accordingly it does not need a copy of a run-time system.

Communication between active partitions is via remote procedure calls on RCI units. Such remote calls are processed by stubs at each end of the communication; parameters and results are passed as streams. This is all done automatically by the partition communication subsystem (PCS) and need not concern the user.

Thus to do a remote call from planet Earth to the spaceship StarTrek we might have one partition containing

```
package StarTrek is                          -- in space
   pragma Remote_Call_Interface(StarTrek);
   procedure Command(S: String);
end;
```

and then in a different partition

```
with StarTrek;
package Earth_Station is                      -- on terra firma
   ...
      StarTrek.Command("Invade Jupiter");
   ...
end;
```

so that the call of StarTrek.Command is all done by magic. Note incidentally that each partition has its own package Calendar so there are no relativistic problems regarding simultaneity.

The means of dividing the system up into partitions is not defined by the language and is done by some appropriate post-compilation tools.

22.4   Information Systems

This annex addresses material typically associated with COBOL programs.

The rules about decimal types follow those for fixed point types in general. In addition, the package Ada.Decimal declares a number of constants giving limits on the values of delta and digits supported plus a generic procedure for doing division giving both quotient and remainder in one operation. The constant Max_Decimal_Digits gives the largest digits value supported by the implementation; it has to be at least 18.

A major concern in information system processing is the format of human-readable output. Extensive facilities are provided by the package Ada.Text_IO.

Editing. This defines a private type Picture for the control of format and subprograms to manipulate and create pictures from strings. There is also a generic package Decimal_Output for the output of decimal values according to the format specified by a picture. Means are provided for localizing the currency symbol, filler character, digits separator and radix mark.

22.5   Numerics

This annex contains the definitions of packages for complex arithmetic, accuracy requirements for floating and fixed point arithmetic (the former based on the concept of model numbers) and accuracy requirements for the various predefined packages.

The predefined generic packages for complex arithmetic are

```
Numerics.Generic_Complex_Types
Numerics.Generic_Complex_Elementary_Functions
Text_IO.Complex_IO
```

plus nongeneric forms such as

```
Numerics.Complex_Types                        -- for Float
Numerics.Long_Complex_Types                   -- for Long_Float
Numerics.Complex_Elementary_Functions         -- for Float
Numerics.Long_Complex_Elementary_Functions    -- for Long_Float
```

although there are no nongeneric forms for Complex_IO.

In earlier chapters in this book we have discussed a hypothetical package Generic_Complex_Numbers in which the type Complex was private plus various child packages. This was introduced purely as an illustration largely because the concept of complex numbers and the possibility of implementing them in different ways is common knowledge. However, in practice, complex numbers are inevitably implemented in cartesian forms and the package defined in this annex thus declares the type Complex as a visible record type

```
type Complex is
   record
      Re, Im: Real'Base;
   end record;
```

where Real is the formal generic parameter. This has the advantage that record aggregates can be used in a natural way to provide complex literals.

Moreover, there is also a type Imaginary which is private and whose full declaration is

```
type Imaginary is new Real'Base;
```

and this type has values representing pure imaginary numbers. Constants i (and j for engineers) having the appropriate value are also defined. This enables complex expressions to be written in a very natural way such as

```
X, Y: Real;
Z: Complex;
...
Z := X + i*Y;
```

The four operators "=", "–", "*" and "/" are provided for all combinations of the types Real'Base, Imaginary and Complex. The operator "**" is provided for a first parameter of the type Imaginary or Complex and a second parameter of type Integer as usual.

Constructor and destructor functions are also provided with names Re, Im, Compose_From_Cartesian and Modulus, Argument, Compose_From_Polar. Although somewhat redundant since the type Complex is not private they might be useful as generic actual parameters. Compose_From_Cartesian takes one or two real parameters or one imaginary parameter. Compose_From_Polar and Argument take an optional Cycle parameter like the trigonometric functions. There are also functions "abs" and Conjugate with appropriate specifications.

The specification of the generic package for complex elementary functions has the form

```
with Ada.Numerics.Generic_Complex_Types;
generic
  with package Complex_Types is
       new Ada.Numerics.Generic_Complex_Types(<>);
  use Complex_Types;
package Ada.Numerics.Generic_Complex_Elementary_Functions is
    ...
  function Sqrt(X: Complex) return Complex;
  -- similarly for Log, Exp, Sin, Cos, Tan,
  -- Acrsin, Arccos, Arctan, Arccot,
  -- Sinh, Cosh, Tanh, Coth,
  -- Arcsinh, Arccosh, Arctanh, Arccoth
end;
```

and also includes Exp taking an imaginary parameter and "**" taking combinations of real and complex parameters.

Note that this package has a formal package parameter which has to be an instantiation of Generic_Complex_Types. This technique was discussed in Section 17.4. However, unlike the hypothetical package Generic_Complex_ Functions of that section, this annex package does not also import (an instantiation of) the real elementary functions since algorithms other than those we hypothesized are likely to be used in the implementation; moreover, they are not needed for the specification of the package and can always be imported by the body.

The package Complex_IO also takes an instantiation of Generic_Complex_ Types as its only parameter. It provides various Put and Get procedures with similar specifications to those in Text_IO.Float_IO except that they take a parameter of type Complex rather than Num. Put outputs the values of the real and imaginary parts as a pair of real values in the corresponding format separated by a comma and all enclosed in parentheses. Get accepts the same format but the parentheses and comma may be omitted.

The reader may recall that the behaviour of floating and fixed point types in Ada 83 was defined in terms of model and safe numbers; in the case of floating point the model numbers related to the requested number of digits whereas the safe numbers related to the implemented number of digits. However, few people seemed to understand this stuff and so the concepts were reconsidered for Ada 95.

Floating point in Ada 95 continues to be defined in terms of model numbers but these relate to the implemented properties and so roughly correspond to the safe numbers of Ada 83 (there are no safe numbers in Ada 95). Moreover, whereas the Ada 83 model was in terms of a binary exponent, the Ada 95 model is in terms of the exponent of the machine which might for example be hexadecimal. Otherwise the model works in much the same way.

The canonical model and the various attributes were outlined in Section 15.4. The model numbers are zero plus all values of the canonical form where the mantissa has Model_Mantissa digits and the exponent is greater than or equal to Model_Emin. Note that there is no upper bound and so no attribute Model_Emax. The general principle is that associated with each value is a model interval. If a value is a model number then the model interval is simply the model number. Otherwise it is the interval defined by the two model numbers surrounding the value.

When an operation is performed, the bounds of the result are given by the smallest model interval that can arise as a consequence of operating upon any values in the model intervals of the operands. The relational operators are also defined in terms of model intervals. If the result is the same, whatever values are chosen in the intervals, then its value is clearly not in dispute. If, however, the result depends upon which values in the intervals are chosen then the result is undefined.

Some care is needed in the interpretation of these principles. Although we may not know where a value lies in a model interval, nevertheless it does have a specific value and should not be treated in a stochastic manner. For example $X = X$ is always true even if we do not know the specific value of X. There is perhaps some philosophical analogy here with Quantum Mechanics – the execution of the program equates to performing an observation on X and the knowing of the specific value is the collapse of the wave packet!

One tiny example must suffice. Consider a hypothetical binary machine with a type Rough that has just 5 bits in the mantissa, 3 bits in the exponent and a sign bit (we can squeeze this into a byte because the leading mantissa bit need not be stored). The model numbers around one are

$$..., \ ^{30}/_{32}, \ ^{31}/_{32}, \ 1, \ 1^1/_{16}, \ 1^2/_{16}, \ 1^3/_{16}, \ ...$$

Now suppose that R of type Rough has the value $1^1/_8$ and consider the values of $((R*R)*R)*R$ and $(R*R)*(R*R)$. The final model intervals are $[1^1/_2, 1^{11}/_{16}]$ and $[1^9/_{16}, 1^3/_4]$ respectively. The upper bound of the latter interval is outside the former interval and so the optimization of computing R**4 by repeated squaring actually gives a different result. However, the language definition allows this optimization anyway since it does not prescribe any order to the association of the multiplications for exponentiation as mentioned in Section 6.5.

This annex thus prescribes the accuracy of floating point operations in terms of model numbers; it also gives accuracy and performance requirements for the various packages. Some awkward hardware might not be able to meet these requirements for built-in implementations of certain functions (such as Sin) and rather than exclude such implementations from conformance to this annex altogether, it is instead possible to conform in either a relaxed or strict mode. In the relaxed mode, the accuracy requirements do not have to be met. For further details consult the *ARM*.

Fixed point in Ada 95 is defined entirely in terms of *small* and does not use the concept of model numbers at all.

22.6 Safety and Security

This annex provides a number of pragmas which can be used to aid the analysis of a program to ensure that it is correct.

The configuration pragma Normalize_Scalars ensures that all otherwise uninitialized objects have an initial value. This reduces the dangers of bounded errors.

The configuration pragma Reviewable directs the compiler to generate code and listings enabling an understandable mapping between the source code and the object code.

The pragma Inspection_Point takes a list of object names and ensures that at each point where it is written the named objects are in sensible places from which their values can be obtained for analysis or debugging.

The pragma Restrictions has additional arguments defined in this annex which can be used to ensure that the program uses only simple and consequently formally analysable features of the language.

23 Finale

23.1 Names and expressions	23.4 Visibility and composition
23.2 Type equivalence	23.5 Portability
23.3 Overall program structure	23.6 Program design

This final chapter covers various overall aspects of Ada. The first four sections consider in more detail and consolidate some important topics which have of necessity been introduced in stages throughout the book. There is then a section on the important issue of portability. Finally, we discuss the general topic of program design as it relates to Ada.

23.1 Names and expressions

The idea of a name should be carefully distinguished from that of an identifier. An identifier is a syntactic form such as Fred which is used for various purposes including introducing entities when they are declared. An operator has a similar status to an identifier; operators and identifiers are collectively referred to as direct names in the syntax. A name, on the other hand, may be more complex and is the form used to denote entities in general.

Syntactically, a name typically starts with an identifier such as Fred or an operator symbol such as "+" and can then be followed by one or more of the following in an arbitrary order

- one or more index expressions in brackets; this denotes a component of an array,

- a discrete range in brackets; this denotes a slice of an array,

Table 23.1 Predefined operations.

Operator	Operand(s)		Result
and or xor	Boolean		same
	one-dimensional Boolean array		same
	modular		same
and then or else	Boolean		same
= /=	any, not limited		Boolean
< <= > >=	scalar		Boolean
	one-dimensional discrete array		Boolean
in not in	scalar	range	Boolean
	any	subtype mark	Boolean
+ – (binary)	numeric		same
&	one-dimensional array | component		same array
+ – (unary)	numeric		same
*	integer	integer	same
	fixed	Integer	same fixed
	Integer	fixed	same fixed
	univ fixed	univ fixed	univ fixed
	floating	floating	same
	root real	root integer	root real
	root integer	root real	root real
/	integer	integer	same
	fixed	Integer	same fixed
	univ fixed	univ fixed	univ fixed
	floating	floating	same
	root real	root integer	root real
mod rem	integer	integer	same
**	integer	Natural	same integer
	floating	Integer	same floating
not	Boolean		same
	one-dimensional Boolean array		same
	modular		same
abs	numeric		same

- a dot followed by an identifier, operator or **all**; this denotes a record component, an object designated by an access value, or an entity in a package, task, protected object, subprogram, block or loop,
- a prime and then an identifier, possibly indexed; this denotes an attribute,
- an actual parameter list in brackets; this denotes a function call.

Type conversions and character literals are also treated as names in the syntax. Character literals are considered to be parameterless functions and can be renamed.

Names are just one of the primary components of an expression. The others are literals (numeric literals, strings and **null**), aggregates, allocators and qualified expressions as well as expressions in brackets. Expressions involving scalar operators were summarized in Section 6.9.

For convenience, all the operators and their predefined uses are shown in Table 23.1. They are grouped according to precedence level. We have also included the short circuit forms **and then** and **or else** and the membership tests **in** and **not in** although these are not technically classed as operators (they cannot be overloaded).

Note the careful distinction between Boolean which means the predefined type and 'Boolean' which means Boolean or any type derived from it. Similarly Integer means the predefined type and 'integer' means any integer type (including root integer). Also 'floating' means any floating type plus root real.

Observe that the membership tests apply to any type and not just scalar types which were discussed in Section 6.9. Thus we can check whether an array or record has a particular subtype by using a membership test rather than testing the bounds or discriminant. So we can write

> V **in** Vector_5   -- true, see Section 8.2
> John **in** Woman   -- false, see Section 16.5

rather than

> V'First = 1 **and** V'Last = 5
> John.Sex = Female

which are equivalent.

Finally, remember that & can take either an array or a component for both operands so four cases arise.

The observant reader will notice that the syntax in Appendix 3 uses the syntactic form 'simple_expression' in some cases where 'expression' might have been expected. One reason for this is to avoid a potential ambiguity regarding the use of **in** as a membership test with ranges.

From time to time we have referred to the need for certain expressions to be static. As explained in Chapter 2 this means that they have to be evaluated at compile time. An expression is static if all its constituents are one of the following

* a numeric, enumeration, character or string literal,
* a named number,
* a constant initialized by a static expression,
* a predefined operator with scalar parameters and result,
* a predefined concatenation operator returning a string,
* a membership test or short circuit form,
* a static attribute or a functional attribute with static parameters,

- a type conversion provided that any constraint involved is static,
- a qualified static expression provided that any constraint involved is static.

Note that renaming preserves staticness so a renaming of one of the above (for which renaming is allowed) is also an allowed constituent of a static expression. Observe that apart from the ability to build up static strings by concatenation, staticness only applies to scalar expressions and that all intermediate subexpressions must also be scalar. Thus although 'a'&'b' is a static string nevertheless 'a'&'b'='c'&'d' is not static although the result is scalar. However, the bounds, length and range of a static array are static. The main purpose of static strings is as parameters for pragmas.

It is an important point that staticness is an intrinsic property of an expression and does not depend upon its context. Thus 2 + 3 is always statically evaluated to give 5 irrespective of whether the context demands a static expression.

EXERCISE 23.1

1   Given

```
L: Integer := 6;
M: constant Integer := 7;
N: constant := 8;
```

then classify the following as static or dynamic expressions and give their type.

(a) L+1   (b) M+1   (c) N+1

23.2   Type equivalence

It is perhaps worth emphasizing the rules for type equivalence. The basic rule is that every type definition introduces a new type. Remember the difference between a type definition and a type declaration. A type definition introduces a type whereas a type declaration also introduces an identifier referring to it. Thus

type T **is** (A, B, C);

is a type declaration whereas

(A, B, C)

is a type definition.

The language rules are such that, strictly speaking, types never have names; it is subtypes that have names. Thus T is the name of an unconstrained subtype of an unnamed type; T is known as the first subtype. This nicety need rarely concern the user but explains why the *ARM* usually refers to subtypes and never has to say 'type or subtype'. We should thus really say 'the type of T' meaning the type of which T is the name of the unconstrained subtype. But of course we just loosely say 'the type T'. Note that the attribute **Base** does not give the type but simply an unconstrained subtype of the type.

Most subtypes have names but in a few cases even all subtypes may be anonymous. The obvious cases occur with the declarations of arrays, tasks and protected objects. Thus

```
A: array (I range L .. R) of C;
```

is essentially short for

```
type anon is array (I range <>) of C;
A: anon(L .. R);
```

and

```
task T is ...
```

is essentially short for

```
task type anon is ...
T: anon;
```

In such cases we say that A and T are of anonymous types.

In some cases the first subtype is constrained. This occurs with array types, derived types and numeric types and so

```
type T is array (I range L .. R) of C;
```

is essentially short for

```
subtype index is I range L .. R;
type anon is array (index range <>) of C;
subtype T is anon(L .. R);
```

and

```
type S is new T constraint;
```

is essentially short for

```
type anon is new T;
subtype S is anon constraint;
```

and

```
type T is range L .. R;
```

is essentially short for

```
type anon is new some_integer_type;
subtype T is anon range L .. R;
```

where some_integer_type corresponds to an underlying implemented type. Similar expansions apply to floating and fixed types.

When interpreting the rule that each type definition introduces a new type, remember that generic instantiation is equivalent to text substitution in this respect. Thus each instantiation of a package with a type definition in its specification introduces a distinct type. It will be remembered that a similar rule applies to the identification of different exceptions. Each textually distinct exception declaration introduces a new exception; an exception in a recursive procedure is the same for each incarnation but generic instantiation introduces different exceptions.

Remember also that multiple declarations are equivalent to several single declarations written out explicitly. Thus if we have

```
A, B: array (I range L .. R) of C;
```

then A and B are of different anonymous types.

In summary then, Ada has named equivalence rather than the weaker structural equivalence used for some types in C++. As a consequence Ada gives greater security in the sense that more errors can be found during compilation. However, the overzealous use of lots of different types can lead to trouble and there are stories of programs that could never be got to compile.

An obvious area of caution is with numeric types (a novice programmer often uses lots of numeric types with great glee). Attempts to use different numeric types to separate different units of measurement (for example the lengths and areas of Exercise 11.3(**1**)) can lead to messy situations where either lots of overloadings of operators have to be introduced or so many type conversions are required that the clarity sought is lost by the extra clutter. Another problem is that each different numeric type will require a separate instantiation of the relevant package in Text_IO if input–output is required. An example of possible overuse of numeric types is in Text_IO itself where the distinct integer type Count (used for counting characters, lines and pages) is a frequent irritant.

So too many types can be unwise. However, the use of appropriate constraints (as explicit subtypes or directly) always seems to be a good idea. Remember that subtypes are merely shorthand for a type plus constraint and as a consequence have structural equivalence. Thus, recalling an example in Section 6.4, we can declare

```
subtype Day_Number is Integer range 1 .. 31;
subtype Feb_Day is Day_Number range 1 .. 29;
D1: Integer range 1 .. 29;
D2: Day_Number range 1 .. 29;
D3: Feb_Day;
```

and then D1, D2 and D3 all have exactly the same subtype.

When to use a subtype and when to use a new type is a matter of careful judgement. The guidelines must be the amount of separation between the abstract concepts. If the abstractions are quite distinct then separate types are justified but if there is much overlap and thus much conversion then subtypes are probably appropriate. Thus we could make a case for Day_Number being a distinct type

```
type Day_Number is range 1 .. 31;
```

but we would find it hard to justify making Feb_Day not simply a subtype of Day_Number.

Another important distinction between types and subtypes is in their representation. The basic rule is that a subtype has the same representation as the base type whereas a derived type can have a different representation. Of course, the compiler can still optimize, but that is another matter.

It should also be remembered that checking subtype properties is generally a run-time matter. Thus

```
S: String(1 .. 4) := "ABC";
```

raises Constraint_Error although we can expect that any reasonable compiler would pick this up during compilation.

However, although checking that a value lies within a subtype is a run-time matter, static matching is generally required between two subtypes. Examples are matching the component subtypes in array conversions (Section 8.2), the matching in deferred constants (Section 11.2) and subtype conformance rules for renaming subprogram bodies (Section 12.6).

23.3   Overall program structure

Ada has five structural units in which declarations can occur; these are blocks, subprograms, packages, tasks and protected units. They can be classified in various ways. First of all packages, tasks and protected units have separate specifications and bodies; for subprograms this separation is optional; for blocks it is not possible or relevant since a block has no specification. We can also consider separate compilation: packages, tasks, protected units and subprogram bodies can all be subunits but only packages and subprograms can be library units including child library units. Note also that only packages and subprograms can be generic. Finally, tasks, subprograms and blocks can have dependent tasks; packages cannot since they are only passive scope control units and declaring a task in a protected unit is not allowed since it is a potentially blocking operation (see Section 18.4). These various properties of units are summarized in Table 23.2.

We can also consider the scope and nesting of these five structural units. (Note that a block is a statement whereas the others are declarations.) Each unit can generally appear inside any of the other units and this lexical nesting can

Table 23.2   Properties of units.

Property	Blocks	Subprograms	Packages	Tasks	Protected
Separation	no	optional	yes	yes	yes
Subunits	no	yes	yes	yes	yes
Library units	no	yes	yes	no	no
Generic units	no	yes	yes	no	no
Dependent tasks	yes	yes	no	yes	no

in principle go on indefinitely, although in practical programs a depth of three will not often be exceeded. The only restrictions to this nesting are that a block, being a statement, cannot appear in a package specification but only in its body (and directly only in the initialization sequence); none of these units can appear in a task specification but only in its body; similarly none can appear in a protected specification although they can appear inside the bodies of entries and subprograms of the unit. In practice, however, some of the combinations will arise rarely. Blocks will usually occur inside subprograms and task bodies and occasionally inside other blocks. Subprograms will occur as library units and inside packages and protected units and less frequently inside tasks and other subprograms. Packages will usually be library units or inside other packages. Tasks will probably nearly always be inside packages and occasionally inside other tasks or subprograms. Protected units will usually be inside packages.

The *ARM* does not prescribe how the program is to be started but as discussed in Sections 4.4 and 12.1 we can imagine that one of the library units which is a subprogram (or an instance of a generic subprogram) is called by some magic outside the language itself. Moreover, we must imagine that this originating flow of control is associated with an anonymous task; this is called the environment task. The priority of this task can be set by the pragma Priority in the outermost declarative part of this main subprogram.

A further point is that whether a main subprogram can have parameters or not or whether there are restrictions on their types and modes or indeed whether the main subprogram can be a function is dependent on the implementation. It may indeed be very convenient for a main subprogram to have parameters, and for the calling and parameter passing to be performed by the magic associated with the interpretation of a statement in some non-Ada command language. On the other hand any such parameters may be accessible through the package Command_Line discussed in Section 20.7.

The general effect is illustrated by the following simple model

```
task Environment_Task;

task body Environment_Task is
    -- all the library units, including Standard are declared here in
    -- some order consistent with the elaboration requirements
begin
```

```
    -- call the main subprogram, if any
  end;
```

This model also illustrates that

- Delay statements executed by the environment task during the elaboration of a library package delay the environment task.

- Tasks that depend on a library unit (and that are not designated by an access value) are started before the main subprogram is called.

- After normal termination of the main subprogram the environment task must wait for all library tasks to terminate. If all library tasks terminate, then the program as a whole terminates.

If the main subprogram terminates abnormally by the propagation of an exception or the environment task terminates abnormally, then the implementation should wait for library tasks to terminate. However, it is permitted to abort such tasks.

If any external files are used by statements executed in library package bodies, then such operations are performed before execution of the main subprogram begins. If external files are used by library tasks, then these files are processed in accordance with normal Ada semantics, whether or not execution of the main subprogram has begun or has finished. After the main subprogram and all library tasks have terminated (or if execution of the main subprogram is abandoned because of an unhandled exception), any further effects on the external files are not specified; in particular, any files that have been left open may (but need not) be closed.

The model just discussed corresponds to an active partition. A passive partition has no environment task and so all library units are preelaborated.

23.4 Visibility and composition

The visibility and scope rules have been introduced by stages. The basic rules applicable to the simple block structure were introduced in Section 6.2 and further discussed in Section 9.6 when we considered the use of the dotted notation to provide visibility of an outer identifier which had been hidden by an inner redeclaration. The overloading rules were discussed in Section 9.2 and we recall from Section 9.5 that the use of identifiers fell into two categories: overloadable (subprograms) and not overloadable (the rest). We then considered the impact of packages in Section 12.5 and the rules regarding the use clause. We also noted in Section 14.5 that exceptions had some special characteristics. We do not intend to repeat all these rules here but rather to illustrate some of their effects particularly with regard to building programs from components.

We begin by recalling from Section 9.5 that enumeration literals behave much like parameterless functions. We could not therefore declare both an enumeration type and a parameterless function returning that type and with the same identifier as one of the literals in the same declarative region thus

```
type Colour is (Red, Amber, Green);
function Red return Colour;                          -- illegal
```

although we could of course declare the function Red in an inner scope where it would hide the literal Red. A more subtle illustration is given by

```
package P is
   type Light is new Colour;
   function Red return Light;
end;
```

where (assuming Colour as above) the function Red replaces the literal Red of the derived type Light. So if we then declared

```
type More_Light is new Light;
```

then More_Light would inherit the function Red rather than the literal Red.

We will now discuss the visibility rules and similar properties of generic packages in more detail. Reconsider the package Set_Of from Section 17.2

```
generic
   type Base is (<>);
package Set_Of is
   type Set is private;
   type List is array (Positive range <>) of Base;
   ...
end;
```

It is very important to grasp the difference between the rules for the template (the generic text as written) and an instance (the effective text after instantiation).

The first point is that the generic package is not a genuine package and in particular does not export anything. So no meaning can be attached to Set_Of.List outside the generic package and nor can Set_Of appear in a use clause. Of course, inside the generic package we can indeed write Set_Of.List if we wished to be pedantic or had hidden List by an inner redeclaration.

If we now instantiate the generic package thus

```
package Character_Set is new Set_Of(Character);
```

then Character_Set is a genuine package and so we can refer to Character_Set.List outside the package and Character_Set can appear in a use clause. In this case there is no question of writing Character_Set.List *inside* the package because the inside text is quite ethereal.

Another very important point concerns the properties of an identifier such as List. Inside the generic template we can only use the properties common to all possible actual parameters as expressed by the formal parameter notation. Outside we can additionally use the properties of the particular instantiation. So, inside we cannot write

```
S: List(1 .. 6) := "String";
```

because we do not know that the actual type is going to be a character type – it could be an integer type. However, outside we can indeed write

```
S: Character_Set.List(1 .. 6) := "String";
```

because we know full well that the actual type is, in this instance, a character type.

Constructing a total program requires putting together various software components whose interfaces match much as we can put together hardware components by the use of various plugs and sockets. In order for an entity from one component to be used by another, its name must be exported from the component declaring it and then imported into the component using it. Our normal component is naturally a library package which will often be generic. The various tools at our disposal are

- Entities are exported by being in the visible part of a package.
- Entities are imported by being generic parameters.
- Entities are also imported through with clauses. Direct visibility is given by use clauses.

We have also seen that generic actual parameters can be imported into a package and then used to create entities that are exported (the example List above); we also noted that specific properties of the actual parameters were reexported but not visible internally (the fact that the actual type was a character type).

The Ada export and import rules work on groups of entities rather than individual entities as in some languages. The Ada technique avoids clutter and is very appropriate when the entities are highly cohesive (that is are strongly related). However, if they are not cohesive then the coarse grouping is a nuisance; there are various techniques that can be used to give finer control.

An obvious technique for giving finer control of entities exported from the visible part of a package is simply to declare a hierarchical set of nested packages

```
package Outer is
  package Inner1 is
    ...
  end;

  package Inner2 is
    ...
  end;
end;
```

We could then write

```
with Outer;
package User is
  use Outer.Inner1;
```

and then Inner2 and its internal entities will not be directly visible. Note that we cannot put the use clause immediately after the with clause because a use clause in such a position can only refer to the packages mentioned in the with clause itself.

Rather better control is provided by child packages

```
package Parent is
  ...
end;

package Parent.Child1 is
  ...
end;

package Parent.Child2 is
  ...
end;
```

and then we can have with and use clauses for one child and not the other.

There is no directly corresponding technique for grouping imported generic parameters. Sometimes we would like to only partially instantiate a generic package. Consider the more general function Integrate of Section 17.3

```
generic
  type Floating is digits <>;
  with function F(X: Floating) return Floating;
function Integrate(A, B: Floating) return Floating;
```

If we want to do lots of different integrations but all with the same floating type then it would be rather nice to fix the type parameter once and then only have to bother with the function parameter thereafter. This could be done if our generic function were rewritten as a nested generic thus

```
generic
  type Floating is digits <>;
package Generic_Integrate is
  generic
    with function F(X: Floating) return Floating;
  function Integrate(A, B: Floating) return Floating;
end Generic_Integrate;
```

We can then write

```
package Float_Integrate is new Generic_Integrate(Float);
use Float_Integrate;
```

and now we can instantiate the inner generic with our actual function G as in Section 17.3. This technique obviously works but we do have to impose a predetermined order on our partial parameterization.

Another approach is to use generic package parameters. We saw in Section 17.4 how the group of three related parameters were bundled together as the package General_Vector.

Renaming is a useful (although somewhat heavy) tool for filtering visibility. We can import some entities into a package and then just rename those that we wish to reexport. As an example consider again the package Set_Of. Suppose we wish to instantiate this for type Character but only want the user to have access to Make_Set on single values, "+", "−" and Size on the grounds that the other operations are superfluous. (This is only an example!) We write

```
with Set_Of;
package XYZ is new Set_Of(Character);
```

and then

```
with XYZ;
package Character_Set is
   subtype Set is XYZ.Set;
   function Make_Set(X: Character) return Set renames
                                          XYZ.Make_Set;
   function "+" (X, Y: Set) return Set renames XYZ."+";
   function "−" (X, Y: Set) return Set renames XYZ."−";
   function Size(X: Set) return Natural renames XYZ.Size;
end Character_Set;
```

The user can now access the reexported facilities from the package Character_Set without having visibility of the facilities of XYZ. Of course the user could still write **with** XYZ; and this would defeat the object of the exercise. However, it might be that our program library has additional tools which can hide library units without deleting them.

Note also that we had to use a subtype because we cannot rename a type. The subtype declaration also makes available the intrinsic ability to declare objects and perform assignment. However, if we wish to do equality comparisons then we must explicitly rename "=" as well thus

```
function "=" (Left, Right: Set) return Boolean renames XYZ."=";
```

This also makes "**/**=" available as one would expect. The general rule therefore is that predefined operators can be imported by renaming but intrinsic properties which cannot be dealt with that way are available automatically. In order to properly comprehend the mechanism it must be realized that predefined operators such as "=" are implicitly declared immediately after the declaration of the type to which they refer.

Another example is provided by enumeration types; if we want to have

Table 23.3   Compilation units.

Unit	Dependency
package spec	may need a body
package body	depends on: [generic] package spec
subprogram spec	needs a body
subprogram body	may depend on: [generic] subprogram spec
gen package spec	may need a body
gen subprogram spec	needs a body
subunit	depends on: package body | subprogram body | subunit
child spec	depends on: package spec
gen package instance	all in one lump
gen subprogram instance	all in one lump

visibility of the literals then they have to be renamed. So writing

```
package C is
   type Colour is (Red, Amber, Green);
   -- predefined operators such as = and < applying to the
   -- type Colour are implicitly declared here
end;

with C;
package P is
   subtype Light is C.Colour;
   function Red return Light renames C.Red;
   function Amber return Light renames C.Amber;
   function "<" (Left, Right: Light) return Boolean renames C."<";
end;
```

will provide visibility (from P) of the literals Red and Amber but not Green and also of "<" but none of the other relational operators. But this does not apply to character literals; they are always 'visible' in the same way that numeric literals are visible. Further details can be found in the *ARM*.

Rather simpler examples of the renaming technique for controlling visibility are given by the renaming of the exceptions declared in IO_Exceptions at the end of the input–output packages.

Note that derived types are often better than subtypes for giving a new name to a type as we saw when discussing how to give the name Colour to the exported type Set in Section 17.2.

We continue by reconsidering the rules for order of compilation and recompilation of the units in a program library. The various different units are summarized in Table 23.3 which also shows their basic interrelationships. Remember also that renaming is permitted at the library level so that a library item can simply be the renaming of another library item.

The reader will recall from Chapter 12 that the compilation order is determined by the dependency relationships. A unit cannot be compiled unless all the units on which it depends have already been entered into the library. And similarly, if a unit is changed then all units depending upon it also have to be recompiled. The basic rules for dependency are

- A body is dependent on its specification.
- A child is dependent upon its parent's specification.
- A subunit is dependent on its parent body or subunit.
- A unit is dependent on the specifications of units given in its with clauses.

In addition, an implementation may impose the following auxiliary rule

- If a subprogram call is inlined using the pragma Inline (see Appendix 1) then the calling unit will be dependent upon the called subprogram body (as well as the specification).

The language definition is very careful not to impose unnecessary restrictions on how the compilation process actually works. At the end of the day there is really only the one requirement that a linked partition be consistent. The discussion here must thus be interpreted as the sort of way in which a library environment might work rather than how it must work.

The basic rules for compilation are as follows. A new library unit will replace an existing library unit (of any sort) with the same name. A unit will be rejected unless there already exists all those units on which it depends; thus a body is rejected unless its specification exists and a subunit is rejected unless its parent body or subunit exists. If a unit is replaced then all units dependent on it need to be compiled.

These fairly straightforward rules are complicated by the fact that a subprogram need not have a distinct specification and a package may not need a body.

If we start with an empty library and compile a procedure body P, then it will be accepted as a library unit (and not needing a distinct specification). If we subsequently compile a new version of the body then it will replace the previous library unit. If, however, we subsequently enter and compile just the specification of P, then it will make the old body obsolete and we must then compile a new body which will now be classed as dependent upon the separate specification. In other words we cannot add the specification as an afterthought and then provide a new body perhaps in the expectation that units dependent just on the specification could avoid recompilation. Moreover, once we have a distinct specification and body we cannot join them up again – if we provide a new body which matches the existing distinct specification then it will replace the old body, if it does not match the specification then it will be rejected.

A library package cannot have a body unless it needs one to satisfy language rules. This prevents the inadvertent loss of a body when a specification is replaced since otherwise the system would link without the body. The pragma Elaborate_Body can be used to force a body to be required as mentioned in Section 12.7.

Generics also have to be considered and we need to take care to distinguish between generic units and their instantiations. A generic subprogram always has a distinct specification but a generic package may not need a body. Note carefully that the body of a generic package or subprogram looks just like the body of a plain package or subprogram. It will be classed as one or the other according to the category of the existing specification (a body is rejected if there is no existing specification except in the case of a subprogram which we discussed above). An instantiation however is all in one lump, it is classed as a single library unit in its own right and the separation of specification and body does not occur. The notional body of a generic instance cannot be replaced by a newly compiled plain body. For example, suppose we first compile

```
generic
procedure GP;

procedure GP is
begin ... end GP;
```

and then separately compile

```
with GP;
procedure P is new GP;
```

and then submit

```
procedure P is
begin ... end P;
```

The result is that the new unit P will be accepted. However, it will be classed as a nongeneric library unit and completely replace the existing instantiation. It cannot be taken as a new body for the generic instance since the instantiation is treated as one lump.

We conclude by emphasizing that we have been discussing a possible implementation of the program library. Some implementations may insist that compilation is only possible if all units on which a unit depends have already been compiled; other implementations may merely insist that just the source of the units be present. The above discussion must thus be interpreted in an appropriate manner. We can expect an implementation to provide utility programs which manipulate the library in additional ways. Any such facilities are outside the scope of this book and we must hence refer the reader to the documentation for the implementation concerned.

23.5 Portability

An Ada program may or may not be portable. In many cases a program will be intimately concerned with the particular hardware on which it is running; this is particularly true of embedded applications. Such a program cannot be transferred to another machine without significant alteration. On the other hand it is highly desirable to write portable software components so that they can be reused in different applications. In some cases a component will be totally portable; more often it will make certain demands on the implementation or be parameterized so that it can be tailored to its environment in a straightforward manner. This section contains general guidelines on the writing of portable Ada programs.

One thing to avoid is programs with bounded errors and those whose behaviour depends upon some order of evaluation which is not specified. They can be insidious. A program may work quite satisfactorily on one implementation and may seem superficially to be portable. However, if it happens to depend upon some unspecified feature then its behaviour on another implementation cannot be guaranteed. A common example in most programming languages occurs with variables which accidentally are not initialized. It is often the case that the intended value is zero and furthermore many operating systems clear the program area before loading the program. Under such circumstances the program will behave correctly but may give surprising results when transferred to a different implementation. In the previous chapters we have mentioned various causes of such doubtful programs. For convenience we summarize them here.

An important group of situations concerns the order of evaluation of expressions. Since an expression can include a function call and a function call can have side effects, it follows that different orders of evaluation can sometimes produce different results. The order of evaluation of the following is not specified

- the operands of a binary operator,
- the destination and value in an assignment,
- the components in an aggregate,
- the parameters in a subprogram or entry call,
- the index expressions in a multidimensional name,
- the expressions in a range,
- the barriers in a protected object
- the guards in a select statement.

There is an important situation where a junk value can arise

- reading an uninitialized variable before assigning to it.

There are situations where the language mechanism is not specified

- the passing of array and record parameters,
- the algorithm for choosing a branch of a select statement or between several queues in protected units.

But note that the last can be specified by the pragma Queuing_Policy if the Real-Time Systems annex is implemented.

There are also situations where the programmer is given extra freedom to overcome the stringency of the type model; abuse of this freedom can lead to erroneous programs. Examples are

* suppressing exceptions,
* unchecked access,
* unchecked deallocation,
* unchecked conversion.

Finally, we recall from Section 12.7 that the order of elaboration of library units is not fully determined.

Numeric types are another important source of portability problems. The reason is, of course, the compromise necessary between achieving absolutely uniform behaviour on all machines and maximizing efficiency. Ada gives the user various options in choosing an appropriate compromise as discussed in Section 15.1.

There are various attributes which, if used correctly, can make our programs more portable. Thus we can use Base to find out what is really going on and Machine_Overflows to see whether Constraint_Error will occur or not. But the misuse of these attributes can lead to very non-portable programs.

There is, however, one simple rule that can be followed. We should always declare our own floating point types and not directly use the predefined types such as Float. A similar approach should be taken with integer types, although the language does encourage us to assume that the predefined type Integer has a sensible range.

Another area to consider is tasking. Any program that uses tasking is likely to suffer from portability problems because instruction execution times vary from machine to machine. In some cases a program may not be capable of running at all on a particular machine because it does not have adequate processing power. Hard guidelines are almost impossible to give but the following points should be kept in mind.

Take care that the type Duration is accurate enough for the application. Remember that regular loops (that is, at uniform intervals) cannot easily be achieved if the interval required is not a multiple of small.

Avoid the unsynchronized use of shared variables as far as possible. Sometimes, timing considerations demand quick and dirty techniques. In simple cases the pragma Atomic may be able to prevent interference between tasks.

The use of the abort statement will also give portability problems because of its asynchronous nature.

And finally, different machines have different sizes and so a program that runs satisfactorily on one machine might raise Storage_Error on another. Moreover, different implementations may use different storage allocation strategies for access types and task data. We have seen how representation clauses can be used to give control of storage allocation and thereby reduce portability problems.

EXERCISE 23.5

1   The global variable I is of type Integer and the function F is

```
function F return Integer is
begin
   I := I + 1;
   return I;
end F;
```

Explain why the following fragments of program are unwise. Assume in each case that I is reset to 1.

(a) I := I + F;   (b) A(I) := F;   (c) AA(I, F) := 0;

23.6   Program design

This final section considers the question of designing Ada programs. As stated in Section 1.5, this book does not claim to be a treatise on program design. Indeed, program design is still largely an art and the value of different methods of design is often a matter of opinion rather than a matter of fact. We have therefore tried to stick to the facts of Ada and to remain neutral regarding design. Nevertheless much has been learnt about design methods over the last decade and many millions of lines of Ada programs have been designed and written. In particular, Object Oriented Design, which matches Ada well, has gained popularity.

Perhaps the most important aspect of design is ensuring that software can be reused. In a broad sense this includes maintenance. This means that the external behaviour should be clearly specified and that the internal structure should be understandable. It is not possible to say much in the space available but the following thoughts might be helpful.

There are various low level and stylistic issues which are perhaps obvious. Identifiers should be meaningful. The program should be laid out neatly – the style used in this book is based on that recommended from the syntax in the *ARM*. Useful comments should be added. The block structure should be used to localize declarations to their use. Whenever possible a piece of information should only be written once; thus number and constant declarations should be used rather than explicit literals. And so on.

Programming is really all about abstraction and the mapping of the problem onto constructions in the programming language. We recall from Section 1.3 that the development of programming languages has been concerned with the introduction of various levels of abstraction and that Ada includes means for abstraction not present in other practically used languages.

An important concept in design and the use of abstractions is information hiding. Information should only be accessible to those parts of a program that need to know. The use of packages and private data types to hide unnecessary detail is the cornerstone of good Ada programming.

Designing an Ada program is therefore largely concerned with designing groups of packages and the interfaces between them. A group can often be organized as a child hierarchy. Often we will hope to use existing packages. For this to be possible it is clear that they must have been designed with consistent, clean and sufficiently general interfaces. The difficulties are perhaps in deciding what items are sufficiently related or fundamental to belong together in a package and also how general to make the package. If a package is too general it might be clumsy and inefficient; if not general enough it will not be as useful as it might.

A very simple form of package is one which merely consists of a group of related types and constants and has no body. The packages System and Characters.Latin_1 are in this category. Other examples might be packages of related mathematical constants, conversion constants (metric to imperial say), tables of physical and chemical constants and so on. The last could be

```
package Elements is
   type Element is (H, He, Li, ... );
      -- beware of Indium - In is reserved!
      -- so is At for the elusive Astatine!!
   Atomic_Weight: constant array (Element) of Float :=
            (1.008, 4.003, 6.940, ... );
   ...
end Elements;
```

An important use of packages is to provide Abstract Data Types. Obvious examples are the packages Rational_Numbers (Exercise 11.2(**3**)) and Queues (Exercise 11.5(**3**)). In such cases the use of private types enables us to separate the representation of the type from the operations upon it. In a way the new types can be seen as natural extensions to the language. Indeed, the whole essence of Object Oriented Programming is the reuse and composition of abstract data types through extension and inheritance.

There is the question of what to do when something goes wrong. The use of exceptions needs care. In Chapter 14 we warned against the unnecessary use of exceptions and in particular the casual raising of the predefined exceptions since we have no guarantee, when handling such an exception, that it was raised for the reason we had in mind.

As an example, consider the factorial function and the action to be taken when the parameter is incorrect. We could consider

- returning a default value,
- returning a status via a Boolean parameter,
- raising an exception.

Returning a default value such as −1 as in Exercise 14.1(**2**) is not satisfactory since there is no guarantee that the user will check for this default value upon return. If we could rely upon the user doing so then we could equally rely upon the user checking the parameter of the function before calling it in the first place. Returning an auxiliary status value via another parameter also relies upon the caller checking the value and also forces us to use a procedure rather than a function.

There are only two ways out of a subprogram in Ada; back to the point of call or by a propagated exception. We seem to have eliminated the possibility of returning to the point of call as not reliable and so have to come to the conclusion that the raising of an exception is the appropriate solution.

The raising of exceptions is, however, not a panacea. We cannot sweep the problem under the carpet. The exception must be handled somewhere otherwise the program will terminate. In fact this is one of their advantages – if the user does nothing then the program will terminate safely, whereas if we return status values and the user does nothing then the program will probably ramble on in a fruitless way.

The indiscriminate use of **others** in an exception handler should be avoided. If we write **others** we are really admitting that anything could have gone wrong and we should take appropriate action; we should not use **others** as shorthand for the exceptions we anticipate.

Object Oriented Programming raises interesting issues. It is clear that Object Oriented Design is an excellent concept but it is not at all clear that the programming techniques of inheritance, polymorphism and dispatching are the panacea some would claim. It is clear that the overuse of inheritance can lead to very obscure programs. Luckily, Ada very clearly separates the concept of a specific type from a class of types with the result that one can always find out the specific type of an object. Thus in Section 13.5 we were able to ensure that the Posh passenger always gets a decent meal. Another good point with Ada is that the deliberate omission of linguistic multiple inheritance forces more explicit programming.

The problem with inheritance is that it provides properties that are not directly stated. In fact it is almost the opposite of information hiding. Good abstraction is about hiding irrelevant detail; the trouble with inheritance is that it hides (or at least obscures) relevant detail.

Another major design area concerns the use of tasks. It is usually fairly clear that a problem needs a solution involving tasks but it is not always clear how the various activities should be allocated to individual tasks.

There are perhaps two major problems to be solved regarding the interactions between tasks. One concerns the transmission of messages between tasks, the other the controlling of access to common data by several tasks.

The rendezvous provides a natural mechanism for the closely coupled transmission of a message; examples are provided by the interaction between mother and the other members of her family in the procedure Shopping in Section 18.2 and by the interaction between the server and the customer in the package Cobblers of Exercise 18.10(**1**).

Controlled access to common data is done using protected objects. These are very efficient since task switching is kept to a minimum. Examples are the object Variable and the type Buffering in Section 18.4.

It is emphasized that the abort statement is for extreme situations only. One possible use is in a supervisory task where it may be desirable to close down a complete subsystem in response to a command from a human operator. The asynchronous select statement of Section 18.8 provides the effect of abort in a controlled manner and should be used if possible.

A multitasking Ada program will often be seen as a set of cooperating tasks designed together. In such circumstances we can rely on the calling tasks to obey the necessary protocols and the design of servers is then simplified.

Finally, there are generics and the whole question of parameterization and reuse. Genericity provides static polymorphism whereas type extension and the associated dispatching provide dynamic polymorphism. The two often work together and provide various means of parameterization and composition as illustrated by the discussion on iterators in Section 19.4. The degree to which parameterization should be applied is a matter for debate and indeed the techniques of that section are simply illustrations of what can be done rather than necessarily what should be done.

And so, in some imagined future market for software components it is likely that packages of all sorts of generalities and performance will be available. We conclude by imagining a future conversation in our local software store.

Customer: Could I have a look at the reader–writer package you have in the window?

Server: Certainly. Would you be interested in this robust version – proof against abort? Or we have this slick version for trusty callers. Just arrived this week.

Customer: Well – it's for a cooperating system so the new one sounds good. How much is it?

Server: It's 250 Eurodollars but as it's new there is a special offer with it – a free copy of this random number generator and 10% off your next certification.

Customer: Great. Is it validated?

Server: All our products conform to the highest standards. The parameter mechanism conforms to ES98263 and it has the usual international multitasking certificate.

Customer: OK, I'll take it.

Server: Will you take it as it is or shall I instantiate it for you?

Customer: As it is please. I prefer to do my own instantiation.

               ...

On this fantasy note we come to the end of this book. It is hoped that the reader will have gained some general understanding of the principles of Ada as well as a lot of the detail. Further understanding will come with use and the author hopes that he has in some small way prepared the reader for the successful use of a very good programming language.

Appendix 1

Reserved Words, Attributes and Pragmas

This appendix lists the reserved words and predefined attributes and pragmas. An implementation may define additional attributes and pragmas but not additional reserved words.

A1.1 Reserved words

The following words are reserved; the index contains references to the places where their use is described.

abort	declare	goto	out	select
abs	delay			separate
abstract	delta	if	package	subtype
accept	digits	in	pragma	
access	do	is	private	tagged
aliased			procedure	task
all	else	limited	protected	terminate
and	elsif	loop		then
array	end		raise	type
at	entry	mod	range	
	exception		record	until
begin	exit	new	rem	use
body		not	renames	
	for	null	requeue	when
case	function		return	while
constant	generic	of	reverse	with
		or		
		others		xor

The reserved words **access**, **delta**, **digits** and **range** are also used as attributes; there is no conflict.

569

A1.2   Predefined attributes

This section lists all the predefined attributes. Most attributes are dealt with in detail in the body of this book and so the descriptions are generally brief.

X'Access: Applies to an object or subprogram. Denotes an access value designating the entity. (See 10.4, 10.7)

X'Address: Applies to an object, program unit or label. Denotes the address of the first storage element associated with the entity. Of type System.Address. (See 21.1)

S'Adjacent: Applies to a floating point subtype S of a type T and denotes
  function S'Adjacent(X, Towards: T) **return** T;
which returns the machine number adjacent to X in the direction of Towards.

S'Aft: Applies to a fixed point subtype. Yields the number of decimal digits needed after the point to accommodate the subtype S, unless the delta of the subtype S is greater than 0.1, in which case it yields the value one. (S'Aft is the smallest positive integer N for which $(10**N)*S'Delta$ is greater than or equal to one.) Of type universal integer. (See 20.5)

X'Alignment: Applies to a subtype or object. The Address of an object is an integer multiple of this attribute. Of type universal integer.

S'Base: Applies to a subtype S and denotes an unconstrained subtype of its type. (See 23.2)

S'Bit_Order: Applies to a record subtype and denotes the bit ordering. Of type System.Bit_Order. (See 21.1)

P'Body_Version: Applies to a program unit and returns a String. (Distributed)

T'Callable: Applies to a task. Yields true unless the task is completed, terminated, or abnormal. Of type Boolean. (See 18.8)

E'Caller: Applies to an entry. Yields the identity of the task calling the entry body or accept statement. Of type Task_Identification.Task_ID. (Systems)

S'Ceiling: Applies to a floating point subtype S of a type T and denotes
  function S'Ceiling(X: T) **return** T;
which returns the algebraically smallest integral value not less than X.

S'Class: Applies to a tagged subtype. Denotes its class wide type. (See 13.2)

X'Component_Size: Applies to an array subtype or object. Denotes the size in bits of components of the type. Of type universal integer. (See 21.1)

S'Compose: Applies to a floating point subtype S of a type T and denotes
  function S'Compose(Fraction: T; Exponent: *universal_integer*) **return** T;
which in essence is Fraction but with its exponent replaced by Exponent.

A'Constrained: Applies to an object of a discriminated type. Yields true if A is a constant or is constrained. (See 16.2)

S'Copy_Sign: Applies to a floating point subtype S of a type T and denotes
  function S'Copy_Sign(Value, Sign: T) **return** T;
which returns the magnitude of Value with the sign of Sign. (See 15.4)

E'Count: Applies to an entry. Yields the number of tasks queued on the entry. Of type universal integer. (See 18.4, 18.5)

S'Definite: Applies to a formal indefinite subtype. Yields true if the actual subtype is definite. Of type Boolean. (See 17.2)

S'Delta: Applies to a fixed point subtype. Yields the value of the delta of the subtype. Of type universal real. (See 15.5)

S'Denorm: Applies to a floating point subtype. Yields true if every denormalized number is a machine number. Of type Boolean.

P'Digits: Applies to a floating point or decimal subtype. Yields the requested number of decimal digits. Of type universal integer. (See 15.4, 15.6)

S'Exponent: Applies to a floating point subtype S of a type T and denotes
  function S'Exponent(X: T) **return** T;
which returns the normalized exponent of X. (See 15.4)

S'External_Tag: Applies to a tagged subtype. Yields an external representation of the tag. Of type String. (See 20.6)

A'First(N): Applies to an array object or constrained subtype. Denotes the lower bound of the nth index range. Of the type of the bound. (See 8.1, 8.2)

A'First: Same as A'First(1).

S'First: Applies to a scalar subtype. Yields the lower bound of the range of S. Of the same type as S. (See 6.8)

R.C'First_Bit: Applies to a component C of a composite, non-array object R. Yields the offset, measured in bits, from the start of the first of the storage elements occupied by C, of the first bit occupied by C. Of type universal integer. (See 21.1)

S'Floor: Applies to a floating point subtype S of a type T and denotes
  function S'Floor(X: T) **return** T;
which returns the algebraically largest integral value not greater than X.

S'Fore: Applies to a fixed point subtype. Yields the minimum number of characters needed before the decimal point for the decimal representation of any value of the subtype S, assuming that the representation does not include an exponent, but includes a one character prefix that is either a minus sign or a space. (This minimum number does not include superfluous zeros or underlines; and is at least two.) Of the type universal integer. (See 20.5)

S'Fraction: Applies to a floating point subtype S of a type T and denotes
  function S'Fraction(X: T) **return** T;
which in essence is the number X with exponent replaced by zero. (See 15.4)

E'Identity: Applies to an exception. Yields the identity of the exception. Of type Exceptions.Exception_ID. (See 14.4)

T'Identity: Applies to a task. Yields the identity of the task. Of type Task_Identification.Task_ID. (Systems)

S'Image: Applies to a scalar subtype and denotes
  function S'Image(Arg: S'Base) **return** String;
The result is the image of the value of Arg, that is, a sequence of characters representing the value in display form. The image of an integer value is the corresponding decimal literal; without underlines, leading zeros, exponent,

or trailing spaces; but with a one character prefix that is either a minus sign or a space. The image of a real value is as for the corresponding Put with default format (see 20.5). The image of an enumeration value is either the corresponding identifier in upper case or the corresponding character literal (including the two apostrophes); neither leading nor trailing spaces are included. The image of a nongraphic character is the corresponding name in upper case such as NUL.

S'Class'Input: Applies to a subtype S'Class of a class wide type T'Class and denotes
> **function** S'Class'Input(Stream: **access**
> Ada.Streams.Root_Stream_Type'Class) **return** T'Class;

Reads the external tag from Stream, determines the corresponding internal tag and then dispatches to the Input attribute. (See 20.6)

S'Input   Applies to a subtype S of a specific type T and denotes
> **function** S'Input(Stream: **access**
> Ada.Streams.Root_Stream_Type'Class) **return** T;

Reads and returns one value from the stream. (See 20.6)

A'Last(N): Applies to an array object or constrained subtype. Denotes the upper bound of the nth index range. Of the type of the bound. (See 8.1, 8.2)

A'Last: Same as A'Last(1).

S'Last: Applies to a scalar subtype. Yields the upper bound of the range of S. Of the same type as S. (See 6.8)

R.C'Last_Bit: Applies to a component C of a composite, non-array object R. Yields the offset, in bits, from the start of the first storage element occupied by C, of the last bit occupied by C. Of type universal integer. (See 21.1)

S'Leading_Part: Applies to a floating point subtype S of a type T and denotes
> **function** S'Leading_Part(X: T; D: *universal_integer*) **return** T;

which in essence is the number X but with all except the first D digits in the mantissa set to zero.

A'Length(N): Applies to an array object or constrained subtype. Denotes the number of values of the nth index range (zero for a null range). Of type universal integer. (See 8.1, 8.2)

A'Length: Same as A'Length(1).

S'Machine: Applies to a floating point subtype S of a type T and denotes
> **function** S'Machine(X: T) **return** T;

which is X if it is a machine number and otherwise one adjacent to X.

S'Machine_Emax: Applies to a floating point subtype. Yields the largest value of *exponent* in the canonical representation for which all numbers are machine numbers. Of type universal integer. (See 15.4)

S'Machine_Emin: Applies to a floating point subtype. Yields the smallest value of *exponent* in the canonical representation for which all numbers are machine numbers. Of type universal integer. (See 15.4)

S'Machine_Mantissa: Applies to a floating point subtype. Yields the largest number of digits in the mantissa in the canonical representation for which all numbers are machine numbers. Of type universal integer. (See 15.4)

S'Machine_Overflows: Applies to a floating or fixed point subtype. Yields true if overflow and divide by zero raise Constraint_Error for every predefined operation returning a value of the base type of S. Of type Boolean. (See 15.4, 15.5)

S'Machine_Radix: Applies to a floating or fixed point type. Yields the radix used by the machine representation of the base type of S. Of the type universal integer. (See 15.4, 15.5, 15.6)

S'Machine_Rounds: Applies to a floating or fixed point type. Yields true if rounding is performed on inexact results of every predefined arithmetic operation returning a value of the base type of S. Of type Boolean.

S'Max: Applies to a scalar type and denotes
    function Max(Left, Right: S'Base) **return** S'Base;
The result is the greater of the parameters. (See 6.8)

S'Max_Size_In_Storage_Elements: Applies to any subtype. Denotes the maximum value for Size_In_Storage_Elements that will be requested by Allocate for an access type designating the subtype S. (See 21.1)

S'Min: Applies to a scalar type and denotes
    function Min(Left, Right: S'Base) **return** S'Base;
The result is the lesser of the parameters. (See 6.8)

S'Model: Applies to a floating point subtype S of a type T and denotes
    function S'Model(X: T) **return** T;
which is X if it is a model number and otherwise one adjacent to X. This attribute and Model_Emin, Model_Epsilon, Model_Mantissa and Model_Small concern the floating point model. (See 15.4)

S'Modulus: Applies to a modular subtype. Yields its modulus. Of type universal integer. (See 15.2)

S'Class'Output: Applies to a subtype S'Class of a class wide type T'Class and denotes
    procedure S'Class'Output(Stream: **access**
                Ada.Streams.Root_Stream_Type'Class; Item: **in** T'Class);
Writes the external tag of Item to the Stream, and then dispatches to the Output attribute. (See 20.6)

S'Output: Applies to a subtype S of a specific type T and denotes
    procedure S'Output (Stream: **access**
                Ada.Streams.Root_Stream_Type'Class; Item: **in** T);
Writes the value of Item to the stream including bounds and discriminants. (See 20.6)

D'Partition_ID: Applies to a library level declaration (not pure). Denotes the partition in which the entity was elaborated. Of type universal integer. (Distributed)

S'Pos: Applies to a discrete subtype and denotes
    function S'Pos(Arg: S'Base) **return** *universal_integer*;
Returns the position number of Arg. (See 6.8)

R.C'Position: Applies to a component C of a composite, non-array object R. Yields R.C'Address − R'Address. Of type universal integer. (See 21.1)

S'Pred: Applies to a scalar subtype and denotes
> **function** S'Pred(Arg: S'Base) return S'Base;

For a discrete subtype, returns the value whose position number is one less than that of Arg. For a fixed type, returns the result of subtracting small from Arg; for a floating type returns the machine number below Arg. The exception Constraint_Error is raised if appropriate. (See 6.8)

A'Range(N): Applies to an array object or constrained subtype. Is equivalent to A'First(N) .. A'Last(N). (See 8.1, 8.2)

A'Range: Same as A'Range(1).

S'Range: Applies to a scalar subtype. Equivalent to S'First .. S'Last. (See 6.8)

S'Class'Read: Applies to a subtype S'Class of T'Class and denotes
> **procedure** S'Class'Read(Stream: **access**
> Ada.Streams.Root_Stream_Type'Class; Item: **out** T'Class);

Dispatches to the Read attribute according to the tag of Item. (See 20.6)

S'Read: Applies to a subtype S of a specific type T and denotes
> **procedure** S'Read(Stream:
> **access** Ada.Streams.Root_Stream_Type'Class; Item: **out** T);

Reads the value of Item from the stream. (See 20.6)

S'Remainder: Applies to a floating point subtype S of a type T and denotes
> **function** S'Remainder(X, Y: T) **return** T;

Essentially returns $V = X - nY$ where n is the integer nearest to X/Y. (n is even if midway.)

S'Round: Applies to a decimal fixed point subtype and denotes
> **function** S'Round(X: *universal_real*) return S'Base;

Returns the value obtained by rounding X (away from zero if X is midway between values of S'Base). (See 15.6)

S'Rounding: Applies to a floating point subtype S of a type T and denotes
> **function** S'Rounding(X: T) **return** T;

Returns the integral value obtained by rounding X (away from zero for exact halves).

P'Safe_First: Applies to a floating point subtype S of a type T. Yields the lower bound of the safe range of T. Of type universal real. (See 15.4)

P'Safe_Last: Applies to a floating point subtype S of a type T. Yields the upper bound of the safe range of T. Of type universal real. (See 15.4)

S'Scale: Applies to a decimal fixed point subtype. Yields N such that S'Delta = 10.00**(−N). Of type universal integer. (See 15.6)

S'Scaling: Applies to a floating point subtype S of a type T and denotes
> **function** S'Scaling(X: T; Adjustment: *universal_integer*) **return** T;

which in essence is the number X but with its exponent increased by Adjustment.

S'Signed_Zeros: Applies to a floating point subtype S of a type T. Returns true if the hardware representation for T supports signed zeros. Of type Boolean. (See 15.4)

S'Size: Applies to any subtype. For a definite subtype gives the size in bits of a packed record component of the subtype; for an indefinite subtype is implementation defined. Of type universal integer. (See 21.1)

X'Size: Applies to an object. Denotes its size in bits. Of type universal integer. (See 21.1)

S'Small: Applies to a fixed point subtype. Denotes its *small*. Of type universal real. (See 15.5)

S'Storage_Pool: Applies to an access subtype. Denotes its storage pool. Of type System.Storage_Pools.Root_Storage_Pool'Class. (See 21.3)

S'Storage_Size: Applies to an access subtype. Yields a measure of the number of storage elements reserved for its pool. Of type universal integer. (See 21.1)

T'Storage_Size: Applies to a task. Yields the number of storage elements reserved for the task. Of type universal integer. (See 21.1)

S'Succ: Applies to a scalar subtype and denotes
    function S'Succ(Arg: S'Base) **return** S'Base;
For a discrete subtype, returns the value whose position number is one more than that of Arg. For a fixed type, returns the result of adding small to Arg; for a floating type returns the machine number above Arg. The exception Constraint_Error is raised if appropriate. (See 6.8)

S'Tag: Applies to a subtype S of a tagged type T. Denotes the tag of T. Of type Ada.Tags.Tag. (See 13.4)

X'Tag: Applies to an object of a class wide type. Denotes the tag of X. Of type Ada.Tags.Tag. (See 13.4)

T'Terminated: Applies to a task. Yields true if the task is terminated. Of type Boolean. (See 18.8)

S'Truncation: Applies to a floating point subtype S of a type T and denotes
    function S'Truncation(X: T) **return** T;
Returns the integral value obtained by truncation towards zero.

S'Unbiased_Rounding: Applies to a floating point subtype S of a type T and denotes
    function S'Unbiased_Rounding(X: T) **return** T;
Returns the integral value nearest to X choosing the even value if X is an exact half.

X'Unchecked_Access: Applies to an aliased view of an object. As for X'Access but as if X were at the library level. (See 10.5)

S'Val: Applies to a discrete subtype and denotes.
    function S'Val(Arg: *universal_integer*) **return** S'Base;
Returns the value of S with position number Arg. (See 6.8)

X'Valid: Applies to a scalar object. Yields true if X is normal and has a valid representation. Of type Boolean. (See 21.2)

S'Value: Applies to a scalar subtype and denotes
    function S'Value(Arg: String) **return** S'Base;

Returns the value corresponding to the given image, ignoring any leading or trailing spaces.

P'Version: Applies to a program unit and returns a String. (Distributed)

S'Wide_Image: Similar to Image but returns a Wide_String.

S'Wide_Value: Similar to Value but applies to a Wide_String.

S'Wide_Width: Similar to Width for Wide_Image and Wide_String.

S'Width: Applies to a scalar subtype. Yields the length of a String returned by S'Image over all values of the subtype. Of type universal integer. (See 20.5)

S'Class'Write: Applies to a subtype S'Class of a class wide type T'Class and denotes
      procedure S'Class'Write(Stream: **access**
                  Ada.Streams.Root_Stream_Type'Class; Item: **in** T'Class);
  Dispatches to the Write attribute according to the tag of Item. (See 20.6)

S'Write: Applies to a subtype S of a specific type T and denotes
      procedure S'Write(Stream: **access**
                  Ada.Streams.Root_Stream_Type'Class; Item: **in** T);
  Writes the value of Item to the stream. (See 20.6)

A1.3   Predefined pragmas

Pragmas are of various categories. Configuration pragmas apply to the whole partition and appear at the beginning of a compilation. Program unit pragmas immediately follow or are immediately within the unit to which they apply; in the latter case the argument is optional. Library unit pragmas similarly apply to library units. Representation pragmas apply to a preceding entity in the same declarative region or to an immediately preceding compilation unit.

The following pragmas are predefined in the core language. The syntax of the parameters is given in the same style as the general syntax in Appendix 3.

pragma Controlled(*first_subtype*_local_name);
  Applies to a non-derived access subtype. This is a representation pragma. Specifies that garbage collection is not to be performed for objects in a standard storage pool for the type. (See 21.2)

pragma Convention([Convention =>] *convention*_identifier,
      [Entity =>] local_name);
  Applies typically to types and subprograms. This is a representation pragma. Specifies the convention for the entity. (See 21.4)

pragma Elaborate(*library_unit*_name {, *library_unit*_name});
  This pragma is only allowed in the context clause of a compilation unit. Each argument must be the name of a library unit mentioned by the context clause. This pragma specifies that the corresponding library unit bodies must be elaborated before the current compilation unit. (See 12.7)

pragma Elaborate_All(*library_unit*_name {, *library_unit*_name});

As Elaborate but is transitive and specifies that every unit needed by the named units is elaborated before the current unit. (See 12.7)

pragma Elaborate_Body[(*library_unit_*name)];
This is a library unit pragma. Specifies that the body of the unit is to be elaborated immediately after its declaration (spec). (See 12.7)

pragma Export([Convention =>] *convention_*identifier,
  [Entity =>] local_name
  [, [External_Name =>] *string_*expression]
  [, [Link_Name =>] *string_*expression]);
Applies typically to subprograms and objects. Specifies that the entity be made accessible to a foreign language. (See 21.4)

pragma Import(...);
Similar to Export. Specifies that the entity is external to the Ada program. (See 21.4)

pragma Inline(name {, name});
Applies to subprograms, entries and generic subprograms. This is a program unit pragma. Specifies that inline expansion is requested for all calls. (See 21.1)

pragma Linker_Options(*string_*expression);
Applies to the immediately enclosing compilation unit. The string is passed to the system linker for partitions including the unit. The effect is implementation-defined.

pragma List(identifier);
Takes one of the identifiers On or Off as argument. Specifies that listing of the compilation is to be continued or suspended until a List pragma with the opposite argument is given within the same compilation. The pragma itself is always listed if the compiler is producing a listing.

pragma Optimize(identifier);
Takes one of the identifiers Time, **Space** or Off as argument. Specifies whether time or space is the primary optimization criterion or that optimization should be turned off. It applies until the end of the immediately enclosing declarative region or the end of the compilation. (See 2.7)

pragma Pack(*first_subtype_*local_name);
Applies to a composite subtype. This is a representation pragma. Specifies that storage minimization should be the main criterion when selecting the representation of the type. For a type extension only applies to the extension part. (See 21.1)

pragma Page;
Specifies that the program text which follows the pragma should start on a new page (if the compiler is currently producing a listing).

pragma Preelaborate[(*library_unit_*name)];
Specifies that the unit is to be preelaborated. (See 12.7)

pragma Pure[(*library_unit_*name)];
Specifies that the unit is pure. (See 12.7)

pragma Restrictions(restriction {, restriction});
　　where:　restriction ::= *restriction*_identifier
　　　　　　　　　　　　| *restriction_parameter*_identifier => expression
Asserts that the restrictions given apply to the partition concerned. This is
a configuration pragma. Used by the Real-Time and Safety and Security
annexes. (See 22.2 and 22.6)

pragma Storage_Size(expression);
　　Applies to the task definition in which it is immediately enclosed.
Specifies the storage requested for a task object. (See 21.1)

pragma Suppress(identifier [, [On =>] name]);
　　Applies to the identifier of a check and optionally also to the name of some
entity. Allowed as a configuration pragma or immediately within a
declarative part or immediately within a package specification. In the last
case, the only allowed form is with a name that denotes an entity (or several
overloaded subprograms) declared immediately within the package
specification. Permission to omit the given check extends from the place of
the pragma to the end of the declarative region associated with the innermost
enclosing block statement or program unit. For a pragma given in a package
specification, the permission extends to the end of the scope of the named
entity. If the pragma includes a name, the permission applies only for
operations concerning the entity or objects and values of its type. (See 21.1)

The following additional pragmas are defined in the specialized annexes.

pragma All_Calls_Remote[(*library_unit*_name)]; (Distributed)

pragma Asynchronous(local_name); (Distributed)

pragma Atomic(local_name); (Systems)

pragma Atomic_Components(*array*_local_name); (Systems)

pragma Attach_Handler(*handler*_name, expression); (Systems)

pragma Discard_Names[(([On =>] local_name)]; (Systems)

pragma Inspection_Point[(object_name {, object_name})]; (Safety and Security)

pragma Interrupt_Handler(*handler*_name); (Systems)

pragma Interrupt_Priority[(expression)]; (Real-Time)

pragma Locking_Policy(*policy*_identifier); (Real-Time)

pragma Normalize_Scalars; (Safety and Security)

pragma Priority(expression); (Real-Time)

pragma Queuing_Policy(policy_identifier); (Real-Time)

pragma Remote_Call_Interface[(*library_unit*_name)]; (Distributed)

pragma Remote_Types[(*library_unit*_name)]; (Distributed)

pragma Reviewable; (Safety and Security)

pragma Shared_Passive[(*library_unit*_name)]; (Distributed)

pragma Task_Dispatching_Policy(policy_identifier); (Real-Time)

pragma Volatile(local_name); (Systems)

pragma Volatile_Components(array_local_name); (System)

Appendix 2

Glossary

The following glossary is adapted from Annex N of the *ARM*.

Access type   An access type has values that designate aliased objects. Access types correspond to 'pointer types' or 'reference types' in some other languages.

Aliased   An aliased view of an object is one that can be designated by an access value. Objects allocated by allocators are aliased. Objects can also be explicitly declared as aliased with the reserved word **aliased**. The Access attribute can be used to create an access value designating an aliased object.

Array type   An array type is a composite type whose components are all of the same type. Components are selected by indexing.

Character type   A character type is an enumeration type whose values include characters.

Class   A class is a set of types that is closed under derivation, which means that if a given type is in the class, then all types derived from that type are also in the class. The set of types of a class share common properties, such as their primitive operations.

Compilation unit   The text of a program can be submitted to the compiler in one or more compilations. Each compilation is a set of compilation units. A compilation unit contains either the declaration, the body, or a renaming of a program unit.

Composite type   A composite type has components.

Construct   A construct is a piece of text (explicit or implicit) that is an instance of a syntactic category.

Controlled type   A controlled type supports user defined assignment and finalization. Objects are always finalized before being destroyed.

Declaration   A declaration is a language construct that associates a name with (a view of) an entity. A declaration may appear explicitly in the program text (an explicit declaration), or may be supposed to occur at a given place in the text as a consequence of the semantics of another construct (an implicit declaration).

Definition   All declarations contain a definition for a view of an entity. A view consists of an identification of the entity (the entity of the view), plus specific characteristics that effect the use of the entity through that view (such as mode of access to an object, formal parameter names and defaults for a subprogram, or visibility to components of a type). In most cases, a declaration also contains the definition for the entity itself (a renaming declaration is an example of a declaration that does not define a new entity, but instead defines a view of an existing entity).

Derived type   A derived type is a type defined in terms of another type, which is the parent type of the derived type. Each class containing the parent type also contains the derived type. The derived type inherits properties such as components and primitive operations from the parent. A type and the types derived from it (directly or indirectly) together form a derivation class.

Discrete type   A discrete type is either an integer type or an enumeration type. Discrete types may be used, for example, in case statements and as array indexes.

Discriminant   A discriminant is a parameter of a composite type. It can control, for example, the bounds of a component of the type if that type is an array type. A discriminant of a task type can be used to pass data to a task of the type upon creation.

Elementary type   An elementary type does not have components.

Enumeration type   An enumeration type is defined by an enumeration of its values, which may be named by identifiers or character literals.

Exception   An exception represents a kind of exceptional situation; an occurrence of such a situation (at run time) is called an exception occurrence. To *raise* an exception is to abandon normal program execution so as to draw attention to the fact that the corresponding situation has arisen. Performing some actions in response to the arising of an exception is called handling the exception.

Execution   The process by which a construct achieves its run-time effect is called an execution. Execution of a declaration is also called elaboration. Execution of an expression is also called evaluation.

Generic unit   A generic unit is a template for a (nongeneric) program unit; the template can be parameterized by objects, types, subprograms, and packages. An instance of a generic unit is created by a generic instantiation. The rules of the language are enforced when a generic unit is compiled, using a generic contract model; additional checks are performed upon instantiation to verify the contract is met. That is the declaration of a generic unit represents a contract between the body of the generic and instances of the generic. Generic units can be used to perform the role that macros sometimes play in other languages.

Integer type   Integer types comprise the signed integer types and the modular types. A signed integer type has a base range that includes both positive and negative numbers, and has operations that may raise an exception when the result is outside the base range. A modular type has a base range whose lower bound is zero, and has operations with 'wraparound' semantics. Modular types subsume what are called 'unsigned types' in some languages.

Library unit   A library unit is a separately compiled program unit, and is always a package, subprogram, or generic unit. Library units may have other (logically nested) library units as children, and may have other program units physically nested within them. A root library unit, together with its children and grandchildren and so on, forms a subsystem.

Limited type   A limited type is (a view of) a type for which the assignment operation is not allowed. A nonlimited type is (a view of) a type for which the assignment operation is allowed.

Object   An object is either a constant or a variable. An object contains a value. An object is created by an object declaration or by an allocator. A formal parameter is (a view of) an object. A subcomponent of an object is an object.

Package   Packages are program units that allow the specification of groups of logically related entities. Typically a package contains the declaration of a type (often a private type or private extension) along with the declarations of primitive subprograms of the type, which can be called from outside the package, while their inner workings remain hidden from outside users.

Partition   A partition is a part of a program. Each partition consists of a set of library units. Each partition may run in a separate address space, possibly on a separate computer. A program may contain just one partition. A distributed program typically contains multiple partitions, which can execute concurrently.

Pragma   A pragma is a compiler directive. There are language defined pragmas that give instructions for optimization, listing control, etc. An implementation may support additional (implementation-defined) pragmas.

Primitive operations   The primitive operations of a type are the operations (such as subprograms) declared together with the type declaration. They are inherited by other types in the same class of types. For a tagged type, the primitive subprograms are dispatching subprograms, providing run-time polymorphism. A dispatching subprogram may be called with statically tagged operands, in which case the subprogram body invoked is determined at compile time. Alternatively, a dispatching subprogram may be called using a dispatching call, in which case the subprogram body invoked is determined at run time.

Private extension A private extension is like a record extension, except that the components of the extension part are hidden from its clients.

Private type A private type is a partial view of a type whose full view is hidden from its clients.

Program unit A program unit is either a package, a task unit, a protected unit, a protected entry, a generic unit, or an explicitly declared subprogram other than an enumeration literal. Certain kinds of program units can be separately compiled. Alternatively, they can appear physically nested within other program units.

Program A program is a set of partitions, each of which may execute in a separate address space, possibly on a separate computer. A partition consists of a set of library units.

Protected type A protected type is a composite type whose components are protected from concurrent access by multiple tasks.

Real type A real type has values that are approximations of the real numbers. Floating point and fixed point types are real types.

Record extension A record extension is a type that extends another type by adding additional components.

Record type A record type is a composite type consisting of zero or more named components, possibly of different types.

Scalar type A scalar type is either a discrete type or a real type.

Subtype A subtype is a type together with a constraint, which constrains the values of the subtype to satisfy a certain condition. The values of a subtype are a subset of values of its type.

Tagged type The objects of a tagged type have a run-time type tag, which indicates the specific type with which the object was originally created. An operand of a class wide tagged type can be used in a dispatching call; the tag indicates which subprogram body to invoke. Non-dispatching calls, in which the subprogram body to invoke is determined at compile time are also allowed. Tagged types may be extended with additional components.

Task type A task type is a composite type whose values are tasks, which are active entities that may execute concurrently with other tasks. The top level task of a partition is called the environment task.

Type Each object has a type. A type has an associated set of values, and a set of primitive operations which implement the fundamental aspects of its semantics. Types are grouped into classes. The types of a given class share a set of primitive operations. Classes are closed under derivation; that is, if a type is in a class, then all of its derivatives are in that class.

Appendix 3

Syntax

The following syntax rules are taken from Annex P of the *ARM*. The rules have been reordered to correspond to the order of introduction of the topics in this book but individual rules have not been changed.

It should be noted that the rules for the construction of lexical elements, which are under the subheading of Chapter 5, have a slightly different status to the other rules since spaces and newlines may be freely inserted between lexical elements but not within lexical elements.

The rules have been sequentially numbered for ease of reference; an index to them will be found in Section A3.2. Note that in rules 74, 95, 175 and 196 the vertical bar stands for itself and is not a metasymbol.

A3.1 Syntax rules

Chapter 2

1 pragma ::= **pragma** identifier [(pragma_argument_association
                                    {, pragma_argument_association})];

2 pragma_argument_association ::=
          [*pragma_argument_*identifier =>] name
        | [*pragma_argument_*identifier =>] expression

Chapter 5

3 graphic_character ::= identifier_letter | digit
          | space_character | special_character

4 character ::= graphic_character | format_effector | other_control_function

5 identifier ::= identifier_letter {[underline] letter_or_digit}

6 letter_or_digit ::= identifier_letter | digit

7 numeric_literal ::= decimal_literal | based_literal

8 decimal_literal ::= numeral [. numeral] [exponent]

9 numeral ::= digit {[underline] digit}

10 exponent ::= E [+] numeral | E – numeral

11 based_literal ::= base # based_numeral [. based_numeral] # [exponent]

12 base ::= numeral

13 based_numeral ::= extended_digit {[underline] extended_digit}

14 extended_digit ::= digit | A | B | C | D | E | F

15 character_literal ::= 'graphic_character'

16 string_literal ::= "{string_element}"

17 string_element ::= "" | *non_qotation_mark*_graphic_character

18 comment ::= –– {*non_end_of_line*_character}

Chapter 6

19 basic_declaration ::=

type_declaration	| subtype_declaration
| object_declaration	| number_declaration
| subprogram_declaration	| package_declaration
| generic_declaration	| exception_declaration
| generic_instantiation	| renaming_declaration
| abstract_subprogram_declaration	

20 object_declaration ::=
      defining_identifier_list :
        [aliased] **[constant]** subtype_indication [:= expression];
      | defining_identifier_list :
        [aliased] **[constant]** array_type_definition [:= expression];
      | single_task_declaration
      | single_protected_declaration

21 number_declaration ::=
      defining_identifier_list : **constant** := *static*_expression;

22 defining_identifier_list ::= defining_identifier {, defining_identifier}

23 defining_identifier ::= identifier

24 assignment_statement ::= *variable*_name := expression;

25 block_statement ::= [*block*_statement_identifier :]
      [**declare**
        declarative_part]
      begin
        handled_sequence_of_statements
      end [*block*_identifier];

26 statement_identifier ::= direct_name

27 type_declaration ::=
         full_type_declaration | incomplete_type_declaration
         | private_type_declaration | private_extension_declaration

28 full_type_declaration ::=
         type defining_identifier [known_discriminant_part]
                                  is type_definition;
         | task_type_declaration
         | protected_type_declaration

29 type_definition ::=
         enumeration_type_definition | integer_type_definition
         | real_type_definition | array_type_definition
         | record_type_definition | access_type_definition
         | derived_type_definition

30 subtype_declaration ::=
         subtype defining_identifier **is** subtype_indication;

31 subtype_indication ::= subtype_mark [constraint]

32 subtype_mark ::= *subtype*_name

33 constraint ::= scalar_constraint | composite_constraint

34 scalar_constraint ::=
         range_constraint | digits_constraint | delta_constraint

35 composite_constraint ::= index_constraint | discriminant_constraint

36 range_constraint ::= **range** range

37 range ::= range_attribute_reference
         | simple_expression .. simple_expression

38 enumeration_type_definition ::=
         (enumeration_literal_specification
                          {, enumeration_literal_specification})

39 enumeration_literal_specification ::=
         defining_identifier | defining character_literal

40 defining_character_literal ::= character_literal

41 name ::= direct_name | explicit_dereference | indexed_component
         | slice | selected_component | attribute_reference
         | type_conversion | function_call | character_literal

42 direct_name ::= identifier | operator_symbol

43 prefix ::= name | implicit_dereference

44 explicit_dereference ::= name . **all**

45 implicit_dereference ::= name

46 attribute_reference ::= prefix ' attribute_designator

47 range_attribute_reference ::= prefix ' range_attribute_designator

48 attribute_designator ::= identifier [(*static*_expression)]
        | **Access** | **Delta** | **Digits**

49 range_attribute_designator ::= **Range** [(*static*_expression)]

50 expression ::=
        relation {**and** relation}
        | relation {**and then** relation}
        | relation {**or** relation}
        | relation {**or else** relation}
        | relation {**xor** relation}

51 relation ::=
        simple_expression [relational_operator simple_expression]
        | simple_expression [**not**] **in** range
        | simple_expression [**not**] **in** subtype_mark

52 simple_expression ::=
        [unary_adding_operator] term {binary_adding_operator term}

53 term ::= factor {multiplying_operator factor}

54 factor ::= primary [** primary] | **abs** primary | **not** primary

55 primary ::= numeric_literal | **null** | string_literal | aggregate | name
        | qualified_expression | allocator | (expression)

56 logical_operator ::= **and** | **or** | **xor**

57 relational_operator ::= = | **/=** | < | <= | > | >=

58 binary_adding_operator ::= + | – | &

59 unary_adding_operator ::= + | –

60 multiplying_operator ::= * | **/** | **mod** | **rem**

61 highest_precedence_operator ::= ** | **abs** | **not**

62 type_conversion ::=
        subtype_mark (expression) | subtype_mark (name)

63 qualified_expression ::=
        subtype_mark ' (expression) | subtype_mark ' aggregate

Chapter 7

64 sequence_of_statements ::= statement {statement}

65 statement ::= {label} simple_statement | {label} compound_statement

66 simple_statement ::=
        null_statement | assignment_statement
        | exit_statement | goto_statement
        | procedure_call_statement | return_statement
        | entry_call_statement | requeue_statement
        | delay_statement | abort_statement
        | raise_statement | code_statement

67 compound_statement ::=

         if_statement | case_statement

         | loop_statement | block_statement

         | accept_statement | select_statement

68 label ::= <<*label*_statement_identifier>>

69 null_statement ::= **null**;

70 if_statement ::=

       if condition **then**

         sequence_of_statements

       {**elsif** condition **then**

         sequence_of_statements}

       [**else**

         sequence_of_statements]

       end if;

71 condition ::= *boolean*_expression

72 case_statement ::=

       case expression **is**

         case_statement_alternative

         {case_statement_alternative}

       end case;

73 case_statement_alternative ::=

       when discrete_choice_list => sequence_of_statements

74 discrete_choice_list ::= discrete_choice { | discrete_choice}

75 discrete_choice ::= expression | discrete_range | **others**

76 discrete_range ::= *discrete*_subtype_indication | range

77 loop_statement ::= [*loop*_statement_identifier :]

       [iteration_scheme] **loop**

         sequence_of_statements

       end loop [*loop*_identifier];

78 iteration_scheme ::=

       while condition | **for** loop_parameter_specification

79 loop_parameter_specification ::=

       defining_identifier **in** [**reverse**] discrete_subtype_definition

80 exit_statement ::= **exit** [*loop*_name] [**when** condition];

81 goto_statement ::= **goto** *label*_name;

Chapter 8

82 array_type_definition ::=

       unconstrained_array_definition | constrained_array_definition

83 unconstrained_array_definition ::=
      array (index_subtype_definition
            {, index_subtype_definition}) **of** component_definition

84 constrained_array_definition ::=
      array (discrete_subtype_definition
            {, discrete_subtype_definition}) **of** component_definition

85 index_subtype_definition ::= subtype_mark **range** <>

86 discrete_subtype_definition ::= *discrete*_subtype_indication | range

87 component_definition ::= [**aliased**] subtype_indication

88 index_constraint ::= (discrete_range {, discrete_range})

89 indexed_component ::= prefix (expression {, expression})

90 slice ::= prefix (discrete_range)

91 aggregate ::= record_aggregate | extension_aggregate | array_aggregate

92 record_aggregate ::= (record_component_association_list)

93 record_component_association_list ::=
      record_component_association {, record_component_association}
    | **null record**

94 record_component_association ::=
      [component_choice_list =>] expression

95 component_choice_list ::=
      *component*_selector_name{ | *component*_selector_name}
    | **others**

96 array_aggregate ::=
      positional_array_aggregate | named_array_aggregate

97 positional_array_aggregate ::=
      (expression , expression {, expression})
    | (expression {, expression} , **others** => expression)

98 named_array_aggregate ::=
      (array_component_association {, array_component_association})

99 array_component_association ::=
      discrete_choice_list => expression

100 record_type_definition ::=
      [[**abstract**] **tagged**] [**limited**] record_definition

101 record_definition ::=
      record
        component_list
      end record
    | **null record**

102 component_list ::=
        component_item {component_item}
        | {component_item} variant_part
        | **null**;

103 component_item ::= component_declaration | representation_clause

104 component_declaration ::= defining_identifier_list :
                component_definition [:= default_expression];

105 default_expression ::= expression

106 selected_component ::= prefix . selector_name

107 selector_name ::= identifier | character_literal | operator_symbol

Chapter 9

108 subprogram_declaration ::= subprogram_specification;

109 subprogram_specification ::=
        procedure defining_program_unit_name parameter_profile
        | **function** defining_designator parameter_and_result_profile

110 parameter_profile ::= [formal_part]

111 parameter_and_result_profile ::= [formal_part] **return** subtype_mark

112 designator ::= [parent_unit_name .] identifier | operator_symbol

113 defining_designator ::=
        defining_program_unit_name | defining_operator_symbol

114 defining_program_unit_name ::=
        [parent_unit_name .] defining_identifier

115 parent_unit_name ::= name

116 operator_symbol ::= string_literal

117 defining_operator_symbol ::= operator_symbol

118 formal_part ::= (parameter_specification {; parameter_specification})

119 parameter_specification ::=
        defining_identifier_list : mode subtype_mark
                    [:= default_expression]
        | defining_identifier_list : access_definition
                    [:= default_expression]

120 mode ::= [**in**] | **in out** | **out**

121 subprogram_body ::=
        subprogram_specification **is**
          declarative_part
        begin
          handled_sequence_of_statements
        end [designator];

122 procedure_call_statement ::=
        *procedure*_name; | *procedure*_prefix actual_parameter_part;

123 function_call ::=
        *function*_name | *function*_prefix actual_parameter_part

124 actual_parameter_part ::=
        (parameter_association {, parameter_association})

125 parameter_association ::=
        [*formal_parameter*_selector_name =>] explicit_actual_parameter

126 explicit_actual_parameter ::= expression | *variable*_name

127 return_statement ::= **return** [expression];

Chapter 10

128 access_type_definition ::=
        access_to_object_definition
        | access_to_subprogram_definition

129 access_to_object_definition ::=
        access [general_access_modifier] subtype_indication

130 general_access_modifier ::= **all** | **constant**

131 access_to_subprogram_definition ::=
        access [**protected**] **procedure** parameter_profile
        | **access** [**protected**] **function** parameter_and_result_profile

132 access_definition ::= **access** subtype_mark

133 incomplete_type_declaration ::=
        type defining_identifier [discriminant_part];

134 allocator ::= **new** subtype_indication | **new** qualified_expression

Chapter 11

135 package_declaration ::= package_specification;

136 package_specification ::=
        package defining_program_unit_name **is**
         {basic_declarative_item}
        [**private**
         {basic_declarative_item}]
        end [[parent_unit_name .] identifier]

137 package_body ::=
        package body defining_program_unit_name **is**
         declarative_part
        [**begin**
         handled_sequence_of_statements]
        end [[parent_unit_name .] identifier];

138 declarative_part ::= {declarative_item}

139 declarative_item ::= basic_declarative_item | body

140 basic_declarative_item ::=
      basic_declaration | representation_clause | use_clause

141 body ::= proper_body | body_stub

142 proper_body ::= subprogram_body | package_body | task_body
      | protected_body

143 use_clause ::= use_package_clause | use_type_clause

144 use_package_clause ::= **use** *package*_name {, *package*_name};

145 use_type_clause ::= **use type** subtype_mark {, subtype_mark};

146 private_type_declaration ::= **type** defining_identifier
      [discriminant_part] **is** [[**abstract**] **tagged**] [**limited**] **private**;

147 derived_type_definition ::=
      [**abstract**] **new** *parent*_subtype_indication [record_extension_part]

Chapter 12

148 compilation ::= {compilation_unit}

149 compilation_unit ::=
      context_clause library_item | context_clause subunit

150 library_item ::=
      [**private**] library_unit_declaration | library_unit_body
      | [**private**] library_unit_renaming_declaration

151 library_unit_declaration ::=
      subprogram_declaration | package_declaration
      | generic_declaration | generic_instantiation

152 library_unit_renaming_declaration ::=
      package_renaming_declaration
      | generic_renaming_declaration
      | subprogram_renaming_declaration

153 library_unit_body ::= subprogram_body | package_body

154 context_clause ::= {context_item}

155 context_item ::= with_clause | use_clause

156 with_clause ::= **with** *library_unit*_name {, *library_unit*_name};

157 body_stub ::= subprogram_body_stub | package_body_stub
      | task_body_stub | protected_body_stub

158 subprogram_body_stub ::= subprogram_specification **is separate**;

159 package_body_stub ::=
      package body defining_identifier **is separate**;

160 task_body_stub ::= **task body** defining_identifier **is separate**;

161 protected_body_stub ::=
    protected body defining_identifier **is separate**;

162 subunit ::= **separate** (parent_unit_name) proper_body

163 renaming_declaration ::=
    object_renaming_declaration
    | exception_renaming_declaration
    | package_renaming_declaration
    | subprogram_renaming_declaration
    | generic_renaming_declaration

164 object_renaming_declaration ::=
    defining_identifier : subtype_mark **renames** *object*_name;

165 exception_renaming_declaration ::=
    defining_identifier : **exception renames** *exception*_name;

166 package_renaming_declaration ::=
    package defining_program_unit_name **renames** *package*_name;

167 subprogram_renaming_declaration ::=
    subprogram_specification **renames** *callable_entity*_name;

168 generic_renaming_declaration ::=
    generic package defining_program_unit_name
      renames *generic_package*_name;
    | **generic procedure** defining_program_unit_name
      renames *generic_procedure*_name;
    | **generic function** defining_program_unit_name
      renames *generic_function*_name;

Chapter 13

169 record_extension_part ::= **with** record_definition

170 extension_aggregate ::=
    (ancestor_part **with** record_component_association_list)

171 ancestor_part ::= expression | subtype_mark

172 abstract_subprogram_declaration ::=
    subprogram_specification **is abstract**;

173 private_extension_declaration ::=
    type defining_identifier [discriminant_part] **is**
      [**abstract**] **new** *ancestor*_subtype_indication **with private**;

Chapter 14

174 handled_sequence_of_statements ::=
    sequence_of_statements
    [**exception**
      exception_handler
      {exception_handler}]

175 exception_handler ::= **when** [choice_parameter_specification :]
              exception_choice { | exception_choice} =>
                                       sequence_of_statements

176 choice_parameter_specification ::= defining_identifier

177 exception_choice ::= *exception*_name | **others**

178 exception_declaration ::= defining_identifier_list : **exception**;

179 raise_statement ::= **raise** [*exception*_name];

Chapter 15

180 integer_type_definition ::=
              signed_integer_type_definition | modular_type_definition

181 signed_integer_type_definition ::=
              range *static*_simple_expression .. *static*_simple_expression

182 modular_type_definition ::= **mod** *static*_expression

183 real_type_definition ::=
              floating_point_definition | fixed_point_definition

184 floating_point_definition ::=
              digits *static*_expression [real_range_specification]

185 real_range_specification ::=
              range *static*_simple_expression .. *static*_simple_expression

186 fixed_point_definition ::=
              ordinary_fixed_point_definition | decimal_fixed_point_definition

187 ordinary_fixed_point_definition ::=
              delta *static*_expression real_range_specification

188 decimal_fixed_point_definition ::=
              delta *static*_expression **digits** *static*_expression
                                       [real_range_specification]

189 digits_constraint ::= **digits** *static*_expression [range_constraint]

190 delta_constraint ::= **delta** *static*_expression [range_constraint]

Chapter 16

191 discriminant_part ::=
              unknown_discriminant_part | known_discriminant_part

192 unknown_discriminant_part ::= (<>)

193 known_discriminant_part ::=
              (discriminant_specification {; discriminant_specification})

194 discriminant_specification ::=
          defining_identifier_list : subtype_mark [:= default_expression]
        | defining_identifier_list : access_definition [:= default_expression]

195 discriminant_constraint ::=
      (discriminant_association {, discriminant_association})

196 discriminant_association ::=
    [*discriminant*_selector_name { | *discriminant*_selector_name} =>]
                                        expression

197 variant_part ::=
      case *discriminant*_direct_name **is**
        variant
        {variant}
      end case;

198 variant ::= **when** discrete_choice_list => component_list

Chapter 17

199 generic_declaration ::=
      generic_subprogram_declaration | generic_package_declaration

200 generic_subprogram_declaration ::=
      generic_formal_part subprogram_specification;

201 generic_package_declaration ::=
      generic_formal_part package_specification;

202 generic_formal_part ::=
      generic {generic_formal_parameter_declaration | use_clause}

203 generic_formal_parameter_declaration ::=
        formal_object_declaration
      | formal_type_declaration
      | formal_subprogram_declaration
      | formal_package_declaration

204 formal_object_declaration ::=
      defining_identifier_list : mode subtype_mark
                              [:= default_expression];

205 formal_type_declaration ::=
      type defining_identifier [discriminant_part] **is**
                              formal_type_definition;

206 formal_type_definition ::=
        formal_private_type_definition
      | formal_derived_type_definition
      | formal_discrete_type_definition
      | formal_signed_integer_type_definition
      | formal_modular_type_definition
      | formal_floating_point_definition
      | formal_ordinary_fixed_point_definition
      | formal_decimal_fixed_point_definition
      | formal_array_type_definition
      | formal_access_type_definition

207 formal_private_type_definition ::=
            [[**abstract**] **tagged**] [**limited**] **private**

208 formal_derived_type_definition ::=
            [**abstract**] **new** subtype_mark [**with private**]

209 formal_discrete_type_definition ::= (<>)

210 formal_signed_integer_type_definition ::= **range** <>

211 formal_modular_type_definition ::= **mod** <>

212 formal_floating_point_definition ::= **digits** <>

213 formal_ordinary_fixed_point_definition ::= **delta** <>

214 formal_decimal_fixed_point_definition ::= **delta** <> **digits** <>

215 formal_array_type_definition ::= array_type_definition

216 formal_access_type_definition ::= access_type_definition

217 formal_subprogram_declaration ::=
            with subprogram_specification [**is** subprogram_default];

218 subprogram_default ::= default_name | <>

219 default_name ::= name

220 formal_package_declaration ::= **with package** defining_identifier **is**
            new *generic_package_*name formal_package_actual_part;

221 formal_package_actual_part ::= (<>) | [generic_actual_part]

222 generic_instantiation ::=
            package defining_program_unit_name **is**
            new *generic_package_*name [generic_actual_part];
         | **procedure** defining_program_unit_name **is**
            new *generic_procedure_*name [generic_actual_part];
         | **function** defining_designator **is**
            new *generic_function_*name [generic_actual_part];

223 generic_actual_part ::= (generic_association {, generic_association})

224 generic_association ::=
            [*generic_formal_parameter_*selector_name =>]
                                    explicit_generic_actual_parameter

225 explicit_generic_actual_parameter ::= expression | *variable_*name
            | *subprogram_*name | *entry_*name | subtype_mark
            | *package_instance_*name

Chapter 18

226 task_type_declaration ::=
            task type defining_identifier [known_discriminant_part]
                                    [**is** task_definition];

227 single_task_declaration ::= **task** defining_identifier [**is** task_definition];

228 task_definition ::=
      {task_item}
    [**private**
      {task_item}]
    end [*task*_identifier]

229 task_item ::= entry_declaration | representation_clause

230 task_body ::=
    task body defining_identifier **is**
      declarative_part
    begin
      handled_sequence_of_statements
    end [*task*_identifier];

231 entry_declaration ::= **entry** defining_identifier
                [(discrete_subtype_definition)] parameter_profile;

232 entry_call_statement ::= *entry*_name [actual_parameter_part];

233 accept_statement ::=
    accept *entry*_direct_name [(entry_index)] parameter_profile [**do**
      handled_sequence_of_statements
    end [*entry*_identifier]];

234 entry_index ::= expression

235 delay_statement ::= delay_until_statement | delay_relative_statement

236 delay_until_statement ::= **delay until** *delay*_expression;

237 delay_relative_statement ::= **delay** *delay*_expression;

238 protected_type_declaration ::=
    protected type defining_identifier [known_discriminant_part]
                      is protected_definition;

239 single_protected_declaration ::=
    protected defining_identifier **is** protected_definition;

240 protected_definition ::=
      {protected_operation_declaration}
    [**private**
      {protected_element_declaration}]
    end [*protected*_identifier]

241 protected_operation_declaration ::= subprogram_declaration
    | entry_declaration | representation_clause

242 protected_element_declaration ::=
    protected_operation_declaration | component_declaration

243 protected_body ::=
    protected body defining_identifier **is**
      {protected_operation_item}
    end [*protected*_identifier];

244 protected_operation_item ::=
            subprogram_declaration | subprogram_body
            | entry_body | representation_clause

245 entry_body ::=
            entry defining_identifier entry_body_formal_part entry_barrier **is**
              declarative_part
            begin
              handled_sequence_of_statements
            end [*entry_*identifier];

246 entry_body_formal_part ::=
            [(entry_index_specification)] parameter_profile

247 entry_barrier ::= **when** condition

248 entry_index_specification ::=
            for defining_identifier **in** discrete_subtype_definition

249 select_statement ::= selective_accept | timed_entry_call
            | conditional_entry_call | asynchronous_select

250 selective_accept ::=
             select
              [guard]
               select_alternative
            {**or**
              [guard]
               select_alternative}
            [**else**
              sequence_of_statements]
            end select;

251 guard ::= **when** condition =>

252 select_alternative ::= accept_alternative
            | delay_alternative | terminate_alternative

253 accept_alternative ::=
            accept_statement [sequence_of_statements]

254 delay_alternative ::=
            delay_statement [sequence_of_statements]

255 terminate_alternative ::= **terminate**;

256 conditional_entry_call ::=
             select
              entry_call_alternative
             else
              sequence_of_statements
             end_select;

257 entry_call_alternative ::=
            entry_call_statement [sequence_of_statements]

258 timed_entry_call ::=
      select
         entry_call_alternative
      or
         delay_alternative
      end select;

259 abort_statement ::= **abort** *task_*name {, *task_*name};

260 asynchronous_select ::=
      select
         triggering_alternative
      then abort
         abortable_part
      end select;

261 triggering_alternative ::=
      triggering_statement [sequence_of_statements]

262 triggering_statement ::= entry_call_statement | delay_statement

263 abortable_part ::= sequence_of_statements

264 requeue_statement ::= **requeue** *entry_*name [**with abort**];

Chapter 21

265 representation_clause ::=
      attribute_definition_clause
      | enumeration_representation_clause
      | record_representation_clause
      | at_clause

266 local_name ::= direct_name | direct_name ' attribute_designator
      | *library_unit_*name

267 attribute_definition_clause ::=
      for local_name ' attribute_designator **use** expression;
      | **for** local_name ' attribute_designator **use** name;

268 enumeration_representation_clause ::=
      for *first_subtype_*local_name **use** enumeration_aggregate;

269 enumeration_aggregate ::= array_aggregate

270 record_representation_clause ::=
      for *first_subtype_*local_name **use**
        record [mod_clause]
         {component_clause}
        end record;

271 mod_clause ::= **at mod** *static_*expression;

272 component_clause ::= *component_*local_name **at**
                       position **range** first_bit .. last_bit;

273 position ::= *static*_expression

274 first_bit ::= *static*_simple_expression

275 last_bit ::= *static*_simple_expression

276 at_clause ::= **for** direct_name **use at** expression;

277 code_statement ::= qualified_expression;

A3.2   Syntax index

This index lists the syntactic categories in alphabetical order and gives the number of their definition in the previous section and also the numbers of the categories in which each is used. Categories for which there is no definition number are terminal.

Category	Definition number	Used in number		
abortable_part	263	260		
abort_statement	259	66		
abstract_subprogram_declaration	172	19		
accept_alternative	253	252		
accept_statement	233	67	253	
access_definition	132	119	194	
access_to_object_definition	129	128		
access_to_subprogram_definition	131	128		
access_type_definition	128	29	216	
actual_parameter_part	124	122	123	232
aggregate	91	55	63	
allocator	134	55		
ancestor_part	171	170		
array_aggregate	96	91	269	
array_component_association	99	98		
array_type_definition	82	20	29	215
assignment_statement	24	66		
asynchronous_select	260	249		
at_clause	276	265		
attribute_definition_clause	267	265		
attribute_designator	48	46	266	267
attribute_reference	46	41		
base	12	11		
based_literal	11	7		
based_numeral	13	11		
basic_declaration	19	140		
basic_declarative_item	140	136	139	

Category	Definition number	Used in number				
binary_adding_operator	58	52				
block_statement	25	67				
body	141	139				
body_stub	157	141				
case_statement	72	67				
case_statement_alternative	73	72				
character	4	18				
character_literal	15	40	41	107		
choice_parameter_specification	176	175				
code_statement	277	66				
comment	18					
compilation	148					
compilation_unit	149	148				
component_choice_list	95	94				
component_clause	272	270				
component_declaration	104	103	242			
component_definition	87	83	84	104		
component_item	103	102				
component_list	102	101	198			
composite_constraint	35	33				
compound_statement	67	65				
condition	71	70	78	80	247	251
conditional_entry_call	256	249				
constrained_array_definition	84	82				
constraint	33	31				
context_clause	154	149				
context_item	155	154				
decimal_fixed_point_definition	188	186				
decimal_literal	8	7				
declarative_item	139	138				
declarative_part	138	25	121	137	230	245
default_expression	105	104	119	194	204	
default_name	219	218				
defining_character_literal	40	39				
defining_designator	113	109	222			
defining_identifier	23	22	28	30	39	79
		114	133	146	159	160
		161	164	165	173	176
		205	220	226	227	230
		231	238	239	243	245
		248				
defining_identifier_list	22	20	21	104	119	178
		194	204			
defining_operator_symbol	117	113				
defining_program_unit_name	114	109	113	136	137	166

Category	Definition number	Used in number				
		182	184	187	188	189
		190	196	225	234	236
		237	267	271	273	276
extended_digit	14	13				
extension_aggregate	170	91				
factor	54	53				
first_bit	274	272				
fixed_point_definition	186	183				
floating_point_definition	184	183				
formal_access_type_definition	216	206				
formal_array_type_definition	215	206				
formal_decimal_fixed_point_definition	214	206				
formal_derived_type_definition	208	206				
formal_discrete_type_definition	209	206				
formal_floating_point_definition	212	206				
formal_modular_type_definition	211	206				
formal_object_declaration	204	203				
formal_ordinary_fixed_point_definition	213	206				
formal_package_actual_part	221	220				
formal_package_declaration	220	203				
formal_part	118	110	111			
formal_private_type_definition	207	206				
formal_signed_integer_type_definition	210	206				
formal_subprogram_declaration	217	203				
formal_type_declaration	205	203				
formal_type_definition	206	205				
format_effector	-	4				
full_type_declaration	28	27				
function_call	123	41				
general_access_modifier	130	129				
generic_actual_part	223	221	222			
generic_association	224	223				
generic_declaration	199	19	151			
generic_formal_parameter_declaration	203	202				
generic_formal_part	202	200	201			
generic_instantiation	222	19	151			
generic_package_declaration	201	199				
generic_renaming_declaration	168	152	163			
generic_subprogram_declaration	200	199				
goto_statement	81	66				
graphic_character	3	4	15	17		
guard	251	250				
handled_sequence_of_statements	174	25	121	137	230	233
		245				

Category	Definition number	Used in number				
highest_precedence_operator	61					
identifier	5	1	2	23	25	42
		48	77	107	112	136
		137	228	230	233	240
		243	245			
identifier_letter	-	3	5	6		
if_statement	70	67				
implicit_dereference	45	43				
incomplete_type_declaration	133	27				
index_constraint	88	35				
index_subtype_definition	85	83				
indexed_component	89	41				
integer_type_definition	180	29				
iteration_scheme	78	77				
known_discriminant_part	193	28	191	226	238	
label	68	65				
last_bit	275	272				
letter_or_digit	6	5				
library_item	150	149				
library_unit_body	153	150				
library_unit_declaration	151	150				
library_unit_renaming_declaration	152	150				
local_name	266	267	268	270	272	
logical_operator	56					
loop_parameter specification	79	78				
loop_statement	77	67				
mod_clause	271	270				
mode	120	119	204			
modular_type_definition	182	180				
multiplying_operator	60	53				
name	41	2	24	32	43	44
		45	55	62	80	81
		115	122	123	126	144
		156	164	165	166	167
		168	177	179	219	220
		222	225	232	259	264
		266	267			
named_array_aggregate	98	96				
null_statement	69	66				
number_declaration	21	19				
numeral	9	8	10	12		
numeric_literal	7	55				
object_declaration	20	19				

Category	Definition number	Used in number			
object_renaming_declaration	164	163			
operator_symbol	116	42	107	112	117
ordinary_fixed_point_definition	187	186			
other_control_function	-	4			
package_body	137	142	153		
package_body_stub	159	157			
package_declaration	135	19	151		
package_renaming_declaration	166	152	163		
package_specification	136	135	201		
parameter_and_result_profile	111	109	131		
parameter_association	125	124			
parameter_profile	110	109	131	231	233	246
parameter_specification	119	118			
parent_unit_name	115	112	114	136	137	162
position	273	272			
positional_array_aggregate	97	96			
pragma	1				
pragma_argument_association	2	1			
prefix	43	46	47	89	90	106
		122	123		
primary	55	54			
private_extension_declaration	173	27			
private_type_declaration	146	27			
procedure_call_statement	122	66			
proper_body	142	141	162		
protected_body	243	142			
protected_body_stub	161	157			
protected_definition	240	238	239		
protected_element_declaration	242	240			
protected_operation_declaration	241	240	242		
protected_operation_item	244	243			
protected_type_declaration	238	28			
qualified_expression	63	55	134	277	
raise_statement	179	66			
range	37	36	51	76	86
range_attribute_designator	49	47			
range_attribute_reference	47	37			
range_constraint	36	34	189	190	
real_range_specification	185	184	187	188	
real_type_definition	183	29			
record_aggregate	92	91			
record_component_association	94	93			
record_component_association_list	93	92	170		
record_definition	101	100	169		

Category	Definition number	Used in number			
record_extension_part	169	147			
record_representation_clause	270	265			
record_type_definition	100	29			
relation	51	50			
relational_operator	57	51			
renaming_declaration	163	19			
representation_clause	265	103	140	229	241	244
requeue_statement	264	66			
return_statement	127	66			
scalar_constraint	34	33			
select_alternative	252	250			
select_statement	249	67			
selected_component	106	41			
selective_accept	250	249			
selector_name	107	95	106	125	196	224
sequence_of_statements	64	70	73	77	174	175
		250	253	254	256	257
		261	263			
signed_integer_type_definition	181	180			
simple_expression	52	37	51	181	185	274
		275				
simple_statement	66	65			
single_protected_declaration	239	20			
single_task_declaration	227	20			
slice	90	41			
space_character	-	3			
special_character	-	3			
statement	65	64			
statement_identifier	26	25	68	77		
string_element	17	16			
string_literal	16	55	116			
subprogram_body	121	142	153	244		
subprogram_body_stub	158	157			
subprogram_declaration	108	19	151	241	244	
subprogram_default	218	217			
subprogram_renaming_declaration	167	152	163			
subprogram_specification	109	108	121	158	167	172
		200	217			
subtype_declaration	30	19			
subtype_indication	31	20	30	76	86	87
		129	134	147	173	
subtype_mark	32	31	51	62	63	85
		111	119	132	145	164
		171	194	204	208	225
subunit	162	149			

Category	Definition number	Used in number		
task_body	230	142		
task_body_stub	160	157		
task_definition	228	226	227	
task_item	229	228		
task_type_declaration	226	28		
term	53	52		
terminate_alternative	255	252		
timed_entry_call	258	249		
triggering_alternative	261	260		
triggering_statement	262	261		
type_conversion	62	41		
type_declaration	27	19		
type_definition	29	28		
unary_adding_operator	59	52		
unconstrained_array_definition	83	82		
underline	-	5	9	13
unknown_discriminant_part	192	191		
use_clause	143	140	155	202
use_package_clause	144	143		
use_type_clause	145	143		
variant	198	197		
variant_part	197	102		
with_clause	156	155		

Answers to Exercises

Specimen answers are given to all the exercises. In some cases they do not necessarily represent the best technique for solving a problem but merely one which uses the material introduced at that point in the discussion.

Answers 2

Exercise 2.2

1
```
package Simple_Maths is
    function Sqrt(F: Float) return Float;
    function Log(F: Float) return Float;
    function Ln(F: Float) return Float;
    function Exp(F: Float) return Float;
    function Sin(F: Float) return Float;
    function Cos(F: Float) return Float;
end Simple_Maths;
```

The first few lines of our program Print_Roots could now become

```
with Simple_Maths, Simple_IO;
procedure Print_Roots is
    use Simple_Maths, Simple_IO;
```

Exercise 2.4

1
```
type Month_Name is (Jan, Feb, Mar, Apr, May, Jun, Jul, Aug, Sep, Oct, Nov, Dec);
```

Exercise 2.5

1
```
for I in 0 .. N loop
    Pascal(I) := Next(I);
end loop;
```

2
```
for N in 0 .. 10 loop
    Pascal2(N, 0) := 1;
    for I in 1 .. N-1 loop
        Pascal2(N, I) := Pascal2(N-1, I-1) + Pascal2(N-1, I);
    end loop;
```

```
      Pascal2(N, N) := 1;
   end loop;
```

3   **type** Date **is**
    record
       Day: Integer;
       Month: Month_Name;
       Year: Integer;
    end record;

Today: Date;
...
Today := (24, May, 1819);

Answers 3

Exercise 3.1

1   **package** Buffer_System **is**   -- visible part

```
   type Buffer is private;
   Error: exception;
   procedure Load(B: in out Buffer; S: in String);
   procedure Get(B: in out Buffer; C: out Character);
   function Is_Empty(B: Buffer) return Boolean;
private                                              -- private part
   Max: constant Integer := 80;
   type Buffer is
      record
         Data: String(1 .. Max);
         Start: Integer := 1;
         Finish: Integer := 0;
      end record;
end Buffer_System;

package body Buffer_System is
   procedure Load(B: in out Buffer; S: in String) is
   begin
      if S'Length > Max or B.Start <= B.Finish then
         raise Error;
      end if;
      B.Start := 1;
      B.Finish := S'Length;
      B.Data(B.Start .. B.Finish) := S;
   end Load;

   procedure Get(B: in out Buffer; C: out Character) is
   begin
      if B.Start > B.Finish then
         raise Error;
      end if;
      C := B.Data(B.Start);
      B.Start := B.Start + 1;
   end Get;

   function Is_Empty(B: Buffer) return Boolean is
   begin
      return B.Start > B.Finish;
   end Is_Empty;
end Buffer_System;
```

The parameter Buffer of Load now has to be **in out** because the original value is read. Also, we could replace the test in Get by

> **if** Is_Empty(B) **then**

Exercise 3.2

1   **package** Objects **is**
  type Object **is tagged**
   record
    X_Coord: Float;
    Y_Coord: Float;
   end record;

  function Distance(O: Object) **return** Float;
  function Area(O: Object) **return** Float;
 end Objects;

 package body Objects **is**
  function Distance(O: Object) **return** Float **is**
  begin
   return Sqrt(O.X_Coord**2 + O.Y_Coord**2);
  end Distance;

  function Area(O: Object) **return** Float **is**
  begin
   return 0.0;
  end Area;
 end Objects;

 with Objects; **use** Objects;
 package Shapes **is**
  type Point **is new** Object **with null record**;

  type Circle **is new** Object **with**
   record
    Radius: Float;
   end record;

  function Area(C: Circle) **return** Float;

  type Triangle **is new** Object **with**
   record
    A, B, C: Float;
   end record;

  function Area(T: Triangle) **return** Float;
 end Shapes;

 package body Shapes **is**
  function Area(C: Circle) **return** Float **is**
  begin
   return Pi*C.Radius**2;
  end Area;

  function Area(T: Triangle) **return** Float **is**
   S: **constant** Float := 0.5 * (T.A + T.B + T.C);
  begin
   return Sqrt(S * (S – T.A) * (S – T.B) * (S – T.C));
  end Area;
 end Shapes;

Note that we can put the use clause for Objects immediately after the with clause.

Exercise 3.3

1
```
procedure Add_To_List(List: in out Cell_Ptr; Obj_Ptr: Pointer) is
   Local: Cell_Ptr := new Cell;
begin
   Local.Element := Obj_Ptr;
   Local.Next := List;
   List := Local;
end Add_To_List;
```

or more briefly using a form of allocation with initial values

```
procedure Add_To_List(List: in out Cell_Ptr; Obj_Ptr: Pointer) is
begin
   List := new Cell'(Obj_Ptr, List);
end Add_To_List;
```

2
```
package body Objects is
   function Distance(O: Object) return Float is
   begin
      return Sqrt(O.X_Coord**2 + O.Y_Coord**2);
   end Distance;
end Objects;
```

3   We have to add the function Area for the type Point thus

```
with Objects; use Objects;
package Shapes is
   type Point is new Object with null record;
   function Area(P: Point) return Float;
   ...
end Shapes;
```

```
package body Shapes is
   function Area(P: Point) return Float is
   begin
      return 0.0;
   end Area;
   ...
end Shapes;
```

4   We cannot declare the function Moment for the abstract type Object because it contains a call of the abstract function Area.

5
```
function MO(OC: Object'Class) return Float is
begin
   return MI(OC) + Area(OC) * Distance(OC)**2;
end MO;
```

Answers 4

Exercise 4.2

1   The default field is 6 for a 16-bit type Integer and 11 for a 32-bit type Integer so

```
Put(123);                      -- "sss123"  and  "ssssssss123"
Put(-123);                     -- "ss-123"  and  "sssssss-123"
```

Exercise 4.4

1   ```
    with Ada.Text_IO, Ada.Integer_Text_IO;
    use Ada.Text_IO, Ada.Integer_Text_IO;
    procedure Multiplication_Table is
    begin
       for Row in 1 .. 10 loop
          for Column in 1 .. 10 loop
             Put(Row * Column, 5);
          end loop;
          New_Line;
       end loop;
    end Multiplication_Table;
    ```

2   ```
    with Ada.Text_IO, Etc;
    use Ada.Text_IO, Etc;
    procedure Table_Of_Square_Roots is
       use My_Float_IO, My_Elementary_Functions;
       Last_N: Integer;
       Tab: Count;
    begin
       Tab := 10;
       Put("What is the largest value please? "); Get(Last_N);
       New_Line(2);
       Put("Number"); Set_Col(Tab); Put("Square root");
       New_Line(2);
       for N in 1 .. Last_N loop
          Put(N, 4); Set_Col(Tab); Put(Sqrt(My_Float(N)), 3, 6, 0);
          New_Line;
       end loop;
    end Table_Of_Square_Roots;
    ```

3   ```
    with Ada.Text_IO;
    package My_Numerics.My_Float_IO is
        new Ada.Text_IO.Float_IO(My_Float);

    with Ada.Text_IO;
    package My_Numerics.My_Integer_IO is
        new Ada.Text_IO.Integer_IO(My_Integer);

    with Ada.Numerics.Generic_Elementary_Functions;
    package My_Numerics.My_Elementary_Functions is
        new Ada.Numerics.Generic_Elementary_Functions(My_Float);
    ```

4   ```
    with Ada.Text_IO, Ada.Integer_Text_IO;
    use Ada.Text_IO, Ada.Integer_Text_IO;
    with Ada.Numerics.Discrete_Random;
    procedure Sundays is
       type Day is (Mon, Tue, Wed, Thu, Fri, Sat, Sun);
       package Random_Day is new Ada.Numerics.Discrete_Random(Day);
       use Random_Day;
       G: Generator;
       D: Day;
       Number_Of_Sundays: Integer;
    begin
       Number_Of_Sundays := 0;
       for I in 1 .. 100 loop
          D := Random(G);
    ```

```
        if D = Sun then
            Number_Of_Sundays := Number_Of_Sundays + 1;
        end if;
    end loop;
    Put("Percentage of Sundays in random selection was ");
    Put(Number_Of_Sundays);
    New_Line;
end Sundays;
```

5
```
with Ada.Text_IO, Ada.Integer_Text_IO;
use Ada.Text_IO, Ada.Integer_Text_IO;
procedure Triangle is
    Size: Integer;
begin
    Put("Size of triangle please: ");  Get(Size);
    declare
        Pascal: array (0 .. Size) of Integer;
        Tab: Count;        -- indentation at start of row
    begin
        Tab := Count(2*Size + 1);
        Pascal(0) := 1;
        for N in 1 .. Size loop
            Pascal(N) := 1;
            for I in reverse 1 .. N-1 loop
                Pascal(I) := Pascal(I-1) + Pascal(I);
            end loop;
            Tab := Tab - 2;
            New_Line(2);  Set_Col(Tab);
            for I in 0 .. N loop
                Put(Pascal(I), 4);
            end loop;
        end loop;
        New_Line(2);
        if 2*Size > 8 then
            Set_Col(Count(2*Size - 8));
        end if;
        Put("The Triangle of Pascal");
        New_Line(2);
    end;
end Triangle;
```

It is instructive to consider how this should be written to accommodate larger values of Size in a flexible manner and thereby avoid the confusing repetition of the literal 2. A variable Half_Field might be declared with the value 2 in the above but would need to be 3 for values of Size up to 19 which will go off the screen anyway. Care is needed with variables of type Count which are not allowed to take negative values.

Answers 5

Exercise 5.3

1   The following are not legal identifiers

(b) contains &
(c) contains hyphens not underlines
(e) adjacent underlines
(f) does not start with a letter

(g) trailing underline
(h) this is two legal identifiers
(i) this is legal – but it is a reserved word
     and not an identifier

Note that (a) is of course a legal identifier but it would be unwise to declare our own variable called Ada because it would conflict with the predefined package of that name.

Exercise 5.4

1 (a) legal – real
(b) illegal – no digit before point
(c) legal – integer
(d) illegal – integer with negative exponent
(e) illegal – closing # missing
(f) legal – real
(g) illegal – C not a digit of base 12
(h) illegal – no number before exponent
(i) legal – integer – case of letter immaterial
(j) legal – integer
(k) illegal – underline at start of exponent
(l) illegal – integer with negative exponent

2 (a) $224 = 14 \times 16$ (c) 4095.0
(b) $6144 = 3 \times 211$ (d) 4095.0

3 (a) 32 ways

41, 2#101001#, 3#1112#, ... 10#41#, ... 16#29#
41E0, 2#101001#E0, ... 16#29#E0

(b) 40 ways. As for example (a) plus, since 150 is not prime but $2 \times 3 \times 5^2 = 150$ also

2#1001011#E1, 3#1212#E1, 5#110#E1, 5#11#E2, 6#41#E1, 10#15#E1
15#A#E1, 15E1

Exercise 5.5

1 (a) 7   (c) 1
(b) 1   (d) 12

2 (a) This has 3 elements
         the identifier   delay
         the literal   2.0
         the single symbol   ;

(b) This has 4 elements
         the identifier   delay2
         the single symbol   .
         the literal   0
         the single symbol   ;

Case (a) is a legal delay statement, (b) is just a mess.

Answers 6

Exercise 6.1

1 F: Float := 1.0;

2 Zero: **constant** Float := 0.0;
One: **constant** Float := 1.0;

but it might better to write real number declarations

Zero: **constant** := 0.0;
One: **constant** := 1.0;

3 (a) **var** is illegal – this is Ada not Pascal
   (b) terminating semicolon is missing
   (c) a constant declaration must have an initial value
   (d) no multiple assignment – this is Ada not Algol
   (e) nothing – assuming M and N are of integer type
   (f) 2Pi is not a legal identifier

Exercise 6.2

1 There are four errors

   (1) semicolon missing after declaration of J, K
   (2) K used before a value has been assigned to it
   (3) = instead of := in declaration of P
   (4) Q not declared and initialized

Exercise 6.4

1 It is assumed that the values of all variables originally satisfy their constraints.

   (a) the ranges of I and J are identical so no checks are required and consequently Constraint_Error cannot be raised,

   (b) the range of J is a subset of that of K and again Constraint_Error cannot be raised,

   (c) in this case a check is required since if K > 10 it cannot be assigned to J in which case Constraint_Error will be raised.

Exercise 6.5

1 (a) −105   (d) −3   (g) −1
   (b) −3   (e) −3   (h) 2
   (c) 0   (f) illegal

2 All variables are of type Float

   (a) M*R**2
   (b) B**2 − 4.0*A*C
   (c) (4.0/3.0)*Pi*R**3   -- brackets not necessary
   (d) (P*Pi*A**4) / (8.0*L*Eta) -- brackets are necessary

Exercise 6.6

1 (a) Sat
   (b) Sat   note that Succ applies to the base type
   (c) 2

2 (a) **type** Rainbow **is** (Red, Orange, Yellow, Green, Blue, Indigo, Violet);
   (b) **type** Fruit **is** (Apple, Banana, Orange, Pear);

3 Groom'Val((N−1) **mod** 8)

   or perhaps better

   Groom'Val((N−1) **mod** (Groom'Pos(Groom'Last) + 1))

4   D := Day'Val((Day'Pos(D) + N − 1) **mod** 7);

5   If X and Y are both overloaded literals then X < Y will be ambiguous. We would have
to use qualification such as T'(X) < T'(Y).

Exercise 6.7

1   T: **constant** Boolean := True;
F: **constant** Boolean := False;

2   The values are True and False, not T or F which are the names of constants.

(a) False   (c) True   (e) False
(b) True   (d) True

3   The expression is always True. The predefined operators **xor** and **/=** operating on
Boolean values are the same. But see the note at the end of Section 11.3.

Exercise 6.8

1   (a) False   (b) Sat

Exercise 6.9

1   All variables are of type Float except for N in example (c) which is Integer.

(a)   2.0*Pi*Sqrt(L/G)
(b)   M_0/Sqrt(1.0−(V/C)**2)
(c)   Sqrt(2.0*Pi*Float(N)) * (Float(N)/E)**N

2   Sqrt(2.0*Pi*X) * Exp(X*Ln(X)−X)

Answers 7

Exercise 7.1

1
```
declare
   End_Of_Month: Integer;
begin
   if Month = Sep or Month = Apr or Month = Jun or Month = Nov then
      End_Of_Month := 30;
   elsif Month = Feb then
      if Year mod 4 = 0 then
         End_Of_Month := 29;
      else
         End_Of_Month := 28;
      end if;
   else
      End_Of_Month := 31;
   end if;
   if Day /= End_Of_Month then
      Day := Day + 1;
   else
      Day := 1;
      if Month /= Dec then
         Month := Month_Name'Succ(Month);
      else
```

```
                Month := Jan;
                Year := Year + 1;
            end if;
        end if;
    end;
```

If today is 31 Dec 2099 then Constraint_Error will be raised on attempting to assign 2100 to Year. Note that the range 1901 .. 2099 simplifies the leap year calculation.

2
```
    if X < Y then
        declare
            T: Float := X;
        begin
            X := Y;  Y := T;
        end;
    end if;
```

Exercise 7.2

1
```
    declare
        End_Of_Month: Integer;
    begin
        case Month is
            when Sep | Apr | Jun | Nov =>
                End_Of_Month := 30;
            when Feb =>
                if Year mod 4 = 0 then
                    End_Of_Month := 29;
                else
                    End_Of_Month := 28;
                end if;
            when others =>
                End_Of_Month := 31;
        end case;
        -- then as before
        ...
    end;
```

2
```
    subtype Winter is Month_Name range Jan .. Mar;
    subtype Spring is Month_Name range Apr .. Jun;
    subtype Summer is Month_Name range Jul .. Sep;
    subtype Autumn is Month_Name range Oct .. Dec;
    ...
    case M is
        when Winter => Dig;
        when Spring => Sow;
        when Summer => Tend;
        when Autumn => Harvest;
    end case;
```

Note that if we wished to consider winter as December to February then we could not declare a suitable subtype.

3
```
    case D is
        when 1 .. 10 => Gorge;
        when 11 .. 20 => Subsist;
        when others => Starve;
    end case;
```

We cannot write 21 .. End_Of_Month because it is not a static range. In fact **others** covers all values of type Integer because although D is constrained, nevertheless the constraints are not static.

Exercise 7.3

1   **declare**
      Sum: Integer := 0;
      I: Integer;
    begin
      loop
        Get(I);
        exit when I < 0;
        Sum := Sum + I;
      end loop;
    end;

2   **declare**
      Copy: Integer := N;
      Count: Integer := 0;
    begin
      while Copy **mod** 2 = 0 **loop**
        Copy := Copy **/** 2;
        Count := Count + 1;
      end loop;
      ...
    end;

3   **declare**
      G: Float := −Ln(Float(N));
    begin
      for P **in** 1 .. N **loop**
        G := G + 1.0/Float(P);
      end loop;
      ...
    end;

We assume that Ln is the function for natural logarithm.

Answers 8

Exercise 8.1

1   **declare**
      F: **array** (0 .. N) **of** Integer;
    begin
      F(0) := 0; F(1) := 1;
      for I **in** 2 .. F'Last **loop**
        F(I) := F(I−1)+F(I−2);
      end loop;
      ...
    end;

2   **declare**
      Max_I: Integer := A'First(1);
      Max_J: Integer := A'First(2);
      Max: Float := A(Max_I, Max_J);

```
begin
  for I in A'Range(1) loop
    for J in A'Range(2) loop
      if A(I, J) > Max then
        Max := A(I, J);
        Max_I := I;  Max_J := J;
      end if;
    end loop;
  end loop;
  -- Max_I, Max_J now contain the result
end;
```

3 **declare**
```
    Days_In_Month: array (Month_Name) of Integer :=
        (31, 28, 31, 30, 31, 30, 31, 31, 30, 31, 30, 31);
    End_Of_Month: Integer;
begin
    if Year mod 4 = 0 then
        Days_In_Month(Feb) := 29;
    end if;
    End_Of_Month := Days_In_Month(Month);

    -- then as Exercise 7.1(1)

end;
```

4 Yesterday: **constant array** (Day) **of** Day := (Sun, Mon, Tue, Wed, Thu, Fri, Sat);

5 Bor: **constant array** (Boolean, Boolean) **of** Boolean :=
              ((False, True), (True, True));

6 Unit: **constant array** (1 .. 3, 1 .. 3) **of** Float :=
              ((1.0, 0.0, 0.0),
               (0.0, 1.0, 0.0),
               (0.0, 0.0, 1.0));

Exercise 8.2

1 **type** Bbb **is array** (Boolean, Boolean) **of** Boolean;

2 **type** Ring5_Table **is array** (Ring5, Ring5) **of** Ring5;

Add: **constant** Ring5_Table :=
              ((0, 1, 2, 3, 4),
               (1, 2, 3, 4, 0),
               (2, 3, 4, 0, 1),
               (3, 4, 0, 1, 2),
               (4, 0, 1, 2, 3));

Mult: **constant** Ring5_Table :=
              ((0, 0, 0, 0, 0),
               (0, 1, 2, 3, 4),
               (0, 2, 4, 1, 3),
               (0, 3, 1, 4, 2),
               (0, 4, 3, 2, 1));

A, B, C, D: Ring5;

...

D := Mult(Add(A, B), C));

Exercise 8.3

1   Days_In_Month: **array** (Month_Name) **of** Integer :=
          (Sep | Apr | Jun | Nov => 30, Feb => 28, **others** => 31);

2   Zero: **constant** Matrix := (1 .. N => (1 .. N => 0.0));

3   This cannot be done with the material at our disposal at the moment. See Exercise
       9.1(**6**).

4   **type** Molecule **is** (Methanol, Ethanol, Propanol, Butanol);
       type Atom **is** (H, C, O);

       Alcohol: **constant array** (Molecule, Atom) **of** Integer :=
                (Methanol => (H =>   4, C => 1, O => 1),
                 Ethanol => (6,   2,   1),
                 Propanol => (8,   3,   1),
                 Butanol => (10,   4,   1));

       Note the danger in the above. We have used named notation in the first inner
       aggregate to act as a sort of heading but omitted it in the others to avoid clutter.
       However, if we had written H; C and O in other than positional order then it would
       have been very confusing because the positional aggregates would not have had the
       meaning suggested by the heading.

Exercise 8.4

1   Roman_To_Integer: **constant array** (Roman_Digit) **of** Integer :=
          (1, 5, 10, 50, 100, 500, 1000);

2   **declare**
          V: Integer := 0;
       begin
          for I **in** R'Range **loop**
             if I /= R'Last **and then**
                Roman_To_Integer(R(I)) < Roman_To_Integer(R(I+1)) **then**
                V := V – Roman_To_Integer(R(I));
             else
                V := V + Roman_To_Integer(R(I));
             end if;
          end loop;
          ...
       end;

       Note the use of **and then** to avoid attempting to access R(I+1) when I = R'Last.

Exercise 8.5

1   AOA(1 .. 2) := (AOA(2), AOA(1));

2   Farmyard: String_3_Array(1 .. 6) := ("pig", "cat", "dog", "cow", "rat", "ass");
       ...
       Farmyard(4)(1) := 's';

3   **if** R'Last >= 2 **and then** R(R'Last–1 .. R'Last) = "IV" **then**
          R(R'Last–1 .. R'Last) := "VI";
       end if;

Exercise 8.6

1   White, Blue, Yellow, Green, Red, Purple, Orange, Black

2   (a)   Black   (b)   Green   (c)   Red

3   **not** (True **xor** True) = True
    not (True **xor** False) = False

    the result follows.

4   An aggregate of length one must be named.

5   "123", "ABC", "Abc", "aBc", "abC", "abc"

6   (a)   1   (b)   5   (c)   5

    We note therefore that & like **and, or** and **xor** is not strictly commutative.

7   (a)   1 .. 10   (c)   6 .. 15
    (b)   1 .. 10   (d)   0 .. 9

Exercise 8.7

1   C1, C2, C3: Complex;
    (a)   C3 := (C1.Rl+C2.Rl, C1.Im+C2.Im);
    (b)   C3 := (C1.Rl*C2.Rl – C1.Im*C2.Im, C1.Rl*C2.Im + C1.Im*C2.Rl);

2   **declare**
        Index: Integer;
    begin
        for I **in** People'Range **loop**
            if People(I).Birth.Year >= 1950 **then**
                Index := I;
                exit;
            end if;
        end loop;
        -- we assume that there is such a person
    end;

Answers 9

Exercise 9.1

1   **function** Even(X: Integer) **return** Boolean **is**
    begin
        return X **mod** 2 = 0;
    end Even;

2   **function** Factorial(N: Natural) **return** Positive **is**
    begin
        if N = 0 **then**
            return 1;
        else
            return N*Factorial(N–1);
        end if;
    end Factorial;

3   **function** Outer(A, B: Vector) **return** Matrix **is**
   C: Matrix(A'Range, B'Range);
begin
  for I **in** A'Range **loop**
    for J **in** B'Range **loop**
      C(I, J) := A(I)*B(J);
    end loop;
  end loop;
  return C;
end Outer;

4   **type** Primary_Array **is array** (Integer **range** <>) **of** Primary;

  function Make_Colour(P: Primary_Array) **return** Colour **is**
   C: Colour := (F, F, F);
begin
  for I **in** P'Range **loop**
    C(P(I)) := T;
  end loop;
  return C;
end Make_Colour;

Note that multiple values are allowed so that Make_Colour((R, R, R)) = Red.

5   **function** Inner(A, B: Vector) **return** Float **is**
   Result: Float := 0.0;
begin
  if A'Length /= B'Length **then**
    raise Constraint_Error;
  end if;
  for I **in** A'Range **loop**
    Result := Result + A(I)*B(I+B'First–A'First);
  end loop;
  return Result;
end Inner;

6   **function** Make_Unit(N: Natural) **return** Matrix **is**
   M: Matrix(1 .. N, 1 .. N);
begin
  for I **in** 1 .. N **loop**
    for J **in** 1 .. N **loop**
      if I = J **then**
        M(I, J) := 1.0;
      else
        M(I, J) := 0.0;
      end if;
    end loop;
  end loop;
  return M;
end Make_Unit;

We can then declare

Unit: **constant** Matrix := Make_Unit(N);

7   **function** GCD(X, Y: Natural) **return** Natural **is**
begin
  if Y = 0 **then**
    return X;

```
        else
            return GCD(Y, X mod Y);
        end if;
    end GCD;
```

Exercise 9.2

1
```
    function "<" (X, Y: Roman_Number) return Boolean is
        function Value(R: Roman_Number) return Integer is
            V: Integer := 0;
        begin
            ...   -- then loop as in Exercise 8.4(2)
            return V;
        end Value;
    begin
        return Value(X) < Value(Y);
    end "<";
```

2
```
    function "+" (X, Y: Complex) return Complex is
    begin
        return (X.RI + Y.RI, X.Im + Y.Im);
    end "+";

    function "*" (X, Y: Complex) return Complex is
    begin
        return (X.RI*Y.RI – X.Im*Y.Im, X.RI*Y.Im + X.Im*Y.RI);
    end "*";
```

3
```
    function "<" (P: Primary; C: Colour) return Boolean is
    begin
        return C(P);
    end "<";
```

4
```
    function "<=" (X, Y: Colour) return Boolean is
    begin
        return (X and Y) = X;
    end "<=";
```

5
```
    function "<" (X, Y: Date) return Boolean is
    begin
        if X.Year /= Y.Year then
            return X.Year < Y.Year;
        elsif X.Month /= Y.Month then
            return X.Month < Y.Month;
        else
            return X.Day < Y.Day;
        end if;
    end "<";
```

Exercise 9.3

1
```
    procedure Swap(X, Y: in out Float) is
        T: Float;
    begin
        T := X;  X := Y;  Y := T;
    end Swap;
```

2
```
procedure Rev(A: in out Vector) is
   R: Vector(A'Range);
begin
   for I in A'Range loop
      R(I) := A(A'First + A'Last – I);
   end loop;
   A := R;
end Rev;
```

or maybe

```
procedure Rev(A: in out Vector) is
begin
   for I in A'First .. A'First + A'Length/2 – 1 loop
      Swap(A(I), A(A'First + A'Last – I));
   end loop;
end Rev;
```

This procedure can be applied to an array R of type Row by

Rev(Vector(R));

3 The fragment is not portable because the outcome depends upon whether the parameter is passed by copy or by reference. If it is copied then A(1) ends up as 2.0; if it is passed by reference then A(1) ends up as 4.0.

Exercise 9.4

1
```
function Add(X: Integer; Y: Integer := 1) return Integer is
begin
   return X + Y;
end Add;
```

The following 6 calls are equivalent

Add(N)	Add(N, 1)
Add(X => N, Y => 1)	Add(X => N)
Add(N, Y => 1)	Add(Y => 1, X => N)

2
```
function Favourite_Spirit return Spirit is
begin
   case Today is
      when Mon .. Fri => return Gin;
      when Sat | Sun => return Vodka;
   end case;
end Favourite_Spirit;

procedure Dry_Martini(Base: Spirit := Favourite_Spirit;
                      How: Style := On_The_Rocks;
                      Plus: Trimming := Olive);
```

This example illustrates that defaults are evaluated each time they are required and can therefore be changed from time to time.

Exercise 9.5

1 The named form of call

Sell(C => Jersey);

is unambiguous since the formal parameter names are different.

Answers 10

Exercise 10.2

```
1   procedure Append(First: in out Cell_Ptr; Second: in Cell_Ptr) is
       L: Cell_Ptr := First;
    begin
       if First = null then
          First := Second;
       else
          while L.Next /= null loop
             L := L.Next;
          end loop;
          L.Next := Second;
       end if;
    end Append;

2   function Size(T: Node_Ptr) return Integer is
    begin
       if T = null then
          return 0;
       else
          return Size(T.Left)+Size(T.Right)+1;
       end if;
    end Size;

3   function Copy(T: Node_Ptr) return Node_Ptr is
    begin
       if T = null then
          return null;
       else
          return new Node'(T.Value, Copy(T.Left), Copy(T.Right));
       end if;
    end Copy;
```

Exercise 10.3

```
1   function "+" (A: A_String) return String is
    begin
       return A.all;
    end "+";
```

and then Put(+Zoo(3)); will output the string "camel".

```
2   function "&" (X, Y: A_String) return A_String is
    begin
       return new String'(X.all & Y.all);
    end "&";
```

Exercise 10.4

```
1   type G_String is access constant String;
    type G_String_Array is array (Positive range <>) of G_String;
```

Aardvark: **aliased constant** String := "aardvark";
Baboon: **aliased constant** String := "baboon";
...
Zebra: **aliased constant** String := "zebra";

```
Zoo: constant G_String_Array :=
        (Aardvark'Access, Baboon'Access, ..., Zebra'Access);
```

2   ```
    N: Integer := ... ;
    M: Integer := ... ;
    World: array (1 .. N, 1 .. M) of Cell;
    Abyss: constant Cell := (0, 0, (1 .. 8 => null));
    ...
    -- offsets of 8 neighbours starting at North
    type Offset is array (1 .. 8) of Integer;
    H_Off: Offset := (+0, +1, +1, +1, +0, -1, -1, -1);
    V_Off: Offset := (+1, +1, +0, -1, -1, -1, +0, +1);

    -- now link up the cells
    for I in 1 .. N loop
      for J in 1 .. M loop
        -- link to eight neighbours except on boundary
        declare
          H_Index, V_Index: Integer;
        begin
          for N_Index in 1 .. 8 loop
            H_Index := I + H_Off(N_Index);
            V_Index := J + V_Off(N_Index);
            if H_Index in 1 .. N and V_Index in 1 .. M then
              World(I, J).Neighbour_Count(N_Index) :=
                    World(H_Index, V_Index).Life_Count'Access;
            else
              -- edge of world, link to abyss
              World(I, J).Neighbour_Count(N_Index) :=
                    Abyss.Life_Count'Access;
            end if;
          end loop;
        end;
      end loop;
    end loop;
    ```

Clearly the repetition of World(I, J) could be eliminated by introducing an access type
to the cell itself. Or we could use renaming as described in Section 12.6. It would be
better if we did not have so many occurrences of the literal 8. Indeed, the enthusiastic
reader might like to consider how this example might be extended to three or more
dimensions. In three dimensions of course the number of neighbours is $3^3 - 1 = 26$.

3   ```
    type Cell;
    type Ref_Cell is access constant Cell;
    type Ref_Cell_Array is array (Integer range <>) of Ref_Cell;
    type Cell is
      record
        Life_Count: Integer range 0 .. 1;
        Total_Neighbour_Count: Integer range 0 .. 8;
        Neighbour: Ref_Cell_Array(1 .. 8);
      end record;
    ...
    C.Total_Neighbour_Count := 0;
    for I in C.Neighbour'Range loop
      C.Total_Neighbour_Count :=
          C.Total_Neighbour_Count + C.Neighbour(I).Life_Count.all;
    end loop;
    ```

The other changes are that World and Abyss have to be declared as aliased

World: **array** (1 .. N, 1 .. M) **of aliased** Cell;
Abyss: **aliased constant** Cell := (0, 0, (1 .. 8 => **null**));

and the expressions assigned to the neighbours omit Life_Count as in

World(I, J).Neighbour(N_Index) := Abyss'Access;

4   Conversions are allowed from any type to Const_Int_Ptr, from Ref_Int_A to Int_Ptr, and from Ref_Int_B to Int_Ptr.

Exercise 10.6

1   The conversion to Ref1 is checked dynamically; it passes for the call of P with X1'Access and fails with X2'Access. The conversion to Ref2 is checked statically and passes.

2   The conversion to Ref1 is checked dynamically; it passes for X1 and fails for X2 and X3. The conversion to Ref2 is checked dynamically and passes in all cases. The conversion to Ref3 is checked statically and passes.
    Note that the case of X3 and Ref2 is where the accessibility is adjusted on the chained call; without this adjustment it would unnecessarily fail. The point is that considering P1 as a whole, since the type A2 is inside, the conversion is always safe. But since the type A2 is outside P2 which actually does the conversion, it has to be checked dynamically; the adjustment ensures that it always passes.

Exercise 10.7

1
```
function G(T: Float) return Float is
begin
   return Exp(T) * Sin(T);
end G;
...
Answer: Float := Integrate(G'Access, 0.0, P);
```

2
```
type Operand is access function (X: Float) return Float;

function Solve(F: Operand) return Float;
...
function G(X: Float) return Float is
begin
   return Exp(X) + X - 7.0;
end G;
...
Answer := Solve(G'Access);
```

3
```
procedure This;
procedure That;
type Action is access procedure;
P: Action := This'Access;

procedure This is
begin
   P := That'Access;
   ...
end This;

procedure That is
begin
```

```
      P := This'Access;
      ...
   end That;
```

An alternative approach which does not impact on the body of This and That is to use two intermediate procedures This_Shell and That_Shell which call This and That.

Answers 11

Exercise 11.1

1
```ada
   package Random is
      Modulus: constant := 2**13;
      subtype Small is Integer range 0 .. Modulus;
      procedure Init(Seed: Small);
      function Next return Small;
   end;

   package body Random is
      Multiplier: constant := 5**5;
      X: Small;

      procedure Init(Seed: Small) is
      begin
         X := Seed;
      end Init;

      function Next return Small is
      begin
         X := X*Multiplier mod Modulus;
         return X;
      end Next;
   end Random;
```

2
```ada
   package Complex_Numbers is
      type Complex is
         record
            RI, Im: Float := 0.0;
         end record;

      I: constant Complex := (0.0, 1.0);

      function "+" (X: Complex) return Complex;       -- unary +
      function "–" (X: Complex) return Complex;       -- unary –

      function "+" (X, Y: Complex) return Complex;
      function "–" (X, Y: Complex) return Complex;
      function "*" (X, Y: Complex) return Complex;
      function "/" (X, Y: Complex) return Complex;
   end;

   package body Complex_Numbers is

      function "+" (X: Complex) return Complex is
      begin
         return X;
      end "+";

      function "–" (X: Complex) return Complex is
      begin
         return (–X.RI, –X.Im);
      end "–";
```

```
function "+" (X, Y: Complex) return Complex is
begin
   return (X.RI + Y.RI, X.Im + Y.Im);
end "+";

function "–" (X, Y: Complex) return Complex is
begin
   return (X.RI – Y.RI, X.Im – Y.Im);
end "–";

function "*" (X, Y: Complex) return Complex is
begin
   return (X.RI*Y.RI – X.Im*Y.Im, X.RI*Y.Im + X.Im*Y.RI);
end "*";

function "/" (X, Y: Complex) return Complex is
   D: Float := Y.RI**2 + Y.Im**2;
begin
   return ((X.RI*Y.RI + X.Im*Y.Im)/D, (X.Im*Y.RI – X.RI*Y.Im)/D);
end "/";

end Complex_Numbers;
```

Exercise 11.2

1   Inside the package body we could write

```
function "*" (X: Float; Y: Complex) return Complex is
begin
   return (X*Y.RI, X*Y.Im);
end "*";
```

but outside we could only write

```
function "*" (X: Float; Y: Complex) return Complex is
   use Complex_Numbers;
begin
   return Cons(X, 0.0)*Y;
end "*";
```

and similarly with the operands interchanged.

2
```
declare
   C, D: Complex_Numbers.Complex;
   F: Float;
begin
   C := Complex_Numbers.Cons(1.5, –6.0);
   D := Complex_Numbers."+" (C, Complex_Numbers.I);
   F := Complex_Numbers.RI_Part(D) + 6.0;
   ...
end;
```

3
```
package Rational_Numbers is
   type Rational is private;

   function "+" (X: Rational) return Rational;      -- unary +
   function "–" (X: Rational) return Rational;      -- unary –

   function "+" (X, Y: Rational) return Rational;
   function "–" (X, Y: Rational) return Rational;
   function "*" (X, Y: Rational) return Rational;
   function "/" (X, Y: Rational) return Rational;
```

```ada
function "/" (X: Integer; Y: Positive) return Rational;
function Numerator(R: Rational) return Integer;
function Denominator(R: Rational) return Positive;
private
  type Rational is
    record
      Num: Integer := 0;          -- numerator
      Den: Positive := 1;         -- denominator
    end record;
end;

package body Rational_Numbers is

  function Normal(R: Rational) return Rational is
    -- cancel common factors
    G: Positive := GCD(abs R.Num, R.Den);
  begin
    return (R.Num/G, R.Den/G);
  end Normal;

  function "+" (X: Rational) return Rational is
  begin
    return X;
  end "+";

  function "-" (X: Rational) return Rational is
  begin
    return (-X.Num, X.Den);
  end "-";

  function "+" (X, Y: Rational) return Rational is
  begin
    return Normal((X.Num*Y.Den + Y.Num*X.Den, X.Den*Y.Den));
  end "+";

  function "-" (X, Y: Rational) return Rational is
  begin
    return Normal((X.Num*Y.Den - Y.Num*X.Den, X.Den*Y.Den));
  end "-";

  function "*" (X, Y: Rational) return Rational is
  begin
    return Normal((X.Num*Y.Num, X.Den*Y.Den));
  end "*";

  function "/" (X, Y: Rational) return Rational is
  begin
    return Normal((X.Num*Y.Den, X.Den*Y.Num));
  end "/";

  function "/" (X: Integer; Y: Positive) return Rational is
  begin
    return Normal((X, Y));
  end "/";

  function Numerator(R: Rational) return Integer is
  begin
    return R.Num;
  end Numerator;

  function Denominator(R: Rational) return Positive is
  begin
```

```
        return R.Den;
      end Denominator;

    end Rational_Numbers;
```

4   Although the parameter types are both Integer and therefore the same as for predefined integer division, nevertheless the result types are different. The result types are considered in the hiding rules for functions. See Section 9.5.

Exercise 11.3

1
```
    package P is
      type Length is new Float;
      type Area is new Float;
      function "*" (X, Y: Length) return Length;
      function "*" (X, Y: Length) return Area;
      function "*" (X, Y: Area) return Area;
    end;

    package body P is

      function "*" (X, Y: Length) return Length is
      begin
        raise Constraint_Error;
      end "*";

      function "*" (X, Y: Length) return Area is
      begin
        return Area(Float(X)*Float(Y));
      end "*";

      function "*" (X, Y: Area) return Area is
      begin
        raise Constraint_Error;
      end "*";

    end P;
```

Exercise 11.4

1
```
    package Stacks is
      type Stack is private;
      Empty: constant Stack;
      ...
    private
      ...
      Empty: constant Stack := ((1 .. Max => 0), 0);
    end;
```

Note that Empty has to be initialized because it is a **constant** despite the fact that Top which is the only component whose value is of interest is automatically initialized anyway. We could alternatively have declared a function Empty. This would have the advantage of being a primitive operation of Stack and thus inherited if we ever derived from Stack.

2
```
    function Is_Empty(S: Stack) return Boolean is
    begin
      return S.Top = 0;
    end Is_Empty;

    function Is_Full(S: Stack) return Boolean is
```

```
begin
   return S.Top = Max;
end Is_Full;
```

Although Is_Empty is good for testing whether a stack is empty it cannot be used to set a stack empty. A constant or function Empty combined with equality can do both.

3   ```
    function "=" (S, T: Stack) return Boolean is
    begin
       return S.S(1 .. S.Top) = T.S(1 .. T.Top);
    end "=";
    ```

4   ```
    function "=" (A, B: Stack_Array) return Boolean is
    begin
       if A'Length /= B'Length then
          return False;
       end if;
       for I in A'Range loop
          if A(I) /= B(I + B'First – A'First) then
             return False;
          end if;
       end loop;
       return True;
    end "=";
    ```

Note that this uses the redefined = (via /=) applying to the type Stack. This pattern of definition of array equality clearly applies to any type. Beware that we cannot use slice comparison (as in the previous answer) because that would call the function being declared and so recurse infinitely.

Equality and inequality returning Boolean arrays might be

```
type Boolean_Array is array (Integer range <>) of Boolean;
```

```
function "=" (A, B: Stack_Array) return Boolean_Array is
   Result: Boolean_Array(A'Range);
begin
   if A'Length /= B'Length then
      return (A'Range => False);
   end if;
   for I in A'Range loop
      Result(I) := A(I) /= B(I + B'First – A'First);
   end loop;
   return Result;
end "=";
```

```
function "/=" (A, B: Stack_Array) return Boolean_Array is
begin
   return not (A = B);
end "/=";
```

Recall from Section 8.6 that **not** can be applied to all one-dimensional Boolean arrays.

5   ```
    package Stacks is
       type Stack is private;
       procedure Push(S: in out Stack; X: in Integer);
       procedure Pop(S: in out Stack; X: out Integer);
    private
       Max: constant := 100;
       Dummy: constant Integer := 0;
       type Integer_Vector is array (Integer range <>) of Integer;
    ```
    ```

```
      type Stack is
        record
          S: Integer_Vector(1 .. Max) := (1 .. Max => Dummy);
          Top: Integer range 0 .. Max := 0;
        end record;
    end;

    package body Stacks is
      procedure Push(S: in out Stack; X: in Integer) is
      begin
        S.Top := S.Top + 1;
        S.S(S.Top) := X;
      end;

      procedure Pop(S: in out Stack; X: out Integer) is
      begin
        X := S.S(S.Top);
        S.S(S.Top) := Dummy;
        S.Top := S.Top − 1;
      end;
    end Stacks;
```

Note the use of Dummy as a default Integer value for unused components of the stack.

6   ```
    function "=" (X, Y: Rational) return Boolean is
    begin
      return X.Num * Y.Den = X.Den * Y.Num;
    end "=";
    ```

A formulation of rational numbers not using reduction after each operation would soon overflow and so would not be sensible.

*Exercise 11.5*

1   In the case of the access formulation, although Is_Empty is straightforward, it is difficult to write an appropriate function Is_Full; we will return to this when exceptions are discussed in detail in Chapter 14.

```
    function Is_Empty(S: Stack) return Boolean is
    begin
      return S = null;
    end Is_Empty;
```

2   ```
    function "=" (S, T: Stack) return Boolean is
        SL: Cell_Ptr := Cell_Ptr(S);
        TL: Cell_Ptr := Cell_Ptr(T);
    begin
      while SL /= null and TL /= null loop
        if SL.Value /= TL.Value then
          return False;
        end if;
        SL := SL.Next;
        TL := TL.Next;
      end loop;
      return SL = TL;
    end "=";
    ```

3   ```
    package Queues is
        Empty: exception;
    ```
    ```

```
    type Queue is limited private;
    procedure Join(Q: in out Queue; X: in Item);
    procedure Remove(Q: in out Queue; X: out Item);
    function Length(Q: Queue) return Integer;
private
  type Cell;
  type Cell_Ptr is access Cell;
  type Cell is
    record
      Data: Item;
      Next: Cell_Ptr;
    end record;
  type Queue is
    record
      Count: Integer := 0;
      First, Last: Cell_Ptr;
    end record;
end;
package body Queues is
  procedure Join(Q: in out Queue; X: in Item) is
    L: Cell_Ptr;
  begin
    L := new Cell'(Data => X, Next => null);
    if Q.Count = 0 then         -- queue was empty
      Q.First := L;
      Q.Last := L;
    else
      Q.Last.Next := L;
      Q.Last := L;
    end if;
    Q.Count := Q.Count + 1;
  end Join;

  procedure Remove(Q: in out Queue; X: out Item) is
  begin
    if Q.Count = 0 then
      raise Empty;
    end if;
    X := Q.First.Data;
    Q.First := Q.First.Next;
    Q.Count := Q.Count - 1;
  end Remove;

  function Length(Q: Queue) return Integer is
  begin
    return Q.Count;
  end Length;
end Queues;
```

It would be tidy to assign **null** to Q.Last in the case when the last value is removed but it is not strictly necessary.

Exercise 11.6

1 **private**
```
    Max: constant := 1000;      -- no of accounts
    type Key_Code is new Integer range 0 .. Max;
```

```
        type Key is
          record
            Code: Key_Code := 0;
          end record;
    end;

    package body Bank is
        Balance: array (Key_Code range 1 .. Key_Code'Last) of Money := (others => 0);
        Free: array (Key_Code range 1 .. Key_Code'Last) of Boolean := (others => True);

        function Valid(K: Key) return Boolean is
        begin
            return K.Code /= 0;
        end Valid;

        procedure Open_Account(K: in out Key; M: in Money) is
        begin
            if K.Code = 0 then
              for I in Free'Range loop
                if Free(I) then
                   Free(I) := False;
                   Balance(I) := M;
                   K.Code := I;
                   return;
                end if;
              end loop;
            end if;
        end Open_Account;

        procedure Close_Account(K: in out Key; M: out Money) is
        begin
            if Valid(K) then
              M := Balance(K.Code);
              Free(K.Code) := True;
              K.Code := 0;
            end if;
        end Close_Account;

        procedure Deposit(K: in Key; M: in Money) is
        begin
            if Valid(K) then
              Balance(K.Code) := Balance(K.Code) + M;
            end if;
        end Deposit;

        procedure Withdraw(K: in out Key; M: in out Money) is
        begin
            if Valid(K) then
              if M > Balance(K.Code) then
                Close_Account(K, M);
              else
                Balance(K.Code) := Balance(K.Code) - M;
              end if;
            end if;
        end Withdraw;

        function Statement(K: Key) return Money is
        begin
            if Valid(K) then
              return Balance(K.Code);
```

      end if;
    end Statement;

  end Bank;

Various alternative formulations are possible. It might be neater to declare a record type representing an account containing the two components Free and Balance.
    Note that the function Statement will raise Program_Error if the key is not valid. Alternatively we could return a dummy value of zero but it might be better to raise our own exception as described in Chapter 14.

2   An alternative formulation which represents the home savings box could be that where the limited private type is given by

    type Box **is**
      record
        Code: Box_Code := 0;
        Balance: Money;
      end record;

In this case the money is kept in the variable declared by the user. The bank only knows which boxes have been issued but does not know how much is in a particular box. The details are left to the reader.

3   Since the parameter is of a record type, it is not defined whether the parameter is passed by copy or by reference. If it is passed by copy then the call of Action will succeed whereas if it is passed by reference it will not. The program is therefore not portable in this respect. However this does not seem a very satisfactory answer and might be considered a loophole in the design of the system.
    The problem can be overcome by using a type that is always passed by reference. As we will see in Chapter 13, a tagged record type is always passed by reference and so we can simply make the type Key into a tagged record type. Another approach is to use an access type to point at the keys and then we can rely upon the access type itself always being passed by copy.

4   He is thwarted because of the rule mentioned in Section 9.3 that a record type with any default initialized components is always copied in precisely so that junk values cannot be created.

Answers 12

Exercise 12.1

1   The number of possible orders of compilation is (a) 120, (b) 18. The source model thus gives the programmer much more flexibility.

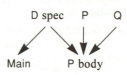

Exercise 12.2

1   The number of possible orders of compilation is (a) 120, (b) 8. The source model again is much more flexible. Indeed the number of combinations for the source model is always *n*! (where *n* is the number of units) irrespective of the dependency structure.

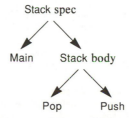

Exercise 12.3

1   **package** Complex_Numbers **is**
      type Complex **is private**;
      ...
      function "+" (X, Y: Complex) **return** Complex;
      ...
    private
      ...
    end Complex_Numbers;

    package Complex_Numbers.Cartesian **is**
      function Cons(R, I: Float) **return** Complex;
      function RI_Part(X: Complex) **return** Float;
      function Im_Part(X: Complex) **return** Float;
    end Complex_Numbers.Cartesian;

    package Complex_Numbers.Polar **is**
      -- as before
    end Complex_Numbers.Polar;

    The bodies are as expected.

2   We have used the abbreviation C_N for Complex_Numbers.

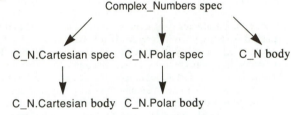

Complex_Numbers spec

C_N.Cartesian spec   C_N.Polar spec   C_N body

C_N.Cartesian body   C_N.Polar body

3   The only subprograms inherited are the arithmetic operations in the package Complex_Numbers. Those in the child packages are not primitive operations of the type Complex and so are not inherited.

Exercise 12.4

1   **private package** Rational_Numbers.Slave **is**
      function Normal(R: Rational) **return** Rational;
    end;

    package body Rational_Numbers.Slave **is**
      function GCD ... etc.

      function Normal(R: Rational) **return** Rational **is**
        G: Positive := GCD(**abs** R.Num, R.Den);
      begin
        return (R.Num/G, R.Den/G);
      end Normal;
    end Rational_Numbers.Slave;

    with Rational_Numbers.Slave;
    package body Rational_Numbers **is**
      use Slave;
      -- as before without the function Normal
    end Rational_Numbers;

2   **package** Complex_Numbers.Trig **is**
      function Sin(X: Complex) **return** Complex;
      function Cos(X: Complex) **return** Complex;

```
     ...
   end;

   private function Complex_Numbers.Trig.Sin_Cos(X: Complex) return Complex is
   begin
     ...
   end;

   with Complex_Numbers.Trig.Sin_Cos;
   package body Complex_Numbers.Trig is
     ...
   end Complex_Numbers.Trig;
```

The function Sin_Cos can be called directly as such within the body of Trig without a use clause.

Exercise 12.6

1   **function** Monday **return** Diurnal.Day **renames** Diurnal.Mon;

2   This cannot be done because Next_Work_Day is of an anonymous type.

3   Pets: String_3_Array **renames** Farmyard(2 .. 3);

    Note that the bounds of Pets are 2 and 3.

4   **function** "+" (X, Y: Complex_Numbers.Complex) **return** Complex_Numbers.Complex
        renames Complex_Numbers."+";

5   This_Cell: Cell **renames** World(I, J);

Answers 13

Exercise 13.1

1   P: Point := (Object(C) **with null record**);

2   R: Reservation:
```
   ...
   R.Flight_Number := 77;
   R.Date_Of_Travel := (5, Nov, 2007);
   ...
   NR: Nice_Reservation := (R with Window, Green);
```

3   **package** Reservation_System.Supersonic **is**
```
      type Supersonic_Reservation is new Reservation with
        record
          ...
        end record;

      procedure Make(SR: in out Supersonic_Reservation);
      ...
   end Reservation_System.Supersonic;
```

Exercise 13.2

1   **procedure** Print_Area(OC: Object'Class) **is**
    begin
      Put(Area(OC));   -- dispatch to appropriate Area
    end;

2   **type** Person **is tagged**
      record
          Birth: Date;
      end record;

    type Man **is new** Person **with**
      record
          Bearded: Boolean;
      end record;

    type Woman **is new** Person **with**
      record
          Children: Integer;
      end record;

3   **procedure** Print_Details(P: **in** Person) **is**
    begin
        Print_Date(P.Birth);
    end;

    procedure Print_Details(M: **in** Man) **is**
    begin
        Print_Details(Person(M));
        Print_Boolean(M.Beard);
    end;

    procedure Print_Details(W: **in** Woman) **is**
    begin
        Print_Details(Person(W));
        Print_Integer(W.Children);
    end;

    procedure Analyse_Person(PC: Person'Class) **is**
    begin
        Print_Details(PC);   -- dispatch
    end;

4   **package body** Queues **is**

        procedure Join(Q: **access** Queue; E: **in** Element_Ptr) **is**
        begin
            if E.Next /= **null then**   -- already on a queue
                raise Queue_Error;
            end if;
            if Q.Count =0 **then**   -- queue was empty
                Q.First := E;
                Q.Last := E;
            else
                Q.Last.Next := E;
                Q.Last := E;
            end if;
            Q.Count := Q.Count + 1;
        end Join;

        function Remove(Q: **access** Queue) **return** Element_Ptr **is**
            Result: Element_Ptr;
        begin
            if Q.Count = 0 **then**
                raise Queue_Error;
            end if;

```
              Result := Q.First;
              Q.First := Result.Next;
              Result.Next := null;
              Q.Count := Q.Count - 1;
              return Result;
           end Remove;

           function Length(Q: Queue) return Integer is
           begin
              return Q.Count;
           end Length;

        end Queues;
```

Exercise 13.3

1
```
    package Objects is
       type Object is abstract tagged null record;

       function Distance(O: Object) return Float;
       function Area(O: Object) return Float is abstract;
    end Objects;

    with Objects; use Objects;
    package Shapes is
       type Point is new Object with
          record
             X_Coord: Float;
             Y_Coord: Float;
          end record;

       function Distance(P: Point) return Float;
       function Area(P: Point) return Float;

       type Circle is new Point with
          record
             Radius: Float;
          end record;

       function Area(C: Circle) return Float;

       -- etc.
    end Shapes;
```

2
```
    function Further(X, Y: Object) return Object is
    begin
       if Distance(X) > Distance(Y) then
          return X;
       else
          return Y;
       end if;
    end Further;
```

Since it returns the type Object it becomes abstract when inherited by Point and Circle
and so has to be overridden. This is somewhat frustrating because the text is
essentially unchanged.

3
```
    function Further(X, Y: Object'Class) return Object'Class is
    begin
       if Distance(X) > Distance(Y) then
          return X;
```

```
    else
        return Y;
    end if;
end Further;
```

This does not suffer from the problems of the previous exercise. It dispatches to the appropriate functions Distance and can be applied to all objects without change.

4   The function Bigger cannot be written for the type Object because it would contain a call of the abstract function Area. Functions could of course be written for Circle and Point but would need to be written out for each. A better solution is to use class wide parameters as in

```
function Bigger(X, Y: Object'Class) return Object'Class is
begin
    if Area(X) > Area(Y) then
        return X;
    else
        return Y;
    end if;
end Bigger;
```

Two general points can be deduced from these exercises. One is that it would be better to manipulate references to the objects rather than the objects themselves. Indeed if we wish to know which is bigger we don't really want to be given a copy of the bigger one, we want an access value referring to it. The extension problems with the function results would then all go away. The other point is that operations which by their nature will not need overriding should be class wide. Indeed the function Distance should perhaps be class wide and not primitive.

5
```
package body Reservation_System.Subsonic is

    procedure Make(BR: in out Basic_Reservation) is
        Select_Seat(BR);
    end Make;

    procedure Make(NR: in out Nice_Reservation) is
        Make(Basic_Reservation(NR));
        Order_Meal(NR);
    end Make;

    procedure Make(PR: in out Posh_Reservation) is
        Make(Nice_Reservation(PR));
        Arrange_Limo(PR);
    end Make;
    ...
end Reservation_System.Subsonic;
```

Exercise 13.4

1
```
function "=" (C, D: Circle) return Boolean is
begin
    return Object(C) = Object(D) and abs(C.Radius − D.Radius) < Delta;
end "=";
```

2
```
function "=" (C, D: Circle) return Boolean is
begin
    return Standard."="(Object(C), Object(D)) and abs(C.Radius − D.Radius) < Delta;
end "=";
```

3   This only swaps the Object part of a Circle or any other type derived from Object. Remember that inheritance only applies to the parameter profile. One possibility is to write

```
procedure Swap(X, Y: in out Object'Class) is
   T: Object'Class := X;
begin
   X := Y;  Y := T;
end Swap;
```

in which case the assignments are effectively done by dispatching. Being a class wide operation it cannot be overridden. Alternatively

```
procedure Swap(X, Y: in out Object) is
   T: Object'Class := Object'Class(X);
begin
   Object'Class(X) := Object'Class(Y);
   Object'Class(Y) := T;
end Swap;
```

can be overridden if desired and again does the assignments according to the specific type. Both solutions work if Object is abstract whereas the original would not even compile in that case.

Exercise 13.5

1   It would fail to compile because, as mentioned in Section 13.2, Order_Meal is not a primitive operation of all types in the class rooted at Reservation.

2
```
procedure Select_Seat(NR: in out Nice_Reservation) is
begin
   if NR.Seat_Sort = Aisle then
      -- choose aisle seat
   else
      -- choose window seat
   end if;
end Select_Seat;
...
procedure Make(R: in out Reservation) is
begin
   Select_Seat(Reservation'Class(R));       -- redispatch
end Make;
```

Observe that we know that the component NR.Seat_Sort must exist because this is a nice reservation or derived from it. Naturally enough all seats are window or aisle seats in nice and posh categories.

Exercise 13.6

1   We could not declare the function Further with Shape as parameter and result because it has a controlling result and would prevent further extension from the partial view. But the class wide version taking Shape'Class would be allowed.

Exercise 13.7

1
```
procedure Adjust(Object: in out Thing) is
begin
   The_Count := The_Count + 1;
end Adjust;
```

The procedures Initialize and Finalize are as before.

2   **package** Tracked_Things **is**
    type Intermediate **is abstract new** Controlled **with**
      record
        -- visible data
      end record;
    end Tracked_Things;

    package Tracked_Things.User_View **is**
      type Thing **is new** Intermediate **with private**;

      procedure Initialize...
    -- etc.
    private
      type Thing **is new** Intermediate **with**
        record
          Identity_Number: Integer
        end record;
    end Tracked_Things.User_View;

Again the intermediate type is abstract so that the user cannot declare objects of the type. But somehow this solution does not feel so good.

3   The type Key and the control procedures could be

    type Key **is new** Limited_Controlled **with**
      record
        Code: Key_Code;
      end record;

    procedure Initialize(K: **in out** Key) **is**
    begin
      K.Code := 0;
    end Initialize;

    procedure Finalize(K: **in out** Key) **is**
    begin
      Return_Key(K);
    end Finalize;

We have chosen to use Initialize to set the initial value but we could have left this to be done by the default mechanism as before.

Exercise 13.8

1   (a)   legal – both tags statically the same
    (b)   illegal – tags statically different
    (c)   illegal – cannot mix static and dynamic cases
    (d)   legal – but tags checked at run time

2   **procedure** Convert(From: **in** Set'Class; To: **out** Set'Class) **is**
    begin
      if From'Tag = To'Tag **then**
        To := From;
      else
       declare
         Temp: Set'Class := From;
          -- and so on
       end;

```
   end if;
 end Convert;
```

3
```
package Abstract_Stacks is
  type Stack is abstract tagged null record;
  function Empty return Stack is abstract;
  procedure Push(S: in out Stack; E: in Element) is abstract;
  procedure Pop(S: in out Stack; E: out Element) is abstract;
end Abstract_Stacks;

procedure Convert(From: in Stack'Class; To: out Stack'Class) is
  Temp: Stack'Class := From;
  E: Element;
begin
  To := Empty;
  while Temp /= Empty loop
    Pop(Temp, E);
    Push(To, E);
  end loop;
end Convert;
```

This doesn't quite work because the elements are now in the reverse order. We leave the reader to sort out this irritating problem. The linked stack might be

```
type Linked_Stack is new Abstract_Stacks.Stack with
  record
    Component: Inner;
  end record;
```

where Inner is as for the Linked_Set. The deep copy mechanism is thus identical. Following the answer to Exercise 11.5(**2**), equality can be defined as

```
function "=" (S, T: Linked_Stack) return Boolean is
  SL: Cell_Ptr := S.Inner.The_Set;
  TL: Cell_Ptr := S.Inner.The_Set;
begin
  ... -- as Exercise 11.5(2)
end "=";
```

The array stack might be

```
type Array_Stack is new Abstract_Stacks.Stack with
  record
    S: Item_Vector(1 .. Max);
    Top: Integer range 0 .. Max := 0;
  end record;
```

with equality as in Section 11.4.

Answers 14

Exercise 14.1

1
```
procedure Quadratic(A, B, C: in Float;
              Root_1, Root_2: out Float; OK: out Boolean) is
  D: constant Float := B**2 - 4.0*A*C;
begin
  Root_1 := (-B+Sqrt(D)) / (2.0*A);
  Root_2 := (-B-Sqrt(D)) / (2.0*A);
  OK := True;
exception
```

```ada
         when Constraint_Error =>
            OK := False;
      end Quadratic;
```

2 ```ada
   function Factorial(N: Integer) return Integer is

      function Slave(N: Natural) return Positive is
      begin
         if N = 0 then
            return 1;
         else
            return N * Slave(N-1);
         end if;
      end Slave;

   begin
      return Slave(N);
   exception
      when Constraint_Error | Storage_Error =>
         return -1;
   end Factorial;
   ```

*Exercise 14.2*

1  ```ada
   package Random is
      Bad: exception;
      Modulus: constant := 2**13;
      subtype Small is Integer range 0 .. Modulus;
      procedure Init(Seed: Small);
      function Next return Small;
   end;

   package body Random is
      Multiplier: constant := 5**5;
      X: Small;

      procedure Init(Seed: Small) is
      begin
         if Seed mod 2 = 0 then
            raise Bad;
         end if;
         X := Seed;
      end Init;

      function Next return Small is
      begin
         X := X * Multiplier mod Modulus;
         return X;
      end Next;
   end Random;
   ```

2 ```ada
   function Factorial(N: Integer) return Integer is

      function Slave(N: Natural) return Positive is
      begin
         if N = 0 then
            return 1;
         else
            return N * Slave(N-1);
         end if;
   ```
   ```

```
      end Slave;
  begin
    return Slave(N);
  exception
    when Storage_Error =>
      raise Constraint_Error;
  end Factorial;
```

3
```
  function "+" (X, Y: Vector) return Vector is
    R: Vector(X'Range);
  begin
    if X'Length /= Y'Length then
      raise Constraint_Error;
    end if;
    for I in X'Range loop
      R(I) := X(I) + Y(I + Y'First – X'First);
    end loop;
    return R;
  end "+";
```

4   No. A malevolent user could write **raise** Stack.Error; outside the package. It would be nice if the language provided some sort of 'private' exception that could be handled but not raised explicitly outside its defining package.

5
```
  procedure Push(S: in out Stack; X: in Integer) is
  begin
    S := new Cell'(X, S);
  exception
    when Storage_Error =>
      raise Error;
  end;

  procedure Pop(S: in out Stack; X: out Integer) is
  begin
    if S = null then
      raise Error;
    else
      X := S.Value;
      S := S.Next;
    end if;
  end;
```

Exercise 14.3

1   Three checks are required. The one inserted by the user plus the two for the assignment to S(Top) which cannot be avoided since we can say little about the value of Top (except that it is not equal to Max). So this is the worst of all worlds thus emphasizing the need to give appropriate constraints.

Exercise 14.4

1   The subprograms become

```
  procedure Push(X: Integer) is
  begin
    if Top = Max then
      Raise_Exception(Error'Identity, "stack overflow");
```

```
      end if;
      Top := Top + 1;
      S(Top) := X;
   end Push;

   function Pop return Integer is
   begin
      if Top = 0 then
         Raise_Exception(Error'Identity, "stack underflow");
      end if;
      Top := Top - 1;
      return S(Top + 1);
   end Pop;
```

and the handler might become

```
   when Event: Error =>
      Put("Stack used incorrectly because of ");
      Put(Exception_Message(Event));
      Clean_Up;
```

Exercise 14.5

1   ```
     package Bank is
        Alarm: exception;
        subtype Money is Natural;
        type Key is limited private;
        -- as before
     private
        -- as before
     end;

     package body Bank is
        Balance: array (Key_Code range 1 .. Key_Code'Last) of Money := (others => 0);
        Free: array (Key_Code range 1 .. Key_Code'Last) of Boolean := (others => True);

        function Valid(K: Key) return Boolean is
        begin
           return K.Code /= 0;
        end Valid;

        procedure Validate(K: Key) is
        begin
           if not Valid(K) then
              raise Alarm;
           end if;
        end Validate;

        procedure Open_Account(K: in out Key; M: in Money) is
        begin
           if K.Code = 0 then
              for I in Free'Range loop
                 if Free(I) then
                    Free(I) := False;
                    Balance(I) := M;
                    K.Code := I;
                    return;
                 end if;
              end loop;
           else
     ```
     ```

```
      raise Alarm;
   end if;
end Open_Account;

procedure Close_Account(K: in out Key; M: out Money) is
begin
   Validate(K);
   M := Balance(K.Code);
   Free(K.Code) := True;
   K.Code := 0;
end Close_Account;

procedure Deposit(K: in Key; M: in Money) is
begin
   Validate(K);
   Balance(K.Code) := Balance(K.Code) + M;
end Deposit;

procedure Withdraw(K: in out Key; M: in out Money) is
begin
   Validate(K);
   if M > Balance(K.Code) then
      raise Alarm;
   else
      Balance(K.Code) := Balance(K.Code) – M;
   end if;
end Withdraw;

function Statement(K: Key) return Money is
begin
   Validate(K);
   return Balance(K.Code);
end Statement;
```

end Bank;

For convenience we have declared a procedure Validate which raises the alarm in most cases. The Alarm is also explicitly raised if we attempt to overdraw but as remarked in the text we cannot also close the account (we could if the key were a tagged type). An attempt to open an account with a key which is in use also causes Alarm to be raised. We do not however raise the Alarm if the bank runs out of accounts but have left it to the user to check with a call of Valid that he was issued a genuine key; the rationale is that it is not the user's fault if the bank runs out of keys.

2   Suppose N is 2. Then on the third call, P is not entered but the exception is raised and handled at the second level. The handler again calls P without success but this time, since an exception raised in a handler is not handled there but propagated up a level, the exception is handled at the first level. The pattern then repeats but the exception is finally propagated out of the first level to the originating call. In all there are three successful calls and four unsuccessful ones. The diagram may help.

An * indicates an unsuccessful call, H indicates a call from a handler.

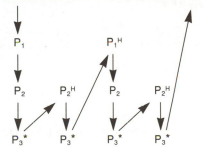

More generally suppose C_n is the total number of calls for the case $N = n$. Then by induction

$$C_{n+1} = 2C_n + 1$$

with the initial condition $C_0 = 1$ since in the case $N = 0$ it is obvious that there is only one call which fails. It follows that the total number of calls C_N is $2^{N+1} - 1$. Of these 2^N are unsuccessful and $2^N - 1$ are successful.

I am grateful to Bob Bishop for this example.

Answers 15

Exercise 15.1

1   P: on A: like Integer, on B: like Short_Integer
.   Q: on A: like Long_Integer, on B: like Integer
    R: on A: cannot be implemented, on B: like Long_Integer

2   No, the only critical case is type Q on machine A. Changing to one's complement changes the range of Integer to

    −32767 .. +32767

    and so only Integer'First is altered.

3   (a)   Integer'Base   (d)   Integer'Base
    (b)   illegal – need explicit conversion   (e)   root integer
    (c)   My_Integer'Base   (f)   My_Integer'Base

4   **type** Longest_Integer **is range** System.Min_Int .. System.Max_Int;

Exercise 15.2

1   (a)   16#EF#   (c)   222
    (b)   120   (d)   239

2   **type** Ring5 **is mod** 5;
    A, B, C, D: Ring5;

    ...

    D := (A + B) * C;

3   (a)   4   (b)   1

    DeMorgan's theorem that **not** (A **and** B) = **not** A **or not** B does not hold if the modulus is not a power of two.

Exercise 15.3

1   (a)   illegal   (c)   root real   (e)   root real
    (b)   Integer'Base   (d)   Integer'Base   (f)   root integer

2   R: **constant** := N * 1.0;

Exercise 15.4

1   **type** Real **is digits** 7;
    type Real_Vector **is array** (Integer **range** <>) **of** Real;

```
function Inner(A, B: Real_Vector) return Real is
   type Long_Real is digits 14;
   Result: Long_Real := 0.0;
begin
   for I in A'Range loop
      Result := Result + Long_Real(A(I)) * Long_Real(B(I));
   end loop;
   return Real(Result);
end Inner;
```

Exercise 15.5

1   The literal 0.5 is universal real and this matches universal fixed.

2
```
function "**" (X: Complex; N: Integer) return Complex is
   Result_Theta: Angle := 0.0;
begin
   for I in 1 .. abs N loop
      Result_Theta := Normal(Result_Theta + X.Theta);
   end loop;
   if N < 0 then Result_Theta := -Result_Theta; end if;
   return (X.R**N, Result_Theta);
end "**";
```

We cannot simply write

```
   return (X.R**N, Normal(X.Theta * N));
```

because if **abs** N is larger than 3 the multiplication is likely to overflow; so we have to repeatedly normalize. A clever solution which is faster for all but the smallest values of **abs** N is

```
function "**" (X: Complex; N: Integer) return Complex is
   Result_Theta: Angle := 0.0;
   Term: Angle := X.Theta;
   M: Integer := abs N;
begin
   while M > 0 loop
      if M rem 2 /= 0 then
         Result_Theta := Normal(Result_Theta + Term);
      end if;
      M := M / 2;
      Term := Normal(Term * 2);
   end loop;
   if N < 0 then Result_Theta := -Result_Theta; end if;
   return (X.R**N, Result_Theta);
end "**";
```

This is a variation of the standard algorithm for computing exponentials by decomposing the exponent into its binary form and doing a minimal number of multiplications. In our case it is the multiplier N which we decompose and then do a minimal number of additions.

    Recognizing that our repeated addition algorithm is essentially the same as for exponentiation, we can in parallel compute X.R**N by the same method. A little manipulation soon makes us realize that we might as well write

```
function "**" (X: Complex; N: Integer) return Complex is
   One: constant Complex := Cons(1.0, 0.0);
   Result: Complex := One;
   Term: Complex := X;
```

```
          M: Integer := abs N;
      begin
          while M > 0 loop
              if M rem 2 /= 0 then
                  Result := Result * Term;   -- Complex *
              end if;
              M := M / 2;
              Term := Term * Term;         -- Complex *
          end loop;
          if N < 0 then Result := One / Result; end if;
          return Result;
      end "**";
```

This brings us back full circle. This is indeed the standard algorithm for computing exponentials and we are now applying it in the abstract to our type Complex. Note the calls of the functions "*" and "/" applying to the type Complex. This version of "**" can be declared outside the package Complex_Numbers and is quite independent of the internal representation (but it will be very inefficient unless the internal representation is polar).

3
```
      private
          type Angle is delta 0.05 range -720.0 .. 720.0;
          for Angle'Small use 2**(-5);
          type Complex is
              record
                  R: Float;
                  Theta: Angle range 0.0 .. 360.0;
              end record;
          I: constant Complex := (1.0, 90.0);
      end;
          ...
      function Normal(A: Angle) return Angle is
      begin
          if A >= 360.0 then
              return A - 360.0;
          elsif A < 0.0 then
              return A + 360.0;
          else
              return A;
          end if;
      end Normal;
```

The choice of delta and small is derived as follows. We need 10 bits to cover the range 0 .. 720 plus one bit for the sign thus leaving 5 bits after the binary point. So *small* will be 2^{-5} and thus any value of delta greater than that will do. We have chosen 0.05.

Answers 16

Exercise 16.1

1   Trace((M'Length, M))

If the two dimensions of M were not equal then Constraint_Error would be raised. Note that the lower bounds of M do not have to be 1; all that matters is that the number of components in each dimension is the same since sliding is permitted when building the aggregate.

2   **package** Stacks **is**
   type Stack(Max: Natural) **is private**;
   Empty: **constant** Stack;
    ...
  private
   type Integer_Vector **is array** (Integer **range** <>) **of** Integer;
   type Stack(Max: Natural) **is**
    record
      S: Integer_Vector(1 .. Max);
      Top: Integer := 0;
    end record;
   Empty: **constant** Stack(0) := (0, (**others** => 0), 0);
  end;

We have naturally chosen to make Empty a stack whose value of **Max** is zero. Note that the function "=" only compares the parts of the stacks which are in use. Thus we can write S = Empty to test whether a stack S is empty irrespective of its value of **Max**.

3   **function** Is_Full(S: Stack) **return** Boolean **is**
  begin
   return S.Top = S.Max;
  end Full;

4   S: **constant** Square := (N, Make_Unit(N));

Exercise 16.2

1   Z: Polynomial := (0, (0 => 0));

The named notation has to be used because the array has only one component.

2   **function** "*" (P, Q: Polynomial) **return** Polynomial **is**
   R: Polynomial(P.N+Q.N) := (P.N+Q.N, (**others** => 0));
  begin
   for I **in** P.A'Range **loop**
    for J **in** Q.A'Range **loop**
     R.A(I+J) := R.A(I+J) + P.A(I)*Q.A(J);
    end loop;
   end loop;
   return R;
  end "*";

It is largely a matter of taste whether we write P.A'Range rather than 0 .. P.N.

3   **function** "–" (P, Q: Polynomial) **return** Polynomial **is**
   Size: Integer;
  begin
   if P.N > Q.N **then**
    Size := P.N;
   else
    Size := Q.N;
   end if;
   declare
    R: Polynomial(Size);
   begin
    for I **in** 0 .. P.N **loop**
     R.A(I) := P.A(I);
    end loop;

```
          for I in P.N+1 .. R.N loop
             R.A(I) := 0;
          end loop;
          for I in 0 .. Q.N loop
             R.A(I) := R.A(I) – Q.A(I);
          end loop;
          return Normal(R);
       end;
    end "–";
```

There are various alternative ways of writing this function. We could initialize R.A by using slice assignments

```
R.A(0 .. P.N) := P.A;
R.A(P.N+1 .. R.N) := (P.N+1 .. R.N => 0);
```

or even more succinctly by

```
R.A := P.A & (P.N+1 .. R.N => 0);
```

4   **procedure** Truncate(P: **in out** Polynomial) **is**
     begin
        if P'Constrained **then**
           raise Truncate_Error;
        else
           P := (P.N–1, P.A(0 .. P.N–1));
        end if;
     end Truncate;

5   Any unconstrained Polynomial could then include an array whose range is 0 .. Integer'Last. This will take a lot of space. Since most implementations are likely to adopt the strategy of setting aside the maximum possible space for an unconstrained record it is thus wise to keep the maximum to a practical limit by the use of a suitable subtype such as Index.

6   **function** F(N: Integer) **return** Integer_Vector;

     type Polynomial(N: Index := 0) **is**
        record
           A: Integer_Vector(0 .. N) := F(N);
        end record;

        ...

     function F(N: Integer) **return** Integer_Vector **is**
        R: Integer_Vector(0 .. N);
     begin
        for I **in** 0 .. N–1 **loop**
           R(I) := 0;
        end loop;
        R(N) := 1;
        return R;
     end;

We have assumed that the type Polynomial is declared in the private part of a package and that the function specification is also in the private part with the function body in the package body. It does not matter that F is referred to before its body is elaborated provided that it is not actually called. Thus if we declared a polynomial (without an initial value) before the body of F then Program_Error would be raised.

```
7    package Rational_Polynomials is
       Max: constant := 10;
       subtype Index is Integer range 0 .. Max;
       type Rational_Polynomial(N, D: Index := 0) is private;

       function "+" (X: Rational_Polynomial) return Rational_Polynomial;
       function "–" (X: Rational_Polynomial) return Rational_Polynomial;

       function "+" (X, Y: Rational_Polynomial) return Rational_Polynomial;
       function "–" (X, Y: Rational_Polynomial) return Rational_Polynomial;
       function "*" (X, Y: Rational_Polynomial) return Rational_Polynomial;
       function "/" (X, Y: Rational_Polynomial) return Rational_Polynomial;

       function "/" (X, Y: Polynomial) return Rational_Polynomial;
       function Numerator(R: Rational_Polynomial) return Polynomial;
       function Denominator(R: Rational_Polynomial) return Polynomial;
     private
       function Zero(N: Index) return Polynomial;
       function One(N: Index) return Polynomial;

       type Rational_Polynomial(N, D: Index := 0) is
         record
            Num: Polynomial(N) := Zero(N);
            Den: Polynomial(D) := One(D);
         end record;
     end;
```

The functions Zero and One are required in order to supply appropriate safe initial
values. It is not possible to write a suitable aggregate for One although it is for Zero.
Nevertheless the function Zero is written for symmetry

```
     function Zero(N: Index) return Polynomial is
     begin
        return (N, (0 .. N => 0));      -- all coefficients zero
     end;

     function One(N: Index) return Polynomial is
        R: Polynomial(N) := Zero(N);
     begin
        R.A(0) := 1;                    -- coefficient of x**0 is one
        return R;
     end;
```

We make no attempt to impose any special language constraint on the denominator as
we did in the type Rational where the denominator has subtype Positive.

```
8    function "&" (X, Y: V_String) return V_String is
     begin
        return (X.N + Y.N, X.S & Y.S);
     end "&";
```

Exercise 16.3

```
1    procedure Shave(P: in out Person) is
     begin
        if P.Sex = Female then
           raise Shaving_Error;
        else
           P.Bearded := False;
        end if;
     end Shave;
```

2   ```
     procedure Sterilize(M: in out Mutant) is
     begin
        if M'Constrained and M.Sex /= Neuter then
           raise Sterilize_Error;
        else
           M := (Neuter, M.Birth);
        end if;
     end Sterilize;
     ```

3    ```
     type Figure is (Point, Circle, Triangle);

     type Object(Shape: Figure) is
        record
           X_Coord: Float;
           Y_Coord: Float;
           case Shape is
              when Point =>
                 null;
              when Circle =>
                 Radius: Float;
              when Triangle =>
                 A, B, C: Float;
           end case;
        end record;
     ```

4   ```
     function Area(X: Object) return Float is
     begin
        case X.Shape is
           when Point =>
              return 0.0;
           when Circle =>
              return Pi * X.Radius**2;
           when Triangle =>
              return ... ;
        end case;
     end Area;
     ```

Note the similarity between the case statement in the function Area and the variant part of the type Object.

5    ```
     type Category is (Basic, Nice, Posh);
     type Position is (Aisle, Window);
     type Meal_Type is (Green, White, Red);

     type Reservation(C: Category) is
        record
           Flight_Number: Integer;
           Date_Of_Travel: Date;
           Seat_Number: String(1 .. 3) := "   ";
           case C is
              when Basic => null;
              when Nice | Posh =>
                 Seat_Sort: Position;
                 Food: Meal_Type;
                 case C is
                    when Basic | Nice => null;
                    when Posh =>
                       Destination: Address;
     ```

```
      end case;
    end case;
  end record;
```

Note the curiously nested structure which is forced upon us by the fact that the individual components must have distinct names.

Exercise 16.4

1   **type** Boxer(W: Weight; Sex: Gender) **is new** Person(Sex => Sex) **with**
    record
        ...
    end record;

We have chosen to give the new discriminant Sex the same name as the old one.

Exercise 16.5

1   **function** Heir(P: Person_Name) **return** Person_Name **is**
      Mother: Womans_Name;
    begin
      if P.Sex = Male **then**
        Mother := P.Wife;
      else
        Mother := P;
      end if;
      if Mother = **null or else** Mother.First_Child = **null then**
        return null;
      end if;
      declare
        Child: Person_Name := Mother.First_Child;
      begin
        while Child.Sex = Female **loop**
          if Child.Next_Sibling = **null then**
            return Mother.First_Child;
          end if;
          Child := Child.Next_Sibling;
        end loop;
        return Child;
      end;
    end Heir;

2   **procedure** Divorce(W: Womans_Name) **is**
    begin
      if W.Husband = **null or** W.First_Child /= **null then**
        return;   -- divorce not possible
      end if;
      W.Husband.Wife := **null**;
      W.Husband := **null**;
    end Divorce;

3   **procedure** Marry(Bride: Womans_Name; Groom: Mans_Name) **is**
    begin
      if Bride.Father = Groom.Father **then**
        raise Incest;
      end if;
      -- then as before
    end Marry;
```
```

Note that there is no need to check for marriage to a parent because the check for bigamy will detect this anyway. Our model does not allow remarriage.

4   Marry is unchanged. Note however that calls of Marry with parameters of the wrong sex will be detected at compile time whereas with variants this is detected at run time.

5   ```
function Spouse(P: Person_Name) return Person_Name is
begin
   if P in Man then
      return Mans_Name(P).Wife;
   else
      return Womans_Name(P).Husband;
   end if;
end Spouse;
```

This is not good because not only is there a check required in doing the membership test but also a conversion to the appropriate specific type so that the component can be selected; this conversion requires yet another check (which always passes).

A better solution is to make Spouse a primitive abstract operation of Person with an access parameter

```
function Spouse(P: access Person) return Person_Name is abstract;
```

and then to provide specific functions for each sex

```
function Spouse(P: access Man) return Person_Name is
begin
   return P.Wife;
end Spouse;
```

```
function Spouse(P: access Woman) return Person_Name is
begin
   return P.Husband;
end Spouse;
```

A call of Spouse will then resolve at compile time to the correct function if the parameter is of a specific type (Mans_Name or Womans_Name) or will dispatch if it is class wide (Person_Name); this gives the best of all worlds.

6   ```
function New_Child(Mother: Womans_Name; Boy_Or_Girl: Gender;
                   Birthday: Date) return Person_Name is
   Child: Person_Name;
begin
   if Mother.Husband = null then
      raise Out_Of_Wedlock;
   end if;
   case Boy_Or_Girl is
      when Male =>
         Child := new Man;
      when Female =>
         Child := new Woman;
   end case;
   Child.Birth := Birthday;
   ... -- and so on as before
end New_Child;
```

This feels most uncomfortable. It seems unnatural to have a parameter giving the sex because we have not otherwise had to introduce the type Gender. We could pass the tag (such as Man'Tag) as a parameter T but that seems really dirty and anyway we would still have to write a conditional statement

```
if T = Man'Tag then
   Child := new Man;
else
   Child := new Woman;
end if;
```

This example illustrates a common problem with polymorphism; it all works fine for output when we know what we have but it is difficult with input when we do not.

Exercise 16.6

1   If the user declared a constrained key with a nonzero discriminant thus

K: Key(7);

then he will have bypassed Get_Key and be able to call the procedure Action without authority. Note also that if he calls Return_Key then Constraint_Error will be raised on the attempt to set the code to zero because the key is constrained.

Hence forged keys can be recognized since they are constrained and so we could rewrite Valid to check for this

```
function Valid(K: Key) return Boolean is
begin
   return not K'Constrained and K.Code /= 0;
end Valid;
```

We must also insert calls of Valid into Get_Key and Return_Key.

Exercise 16.7

1   The first assignment is illegal because there is a type mismatch, the second inserts the appropriate conversion but still fails because of the dynamic accessibility check. The third is illegal because the type is limited.

Answers 17

Exercise 17.1

1
```
generic
   type Item is private;
package Stacks is
   type Stack(Max: Natural) is private;
   procedure Push(S: in out Stack; X: in Item);
   procedure Pop(S: in out Stack; X: out Item);
   function "=" (S, T: Stack) return Boolean;
private
   type Item_Array is array (Integer range <>) of Item;
   type Stack(Max: Natural) is
      record
         S: Item_Array(1 .. Max);
         Top: Integer := 0;
      end record;
end;
```

The body is much as before. To declare a stack we must first instantiate the package.

```
package Boolean_Stacks is new Stacks(Item => Boolean);
use Boolean_Stacks;
S: Stack(Max => 30);
```

```
2   generic
       type Thing is private;
    package P is
       procedure Swap(A, B: in out Thing);
       procedure Cab(A, B, C: in out Thing);
    end P;

    package body P is
       procedure Swap(A, B: in out Thing) is
          T: Thing;
       begin
          T := A;  A := B;  B := T;
       end;

       procedure Cab(A, B, C: in out Thing) is
       begin
          Swap(A, B);  Swap(A, C);
       end;
    end P;
```

Exercise 17.2

```
1   function "not" is new Next(Boolean);

2   generic
       type Number is range <>;
    package Rational_Numbers is
       type Rational is private;
       function "+" (X: Rational) return Rational;
       function "–" (X: Rational) return Rational;
       function "+" (X, Y: Rational) return Rational;
       function "–" (X, Y: Rational) return Rational;
       function "*" (X, Y: Rational) return Rational;
       function "/" (X, Y: Rational) return Rational;

       subtype Positive_Number is Number range 1 .. Number'Last;
       function "/" (X: Number; Y: Positive_Number) return Rational;
       function Numerator(R: Rational) return Number;
       function Denominator(R: Rational) return Positive_Number;
    private
       type Rational is
          record
             Num: Number := 0;
             Den: Positive_Number := 1;
          end record;
    end;

3   generic
       type Index is (<>);
       type Floating is digits <>;
       type Vec is array (Index range <>) of Floating;
       type Mat is array (Index range <>, Index range <>) of Floating;
    function Outer(A, B: Vec) return Mat;

    function Outer(A, B: Vec) return Mat is
       C: Mat(A'Range, B'Range);
    begin
       for I in A'Range loop
          for J in B'Range loop
```

```
            C(I, J) := A(I) * B(J);
        end loop;
    end loop;
    return C;
end Outer;

function Outer_Vector is new Outer(Integer, Float, Vector, Matrix);
```

4   **package body** Set_Of **is**

```
    function Make_Set(L: List) return Set is
        S: Set := Empty;
    begin
        for I in L'Range loop
            S(L(I)) := True;
        end loop;
        return S;
    end Make_Set;

    function Make_Set(E: Element) return Set is
        S: Set := Empty;
    begin
        S(E) := True;
        return S;
    end Make_Set;

    function Decompose(S: Set) return List is
        L: List(1 .. Size(S));
        I: Positive := 1;
    begin
        for E in Set'Range loop
            if S(E) then
                L(I) := E;
                I := I + 1;
            end if;
        end loop;
        return L;
    end Decompose;

    function "+" (S, T: Set) return Set is
    begin
        return S or T;
    end "+";

    function "*" (S, T: Set) return Set is
    begin
        return S and T;
    end "*";

    function "-" (S, T: Set) return Set is
    begin
        return S xor T;
    end "-";

    function "<" (E: Element; S: Set) return Boolean is
    begin
        return S(E);
    end "<";

    function "<=" (S, T: Set) return Boolean is
    begin
```

```
         return (S and T) = S;
      end "<=";

      function Size(S: Set) return Natural is
         N: Natural := 0;
      begin
         for E in Set'Range loop
            if S(E) then
               N := N + 1;
            end if;
         end loop;
         return N;
      end Size;

   end Set_Of;
```

5   ```
     private
        type Element_Array is array (Element) of Boolean;
        type Set is
           record
              Value: Element_Array := (Element => False);
           end record;

        Empty: constant Set := (Value => (Element => False));
        Full: constant Set := (Value => (Element => True));
     end;
     ```

We have to make the full type into a record containing the array as a single component
so that we can give it a default initial expression. Unfortunately, this means that the
body needs rewriting and moreover the functions become rather untidy. Sadly we
cannot write the default expression as Empty.Value. This is because we cannot use the
component name Value in its own declaration. In general, however, we can use a
deferred constant as a default value before its full declaration. Note also that we have
to use the named notation for the single component record aggregates.

*Exercise 17.3*

1    First we have to declare our function "<" which we define as follows: if the
     polynomials have different degrees, the one with the lower degree is smaller; if the
     same degree, then we compare coefficients starting at the highest power. So

```
function "<" (X, Y: Polynomial) return Boolean is
begin
   if X.N /= Y.N then
      return X.N < Y.N;
   end if;
   for I in reverse 0 .. X.N loop      -- or X.A'Range
      if X.A(I) /= Y.A(I) then
         return X.A(I) < Y.A(I);
      end if;
   end loop;
   return False;      -- they are identical
end "<";

procedure Sort_Poly is new Sort(Integer, Polynomial, Poly_Array);
```

2   ```
     type Mutant_Array is array (Integer range <>) of Mutant;

     function "<" (X, Y: Mutant) return Boolean is
     begin
     ```

```
      if X.Sex /= Y.Sex then
         return X.Sex > Y.Sex;
      else
         return Y.Birth < X.Birth;
      end if;
   end "<";
```

procedure Sort_Mutant **is new** Sort(Integer, Mutant, Mutant_Array);

Note that the order of sexes asked for is precisely the reverse order to that in the type Gender and so we can directly use ">" applied to that type. Similarly, younger first means later birth date first and so we use the function "<" we have already defined for the type Date but with the arguments reversed.

We could not sort an array of type Person because we cannot declare such an array anyway since Person is indefinite.

3   We cannot do this because the array is of an anonymous type.

4   We might get Constraint_Error. If C'First = Index'First then the attempt to evaluate Index'Pred(C'Last) will raise Constraint_Error. Considerable care can be required to make such extreme cases foolproof. The easy way out in this case is simply to insert

if C'Length < 2 **then return**; **end if**;

5   The generic body corresponds closely to the procedure Sort in Section 10.2. The type Vector is replaced by Collection. I is of type Index. The types Node and Node_Ptr are declared inside Sort because they depend on the generic type Item. The incrementing of I cannot be done with "+" since the index type may not be an integer and so we have to use Index'Succ. Care is needed not to cause Constraint_Error if the array embraces the full range of values of Index. However, the important thing is that the generic specification is completely unchanged and so we see how an alternative body can be sensibly supplied.

6   **type** Boolean_Array **is array** (Integer **range** <>) **of** Boolean;

function And_All **is new** Apply(Integer, Boolean, Boolean_Array, "and");

7   A further generic parameter is required to supply a value for zero.

```
generic
   type Index is (<>);
   type Item is private;
   Zero: in Item;
   type Vec is array (Index range <>) of Item;
   with function "+" (X, Y: Item) return Item;
function Apply(A: Vec) return Item;

function Apply(A: Vec) return Item is
   Result: Item := Zero;
begin
   for I in A'Range loop
      Result := Result + A(I);
   end loop;
   return Result;
end Apply;
```

and then

function And_All **is new** Apply(Integer, Boolean, True, Boolean_Array, "and");

8   **generic**
    type Item **is private**;
    type Vector **is array** (Integer **range** <>) **of** Item;
    with function "=" (X, Y: Item) **return** Boolean **is** <>;
    function Equals(A, B: Vector) **return** Boolean;

    function Equals(A, B: Vector) **return** Boolean **is**
    begin
      -- body exactly as for Exercise 11.4(4)
    end Equals;

We can instantiate by

    function "=" **is new** Equals(Stack, Stack_Array, "=");

or simply by

    function "=" **is new** Equals(Stack, Stack_Array);

in which case the default parameter is used.

    Note that it is esential to pass "=" as a parameter otherwise predefined equality would be used and the whole point is that we have redefined "=" for the type Stack.

9   **generic**
    type Floating **is digits** <>;
    with function F(X: Floating) **return** Floating;
    function Solve **return** Floating;

    function G(X: Float) **return** Float **is**
    begin
      return Exp(X) + X – 7.0;
    end;
    ...
    function Solve_G **is new** Solve(Float, G);
    ...
    Answer: Float := Solve_G;

Exercise 17.4

1   **package body** Generic_Complex_Functions **is**
    use Elementary_Functions;

    function Sqrt(X: Complex) **return** Complex **is**
    begin
      return Cons_Polar(Sqrt(**abs** X), 0.5*Arg(X)));
    end Sqrt;

    function Log(X: Complex) **return** Complex **is**
    begin
      return Cons(Log(**abs** X), Arg(X));
    end Log;

    function Exp(X: Complex) **return** Complex **is**
    begin
      return Cons_Polar(Exp(Rl_Part(X)), Im_Part(X));
    end Exp;

    function Sin(X: Complex) **return** Complex **is**
      Rl: Float_Type := Rl_Part(X);
      Im: Float_Type := Im_Part(X);
    begin
      return Cons(Sin(Rl)*Cosh(Im), Cos(Rl)*Sinh(Im));
    end Sin;

```
   function Cos(X: Complex) return Complex is
      RI: Float_Type := RI_Part(X);
      Im: Float_Type := Im_Part(X);
   begin
      return Cons(Cos(RI)*Cosh(Im), –Sin(RI)*Sinh(Im));
   end Cos;

end Generic_Complex_Functions;
```

2   ```
package Poly_Vector is new General_Vector(Integer, Polynomial, Poly_Array);
```

```
procedure Sort_Poly is new Sort(Poly_Vector);
```

```
package Boolean_Vector is new General_Vector(Integer, Boolean, Boolean_Array);
```

```
function And_All is new Apply(Boolean_Vector, "and");
```

3   ```
generic
   with package Signature is new Group(<>);
   use Signature;
function Power(E: Element; N: Integer) return Element;
```

```
function Power(E: Element; N: Integer) return Element is
   Result: Element := Identity;
begin
   for I in 1 .. abs N loop
      Result := Op(Result, E);
   end loop;
   if N < 0 then Result := Inverse(Result); end if;
   return Result;
end Power;
```

```
package Integer_Addition_Group is
   new Group(Element => Integer, Identity => 0, Op => "+", Inverse => "–");
```

```
function Multiply is new Power(Integer_Addition_Group);
```

4   ```
generic
   type Element is (<>);
   Identity: in Element;
   with function Op(X, Y: Element) return Element;
   with function Inverse(X: Element) return Element;
package Finite_Group is end;
```

```
generic
   with package Signature is new Finite_Group(<>);
   use Signature;
function Is_Group return Boolean;
```

```
function Is_Group return Boolean is
begin
   -- check closed, actual parameter could be constrained
   for E in Element'Range loop
      for F in Element'Range loop
         declare
            Result: Element;
         begin
            Result := Op(E, F);
         exception
            when Constraint_Error =>
               return False;
```
```

```
            end;
          end loop;
        end loop;
        -- check identity is OK
        for E in Element'Range loop
          if Op(E, Identity) /= E or Op(Identity, E) /= E then
            return False;
          end if;
        end loop;
        -- check inverse is OK
        for E in Element'Range loop
          if Op(E, Inverse(E)) /= Identity or Op(Inverse(E), E) /= Identity then
            return False;
          end if;
        end loop;
        -- check associative law OK
        for E in Element'Range loop
          for F in Element'Range loop
            for G in Element'Range loop
              if Op(E, Op(F, G)) /= Op(Op(E, F), G) then
                return False;
              end if;
            end loop;
          end loop;
        end loop;
        return True;
      end Is_Group;
```

Exercise 17.5

1
```
    with Ada.Numerics.Generic_Elementary_Functions;
    use Ada.Numerics;
    with Generic_Complex_Numbers;
    with Generic_Complex_Numbers.Cartesian;
    with Generic_Complex_Numbers.Polar;
    generic
      with package Elementary_Functions is
          new Generic_Elementary_Functions(<>);
      with package Complex_Numbers is
          new Generic_Complex_Numbers(Elementary_Functions.Float_Type);
      with package Cartesian is new Complex_Numbers.Cartesian;
      with package Polar is new Complex_Numbers.Polar;
    package Generic_Complex_Functions is
      use Complex_Numbers, Cartesian, Polar;

      function Sqrt(X: Complex) return Complex;
      ...
    end Generic_Complex_Functions;
```

Note that the generic formals ensure that the packages passed as actuals are correctly related. For example if we did two instantiations of the hierarchy (one for Float and one for Long_Float) then we need to ensure that we do not use the parent from one with a child from the other. However, there is no such guarantee if the hierarchy has a generic subprogram as a child since we can only express the requirement that the profile is correct; this will be enough in most cases but is not foolproof. Of course the program would not crash, just do something silly.

2 This raises the question of how the body is to obtain access to the required elementary functions. The package Generic_Elementary_Functions could be instantiated inside the body; this is straightforward but wasteful if there is already an instantiation in existence. The required instantiation could alternatively be passed as a package parameter so that the specification becomes

```
with Ada.Numerics.Generic_Elementary_Functions;
use Ada.Numerics;
generic
   with package Elementary_Functions is
      new Generic_Elementary_Functions(Floating);
package Generic_Complex_Numbers.Polar is
   ...
```

Note carefully that the instantiation must be with the type Floating which is the formal parameter of the parent package. The answer to the previous exercise would then need modification. The essence of the body is

```
package body Generic_Complex_Numbers.Polar is
   use Elementary_Functions;

   function Cons_Polar(R, Theta: Floating) return Complex is
   begin
      return (R*Cos(Theta), R*Sin(Theta));
   end Cons_Polar;

   function "abs" (X: Complex) return Floating is
   begin
      return Sqrt(X.Rl**2 + X.Im**2);
   end "abs";

   function Arg(X: Complex) return Floating is
      return Arctan(X.Im, X.Rl);
   end Arg;

end Generic_Complex_Numbers.Polar;
```

Numerical analysts will writhe at the poor implementation of **abs** which can unnecessarily overflow in computing the parameter of Sqrt. This can be avoided by suitable rescaling.

Answers 18

Exercise 18.1

1
```
procedure Shopping is

   task Get_Salad;

   task body Get_Salad is
   begin
      Buy_Salad;
   end Get_Salad;

   task Get_Wine;

   task body Get_Wine is
   begin
      Buy_Wine;
   end Get_Wine;

   task Get_Meat;
```

```
        task body Get_Meat is
        begin
            Buy_Meat;
        end Get_Meat;

    begin
        null;
    end Shopping;
```

Exercise 18.2

1
```
    task body Char_To_Line is
        Buffer: Line;
    begin
        loop
            for I in Buffer'Range loop
                accept Put(C: in Character) do
                    Buffer(I) := C;
                end;
            end loop;
            accept Get(L: out Line) do
                L := Buffer;
            end;
        end loop;
    end Char_To_Line;
```

Exercise 18.3

1
```
    with Calendar;
    generic
        First_Time: Calendar.Time;
        Interval: Duration;
        Number: Integer;
        with procedure P;
    procedure Call;

    procedure Call is
        use type Calendar.Time;
        Next_Time: Calendar.Time := First_Time;
        Now: Time := Calendar.Clock;
    begin
        if Next_Time < Now then
            Next_Time := Now;
        end if;
        for I in 1 .. Number loop
            delay until Next_Time;
            P;
            Next_Time := Next_Time + Interval;
        end loop;
    end Call;
```

2   The type Duration requires at least 24 bits.

3   The trouble with writing **delay** Next_Time – Clock; is that the task might be temporarily suspended between calling Clock and issuing the delay; the delay would then be wrong by the amount of time for which the task did not have a processor.

```
4   use Calendar;
    Date: Time;
    Y: Year_Number;
    M: Month_Number;
    D: Day_Number;
    S: Day_Duration;
    High_Noon: Time;
    ...
    Split(Clock, Y, M, D, S);
    High_Noon := Time_Of(Y, M, D, 43_200.0);
    if S > 43_200.0 then            -- afternoon, so add a day
      High_Noon := High_Noon + 86_400.0;
    end if;
```

Exercise 18.4

```
1   protected Variable is
       entry Read(Value: out Item);
       procedure Write(New_Value: in Item);
    private
       Data: Item;
       Value_Set: Boolean := False;
    end Variable;

    protected body Variable is
       entry Read(Value: out Item) when Value_Set is
       begin
         Value := Data;
       end Read;

       procedure Write(New_Value: in Item) is
       begin
         Data := New_Value;
         Value_Set := True;          -- clear the barrier
       end Write;
    end Variable;
```

The problem with this solution is that it no longer allows multiple readers because the function has been replaced by an entry.

2   This is a bit of a trick question. It cannot be done because a discriminant is not static and therefore cannot be used to declare the type Index. One possible alternative is to make the index type of the array and the type of the variables I and J to be type Integer and to use the **mod** operator to do the cyclic arithmetic. The structure would then be

```
    generic
       type Item is private;
    package Buffers is
       type Item_Array is array (Integer range <>) of Item;
       protected type Buffering(N: Integer) is
         -- and so on
       end Buffering;
    end Buffers;
```

```
3   protected Buffer is
       entry Put(X: in Item);
       entry Get(X: out Item);
    private
       V: Item;
```

```
          Is_Set: Boolean := False;
      end;

      protected body Buffer is
          entry Put(X: in Item) when not Is_Set is
          begin
              V := X;
              Is_Set := True;
          end Put;

          entry Get(X: out Item) when Is_Set is
          begin
              X := V;
              Is_Set := False;
          end Get;
      end Buffer;
```

4   ```
     protected Char_To_Line is
         entry Put(C: in Character);
         entry Get(L: out Line);
     private
         Buffer: Line;
         Count: Integer := 0;   -- number of items in the buffer
     end;

     protected body Char_To_Line is
         entry Put(C: in Character) when Count < Buffer'Last is
         begin
             Count := Count + 1;
             Buffer(Count) := C;
         end Put;

         entry Get(L: out Line) when Count = Buffer'Last is
         begin
             Count := 0;
             L := Buffer;
         end Get;
     end Char_To_Line;
     ```

*Exercise 18.7*

1    ```
     protected type Mailbox is
         entry Deposit(X: in Item);
         entry Collect(X: out Item);
     private
         Full: Boolean := False;
         Local: Item;
     end;

     protected body Mailbox is
         entry Deposit(X: in Item) when not Full is
         begin
             Local := X;
             Full := True;
         end Deposit;

         entry Collect(X: out item) when Full is
         begin
             X := Local;
             Full := False;
     ```

    end Collect;
end Mailbox;

This mailbox is reusable whereas the task version was not (indeed the task just terminated after use). We could prevent the protected object from being reused by further state variables.

    The advantages of the protected object are that there need be no concern with termination in the event of it not being used and it is of course much more efficient. A possible disadvantage is that the closely coupled form is not possible.

Exercise 18.8

1   **task** Buffering **is**
      entry Put(X: **in** Item);
      entry Finish;
      entry Get(X: **out** Item);
    end;

    task body Buffering **is**
      N: **constant** := 8;
      type Index **is mod** N;
      A: **array** (Index) **of** Item;
      I, J: Index := 1;
      Count: Integer **range** 0 .. N := 0;
      Finished: Boolean := False;
    begin
      loop
        select
          when Count < N =>
          accept Put(X: **in** Item) **do**
            A(I) := X;
          end;
          I := I + 1; Count := Count + 1;
        or
          accept Finish;
          Finished := True;
        or
          when Count > 0 =>
          accept Get(X: **out** Item) **do**
            X := A(J);
          end;
          J := J + 1; Count := Count − 1;
        or
          when Count = 0 **and** Finished =>
          accept Get(X: **out** Item) **do**
            raise Done;
          end;
        end select;
      end loop;
    exception
      when Done =>
        null;
    end Buffering;

This curious example illustrates that there may be several accept statements for the same entry in the one select statement. The exception Done is propagated to the caller and also terminates the loop in Buffering before being quietly handled. Of course the exception need not be handled by Buffering because exceptions propagated out of tasks are lost, but it is cleaner to do so.

2   The server aborts the caller during the rendezvous thereby placing the caller into an abnormal state. Although the caller cannot be properly completed until after the rendezvous is finished (the server might have access to the caller's data space via a parameter), nevertheless the caller is no longer active and does not receive the exception Havoc.

3
```
select
    Trigger.Wait;
then abort
    loop
        -- compute next estimate in Z
        -- then store it in the protected object
        Result.Put_Estimate(Z);
        -- loop back to improve estimate
    end loop;
end select;
```

Exercise 18.9

1   If we wrote

requeue Reset **with abort**;

then there would be a risk that the task that called Signal was aborted before it could clear the occurred flag. The system would then be in a real mess since subsequent tasks calling Wait would be able to proceed without waiting for the next signal.

2
```
protected Event is
    entry Wait;
    procedure Signal;
private
    Occurred: Boolean := False;
end Event;

protected body Event is
    entry Wait when Occurred is
    begin
        if Wait'Count = 0 then
            Occurred := False;
        end if;
    end Wait;

    procedure Signal is
    begin
        if Wait'Count > 0 then
            Occurred := True;
        end if;
    end Signal;
end Event;
```

The last of the waiting tasks to be let go clears the occurred flag back to false (the last one out switches off the light). It is important that the procedure Signal does not set the occurred flag if there are no tasks waiting since in such a case there is no waiting task to clear it and the signal would persist (remember this is a model of a transient signal).

An amazing alternative solution is

```
protected Event is
    entry Wait;
    entry Signal;
end Event;
```

```
protected body Event is
  entry Wait when Signal'Count > 0 is
  begin
    null;
  end Wait;

  entry Signal when Wait'Count = 0 is
  begin
    null;
  end Signal;
end Event;
```

This works because joining an entry queue is a protected action and results in the evaluation of barriers (just as they are evaluated when a protected procedure or entry body finishes). Note that there is no protected data (and hence no private part) and that both entry bodies are null; in essence the protected data is the Count attributes and these therefore behave properly. In contrast, the Count attributes of task entries are not reliable because joining and leaving task entry queues are not protected in any way.

3

```
task Controller is
  entry Sign_In(P: Priority; D: Data);
private
  entry Request(P: Priority) (P: Priority; D: Data);
end;

task body Controller is
  Total: Integer := 0;
begin
  loop
    if Total = 0 then
      accept Sign_In(P: Priority; D: Data) do
        Total := 1;
        requeue Request(P);
      end;
    end if;
    loop
      select
        accept Sign_In(P: Priority; D: Data) do
          Total := Total + 1;
          requeue Request(P);
        end;
      else
        exit;
      end select;
    end loop;

    for P in Priority loop
      select
        accept Request(P) (P: Priority; D: Data) do
          Action(D);
        end;
        Total := Total - 1;
        exit;
      else
        null;
      end select;
    end loop;
  end loop;
end Controller;
```

The variable Total records the total number of requests outstanding. Each time round the outer loop, the task waits for a call of Sign_In if no requests are in the system, it then services any outstanding calls of Sign_In. The calls to Sign_In requeue onto the appropriate member of the entry family Request. The task then deals with a request of the highest priority. Observe that we had to make P a parameter of the entry family as well as the index; this is because requeue can only be to an entry with the same parameter profile (or parameterless).

Note that the solution works if a calling task is aborted; this is because the requeue does not specify **with abort** and so is considered as part of the abort deferred region of the original rendezvous.

```
4    package Monitor is
        protected Call is
           entry Job(D: Data);
        end;
     private
        task The_Task is
          entry Job(D: Data);
        end;
     end;

     package body Monitor is
        protected body Call is
           entry Job(D: Data) when True is
           begin
              Log_The_Call(Calendar.Clock);
              requeue The_Task.Job;
           end Job;
        end Call;
        ...
     end Monitor;
```

Exercise 18.10

```
1    package Cobblers is
        procedure Mend(A: Address; B: Boots);
     end;

     package body Cobblers is
        type Job is
           record
              Reply: Address;
              Item: Boots;
           end record;

        package P is new Buffers(Job);
        use P;
        Boot_Store: Buffer(100);

        task Server is
           entry Request(A: Address; B: Boots);
        end;

        task type Repairman;
        Tom, Dick, Harry: Repairman;

        task body Server is
           Next_Job: Job;
        begin
           loop
```

```
      accept Request(A: Address; B: Boots) do
         Next_Job := (A, B);
      end;
      Put(Boot_Store, Next_Job);
   end loop;
end Server;

task body Repairman is
   My_Job: Job;
begin
   loop
      Get(Boot_Store, My_Job);
      Repair(My_Job.Item);
      My_Job.Reply.Deposit(My_Job.Item);
   end loop;
end Repairman;

procedure Mend(A: Address; B: Boots) is
begin
   Server.Request(A, B);
end;
end Cobblers;
```

We have assumed that the type Address is an access to a mailbox for handling boots.
Note one anomaly; the stupid server accepts boots from the customer before checking
the store – if it turns out to be full, he is left holding them. In all, the shop can hold
104 pairs of boots – 100 in store, 1 with the server and 1 with each repairman.

2   procedure Gauss_Seidel is

```
   N: constant := 5;
   subtype Full_Grid is Integer range 0 .. N;
   subtype Grid is Full_Grid range 1 .. N-1;
   type Real is digits 7;
   Tolerance: constant Real := 0.0001;
   Error_Limit: constant Real := Tolerance * (N-1)**2;
   Converged: Boolean := False;
   Error_Sum: Real;

   function F(I, J: Grid) return Real is separate;

   task type Iterator is
      entry Start(I, J: in Grid);
   end;

   protected type Point is
      procedure Set_P(X: in Real);
      function Get_P return Real;
      function Get_Delta_P return Real;
      procedure Set_Converged(B: in Boolean);
      function Get_Converged return Boolean;
   private
      Converged: Boolean := False;
      P: Real;
      Delta_P: Real;
   end;

   Process: array (Grid, Grid) of Iterator;
   Data: array (Full_Grid, Full_Grid) of Point;

   task body Iterator is
      I, J: Grid;
```

```
                P: Real;
            begin
              accept Start(I, J: in Grid) do
                  Iterator.I := Start.I;
                  Iterator.J := Start.J;
              end Start;

              loop
                  P := 0.25 * (Data(I-1, J).Get_P + Data(I+1, J).Get_P
                                    Data(I, J-1).Get_P + Data(I, J+1).Get_P - F(I, J));
                  Data(I, J).Set_P(P);
                  exit when Data(I, J).Get_Converged
              end loop;
            end Iterator;

        protected body Point is
            procedure Set_P(X: in Real) is
            begin
              Delta_P := X - P;
              P := X;
            end;

            function Get_P return Real is
            begin
              return P;
            end;

            function Get_Delta_P return Real is
            begin
              return Delta_P;
            end;

            procedure Set_Converged(B: in Boolean) is
            begin
              Converged := B;
            end;

            function Get_Converged return Boolean is
            begin
              return Converged;
            end;
        end Point;

    begin      -- of main subprogram; the tasks are now active
        for I in Grid loop
          for J in Grid loop
            Process(I, J).Start(I, J);      -- tell them who they are
          end loop;
        end loop;

        loop
          Error_Sum := 0.0;
          for I in Grid loop
            for J in Grid loop
              Error_Sum := Error_Sum + Data(I, J).Get_Delta_P**2;
            end loop;
          end loop;

          Converged := Error_Sum < Error_Limit;
          exit when Converged;
        end loop;
```

-- tell the protected objects that the system has converged

```
for I in Grid loop
   for J in Grid loop
      Data(I, J).Set_Converged(True);
   end loop;
end loop;
```

-- output results

end Gauss_Seidel;

Note that there are protected objects on the boundary points but we have not shown how to initialize them. The central computation could be made neater by using renaming in order to avoid repeated evaluation of Data(I, J) and so on; this would also speed things up. Thus we could write

```
function Get_P1 return Real renames Data(I-1, J).Get_P;
function Get_P2 return Real renames Data(I+1, J).Get_P;
...
procedure Set_P(X: in Real) renames Data(I, J).Set_P;
function Get_Converged return Boolean renames Data(I, J).Get_Converged;
```

and then

```
Set_P(0.25 * (Get_P1+Get_P2+Get_P3+Get_P4 – F(I, J)));
exit when Get_Converged;
```

Answers 19

Exercise 19.1

1
```
function Volume(C: Cylinder) return Float is
begin
   return Area(C.Base) * C.Height;
end Volume;

function Area(C: Cylinder) return Float is
begin
   return 2.0*Area(C.Base) + 2.0*Pi*C.Base.Radius*C.Height;
end Area;
```

We cannot apply the function Moment to a cylinder because the type Cylinder is not in Object'Class. We are thus protected from such foolishness.

Exercise 19.2

1
```
generic
   type S is new Object with private;
package Colour_Mixin is
   type Coloured_Object is new S with private;
   procedure Set_Colour(CO: in out Coloured_Object; C: in Colour);
   function Colour_Of(CO: Coloured_Object) return Colour;
private
   type Coloured_Object is new S with
      record
         The_Colour: Colour;
      end record;
end;
```

```
package body Colour_Mixin is
  procedure Set_Colour(CO: in out Coloured_Object: C: in Colour) is
  begin
    if Area(CO) >= 10.0 or C /= Red then
      CO.The_Colour := C;
    end if;
  end Set_Colour;

  function Colour_Of(CO: Coloured_Object) return Colour is
  begin
    return CO.The_Colour;
  end Colour_Of;
end Colour_Mixin;
```

2   ```
     with Ada.Finalization; use Ada;
     generic
       type Raw_Type is tagged private;
     package Tracking is
       type Tracked_Type is new Raw_Type with private;
       function Identity(TT: Tracked_Type) return Integer;
     private
       type Control is new Finalization.Controlled with
         record
           Identity_Number: Integer;
         end record;

       procedure Initialize(C: in out Control);
       procedure Adjust(C: in out Control);
       procedure Finalize(C: in out Control);

       type Tracked_Type is new Raw_Type with
         record
           Component: Control;
         end record;
     end Tracking;

     package body Tracking is
       The_Count: Integer := 0;
       Next_One: Integer := 1;

       function Identity(TT: Tracked_Type) return Integer is
       begin
         return TT.Component.Identity_Number;
       end Identity;

       procedure Initialize(C: in out Control) is
       begin
         The_Count := The_Count + 1;
         C.Identity_Number := Next_One;
         Next_One := Next_One + 1;
       end Initialize;

       procedure Adjust ...
       procedure Finalize ...
     end Tracking;
     ```

3    ```
     with Objects; use Objects;
     with Tracking;
     package Hush_Hush is
       type Secret_Shape is new Object with private;
     ```

```
    function Shape_Identity(SS: Secret_Shape) return Integer;
    ...
private
  package Q is new Tracking(Raw_Type => Object);
  type Secret_Shape is new Q.Tracked_Type with
    record
      ...   -- other hidden components
    end record;
end Hush_Hush;
```

```
package body Hush_Hush is
  function Shape_Identity(SS: Secret_Shape) return Integer is
  begin
    return Identity(SS);
  end Shape_Identity;
  ...
end Hush_Hush;
```

Note carefully that the type Shape_Secret inherits the function Identity from Q.Tracked_Type. Of course we could have laboriously written **return** Q.Identity(Q.Tracked_Type(SS)); however, we do not actually have to write out a body for Shape_Identity but can simply use a renaming thus

```
function Shape_Identity(SS: Secret_Shape) return Integer renames Identity;
```

Exercise 19.3

```
1   package body Lists is
      procedure Insert(After: Cell_Ptr; Item: Cell_Ptr) is
      begin
        if Item = null or else Item.Next /= null then
          raise List_Error;
        end if;
        if After = null then
          raise List_Error;
        end if;
        Item.Next := After.Next;
        After.Next := Item;
      end Insert;

      function Remove(After: Cell_Ptr) return Cell_Ptr is
        Result: Cell_Ptr;
      begin
        if After = null then
          raise List_Error;
        end if;
        Result := After.Next;
        if Result /= null then
          After.Next := Result.Next;
          Result.Next := null;
        end if;
        return Result;
      end Insert;

      function Next(After: Cell_Ptr) return Cell_Ptr is
      begin
        if After = null then
          raise List_Error;
        end if;
```

```
            return After.Next;
         end Next;
      end Lists;
```

Note that we do not have to do anything about a dummy first element. The user has to do that by declaring a list with one cell already in place by for example

```
The_List: Cell_Ptr := new Cell;
```

2   Using access parameters enables most of the checks to be omitted since we know that an access parameter can never be null. The subprograms become

```
      procedure Insert(After: access Cell; Item: access Cell) is
      begin
         if Item.Next /= null then
            raise List_Error;
         end if;
         Item.Next := After.Next;
         After.Next := Item;
      end Insert;

      function Remove(After: access Cell) return Cell_Ptr is
         Result: Cell_Ptr;
      begin
         Result := After.Next;
         if Result /= null then
            After.Next := Result.Next;
            Result.Next := null;
         end if;
         return Result;
      end Remove;

      function Next(After: access Cell_Ptr) return Cell_Ptr is
      begin
         return After.Next;
      end Next;
```

Exercise 19.4

1   ```
    package List_Iteration_Stuff is
       new Iteration_Stuff(Lists.List, Lists.Iterators.Iterator);

    procedure Green_To_Red is
       new Generic_Green_To_Red(I_S => List_Iteration_Stuff);
    ```

2   ```
    package Iterators is
       type Structure is abstract tagged null record;
       type Iterator is abstract tagged null record;
       procedure Iterate(S: Structure; IC: Iterator'Class) is abstract;
       procedure Action(C: in out Colour; I: in out Iterator) is abstract;
    end;

    package Trees is
       type Tree is new Structure with private;
       ...
       procedure Iterate(T: Tree; IC: Iterator'Class);
    private
       type Node;
       type Node_Ptr is access Node;
    ```

```
    type Node is
      record
        C: Colour;
        Left, Right: Node_Ptr;
      end record;
    type Tree is new Structure with
      record
        Root: Node_Ptr;
      end record;
end;

package body Trees is
    ...
    procedure Iterate(T: Tree; IC: Iterator'Class) is
      procedure Inner(N: Node_Ptr) is
      begin
        if N /= null then
          Action(N.C, IC);          -- dispatches on IC
          Inner(N.Left);
          Inner(N.Right);
        end if;
      end Inner;
    begin
      Inner(T.Root);
    end Iterate;

end Trees;
```

The package Iterators has no body. It serves just as a means of establishing the abstract
types and their primitive operations; Iterate is a primitive operation of Structure and
Action is a primitive operation of Iterator. The type Trees is then extended from
Structure but note that an extra level is required in order to hold the pointer to the root
of the tree. A consequence of this is that the recursive walk over the tree has to be
done by a local procedure Inner within Iterate. We can now declare the general
counting function as follows

```
type Count_Iterator is new Iterator with
    record
      Result: Natural;
      The_Colour: Colour;
    end record;

procedure Action(C: in out Colour; I: in out Count_Iterator) is
begin
    if C= I.The_Colour then
      I.Result := I.Result + 1;
    end if;
end Action;

function Count(S: Structure'Class; C: Colour) return Natural is
    I: Count_Iterator;
begin
    I.Result := 0;
    I.The_Colour := C;
    Iterate(S, I);               -- dispatch on S
    return I.Result;
end Count;

Oak: Tree;                       -- declare some tree
    ...                          -- build the tree
N := Count(Oak, Green);
```

The final statement counts how many nodes have the colour Green in the Tree called Oak. Note the double dispatching. The function Count dispatches to the particular Iterate for the tree structure and then that Iterate dispatches to the Action for counting.

Exercise 19.5

1   Yes, dispatching could be used to identify the particular function to be integrated or minimized. Consider

```
generic
   type Floating is digits <>;
package Generic_Integrate is
   type Integrator is abstract tagged null record;
   function Integrand(X: Floating; I: Integrator) return Floating;
   function Integrate(I: Integrator'Class; From, To: Floating; ... );
end Generic_Integrate;
```

and then we have to declare a specific integrator type and associated integrand. Thus in order to perform the integration in the text where the nonlocal array X is used as data for the integrand G we might write

```
package My_Integrate is new Generic_Integrate(My_Float);
use My_Integrate;

type G_Integrator is new Integrator with
   record
      X: Vector(1 .. N);
   end record;

function Integrand(T: My_Float; I: G_Integrator) return My_Float is
begin
   -- compute the function G using the nonlocal array which has been
   -- copied into I.X and the parameter T
end Integrand;
```

and then the function F which is the slave for minimization (which we have assumed is as before) then becomes

```
function F(X: Vector) return My_Float is
   I: G_Integrator;
begin
   I.X := X;                    -- copy the data into the integrator
   Integrate(I, 0.0, T_Final);
end F;
```

Clearly the minimization can be treated in the same way.

Exercise 19.6

1
```
procedure Set_Colour(This: Coloured_Gluon; C: Colour) is
begin
   if Area(This.Obj_Ptr.all) >= 10.0 then
      Set_Colour(Coloured(This), C));
   end if;
end Set_Colour;

procedure Set_Colour(This: Coloured_Gluon; C: Colour) is
   Circle_View: Circle renames Circle(This.Obj_Ptr.all);
begin
   if Circle_View.Radius >= 2.0 then
      Set_Colour(Coloured(This), C);
```

```
  end if;
end Set_Colour;
```

Observe the view conversion in the second case. If the gluon has been applied to an object which is not a Circle (or derived from a Circle) then Constraint_Error is raised.

2   **function** Area(This: Coloured_Circle) **return** Float **is**
         Nominal_Area: Float := Area(Circle(This));
     begin
       if This.Inner.C = Red **then**
          Nominal_Area := Nominal_Area * 2.0;
       end if;
       return Nominal_Area;
     end Area;

3   **type** Circular_Gluon(Col_Ptr: **access** Coloured'Class) **is new** Circle **with null record**;

     type Circular_Colour **is new** Coloured **with**
        record
           Inner: Circular_Gluon(Circular_Colour'Access);
        end record;

The diagram shows a circular colour in a list of colours.

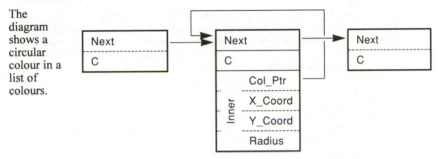

4   **type** Cell_Gluon(Ptr: **access** Garment) **is new** Cell **with null record**;

     type Garment **is limited**
        record
           Style: ... ;
           Pattern: ... ;
           C: Colour;
           S: Size;
           Colour_List, Size_List: Cell_Gluon(Garment'Access);
        end record;

Exercise 19.7

1   **procedure** Handle(CD: **access** Canon_Data; E: Exception_Occurrence) **is**
     begin
       if E = Bang'Identity **then**
          Put_Line("Cannon seems to have exploded.");
          Put("Perhaps ");
          Put(CD.Pounds_Of_Powder);
          Put(" pounds of powder was too much!");
       else
          Put("Some other catastrophe ...");
       end if;
     end Handle;

2   It could be rewritten as follows. Type extension is necesssary to pass the additional data.

```
task type Control(Activity: access Descriptor'Class);

task body Control is
   Next_Time: Calendar.Time := Activity.Start_Time;
begin
   loop
      delay until Next_Time;
      Activity.Action(Activity);              -- indirect call
      Next_Time := Next_Time + Activity.Interval;
      exit when Next_Time > Activity.End_Time;
   end loop;
   Activity.Last_Wishes(Activity);           -- indirect call
exception
   when Event: others =>
      Activity.Handle(Activity, Event);       -- indirect call
end Control;

package Root_Activity is
   type Descriptor;
   type Action_Type is access procedure(D: access Descriptor'Class);
   type Last_Wishes_Type is access procedure (D: access Descriptor'Class);
   type Handle_Type is access procedure (D: access Descriptor'Class;
                                         E: Exception_Occurrence);

   type Descriptor is tagged
      record
         Start_Time, End_Time: Calendar.Time;
         Interval: Duration;
         Action: Action_Type;
         Last_Wishes: Last_Wishes_Type := Null_Last_Wishes'Access;
         Handle: Handle_Type := Default_Handle'Access;
      end record;
end;

package body Root_Activity is
   procedure Null_Last_Wishes(D: access Descriptor'Class) is
   begin
      null;
   end Null_Last_Wishes;

   procedure Default_Handle(D: access Descriptor'Class;
                            E: Exception_Occurrence) is
   begin
      Put_Line("Unhandled exception");
      Put_Line(Exception_Information(Event));
   end Default_Handle;
end Root_Activity;

use Root_Activity;

type Cannon_Data is new Descriptor with
   record
      Pounds_Of_Powder: Integer;
   end record;

procedure Cannon_Action(D: access Descriptor'Class) is
   CD: Cannon_Data := Cannon_Data(D.all);
begin
   Load_Cannon(CD.Pounds_Of_Powder);
```

```
    Fire_Cannon;
  end Cannon_Action;

The_Data: Cannon_Data :=
    (Start_Time => High_Noon;
     End_Time => When_The_Stars_Fade_And_Fall;
     Interval => 24*Hours;
     Action => Cannon_Action'Access;
       ...
     Pounds_Of_Powder => 100);

Cannon_Task: Control(The_Data);
```

So here is a deep point. The access problems are overcome by type extension itself and not by the dispatching. However, the dispatching approach is neater because the default subprograms are automatically inherited and do not clutter the record.

Exercise 19.8

1   The tagged type case is easy; we simply write

```
package People is
  type Person_Name(<>) is private;
  type Mans_Name (<>) is private;
  type Womans_Name(<>) is private;

  function Man_Of(P: Person_Name) return Mans_Name;
  function Woman_Of(P: Person_Name) return Womans_Name;
  function Person_Of(M: Mans_Name) return Person_Name;
  function Person_Of(W: Womans_Name) return Person_Name;
    ...  -- other subprograms
private
  type Person;
    ...
  type Person_Name is access all Person'Class;
  type Mans_Name is access all Man;
    ...
  type Person is abstract tagged ...
    ...
end People;
```

where the private part is exactly as before. The conversion functions are simply

```
function Man_Of(P: Person_Name) return Mans_Name is
begin
  Mans_Name(P);
end;
```

and so on. Remember that conversion is allowed between general access types referring to derived types in the same class. Constraint_Error is raised if we attempt to convert a person to a name of the wrong sex. Conversion in the opposite direction (towards the root) always works.

The variant formulation requires more care. We cannot write, in the private part, something like

```
type Person_Name is access Person;
type Mans_Name is Person_Name(Male);
```

because the full type always has to be a new type. We might try

```
type Person_Name is access all Person;
type Mans_Name is access all Person(Male);
```

where again we have used general access types in the hope that we can convert between them. But this does not work. Conversion between such types is only possible if the constraints statically match or in the case of a conversion to an unconstrained discriminated subtype. So we cannot convert from a Person_Name to a Mans_Name. The only thing to do is to omit the constraint so we also have

type Mans_Name **is access all** Person;

and then perform the necessary checks ourselves.

2   We could have a viewer package thus

```
package People is
   type Person_Name(<>) is limited private;
   -- various interrogative functions
   function Spouse(P: Person_Name) return Person_Name;
   function First_Child(P: Person_Name) return Person_Name;
   function Next_Sibling(P: Person_Name) return Person_Name;
   function Date_Of_Birth(P: Person_Name) return Date;
   ...
private
   type Person;                       -- completed in body
   type Person_Name is access all Person'Class;

package People.Iterators ...
```

There could then be a private child giving the original broader view

```
private package People.Internals is
   type Internal_Person_Name(<>) is private;
   procedure Marry ...
   function Spouse(P: Internal_Person_Name) return Internal_Person_Name;
   ...    -- etc. as before
end People.Internals;
```

The body of People could use this private child

```
with People.Internals; use People.Internals;
package body People is
   type Person is new Internal_Person with null record;
   -- the external functions can then call the internal functions
   -- with appropriate conversions
   ...
end People;
```

The main subprogram could be a child procedure People.Main which creates and builds the model using the view provided by the private child People.Internals. It might call some external procedure which the user writes in order to do the interrogations.

Answers 20

Exercise 20.2

1   Index(S, Decimal_Digit_Set **or** To_Set('.'))

2   " !DEMOS"

3
```
function Make_Map(K: String) return Character_Mapping is
   Key_Set, Non_Key_Set: Character_Set;
   In_letters, Out_Letters: String(1 .. 26);
```

```
begin
   Key_Set := To_Set(To_Upper(K));
   Non_Key_Set := To_Set(('A', 'Z')) – Key_Set;
   In_Letters := To_Sequence(Key_Set) & To_Sequence(Non_Key_Set);
   Out_Letters := To_Sequence(To_Set(('A', 'Z')));
   return To_Mapping(In_Letters & To_Lower(In_Letters),
                     Out_Letters & To_Lower(Out_Letters));
end Make_Map;
   ...
Translate(S, Make_Map("Byron"));
```

4   **function** Decode(Character_Mapping: M) **return** Character_Mapping **is**
```
begin
   return To_Mapping(To_Range(M), To_Domain(M));
end Decode;
   ...
Translate(S, Decode(Make_Map("Byron")));
```

The functions To_Domain and To_Range produce the domain and range of the original mapping and the reverse map is simply created by calling To_Mapping with them reversed. Note that To_Mapping raises Translation_Error anyway if the first argument has duplicates and so no additional check is required.

Exercise 20.3

1   **with** Ada.Numerics.Elementary_Functions;
     use Ada.Numerics;
     package body Simple_Maths **is**

```
   function Sqrt(F: Float) return Float is
   begin
      return Elementary_Functions.Sqrt(F);
   exception
      when Argument_Error =>
         raise Constraint_Error;
   end Sqrt;

   function Log(F: Float) return Float is
   begin
      return Elementary_Functions.Log(F, 10.0);
   exception
      when Argument_Error =>
         raise Constraint_Error;
   end Log;

   function Ln(F: Float) return Float is
   begin
      return Elementary_Functions.Log(F);
   exception
      when Argument_Error =>
         raise Constraint_Error;
   end Ln;

   function Exp(F: Float) return Float is
   begin
      return Elementary_Functions.Exp(F);
   end Exp;

   function Sin(F: Float) return Float is
   begin
```

```
      return Elementary_Functions.Sin(F);
    end Sin;

    function Cos(F: Float) return Float is
    begin
      return Elementary_Functions.Cos(F);
    end Cos;

  end Simple_Maths;
```

We did not write a use clause for Elementary_Functions because it would not have enabled us to write for example **return** Sqrt(F); since this would have resulted in an infinite recursion.

2
```
  type Hand is (Paper, Stone, Scissors);
  type Jacks_Hand is new Hand;
  type Jills_Hand is new Hand;
  type Outcome is (Jack, Draw, Jill);
  Payoff: array (Jacks_Hand, Jills_Hand) of Outcome :=
        ((Draw, Jack, Jill),
         (Jill, Draw, Jack),
         (Jack, Jill, Draw));
  package Random_Hand is new Discrete_Random(Hand);
  use Random_Hand;
  Jacks_Gen: Generator;
  Jills_Gen: Generator;
  Result: Outcome;
  ...
  Reset(Jacks_Gen); Reset(Jills_Gen);
  loop
    Result := Payoff(Jacks_Hand(Random(Jacks_Gen)),
                     Jills_Hand(Random(Jills_Gen)));
    case Result is
      when Jack =>
        ...
      when Draw =>
        ...
      when Jill =>
        ...
    end case;
  end loop;
```

The types Jacks_Hand and Jills_Hand are introduced simply so that the array Payoff cannot be indexed incorrectly. There are clearly lots of different ways of doing this example. A more object oriented approach might be to declare a type Player containing the personal generator and perhaps the player's score.

Exercise 20.4

1
```
  with Ada.Direct_IO;
  generic
    type Element is private;
  procedure Rev(From, To: String);

  procedure Rev(From, To: String) is
    package IO is new Ada.Direct_IO(Element);
    use IO;
    Input: File_Type;
    Output: File_Type;
```

```
      X: Element;
    begin
      Open(Input, In_File, From);
      Open(Output, Out_File, To);
      Set_Index(Output, Size(Input));
      loop
        Read(Input, X);
        Write(Output, X);
        exit when End_Of_File(Input);
        Set_Index(Output, Index(Output)-2);
      end loop;
      Close(Input);
      Close(Output);
    end Rev;
```

Remember that **reverse** is a reserved word. Note also that this does not work if the file is empty (the first call of Set_Index will raise Constraint_Error).

Exercise 20.5

1　The output is shown in string quotes in order to reveal the layout. Spaces are indicated by **s**. In reality of course, there are no quotes and spaces are spaces.

(a)　"Fred"
(b)　"sss120"
(c)　"sssss120"
(d)　"120"
(e)　"-120"

(f)　"ss8#170#"
(g)　"-3.80000E+01"
(h)　"sssss7.00E-2"
(i)　"3.1416E+01"
(j)　"1.0E+10"

2
```
    with Ada.Text_IO;
    with Ada.Float_Text_IO;
    use Ada;
    package body Simple_IO is

      procedure Get(F: out Float) is
      begin
        Float_Text_IO.Get(F);
      end Get;

      procedure Put(F: in Float) is
      begin
        Float_Text_IO.Put(F);
      end Put;

      procedure Put(S: in String) is
      begin
        Text_IO.Put(S);
      end Put;

      procedure New_Line(N: in Integer := 1) is
      begin
        Text_IO.New_Line(Text_IO.Count(N));
      end New_Line;

    end Simple_IO;
```

We have used the nongeneric package Ada.Float_Text_IO. All calls use the full dotted notation to avoid recursion.

The other point of note is the type conversion in New_Line.

Exercise 20.6

```
1    procedure Date_Read(Stream: access Root_Stream_Type'Class;
                                Item: out Date) is
       Month_Number: Integer range 1 .. 12;
     begin
       Integer'Read(Stream, Item.Day);
       Integer'Read(Stream, Month_Number;
       item.Month := Month_Name'Val(Month_Number – 1);
       Integer'Read(Stream, Item.Year);
     end Date_Read;

     for Date'Read use Date_Read;
```

Answers 21

Exercise 21.2

```
1    S: Status;
     for S'Address use 8#100#;
       ...
     if not S'Valid then raise Bad_Data; end if;
```

Answers 23

Exercise 23.1

1   (a) dynamic – Integer   (b) static – Integer   (c) static – root integer

Exercise 23.5

1   (a) The order of evaluation of the operands I and F of "+" is not defined. As a result
         the effect could be either of

```
         I := 1 + 2;                    -- I first, or
         I := 2 + 2;                    -- F first
```

    (b) The order of evaluation of the destination A(I) and the value F is not defined. The
         effect could be either of

```
         A(1) := 2;                     -- I first, or
         A(2) := 2;                     -- F first
```

    (c) The order of evaluation of the two indexes is not defined. The effect could be
         either of

```
         AA(1, 2) := 0;                 -- I first, or
         AA(2, 2) := 0;                 -- F first
```

Bibliography

The following selection for further reading comprises a number of books which the author believes will be found helpful. It is by no means exhaustive and omits many other books which make a valuable contribution to the Ada literature. However, if you are new to Ada and wish to build a library then this list is a good starting point. At the time of writing, there are not many books specifically on Ada 95 and so this list includes some interesting older books on Ada 83 which are still relevant.

Booch, G. (1986). *Software Engineering with Ada*, 2nd edn. Benjamin Cummings

This well-known classic was one of the first books to discuss how to design programs in Ada; it is especially famed for Object Oriented Programming.

Burns, A. and Wellings, A. (1995). *Concurrency in Ada,* Cambridge University Press

This is a very worthy successor to Alan Burns' previous book entitled *Concurrent Programming in Ada* which addressed Ada 83. This new book is a very complete account of tasking in Ada 95 and contains many canonical examples which explore all aspects of concurrency in considerable depth. It naturally includes comprehensive coverage of the Real-Time Systems annex.

Cohen, N. H. (1996). *Ada as a Second Language*, 2nd edn. McGraw-Hill

This is a rather comprehensive account of the Ada language completely updated for Ada 95. It is a large book and contains many examples explored in detail. In particular it covers the specialized annexes in more detail than we have here. It also has myriads of exercises but no solutions (just as well because otherwise it would be 2000 pages!).

Gautier, R. J. and Wallis, P. J. L., eds. (1990). *Software Reuse with Ada.* Peter Peregrinus

This contains a good discussion on how to design reusable software components in Ada 83. It is inevitably somewhat restricted since Ada 95 offers alternative techniques.

Hibbard, P., Hisgen, A., Rosenberg, J., Shaw, M. and Sherman, M. (1983). *Studies in Ada Style*, 2nd edn. Springer-Verlag

This excellent book contains a detailed analysis of a small number of intricate programs which explore important issues of structure. A lot can be learnt from really understanding them.

Jones, Do-While (1989). *Ada in Action*. Wiley

This down-to-earth and amusing book contains some valuable practical advice on using Ada 83. It also contains a number of listings of useful programs.

Pyle, I. P. (1991). *Developing Safety Systems: A Guide using Ada*. Prentice-Hall

It has now been realized that software is a key issue in the development of many life critical systems. This book illustrates the advantages of Ada in this area and is equally applicable to Ada 95.

Shumate, K. (1998). *Understanding Concurrency in Ada*. Intertext Publications

This is a detailed account of tasking in Ada 83. Although clearly somewhat out of date because of the absence of any discussion on protected objects it nevertheless makes good reading. It contains a fascinating discussion of many variations on the cobblers example at the end of Chapter 18.

Software Productivity Consortium, The (1995). *Ada 95 Quality and Style*. Software Productivity Consortium

This is an updated version of the previous 1989 edition which covered Ada 83. It is a valuable guide to writing good Ada programs. Topics covered include portability and reuse as well as stylistic issues. A must for every programmer.

The following books are of a more general nature.

Gibson, W. and Sterling, B. (1991). *The Difference Engine*. Bantam Books

This colourful novel contemplates a Victorian world in which Babbage's engines are in widespread use, Lord Byron becomes Prime Minister of Britain and Ada is known as the Queen of Engines. A good read for a flight to a conference!

Langley Moore, D. (1977). *Ada, Countess of Lovelace*. John Murray

This is a classical biography of Lord Byron's daughter after whom the language is named.

Nabokov, V. (1969). *Ada*. Weidenfeld and Nicolson

The title of this book is an illustration of overloading. It has nothing to do with either Ada the language or the Countess of Lovelace. However, if you are fed up with programming languages, this novel brings light relief and will provoke interesting comment if placed in your library.

Stein, D. (1985). *Ada, A Life and a Legacy*. MIT Press

This biography contains more about Ada's relationship and technical work with Charles Babbage.

Toole, Betty A. (1992). *Ada, the Enchantress of Numbers*. Strawberry Press

This recent biography of Ada is written by someone familiar with the Ada language community and captures more of the spirit of Ada as the first programmer.

Index

Index to Examples

This index lists the more significant examples. The entries give the section numbers where they are declared or referenced; entries followed by the letter e indicate that the reference is to the exercises. Predefined entities such as the type String will be found in the main index.